THE CULTURE OF JAPANESE FASCISM

ASIA-PACIFIC: CULTURE, POLITICS, AND SOCIETY

Editors: Rey Chow, H. D. Harootunian, and Masao Miyoshi

THE CULTURE OF JAPANESE FASCISM

Edited by Alan Tansman

DUKE UNIVERSITY PRESS
DURHAM AND LONDON
2009

Designed by Amy Ruth Buchanan
Typeset in Quadraat by Tseng
Information Systems, Inc.
Library of Congress Cataloging-
in-Publication Data appear on the
last printed page of this book.

Duke University Press gratefully
acknowledges the support of
Columbia University, which
provided funds toward the
production of this book.

CONTENTS

MARILYN IVY

Foreword:
Fascism, Yet?

■ Last week as I was waiting for the subway at Times Square station, I noticed a woman as she was coming off the train, fixed as I was by the enormous purple button pinned to her coat. In large white letters it asked, "Is It Fascism Yet?" I exchanged a knowing glance with a fellow passenger as we pushed into the car. "It's getting there," he said wanly as we pulled away.

Fascism—as name, idea, political system, worldview, culture—seems ever to produce the difficulty of knowing whether or not it has arrived, yet. Historically referencing Germany and Italy circa 1930, ever beholden to particular European times and places, fascism provokes uncertainties about its reach, metaphorical and otherwise. How will we know when it's fascism? Just like the question "Are we having fun yet?" the question "Is it fascism yet?" spurs us to wonder "Well, is it?" ("Well, are we?"). Or, alternatively, of course, with the barb already embedded in the question, we feel sure of the implied irony: we know that it is fascism, already. How much fascism is necessary before one can answer the question in the affirmative? When do we know fascism is fascism?

One possible answer is that we know fascism is fascism when it's too late, always after the fact. What my moment on the subway and others disclose is that fascism is a notion that outstrips its historical reference, one that has a theoretical and reflective afterlife that can allow us to think about a range of problems that weren't, aren't, thinkable otherwise. Like other comparative concepts — *modernity*, for example — the notion of fascism generates comparative frenzy and anxiety, a constant search to find and verify just one more fact that would allow us to claim that Japan, say, was a fascist state. Indeed, as Alan Tansman shows in his introduction to this volume, by the mid-1980s there was a "consensus" that the term *fascism* was not applicable to Japan. That consensus is no longer unbroken (if it ever was); as these essays and others seek to reveal, the arrival of fascism, the fantasy and culture of fascism, is known by its aftereffects and signs, its traces and remainders in domains seemingly distant from that of the political.

I can't think about fascism without thinking about Max Horkheimer and Theodor Adorno and their *Dialectic of Enlightenment* and the legacy of other, related critical theorists — notably, Walter Benjamin, of course, but also Ernst Bloch. For them, fascism had and has everything to do with the limits of capital, with the attempt to overcome those limits through the uncanny twins of gleaming technology and bloody archaism, both made productive through the spectacle of mass culture and its technological reproducibility.

As many have remarked, most vividly Slavoj Žižek in recent years, fascism describes an attempt to have capitalism without capitalism — to have your capitalism and eat it, too, at the same time as it most assuredly devours you. As he states, "The fascist dream is simply to have *capitalism without its 'excess,' without the antagonism that causes its structural imbalance*."[1] What would capitalism be without excess? It would, in a sense, be a "capitalism without capitalism." It would be a capitalism without the specter of class division and all its implications. It would be a capitalism without the terror of labor unrest, of revolution — and the trains would run on time. To erase class divisions by appealing to the nation as an organic community that transcends these divisions while keeping in place existing property relations — that, perhaps, is the core vocation of fascism.

Fascism — or perhaps, if we prefer, the fascist fantasy — comes in to regulate the dangerous excesses of capitalism. It is important to remember, however, that the excessiveness of capitalism is its normal state; there is no time when balance and stasis will be or can be reached. Capitalism utterly depends on unevenness, and its state of normalcy is one of hysterical, excessive production. And that is why a discourse of the Master or Leader—of the Subject presumed to know—emerges repeatedly to regulate excess, to get rid of social antagonisms. At the same time, this dangerous excess is placed outside the social body.

In Japan, the emperor occupied this position of Master, although not in the same modality as Hitler or Mussolini. The emperor, placed at the point of origin, also became the projected, mass-mediated *effect* of an always existing nation, notwithstanding—or perhaps because of—the reality of his distanced and deferred image. The figure of the emperor was thus both origin and projection, both subject and object. Excess was purged, assigned to the outside, as the foreign: the outside as the West, as the source of capitalist excess, of decadent modernity—or the foreign within: Koreans and communists, most notably. The aversion and fear of this excess was not only of the foreign as such but of that which embodies abstract universality, that which can't be contained within the corporatist fantasy of a community in which all participate as fraternalized beings (here, in the embrace of the emperor). The idea that an "individual can directly, irrespective of his or her place within the social organism, participate in the universal" (for example, as upheld in the idea of human rights) was thus anathema.[2] Such abstract universality is the stigmata of Western modernity; thus, it was this modernity that cried out to be overcome in the name of an organically unified nation-culture.[3] Instead of the ceaseless displacement of capitalism, a formation in which everyone would know his own place was theorized to encompass a global hierarchy. Organic community was restored under the gaze of the Master, who also became the effect of the gaze of the national masses (Takashi Fujitani is to be thanked here for elucidating this dimension of emperorship in Japan).[4] What disturbs this organicism was disallowed—modernity itself (although not technology as such)—and could only be definitively eliminated by the drive toward total war, as developed in the writings of Japanese ideologues and philosophers of the period. (Note that this narrative does not engage the question of how the West, for example, entered and perturbed the existing communal space of Japan; German fascists had their memories of oppression to reference, as well. But the question remains as to how these antagonisms constitutive to capitalism were occluded in Japan.)

The "corporatist temptation," the temptation to return to unmediated communal identification, is in fact the "necessary reverse of capitalism," in Žižek's words. Capital always already inscribes the possibility and the *ne-cessity* of this reversal. In its seeming external negation of liberal, capitalist democracy, fascism in fact completes, as its "*internal negation*," the truth of capitalist democracy.[5] That is why Horkheimer and Adorno, generalizing from Auschwitz to the entire Enlightenment project, speak of the dialectical entwinement of myth and enlightenment, of the "wholly enlightened earth . . . radiant with triumphant calamity."[6] And that is why, in their analysis of the American culture industry, they can talk about the virtual fascism of the consumer in the midst of that which many presume to be the obverse of fascism: American liberal democracy. Fascism is the internal negation of capitalism; to negate the negation, something else must occur (in the classic sense, communism). We are ever naive if we think of democracy, that is, as the obverse of fascism.

Japanese fascism (can we call it that?) strove to institute a world where everyone knew his place, while still working to keep capitalist relations of production intact. Thus, the economy had to be subordinated to the ideological-political domain, while the ideological-political domain was stylized through the techniques and technologies of mass cultural pro-duction, in turn subordinated to the aesthetic demands of the "mass orna-ment" and to the codified and singular norms of Japanese beauty.[7]

We see here the contours of a reactionary modernism that was enabled by the spatial bifurcation (one indeed instituted by colonial relations) of the West and the East and the resolution that called for Western technology and Eastern spirit, the Japanese version of the German amalgam of technology and culture. This split position was virtually ordained historically by Japa-nese attempts to form a national unity in the face of the West (a unity that could not be attained without the powers of capital and technology), and this split position is a fundamental armature of the fascist fantasy in Japan. It is a fantasy that emerges with the placing of Japan within the narrative of global capitalist unevenness.

Ernst Bloch was profoundly attuned to this dimension of unevenness in capitalism, to the antagonisms that cannot be sutured, and to the different forms of temporality that then emerge: what he called non-synchronous synchronicity. He was also attuned to the intoxication of fascism, of folk-loric nationalism, and to the spooky repetitions of "old dreams," as he called them. He understood the pleasures to be had in fascist identifica-tions, pleasures that the left could not mobilize.[8] In the archaic revivals of interwar Japan, we find a similar reinscription of ghostliness across the non-contemporaneous contemporaneity of the country and the city, the peasant and the petite bourgeoisie. And we find, as well, machineries of desire that proffered the transferential pleasures of identification with power in the guise of the emperor and in the sacrifices of total war.

If we think of the fascist fantasy as an integral part of the structure of capitalism, as a constitutive moment in the dialectic of enlightenment, then we won't find it illegitimate to think of Japan as permeated with something we could call fascism in the interwar years. Nor would we think it strange to ask, "Is It Fascism Yet?" in any existing capitalist nation. That fantasy is always cultural, to the extent that fantasy is symbolic, but more important, it is the fantasy of culture itself that gives shape to many of the aesthetic and philosophical enterprises circulating around the fascist sign. That is, culture—the notion of culture—emerges as that which *also* works precisely to erase the political (that is, class division and unevenness) and the traumas of capitalism (the commodity form itself). While we can invoke "culture" to signify, most broadly, the aesthetic, an awareness of this other nomination of culture is crucial for an attempt to bring together the notions of culture and fascism. With fascism, what is revealed is what was fascistic about culture to begin with (think of the invocations of "German culture" or "Japanese culture"). Attention to the fascistic potential in the modern notion of culture itself, such that the culture of fascism can also imply the fascism of culture; attention to fascism as the internal negation of capitalism; and attention to the synchronous non-synchronicity of the competing temporalities fascist fantasies strive to collapse: these are three forms of attention that will help us determine whether it really is fascism yet, in Japan or elsewhere, then or now.

Notes

1. Slavoj Žižek, *Tarrying with the Negative: Kant, Hegel, and the Critique of Ideology* (Durham: Duke University Press, 1993), 210. Emphasis in the original.
2. Slavoj Žižek, *The Žižek Reader*. Elizabeth Wright and Edmond Wright, eds. (Malden, Mass.: Blackwell Publishers, 1999), 138.
3. See Harry Harootunian's magisterial *Overcome by Modernity: History, Culture and Community in Interwar Japan* (Princeton, N.J.: Princeton University Press, 2001).
4. Takashi Fujitani, *Splendid Monarchy: Power and Pageantry in Modern Japan* (Berkeley: University of California Press, 1996).
5. Slavoj Žižek, *Tarrying with the Negative*, 210.
6. Max Horkheimer and Theodor Adorno, *Dialectic of Enlightenment: Philosophical Fragments* (Stanford, Calif.: Stanford University Press, 2002), 1.
7. See Siegfried Kracauer, *The Mass Ornament: Weimar Essays* (Cambridge, Mass.: Har-

vard University Press, 2005). On the place of Japanese aesthetics in fascist times, see Leslie Pincus, *Autheticating Culture in Interwar Japan: Kuki Shūzō and the Rise of a National Aesthetic* (Berkeley: University of California Press, 1996).

8. See in particular the essays in Ernst Bloch, *The Heritage of Our Times* (Berkeley: University of California Press, 1996).

ALAN TANSMAN

Introduction:
The Culture of Japanese Fascism

■   The essays in this volume examine the relationship between culture and fascism in Japan in the decades preceding the end of the Pacific War in 1945. Gathering the evidence of a culture of fascism that was not always so named, the authors are more concerned with the diffusion of fascism as ideology and representation than with its origins and consequences as a political movement or regime.

Though a number of essays offer definitions of fascism and explore how Japanese culture and thought in the interwar years can profitably be understood as fascist, the volume as a whole does not present a unified definition of "fascism," or even a uniform picture of Japan in these years. Indeed, some contributors resist applying the term and concept to Japan, even as they find areas of congruence with fascist states and cultural forms elsewhere. As a whole, however, the volume does argue for the presence of a fascist culture in Japan and for the presence of fascistic ways of healing the crisis of interwar modernity. It is an assumption of most of the essays, and of the conception of the volume itself, that to understand the Japanese inflection of fascism, we would benefit more from observing its marks on culture than from comparing political details in the hope of finding a kind of fascism that fits a generic definition across societies. As Mark Neocleous reminds us, focusing on the actual content of policies "obscures the common ideological prescriptions behind them."[1] Kevin Doak sets the tone by examining fascism in the 1930s not as an established political system, but as an ideology that sought to intervene in culture as the first step toward the eventual control of political institutions and ideology.

Until fairly recently, scholars of Japanese history and culture, both inside Japan and out, generally treated the question of fascism in its political manifestations. The debates among these scholars over the very applicability of the term to the Japanese state (was it fascist the way Italy and Germany were?) dampened the possibility not only of analyzing Japan's fascism (if it wasn't fascist like Germany and Italy, then it wasn't fascist), but also of examining its cultural manifestations (if Japan wasn't fascist, it couldn't have had a fascist culture).[2]

There have been exceptions to this rule, of course. It seems that as insistently as American scholars have asserted that Japan should not be considered fascist, Japanese scholars have applied the term more freely—perhaps because, having lived through the 1930s, many of them knew in their bones how the regime differed from other regimes.[3] The groundwork for this understanding of Japan as fascist was established by such scholars, journalists, and writers who lived through fascism and who were attuned to the sphere of culture and language.[4]

According to Richard Torrance's essay in this volume, by the time of Japan's invasion of Manchuria in 1931, the terms *fascism* (*fuashizumu*), *fascist* (*fuassho*), and *fascsistization* (*fuasshoka*) had already been in circulation and were "supported by a body of political theory that seemed to correspond to Japan's social, political, and cultural realities." For the Marxist philosopher Tosaka Jun, in 1937 the debate over the existence of fascism in Japan was over.

Tosaka was perhaps the most penetrating and sustained prewar analyst of the relationship of fascist culture to politics in Japan. He described Japanese fascism as a response to the contradictions of capitalism, suffusing politics, culture, and daily life, generally accepted and experienced by a great breadth of people, knowingly or not, across educational and class lines, including students, politicians, the petite bourgeoisie, farmers, and laborers. Tosaka argued that there was no ideal form of fascism with intrinsic qualities, and that with some differences its inflection in Japan was of a kind with other fascisms in the world.[5] Fascism in Japan may have differed from that of Italy and Germany in its intellectual roots and in its having

ALAN TANSMAN

2

been imposed from above rather than associated with a mass movement from below, but even those differences were fast disappearing as fascism gained momentum. The term itself was important to Tosaka because it allowed him to insist on Japan's kinship to European fascism; to call the Japanese case too "special," he argued, could result in losing the sense in which it was indeed part of global fascism.[6]

Tosaka's understanding of the relationship of culture to fascism was prescient. In his essay "Against the Nazi Control of the Arts" (1937), he likened the silencing of critical thought in Japan to that in Nazi Germany. Central to Japan's fascism, he argued, was the worship of beauty and the government ban on critique.[7] At the heart of fascism, that is, lay the manipulation of representation and language. Tosaka noted that when not only movements such as the antifascist Jinmin Sensen (People's Front), treated extensively by Richard Torrance in this volume, but also the use of the term *people's front* itself, were banned because they were seen to damage the national essence (*kokutai*), problems of language had reached the level of law, and a theory of grammar had become a theory of political control. In "Nihonshugisha no bungakka (Japanism into Literature)" (1937), Tosaka took on the culture critic (*bungei hyōronka*) Kobayashi Hideo, the kind of thinker Tosaka considered fundamental to the functioning of fascism, and whom Harry Harootunian in this volume reveals to have attempted to mystify everyday life by the appeal of the auratic, timeless, fascist moment. Dominating Japanese letters in 1936, critics such as Kobayashi lent their work to smoothing over the economic, political, social, cultural, and class conflicts that wracked Japanese society. To Tosaka, it was no coincidence that such ideological work was being done by literature, and it was particularly dangerous that it was being done so, because literary ideas, he argued, easily became "ideologies of literature (*bungakushugi*)" that rejected positivism and logic and then served up aesthetic models for the social world. The fruit of such literary thinking was "Japanism," by which Tosaka meant the ideology of Japanese fascism. Tosaka saw that "Japanism," first laughed away in the realm of social thought, had worked its way back to society through the realm of literature, which could easily accommodate its mythmaking capacity. Literature thus came to serve the authorities as a "troop of trumpeters" unifying ideology. Tosaka called these literary intellectuals "critics writing in the mode of love and devotion (*aijōteki hyōronka*)." They made fascism palatable to liberal-thinking people who did not like fascism as a "mode" of being or thinking but found it attractive when associated with words like "love," "art," or "tradition."[8]

Tosaka was describing a situation in which private languages became bound, through the combined force of censorship, inculcation, and the threat of punishment, to the words of the state. Fascism was thus the product of an atmosphere seeded by purveyors of culture and also of the inculcation of that atmosphere through official channels. The "culture of fascism," Tosaka argued, was, like atmosphere, there to be sensed, even if denied by those who created it.[9] The government understood how to work atmosphere all too well. It employed what one censor called a "tacit pressure (*mugon no atsuryoku*)" to have ideology accepted "naturally" by "creating atmosphere (*kūkizukuri*)."[10] It was this spell of the atmosphere of fascism—functioning "like the gears of a giant opaque machine," in the words of the critic Aono Suekichi in the 1930s—that the antifascist writers of "the spirit of prose" (discussed by Richard Torrance) warned their readers to guard against.

In the 1930s, Tosaka Jun was already well on his way to discerning the aesthetic dimension of fascism. The general use of the term *fascism* in the 1930s in its transliterated version preserves the etymology of the word, which is to "bind." That original meaning helps us understand the "fascist aesthetic," which reduced messy variety to timeless uniformity. If modernity meant social abstraction resulting from increased urbanization and industrialization, threats of civil strife and economic uncertainty, and the dreadful consequences of mass consumption and commodification, then a discourse of harmony appealed to a timeless culture as an anchor of community and offered a restoration of cultural wholeness by poeticizing fractured daily life into a harmonious, timeless, artistic space untouched by modernity—a mythic space evoked, for example, in the writings of the novelist Kawabata Yasunari, which Nina Cornyetz reveals in this volume to be doing the work of the "fascist aesthetic"—an aesthetic that, in Susan Sontag's description, glorifies surrender, exalts mindlessness, and glamorizes death.[11] Fascist aesthetics attempted to resolve the conflicts of modernity itself, calling for a complete submission either to absolute order or to a violent, undifferentiated, but liberating moment of violence, or what Angus Lockyer here calls an "epiphanic abolition of . . . distance."

Tosaka Jun's work in the 1930s provided one possibility for seeing through this atmosphere. This was a possibility for years left behind. Building on Tosaka, Maruyama Masao began in the late 1940s to analyze Japanese fascism not as a state structure but as a movement. Maruyama, the most influential postwar Japanese analyst of Japanese fascism, argued that what differentiated Japanese fascism from European fascism was that it took hold gradually, as military, political, and bureaucratic forces were stimulated from below by outbursts of radical fascism. The fascist movement from below was then absorbed into the totalitarian transformation that was taking place above, until, finally, the international situation required absolute unity.

To Maruyama, these outbursts from below, inaugurated by intellectuals such as Kita Ikki, who called for constructing a revolutionized Japan, were "movements close to fascism in the true sense of the word."[12] What Maruyama called "radical fascism" became active after the Manchurian Incident in 1931—the unauthorized attack on and seizing of a Chinese garrison by the Japanese field army, leading to the conquest and pacification of Manchuria and the creation of the Japanese puppet state, Manchukuo—eventually resulting in assassinations and attempted assassinations of government officials. Yet, Maruyama argued, the idealism of Japanese fascism never allowed it to develop into a large-scale party capable of concrete action and political control. As for radical fascism "from below," it came to an end in a failed coup by imperial loyalists in 1936, fueled by the thinking of Kita Ikki and intended to effect a spiritual reformation of Japan by restoring the Imperial Way of government.[13]

By seeing fascism in Japan through the prism of European fascisms, and by localizing it in radical fascist groups, Maruyama may have set the stage for its later conceptual dismissal, even as his emphasis on fascism as a movement suggests a shift to the cultural sphere, to the realm of consciousness and belief and, by extension, to representation. Yet as much as Maruyama helps us move in this direction, he does not take us far enough in seeing Japan's fascism as a local inflection of a global, cultural phenomenon—precisely what Tosaka had uncovered.

By 1960, Japanese scholars easily used the word, but more as a talismanic signifier of the bad recent past than as an analytic term. Emphasis was given to the particularity of Japan's fascism, to "Japanese-style fascism (nihongata fasshizumu)" or "emperor-system fascism (tennōsei fashizumu)."[14] Analysis of the "emperor system" as the force behind the mass mobilization that led to war was first articulated by Maruyama and others in the postwar years. The emperor system, it was argued, monolithically imposed obeisance in the name of the mythology of national cause. It was the product of the Meiji government's ideological machinations, in the last decades of the nineteenth century and the first decades of the twentieth century, to mystify the nature of the state, and it made the people submissive to the goals of the state through internal psychological inculcation and external force.[15] For Irokawa Daikichi, the emperor system was a "spiritual structure" controlling people from within, a perfectly functioning ideology, for "once within its confines, the corners of the box obscured in the darkness, the people were unable to see what it was that hemmed them in."[16]

Though the analysis of the emperor system would seem to imply an understanding of Japan as having partaken of global fascism while inflecting it through its own idiom, in fact greater emphasis was given to the emperor side of the phrase, while fascism remained relatively unanalyzed, merely signifying Japan's past of repression and colonialism.[17] In fact, the use of the figure of the emperor system displaced fascism as a lens through which to understand the workings of a more global ideology. It has preserved (among Marxists and non-Marxists alike) a particular category for Japan, rather than seeing it as an inflection of a global phenomenon.

It is an analysis of the cultural sphere that allows Japan to be seen as one of a number of modern, fascist nations in the years between the ends of the two world wars.[18] This is because culture is where fascism gathers its ideological power. As Slavoj Žižek writes, "The ideological power of fascism lies precisely in the feature which was perceived by liberal or leftist critics as its greatest weakness: in the utterly void, formal character of its appeal, in the fact that it demands obedience and sacrifice for their own sake."[19] In recent years, analyzing fascism in its cultural form has become less uncommon than it once was. Making a link between regime and culture during the interwar years in Japan, Leslie Pincus has noted a "fascist turn in cultural discourse." Harry Harootunian has described a "fascist temperament" in the 1930s that fueled a language of renewal and harmony and attempted to recover a spiritual state of culture in order to heal social fissures. This aesthetic discourse aimed at poeticizing everyday life by offering the myth of a harmonious social order and by appealing to a timeless culture and community in the face of a fracturing mass culture of consumption.[20]

Once one's eyes are adjusted by the lens of culture, the terms used to describe European fascism come to work for Japan, as well. Fascism, in Roger Griffin's phrase, converts cultural despair into passionate purpose. It draws its inspiration from the past, not merely in an act of nostalgia, but as a means of providing a this-worldly cure to malaise and anomie by regimenting people's lives and creating consensus through propaganda, indoctrination, repression, and terror directed at internal and external enemies. The "core myth" of fascism provides the possibility for an experience of immediacy and unity that counters the alienation and fragmentation of the modern individual.[21]

We can add to this core myth Neocleous's analysis of the common ideology of fascism that runs through Italian, German, and Spanish fascisms, despite local differences, and that applies to Japan, as well. According to Neocleous, fascism emerged as a reaction to the threats of social and political divisions created in the crisis of capitalism in the years following the First World War. In particular, it was a reaction to the threat of modernity in its political forms, whether Marxism or liberalism. Based on earlier romantic philosophies, fascism promised an end to class division by evoking a myth of a state and a nation unified by the natural bonds of its people through their blood and spirit. Fascism wanted cohesion and offered it in a language of faith that appealed, through images and myths, to feelings rather than ideas, sentiments rather than rational thoughts. It called for a unity that is "natural," like a family's, in which individuals might gain a spontaneous, intuitive grasp of their relationship to a more powerful entity and a feeling for their calling to a higher spiritual unity. Fascism elevated the will to an ideal, praising the intuitive act over the intellectually self-reflective act. In this way, it was an assault on Enlightenment values of rational positivism.[22]

Fascism was, then, an ideology for molding and controlling the masses to nationalize them—or to nationalize them to mold and control them—in the name of a myth of nature—of a "natural" nation with no history but is timeless, like myth, made of individuals connected through bonds of nature.[23] In place of history, fascism emphasized nature; in place of politics, it evoked beauty. In his essay in this volume, Harry Harootunian argues that the cultural critic Kobayashi Hideo partook of the language of fascism by replacing the lived time of history and politics with the timeless space of eternal beauty.

Fascism found a solution to alienation and exploitation not in a radical change in economic systems, but also in policies and rhetoric ostensibly meant to beautify work, the workplace, and everyday life. Such an effort lay behind the proposal for reforming school dormitory life by Japan's largest and most influential folk art organization, the Mingei Kyōkai (Folk-Craft Association), analyzed here by Kim Brandt. Though published in 1941 and never realized, the proposal was, according to Brandt, an exemplary and "recognizably fascist effort to employ aesthetics as a means of increasing industrial productivity for total war":

> In Japan as well as in Germany or Italy or France, one of the central goals of fascist thinkers and policymakers was to create a beautiful new society in which individuality could be both exalted and sublated by the

exquisite discipline of national unity and sacrifice. This vision had very concrete uses in mobilizing national subjects and resources for wartime labor and privation, but it was also held out as an end in and of itself. The ideal of "one hundred million hearts beating as one," as one of the most often quoted slogans of wartime Japan put it, was presented as a source of aesthetic gratification, as well as of virtue and strength.

Ultimately, fascism, argues Neocleous, is the culmination of a conservative revolutionary tradition, with roots in Nietzsche and Bergson and intellectual branches that reached across national boundaries, encompassing modern and modernist writers such as Ezra Pound and Wyndham Lewis in the United States and England, Gottfried Benn in Germany, F. T. Marinetti and Gabriele d'Annunzio in Italy, Georges Sorel in France, and Ernesto Giménez Caballero in Spain. Fascism thus cannot be separated from modernism. An exchange of ideas—both modernist and fascist ideas—across Europe aligned Nazism with Italian fascism, though each employed different ideological mechanisms and styles of rhetoric according to its own traditions.

Japan was part of the same conversation. Japan's confrontation with modernity was coeval with Europe's, and Japanese intellectuals maturing in the 1920s were as likely to know European texts as much as Japanese. By the 1920s, the background of any educated Japanese encompassed modern European literature and philosophy as much as—often more than—Japanese traditions of philosophical and political thought. Modernism and fascism were the lingua franca spoken fluently in Japan and in Europe and, combined with local traditions and European letters, they fueled the organicist thought and rhetoric that underpinned fascism. The social, economic, and cultural conditions that gave birth to European fascism were also shared by Japan, and the solutions, through the state's imposition of mythic thinking that extolled natural bonds of blood and demanded devotion and sacrifice of the individual to the state, nation, or lineage, backed by coercion at home, in the name of the domination of peoples of poorer bloodline abroad, made Japan one among other fascist nations.

Japan's Crisis of Modernity and Fascist Mobilization

In the 1930s, the 1920s ideology of cosmopolitan liberalism and its ideal of the integrity of the free individual were already losing ground to a political ideal of communitarianism and a rhetoric of authenticity that called for restoring a sense of true "Japaneseness."²⁴ Intellectuals argued for the abandonment of the belief in individuality—an abstract, modern notion that festered at the core of the crisis—and searched for an identity grounded in native culture and life or mediated through absolute identification with the "people (minzoku)" and the state.²⁵ The individual was viewed not only as selfish, but also as an inadequate source of meaning, while the "people" and the state became idealized as the sources of meaningful action and identity. Intellectuals critiqued modernity as an insufficient vehicle for either national or personal identity: it had led to a dead end that needed to be overcome.²⁶ The revolt against modernity registered by writers was a revolt of writers betrayed by modernity's promise.

The earthquake that destroyed Tokyo in 1923 left in its wake dramatic physical evidence of the power of destruction, particularly of the fragility of the modern metropolis, feeding both the anxiety and the hope that the city and culture that had been destroyed could be invented anew.²⁷ During the next decade, unemployment in the cities, fear of starvation in the countryside, right-wing assassinations, military coups, and the creation of a Japanese puppet state in Manchuria suffused Japanese life, through government propaganda, popular culture, and the media, with an atmosphere of imminent, dramatic transformation that lent various new ideologies meant to "overcome the modern," as the 1941 symposium of intellectuals was named, a tone of crisis. From 1932 on, this was termed by the government and media a "state of emergency (hijōji)." The rhetoric of "emergency" transformed Japan into a place of eternal crisis, thus providing the atmospheric backing needed, in the name of national survival, to increase the power of the military, rationalize Japanese hegemony over East Asia, and eliminate dissent at home.²⁸

This sense of crisis laid the groundwork for a "politics of despair," which Fritz Stern described as fundamental to the growth of fascism in Germany. The mood of the times was encapsulated by the catch phrases "overcoming the modern (kindai no chōkoku)" and "malaise (fuan)." Malaise—the emotional correlative of the political "emergency"—entered everyday language as a result of the 1934 translation into Japanese of Lev Shestov's Dostoevsky and Nietzsche: The Philosophy of Tragedy (1903), which sold thousands of copies and provoked a flurry of essays by intellectuals who saw in it a statement of their own disillusionment and anxiety. In 1933, the philosopher Miki Kiyoshi had associated Shestov with the word "malaise," which to him meant a vague sense of crisis. Miki cited Martin Heidegger as the philosopher of malaise par excellence and likened the spiritual crisis in Japan—which he said had begun in 1931 with the conquest of Manchuria—to the one that overtook the Europe of Heidegger and Andre Gide.[29]

Only a drastic cure could heal the "confusion of everyday life, the futility and blindness of cultural life," despaired Hirato Renkichi (1893–1922), the translator of F. T. Marinetti's Futurist Manifesto in 1921. The cure, according to Hirato, would take the form of a musical moment of wholeness and the binding together of all things: "the musical condition of Futurism develops into an absolute symphony of the spirit and the skies, a freedom that allows all things to flow into one another, a magnificent orchestra that binds all things together in an organic relationship."[30]

Eight years after Hirato made his pronouncement, the Japanese Dadaist Tsuji Jun (1885–1944) expressed a feeling of creative despair: "Realism, Naturalism, Romanticism, human socialism, bourgeoisie, proletariat, Expressionism, Dada—it makes my head ache just hearing their names. Naturalist novels, Symbolist poems, Romantic dramas, literature awakened to class-consciousness—they should all just do as they please." Whereas Hirato could still envision an escape from modern alienation, Tsuji had lost any sense of authority outside the self, and thus any set of objective ethical or aesthetic values. "Gods, Buddhas, humanity, society, freedom, the nation" were nothing more than a "changing of idols." To Tsuji, all Japanese culture was beyond repair: "the age rushes along, the flow of the currents of thought surges upon us and is greedily sucked up by the fresh minds and the instincts of the new age. Stemming the tide through base and absurd methods is even more pathetic. One might better surrender, helmets removed, the rotting bourgeois castle. It is a great pity that one's eyes only open when the fire is in one's own storehouse."[31]

I quote a Futurist and a Dadaist not to imply any necessary connection between their aesthetics and fascism but to remind us that the "fascist" response to cultural crisis took place across the spectrum of participants in culture. Avant-garde and Futurist artists were as disturbed by the increasing abstraction of language as were neo-traditionalist writers. For both the right and the left, as Harry Harootunian has argued, the task was to overcome the division, disunity, and fragmentation that contemporary society was experiencing. Such cures to the crisis of modernity's fragmentation were laid out in arguments, or evocations, of timeless communities, arts, or artistic practices that aestheticized history and social life by imagining an organic community, apotheosizing the "folk," and waging what the cultural critic Kobayashi Hideo often referred to as an assault against abstraction.

The assault was felt in the shocks of economic depression, military expansion, repressive government intervention in social conflicts (between labor and management), right-wing terror, cultural malaise, and fear of the Anglo-American powers; these provided the context for state-controlled mobilization for what the state called a "holy war (*seisen*)" under the banner of harmony and order at home and expansion and control abroad. This reached a climax in Prime Minister Konoe Fumimaro's outline of a "New Order" in 1940, which, through the Imperial Rule Assistance Association, glorified the national body and called for military hegemony and the creation of an autarchic economic empire. The intellectuals in Konoe's brain trust, the Shōwa Kenkyūkai (Shōwa Research Center),[32] spoke a language close to that of European fascist thinkers and promoted a political structure akin to that found in Italy and Germany, attempting to take charge of all aspects of economic, political, and cultural life and striving to unite "the masses" in an attitude of reverence for one quasi-divine figure (in this case, the emperor). These intellectuals, like their fascist counterparts in Europe, argued for a new society to heal the ills of a crisis in society and saw control of freedom as part of that cure, for through control would be won a higher form of freedom.

The government mobilized collectivism, war, and expansion and promoted a new culture it deemed befitting Japan's history and ethnicity. A combination of restrictive laws and the creation of local organizations set up to repress dissent and inculcate state values on a mass scale was orchestrated by the government's "National Mobilization (*kokka sōdōin*)," whose ultimate goal was to "extinguish oneself through service to the state (*messhi hōkō*)."[33]

The ideological underpinnings of inculcation were kept abstract enough to be flexible—Japanese ideologues could fill fascism with a wide variety of content. The reach of the state extended throughout the realms of education, cultural expression, entertainment, and the media, casting an oppressive pall over expression and action through surveillance, mass propaganda, and censorship, and backed by police repression.[34]

The government attempted to rationalize all aspects of life. How one nurtured the spirit (in worship), trained the body (in exercise), celebrated life's progress (in weddings), created one's image (through clothing or hairstyles, which would match the national spirit and essence), and nurtured one's body (with food and sport) and senses (in the arts) would reflect the directives of centralized organizations. The material side of life was to be restricted and focused throughout the nation, in local control organizations and centralizing forces such as the draft.[35] Appeals would be made to modify the "people's lifestyle (*kokumin seikatsu*)" to invigorate the "people's health (*kokumin kenkō*)," and to limit the more frivolous pleasures of life, summed up by the phrase "erotic grotesque nonsense (*eroguronansensu*)." National mobilization meant the beginning of the end of the pursuit of material comfort and pleasure—the end, that is, of the fun of urban life.[36] The time for play was over, except, perhaps, for spiritual play. Through a reading of the detective fiction of Edogawa Ranpo, James Reichert explores how this impulse to homogeneity and purity represented a stay against the modern mess, against the pleasure of the erotic, grotesque, and nonsensical, and that mess's threatening transgression of fascist ideals. Keith Vincent's examination of the detective novel *The Devil's Disciple* (1929) examines a dizzying narrative of paranoia that displays a desire for the demands of fascist binding even as it exposes and resists it:

> If the modern detective novel finds such clean closure indispensable, its precondition is to be found in another impossible project, described famously by Hirabayashi [Hatsunosuke] in an earlier essay as "the maintenance of the national order through a complete (*kansei sareta*) system of written laws." The use of writing to "complete" a system of laws and to bring a novel to a single closural point is among the most cherished fantasies of modernity. In a culture of fascism it becomes an obsession. The fact that it is a fantasy is a knowledge that most detective and legal fictions work to suppress. Their chronic failure or principled refusal to do so are symptoms of and resistances to a culture of fascism that seeks to cure itself through the production of increasingly implausible fictions.

At the state level, the "cure" for the messiness and harshness of material reality was to come through the elevation of spiritual values. The attempted reach of the state into the realm of the spirit was manifest in the new configuration of labor organizations, organized through the concept of "labor–capital fusion," referring to an ideal unity of purpose, fusing worker and manager with the emperor as one mind and one spirit.[37] (Even baseball was played as a spiritual venture in novels of the time.)[38]

Having a Japanese spirit meant having the authority of Japanese purity. Aaron Skabelund shows how Japanese bureaucrats, with the help of private enthusiasts, projected notions of Japanese purity onto the Japanese dog, then used that dog as a tool of indoctrination. The myth and representation of Hachikō, he argues, "played a prominent role in the culture of fascism as experienced in Japan." The Hachikō phenomenon struck the liberal antifascist critic Hasegawa Nyozekan (1875–1969) in 1935 as sentimentalism gone awry and as an example of "fascism from below"; the public, "influenced by a swirl of rumor, sensational media reports, and theories," had entered a "self-hypnotic, collective psychotic" trance that allowed them to believe things that they had not experienced and that they could not rationally explain. This tendency, Hasegawa worried, "might result in similar delusions about weightier social and political issues with more dangerous consequences than those created by the fervor over Hachikō."

The Representational Vacuum

Fascism converted cultural despair into passionate purpose, providing a cure to malaise and anomie by regimenting people's lives and creating consensus through propaganda, indoctrination, repression, and terror directed at internal and external enemies.[39] The state's control of language, thought, and behavior created a vacuum that the cultural work of fascism filled. The cultural work of fascism was formed in this representational vacuum. It was through censorship codes that language was mediated for Japanese listeners, viewers, and readers. Although censorship of all media began as early as the beginnings of the modern state in the last quarter of the nineteenth century, with a tradition going back two centuries, in the mid-1930s it went even further toward creating an expressive vacuum. After 1937, the producers of newspapers, radio broadcasts, magazines, books, songs, comic books, films, and photographs were all subjected to strict codes, or subjected themselves, out of pragmatic necessity, to self-censorship. Left-wing political organizations and journals were squelched, and language thought to deter from the war effort and the unity of a citizenry behind it came under harsh review. As certain kinds of language were shut out, other kinds were pumped up. National organizations responsible for the dissemination of information or for the content and style of popular entertainment, such as the Jōhō Iinkai (Information Committee), formed in 1931, worked with the industries themselves in the censorship of ideas and language.[40] The hand of propaganda went so far as to reach into the imagination itself.

Beginning in 1937, and increasingly after 1941, popular songs uplifting the spirit of national unity were promoted, while those that did not were controlled. Sensitive to the affective power of aesthetic form, censors assumed that, when censoring songs, they were to focus not on lyrical content but on singing style.[41] In 1936, for example, the pop tune "Wasuretewa iya yo! (Don't Forget Me!)" was considered dangerous because of the singer's lascivious lingering on the final note in the title's phrase. The song's exclamatory "yo!" could, when rendered skillfully, make all too visible the sexualized body of the singer—and along with it a whole world of suppressed, tantalizing, erotic decadence.

In the film industry, as in the other media, censorship intensified in direct proportion to the medium's access to an ever growing audience. Between 1926 and 1934, the film audience, for example, increased by 60 percent—as many as 35 percent of the total moviegoers were fifteen and under, an audience primed for the "decadent" messages of popular culture and for fantasies of foreign lifestyles, as well as, on the opposite extreme, to new state propaganda. Control extended to the lyrics of popular songs thought to corrupt the national language (kokugo) with foreign phrases and expressions. Words themselves were subject to the force of direct ideological pressure. Loan words once written in the phonetic script that could transparently transliterate foreign words would now be changed to Japanese ideograms.[42] So suffused with the marks of twisted truths and of formulated propaganda were the languages absorbed by reading, listening, and watching that it would be no exaggeration to say that all thought and expression were squeezed and molded to fit into state-imposed forms.

The administration of aesthetics meant to make people support war and be willing to persevere stoically in dire conditions as war continued.[43] This effort was dubbed a "war of ideas (shisōsen)." From the time of the failed coup by imperial loyalists in 1936, imperial thought dominated the language of propaganda in phrases such as "eight corners of the world under one roof (hakkō ichiu)." From 1937 on, catch phrases like this one replaced news of casualties on the front. Language prevaricated, or simply lied, and was xenophobic. The new language conjured images of blood and race and heroism, creating what Tsurumi Kazuko calls a "halo of sanctity."[44]

As interventionist as they were, it is worth noting that artistic propaganda policies never attained the level of elaboration they had in Italy, Germany, and even Spain.[45] It is no coincidence that the essays in this volume that treat the visual work of fascist aesthetics are less at ease with the appellation "fascist" than those that examine matters of language and thought. Michael Baskett, for example, shows that the cultural interaction among the Axis powers led to imperfect and sometimes failed results and "did not lead to the successful creation of a collective 'fascist' identity," even though they had goals in common, "including an obsession with the discourse of racial purity and imperialist expansionism, as well as a belief in the ability of the medium of film to create (or destroy) national prestige on a mass level." Aaron Gerow argues that, although the Japanese did produce films meant to inculcate a citizenry with the ideals of the state, and although there was "a discursive framework for the production of stylistically fascistic texts," neither a national cinema nor a national cinematic audience ever developed that could effectively "contribute to the formation of common Japanese imaginaries, fascist or not, or to the effective aesthetic expression of the nation." In part, he argues, this was because of the very hybridity of Japanese film, and in part because of limitations on material resources and the state's unwillingness to nationalize (or lack of interest in nationalizing) mass entertainment.

In the case of architecture, Jonathon Reynolds concurs with Baskett's argument against the existence of a fascist style. The Diet building in Tokyo shared design elements with those of non-fascist states, and, more to the point, architecture and design were not used in Japan as they were in Italy and Germany. Japan never built monumental works capable of transforming urban space on a grand scale.[46] The state was not very interested in architecture and, moreover, lacked materials to execute it on a large scale. Reynolds argues that any political message the Diet building could carry was disrupted by the divisive issue of what Japaneseness meant, the availability of building materials, and arguments over the relationship between style and national identity: "the building was unable to meet the unrealistic demands placed upon it. The Diet building emerged from the war as an unhappy reminder of failed military adventurism and ineffectual political leadership."

In her discussion of the national state-sponsored competitions to choose the best designs for memorial tablets commemorating Japan's war dead, Akiko Takenaka concurs with Reynolds that there was no distinctive fascist design. But Takenaka goes on to show that the design itself, and the successful building and dissemination of actual statues, were less important in the creation of a national aesthetic than was the very process of the competition itself:

> The chūreitō [lit., "tower to the loyal spirits"] functioned like an icon in the civic religion of fascism, which, according to George Mosse, draws "its strength from an already present consensus." . . . Mosse's argument is confined to the visual expressions of fascist culture; the chūreitō project, however, helped create political consensus through its process

of creation, even more so than through its actual appearance. That consensus, fostered through education and mass culture, placed ultimate value on one's sacrifice through death to the emperor and was demonstrated not by the physical appearance of the memorials, but by individuals working throughout the process of design and construction.

Angus Lockyer also examines an aborted attempt at aesthetic management (the Japan World Exhibition to commemorate the two thousand six hundredth year of the Imperial Era, planned for 1940) and finds that no unified aesthetic program could be produced, because as the planning "confronted the lessons of experience, . . . the exhibition entered the world of trade-offs, accounting, and interest." Lockyer is interested in how fascist culture can explain how and why aesthetics and ideology could become regime and suggests that fascist regimes "were distinguished by the extent to which the production of culture became the work of the state, rehearsing these tropes in an attempt to yoke subject to regime." Spectacle, therefore, is "one point at which to connect fascist culture to fascist politics." In this regard, according to Lockyer, Japan was lacking: "it is hard to find such a spectacle in Japan, however."

In his response paper included at the end of the volume, Alejandro Yarza argues that fascist consent in Spain was forged not by a totalizing state project but through diverse means, including the dissemination of Franco's personal film projects; the inner contradictions that weighed down the cultural policies of the various national fascisms did not prevent the powerful forging of such consent, which was effected by what he calls Francoist kitsch and its politics of time. Yarza's description of the Spanish situation resonates with the Japanese, in which consent did not necessarily depend on a unified vision emanating from the state.

For Takenaka, Baskett, and Gerow, it was the very process of attempting to forge a national aestheticizing project—which some in this volume call "fascist"—more than the aesthetic objects themselves that had a political effect. They imply that insisting on seeing fascism only in its relationship to the works of regimes may occlude seeing fascism in its discursive or aesthetic forms. Also potentially occluding our vision of fascism are the ways in which fascist discourses can partake of non-fascist and antifascist discourses or even overtly disavow their own fascism. The folk-art theorist Yanagi Sōetsu, discussed by Noriko Aso, was a cosmopolitan humanist "spreading the message of a beautiful . . . way of life for all people, everywhere." Yanagi made explicitly antifascist arguments: "recently there has been a trend to imitate fascism (*fuassho*). How pitiful that even lovers of the nation (*aikokushugisha*) must learn from the West. No one has a greater unpatriotic sensibility than the Japanese fascists (*fuashisto*). It is disconcerting that Japanese learn the meaning of patriotism from Mussolini."

Japanese nationalists, Yanagi goes so far as to say, have been a cancer responsible for recent troubles. Nevertheless, despite his antifascist claims, Yanagi's aesthetics could be inflected fascistically.[47] Aso finds "striking similarities . . . between his folk-craft discourse and fascistic aesthetics of the wartime era." More broadly, his "discursive ambiguities suggest points of articulation between mid-twentieth century humanist and fascist discourses that made slipping from one to the other all too easy for many Japanese intellectuals at the time." Such slippage lay behind the work of cultural fascism. In Isaiah Berlin's words, "Few things have played a more fatal part in the history of human thought and action than great imaginative analogies from one sphere, in which a particular principle is applicable and valid, to other provinces, where its effect may be exciting and transforming, but where its consequences may be fallacious in theory and ruinous in practice."[48]

Cognizant of such slippage, we can be aware of the appearance of fascism in cultural (or political) work that does not speak fascism's name. In her discussion of the fascist aesthetics of the beautiful fiction of Kawabata Yasunari, Nina Cornyetz writes, "I would go so far as to argue that, even were there no texts by Kawabata that literally voiced support for Japan's 'mission' in Asia, the theoretical analysis of the *signifying system* that underpins Kawabata's aesthetics . . . will reveal aspects shared by the various and different political forms of fascism."

Such slippage, and the fact that fascism need not be so named to do its cultural—or political—work, may account for the political and cognitive motivations for the fascist disavowal of fascism, which plays an important structural role in the working of fascism itself and in the postwar forgetting of Japan's fascist past. This forgetting has been aided by the assumption that fascism is so particularly imposing an ideology that only the most concrete and unambiguous of evidence might sufficiently prove its presence.[49] While reading the evidence given in this volume for the fascism of Japanese culture and thought in the interwar years, we should keep caution against interpreting an ideology's lack of *complete* success as evidence of its weak effect. Imperfect penetration is no guard against a culture's (or even a regime's) work—fascist or otherwise. As Hannah Arendt remarked, "It is quite obvious that mass support for totalitarianism comes neither from ignorance nor from brainwashing."[50]

The essays in this volume are arranged according to broad generic categories. Part I, "Theories of Japanese Fascism," opens with two essays that examine how fascism was understood in Japan in the 1930s. In "Fascism Seen and Unseen: Fascism as a Problem in Cultural Representation," Kevin M. Doak discusses two early influential theorists of Japanese fascism: the Marxist Tosaka Jun and the liberal Christian Imanaka Tsugimaro. In "*The People's Library*: The Spirit of Prose Literature versus Fascism," Richard Torrance continues this discussion from the perspective of the antifascist literary group centered on the journal *Jinmin bunko* (The People's Library). Both essays keep in focus the centrality of culture to the theorization of fascism. In "Constitutive Ambiguities: The Persistence of Modernism and Fascism in Japan's Modern History," Harry Harootunian analyzes the discourse of the everyday in the writings of Tosaka Jun and Kobayashi Hideo, revealing their differing solutions to the "issues of capitalist modernization and the resulting aporias of representation." Kobayashi here emerges as a master fascist re-enchanter of the everyday for both the 1930s and the postwar years.

The essays in part II, "Fascism and Daily Life," reinforce the notion that fascism's solution to alienation and exploitation was found in efforts to beautify work, the workplace, and everyday life. In "The Beauty of Labor: Imagining Factory Girls in Japan's New Order," Kim Brandt discusses how such an effort lay behind the Japanese government's use of the ideas of the Japanese Folk-Craft Movement to create a culture of daily life infused with the beauty of preindustrial Asian objects and practices; Noriko Aso's "Mediating the Masses: Yanagi Sōetsu and Fascism," analyzes how Yanagi's humanist discourse of daily-life amelioration bled into a fascist aesthetics. The government's efforts to instill daily life with an ideology of beauty and purity is shown also in Aaron Skabelund's "Fascism's Furry Friends: Dogs, National Identity, and Purity of Blood in 1930s Japan," which describes how the symbol of a loyal dog acquired pedagogic force for promulgating values of racial purity and national essence.

Daily life was molded by public entertainment and spectacle, the focus of part III, "Exhibiting Fascism." In "Narrating the Nation-ality of a Cinema: The Case of Japanese Prewar Film," Aaron Gerow describes how the formation of a fascist cinema was limited by the conflicts over the very formation of a national cinema. Michael Baskett shows the difficulties—both ideological and commercial—involved in Japan's forming a unified filmic aesthetic with the other Axis powers, in "All Beautiful Fascists? Axis Film Culture in Imperial Japan." The same check on the creation of a singular fascist aesthetic can be seen in the memorial design competitions discussed in Akiko Takenaka's "Architecture for Mass-Mobilization: The Chūreitō Memorial Design Competition, 1939–1945," and in "Japan's Imperial Diet Building in the Debate over Construction of a National Identity," where Jonathan M. Reynolds argues that the Diet Building's symbolic value fell short of what could be called fascistic. Angus Lockyer takes this point further in "Expo Fascism? Ideology, Representation, Economy," in which he argues that the plans for a 1940 exhibition, while displaying some qualities of a fascist aesthetic, could not in the end be deemed fascist. Finally, Ellen Schattschneider, in "The Work of Sacrifice in the Age of Mechanical Reproduction: Bride Dolls and Ritual Appropriation at Yasukuni Shrine," reveals how a newly renovated military history museum in Tokyo might be read as an illustration of fascist aesthetics but also as an example of a resistance to such an aesthetics.

If the essays on visual forms of display argue for the heuristic limits, or complications, of the concept of fascism for the Japanese case, the essays in part IV, "Literary Fascism," have little difficulty locating the fascist aesthetic in the work of language. In "Fascist Aesthetics and The Politics of Representation in Kawabata Yasunari," Nina Cornyetz analyzes the aesthetic discourse of timeless harmony and its relationship to a fascist politics of violence in the writing of Kawabata Yasunari. In "Disciplining the Erotic-Grotesque in Edogawa Ranpo's *Demon of the Lonely Isle*," Reichert reads the detective fiction of Edogawa Rampo to explore how the fascist impulse toward homogeneity and purity represented a resistance to the threatening confusions of modern culture. Such threats belonged to what Keith Vincent calls a culture of paranoia, which he explores in "Hamaosociality: Narrative and Fascism in Hamao Shirō's *The Devil's Discipline*," a novel that reveals the workings of, and against, the drive toward fascism.

While we are interested in how aesthetics of Japanese fascism worked within texts and artifacts, we also want to know how they penetrated real life. James Dorsey's "Literary Tropes, Rhetorical Looping, and the Nine Gods of War: 'Fascist Proclivities' Made Real," makes the connection between culture (as rhetoric) and life (as violence) explicit by showing how true stories about Japanese submariners circulated around various modes of mass entertainment and became a model of action for flesh-and-blood young men hoping to turn hero within a culture of fascism. Their deaths, he writes, had "been rehearsed through the participation—sometimes as active producers and sometimes as passive consumers—in the communal myth." The process of securing that myth required a variegated "saturation" of the cultural sphere even more than a unified propogandistic assault.[51] As Alejandro Yarza argues in the concluding essay of this volume, a "relaxed" Francoist film policy in Spain illuminates the "hybrid and apparently contradictory ways in which fascist regimes attempted to secure ideological hegemony."

In the trenchant foreword that opens the volume, Marilyn Ivy puts a fine point on the cultural work of fascism. The fascist fantasy, she writes, "is always cultural," and "it is the fantasy of culture itself that gives shape to many of the aesthetic and philosophical enterprises circulating around the fascist sign." This volume represents an attempt to suggest the shape to that sign as it marked various works of Japanese culture.

Notes

1. See Mark Neocleous, *Fascism* (Minneapolis: University of Minnesota Press, 1997), 76. Mabel Berezin points out that much writing on European fascism has failed to distinguish between movements and regimes, ideology and state, and political impulse and political institution and has elided questions of culture, which regard "conversion mechanisms" and the assurance of consent. Concerning Franco's regime in Spain, Paul Preston cautions that applying a strict definition of fascism to Spain allows the regime to be understood as not having been fascist, and thereby to be seen as less morally distasteful. See Mabel Berezin, *Making the Fascist Self: The Political Culture of Inter-War Italy* (Ithaca, N.Y.: Cornell University Press, 1997), 9; Paul Preston, *Franco: A Biography* (London: HarperCollins, 1995), 69.

2. Abe Hirozumi's use of the term in his 1975 book exemplifies its common usage as a term of debate in discussing Japan in the 1930s. After four hundred pages of closely parsing debates over fascism in Japan he arrives at no final conclusion about its precise applicability, yet he opens his study by stating that Japan's fascism took hold in 1931—with attempted military coups, the violent takeover in Manchuria, and the formation of radical right-wing organizations—and became regularized in 1936, with the beginning of mass mobilization and mass censorship. See Abe Hirozumi, *Fuashizumu hihan no jōsetsu* (Tokyo: Miraisha, 1975). In the United States, Peter Duus and Daniel I. Okimoto argued that even in the most nuanced discussion of the concept of fascism in Japan had "passed on to the most obvious conclusion: the Japanese case is so dissimilar [to the European] that it is meaningless to speak of Japan in the 1930s as a 'fascist' political system." To them, it was clear that "the hazards of using the fascist paradigm as an analytical

tool are likely to offset its benefits." Duus's and Okimoto's argument seems to have been an effective one. By the mid-1980s, the consensus among American scholars seems to have been that the term *fascism* "must not be applied to Japan" between 1930 and 1941, for it had become analytically useless in both the United States and Japan. See Peter Duus and Daniel Okimoto, "Fascism and the History of Prewar Japan: The Failure of a Concept," *Journal of Asian Studies* (November 1979): 65–76.

3. Walter Laqueur says this about Europeans living under fascism: see Walter Laqueur, *Fascism: Past, Present, Future* (Oxford: Oxford University Press, 1996), 10.

4. On one of the earliest of such analyses, Sassa Hirō argued that Japan's incipient fascism was a response to the economic and social crises of capitalism and, as in Europe, had led to imperialist violence. Sassa hoped to distinguish Japanese from Western forms of fascism, not to strip it of its fascist inflection but to prevent Japan's fascism from going unrecognized in a general description based on a foreign model. But for him, Japanese fascism belonged to a global phenomenon. And as in Europe, in Japan it was unstoppable, even if, unlike its European variety, it had no dictator. Sassa's brave essay is riddled with Xs marking the power of the state—made either by the hand of the censor or by his own self-censoring pen. One can easily imagine that these marks of power, which must have forced Sasa to feel the pressure of the state on his language, allowed him to see the salience of the control of representation to an analysis of fascism. Through the haze created by the censors, he managed to plead with his readers to notice what was happening. "Dear reader, do you feel the rush of the times, the pressing down of its force?": Sassa Hirō, *Nihon fasshizumu no hatten katei* [The Process of Development of Japanese Fascism] (Tokyo: Asano Shoten, 1932), 106–10.

5. Tosaka Jun, "Gendai Tetsugaku Tōwa," in *Tosaka Jun zenshū*, vol. 3 (Tokyo: Keisō Shobō, 1934–37), 213–14.

6. Tosaka makes the interesting comment that the lineage of Nietzsche, Kierkegaard, and Heidegger came to Japan not as fascist thought but as philosophies of cultural freedom: see, *Nihon ideorogiiron*, in *Tosaka Jun zenshū*, vol. 2 (Tokyo: Keisō Shobō, 1966), 434.

7. Idem, "Nihonshugi no bungakka," in *Tosaka Jun zenshū*, vol. 5 (Tokyo: Keisō Shobō, 1967), 82.

8. Ibid., 86.

9. Ibid., 42–45.

10. Minami Hiroshi, "Senden—Senji no taishū sōsa," in *Shōwa Bunka 1925–1945*, Minami Hiroshi and Shakai Shinri Kenkyūjo, eds. (Tokyo: Keisō Shobō, 1987), 364.

11. Susan Sontag, "Fascinating Fascism," in *Under the Sign of Saturn* (New York: Vintage Books, 1972), 91.

12. Maruyama Masao, "The Ideology and Dynamics of Japanese Fascism," trans. Andrew Fraser, in *Thought and Behaviour in Modern Japanese Politics*, expanded ed.,

ed. Ivan Morris (Oxford: Oxford University Press, 1969), 65. Maruyama argued that Japanese fascism shared much with its European counterparts, including a rejection of individualistic liberalism, an opposition to parliamentary politics, the promotion of foreign expansion, the glorification of military buildup, a rejection of class warfare, a struggle against Marxism, and an ideological language of spirituality and idealism. What differentiates Japanese fascism, for Maruyama, is its emphasis on the nation as a family-state, the prominent position of agrarianism, and a rhetoric of the emancipation of Asian peoples from Western colonialism. Maruyama discerned three stages of the fascist movement in Japan: the preparatory period, from after the First World War until the Manchurian Incident in 1931; the period of maturity, from 1931 to the February Incident of 1936, in which a movement among civilians became concretely linked with military power that came to occupy the core of national governance; and the consummation period, in which the military, supporting fascism from above, created a ruling coalition with the bureaucracy, monopoly capital, and the political parties: see ibid., 26–27. Hasegawa Nyozekan coined the phrase "cool fascism" in 1932 to describe fascism born without violent upheaval but through existing government institutions. This was popularized by Maruyama in the 1950s. On Hasegawa, see Andrew Barshay, *State and Intellectual in Imperial Japan: The Public Man in Crisis* (Berkeley: University of California Press, 1988), 193.

13. On February 26, 1,400 troops led by junior army officers acting in the name of the emperor seized central Tokyo and killed the finance minister, the Lord Keeper of the Privy Seal, and the inspector general of the military and attacked the residence of the prime minister. Though supported by some in the military, they were opposed by others and vehemently by the emperor himself. On February 27, martial law was declared, and by February 29, the coup had been put down, and most of the soldiers dispersed. Two committed suicide, and nineteen, including the central ideologue Kita Ikki, were executed. The failed coup followed two others in 1931: the October Incident (*jūgatsu jikken*), in which ultranationalist field officers attempted to install General Sadao as head of the cabinet, eliminate parliamentary politics, and consolidate gains made in Manchuria (all those involved were dismissed); and the May Incident (*sanjūgatsu jikken*), whose plans were exposed and aborted and kept secret by the army. Many of those involved became members of the Kwantung Army and were instrumental in the takeover of Manchuria: see Ben-Ami Shillony, *The Kōdansha Encyclopedia of Japanese History*, vol. 5 (Tokyo: Kōdansha, 1983), 250.

14. See, e.g., Komatsu Shigeo, "Nihongata fasshizumu—Sono taishūteki kisoku," in *Kindai Nihon shisō kōza*, vol. 5 (Tokyo: Chikuma Shobō, 1960), 277–326; Tanaka Sōgoro, *Nihon fashizumushi* (Tokyo: Kawade Shobō, 1960). My own reading of the historiography of fascism in Japan is that Japanese scholars have been far more at ease with the term. In the 1920s, there were no analyses of fascism in Japanese, and the word itself had not entered the lexicon. Since the 1950s, the Marxist literature on fascism has been prolific, but in the 1930s only a few valiantly faced

the topic: see Gavan McCormack, "1930's Japan: Fascist?" in *Bulletin of Concerned Asian Scholars* 14, no. 2 (April–June 1982): 20–33.

15. Carol Gluck, *Japan's Modern Myths: Ideology in the Meiji Period* (Princeton, N.J.: Princeton University Press, 1985), 4–6.

16. Irokawa Daikichi, *The Culture of the Meiji Period*, trans. Marius B. Jansen (Princeton, N.J.: Princeton University Press, 1985), 246. The term itself was coined in the 1930s as an increased discrepancy between ideology and the world it described led to greater ideological rigidity and harsher enforcement of it. This process began its shift into high gear after the Russo-Japanese War of 1904–1905, after which the "national essence (*kokutai*)" became, in Irokawa's view, an un-self-conscious component of popular thinking. Irokawa has argued that the people could indeed resist the power of the emperor system, as the government well knew when it imposed it through a police state: ibid., 245. Irokawa has argued that "the emperor system was organized so that the hard, external side of the power structure—the special higher police, the military police, the Peace Preservation Law, and the other forces used to intimidate and discriminate against the lower classes—was covered up by the gentler side": ibid., 122. Carol Gluck has argued that what *tennōsei* signified was not as monolithic as has often been argued. "In what ways *tennōsei* ideology moved prewar Japanese to act as the state would have them act and in what ways it prevented them from acting differently are questions that must still be asked of the ideological process in the Shōwa period." Gluck, *Japan's Modern Myths*, 285.

17. By the 1980s, Japanese scholars had come to use the term *fascism* to identify Japan's history of repression and imperialism. See, e.g., Ban Bō, *Nihon Fashizumu* (Tokyo: Ōgetsu Shoten, 1981); Nagahama Isao, *Nihon fashizumu kyoshiron* (Tokyo: Akashi Shoten, 1984). This brand of fascism consisted of a system imposed from the top by an Army leadership that was loyal to the emperor. It was anticommunist and restricted, then eliminated, liberal civic and political freedoms by controlling economic, social, and cultural life in the name of an imperialist war whose cause it trumpeted through jingoistic and nativistic rhetoric: see the essays in Eguchi Keiichi, ed., *Nihon fasshizumu no keisei* (Tokyo: Nihonhyōronsha, 1978); Ban Bō, *Nihon fasshizumu no kōbō* (Tokyo: Rokkō Shuppan, 1989), 29–31.

18. A strong dissent against this is in Graham Parkes, "The Putative Fascism of the Kyoto School, and the Political," *Philosophy East and West* 47, no. 3 (1997): 305–36.

19. See Slavoj Žižek, *The Sublime Object of Ideology* (London: Verso, 1989), 82.

20. See Leslie Pincus, *Authenticating Culture in Imperial Japan: Kuki Shūzō and the Rise of National Aesthetics* (Berkeley: University of California Press, 1996), 247. See also Harry Harootunian, "Overcoming Modernity: Fantasizing Everyday Life and the Discourse on the Social in Interwar Japan," *Parallax* 2 (February 1996): 79–84, 88.

21. This "mythic core" can "unleash strong affective energies" through a vision of reality by positing an organic nation in a state of decay that, because it possesses

a lifecycle, can be revitalized through the manipulation of a group psyche, appealing to individuals to sacrifice themselves for a destiny that will bring them greatness: see Roger Griffin, ed., *Fascism* (Oxford: Oxford University Press, 1995), 3–8.

22. Like Marxism, it is also an assault on materialism; fascism uses the socialist language of anti-materialistic revolution shorn of socialism's basic premises: see Neocleous, *Fascism*, 38.

23. Although the German inflection may differ from the Italian—the Germans harking back to a medieval ideal of community and the Italians to a corporate ancient Rome; the Germans forging bonds by race or species and the Italians by corporate group—both (and all fascisms) demand national cohesion in the cause of war and are grounded in a philosophy of violence that forges a healthy body and develops a healthy human spirit out of an ill modern body and its fractured mind. Fascism dips into a mythic past while marching into a technologically advanced future to meld disputing masses, political parties, and economic interests into a unified nation, now deified. An individual's freedom in fascism is a freedom found not within the self but within the nation, whose power is masked as natural and spiritual. Fascism may be revolutionary in its promise to transform politics and to alter the very being and spirit of man by curing the ills caused by modernity (materialism, liberal freedom, the life of the intellect), but fascism is conservative in that it seeks to conserve capitalism, not destroy it. As much as it condemns finance capital for being nonproductive, it needs industrial capital to modernize technologically, to execute war, and to control and administer colonies: ibid., 69.

24. See Harry Harootunian and Tetsuo Najita, "The Japanese Revolt against the West: Political and Cultural Critique in the Twentieth Century," in *The Cambridge Encyclopedia of Japan*, vol. 6, ed. Peter Duus (Cambridge: Cambridge University Press, 1989).

25. Kevin M. Doak provides an overview of how ethnicity and nationalism evolved in the political discourse of early-twentieth-century Japan and became a pressing issue in the 1930s. He translates *minzoku* as "ethnic nation": see Kevin M. Doak, "Ethnic Nationalism and Romanticism in Early Twentieth-Century Japan," *Journal of Japanese Studies* 22, no. 1 (1996): 77–103.

26. In 1942, the "Overcoming Modernity" symposium summed up the period's attempt to break through the aporia to which modernity had led the Japanese. The symposium was attended by a select few, but the argument was joined by philosophers, political thinkers, and literary and cultural critics across the spectrum of political belief: See Hiromatsu Wataru, "*Kindai no chōkoku*" *ron: Showa shisōshi e no ichi shikaku* (Tokyo: Kōdansha, 1989).

27. Edward Seidensticker traces much of the anxiety and hope of the age to the event: see Edward Seidensticker, *Tokyo Rising: The City since the Great Earthquake* (Cambridge, Mass.: Harvard University Press, 1991), 8–13.

28. "Hijōji," in *Nihonkingendaishiji* (Tokyo: Tōyōkeizaishinpōsha, 1978), 573. The lan-

guage of national emergency, which included popular words such as *deadlock* (*yu-kizumari*) and *national emergency* (*jikyoku*), was used throughout the culture, even in advertising. On the language of crisis, see Sandra Wilson, "Bureaucrats and Villages in Japan," *Social Science Japan Journal*, no. 1 (1998). By the 1930s, Japan had already experienced periods of rapid social change and collapse, but the crisis in the 1930s was at a higher pitch: see Kerry Smith, *A Time of Crisis: Japan, the Great Depression, and Rural Revitalization* (Cambridge, Mass.: Harvard University Asia Center, 2001), 2–5, 379. Frederick Dickinson rightly insists on seeing the events of the 1930s as having a history beginning before the 1930s. "The Great War (World War I)," he writes, "offers telling clues of subsequent events," and the dramatic developments of the 1930s "should not be considered more than immediate catalysts to renewed aggression": Frederick Dickinson, *War and National Reinvention: Japan in the Great War, 1914–19* (Cambridge, Mass.: Harvard University Asian Center, 1999), 247–48.

29. See Miki Kiyoshi, "Fuan no Shisō to sono chōkoku," in *Miki Kiyoshi zenshū*, vol. 5 (Tokyo: Iwanami Shoten, 1985), 285–309. Miki critiques the easy acceptance by the Japanese of the language of anxiety as another example of a fascination with new European ideas that have no grounding in Japanese conditions; he then recognizes that Japan is, indeed, approaching those conditions: see ibid., esp. 285–86. Kakiwara Osamu discusses the "boom" in essays by the Marxists and non-Marxists Miki Kiyoshi, Kobayashi Hideo, Masamune Hakuchō, Yokomitsu Ryūichi, Aono Suekichi, Tosaka Jun, Kamei Katsuichirō, and others: see Kakiwara Osamu, "'Haikyo' to 'Fuan'—Shestovteki fuan," in *Kōza Shōwa Bungaku shi*, vol. 2 (Tokyo: Yūseido, 1988), 124–35. See also Kevin M. Doak, *Dreams of Difference: The Japan Romantic School and the Crisis of Modernity* (Berkeley: University of California Press, 1994), xx–xxi, 90–95.

30. Hirato Renkichi, "Watashi no miraishugi to jikko," in *Gendai bungaku no hakken—Saisho no shōtotsu* (Tokyo: Gakugeishorin, 1968), 204. Marjorie Perloff argues that Futurism can, but does not necessarily, lend itself to fascism: see Marjorie Perloff, *The Futurist Moment: Avant-garde, Avant Guerre, and the Language of Rupture* (Chicago: University of Chicago Press, 1986), 30; Cinzia Blum, *The Other Modernism: F. T. Marinetti's Futurist Fiction of Power* (Berkeley: University of California Press, 1996).

31. Tsuji Jun, "Despera," in *Gendai bungaku no hakken*, vol. 1 (Tokyo: Gakugeishorin, 1967), 8, 18, 123.

32. Rōyama Masamichi (1895–1945), Ryū Shōtarō (1900–67), and Miki Kiyoshi (1895–1945): see Valerie F. Fletcher, *Dreams and Nightmares: Utopian Visions in Modern Art*. (Washington, D.C.: Smithsonian Institution Press, 1983), 3, 156.

33. Beginning in 1925, the Peace Preservation Law gave legal leverage to crush opposition to the government; in 1928 (the year 1,600 communists or sympathizers were arrested in one crackdown), the law was amended to include the death penalty for seditious activities: Irokawa, *The Culture of the Meiji Period*, 15. Gavan McCormack gives an excellent survey of arguments about fascism in Japan from

the 1930s to the 1970s: see Gavan McCormack, "Nineteen-Thirties Japan: Fascism?" *Social Analysis* (1981): 20–30.

34. The fact that the Imperial Rule Assistance Association was not a political party pulling the strings of government but what one scholar describes as a tool of administrative mass mobilization has led to the view that it—and, by extension, the Japanese government—was neither fascist nor totalitarian, even if Japan did create a propaganda network more effective than Goebbels's own in shaping public opinion: see Ben-Ami Shillony, *Politics and Culture in Wartime Japan* (Oxford: Oxford University Press, 1981), 3–12; Thomas R. H. Havens, *Valley of Darkness: The Japanese People and World War II* (New York: W. W. Norton, 1978), 72–79, 197; Gregory Kasza, "Fascism from Below? A Comparative Perspective on the Japanese Right, 1931–36," *Journal of Contemporary History* 19 (1984): 286–90.

35. Minami and Shakai, *Shōwa Bunka 1925–1945*, 131–34, 83.

36. Ibid., 66–78.

37. Andrew Gordon, *Labor and Imperial Democracy in Prewar Japan* (Berkeley: University of California Press, 1991), 237, 327–28, 259. See also Sheldon Garon, *Molding Japanese Minds: The State in Everyday Life* (Princeton, N.J.: Princeton University Press, 1997), 5–13.

38. Minami and Shakai, *Shōwa Bunka 1925–1945*, 517–24.

39. See Griffin, *Fascism*, 3–8.

40. From its inception, radio was tied to state power and under the aegis of government control. Hundreds of thousands of listeners would hear reports from the war front. These reports, of course, were not given through the transparent medium of radio from actual places to listeners in the form of truth. News was mediated through the state—that is, through censorship codes: Minami and Shakai, *Shōwa Bunka 1925–1945*, 313, 315, 331.

41. Kirsten Cather's dissertation, "The Great Censorship Trials of Literature and Film in Postwar Japan, 1950–1983" (University of California, Berkeley, 2004), shows that censors also functioned as cultural critics.

42. Minami and Shakai, *Shōwa Bunka 1925–1945*, 190, 315, 399.

43. I take the phrase from Richard Burt, ed., *The Administration of Aesthetics: Censorship, Political Criticism, and the Public Sphere* (Minneapolis: University of Minnesota Press, 1994).

44. Kasuko Tsurumi, *Social Change and the Individual: Japan before and after Defeat in World War II* (Princeton, N.J.: Princeton University Press, 1970), 120. See also Minami and Shakai, *Shōwa Bunka 1925–1945*, 355–83.

45. No Japanese leader ever wrote a script and had a film made from it, as did Franco; nor was any so influenced by and immersed in the arts of music and architecture as was Hitler; and none was so directly influenced by men of literature (Futurists such as Marinetti) as was Mussolini. The mesmerizing rhetoric that emerges from these leaders' speeches and from iconic texts such as Hitler's *Mein Kampf* and Mussolini's autobiographies did not emanate from the mouth of the emperor, though the artistry of imperial pageantry and the diffusion through mass

media of the emperor's sanctified image did indeed transform him into a "visible symbol" representing the national totality: see Takashi Fujitani, *Splendid Monarchy: Power and Pageantry in Modern Japan* (Berkeley: University of California Press, 1996), 24, 236. Japan's political leaders did, of course, make speeches, but their speechifying was not as central to the propaganda effort as it was in Europe. The Japanese state did not employ the services of a genius of propaganda like Joseph Goebbels, of an architect like Albert Speer to transform physical space, of a philosopher like Albert Rosenberg to change the shape of the arts, or of a filmmaker like Leni Riefenstahl to make those newly designed artistic spaces available to mass audiences.

46. Plans for a sublime capital in Japanese-occupied Manchuria, for example, were called for but never executed, and the power of design was to be limited to the small numbers of people who saw the plans exhibited: Inoue Shōichi, *Senjika Nihon no kenchikuka: Ato, kitchu, japanesuku* (Tokyo: Asahi Sensho, 1995), 1–16, 88–94, 128.

47. Yanagi Muneyoshi, "Nihon o aisuru," in *Yanagi Muneyoshi zenshū*, vol. 17 (Tokyo: Chikuma Shobō, 1980), 597. Yanagi also argued against the government's attempt to standardize Okinawan dialects in 1940, out of his desire to preserve provincial differences. See his "Chihōsei no bunkateki kachi," in *Yanagi Muneyoshi zenshū*, vol. 8, 224.

48. Isaiah Berlin, *The Crooked Timber of Humanity: Chapters in the History of Ideas* (London: John Murray, 1990), 197.

49. In *Kusa no ne no fashizumu: Nihon minshū no sensō taiken* (Tokyo: Tokyo Daigaku Shuppankai, 1987), Yoshimi Yoshiaki suggests that propagandistic clichés such as the "holy war (*seisen*)" and "extinguish oneself through service to the state (*messhi hōkō*)," while infiltrating the language and thoughts of Japanese men and women struggling through their everyday lives during the war years, only imperfectly penetrated their minds. Some young men who expressed passionate support for the "holy war" before being drafted expressed only visceral fear after; some who felt regret, or sadness even, for not being drafted at all quickly were relieved of their sentiments by the fear that set in with the reality of going to war: ibid., 92, 95. As the war progressed, exhaustion set in, and surrender soon became the most desirable option. Some were transformed from peace-loving to violently anti-Chinese; others felt empathy with the Chinese on the battlefront as fellow farmers or as the bearers of a great civilization, though this fellow feeling could strengthen one's belief in Japan's role as the protector of Asia: ibid., 39, 41, 52, 63. At home, many may have felt joy in the work being done in Manchuria, rendered unaware by censorship and propaganda of the project there as one of theft and violence: ibid., 110. Indeed, the goodwill of believers in the war as holy and in Japan as protector and liberator of Asia may have prevented them from seeing the more complicated truth of events. Yoshimi's reading of hundreds of letters, diaries, and surveys reveals that the language of ideology shifted according to the practical exigencies of daily life, and its reception depended on a multitude

of factors, including economic class, education, age, gender, and locale. However, those with a measure of material comfort had the luxury to be thrilled at the prospect of a "holy war," while those in a more fragile economic condition were more pragmatic and tended to view the war in terms of its effects on their daily lives: ibid., 1–17.

50. Hannah Arendt, *Totalitarianism: Part Three of The Origins of Totalitarianism* (San Diego: Harcourt Brace, 1979 [1968]), 5.

51. See Claudia Koonz, *The Nazi Conscience* (Cambridge, Mass.: Harvard University Press, 2003), 271.

PART I

THEORIES OF JAPANESE FASCISM

KEVIN M. DOAK

Fascism Seen and Unseen:
Fascism as a Problem in Cultural Representation

> Just as romanticism was the illusion of the nineteenth century, fascism is
> the illusion of our time.
> —Imanaka Tsugimaro, *Fuashizumu undō ron*, 78–79.

■ Retrospection has advantages, but it also has its risks. Nowhere is this more so than in the never-ending debate over whether, when, and how Japan was fascist. Unlike Mussolini's Italy, where fascism was undeniable, or Hitler's Germany, where (with a bit of conceptual revision) National Socialism could be made to play the role of a "fascist" revolution, wartime Japan never experienced an overthrow of the monarchical constitutional order established in the late nineteenth century. Nonetheless, the rise of militarist influences with the escalation of war on the Asian continent, Japan's joining with fascist Italy and Nazi Germany in the anti-Comintern pact in 1936, then the Tripartite Pact in 1940 all have given postwar historians cause to lump Japan in the same "fascist" category as its wartime allies. The fascist label has been particularly appealing for two broad groups of critics: Marxists, who could draw from their wartime comrades who considered Japan's wartime crackdown on communism as "fascist"; and postwar nationalists (both Japanese as well as citizens of Japan's wartime enemy states), who simply use the term to excoriate anything connected with wartime Japan.[1] Often lost in the recriminations and political posturings over Japanese "fascism" are serious and troubling questions. Was the dominant political structure, or even the cultural tendencies, of wartime Japan really "fascist"? And if so, what does this "fascism" refer to? How was fascism reconciled with Japanese imperialism? Finally—and, I believe, most important—what did Japanese at the time understand fascism to be, and to what extent did they consider their own political and cultural forms to be "fascist"?

The problem of identifying how fascism works as a cultural ideology is not a simple one. Complicating the question is the difficulty in determining a "fascist" culture style. As Walter Laqueur points out in his authoritative *Fascism: Past, Present and Future*, the fascist "cultural malaise was most acutely felt in literature and the visual arts. . . . [yet] political indoctrination in culture was, on the whole, limited to prohibitions; there was no Nazi style in literature comparable to 'Socialist realism.'" Further, Laqueur notes, even Hitler's preference for monumentalism in the visual arts was not shared in Mussolini's fascist Italy.[2] It may not be possible in the end to identify a single fascist theory of culture, in this sense. Moreover, underlying Laqueur's interrogation is the liberal understanding of culture as a broad—perhaps even undefinable—field of human creativity. Given this assumption about culture, it is not at all surprising that Laqueur finds it impossible to identify a specific Nazi or fascist cultural style. This failure to identify a universal fascist style aside, Laqueur's point about literature's historical relationship to fascism in particular seems especially fruitful in identifying how fascism and culture intersected in wartime Japan.

When joined by the postwar reflections of Maruyama Masao, Laqueur's emphasis on literature as a key site for fascist culture takes on added value in determining the place of fascist culture in wartime Japan. Maruyama was not only one of postwar Japan's most important commentators on the political culture of wartime Japan. He was also a witness to historical fascism in Japan, having lived through the period while struggling to continue his work in comparative political theory. His reflections on the impact of fascism among intellectuals are an important starting point in trying to capture the precise ways in which fascism and culture intersected in wartime Japan. Maruyama identified a double response in literary culture to the pressures of fascism when he described the "typhoon" that swept up writers in the early 1930s:

> There was another important shift in the basic circumstances surrounding politics and literature. This was of course the development of Japan's continental policy which followed from the establishment of Manchu-

kuo and the escalation into all-out war between Japan and China that occurred as its historical consequence. This brought the problem of "national trends (kokusei)" once again front and center into literature. . . . One group among the tenkō writers folded their earlier image of keeping pace with politics — what had been for them a movement — into this new "politics" without any revision at all. Look how far politics has come, literature must not be left behind! (This was the direction of what was called state-policy literature, or continental literature.) Yet another group discovered in the myth of ethnic nationality (minzoku) and the emperor the ir-rationality [sic] which had been rejected in the previous clamor over "the supremacy of politics." They tried very hard to burn up their literary selves in the totality of irrationality which was the flip side of the totality of rationality.[3]

Together, Laqueur's and Maruyama's analyses suggest that too little attention has been given to literary texts, where fascist views were often espoused in terms of a return to ethnic national culture. In short, what is needed today is a different approach that, instead of uncritically ingesting postwar assumptions about Japanese fascism as the characteristic mode of wartime state power, seeks to uncover the place of fascism within and against dominant retrospective views by turning back to what was actually said about fascism by its critics during the time when fascism began to appear as a cultural movement in Japan.

Two of the most influential critics of fascism who wrote during the 1930s and early 1940s were Imanaka Tsugimaro (1893–1980) and Tosaka Jun (1900–45). These two men might be seen as a study in contrasts. Imanaka was a liberal Christian who resigned his post at Kyushu Imperial University in 1942 to take a position in the wartime government, whereas Tosaka was a Marxist who was arrested in 1938 and died in prison at the end of the war. Moreover, Imanaka's studies drew attention to the historical connections between fascist movements and workers' movements, while Tosaka emphasized fascism as an ideology linked to capitalism and liberal intellectuals. Yet they shared a deep concern about the rise of fascism in Japan and believed that the foundations for fascism stemmed from transformations that followed the First World War. Read together, their writings on fascism provide an important illumination on how fascism was seen, and subsequently "unseen" — a complex process of shifting signification that has had a lasting impact on the debate over Japanese fascism today. Most important, as we shall see, their works reveal how many postwar retrospectives came to "unsee" fascism by discounting the centrality of an ethnic concept of national cultural identity (minzoku) and instead represented Japanese fascism as a top-down ideology driven by the state and social elites. As I will note, this postwar unseeing of historical fascism has served to legitimate a new ideology of ethnic national culture whose contemporary adherents often claim to be the most virulent critics of wartime "fascism" even as they adopt a political position whose ultimate target is not limited to the ghosts of the wartime state but may even extend to the postwar liberal-democratic Japanese state.

Back to the Future: Imanaka Tsugimaro
and Tosaka Jun's Wartime Theories on Fascism

Imanaka Tsugimaro is a rewarding place to begin a reconsideration of cultural fascism in Japan. Although not widely known in the English literature on Japanese fascism, Imanaka's wartime studies are among the most important works on fascism in Japan during the 1930s and served as very early warnings of the dangers of fascism in Japan.[4] In his first major work on fascism, On the Fascist Movement (February 1932), Imanaka confronted the problem of particular differences within any universal theory of fascism. Imanaka stated that the book would focus exclusively on the fascist movement in Italy, but he added two important qualifications. First, he noted that he considered "movements like Hitler's to be essentially the same" as the fascism in Italy. And second, he added that his major objective in the work was to focus on fascist movements rather than fascist states, "because I have been thinking about its [fascism's] contemporary political significance for Japan."[5] At issue was whether Imanaka could articulate a theory of fascism that could suture the differences in Italian, German, French, Swiss, Japanese, and other fascist movements. And whether he could do so rested on how he conceived of fascism as a general problem.

Imanaka arrived at a universal understanding of fascism first from a historical reading of the movement's origins in Italy and second through a conceptual analysis that tried to isolate those elements of fascism that were common to all fascist movements. His analysis of the historical development of fascism in Italy in three stages (Revolutionary Fascism of 1914; Combative Fascism of 1919; and Party Fascism after 1921) emphasized the social, economic, and cultural dislocations of the First World War as the universal conditions for the rise of fascism as a general phenomenon.[6] Imanaka's focus on the crisis of 1914 led him to confront the relationship of fascism to the middle class and, especially, to understand the historical and theoretical ties between fascist and communist movements. He concluded that fascism was not merely a "reactionary" but also in some senses a "revolutionary" movement whose origins were found in self-articulations by fascists whose revolutionary beliefs had been honed within socialist movements. The implications for cultural ideology were significant. Fascism was both revolutionary and reactionary, both a middle-class ideology and a force that went far beyond the middle class, ultimately betraying middle-class hopes. Here, Imanaka was quite close to Walter Laqueur's point that "fascism thought of itself as a movement of cultural revolution."[7] What they shared was a sense that fascism aimed at revolution, a breaking out of the restraints of constitutional politics to something entirely new and different. But what kind of revolution was the fascist revolution? And what role, if any, did culture play in addressing the social and economic dislocations that flowed from the First World War?

The key to grasping the apparently paradoxical nature of fascism was to recognize that the First World War had unleashed a historically specific form of nationalism (minzokushugi) centered on an ethnic appropriation of cultural identity. Defining culture as the culture of ethnic nations appealed to growing numbers of people, especially but not exclusively among the middle class, who turned to ethnic nationalism to address what existing political structures seemed incapable of resolving: the oppression suffered by "weak" capitalist economies at the hands of the stronger established capitalist states. Skirting a theory of historical backwardness, Imanaka preferred to describe these economic inequalities between nations in terms of whether their economic base was "fragile" or "sound." In advanced capitalist states with a "fragile" economic base (e.g., interwar Italy), the influx of capital from advanced "sound" capitalist economies (e.g., England, the United States, Germany) is seen as a threat to their national survival.[8] Imanaka's point was that any attempt to understand fascism theoretically must consider these international relations of power, or what was really a theory of global imperialism, in addition to issues of domestic oppression.

For Imanaka's theory of fascism, the most significant point about these dislocations of imperialist capitalism was that, beginning around the First World War, it was the middle class in countries where capitalism had a fragile base who were the most seriously afflicted. In those economies, the middle class found its relative advantage over the working class—and its dreams of approximating the upper class—quickly disappearing. Fascism arose as a recognition by middle-class people in these "fragile" capitalist countries that capitalist methods had failed them, and they were easily seduced by fascism's promise of a "third way," imaginative (and thoroughly imagined) hopes for a social solution that would overcome capitalism itself. In this sense, Imanaka concluded that "fascism is not a concept that can be completely subsumed under the category of a capitalist reactionary movement."[9] Indeed, he pointed to fascism's origins in working-class movements in both Italy and Germany, noting the paradox that fascism was more influential in countries with active socialist politics than it was in England, France, and the United States, where socialists and communists had enjoyed much less success as organized players in national politics. One defining feature of fascism, for Imanaka, was its anti-capitalist nature.

Thus, a major problem confronting any global theory of fascism was the historical relationship between communism and fascism as forms of anti-capitalism. As Imanaka put it, "The parallel direction in the force of fascism and communism is a fact difficult to ignore, but [the real problem is] how to explain this fact."[10] Imanaka rejected the notion that the turn to fascism was merely a "strategic mistake" by leaders of the communist movement, pointing instead to the longstanding influence of "nationalism (minzoku-shugi)" among the Italian intellectual class. Those in the communist movement who labeled fascism a "reactionary" force were simply reflecting the reality that middle-class socialists eventually turned against the communist movement. For those who did and became national socialists, the crisis of international capitalism meant their own position as a middle class was endangered and, unable to identify with an international proletariat due to their nationalistic education, they increasingly turned to the state. Imanaka's underlying point was that fascism arose not as an ideology for, by, or of a state that was already supreme, but from an endangered middle class that turned to the state to shore up the fragile capitalist base of its own nation. For this reason, Imanaka concluded that fascism was not simply the logic of reaction, but an extension of the revolutionary sentiment of the working class transferred by the nationalist middle class into a revolution by the "social mass."[11] His conclusions take on a prophetic tone when read in the light of the conversions to national socialism the following year by Sano Manabu and Nabeyama Sadachika, members of the Japan Communist Party's Central Committee. Fascism, like communism, was a revolutionary movement against capitalism, but it sought its revolutionary subject not in a class-bound entity like the proletariat, but in the mass-based subjectivity of minzoku, or ethnic nationality.

Revolutionary fascism, then, had to involve cultural considerations and should not be merely reduced to an analysis of political institutions. Some theory of cultural identity was necessary to account for the dynamics that led the middle class to reject class-consciousness in favor of a "social mass" conceived as the embodiment of the ethno-cultural nation. Why should the social masses be signified in ethnic national terms? On this question, Imanaka's comparative theory of fascism faltered. He did not sufficiently explore the cultural implications of fascism, except to note the power of this revolutionary ethnic nationalism (minzokushugi) that had emerged around the First World War and that had transformed socialist movements around the world. One might have expected Imanaka to develop a cultural theory of fascism when, a few months later, he offered a monograph on the rise of the national socialist movement in Germany, a movement that in mid-1932 was a striking example of "bottom-up" fascism rather than "top-down" fascism growing out of a state. Here was a prime opportunity for Imanaka to explain how socialists, middle-class professionals, and especially the young were being enticed to join a movement that he argued would never serve their real interests. Surely, some form of culturalist ideology was the key. But in the end, Imanaka retreated from the cultural implications of his work, concluding only that the source of fascism's power could not be found in any theory, cultural or otherwise.[12] Fascism was merely a "movement" and could only be studied as such.

Imanaka's disavowal of the significance of cultural representation is perhaps the most important legacy of his approach to understanding what fascism is. It was an ironic disavowal, given that Imanaka implicitly recognized the ethnic cultural ideology at the core of the fascist movements he described. In On National Socialism (June 1932), he rendered the concept of "nation" in both the Italian Partito Nationale Fascista and the German Nationalsozialistische movement as "minzoku."[13] Imanaka thereby captured the ethno-cultural nationalism that he believed linked both movements together in their fascism. This conceptualization is revealing, not only for Imanaka's subsequent disavowal of ethno-cultural elements in fascism, but also for the ways this contemporary perception of fascism has given way to postwar emphases on statism. In their postwar "unseeing" of fascism, most historians of Japanese fascism have rendered national socialism with an emphasis on the state (kokka shakaishugi), displacing the populist, ethnic sense of nation (minzoku) that emerges in the pages of Imanaka's text as a witness to how contemporary theorists located the core cultural ideology of fascism in ethnic movements that rose up against existing states. In this indirect revelation of ethnic nationalism as the key element in fascism's cultural ideology, Imanaka's theory makes two contributions to understanding the rise of fascism: it located the historical origins of fascism in the anti-imperialist ethnic nationalism of the First World War period, and it suggested how bottom-up nationalist fervor had mobilized Japanese fascists to commit acts of terrorism against the multiethnic Japanese state, to even assassinate Prime Minister Inukai in May 1932.[14]

Unfortunately, an institutional bias that reduced the question of liberal democracy to parliament precluded a completion of the cultural theory opened up by the problem of ethnic nationality that Imanaka's study of fascism had stumbled on. Instead of revealing the claims ethnic forms of nationalism make on national culture, Imanaka settled on an a-cultural theory of racism in the crudest biologically determinist mode. Imanaka simply wrote off Nazi cultural ideology as a form of biological racial consciousness (jinshu ishiki) and racial passion (jinshu kanjō) that extended beyond ethnic German identity to encompass almost all white, non-Jewish Europeans (notably absent from the list were Italians).[15] This determination to see (German) fascism in terms of biological race, rather than as part of the interwar turn to ethnic forms of national culture, required Imanaka to return to one of the central issues of interwar political discourse: the question of how to define this newly emergent form of ethno-cultural identity called minzoku.

Imanaka's discussion of the problem of nationality (minzoku) in relation to fascism is the most important site for understanding his retreat from a cultural theory adequate to account for the object of his study. The entire discussion was little more than an exercise in anti-theory. He began his discussion on "the concept of minzoku" with a statement that theories and concepts are of little value in understanding fascism before adding for safe measure that "the word minzoku has yet to be given a precise concept in political science"(although he gave it his own, rather straightforward definition as "nation").[16] Yet his discussion made it clear that Imanaka was in fact drawing implicitly on a body of specific theoretical discourse on nationality that equated minzoku with an ethnological concept of national identity (nasci) that posited the ethnic group as a natural body, distinct from both the modern state and constitutional forms of nationality.[17] Marching ahead, oblivious to the ground he trod, Imanaka made a conceptual leap, applying this concept of "nation" to render Gobineau's and Gumplowicz's concepts of "race," Walter Bagehot's concept of nationality, as well as Ratzer's concept of "territory." Having dissimulated the concepts of minzoku and nation by applying them inconsistently across nineteenth-century European discourses, Imanaka then turned to what he called the three dominant understandings of minzoku in his day: the cultural identity referred to by both Renan's concept of nation and Herder's concept of *Volk* (Imanaka's amalgamation of these two only reveals his failure to grasp what Renan was arguing against); Harry Elmore Barnes's concept of national consciousness; and the "orthodox school of Marxism's concept of nation."[18] Recent allegations by some theorists of Japanese culture about the "multivalence" of the concept of minzoku notwithstanding, it is clear that all three of these traditions were really concerned with the same subject: how to understand the problem of the nation (*minzoku*), especially as a question of ethno-cultural identity.

What ultimately underwrote this disavowal of the repressive cultural functions inherent in ethnic nationalism was Stalin's economic argument in favor of a utilitarian embrace of this revolutionary (ethnic) nationalism in the struggle against imperialism.[19] But to redeem this concept of minzoku for progressive purposes, it was necessary to sever, however disingenuously, its connection to racism. Citing Stalin's position that the nation was a product of history rather than culture, Imanaka concluded, "I think it is best to put other ethnic (*minzoku-teki*) concepts that exist in a different relationship to the ethnic nation-state (*minzoku kokka*) under other conceptual headings. For example, forms of social community that spring from such identities as clan, tribe, race (*jinshu*), language, religion, and life environment are something other than ethnic nationality (*minzoku*)."[20] In short, Imanaka followed Stalin's utilitarian approach to ethnic nationalism while at the same time trying to exempt the cultural elements of ethnic nationality from consideration.

As the core of fascist social ideology, minzoku now signified race in a strictly biological mode (even though, as Imanaka admitted, fascists themselves often hotly rejected the suggestion that their understanding of the nation was coterminous with a biological concept of race).[21] But when discovered in the hands of those thought not to be fascists, minzoku had to be put under some "other conceptual heading"—an implicit theory of ethnic culture long before ethnicity became an explicit concept in cultural theory. And yet, as with Stalin, it was Imanaka's failure to consider culture as more than a superstructure for an economically determined base that caused him to overlook the oppressive cultural features of ethnic nationalism and to turn instead to a reductive definition of biological race. Or perhaps one can say it was his liberal affinity for national culture that led him to reconfigure the minzokushugi of fascism as a form of racism rather than the histori-cally specific, culturally informed mode of ethnic nationalism that he had earlier identified it as being.

Once the minzoku of Hitler's and Mussolini's nationalism was arrested in this racial lens, Japanese minzoku ideology could be exempted from fas-cism as long as it was not affiliated with this biological racialism. And in-deed, after demonstrating the centrality of minzoku ideology in European fascism, Imanaka explained the rise of fascist movements in Japan with no reference to the influence of this minzoku social identity, whether con-ceived as "race" or "ethnic nationality." Still, Imanaka's analysis of Japa-nese fascism remains interesting for several other reasons, not the least of which is his detailed history of Japanese fascism as a movement that, like Hitler's and Mussolini's movements, was an effort at revolution from below. After first noting the blow to parliamentary democracy with the at-tack on Prime Minister Hamaguchi in November 1930, Imanaka traced the rise of fascism back to longstanding tensions between party politicians and a coalition of bureaucrats and military officers. He then gave careful at-tention to the platforms and declarations of three fascist movements: the Japan Socialism group inspired by Takabatake Motoyuki's state socialism; the Great Japan Production Party and its supporters in populist religious groups such as ōmotokyō; and the Japan National Social Party, especially Shimonaka Yasaburō and his "Economic Problems Study Group."[22] Ima-naka was not mistaken: these men and their groups were indeed inspired by fascist ideals. Nor was he wrong about the connection between these fascists and the socialist and labor movement in Japan. But in approach-ing the issue of fascism from his socioeconomic perspective, and having reduced the problem of ethnic nationalism to simply a matter of biological race, he had divested his argument of the broader cultural implications of the fascist agenda.

This disavowal of the ethno-culturalism inherent in the fascist agenda had important consequences in encouraging Imanaka to personally draw closer to the Japanese state at the height of the war, as I will discuss later. In the end, Imanaka's ultimate conclusion that fascism was merely a form of political dictatorship, along with his tendency to emphasize biological race over culture, determined his conviction that culture—and cultural inflec-tions of the nation—could be dispensed with as insignificant factors in the rise of fascist movements, both in Japan and elsewhere.[23] This exemption of culture from Imanaka's theory of fascism laid the foundations for later approaches that followed Imanaka by exempting ethnic culture from explanations of fascism and substituting for ethnic national culture notions of biological race or by dismissing the question of fascism entirely, since Japan did not "go fascist," as the Diet functioned throughout the war, and Japan never operated concentration camps as the Nazis did. In either case, the result was a theoretical failure to identify the place and power of ethnicity in nationalist ideology.

In contrast to Imanaka's institutional approach, Tosaka Jun's theoretical approach emphasized fascism as a specific form of cultural ideology. Tosaka's cultural critique of Japanese fascism was presented in *Nippon ideorogii* (revised edition, 1936) but stemmed from essays written between 1929 and 1934. The timing is significant. Whereas Imanaka's theories of fascism reflected influential events of the early 1930s (military actions in Manchuria and the fall of party government at home), Tosaka was able to reflect on the cultural and literary movements that had begun to change national discourse by the mid-1930s. As Watanabe Kazutami has noted, the year 1935 was a turning point in Japanese cultural discourse.[24] In that year, Yokomitsu Riichi's call for a "return to minzoku" by literary writers was simultaneously echoed in the formation of the Japan Romantic School, while Shimazaki Tōson's *Before the Dawn* (1932) and the prominent discussions on it in the Japanese press reinforced the move toward minzoku as the foundation of a new beginning for Japanese national identity.[25] In addition, the mass exodus from the Communist Party following the "conversions" of Sano Manabu and Nabeyama Sadachika in 1933 made it clear that the communist movement in Japan was in no way immune to the seductive appeal of minzoku.[26] Throughout this period, Tosaka grew increasingly concerned that the abandonment of the political left and the turn toward fascism could not be explained without attention to these cultural developments, and he sought to identify the culturalist ideology of fascism that was crippling the Marxist movement.

Tosaka made a substantial improvement over Imanaka's theory in identifying the cultural ideology of fascism that was increasingly becoming visible in his day. He found the core of this culturalist ideology in the "cultural renaissance (*bungei fukkō*)" that former proletarian writers such as Hayashi Fusao had loudly proclaimed in the early 1930s. Tosaka placed this ostensible "cultural renaissance" in the broader context of a fascistic desire for "restoration (*fukko*)" of the past, an impulse that inevitably saw in the past a family system that was the essence of the Japanese ethnic way of life (*nihon minzoku seikatsu no honshitsu*).[27] In contrast to Imanaka, whose liberalism sought to retain the culturalism of a progressive ethnic nationalism by reducing fascism to political dictatorship and "race," Tosaka emphasized the ideological functions of fascism that were centrally concerned with the ethno-cultural expressions of national identity often favored by Japanese liberals and writers. Tosaka's major concern was in outlining the cultural ideological relations between fascism and liberalism. His characterization of the "cultural renaissance" as merely a "renaissance of pure literature" was a direct refutation of Yokomitsu's call for a new literature of and by the entire ethnic nation.[28] For Tosaka, the belief in a literature that was not defined by class identity was the most direct expression of what he called "fascism," a term he used to characterize liberals and anyone who invoked a national culture that was not divided along class lines.[29]

Under the pressures of the moment (when, it should be noted, there was at best only a weak liberal influence in Japanese intellectual and culture circles), Tosaka found it all too easy to equate any group, idea, or cultural work that was not Marxist with fascism. Indeed, any fair assessment of Tosaka's theory of fascism must begin with an awareness that Tosaka was writing from a sense of frustration that, by the mid-1930s, the proletarian cultural movement was dead and its death had been hastened by a number of desertions from the Marxist movement. Again, the contrast to Imanaka is illustrative. Imanaka saw fascism as a "bottom-up" movement that was destabilizing parliamentary democracy around the world. Tosaka saw fascism as a "top-down" oppression of the proletarian movement, and he imagined historical parallels between Japan in the 1930s and Europe in the 1850s. He explicitly cited Marx's *German Ideology* as the inspiration of his own *Nippon ideorogii*, and like Marx, he traced the repression of the masses to a romantic, idealist ideology of national essence that he called "Japanism."[30] Like Marx, Tosaka was really writing to condemn those who had abandoned the populist movement, and his ire was especially reserved for those who had wrapped themselves in the mantle of "liberalism."

Tosaka's approach—through Marx's critique of philosophical idealism—led him to describe the cultural ideology of fascism in terms of a Japanism that was ultimately defined by its idealist approximation of culture. Here, he came closer than most to grasping the cultural ideology that was often associated with fascism during the 1930s. As Harry Harootunian has pointed out, "Tosaka saw in contemporary Japanism . . . representations of this effort to transmute culture at a fixed moment in archaic times into nature and, thereby, fix, for all times to come, the essence of what it meant to be Japanese."[31] The key to this "Japanism" was a theory of ethnic nationality (*minzoku*) that Tosaka bemoaned for displacing the rising potential of a proletarian culture. But the deployment of a bifurcated logic of idealism and materialism to represent the cultures of fascism and progressivism, respectively, precluded Tosaka from recognizing the role played by leftists within the Japanese fascist movement. Between 1934 and 1935, the Japanist movement had split between the "idealists" and the "progressives," and in the following years it was in fact the progressive wing, not the idealists, who came to dominate the Japanist movement.[32] To his credit, Tosaka was able to capture the contributions many liberals had made in making fascism seem acceptable through his approach, which emphasized fascism as a form of idealism that sought to restrict the meaning of being Japanese in ethno-cultural terms. Yet he was unable from this perspective to address the fascism of the "right-wing nationalist labor unions," although Tosaka closed Nippon ideorogii by recognizing these unions as factors within the fascist movement.[33] Whereas Imanaka had identified the historical links between socialist and fascist groups in Europe, Tosaka was unable to accept the possibility that socialism and National Socialism might have something in common. At the same time, Tosaka was far more sensitive than Imanaka to the cultural theory behind Japanese fascism, an effort to supplant class with ethnicity in the interest of projecting a single identity that would separate "true" Japanese from those who were deemed, on ethnic grounds, not to belong. Tosaka understood better than most the viciousness of ethnic identity posing as culture.

The divergent fortunes of Tosaka and Imanaka at the height of wartime Japan offers a seductive, if superficial, way to sort out the value of their theories on fascism. Tosaka was arrested in a major crackdown on Marxists in November 1938 and released on bail in 1940. However, he was sent back to prison in 1944, where he died from illness the following year, just before the end of the war. Tosaka's tragic end provides powerful material for those who would validate his theories by appealing to the notion of martyrdom (if not by outright accusing the capitalist Occupation forces of complicity with his "fascist executioners"). His imprisonment and death in jail seem to bear out his conclusions that wartime Japan was fascist, especially if one accepts that he was imprisoned for his antifascism.

But Tosaka was not merely a foe of fascism: he wrote equally vitriolic attacks on liberalism. Tosaka's fate must be considered alongside that of Imanaka, also an implacable foe of fascism but a supporter of constitutional liberalism. In contrast to Tosaka, Imanaka found his fortunes improved as the war intensified. Even after 1942, when Imanaka accepted a position in the government under the supervision of the Cabinet Planning Board, nobody accused him of sympathy for fascism. The wartime state did persecute suspected communists, but given its warm reception of the antifascist liberal Imanaka, and the close ties between socialism and fascism in Japan of the 1930s,[34] it is not clear that the anticommunism of the wartime Japanese state is sufficient grounds ipso facto to render it "fascist."

The Ambivalent Legacies of Fascism as Cultural Ideology

Assertions of wartime Japan as "fascist" need to account for the divergent experiences of these two critics of fascism at the hands of the wartime state. If they do not, then it is not clear what it means to call Japan at this time "fascist." In assessing wartime Japan as fascist, it is important to recall not only Tosaka's imprisonment and death, but also the wartime state's embrace of Imanaka, a leading liberal, Christian antifascist. While it would be tempting to conclude with Tosaka's defenders that Imanaka's wartime fortunes only illustrate the complicity of liberalism and fascism, such a conclusion is premature, if not overly partisan. We must first give careful consideration to the different ways Tosaka and Imanaka understood the cultural impact of "fascism" and the relationship between culture and politics. Given the wartime state's warm reception of liberal antifascists such as Imanaka, it is not at all clear that Tosaka's imprisonment warrants concluding that his antifascism was what offended officials of Imperial Japan. Rather, the official reason for his original arrest in 1938 was suspicion of violating the 1925 Peace Preservation Law, which targeted those who espoused overthrowing Japan's political system and the rights of private property. And as Imanaka's writings had already made clear, there was a fine and not always distinct line separating communists from national socialists among those who sought to overthrow constitutional governments and capitalist economies.

There is no question that wartime Japan turned increasingly authoritarian and conservative. There is, however, plenty of room for questioning whether the imperial state was "fascist." Careful attention to the history of the Special Higher Police, and particularly to their use by Prime Minister Tōjō Hideki against his enemies even further to his political right, reveals that extreme rightists, fascists, and practically anyone deemed to pose a threat to the Meiji constitutional order were at risk.[35] Imanaka, a consistent foe of fascism, was at the same time a strong defender of constitutional government, and his sense that constitutional government faced a crisis explains his decision to join the Tōjō government better than any latent fascist proclivities on his part. Like conservative authoritarians in Germany (Paul von Hindenburg, Heinrich Brüning), Tōjō's cabinet had turned against the idealists and populists, rejecting Konoe's Shōwa Research Association and purging the "reform bureaucrats" and other openly fascist groups.

For Imanaka's career, the key moment came in March 1941. In what became known as the "Cabinet Planning Board Incident," Wada Hiroo, Katsumada Seiichi, and fifteen other members of the Cabinet Planning Board were arrested on suspicion of violating the Peace Preservation Law—the same charge that had been leveled against Tosaka. They were not suspected of being communists themselves, but the rationale for their arrest is material to understanding the manner in which fascism and communism were seen by the wartime government. The charge was that Wada and his group were members of the "reform bureaucrats" whose national-socialist tendencies would aid in the realization of the Japanese Communist Party's ultimate objective of overthrowing the constitutional order. Thus, it is significant that Imanaka joined the East Asia Institute (which had been founded in 1938 and placed under the supervision of the Cabinet Planning Board) in July 1942 as part of Prime Minister Tōjō's effort to remove national socialist ("fascist") elements from the government bureaucracy. Imanaka remained a policy analyst for the East Asia Institute until June 1945, convinced that he was best able to resist fascist movements from that official post. He dedicated his efforts during the war to defending constitutional government, and his suggestions for reform of the capitalist economy were designed to avoid the more extreme proposals of the fascist foes of capitalism. In light of these facts, Gregory Kasza's application of Stanley Payne's characterization of "conservative authoritarian" rather than fascist to the wartime Japanese political structure seems a very apt one.[36]

Conceding that the political system in wartime Japan never fully embraced fascism still does not answer the more troubling question: Was there fascist culture in Japan and, if so, how do we understand what it was and where it operated most strongly? Tosaka provides one sure guide to the presence and scope of fascist culture in 1930s Japan. He quickly grasped the political significance of the cultural renaissance that was being conducted under the sign of "minzoku," although tragically he was less capable, or less willing, to recognize the inroads this ethnic cultural ideology had also made among socialist leaders and movements, transforming many of them to national socialism. Yet he was practically alone in connecting this ethnic national ideology with liberalism in Japan. Tosaka's efforts to identify cultural "Japanism," when read alongside Imanaka's focus on fascism

as a revolutionary movement "from below," raises an important cautionary note: too heavy a reliance on "fascism" to explain the political culture
of wartime Japan can render the fascist cultural ideology of minzoku invisible by simply rendering political oppression as a function of the wartime
state rather than as the result of specific social and cultural movements
that began to gather after 1918. As Harootunian has pointed out, the re-
narrativization of wartime fascism by both liberals and Marxists in the early
postwar years was made possible by "a generally widespread denunciation
of the wartime state for being the responsible agent in causing Japan's defeat and destruction."[37] Condemning "fascism" has appealed to many in
postwar Japan who have found it a useful means for legitimating their own
anti-state ideologies, which, it is important to add, are not always on the
political left.

An important caution against this postwar rendering of cultural fascism
invisible through a single-minded pursuit of the fascist state has been made
by the leading cultural critic Karatani Kōjin. Karatani's focus is on fascism
as a cultural theory, especially as a cultural theory that seeks to negate representation. He locates the origins of this rejection of representation in
Japan in the prewar parliamentary system and how its "representatives"
excluded some (lower) social strata from political representation, leaving
those left out of parliamentary representation to turn to the transcendental
emperor for their own cultural representation.[38] Karatani's analysis is rich
with suggestions for any effort to rethink fascism, past or present, in Japan
or elsewhere. His identification of the social origins of fascism in Japan
as arising from within the lower classes that were excluded from liberal-
democratic institutions is not only historically accurate but is also supported by postwar historical research that has uncovered the "grassroots"
of fascism in wartime Japan.[39] This complex, dynamic approach helps us
see how fascism was both a populist movement and a cultural ideology that
drew from the ethnic revision of national identity that had emerged after
the First World War and that took ethnicity to be the key to expanding the
cultural, and eventually the political, franchise of the masses. In this sense,
fascism was not a rejection of modernity but a kind of hypermodernity that
sought to complete the democratic national vision unleashed by the French
Revolution. But most important, it sought to do so at all costs.

Karatani's caution about the widespread use and abuse of the term *fascism* with regard to Japan has significant implications for cultural theory.[40]
Most historical accounts of fascism in Japan have been focused on the
image of a totalitarian, militarist state, but the cost of this state-centered

approach to fascism often has been to overlook fascism as a cultural theory of anti-representation. This is not to say that fascist cultural theory has not offered its own peculiar theory of cultural representation. Whether in Hitler's version or that of Japanese fascists such as Kamei Kan'ichirō, a theory of cultural representation centered on the ethnic collective lies at the heart of many fascist or national socialist cultural theories. Ethnic nationalism is often couched in terms of resistance to darker forces, frequently but not always imagined as coming from the outside, that would extinguish the ethnic *Gemeinschaft* (organic community). But as Karatani's analysis suggests, this cultural theory of ethnic social totality merely negates a host of other internal efforts at social representation while ultimately serving as a form of what Pierre Bourdieu calls "symbolic violence."[41]

In contemporary Japan, this anti-representational stance serves to rehabilitate fascism, not openly by name, but through a more sophisticated ideology that displaces fascism by rendering it unseen while trying to establish lines of historical continuity that do not exist and erasing historical discontinuities that have occurred. Advocates of what must remain an unseen and unnamed fascism often themselves return to fascism's modern, populist origins while simultaneously and, most importantly, shifting the source of fascist violence from the symbolic violence of cultural totality to the presumed physical violence of the constitutional state. In the process, fascism's central cultural theory of an ethnically cleansed social totality is given a new lease on life as a form of resistance to the presumed cultural colonization of (an equally totalized representation of) "the West."

In the face of this new ideology that renders fascism unseen while effecting an ersatz image of fascism in the militarist state, we can no longer be satisfied merely to ask whether fascism has outlived its usefulness as a concept for understanding wartime Japan. Such a question is simply unanswerable without first addressing the logic of cultural essentialism that informs fascist sensibilities (e.g., as manifested in the question of whether "Japan" is fascist or not). Beyond the generic risks of this kind of cultural essentialism, we must confront the possibility that fascism has found a new purpose and a new meaning in postwar Japan. To the degree that debates over wartime Japan as fascist have been indebted to the theoretical influence of Imanaka, a single-minded pursuit of fascism in political and military institutions has allowed historians to exempt from critical attention the broader social and cultural forces—especially those expressed in ethnic national terms—that challenged the politics of the center, while informing the liberationist ideologies of the periphery, of the wartime Japanese empire.

Yet, alternatively, theorists following Tosaka (and there have not been many) have either discussed Japanism in such culturally particular terms that they remain at best remote from a general theory of Japanese fascism, or they have distorted the destabilizing functions of national-socialist movements in wartime Japan by conflating them with the state-supremacy model of Italian fascism. At best, they concede ethnic nationalism could be a kind of fascism, but only if it is conjoined to the (capitalist) state (thus conveniently excusing the cultural fascism of leftist ethnic nationalist movements). In these eyes, the capitalist state remains the ultimate barometer of fascism, and culture can only be considered a fascist problem to the extent that it is an expression of state power. If we are still so deeply enmeshed in this assumption that the state is the ultimate agency of fascism (including national socialism and ethnic nationalism), perhaps deeper reflection on cultural fascism is long overdue. Then we can recover the significance of the question of fascism in Japan, but with a new twist. More attention to the ideology of ethnic culture and less obsession with this overwrought concept "fascism" as the cultural politics of the state would be a useful starting point in capturing the dynamics of wartime Japan and its legacies for the postwar society.

To continue this disavowal of the oppression of ethnic culturalist ideology is not simply a misrepresentation of the past. Rather, it perpetuates a culture of denial about the broader influence of the ethnic nationalism that underlay the fascist, national-socialist, and other repressive movements in wartime and postwar Japan. Ironically, this culture of denial may been seen, at least in part, as a result of the combined weight of Imanaka's and Tosaka's representations of fascism. While historians who follow Tosaka tend to overemphasize a top-down interpretation of fascism, Imanaka's legacy has been to exempt ethnic ideology from the critical attention given to fascist movements of the wartime period and later.

Yet what is most striking about wartime and postwar illiberal continuities is not "fascism" as understood in these narrow frameworks. Rather, it is the ethnic cultural theories that have flourished in the postwar era. As Harumi Befu has noted, "What is common to the wartime Nihonjinron and postwar neo-Nihonjinron is that both rely heavily on primordial sentiments inherent in the presumed 'ethnic essence' of the Japanese."[42] Far more than continuities between the wartime and postwar state, the survival of the "reform bureaucrats," or militarism in postwar Japan's armed forces, it is the continuity of a discourse on ethnic culture that connects the period of "historical fascism" to our present. In other words, it is the specific form of nationalism anchored in a social imaginary of the minzoku that presents the most pressing danger to the practice of democratic politics and culture in contemporary Japan. Yet ethnic nationalism has largely escaped critical attention in debates on Japanese fascism because many on the left have yet to extract themselves from the seductions of ethnic national culture and remain deeply enmeshed in the appeal of ethnic nationalism as the best hope of an anti-imperialist, anti-capitalist social revolution.[43] For them, continuing the focus on fascism within its received modes of representation ("the capitalist state") is a useful means of preventing their own ethnic nationalism from being rendered visible and thus from being held accountable for various acts of oppression, both during the war and after.

These are some of the reasons that those who wish to adopt a critical perspective on culture in Japan must take a broader view that incorporates concerns over the relationship between culture and national formation, concerns that often have been left unaddressed in the visible discourse on fascism. Nishikawa Nagao is one leader in this critical effort to make the unseen seen again, and his alternative to the tired debate over whether Japan is/was/will again be fascist is worthy of serious consideration. For Nishikawa, the problem of culture and political extremism in pre-1945 Japan is less a function of Japanese fascism than a reflection of the broader issue of modern nation-state formation and its impact on cultural identity.[44] One advantage of Nishikawa's approach is that, by situating the problem of culture in terms of nation-state formation instead of merely in relation to fascism, it avoids the cultural particularism that often seeps into attempts to describe Japanese fascism. Another advantage is that it provides a broader theoretical framework within which to think about similar responses to modernity in such divergent nation-states as Japan, the United States, the People's Republic of China, and the (former) Soviet Union. Nishikawa has opened up a new line of inquiry with respect to the problem of cultural nationalism in contemporary Japan, as well, particularly in his provocative suggestion that while emancipation from the "state" has proceeded quite far in postwar Japan, emancipation from the concept of "ethnic nationality (minzoku)" has not.[45] By exploring the relationship of culture and fascism, it should become apparent that this underlying cultural theory of minzoku has largely escaped critical attention under the cover of an obsessive focus on the evils of the state. It should not be allowed to do so any longer.

Notes

Epigraph: *Fuashizumu undō ron*. (Originally published as volume three in *Dokusai seijiron sōsho* [Essays on Political Dictatorship Series]. Tokyo: Ōhata Shoten, 1932.) Reprinted in *Imanaka Tsugimaro seijigaku ronshū* (hereafter: *ITs*), Tanaka Hiroshi, Takehara Yoshifumi, Hanzawa Takamaro, Yasu Seishū, Matsutomi Hiroshi, and Imanaka Hiroshi, eds., 3:1–81, epigraph from pp. 78–79.

1. Needless to say, I am not restricting this analytic distinction to Japanese writers (although Maruyama's appeal to the kokumin nation as the foundation for a postwar democratic society puts him in the later camp). Nor can any such analytic category be asked to cover the entire range of scholarship with equal applicability. But in broad terms, it does capture the main postures and limitations in the literature on Japanese fascism, both in Japanese and Western languages. As an analytic distinction, it opens up a new perspective, which I develop later, on what kind of Japanese "fascism" has been left unseen by this scholarship.

2. Walter Laqueur, "Fascist Culture," in *Fascism: Past, Present, and Future* (Oxford: Oxford University Press, 1996), 62–63.

3. Maruyama Masao, "Kindai nihon shisō to bungaku" (1961), in *Nihon no shisō* (Tokyo: Iwanami Shoten, 2000), 105–6.

4. Imanaka's works are ranked along with Hasegawa Nyozekan's and Ōyama Ikuo's as the most important sources on fascism in Japanese: see Tanaka Hiroshi et al., "Kankō no kotoba," in *ITs*, 2, (Tokyo: Ochanomizu Shobō, 1978), iii.

5. Imanaka Tsugimaro, *Fuashizumu undō ron*, in *ITs*, 3, (Tokyo: Ochanomizu Shobō, 1981), xi.

6. The heart of Imanaka's *Fuashizumu undō ron* is composed of three chapters that analyze in detail each of these stages: cf. *ITs*, 3:12–64. The work then concludes with a section on the essence of fascism. Imanaka's three-stage-development of fascism has been adopted by postwar scholars, most notably Abe Hirozumi, who has applied the approach to the rise of fascism in Japan: the transitional period, 1931–36; the formative period, 1936–40; and the establishment and fall of fascism, 1940–45. See Abe Hirozumi, *Nihon fuashizumu ron* (Tokyo: Eishobō, 1996), 71–86.

7. Laqueur, *Fascism*, 60.

8. *ITs*, 3:68–70. Imanaka's inclusion of Germany on the side of "sound" advanced capitalist nations reflects his careful historical research (he points to the reaction of Italian fascists to the German Banca Commerciale Italiana) and his theoretical ambivalence at the time over Germany's potential for fascism: see ibid., 80–81). Of course, this misplaced optimism about Germany's ability to control fascism led him to immediately address the problem of German fascism in his next book, *Minzoku-teki shakaishugi ron*. (Originally published as volume four in *Dokusai seijiron sōsho* [Essays on Political Dictatorship Series]. Tokyo: Ōhata Shoten, 1932.) Reprinted in *ITs*, 3: 83–271.

9. *ITs*, 3:74.

10. Ibid., 75.

11. Ibid., 76–77. Imanaka's emphasis on the "social masses" as the agent of the fascist revolution, and his concern over the terrorism that connected revolutionary fascism and revolutionary socialism are best appreciated when seen in light of the development of fascism and revolutionary terrorism in Japan. Consider, for example, the connection of revolutionary socialism and populist nationalism with Kita Ikki and his followers and its impact on violent acts of terrorism in the 1930s, as well as the close relationship between many self-avowed fascists such as Kamei Kan'ichirō and the Social Masses Party, founded in 1932.

12. Imanaka, Minzoku-teki shakaishugi ron, 3:229.

13. Cf. Imanaka's translation of Partito Nationale Fascista as Minzoku fuashisuta seitō: ITs, 3:11, 37–64. For his translation of Hitler's Nationalsozialistische Arbeiterpartei as Minzoku-teki shakaishugi rōdō tō, see ibid., 123. Also consider the title of the book, Minzoku-teki shakaishugi ron (On Ethnic-National Socialism), which is exclusively on the German Nazi movement. Imanaka himself at times recognized this fundamental difference between Italian fascism's rejection of a purely biological racial concept of the nation and German national socialism's emphasis on an ethnicized, or "racialized," national Volk: see ibid., 2:92–93. His insistence on a general theory of fascism that subsumed these differences required more attention to the problem of how to understand minzoku, as discussed later.

14. One need not merely surmise the connection. In his introduction to Minzoku-teki shakaishugi ron, 85, Imanaka explicitly raises the catastrophe of the assassination of Prime Minister Inukai as evidence that the fascist movements he had worried about were gaining force in Japan and threatening constitutional government.

15. For Imanaka's brief reduction of Nazi cultural policy to biological race, see ITs, 2:93–96, 3:246. His confusion of the concepts of jinshu and minzoku in Nazi ideology is more explicit earlier (on 3:106–108), and he argues that Nazi ideology was trans-ethnic, transnational, and truly racial (on 3:257).

16. Ibid., 2:69.

17. Ibid., 69–70. For two contemporary sources that largely parallel Imanaka's theory of minzoku, see Ōyama Ikuo, Seiji no shakai-teki kiso (1923), in Ōyama Ikuo Zenshū (Chūō Kōronsha, 1947), vol. 1, 217–37; Yanaihara Tadao, "Minzoku to kokka" (1937), in Yanaihara Tadao zenshū (Tokyo: Iwanami Shoten, 1965), vol. 18, 278–79.

18. ITs, 2:71. Barnes, a professor of sociology at Smith College, understood nationality "as psychic and cultural rather than a political fact" and emphasized the important impact of the First World War on national consciousness: see Harry E. Barnes, Sociology and Political Theory (New York: Alfred A. Knopf, 1924), 189. Imanaka misidentifies him as "Henry" Barnes.

19. Imanaka drew explicitly from Lenin's "Ursprunglicher Entwurf der Thesen zur nationalen und kolonialen Frage" and "Die sozialistische Revolution und das Selbstbestimmungsrecht der Nationen." From Stalin, he drew on Probleme des Leninismus and "Marxism and the National-Colonial Question," which had been translated into Japanese as "Marukusushugi to minzoku mondai" and was in-

cluded in volume 14 of the *Sutārin Buhārin chosakushū*, Sano Manabu and Nishi Masao, eds. (Tokyo: Kaizō Sha, 1930). He also reviewed the major contributions toward a Marxist definition of nationality by Otto Bauer and Karl Kautsky: see *ITs*, 2:69–95.

20. Ibid., 81.

21. Ibid., 93.

22. See Imanaka Tsugimaro, "Waga kuni no fuashizumu undō," in *ITs*, 2:288–307.

23. Here, some attention to the influence of Carl Schmitt on Imanaka's approach to democracy and fascism is important. Schmitt's *Die Diktatur* (1927) framed Imanaka's entire approach to the problem of fascism, which Imanaka then saw in terms of a middle-class movement to uproot parliamentary democracy in the name of a populist dictator: see *ITs*, 2:3–10. Schmitt's influence extended to Imanaka's interpretation of the relationship of fascism to religion, a topic where Imanaka does come close to a cultural theory. A discussion of Imanaka's theories of religion and dictatorship will have to await another opportunity. On Schmitt's wide-ranging influence among prewar Japanese political and legal theorists, see Yamashita Takeshi, *Kāru Shumitto Kenkyū* (Tokyo: Nansō Sha, 1986), esp. the bibliography on 216–85, which lists many of Schmitt's works in Japanese translation by 1939. I thank Professor Takano Kiyohiro of Konan University Law Faculty for this source. Professor Takano added his own testimony to the influence of Carl Schmitt on prewar Japanese political discourse.

24. Watanabe Kazutami, "1935 zengo: Hayashi Tatsuo no tenkō megutte," *Bungaku* 54, no. 9 (November 1986): 1–24.

25. See Seiji M. Lippit, *Topographies of Japanese Modernism* (New York: Columbia University Press, 2002), esp. 199–228. In Japanese, see Bungaku shisō konwakai, eds., *Kindai no yume to chisei: Bungaku shisō no shōwa 10 nen zengo* (Tokyo: Kanrin Shobō, 2000).

26. For evidence of the centrality of minzoku nationalism in Sano's and Nabeyama's thinking, see their jointly written tenkō declaration "Yo wa naze ni kyōsantō o satta ka" (1933), in Sano Manabu chosakushū kankōkai, eds., *Sano Manabu chosakushū*, vol. 1, 1–37. Sano's and Nabeyama's national socialism is most explicit in their conclusion that "minzoku is none other than the majority, that is, the laborers": ibid., 12.

27. Tosaka Jun, *Nippon ideorogii ron* (1936; hereafter *NI*), in *Tosaka Jun zenshū*, vol. 2 (Tokyo: Keisō Shobō, 1966), 310–11, 316–67.

28. Ibid., 367.

29. Tosaka's unstinting critique of Kawai Eijirō is particularly important in this context: see ibid., 398–400. Kawai, a notable defender of Taishō collectivist liberalism and the darling of the "fascism equals militarism" camp, exposes in his wartime thought and writings the centrality of ethnic identity among the "liberals" of his day.

30. *NI*, 255, 392–424.

31. Harootunian, "The Postwar Genealogy of Fascism and Tosaka Jun's Prewar Cri-

KEVIN M. DOAK

52

tique of Liberalism," *Journal of Pacific Asia* 2 (1995): 108. As Harootunian notes, one of the key sites where Tosaka saw this fixation occuring was in "folkism," Harootunian's rendering of *minzokushugi*.

32. The split in Japanism and rise of the "progressive (*shinpo-teki*)" faction were noted at the time by bureaucrats in the Home Ministry's Criminal Affairs Bureau, who were in charge of monitoring the fascist movement: see Gregory Kasza, "Fascism from Below? A Comparative Perspective on the Japanese Right, 1931–1936," *Journal of Contemporary History* 19, no. 4 (1984): 613–14. Kasza also points out that the progressives were more directly influenced by fascist ideas than were the idealists. The split between idealist and progressives in the Japanist movement foreshadows the division Tōyama Shigeki would draw early in the postwar period between "reactionary" and "progressive" forms of Japanese nationalism: see Kevin M. Doak, "Ethnic Nationalism and Romanticism in Early Twentieth-Century Japan," in *Shōwa Japan: Political, Economic, and Social History, 1926–1989*, ed. Stephen S. Large (London: Routledge, 1998), 300–301. For both Tōyama and the progressive Japanists, the preferred expression of this nationalism was *minzokushugi* (ethnic nationalism).

33. *NI*, 437.

34. See Itō Takashi, *Nihon no uchi to soto* (Tokyo: Chūō Kōronsha, 2001), esp. 266–313, 451.

35. It was well known that Tōjō "made excessive use of the police to curb dissent" (Stephen S. Large, "Emperor Hirohito and Early Shōwa Japan," in idem, *Shōwa Japan*, 253), but this dissent was not always from Marxists or liberals. Consider Nakano Seigō, a self-avowed admirer of Mussolini who committed suicide in 1943 after his criticism of Tōjō led to his hounding by the Special Higher Police. Nakano's friend Matsumae Shigeyoshi, head of the general affairs division of the Imperial Rule Assistance Association and a supporter of Konoe, believed he was persecuted by Tōjō for his support of Konoe's New Order in East Asia. Significantly, Matsumae was elected to the postwar Diet as a (right-wing) member of the Socialist Party while remaining founder and president of Tokai University: see Matsumae Shigeyoshi, *Matsumae Shigeyoshi waga jinsei* (Tokyo: Kōdansha, 1980), 115–131, 140–63. Also, Yasuda Yojūrō, a foe of Marxists and liberals (as Richard Torrance notes in this volume), was constantly harassed by the Special Higher Police. Tōjō was scornful also of the ethnic idealism of Ishiwara Kanji, with whom he frequently clashed until Ishiwara's military status was deactivated in 1941. On the relationship between Tōjō and Ishiwara, see Miyazawa Eriko, *Kenkoku daigaku to minzoku kyōwa* (Tokyo: Fūma Shobō, 1997). The differences between Tōjō and Konoe are given detailed treatment in Itō Takashi, *Nihon no uchi to soto*, and Itō, *Shōwaki no seiji*.

36. Kasza, "Fascism from Below?" 624.

37. Harootunian, "The Postwar Genealogy of Fascism and Tosaka Jun's Prewar Critique of Liberalism," 95.

38. Karatani Kōjin, *'Senzen' no shikō* (Tokyo: Kōdansha, 2001), 65–66.

39. Cf. Yoshimi Yoshiaki, *Kusa no ne no fuashizumu* (Tokyo: University of Tokyo Press, 1987).

40. Karatani has been one victim of this freewheeling use of "fascism" as an invective to hurl against one's opponents. A "live report" called "Cultural Fascism" argues that contemporary cultural fascism in Japan is best represented by Karatani himself. The author of this diatribe is a prime example of the inability to see beyond Imanaka's theory of "dictatorship" and, indeed, uses this "dictatorship" theory of fascism to settle personal grievances against Karatani and his New Associationist Movement (NAM) organization: see Hisamoto Yoshiko, *Bunka Fuashizumu* (Tokyo: Editor Shop, 2001).

41. See Pierre Bourdieu, *The Field of Cultural Production* (New York: Columbia University Press, 1993), 112–41. In applying Bourdieu's concept of "symbolic violence" to cultural fascism in Japan, however, one should be careful not to overplay Bourdieu's Weberian emphasis on the state ("the monopoly of legitimate symbolic violence": ibid., 250).

42. Harumi Befu, "Symbols of Nationalism and Nihonjinron," in *Ideology and Practice in Modern Japan*, ed. Roger Goodman and Kirsten Refsing (London: Routledge, 1992).

43. On the leftist supporters of ethnic national culture in postwar Japan, see Kevin M. Doak, "What Is a Nation and Who Belongs? National Narratives and the Ethnic Imagination in Twentieth-Century Japan," *American Historical Review* 102, no. 3 (April 1997): 288–309; Curtis Anderson Gayle, "Progressive Representations of the Nation: Early Postwar Japan and Beyond," *Social Science Japan Journal* 4, no. 1 (2001): 1–19; Amino Yoshihiko, *Rekishi to shite no sengo shigaku* (Tokyo: Nihon Editor School, 2000), esp. 13–55. On the strange partnership between the left-wing and right-wing minzokushugi movements, see Ino Kenji (a proponent from the right of unification of the minzokushugi movements), "Uyoku minzoku-ha undō o tenbō suru," in *Uyoku minzoku-ha sōran*, ed. Ino Kenji (Tokyo: Nijūisseki Shoin, 1990).

44. See Nishikawa Nagao, "Nihon-gata kokumin kokka no keisei: Hikakushi-teki shiten kara," in *Bakumatsu meijiki no kokumin kokka keisei to bunka hen'yō*, ed. Nishikawa Nagao and Matsumiya Hideharu (Tokyo: Shin'yokusha, 1995), 3–42.

45. Idem, "Two Interpretations of Japanese Culture," trans. Mikiko Murata and Gavan McCormack, in *Multicultural Japan: Palaeolithic to Post-modern*, Donald Denoon, et al., eds., (New York: Cambridge University Press, 1997), 247–48. Nishikawa's assertion that an emancipation from the state has been largely completed in postwar Japan may be at first difficult to accept. But there is in fact an undeniable, strong anti-state sentiment among the Japanese public, and it even extends to those working for the state. An editorial from 2001 in the *Daily Yomiuri* reported that Japanese bureaucrats' attitudes are often described in such phrases as "bureaus come before ministries" and "there are ministries, but there is no state": see "Bureaucrats Must Change Attitudes" editorial, *Daily Yomiuri*, January 7, 2001, 6A. The editorial was responding to the reorganization of the Japanese national

political system on January 6, 2001, under Prime Minister Mori, especially the creation of a new Cabinet Office and the reduction of the number of ministries and agencies from twenty-two to twelve, a step widely recognized as part of an effort to build a stronger state that could resist the centrifugal forces of bureaucratic infighting. While some might like to see this reorganization as part of a neo-statist agenda, most commentators understand it as part of a larger process of trying to secure democracy by curtailing the powers of bureaucrats and special interest groups and thereby enhancing Japan's ability to make meaningful commitments to international peacekeeping operations. The problem of a weak state, rather than a strong state, coexists strangely in Japanese public opinion with a broad antigovernment, even anti-statist, populism.

RICHARD TORRANCE

The People's Library:
The Spirit of Prose Literature versus Fascism

■   In 1936, in the literary journal *Bungakkai* (Literary World),
Takeda Rintarō declared, "Our primary obligation is to take action in opposition [to fascism]."[1] He was already in the process of establishing *Jinmin
bunko* (The People's Library), a monthly literary journal that was funded by
his own, not inconsiderable earnings for works appearing in more popular
publications. Although Takeda maintained ultimate editorial control, the
managing editor was Honjō Mutsuo, a secret member of the by then clan-
destine Communist Party. Almost all of the fifty or so contributors were
leftists who had been arrested for their political activities. "We are the leftist
survivors," Naka Kōhei, a regular contributor, declared.[2] In a public reply to
a letter from Jean-Richard Bloch, secretary of the International Association
of Writers for the Defense of Culture, Takeda formally aligned the journal,
in July 1936 with the International Popular Front against Fascism (JB 1:7:2–
3).[3] This alliance of the group with the international antifascist movement
was formally accepted in a letter signed by the secretaries of the International Association of Writers for the Defense of Culture: Louis Aragon, André Malraux, André Chamson, and Jean-Richard Bloch (JB 1:9:2–4).

From the time of the first issue of *The People's Library* in March 1936 until its demise in January 1938, the journal served as Japan's most articulate, organized, and popular literary opposition to fascism.[4] Yet the pages of the journal contain no sustained definitions or theoretical formulations of fascism. Instead, one reads attacks on concrete targets: the *Bungei Konwakai* (Literary Harmonious Discussion Society), those associated with the neoromantic movement, or popular writers of historical fiction. To understand what fascism meant for the writers and readers of *The People's Library* from 1936 to 1938, it is first necessary to review what the concept of fascism signified in Japan in its historical context.

Conceptualizations of Fascism before *The People's Library*

One can discern three broad phases in the development of the discussion of fascism in Japan of the 1930s by Japanese literary figures. Writers and journalists first conceptualized in theoretical terms the possibility of a Japanese fascism in periodicals and books oriented toward a liberal intelligentsia. They were particularly acute in their descriptions of the affinities between political, social, and cultural trends in Japan and those in Italy and other nations that had strong fascist movements. The concept of fascism as defined for the intelligentsia was next taken up by the mass media, which used the term to refer to specific cliques and alliances within military and political circles and to literary and political associations that identified themselves with fascism. Third, as repression of liberal and leftist ideas became more intense from the mid-1930s on, the term, which had generally been used in a derogatory or patronizing manner, fell out of use in the mass media, and it and its variants came to be used as a weapon by remnants of the left—notably, those associated with *The People's Library*—in a fight with an increasingly sophisticated and respectable "new ultranationalism."

With few exceptions, after 1938, the term *fascism* ceased to be used in any sort of critical way, and consideration of Japanese ultranationalism in the 1930s as one manifestation of an international movement to the right would have to wait until after 1945, when the existence of a "Japanese fascism" could once again be discussed freely. What should be borne in mind in the ensuing discussion is that if the concept of fascism seems ill-defined in the mid-1930s when used to characterize the political opponents of the left, this is in part due to increased political repression that did not allow for the same sustained critique of Japanese society carried out by intellectuals in the early 1930s, but it is also because later writers and critics were referring to a term that had already been defined in the early 1930s.

From 1931 until 1935 or so, the question of whether Japan was, or was becoming, a fascist country was extensively debated among Japanese journalists, academics, writers, and literary critics. Japanese liberal intellectuals in particular perceived analogies between trends in Japan and the growing power of ultranationalism in Europe—police brutality, violent suppression of freedom of assembly and association, increasingly severe censorship, a high degree of central control based on dogmatic morality enforced throughout the school system—and they began to speculate about the possibility of fascism in Japan, a possibility that had formerly seemed remote, if not absurd.

In March 1931, in the journal *Hihan* (The Critique), the novelist and journalist Hasegawa Nyozekan began publishing a series of articles warning of the prospect of a Japanese fascism. This series is remarkable not only because Hasegawa was one of the first non-communist liberals in Japan to recognize fascism as a dangerous international phenomenon but also because he was the first to apply a conceptualization of fascism to distinctively Japanese conditions.[5] Hasegawa saw fascism as the product of underdeveloped capitalism in countries where the modern state was of recent origin. It arose because of economic depression, when confidence was shaken in large-scale bourgeois capitalism and its institutions, primarily bourgeois democracy. Since in Italy, as in Japan, politics represents the interests of middling and small capital, fascism is a movement of the middle class, which counters the organization and violence of the proletariat with organization and violence of its own: "Generally overlooked is the fact that the motor of the fascist movement is middle class violence," Hasegawa wrote.[6] Though fascists saw international socialism as their implacable enemy, they nonetheless incorporated the methods of the communists, especially in regard to the establishment of dictatorship: "just as violence is a requisite of the socialistic 'dictatorship,' so too is violence the sine qua non of the process of the formation of the fascist dictatorship."[7]

Fascism, however, argued Hasegawa, tends to legitimize itself over time. On the one hand, when the fascist regime gains power, it needs large-scale capitalism to make the economy function. On the other hand, it deflects internal protest by channeling it into external aggression against foreign enemies and against internal enemies, particularly leftists. "Thus," he wrote, "internationally, fascism has become another name for the dictatorship of the bourgeoisie."[8]

Hasegawa next speculated on whether fascism was possible in Japan. In terms of the economic conditions that give rise to fascism, Hasegawa maintained that Japan fit the model. Ironically, he believed that, in terms of the underdevelopment of its capitalist system, Japan was more prone to fascism than Germany, which had a more highly developed industrial base. Japan was also prone to fascism in respect to the persistence of a feudal ideology: "the ideological concepts based on the economic positions of small and medium capital are essentially reactionary—racialism, nationalism, feudal morality, and so on. In other words, these constitute the 'spirit of fascism.'"[9]

Japan also conformed with the model in having an essentially reactionary middle class. Given the weakness of the capitalist system in Japan, its middle class was dominated by small and middling capital and people in the public employ, including military officers, bureaucrats, and others in the vast state sector in Japan. The ideology of the middle class was not that of laissez-faire capitalism: "in order to garner the votes of the middle class, the political parties must adopt bureaucratic, that is to say, middle class social policies. In this sense, Japan is essentially a fascist State."[10]

Extralegal violence aimed at the suppression of the proletariat and dissent in general, according to Hasegawa, was directed by "Japan's bourgeois politicians who control numerous gangs of professional thugs (shokugyō-teki bōryoku dan), thugs who are the advance troops of fascism."[11] In addition, Hasegawa cites at least twenty-five associations with memberships of more than four and a half million. He argues that these reactionary extensions of middle-class morality—slavish faith in religion, unquestioning loyalty to the emperor, belief in a host of other traditional nationalist abstractions— provide more than enough organizational support in terms of numbers for a Japanese fascism.[12]

By the time of the Manchurian Incident of September 1931, then, the terms *fascism* (*fuashizumu*), *fascist* (*fuassho*), and *fascistization* (*fuasshoka*) were already in circulation and were supported by a body of political theory that seemed to correspond to Japan's social, political, and cultural realities. Such political philosophers as Tosaka Jun, Miki Kiyoshi, and Kawai Eijirō, and a number of others continued to refine and expand the concept in the light of Japan's continued militarization. Subsequently, the notion that Japan was becoming "fascist" began to dominate the mass media. A new term was needed to describe the series of shocking and dismal events that occurred in the early 1930s—namely, the right-wing assassinations of Prime Ministers Hamaguchi and Inugai, former Finance Minister Inoue,

RICHARD TORRANCE

and the Mitsui financier Dan Takuma; the several failed attempts at military coups d'état; the mass arrests of leftists; the police torture and murder of the writer Kobayashi Takiji; and so on. In 1932, for example, the *Japan Times*, Japan's authoritative English-language newspaper, would argue on its editorial page, "Fascism contributes a medium whereby the fundamental institutions of the Empire may be preserved and yet certain objectives achieved."[13] Or again, the ideological conversions in prison of Sano Manabu and Nabeyama Sadachika in June 1933 were described as follows in a headline in *Yomiuri Shimbun*: "The Two Leading Figures of the Communist Party, Sano and Nabeyama, Renounce Communism and Convert (*tenkō*) to Fascism."[14]

Organizations soon formed to oppose fascism in Japan. One of the first was begun in 1933 with nationwide student and faculty protests against the dismissal of Takigawa Yukitoki, a Kyoto University law professor who had written extensively on Kropotkin and who was accused by Hatoyama Ichirō, then minister of education, of supporting communism. Alarmed by the government's blatant violation of the university's autonomy, the increasingly severe repression of leftist cultural organizations and the Communist Party, the arbitrariness of censorship, and the Nazi book burnings, two hundred fifty prominent Japanese writers and intellectuals led by Hasegawa Nyozekan, Miki Kiyoshi, and Nii Itaru formed the *Gakugei Jiyū Dōmei* (Alliance for Freedom in Academic Research and the Arts). In July 1933, the well-known novelist Tokuda Shūsei was chosen as president. Membership rose to four hundred, and the group was so effective that the government ordered it disbanded in 1935. In the years following the creation of the Alliance for Freedom in Academic Research and the Arts, numerous scholarly, religious, and political groups, with thousands of members, implicitly or explicitly opposed fascism in Japan. These cannot be enumerated here, but almost all had been suppressed by the state by the end of 1938.[15]

Given the centrality of literature to all cultural endeavors in the Japan of the 1930s, it is not surprising that in 1932 literary periodicals and the literary pages of newspapers were crowded with analyses of the culture of fascism. Hasegawa, a respected novelist and literary critic who was never sympathetic to popular culture, seemed to express the consensus of the literary world in condemning popular culture, especially samurai fiction, for strengthening feudal values that led to fascist tendencies and state control.[16] The identification of popular samurai fiction with fascism was reinforced when the following article appeared in the February 4, 1932, issue of *Yomiuri Shimbun*:

As the political situation becomes daily more severe, the patriotic fervor and energy of people has swelled forth as a wave. . . . In touch with the intellectual tempo of the times, those generals of the right-wing forces in the literary world, namely Naoki Sanjūrō, Kume Masao, Mikami Otokichi, Shirai Kyōji, and Satō Hachirō, have come to advocate "the realization and strengthening of Fascist literature."[17]

The "fascist literati (*fuassho bunshi*)" mentioned in this article, and the other writers who participated in later fascist literary groups, were almost all novelists of popular historical fiction. Their political views seemed to reflect the romantic and combative content of their fiction. In the January 7, 1932, issue of *Yomiuri Shimbun*, Mikami Otokichi, the author of a famous novel about a transvestite samurai assassin, declared that he had been awakened to the magnificence of the Japanese spirit and had concluded that "neither the present capitalism nor Marxism could bring Japan's small-scale farming villages to life." He hoped only to contribute to "bringing about a new racial and national movement in society and to live under a new social order."[18] Naoki Sanjūrō, the man for whom a celebrated literary prize was later named, began a series titled "My Declaration of Fascism" as follows: "to all the nations of the world, I hereby declare . . . that during the period from 1932 to 1933, I am a fascist. . . . During this year of my fascism, I am waging war on all leftists. Attack and I'll cut you down."[19]

It seems to have been the general consensus that this group, and its subsequent incarnations, which came to include such participants as Kikuchi Kan, Japan's most successful literary entrepreneur; Satō Haruo, the famous poet; and Yoshikawa Eiji, whose epic *Miyamoto Musashi* is still popular even in America, were little more than excursions to share a meal with men in uniform and view the latest military technology. Their fascism was said to have had no effective ideology other than a vague ultranationalism, to have been incapable of inspiring radical action, and to have been merely an attempt at self-promotion by opportunistic novelists whose books were not selling well. Writing in the early spring of 1932, Fuwa Shiyō (Osatake Takeshi) best characterized this early "fascist literary movement." First, it consisted of novelists of popular historical fiction who viewed Hitler as about the same as Kiyokawa Hachirō, the heroic but temperamental Restoration-era swordsman who first assassinated enemies of the Restoration and then assassinated enemies of the Tokugawa. In addition, there were those writers who had lost popularity and used fascism as an advertisement to sell their literary works.[20]

As the discussion of fascism in the literary press progressed, motivations in using the term became more complicated. The proletariat writer Tokunaga Sunao, for example, accused his rival Inuta Shigeru and his agrarian literary movement of "being reborn as a fascistic and reactionary movement." Nakamura Murao, a well-known editor and critic who had been carrying on a running battle with the left for about a decade, saw nothing wrong with a fascist literature in Japan. The most splendid traits of the Japanese people, according to Nakamura, were their love of country and loyalty to the emperor; yet modern Japanese literature had not dealt with these at all. A fascist literature would provide a welcome antidote to the vapidity of proletariat literature.[21]

A roundtable discussion held in 1932 reveals other attitudes by writers and critics toward fascism and fascist literature. Kume Masao, primarily known as a writer of autobiographical fiction, stated that fascism was understood by most Japanese as "despotic rule by a military clique." Shirai Kyōji, a popular writer associated with the fascist movement, offered the following definition: "it is said that fascism has no etymology, only results, but in the end, it can be summed up as dictatorial government based on an ultranationalistic, ethnocentric social policy and its philosophy." Chiba Kameo, a leading modernist critic of the day, maintained that "traditionalism is the major ideological artery of fascism. In a certain sense, this traditionalism does not recognize the freedom of the individual . . . , [but] if fascist literature is to become popular, it must align itself with Japanese traditionalism." Iwasaki Junko, one of the few female commentators on fascism, predicted that "a fascist literature [would] first appear as the literature of romanticism."[22]

Individual definitions of a fascist literature appear to have differed little from the writers' attitudes toward popular genres of literature that were occupying more and more pages of magazines and newspapers directed toward a mass audience. It was nationalistic, romantic, and full of heroic martial valor, and it stressed love of family, the emperor, and traditional values. What made the self-proclaimed fascist writers appear particularly sinister was not what they wrote, or their innocuous meetings with military officers, or their pedestrian political ideas, but their enthusiastic cooperation with attempts by the state to use them as the basis for the establishment of a "Literary Academy" that would co-opt all writers into serving the nation and guiding thought in healthy, patriotic directions. It was an age when a number of new technological means for the control and motivation of the masses were coming into existence, and attempts by government authorities to bring these media—radio, movies, mass-circulation entertainment magazines, and popular fiction—under state guidance seemed threatening to writers of progressive fiction, poetry, and essays.

In 1932, Matsumoto Manabu, former governor of Kagoshima Prefecture, was appointed the chief of the Criminal Affairs Bureau in the Ministry of Home Affairs, an office with direct jurisdiction over thought control. He was firmly allied with the so-called new bureaucrats, the reform faction of the bureaucracy with close ties to the elements in the military calling for a radical, antidemocratic, fascist transformation in society. In addition to drafting repressive legislation to control "dangerous ideas," Matsumoto under the auspices of the nationalist *Nihon Bunka Chūō Renmei* (Japan Culture League), showed a prodigious talent for organizing cultural groups to, in his words, "promote domestic enterprises fostering the Japanese spirit and internationally to shine the light of the Japanese spirit throughout the world." The activities Matsumoto promoted outside the Ministry of Home Affairs were funded by the corporations Mitsui and Mitsubishi.[23]

Using the already formed organizations of the "fascist literati" as a core membership, Chief Matsumoto began the groundwork to establish a state-sponsored Academy of Literature. This project took the preliminary form of the Literary Harmonious Discussion Society. For the next decade, writers struggled against this and other state-sponsored attempts to bring literature and the arts under control. In the end, of course, the early presentiments concerning a Japanese fascism—at least for literary people—proved valid. By 1940, in imitation of models adapted from fascist Italy and Germany, all Japanese writers who wished to continue working professionally were forced to join a variety of state organizations.

The People's Library and the Literary Resistance to Fascism

The People's Library was established in the wake of escalating arrests of political dissidents, mostly on the left: 6,124 in 1930; 10,422 in 1931; and approximately 18,000 in 1933. Almost all those put on trial renounced their political beliefs (*tenkō*) rather than serve long prison terms. Having decimated the political left with mass arrests, the Ministry of Home Affairs then began concentrating on cultural organizations and in 1932 arrested approximately 400 leftist cultural activists.[24]

Takeda Rintarō was one of the more important writers on the left, but he had avoided arrest by fleeing to Manchuria and more or less going underground on his return to Japan. He soon grew dissatisfied with the mood of compromise in the chastened literary world, and he resolved to "raise a little ruckus." The magazine he founded soon reached a circulation of about five thousand. Groups throughout the country—notably in Osaka, Nagoya, and Sapporo—were established in support of the periodical. At one point, Takeda could declare, "At present, we are the most widely read literary journal in Japan" (JB 1:3:140).

The objectives of *The People's Library* were made explicit by Takeda at various points in the life of the journal. Takeda wanted the magazine to appeal to "workers in the city and young people in farming villages, those who read for enjoyment and to satisfy a desire for culture, those who read prose fiction as a part of their everyday life" (JB 1:5:160). To this end, Takeda insisted, "This journal has adopted the firm position that prose fiction is our primary reason for existence" (JB 2:9:152). Takeda further envisioned the magazine as an unwavering voice of opposition:

> We have no big money behind us, no one in authority to protect us. These are words we repeat quite often, but we believe this is in the tradition of not only Japanese literature but also, more broadly, the universal tradition of literature. We are determined to bring to life the novelistic act within the tradition of "no money behind us, no one in authority to protect us." To outsiders, it might seem we are doing splendidly, but management of the magazine for a year has been a difficult project. We foresaw the difficulties, and so we can declare with confidence that we shall not waver from our determination. The denunciation of the Literary Harmonious Discussion Society, the development of legitimate realism, the flourishing of prose—such objectives can be summed up as the protection of culture and the popularization of narrative fiction of high quality, and we have exerted all of our meager strength in attempting to accomplish them. (JB 2:4:1)

As we have seen, at this point the widespread use of the term *fascism* in the pages of literary journals and newspapers described most concretely three trends in the literary world: the forcible suppression of the left; government attempts to control, homogenize, and encourage the arts, much as fascism was creating cartels of movie and steel production in Italy; and the reification of a unique Japanese spirit through government sponsorship of popular literature. In addition, there were two other clear aspects of fascism in the arts that came to the fore in the mid-1930s: the denigration of

Japan's tradition of realism and the neo-romantic exaltation of the poetics of the past, especially in regard to a glorification of the aesthetics of hero worship and death.[25]

Opposition to fascism took the following forms. First, in the pages of *The People's Library* and elsewhere, there were frequent appeals to the tradition of the independence of the Japanese literary world, a tradition of writers, in their work, maintaining freedom from support or obligations to church, state, and large moneyed interests. Next, the Literary Harmonious Discussion Society was the object of unflagging hostility. Third, a running battle was carried on with the Japan Romantic School. Fourth, starting with the works of Ihara Saikaku (1642–93), the value of a native Japanese realism was advocated, and realistic prose fiction served as the journal's mainstay. Finally, as an alternative to the mainstream press, the pages of the journal were opened up to a variety of progressive, democratic, and antimilitaristic causes. These "elements of resistance" will be discussed in more detail later.

In 1935, Aono Suekichi, a leftist critic closely affiliated with *The People's Library*, argued:

> Except for a few popular writers, there are probably no novelists in Japan today who are not opposed to fascism. Even among those who hold no firm ideological positions, many are opposed to fascism because of a traditional spirit of the independence of literature built up in this country over a number of years. One can assume that if faced with the clear and present threat of fascism, the instinctive antifascism of most writers would come to the fore, and there would be a great deal of resistance. For example, almost every writer in Japan expressed anger and dismay over the book burnings by the Nazis. But what if it is the case that fascism does not explicitly reveal itself; instead arrives in stealth? . . . If writers, maintaining as they do their instinctive antifascism, were to be drawn into the gears of a gigantic opaque fascist machine, what a calamity it would be![26]

When reading the literary critics of fascism, one cannot help but be impressed by how sensitive they were to their contemporary society and how clearly they foresaw what was coming. In the political story unfolding before them, they recognized something new, a kind of amorphous perversity by which Japan's objective historical situation and contemporary ideological trends seemed to conform to those sweeping much of the rest of the world, yet the authors of a Japanese-style fascism vehemently denied they were fascist. As Hasegawa Nyozekan observed in 1932, though fascism was said to be raising its head in all areas of society, the political parties, the reactionary organizations, the military, the bureaucrats, everyone had declared they were not fascist. Even that personification of Japanese-style fascism, Hiranuma Kiichirō, leader of the new bureaucrats in the Ministry of Home Affairs, had declared that his goal was not fascism but the establishment of national morality. However, Hasegawa concluded, for Hiranuma, the state was "god," and his national morality meant not that the state followed morality but that morality followed the state.[27] Similarly, Aono Suekichi argued that Japanese fascism invoked the Shintō gods as the foundation of the Japanese people, and yet those gods were subordinate to the two new gods, the modern state and the modern concept of race (minzoku).[28]

As we have seen in essays by Takeda and Aono, one rhetorical strategy the writers and critics adopted again and again to resist this "gigantic opaque fascist machine" was to invoke the tradition of a modern Japanese literary world that had developed in opposition to the modern state, without support from outside institutions. This appears to have been particularly effective in the journal's ongoing battle with Matsumoto Manabu's Literary Harmonious Discussion Society. On a number of occasions, almost all of these writers reinforced the idea that a main goal of The People's Library was to oppose and attempt to disrupt literary movements created by government officials or that acted in cooperation with the power structure.[29] Ueno Takeo wrote to the effect that the Literary Harmonious Discussion Society was the shame of Japanese literature (JB 1:1:119). Nitta Jun accused writers who joined the society of "poisoning the literary scene and selling out Japan's pure literary tradition to the bureaucrats and the wealthy" (JB 1:3:98). Kosaka Takiko wrote of the pride she felt as a woman in seeing that no female writers were associated with the Literary Harmonious Discussion Society (JB 1:1:119). Letters from readers contained comments such as, "I have heard that even younger writers and critics are defending the [Literary Harmonious Discussion Society]. Have they no common sense or conscience?" (JB 1:5:3). Or, "I am in full support of The People's Library's bold challenge to the [Literary Harmonious Discussion Society]" (JB 1:8:9). Suspicions of government intentions to bring the arts under state control were undoubtedly justified. It has become clear that Matsumoto Manabu was attempting to control and organize cultural activities in a manner reminiscent of the Nazi Reichsschrifttumskammer (Chamber of Authors). The consistent pressure exerted by The People's Library was probably a factor in disrupting Matsumoto's plans, at least for several years.[30]

The fascism that writers for *The People's Library* perceived in the Japan Romantic School was as much aesthetic and philosophical as it was political. This was natural enough, since the neo-romantics, led by Yasuda Yojūrō, confuted these categories, arguing that "poetry and war are blood relatives"; that "war is just and beautiful even if it is one of aggression"; and that "war is the greatest performance of poetic lyricism."[31] This "wartime aesthetic"—or, from the perspective of *The People's Library*'s writers, the fascist aesthetic, which the Japan Romantic School was constructing from 1936 on—elevated the "poetic spirit" of a unique classical Japanese tradition and denigrated Japanese realism. Unfurling the banner of the "spirit of prose literature (*sanbun seishin*)," the *People's Library* group actively defended prose realism in the context of the Japanese literary tradition and opposed the nationalistic aesthetic of death being formulated by the Japanese romantics. The phrase *sanbun seishin* originated in a 1924 debate between Arishima Takeo, who argued that artists who devoted themselves wholly to their art were superior to those who were distracted by the petty matters of life, and Hirotsu Kazuo, who countered that the "spirit of prose literature" was the highest form of art precisely because it was the most common, immediate, and relevant to human existence.[32]

By the mid-1930s, what had been a debate over aesthetics became, for *The People's Library* and neo-romantic writers, politicized: prose narrative open to extra-literary diversity was either unaesthetic or democratic, while high poetic art forms were symbols of the nation's beauty, or reactionary. The writers for *The People's Library* felt the literature of prose narrative supported democracy, while the obtuse literary criticism and classical and neoclassical poetry that occupied the pages of the Japan Romantic School's journal *Nihon Rōman-ha* (Japan Romantic School) were inherently authoritarian.

Takeda Rintarō understood the "spirit of prose literature" in terms of a native tradition of realistic prose fiction in Japanese history. He traced this tradition from its origin with Ihara Saikaku to Japanese naturalism to his contemporary social realism (JB 1:9:84). The progress of this evolution corresponded to the rise of the bourgeoisie (JB 1:9:83), but social realism had frustrated the spirit of prose literature because in the haste to establish a politically effective ideology, it had succumbed to the seductions of theory and had become too abstract (JB 1:9:71). "Human experience is a vast, fascinating novel," according to Takeda, and attempts to make this experience conform to narrow ideological or generic constructs were counterproductive (JB 1:9:84). The proper subject of the novel was the disorderly lives of ordinary people. *Sanbun seishin* was the spirit of resistance to all authoritarian discourses, but especially to those propagated by the state. Needless to say, this idea of literature was anathema to the Japan Romantic School. The writers for *The People's Library* were labeled proponents of "shit realism" by critics aligned with romanticism.[33]

The ensuing debate between the two groups was the sharpest and most vituperative in the literary world during the years 1936 and 1937. In a confrontation between the *People's Library* group and the Japanese Romantic School staged by *Hōchi Shimbun* in June 1937, there is the following exchange between Nitta Jun, a member of *The People's Library*, and the neo-romantic Kamei Shōichirō:

> Nitta: Since you believe that there is nothing worth protecting in contemporary culture, then it follows that today's culture can be destroyed without great loss. If we follow your reasoning, isn't this a logical conclusion?
>
> Kamei: Yes. On the other hand, there are people who share our views. This is something worth defending.
>
> Nitta: Yeah, that's fascism![34]

Almost all of the writers of *The People's Library* were convinced that the Japan Romantic School represented fascism. In the June 1937 issue, Izu Kimio noted the congruence between the formation of the Hayashi government, with its policy of unity of religion, culture, and politics (*saisei itchi*), and the appearance of fascist cheerleaders for "Japanism" and "uniquely Japanese things," for whom there was an "intoxication with the unique beauty of Japanese traditional culture and enthusiasm for the purity of Japanese blood" (JB 2:7:32–36).[35] Shibukawa Gyō offered the most sustained critique of the Japan Romantic School in his essays serialized in *The People's Library*. He accused the Japan Romantic School of cultural chauvinism, of implicitly approving of Japan's aggressive war, hero worship leading to dictatorship, and amorality (JB 2:6:150–54). Yoshisawa Gen wrote, "Those who advocate a revival of ancient times probably do not consider themselves to be following a fascist line, but, objectively, the power of their ideas derives, more or less, from the ideology of Japanism" (JB 1:7:136).

In keeping with the position taken by *The People's Library* concerning "the spirit of prose literature," fiction occupied most of the pages of the magazine. The journal and its parent company, Jinminsha, published some of the more important fiction and poetry of the latter part of the 1930s. Takami Jun's *Kokyū wasureubeki* (Let Old Acquaintance Be Forgot; 1935–36), one of the most influential novels of the mid-1930s, was serialized in part in *The People's Library* and later published as a book by Jinminsha. The novel concerns a group of former student radicals who were active as labor organizers during the height of the left-wing movement and were subsequently arrested and renounced their political beliefs. One of the former comrades, Sawamura Minoru, has recently committed suicide, and the group has gathered to mourn his death. Shinohara Tatsuya, a former activist turned pleasure seeker, speculates on the reason why Sawamura took his own life:

> The time of our political involvement was for Sawamura, indeed for our generation, a period when we had the most to live for. Then came the day of reckoning. During the five years after his arrest, Sawamura suffered one painful humiliation after another. Finally, he severed his ties with politics and found a good job at a race track. Before that, he eked out a miserable existence as a temporary clerk at the administrative court. Before that, he worked as a cook in a coffee house. Imagine a guy with a degree in economics from Tokyo Imperial University working as a cook. Then, to put it bluntly, just when he found a job that would let him live like a human being, he killed himself.
>
> Shinohara thought this was odd. Sawamura gave up on politics, lived in utter despair, and just when there was light at the end of the tunnel, he committed suicide. Still, Shinohara also thought he understood. . . . When Sawamura suddenly found a secure life, he lost the self that was struggling to survive. His old self died and a new self was born. His old self, a self of "ideas," disappeared and was replaced by a new self, an "ignoble" self. (JB 1:3:124–25)

The novel is a chronicle of the destroyed lives left in the wake of political repressions of the late 1920s and early 1930s.

Mamiya Mosuke's *Aragane* (Ore; 1937–38), which describes in detail the lives of miners, is now considered a classic of Japanese social realism. Takeda Rintarō's *Ihara Saikaku* (1936–37) was well received when it first appeared and has since gained a reputation as one of his finest works. Jinminsha was the first to publish in book form Kaneko Mitsuharu's *Same* (Sharks; 1937) and *Ottosei* (A Seal; 1937), two poems fiercely critical of the sterility, violence, and homogenization of everyday life in a militaristic society (JB 2:10:1).

A Seal
Smelly breath,

Steaming.
Slimy skin, like a tomb.
It makes me sick,
What a disgusting life!
Bodies—
Ponderous air-filled bags.
Sluggish resilience,
Pitiful rubber.
How conceited!
Mediocre!
Pock marks mar their skin:
Huge balls.
Pushed aside by the fishy nauseating crowd.
I have always longed for the opposite direction.[36]

Almost every major writer with a commitment to realism published fiction or poetry in the journal at one point or another.[37] They did so out of a sense of solidarity with the magazine, since none of the contributors were paid for their writing.

The most politically daring fiction seems to have been created by young, relatively unknown writers. Yuasa Katsuei's *Tabako* (Tobacco; 1936 [JB 1:7:34–51]) concerns discrimination against and police persecution of Japan's Korean minority as perceived by a young boy. An anti-war theme is expressed in Hotta Shōichi's *Yanushi no musuko shusseisu* (The Landlord's Son Goes to War; 1937), which is about a wealthy old man left alone, doubting the value of his years of labor and frugality after his son is drafted to fight in China with the outbreak of the Second Sino-Japanese War (JB 2:14:2–18). *Nikutai no tsumi* (Sins of the Flesh; 1936), by Hirabayashi Hyōgo, is an inspired mix of sado-eroticism, spy fiction, and social realism that concerns the suicide, after police torture, of a former prostitute who serves as a liaison between union leaders and strikers on the line (JB 1:4:24–63). Literary works by women—Hirabayashi Taiko, Hayashi Fumiko, Sata Ineko, Miyamoto Yuriko, Ōtani Fujiko, Yada Tsuseko, and several others—were also featured prominently.

In addition to socially committed fiction, the pages of *The People's Library* were open to a variety of progressive causes. Criticism of contemporary political trends tended to be very specific and was quite often carried in letters from readers. Dissatisfaction with government policies was often expressed. One reader wrote, "There are any number of Diet members speechifying about the exhaustion of our farming villages, but I wonder how many really care?" (JB 2:7:9). Another stated, "Rents charged our tenant farmers are the highest in the world. More than 50 percent of the total harvest is taken by the landowner" (JB 2:12:3). The titles of roundtable discussions provide a good indication of the editorial direction of the magazine. "The Emergence of Socialist Literature in Japan" was made up of the "old men" of the left-wing literary movement, writers and critics such as Aono Suekichi, Akita Ujaku, and Eguchi Kan (JB 1:6–8). Working women — a secretary, farmer, reporter, café waitress, textile factory worker, and so on — formed the discussion "This Is How Working Women View Things" (JB 2:1). Working-class men were the main participants in "Ordinary Life and Literature" (JB 2:6) and "Workers Speak Out about Their Lives" (JB 2:9). Clearly, then, the journal was attempting to provide liberal, democratic, and progressive alternatives to the dominant political ideology of the day. Takeda Rintarō had a long history of opposing "imperialistic wars" and the militarization of Japanese society.[38] For example, he wrote in 1933:

> For the first time in many years, I am writing this under the light of a candle. Outside there is the noise of exploding gunpowder, and overhead the constant racket of airplane propellers. When I walk through the neighborhood, everyone is dressed in khaki. Everywhere I go, I seem to be scolded about something. . . . This is the gloomy, overcast mood of fascism, and it is inimical to literature.[39]

Again, shortly after the China Incident of 1937, he wrote:

> I'm shocked at the level of ignorance on the part of journalists about the idea of modern warfare. A rudimentary knowledge of modern science should be sufficient to understand that warfare in the past and the wars of the present and future are completely different organisms. Everyone would acknowledge that it is foolish to equate a whale and a sardine because they both swim in the sea. A few military men have explained their conception of modern chemical warfare. It is a horror beyond the imaginations of novelists. (JB 2:10:47)

However, because of the increasingly severe censorship around the time of the China Incident of 1937, antimilitary sentiment generally had to be expressed euphemistically through historical and literary allusion. For example, parallels were drawn between the present and the time of the Russo-Japanese War, and Shibukawa Gyō would conclude, "The opposition to the militaristic ideology of the Meiji period was much stronger than it is today" (JB 2:6:153). Here and there, an explicitly antiwar statement made it through the censors—for example, the following by Izu Kimio: "the social situation since the beginning of 1937 has undergone a strong tendency toward a fascism intent on full preparation for war, but at the same time this tendency has also given rise to the firm popular determination to oppose it" (JB 2:8:97).

The People's Library writers also saw claims of Japanese uniqueness and hero worship as concomitant to the militarization of Japanese society. Izu Kimio wrote, "It is imperative that we analyze and oppose arguments based on 'uniquely Japanese things' and 'the unique characteristics of our race,' arguments which are repeatedly forwarded by the fascist literati" (JB 2:7:36). Shibukawa Gyō argued that the all-pervasive hero worship in his contemporary society reflected a state of affairs in which power had become the cultural dominant: "the people, who have been stripped of their own sense of heroism, now take delight in being manipulated by heroes forced upon them" (JB 1:5:121).

The management and editing of The People's Library remained consistent with the ideas expressed in the periodical, and this open, democratic editorial policy proved to be remarkably successful. The company was turning a profit and had expanded into book publishing until the state intervened.

The efforts of the authorities to eliminate The People's Library probably stemmed from their overall effort to stamp out the idea of a popular front against fascism. The Criminal Affairs Bureau in the Ministry of Home Affairs was keeping close watch over the ideological dispositions of individual intellectuals; literary, arts, and academic journals; and the groups that supported them. Secret reports were circulated among authorities within the ministry and other relevant agencies, and these recognized that by 1934, because of internal dissension over the extreme politicization of the arts and repeated arrests, the cultural organizations affiliated with the Communist Party—most prominently, the Federacio de Proletaj Kultur Organizoj Japanaj (KOPF)—were on the verge of disintegration.

However, the authorities were newly worried by the idea of a political and cultural strategy forwarded by Georgi Dimitrov, who, with Stalin's approval, called for popular fronts of progressive forces against fascism at the 1935 Seventh World Congress of the Communist International. To counter this threat, the police expanded their supervision and arrests to intellectuals, and the non-communist left. Roundups of people suspected of working to establish the popular front in Japan were carried out in December 1937 and February 1938. In the first of these mass arrests, called the "People's

Front Incident (*Jinmin Sensen jiken*)," four hundred persons were arrested, among them the leaders of the Japan Proletariat and the Socialist Masses parties and the political theorists Yamakawa Hitoshi, Ōmori Gitarō, Inomata Tsunao, and Sakisaka Itsurō. The second People's Front Incident saw the arrests of forty-five persons, including such elite academic economists as Ōuchi Hyōe, Arisawa Hiromi, and Wakimura Yoshitaōr of Tokyo Imperial University; Minobe Ryōkichi and Abe Yūichi of Hōsei University; and Uno Kōzō of Hokkaido University.

While it was easy for the authorities to detect the "danger" of left-of-center ideas in the realms of politics and economics, it seems that in the case of literature, the officials had a more difficult task. To quote from one secret report in 1938:

> Due to the pressures of the times and the increased arrests by the police, cultural organizations have adopted an attitude that they are following national policy, and they do not express their ideology as they did before. Because they appear to have adopted a basic tone of culturalism, it is difficult to distinguish them from ordinary cultural groups. This means we must go to great lengths to prosecute these cases.[40]

The People's Library, which is recorded briefly in 1938 in police records as a proletariat magazine that had failed, survived as long at it did first because the authorities did not perceive the threat of the Popular Front until 1936 or so and were then busy prosecuting the more obvious figures on the left. They only later proceeded to the more difficult to prove cultural cases.[41] Second, there was the craftiness of the editors of *The People's Library*. Although the journal clearly aligned itself with the International Popular Front Against Fascism, it carried this notice and other potentially controversial notices and editorial decisions in small print at the bottom of the page. Moreover, the journal carried many contributions from leftists once associated with KOPF, but editorial policy insisted that its primary focus was literary, and editors refused to carry literary theory or the formulaic political slogans and plots common to the proletariat literature of a few years earlier. Finally, the editors of and contributors to *The People's Library* came up with creative ways to express political ideas: advancing the "spirit of prose literature," as opposed to neo-romanticism; presenting as history the views of socialists active from the Meiji period; and group discussions concerning the "lifestyles" of male and female factory workers.

In the end, though, *The People's Library* was systematically driven out of existence by government authorities. Police insisted on being present at roundtable discussions and at nationwide events in support of the magazine. In the later months of 1937, issue after issue was banned. Takeda incurred huge debts. Regular contributors to the magazine were repeatedly harassed and arrested both individually and when they met in groups. The journal was forced to cease publication in January 1938. Takeda declared that he felt as though his child had died and wrote nothing of significance after 1938. A number of the journal's most determined antifascist writers, including Takeda Rintarō, Hirabayashi Hyōgo, Yada Tsuseko, Honjō Mutsuo, Furusawa Gen, and Kishi Takeo, perished during the Great East Asian War or in its immediate aftermath.

Conclusion

Concerning the actions of Japanese writers in relation to the government during the Greater East Asian War, Donald Keene has written, "There was no resistance to the militarists save for the negative actions of a few authors . . . , who refrained from publishing."[42] This may be true for the period Keene designates, from 1941 to 1945. But it ignores the fact that for a decade before the outbreak of war between Japan and the United States, Japan was in a continual state of domestic and international crisis. The gradual evolution of fascism identified by writers and critics during this decade engendered a great deal of resistance.

Fascism in a Japanese context consisted of a set of generic markers that, taken together, described and analyzed a social structure and historical process functioning at a subconscious level, like "the gears of a giant opaque machine," in Aono Suekichi's words. Those who were creating this fascism, with few exceptions, were intent on not recognizing the universal genre within which they were working. Fascism was a social dynamic that writers and critics had to expose. Japanese fascism was identified by those opposed to the dominant political trends of the 1930s, trends toward total social control.

Intellectuals, political activists, writers, and a large segment of the general public used the term *fascism* from 1931 to 1938 to resist what they saw as unprecedented repression of leftist political dissidents at home; unprecedented military aggression abroad; unprecedented attempts to bring the arts, mass media, and the economy under state control; unprecedented violence and irrationality in the propaganda composed by writers and artists in support of the emperor state; unprecedented extremism in calls for a return to the golden age of Japan's past; and unprecedented measures taken to mobilize the masses for total war. To sum up, in Takeda Rintarō's words, "Every aspect of social life is being forcefully regulated by coercive control from above" (JB 2:8:113). Until the late 1930s, writers and critics resisted this control, many with courage and at great personal sacrifice.

After *The People's Library* was forced to cease publication, a variety of government agencies took up and extended Matsumoto Manabu's initiative to control literature. In the second half of 1938, the Cabinet Information Bureau organized more than twenty writers into two naval squadrons and sent them to the front to report on the Sino-Japanese War. Two months later, the minister of agriculture and forestry initiated the Nōmin Bungaku Konwakai (Agrarian Literature Harmonious Discussion Society). In 1939, the Department of Overseas Affairs organized the Tairiku Kaitaku Bungei Konwakai (Continental Colonial Development Literary Harmonious Discussion Society). So it continued with a plethora of government-sponsored literary societies with the objective of making writers fully aware of their responsibilities to serve the interests of the state, defend the nation through their art, and formulate and accomplish the cultural mission of the Japanese empire. As the literary historian Senuma Shigeki has concluded, the period from 1938 to 1945 was one of subservience of literature to the state, at least in an institutional, if not an individual, sense.[43]

From 1938 to 1945, Japanese literary discourse lost its autonomy, as *The People's Library* writers had feared. It was also in 1938 that the discussion and critique of fascism in public discourse was systematically suppressed by the state, a time when the term was perhaps the most relevant to the description of contemporary social trends.[44] But did fascism really exist in Japan? Close enough, one is tempted to say, at least from the perspectives of the young writers of *The People's Library*. Clearly, the term before the war was used in a variety of contexts in Japan to identify and oppose ultranationalist political, social, and cultural trends that ultimately resulted in the loss not only of academic and literary freedom but also of tens of millions of lives. The more fruitful question to ask is how and why the concept of fascism was used so widely in Japanese contexts and whether those contexts are relevant to our present. As we have seen, the possibility of the emergence and development of fascism served as a cautionary tale by writers and critics of the potential threat to extinguish a relatively free literary world. The fact that this cautionary tale came true, despite such valiant efforts to prevent it, gives the term *Japanese fascism* the substantiality of experience.

Notes

1. "Bungakkai dōjin zadankai," roundtable discussion, Bungakkai, vol. 3, no. 2 (February 1936), 136–37. See also Ōtani Kōichi, Hyōden Takeda Rintarō (Tokyo: Kawade Shobō, 1982), 222.

2. As quoted in Ōtani, Hyōden Takeda Rintarō, 224.

3. Parenthetical citations refer to volume, issue, and page numbers of Jinmin bunko (hereafter, JB; reprint ed. [Tokyo: Fuji Shuppan, 1996]). I was guided to many of these citations by Tsujihashi Saburō's excellent study "Jinmin bunko no shisei: Jūgonen sensō no nagare no naka de," in Senjika teikō no kenkyū, vol. 2, ed. Dōshisha Daigaku Jinbun Kagaku Kenkyūjo (Tokyo: Misuzu Shobō, 1968), 188–238.

4. On The People's Library being almost the last and most effective leftist opposition to fascism, see Shimahirao Naoshi, "Jinmin bunko o yomu," in Tenkō no meian, Bungakushi o yomikaeru series, vol. 3 (Tokyo: Inpakuto Shuppankai, 1999), 59; Naka Kōhei, "Jinmin bunko kara mita Nippon roman-ha," in "Nippon roman-ha" to wa nani ka, ed. Nitta Mitsuo (Tokyo: Yūshōdō Shoten, 1971), 37; Yamazaki Yukio, "Jinmin bunko sōkan rokujūnen," Hongō-dayori, vol. 24 (May 1996), 1; Odagiri Hideo, "Kaisetsu," in Jinmin bunko: kaisetsu, sōmokuji, sakuin (Tokyo: Fuji Shuppan, 1996), 12, 14.

5. After Mussolini took power on October 30, 1922, the initial responses in Japan were of outrage by conservatives that a socialist government had taken over Italy. At first, fascism was not well understood and of little concern in Japan undergoing "Taishō democracy." With the exception of two articles by Tōyama Shirō and Nii Itaru published in Kaizō in 1922, there was not much analysis of the event. On Hasegawa's originality, see Tanaka Hiroshi, "Nyozekan o 'yomu': Sono 'Kokka hihan' no gendai-teki igi," in Hasegawa Nyozekan shū, 12 vols., (Tokyo: Iwanami Shoten, 1990), 5:421. Clearly, Hasegawa's characterization of fascism did not come out of thin air. Similarities can be found among the various theories of fascism that proliferated in Europe from 1922 to 1928: David Beetham, ed., Marxists in Face of Fascism (Manchester: Manchester University Press, 1983). But neither was it a mere derivation. It differed substantially from the Comintern's post-1928 theory of fascism, according to which "all capitalist regimes, whether parliamentary or dictatorial, were defined as fascist": Beetham, Marxists in the Face of Fascism, 17.

6. Hasegawa, Hasegawa Nyozekan shū, 5:236.

7. Ibid., 241.

8. Ibid., 245–46.

9. Ibid., 249.

10. Ibid., 250.

11. Ibid., 253.

12. Ibid., 254–55.

13. As quoted in *The Nation*, vol. 134, no. 3482 (March 30, 1932), 355.

14. As quoted in Tanaka Hiroshi, *Kindai Nihon to riberarizumu* (Tokyo: Iwanami Shoten, 1994), 309–13.

15. Non-communist resistance is documented in detail in Dōshisha Daigaku Jinbun Kagaku Kenkyūjo, ed., *Senjika teikō no kenkyū: Kirisutosha Jiyūsha no baai*, 2 vols. (Tokyo: Misuzu Shobō, 1968–69). Yamada Seizaburō, *Puroretaria bungaku shi*, 2 vols. (Tokyo: Rironsha, 1973), is a good source for organizations on the orthodox literary left. Select bibliographies of more recent research on the topic of literary resistance to fascism and militarism are in vols. 3–4 of the Bungakushi o yomikaeru series: Hasegawa Kei, ed., *Tenkō no meian: Shōwa jūnen zengo no bungaku* (Tokyo: Inpakuto Shuppankai, 1999), and Kimura Kazunobu, ed., *Senjika no bungaku: Kakudaisuru senso kūkan* (Tokyo: Inpakuto Shuppankai, 2000). An excellent select bibliography of works documenting organized resistance more broadly in society as a whole is in Furihata Setsuo, ed., *Senjika no teikō to jiritsu: Sōzōteki sengo e no taidō* (Tokyo: Shakai Hyōronsha, 1989), 309–12. Another excellent study describing resistance to fascism by communist-affiliated and non-communist-affiliated groups is Inumaru Giichi, *Nihon jinmin sensen undōshi* (Tokyo: Aoki Shoten, 1978).

16. Hasegawa Nyozekan, "Taishā bungei, taishā zasshi, nado ni okeru yugamerareta 'taishā,'" *Shinchō*, vol. 29, no. 8 (August 1932), 7.

17. As quoted in Enomoto Takashi, "Bunka no taishā-ka mondai to kokkashugi-teki henkō, I," *Shakai kagaku tōkyū*, vol. 14, no. 3 (March 1969), 29. For another newspaper account of the same meeting, see "Itsuka-kai enki/Bundan-jin to gen'eki shōkō ketsugō no/Fuassho undō kengen," *Asahi Shimbun*, February 6, 1932, 7.

18. As quoted in Enomoto Takashi, "Bungei Konwakai to taishū sakka no ugoki," *Nihon bungaku*, vol. 11, no. 6 (June 1962), 37.

19. As quoted in Ozaki Hotsuki, *Bundan uchisoto* (Tokyo: Chikuma Shobō, 1975), 212.

20. Fuwa Shiyō, "Bungei jihyō," *Shinchō*, vol. 29, no. 4 (April 1933), 106. See also Nii Itaru, "Bungei jihyō," *Shinchō*, vol. 29, no. 3 (March 1932), 110–15; Chikamatsu Shūkō, "Ankanaru fuassho bungaku," *Shinchō*, vol. 29, no. 9 (September 1932), 106–108.

21. Tokunaga Sunao, "Nomoto Renmei-ha no fuassho bungaku," *Shinchō*, vol. 29, no. 5 (May 1932), 116; Nakamura Murao, "Iwayuru fuasshoka no jijitsu no tankyū to puroretaria bungaku no kanzen naru botsuraku," *Shinchō*, vol. 29, no. 4 (April 1932), 64–69.

22. "Fuassho to fuasshizumu bungei ni tsuite," roundtable discussion, *Shinchō*, vol. 29, no. 4 (April 1932), 126, 131, 134.

23. Matsumoto Manabu, quoted in Wada Toshio, *Shōwa bungei-in samatsu ki* (Tokyo: Chikuma Shobō, 1994), 53. For information on the cooperation between the military and writers and on Matsumoto, see ibid., 35–36, 44–45, 98–109. For a list of organizations, including the "new bureaucrat" Kokuikai, under the um-

brella of the Nihon Bunka Renmei, see ibid., 54. On Matsumoto's role in drafting major legislation on thought-control policy and on financial support for his activities, see ibid., 55–56, 202–14.

24. Yamada Seizaburō, "Puroretaria bungaku shōshi," in *Meisaku annai Nihon no puroretaria bungaku*, ed. Eguchi Kan, Tsuboi Shigeji, and Yamda Seizaburō (Tokyo: Aoki Shoten, 1968), 264–78; "Yonichiroku jiken" and "Sanichigo jiken," *Kokushi daijiten* (Tokyo: Yoshikawa Kōbunkan, 1979–97); "Puroretaria bungaku," *Nihon kindai bungaku daijiten* (Tokyo: Kōdansha, 1977–78); Yoshida Seiichi and Inagaki Tatsurō, eds., *Gendai no hatate-tachi*, Nihon bungaku no rekishi series (Tokyo: Kadokawa Shoten, 1968), 12, 73–81, 226–33; Herbert Bix, *Hirohito and the Making of Modern Japan* (New York: HarperCollins, 2000), 280.

25. Tanaka Hiroshi, *Kindai Nihon to riberarizumu* (Tokyo: Iwanami Shoten, 1993), 309–11.

26. Aono Suekichi, "Bungaku bōei ron: Shinpo-teki bungakusha no ketsugō no hitsuyō ni tsuite," *Shinchō*, vol. 32, no. 9 (September 1935), 106.

27. Hasegawa, *Hasegawa Nyozekan shū*, 5:318–19.

28. Aono Suekichi, "Bungaku to minzoku-sei," *Shinchō*, vol. 29, no. 7 (July 1932), 81.

29. Tsujihashi, "Jinmin bunko no shisei," 2:201.

30. Ikeda Hiroshi, "'Taishū' to iu romanteishizumu," in *Taishū no tōjō: Hirō to dokusha no 20–30 nendai*, ed. Ikeda Hiroshi (Tokyo: Inpakuto Shuppankai, 1998), 72. The Reichsschrifttumskammer was a National Socialist professional organization. Membership was compulsory for all writers, publishers, editors, and others working in the print media. Its ostensible purpose was to expedite the writing, publication, and merchandising of the printed materials. It was a sub-agency of the Reichskulturkammer, which supervised all cultural activities and products. Furusawa Gen commented in *The People's Library* that the major difference between Nazi Germany's book burnings, imprisonment, and expulsion of dissident writers and critics, and organization and control of the literati who remained was that, in the case of Japan, "Writers had sensed the hidden agenda of the Bungei Konwakai and had ferociously opposed it, thus causing the politically ignorant writers who joined the group to reflect on their participation" (JB 2:1:6).

31. Quoted in Tatsumi Kōsei, "Nippon Roman-shugi no ideorogiiron, 2," *Bungaku*, vol. 28, no. 5 (May 1960), 78.

32. Hirotsu Kazuo, "Sanbun geijutsu no ichi," *Gendai bungaku ron taikei*, 8 vols. (Tokyo: Kawade Shobō, 1954), 3:262–64; Sekiguchi Yasuyoshi, "Sanbun seishin e no michi," *Nihon bungaku*, vol. 30, no. 12 (December 1981), 1–4.

33. Kamiya Tadataka, "Shōwa jūnendai no 'sanbun seishin' ron," in *Shōwa no bungaku*, ed. Nihon Bungaku Kenkyū Shiryō Kankōkai (Tokyo: Yūseidō, 1981), 102; Tsujihashi, "Jinmin bunko no shisei," 2:231.

34. "Jinmin Bunko/Nippon Roman-ha tōronkai," roundtable discussion, in *Shōwa hihyō taikei* (Tokyo: Banchō Shobō, 1968), 2:416.

35. Matsumoto Manabu promoted the idea of *saisei itchi* saying, "In ancient times, our Nation's ceremonies (*matsuri*) and government (*matsurigoto*) were one and the

same. . . . Matsuri signifies the movement to improve the whole person on both the spiritual and physical plane, and this is exactly what is meant today by 'cultural movement (*bunka undō*).' . . . Today, more than ever, the restoration of the ceremonial is crucial. . . . I advocate the creation of an Imperial Cultural Institute as an organ for the restoration of Matsuri, which is the same thing as culture": Matsumoto Manabu, *Bunka to seiji* (Tokyo: Tōkō Shoin, 1939), 157–58. The quote originally appeared in *Bungei shunjū*, September 1934.

36. Kaneko Mitsuharu, "A Seal," trans. James Morita, *Kaneko Mitsuharu* (Boston: Twayne Publishers, 1980), 63–64.

37. These include Uno Kōji, Enchi Fumiko, Ono Tōzaburō, Tokuda Shūsei, Tsubota Jōji, Hayama Yoshiki, Fujisawa Takeo, Nogami Yaeko, Kataoka Teppei, Hirotsu Kazuo, Tokunaga Sunao, Kawabata Yasunari, Okada Saburō, Shimaki Kensaku, Ozaki Shirō, Sata Ineko, Serizawa Kōjirō, Miyamoto Yuriko, and Nakano Shigeharu.

38. Takeda was a contributor to the anthology *Sensō ni taisuru sensō*, ed. Kurahara Korehito (Tokyo: Nansō Shoin, 1928), the only explicitly antiwar literary anthology published before the Second World War. He was also famous for shouting antiwar slogans at public rallies and getting away with it.

39. Takeda Rintarō, "Fuassho seishin to bungaku," *Yomiuri Shimbun*, August 20, 1933, 4.

40. As quoted in Tsujihashi Saburō, *Shōwa bungaku nōto* (Tokyo: Ōfūsha, 1975), 11.

41. Ibid., 9.

42. Donald Keene, *Appreciations of Japanese Culture* (Tokyo: Kodansha International, 1971), 300.

43. Senuma Shigeki, *Kanpon Shōwa no bungaku* (Tokyo: Tōjusha, 1976), 37–39.

44. In the same year as the suppression of the *The People's Library*, there was also the banning of Kawai Eijirō's *Fuashizumu hihan*, the arrest of Tosaka Jun and the other academics involved with the suppressed journal *Yūbutsuron kenkyū* (Studies in Materialism), and the arrest of Aoki Suekichi. As the political philosopher Arakawa Ikuo has concluded, the critique of Japanese fascism became impossible in legal publications: Arakawa Ikuo, *Shōwa shisō shi: Kuraku kagayakeru 1930 nendai*, Asahi Sensho series, no. 383 (Tokyo: Asahi Shimbunsha, 1989), 115.

HARRY HAROOTUNIAN

Constitutive Ambiguities:
The Persistence of Modernism and
Fascism in Japan's Modern History

The coming extinction of art is prefigured in the increasing
impossibility of representing historical events.
—Theodor Adorno, *Minima Moralia*

The [poet] Masamune Hakuchō said: "Abstract thinking is
like ghosts. While there are many people who fear the ghostly,
there are as many who conspire with it."
—Kobayashi Hideo, *Thought and Real Life*

■ The Specter of Unevenness

Throughout the 1930s in Japan there was widespread agree-
ment among writers and intellectuals that they were living in a time of historical crisis set into motion earlier by the implementation of a program of
capitalist modernization that now confronted most of the industrial world
and had begun to spill over into its colonial domains. World depression
simply supplied the momentary occasion to prompt thoughtful people
everywhere to identify the vast social, economic, political, and cultural
contradictions capitalist modernity had unleashed but had successfully
contained. Discourse privileged the cultural (artistic) domain especially
where the lived contradictions were sharply etched into the fabric of Japanese life and where the manifest ruptures, discontinuities, and different
coexisting temporalities provided the focus for a rigorous assessment and
evaluation to define Japan's modernist moment. This was the recognition
of a crisis that put into question a perceived separation between modes of
cognition and the real and of the necessity of finding adequate and lasting
modes of representation. An earlier tradition of separating the terms of the

relationship had asked whether it was possible to assess the politics of art-works or whether art must serve politics, which in Japan increasingly was expressed in controversies over art for art's sake and "pure literature" as opposed to a committed art. The observation led to demands that attempted to secure a reunion by a call for making either everyday life into art (culture) or art into everyday life (politics). With capitalist modernization, concepts such as culture, representation, and modernity were increasingly recruited to supply mediation in a socio-historic context marked by the production of new forms of economic and cultural unevenness. As a result, the contents of artistic representations or their dismissals were invariably referred to as the modes of perception and consumption of the new industrial world of work and leisure that we call, depending upon our own politics, either capitalism and commodification or modernity and modern life (*modan raifu*). If, in any event, philosophers such as Miki Kiyoshi in the early 1930s gave coherent expression to this observation in his essay "The Philosophy of Crisis" and Kuki Shūzō defined its content in 1937 by warning Japanese that they had not considered the excessively enthusiastic cultural borrowing since the Meiji period, many thoughtful observers before the 1930s had already designated the existence of vast unevenness as a commonsensical reality of Japan's modernization: Marxists pointing to the persistence of feudal fetters in a capitalist society and a more liberalist persuasion complaining of the effects of late development and the supposed consequences of an incomplete modernity prefigured in early Meiji social and economic policies.

Nowhere were the issues of capitalist modernization and the resulting aporias of representation more intensely engaged than in those discussions that articulated, perhaps inadvertently, the connections of modernism and fascism through the texts of the critic Kobayashi Hideo and the Marxist philosopher Tosaka Jun, and in its continuation after the war, as if still constituting unfinished business, in the writings of Mishima Yukio. Because both the question of finding lasting forms of representation proved to be an irresolvable problem and the reunion of art and everyday life remained an illusive fantasy constituted a shared ground for modernism and fascism, the figure of modernity itself appeared to be what T. J. Clark has called "a constitutive ambiguity" that was capable of mobilizing and directing their respective efforts to respond to the challenge it posed for finding the very means of political and cultural (artistic) representation.[1] But it was the crucial role played by the production of unevenness by capitalist modernization in the cultural and political realms, not only apparently separating them but, more important, establishing coexisting different temporalities, that combined to become the principal source of the crisis of modernity and its representational dilemma. While it is the purpose of this essay to explore the often shared epistemological and interpretative dispositions of thinkers like Tosaka and Kobayashi and writers like Mishima in that troubled moment and to draw out some of the lines of the kinship between modernism and fascism (they are not necessarily connected) in Japan and the crucial role played by the recognition of unevenness, the representational crisis must be seen, as Tosaka had proposed (in *Sekai no ittan to shite no Nihon*), as a local inflection of a broader phenomenon found throughout the industrial and industrializing world.

To add force to the observation that Japan was imperiled by wrenching cultural unevenness that promised to undermine the possibility of realizing stable forms of representation, many worried about the effects of an obsessive desire to imitate European culture so unselectively and uncritically. Fearful of unforeseen consequences caused by superficial borrowing, many thinkers began pointing to how the new imports had not yet penetrated the essence of lived reality, which was still mired in the customs of feudal despotism. Implied in this conclusion was the unstated conviction—widespread in the postwar period—that Japan's modernization was still incomplete. But capitalist modernization was always defined by the production of unevenness as its normal condition. "Universal history," Samir Amin has proposed, "is always the history of uneven development."[2] Despite the claims of its logic, capitalism never moves to establish a universal even terrain and must always collide with counter-histories it encounters along its route. What this simply means is that once capital has been freed from fixed representations reflecting its primitive forms of emergence, it rarely leads directly to the establishment of a universal even grounding for all societal negotiations. This presumption has been at the heart of an ideology, most recently incarnated as globalization, which anxiously anticipates eventual realization of even development everywhere. The importance of this recognition of historical unevenness allows us to understand the appearance of fascism at a certain moment in a number of places and explain divergent differences. But it also prevents us from wishing it away now that we have lived through its inaugural forms. Just as the metropole conceals what lies beyond the luster and sheen of its own self-image, which is always projected as universal, suppressing the surrounding countryside in its permanent eclipse, so the world that remained peripheral to the industrial core in

the interwar period remained hidden in the long shadow capitalist industrialization cast over it. But as the histories of both modernism and fascism
show, it is precisely in these concealed regions where the reality of unevenness is probably lived more intensely and whose exposed existence demonstrates the incapacity of capital logic to either veil it or contain its excess.[3]
In this way, it is the irreducible and unwanted remainder of capital's logic.
Where capital confronts its other, so to speak, representation becomes an
irresolvable problem, since it faces the twin demands of capital's reason,
on the one hand, and the claims of a prior culture of reference, on the other
which, like a receding echo, retreats steadily into a remaindered world of
irrationality and ghosts. But the ghosts of a forgotten world and discarded
past tenaciously refused to remain still and returned as unscheduled reve-
nants to destabilize the present by reminding it of what it had repressed.
What modernists aimed to realize in their practice in prewar Japan, and
everywhere else in the capitalist world, thus attested to the impossibility
of representing a historical object or set of events that signify the essential
abstractness of what really happens at the same time they witness the withdrawal of those fixed forms of representation identified with other, prior
modes of existence.[4]

The Modernist Moment

What emerged in the interwar period, the time of modernism, was a
theoretical discourse of modern aesthetics — or a cultural signifier in the
broadest sense — that aspired to displace a politics embedded in abstract
exchange, dominating the social nexus. Ultimately its distrust of representation was condensed in fascism, which itself announced a verdict on all
political attempts to break the logic of reified social existence.[5] Both modernism and fascism faced the problem of trying to find a mode of representation capable of mastering the essential abstractness of what really happens. Modernism found it increasingly difficult to represent fascism itself,
as an object and as a historical entity and as a subject of realistic portrayal.
By the same measure, fascism — Adorno's "coming to itself of society as
such" — defied the task of representation because it, and the subsequent
contemplation of it, derived from the elimination of subjective freedom.[6] If
fascism was an impossible object to represent — and I am clearly referring
to the regime of social abstraction — its cultural manifestation pronounced
the final judgment on all political attempts to break the iron logic of a
reified social existence. Just as modernists sought to find a mode of repre-

sentation not susceptible to capitalist logic (a vocation shared by Marxists, as well)—the ever new in the ever-changing regime of consumer culture, "where everything solid melts into air"—so fascism struggled to promote a politics no longer anchored by the representational categories that had propelled all previous attempts even as they tried to overcome and transform the very political arrangements they had authorized.[7] What modernism and fascism shared was the desire to resuscitate an aura that was no longer available, which often led to embracing myth, and the effort to construct a conception of semblance. Tosaka Jun, perhaps our best guide to both the culture of modernism and the privileged status enjoyed by the category of culture and its relationship to fascism in interwar Japan, charged the literary critic Kobayashi Hideo with being one kind of realist who had forgotten the class struggle, a type that "brandishes emotions without discrimination."[8] Kobayashi was convinced and reassured that since art and culture had come to replace the vacated place of the nineteenth century's historical subject, Marx's proletariat, the poets who had been momentarily banished from *Capital* were now returning with a vengeance. But as I have already suggested, this was by no means a universalizing process, occurring in the same register everywhere capitalism had established a beachhead, but was powerfully mediated by the presence of vast and specific forms of unevenness that could only be understood historically. Because it was impossible to represent an essential abstractness, thinkers like Kobayashi looked to writers like Shiga Naoya and even Kikuchi Kan and the portrayal of the solitary and sensible concreteness of everyday life removed from the social, even though it was clearly embedded in the discernable world of the present, and Tosaka urged a return to the very materiality of everyday space founded on existing productive relations, which, he believed, had been philosophy's original vocation before it was hijacked by Platonic idealism. While Tosaka sought to supply the space of everydayness with a sense of history (the "kernel of the crystal of historical time," as he put it)[9] and thus the identity of a temporal dimension invariably lost in the rhythms of daily routine and recurrence, a veritable chronotope as Bakhtin was already envisaging in the Soviet Union, Kobayashi would strive to spatialize historical temporality altogether, collapsing time into space, in the shape of an unmoving history or culture identified with nature (the law of statics, as he put it) marked by the constant reappearance of commonness. Perhaps the best example of this struggle was expressed in the conflict over the identity of figures such as the "people," the "masses" and the "folk" and the claim of concreteness each was made to command in the contest to eliminate abstraction. For Tosaka, the category of the "Japanese folk" had no reality whatsoever, since it occluded the lived experience of the "people" or the "masses" in the now, whereas for others like Kobayashi or Watsuji or Kuki, the folk constituted concreteness absent in terms such as *minshū* or *taishū*. The masses were intimately linked to the now of everyday life, while the folk derived from an indeterminate past that was always out there, whose temporality had no specificity and daily life remained the frozen sanctuary of its unchanged essence. In Kobayashi's conception of classicism, the folk resembled the unchanging classic of life that folklorists such as Orikuchi Shinobu commemorated as the calling of native ethnology.

What this difference involved was a struggle over the referent.[10] Tosaka endeavored to reconfigure space and time in such a way as to restore history to the world of everyday space—making it a chronotope—and to show the possibility of change and transformation in a society driven by the ever new in the ever same, while Kobayashi abandoned the regime of temporality altogether to secure a timeless aesthetic free from both historical accountability and an order driven by an identity between the rational and the real. It should be pointed out that modernism was always concerned with finding a stable ground, since it had recognized that everything already corresponded only to the agency of capital and its endless movement. But on its part, fascism had already dismissed all politics as afflicted by the same regime of reification, even though its own mission was paradoxically committed to stauching capitalism, in short, saving it from liberalism and itself.

In the contest to resolve the aporias of representation by appealing to competing forms of concreteness, often signified by terms like "reality (*genjitsu*)" or "actuality (*jissai*)," and the respective claims of life (*seikatsu*) and the veracity of representing history, nothing was more important than the status of the referent, which had either disappeared or was seriously put into question because of the installation of capital as agency and its corresponding regime of social abstraction. During the 1930s, especially, this dispute proliferated into attempts to resolve the relationship between life, the emergent domain of everydayness, and history, usually associated with the narrative of the nation-state. While it is difficult to know precisely why this theme was so overstated in discourse, it is evident that by the end of the decade, its centrality had engendered two principal symposia devoted to endorsing their respective claims: the conference on overcoming the modern, whose subject of discussion reflected the experience of everyday life from the prior two decades of accelerated capitalist modernization; and the conference on world history (*Sekaishiteki tachiba to Nippon*), which elaborated on Japan's mission in world history. Both were convened in Kyoto in 1942. Their differences could not have been greater and disclosed the profound disjunction, spatial and temporal, between a material everydayness produced by modernization and a developed Japanese nation-state, which, according to Kyoto philosophers, was now poised to enter the domain of world history and realize its historic mission. The aporetic nature of this problem between everydayness and world history (the domain of the nation-state) had already been conceptualized by Miki Kiyoshi in the early 1930s with the publication of *Rekishi tetsugaku* (1932) and numerous essays concerned with the problem of history.[11] Like so many of his contemporaries, Miki was drawn into discussions aimed at determining what constituted concrete "reality" in a world already dominated by the commodity form and abstract exchange. He was convinced that the answer to the question was to be found in "historicality (*rekishisei*)," echoing prior and parallel debates still taking place in Europe—notably Bergson and Lukacs, who, like Heidegger in *Sein und Zeit* (1926), expressed a growing impatience with and even rejection of a regime based on quantitative, measurable time (clock time, the time of science) for forms of interior and psychological time. In Heidegger's powerful account, this misrecognition of the nature of temporality led to historicism and establishment of a world dominated by the They (*das Man*).

The logic of Miki's intervention was driven by conviction that the real referred to the realm of "actuality (*jissaiteki*)," implying action (*kōiteki*). In this formulation, the actual signifies the meaning of everydayness—specifically, the situation humans find themselves living in the everyday. But Miki's construction failed to conceal an unease with the contradictory claims of historical representation and the presentation of everydayness. To finesse the separation between two domains, he recommended situating action, history's vocation, in the everyday, even though he recognized the distance between the routines of everyday living and the activity of people on the stage of world history, the latter constituting the precinct of eventfulness, the former a realm spare in events and fixed on the repetition of custom. There would be no contradiction, he declared confidently, between an "actual standpoint" and a historical one. Accordingly, the aporia surfaces when the original standpoint of anthropology, which seeks to emphasize everydayness, will be seen to be incompatible with an historical anthropology.[12] History, Miki observed, was invariably understood as opposed to the everyday and concerned principally with events, the great and extraordinary that act on the stage of world history. The question he posed, but never really answered, was how to move from the eventless world of everydayness to the register of an event-filled world history, from the singular experience to the non-experience of the nation, a temporality of the present, mixed and entangled to a linear trajectory heading for a specific destination. Miki plainly grasped history as national narrative, whose content differed significantly from the mundane experience of time in the everyday present. Moreover, history pointed to the individual and unique, while everydayness was the context of averaging and the commonplace, routine and repetition. For this reason, the everyday could never be seen as identical with history, which presumably occurred elsewhere and in a different temporal register. How Miki sought to resolve this knotted contradiction was to link the everyday and world history to a ground called "originary historicality," which authorized the procession of a steady evolution progressing from the first to the third level. The different and mixed temporalities signaled by the everyday and world history were restructured into a narrative succession supposedly illustrating the inevitable maturation of time, its "ripening (zeitigen, kairos)."[13] In other words, Miki sacrificed the temporality associated with the sentient claims of everyday life to the higher necessity and abstraction of narrative movement and the final (Hegelian) revelation of history's meaning. Regardless of his decision to emplot the unity of the three categories in a linear progression representing the achieved "ripening (jijuku, jukusurujikan)" of history's reason — the world historical (the nation-state), he nevertheless said, opened the path to recognizing the aporia of differing and distinct temporalities belonging to the separate spheres of everydayness and world history and the necessity of pursuing historicality from within the precinct of the everyday.[14]

Both Tosaka Jun and Kobayashi Hideo, fully aware of this disjuncture of temporalities and thus the impossibility of representing history, returned to the everyday and resisted its incorporation into the world historical. Prompted by the need to rethink the source of the historical from within the everyday and rejecting Miki's advice to link everydayness to the world historical, which sacrificed concreteness for abstraction in the last instance, Tosaka and Kobayashi discounted historicism (and the kind of philosophic history Miki had enlisted) and the cost of its valorization of continuity. What bothered both was the historical amnesia produced by an interruptive modernity that ultimately induced forgetting the present, as well as a past that had not yet been assimilated to the requirements of a continuity identified with the present. At the same time, Yanagita Kunio was reminding contemporaries that historicism trades remembrance of a historical present for the "re-establishment of an abstract continuity with the past, in a naturalized and merely chronological form."[15] This abstract continuity with a past was supposed to prove how the nation in the modern present derived its identity from an earlier, originating moment in the passage of a naturally chronological and homogeneous time. Yet the decision to return to the everyday as the ground of actual practice and history—the real—and the modern present promised presentation and construction, as such, rather than reconstruction and representation. It also meant seeing in the present the occasion for re-historicizing the experience of the now. While Tosaka abandoned the powerful narratives available to him from the Marxist debate on the nature of capitalism and looked to everyday life for the kernel of history, Kobayashi similarly embraced the present everyday as the site for recalling heritage and unchanging values as embodied in the classics housing the most common sentiments and emotions. For Tosaka, because the everyday resembled and behaved like the commodity form, it was necessary to devise a critical practice capable of releasing the mystery from its hidden side. This operation promised to reveal its concealed history and what might yet come. In Kobayashi's reflections, the past would be gathered up in the present as an instructive and exemplary historical experience reinforcing what had already been there—a sense of commonness destined to continue and remain, unchanged and unaltered, securing an identity between past and present.

Periodizing Forgetfulness

Despite the promise of social democrats to establish a new political subject that was rational and capable of making informed and responsible decisions, postwar Japan reaffirmed the problematic that before the war had sent modernism and fascism on their shared mission to engage in their respective struggles to find a stable ground for representation. In fact, this link was provided by Kobayashi Hideo, who completed his great work on Motoori Norinaga in the 1970s and carried forward an understanding of the problematic of representation he had already articulated in the heated discussions of the 1930s and, to a lesser extent, Mishima Yukio who, though younger, had passed through a kind of apprenticeship in spiritual essentialism in the Nihon Romanha. The importance of this repressed "continuity" and the concealment of what T. J. Clark has called the "constituent ambiguity" unleashed by Japan's capitalist modernity is that it offers a different perspective on the periodization of Japan's modern history from accounts that have seen the war as an interruption separating the postwar from the prewar or those narratives that have persistently envisaged the war as a temporary "derailing" from the true course of modernization and democracy which defeat and the U.S. Military Occupation put back on track. All of these accounts seemed to agree on a periodization that privileges the postwar epoch over its predecessor and include even the most recent attempts of revisionists to retrace the steps leading to war to minimize Japan's role to show the postwar as deformed, different, or discontinuous from a true history now remembered. Proof of its influence is manifest in the virtual disappearance of any consideration of fascism. Whether it was the "modernist party of the enlightenment" (I am referring here to the *kindaishugisha* grouped around Otsuka Hisao after the war who were in reality modernizers) who saw the postwar as a "second chance" or a diverse group of conservatives who felt they had been forcibly cut off from their past and made to forget it to live a deception in their present, the separation has had profound social and political consequences that have scarcely been perceived, much less evaluated. But this announcement of a "second chance" barely concealed the invitation to actually forget the recent past of war and defeat. Even though principal advocate, Maruyama Masao, early seized the opportunity to provide an accounting of Japan's drift into "ultranationalism" and the extent to which its fascism differed from the experiences of Nazi Germany and Mussolini's Italy, thus preparing the way for its eventual downgrading, the effect of this strategy was to remove from contention Tosaka Jun's earlier critique, which linked fascism to liberalism and its valorization of spiritual freedom. Under these circumstances, it is not hard to see why Maruyama's analysis of ultranationalism and fascism concentrated on the question of social composition and the complicit role played by the masses and petit bourgeoisie. It also explains his modernist decision to educate the country in the proper (liberal) form of political subjectivity, equipped with rational knowledge informing responsibility. Strangely absent in this renewed liberal discourse was the status of the restored emperor (Hirohito) and the imperial court and its consequences for the reconfiguration of Japanese society in the postwar period.

Since the end of the Second World War, Japan's history has been held hostage to a periodizing scheme that has marked off what came before 1945 from what occurred after with the effect of transmuting war and defeat into an unbridgeable historical cleft. As a result, prewar Japan has been variously seen as a history of mistakes, a moment historically misunderstood, deformed, dysfunctional, derailed, delayed, and, even, an incomplete modernity; war, defeat, and the installation of the postwar immediately promised a new start and a genuine social democracy, armed now with informed, rational, and responsible political subjects who would be able to avoid the sins of the past. Instead, the *sengo* has turned into an interminable duration that even today shows no sign of ever ending. In the more recent images of the postwar, Japanese are now reminded of how they have lived a deception since 1945, how they still endure under the weight of the American Occupation, transubstantiated into a permanent military base and outpost of the American imperium, and still remain captive to the neo-colonialism of America's culture, which strikingly recalls similar complaints made before the war. If the immediate years after the war were flush with signs of renewal and the hope of realizing what Maruyama Masao described as a "second chance," the years after the 1960s saw this optimism fold into the timeless politics of the Liberal Democratic Party (LDP), which collapsed the future into an endless present at the same moment Japan's economy headed for global hegemony. While the dreams for social democracy and modern subjectivity soon vanished in the din of pronouncements promising higher standards of living, unlimited economic growth, and the conceits of exaggerated bureaucratic efficiency that literally called for the end of politics, Japanese were increasingly reminded that these were only signs of their defeated status and the price they were made to pay for having allowed themselves to be colonized—spiritually and materially—by the United States. This note was early sounded by critics such as Etō Jun, who repetitiously recalled how unconditional surrender forced on Japan a decision to cease being Japanese and has echoed down to the present in the writings of people such as Kato Norihirō, who has characterized the postwar itself as a defeat and a disfiguration, and countless historical revisionists who busily disavow Japan's depredations in Asia.

In their eagerness to restore a truer identity or a more accurate history, Japanese were permitted to forget and repress more of the past—the prewar years—than they have actually remembered of that troubled but seminal time in Japan's modern history. When Kato singled out Dazai Osamu for praise as the one writer who could write about the war experience, he was, perhaps inadvertently, calling attention to prewar modernism and its struggle with the aporias of representation; and when historical revisionists contest prevailing accounts of Japan's conduct in the war, they, too, are recalling prewar arguments that aimed to mask imperialism and colonialism by appeals to cooperation and community. Both, in fact, repeat, in a more muted register, the complex imbrications of modernism and fascism galvanized before the war and the related but mutually exclusive struggle with the crisis of representation Japan's capitalist modernity had precipitated. These battles were immediately ignored in the postwar effort to set the past right in a new present and were ultimately forgotten (repressed) and lost to memory in the long night of *sengo*. During the Cold War, this historical amnesia reached down to penetrate the lowest levels of consciousness, as exemplified by the fate of fascism. While Marxists in Japan continued to keep vigil by incessant and formulaic appeals to emperor-system fascism, the overwhelming attitude in those years was revealed in a steady lessening of interest in the category's claim to either analytic precision or descriptive accuracy. In time, fascism was seen as simply a parenthesis in twentieth-century history rather than one of its constitutive and determining principles inscribed in the social life world of capitalism, the ghost in the machine. With the study of Japan, scholarship rapidly forgot the United States had fought a war against a nation identified with a fascist alliance and in the most recent efforts to assess the postwar fascism is rarely, if ever, mentioned. In fact, whole generations of readers and students have not been told that the very army that occupied Japan after 1945 to inaugurate the postwar had first waged war against a fascist nation.

But if fascism and modernism were momentarily able to renew their leases on life after the war, the advent of a postmodern Japan in the 1970s aimed to bring about its final overcoming. What this entailed was fulfilling the postmodern promise to finally eliminate the specter of unevenness that modernism had sought to displace and hide from view. LDP politics, despite its stranglehold on the bureaucracy, or vice versa, was a "one-party democracy" situated to discourage the replication of fascism in the forms that had dominated the prewar scene. Implied in this remarkable move was the conviction that the kind of society that had evolved in prewar Japan, one in which the bourgeoisie had struggled for cultural self-definition in the face of a lingering agrarian and "feudal" aristocratic other, no longer existed. As a class, according to Roland Barthes, writing about France in the late 1950s, that "did not wish to be named," the bourgeoisie fought for the specific locus of cultural authority and won. War apparently brought an end to this struggle, to be sure, and American-sponsored democratization supposedly did the rest. As the specter of class power faded into the maw of mass consumer society, the need for class struggle and the space for criticism disappeared. By this time the bourgeoisie, like its counterpart in the United States and other industrial "democracies," had become indistinguishable from the political classes and bureaucrats. From the 1970s on, political leaders and intellectuals began to proclaim the final achievement of a society in which everyone belonged to the middle class. New, technological hegemony, the regime of instrumental rationality, robbed modernism of its imaginary—an outside—and processed its language into rapidly moving image circuits that managed to blur distinctions, level them, and turn "every idea . . . into a fifteen second vignette."[16] Finally, modernism's long encounter with revolutionary projects, myths, and challenges to bourgeois society, which powered it, led to a cancellation of political alternatives other than the most conservative or reactionary affirmations pledged to upholding the cultural order of things.

If we imagine from the respective projects of both modernism and fascism a "constitutive ambiguity" toward modernity—capitalism's relentless production of unevenness—and especially the problem it raised for the very means of representation (cultural/artistic and political), added to the visibility and invisibility of the bourgeoisie, its "positivity" but deeper concealment after the war, then it is hard to see how war, defeat, military occupation, and economic and technological superiority actually changed the social geography. Here is Clark: "for what was modernity except that set of forms in which a certain ruling class attempted to universalize its power, by having that power be individual freedom, or technical rationality, or the one as a condition of the other?"[17] And what else was modernism and fascism—as twin modes of temporalization—but the "continual encounter" with precisely those effects of representation that evaded stabilization, permanence in the void of the ever changing but similar commodity form? This was a problem not merely for cultural production but also for politics. Tosaka Jun observed early that Japan was already a liberal and bourgeois society—capitalist order—and that the culture of representation was fusing with political representation to secure the stolidity and stability of both, just as political practice, limited to determining social relations, was beginning to enlist to its cause meanings from the wider domain of mythoculture to risk forfeiting the productive non-identity or separation between culture and politics. Tosaka recognized, with others, that an effective politics respects the asymmetry between its own limits and an expansive culture.[18] Moreover, he saw exactly how modernism (liberalism) led to a cancellation of politics and a new partnership with fascism offering people the prospect of cultural rather than political representation. When we look back on the immense spectacle of postwar Japan, we must, I believe, read its cultural and political text as a reconfiguration of the knotted history that marked Japan's entry into capitalist modernity, a continuation of what had been so constitutive of the prewar experience, rather than either a postmodern departure or a distorted and crooked version of an authentic history—a what might have been.

Experiencing the Present, Re-historicizing the Everyday

One of the major casualties of the postwar desire for selective amnesia was the literal effacement of the memory of Tosaka Jun and his relentless criticism of fascism, cultural liberalism, and defense of an intellectual devotion to the promise of rationality and science for the masses. The irony of this forgetfulness (in part supplemented by the misrecognitions of Marxists, as well) was that it made possible the claim of enlightenmentism by postwar thinkers such as Ōtsuka Hisao, Maruyama Masao, Kawashima Takayoshi, and even, for a time, Shimizu Ikutaro (who later wrote a book advising the necessity of forgetting the Enlightenment) who monopolized its conception of rationality even as these modernizers managed to water it down to fit the contours of a situational pragmatism put into the service of liberal democracy and the autonomous political subject. What this "party of the Enlightenment" managed to accomplish was an inversion of the very goals that had earlier induced Tosaka and others associated with Yuibutsuron Kenkyūkai (Society for the Study of Materialism) to promote the ideals of science and rationality as a way for the masses to liberate themselves. Tosaka saw in science a means to construct a critique against cultural liberalism and academic philosophy, which already were making common cause with fascism in the 1930s by investing in the Enlightenment project, the prospect of disseminating knowledge for the masses. The postwar "party" of modernizers, by contrast, clumsily betraying their received distrust for the masses and failing at the same time to conceal the conceit traditionally accorded to the intellectual elite, deployed the program of Enlightenment as a means to create a rationally autonomous individual, responsible and informed, who, unlike the prewar masses, would possess the capacity to resist voluntary submission to a political leadership promoting an irrational ideology. What they accomplished was simply the reidentification of subjectivity with prewar elitism. If Tosaka envisaged Enlightenment as a way out of capitalism and liberalism, postwar thinkers made it a condition for the modernization of Japanese political society and the final achievement of a liberal-democratic order. Whereas Tosaka, like Antonio Gramsci, valorized a common sense embedded in everyday life as the knowledge base of the masses, the postwar "enlighteners" replaced it with the authority of the average as expressed in the principle of consensus that derived its force from what counted to be seen and what would be visible as against what was not and remained left out. Tosaka's commitment to Enlightenment ideals was thus distended beyond recognition in the postwar effort to shut off the present and the future from the past, casting him and his program to the shadow lands of repression and ghostly occupancy, his critique of fascism (ideology) no longer accessible to a discourse on direct substantive democracy fated to simply reproduce the worst features of its prewar predecessor. Yet the importance of Tosaka's critique, delivered in Nihon ideorogiiron (1935) and devoted to dissembling a perfervid archaism authorized by academic hermeneutic philosophy—what he called cultural liberalism—was its deep commitment to understanding the nature of Japan's modernity and how capitalist modernization had transformed society. It was this approach that enabled the construction of a theory (he called it a science) of criticism and the development of a critique of the everyday that would target both modernism and fascism as effects of Japan's modernity and the crisis of representation provoked by capitalism and the commodity form.

In an early text on the scientific method written in 1929, Tosaka first addressed the changing relationship between method and object (negotiated in the mode of the Kantian dialectic) and proposed that its foundation and growth into a practice corresponds to a "scholarly practice" that must pursue the "acquisition of truthfulness."[19] By the same measure, the acquisition of truthfulness always aims at securing the identity of a problem at the same time it seeks to grasp the proper form of criticism. Echoing Marx, criticism for Tosaka inevitably involved seizing hold of the "roots" of the relationship between self and other. Any criticism, hence, was also an expression of self-criticism, since the observing self's understanding of an object would always enforce a distance between itself and its relation to this other. What this formulation referred to were "social rules" that inevitably link self to the other of its object of inquiry. When learning connects with the social, it discovers its "condition of separation" because society—the practical life of people—is a ceaseless critical negotiation. But since learning is a critical practice striving to uncover the "roots," it must be armed with an ideal of life. In this way, Tosaka reasoned, "learning constitutes a method of everyday living (seikatsu)" that constantly demands the exercise of social self-criticism as the principle of life, resulting in "a method for living."[20] It is interesting to recall, in this connection, that Yanagita Kunio was advancing a similar union of scholarship and practicality capable of

assisting contemporaries to solve everyday problems as the principal vocation of *minzokugaku*. Where Tosaka differed was in his insistence on the primacy of criticism, absent in Yanagita's formulations, and the importance of
taking a critical position to force ideological formations to yield their idealist assumptions and aspirations. The significance of grasping logic itself
as ideological required the arduous labor of "moving upstream until one
reached the headwaters"—the social position—that had distantly "produced the logical position" but whose history now remained concealed from
the present.[21] What seemed to interest Tosaka most was determining the
identity and location of the all-important "characteristic (*seikakuteki*)" that
ultimately made logic logical (as it made history historical) and required a
full understanding of the "problem." Even the selection of a problem appeared to be problematic, he acknowledged, and grasping it was demanded
by historical society. At the heart of the problem hovered the all-important
identity of the "characteristic"—the "problem of the epoch" itself and its
specifically emblematic historical and social conditions. The contemporary
moment confronted the "problem of the present" and engaged the now of
actuality embedded in the space of everyday life as the entry point into all
subsequent reflection.[22] Despite its similarity with Heidegger's identification of reflection and the circumstances of Being's primordial everydayness
and the decisionism demanded by destiny, Tosaka's formulation was atten-
tive to the chronotope of the now and its "thereness (*soko*)" and thus open
to the promise of actualizing a possibility offered by a processional and
historical moment in the present.[23]

Historical reality foregrounds the "practical idea" as the political actualization of history's movement. Hence, the logic of the "characteristic" is
also a political logic, as well. History's movement in the present had already
introduced the primacy of social relations and class as its new content, intensifying the demand for a "massification of science." Since science was
always class-based, it was now immediately necessary and proper to refig-
ure its basis by reorienting it toward the masses. (Tosaka was referring also
to social science.) Convinced that only the masses were in a position to
shoulder the immense power of history's movement, science had to be lib-
erated from its narrow class fetters—the task of criticism—and put into the
service of enlightening the social constituency. Tosaka was clearly calling
for a science capable of assisting the subaltern masses as the great libratory
instrument of self-transformation rather than its mere "popularization" in
the commodified knowledge packaged and circulated by journalism. Both
an aloof science removed from the world and its vulgarization constituted

the two fundamental errors made in the name of the masses that required rectification through the practice of criticism.

In keeping with the general program of the Society for the Study of Materialism, Tosaka's conception of ideological criticism was made to assist the "cultural struggle" against fascism. Yet the critical practice could just as easily have targeted modernism, as well, which, while explicitly eschewing political fascism, more often than not shared its epistemological and hermeneutic presuppositions. Tosaka recognized that the critique necessitated a reconstitution of ideology. Understood in its original eighteenth-century manifestation as a science of ideas but also resembling Miki Kiyoshi's "logic of conceptual power (kōsōryoku no riron)," the concept of ideology now had to be grasped as an effect of consciousness derived from historical and social existence, which "narrates concretely the reflection of existence." Its task was to ferret out the hidden logical and social structure from its concealed recesses of commodified confinement and to display a repressed history that academic philosophy (if not historical studies) and journalism had conspired to efface. Whereas journalism had bonded with the "daily" and contributed to the formation of the ideological basis of the "everyday life of humans," academic philosophy had ignored everydayness altogether in its aspiration to transcend both the movement of the real and contemporary events. If the true vocation of journalism was to report on "real movements" and "contemporary events," disclosing its commitment to practical and political purpose, academic philosophy had feigned devotion to the culture of diverse disciplinary and specialized sciences, a Kantian gesture enabling it to act as a meta-discipline charged with the task of integrating knowledge according to a worldview of unification.[24] Yet both had failed to realize their calling under contemporary capitalism: academic philosophy forfeited its basic function as a meta-discipline, and journalism forswore its obligation to public opinion to submit to the lure of commercialization and the dictates of the commodity form. Hence, journalism deserted its ideological purpose to supply a daily criticism of events, as philosophy fell short of providing positivist evidence and the verification of proof—two moments of the same gesture: "critical proof" and "positivistic criticism."[25] In the vacated terrain, Tosaka, like Gramsci, recommended installing "common sense" and "science"—the world of the immediate and concrete.[26]

In appealing to a return to common sense, Tosaka was repositioning the materiality of everyday space as the temporal and spatial focus of all subsequent reflection. Significantly, he was also recognizing the importance of the immediacy of the now (*ima*) and its thereness (*soko*) as an index of historical movement. On more than one occasion, he dismissed most philosophy precisely because it had evacuated the everyday for some form of religious or theological and transcendental and otherworldly preoccupation, even though thought and reflection always derived from the actuality of everyday life. Because everyday space returned to materiality to form with time a minimal unity of contemporary existence, it was necessary for philosophy to redirect its task to resuscitating its original vocation of uniting with the quotidian. Hence the everyday and the "now" constituted the scene of concrete existence and the place to begin all subsequent analysis of contemporary "custom" and history. It was not the past, as such, that directed the present to act but, rather, the present that authorized its proper history. It is interesting to note, in this connection, that Tosaka's conception of everyday space represented the last moment in a broader inventory of space itself—the physical, mathematical, and psychological dimensions constituting its others modalities. Ultimately, all were reducible to the actuality of everyday space (an obvious glossing of the Husserlian conception of the origins of geometry in everyday usage)—to signal the recall of a pre-Socratic ideal first revealed in materialist philosophy, which had been repressed in a history dominated by the idea. Just as Tosaka managed to recuperate the repressed materialism from the history of philosophy, so he was able to mount a critical assault against the contemporary claims of cultural theorists who had elevated archaic categories as signposts of timeless and unchanging value guiding the present according to the imperatives of an indeterminate past. But the real importance of his recovery of the everyday was its recognition of the primacy attributed to spatiality in modern capitalist society and its success in suppressing signs of its own temporality. Everydayness was not only the spatial location of a critical beginning but also the temporality that, despite its assertion of eternality, signified an instant in history that would forever remain incomplete. Despite the rarely conceded temporal and spatial disjunction separating the everyday and nation-state, especially how the latter constantly tried to assimilate the former to its temporal and spatial matrices, the everyday still offered the occasion for constant re-historicization against the claims of a completed national history.[27] The mark of its—the everyday—temporality was not only its invitation to perceive new social relationships and the emergence of the masses, but also its identification of a distinct colonial space that figured importantly in so many of Tosaka's timely essays on the current situation to exemplify how philosophy and journalism should complement each other.

With the now of a material everydayness as the starting point for seizing hold of the contours of an historicized present against a memorialized and commemorated past envisioned by cultural theorists, Tosaka believed he had located the referent for subsequent analysis and presentation rather than representation, since everyday life was always in the process of showing itself. Philosophy, he wrote in "Tetsugaku no gendai igi," delegates to the everyday the "historical starting point of its speculative reflections."[28] Despite acknowledging that the concrete and abstract have diverse meanings, it is still impossible to reflect on thought without considering first this "concreteness" in the "original meaning" of the word. In fact, thought occurs universally in places that are "plentifully" endowed with everydayness.[29] Compared to literature, whose claim to concreteness derived from the desire to flesh out a narrative (nikutai), thought must first be "concrete thought." Anything less imperiled the difference between philosophy and literature. In this sense, Tosaka's conception of materiality avoided filling the everyday with mere things, accessorizing it, as he accused the urban ethnographer Kon Wajiro and countless native ethnologists of doing, but, rather, linked the everyday to the concrete thinking of the subaltern masses, which had only recently found expression in its voice.

Tosaka was thus persuaded that abstract thought collapses into irresponsibility when it relies on literature for its concreteness. Since literature itself is but an inflection of thought, its "philosophy," its concretization must appear at a different level.[30] The first principle of criticism therefore entails the act of verbal expression, and this meant carefully identifying a relationship between the referent of everyday time and space mediating the lived experiences of the masses and its critical articulation. Once literature and the varieties of culture have been subordinated to the mediation of concrete thought, only the referent and its capacity for denotation remain. It was, I believe, this move that explains Tosaka's difference from Kobayashi Hideo and the clash he represented between "two different kinds of realists," and supplies the basis for understanding his scorching attack on the claims of culture and cultural theory. In his view, cultural theory rested on a form of signification (this is what he undoubtedly meant when he exclaimed that "territory (tochi) exists nowhere in the world without culture"[31]—that is, on the action of connotation rather than an appeal to a specific referent.[32] In a circular move, connotation was the underlying epistemological (and linguistic) principle authorizing spirit itself and empowering all those programs of signification summoned in the name of cultural—spiritual— history, acting as a hidden and unseen ligature that had been able to supply the folk with a sense of shared solidarity since the time of origins. While invoking the authority of space, cultural theorists such as Watsuji and Kuki, especially, literally banished time from their considerations to secure the effect of a timeless and unchanging cultural essence—a maneuver Kobayashi called social "statics." Under this circumstance, culture never called forth a determinate and historical formation as such; it beckoned only an indefinite imaginary that is always out there. Kobayashi especially insisted on the marginal role of denotation, as shown in his dismissal of history and his attempts to assimilate it to a literature that had successfully exceeded time to always express ineffable and eternal values and emotions. If he envisioned an everydayness in his valorization of writers such as Shiga Naoya, it was vastly different from Tosaka's chronotope of daily life because it merely represented an indeterminate, unmoving space of stillness, where a sense of commonness always prevailed to mark Japanese literature since its beginnings rather than the instantaneous suddenness of the modern present. In this regard, Kobayashi believed that writers, like poets, were committed to "employing everyday words" in their compositions, but like those for earlier nativists, this act referred only to mobilizing fresh words to describe the affective life and states of personal emotionality.[33] Rejecting the "necessity of history," which he contrasted to the "necessity" of everyday life, because of its "thinness," he advised the active pursuit of a more intense "experiencing of everyday life," which meant rescuing the residue of feelings and emotions that have remained the same since the beginning.[34] Kobayashi defended "one's culture" against the charges leveled at him by Tosaka, whose conception of criticism proposed to "extract" the abstract from cultural phenomena to lay hold of the very "commonness (kyōtsūsei)" Kobayashi had centered as something "lively"—that is to say, a living form.[35] For Tosaka, the "most dynamic content of cultural logic demands criticism of the several cultures of reality."[36]

Yet Kobayashi managed to fulfill the modernist expectation to distill, like Baudelaire, the eternal from the merely transitory and contingent. With Tosaka, he affirmed an appreciation of the new, to be sure, but departed in his decision to valorize the present, the modern, as the designated stage for enacting living, classic commonness. For Kobayashi, the present was assigned the responsibility of re-presenting classicism. But this recommendation risked realigning modernism to the idea of heritage and cultural treasure promoted by historicism and threatened to undermine an ambition to see in modernity a living form, despite his endorsement of writers such as Shiga and Kikuchi Kan. To counter this criticism, Kobayashi turned to demonstrating how Marxist writers had rejected the mundane as material for fiction. "It was not that young Marxists had lost the feel for everyday life," he wrote, "but that their ideology instructed them to transform the concept of 'life' from the mundane to the 'historical'." In the enthusiastic welcoming of Marxism in Japan and its theory of inevitable progress, he observed, "honest history got lost."[37] But in its place, he recommended a "healthy interest in history," which meant sensitivity to the "sentiment," "sensible," or "feeling" embedded in history; without it, there would be no chance "to inhale such things as the idea of kokutai."[38] This idea of "breathing in the national polity" adds up to a different form of understanding that "dwells within the recesses of love for the history of one's country."

In the essay "Thought and Real Life," he warned that no worthwhile thought is ever separated from real life. There is no thinking separate from real life:[39] "An act of thinking that fails to pursue making sacrifice in real life is lodged only in the head of animals. Social order is nothing more than the sacrifice that real life pays in thought. The [dappled] light and shades of this contemporaneity occurs in proportion to the depth of sacrifice paid. It is there that the word 'tradition' is established . . . [and] thought is nourished according to the habitual sacrifices of everyday reality."[40] Kobayashi complained of the failure of ideas to capture the complexity of real, everyday life and how abstraction, a ghostly apparition, had come to prevail in his present. No writer, he added, was more devoted to transmuting theories of everyday life into art than Shiga. It was precisely because literature was better able to communicate the experience of everyday—the concreteness from which it was shaped—that it was a more superior form of historical narrative, which he saw sliding into unrelieved abstraction and forgetfulness. In this regard, Tosaka's conception of historical temporality driven by the principles of everydayness came close to Kobayashi's own rejection of historical narratives. Yet where Tosaka sought to reconfigure the relationship between space and time to grasp a history that begins in the present, as a constant act of re-historicization showing history's incompleteness, Kobayashi early confessed to an allergy to history altogether and dismissed it as low-grade fiction, at best accidental and contingent, since "men do not actually see historical reality" but only create it by seizing hold of received "historical materials." To see history and to grasp the true and enduring forms of life, it was necessary to possess the "genius of a poet" or to be one who stands in the position to "polish mightily the mirror of the self," an obvious reference to the Buddhist gesture of "polishing the dust from the mirror" to see genuine reality rather than mere desire. Grasping the "true spirit of history" necessitated distinguishing the fixed, unmoving forms, unseen to the naked eye, the constant recurrence of expressions of commonness, which involved exercising the power of "recall," not simply remembering as one does a chronology of events recorded by historians.[41] Only poets like Motoori Norinaga and Kitabatake Chikafusa possessed such powers of direct "intuition" and "insight" with which to penetrate reality or, indeed, the first poets of ancient Japan who were "firmly embraced by the heart of history, as they were enclosed in nature's heart" to see through the distorted explanations that concealed true humanity. In this regard, history was elevated to the status of the "classics."[42] What seems most important about this decision to discard history was the way time disappeared from his considerations and the resulting diminution of political possibility other than one dedicated to affirming the "way things are" — that is to say, maintaining the status quo.

In "History and Literature," written just before the war, Kobayashi vigorously upheld the contention that historical narrative had lost its relationship to the present real life. As a form, it could no longer convey memory and now stood as an ominous figure for modern forgetting by imaging the present as the culmination of progress. Even though he wished to show how history never repeated itself, the incessant circulation of commonness manifest in the art of great poets came closer to a theory of historical repetition than he might have imagined. At its best, history's claim to represent the narrative of progress vocalized a fiction of unimaginable proportions. Rather, Kobayashi was eager to reinforce a view of history completed long before the present, one that had accompanied the inaugural experience of the race. Modernity demands forgetting and forfeits the possibility of realizing commemorative communication, which only literature is in a position to rescue in the present. What is forgotten is particularly the everyday, which, according to Blanchot writing much later, "We cannot help but miss," because it is not yet information. If, for example, the attitude of a mother whose child has died is considered, the historical reality of the event will be different from how it was experienced. Historical reconstruction would stop with a consideration of the causes and conditions. In the process, though, meaning will be lost if the event, exemplified by the loss of the child, is not accompanied by a recognition of the emotion it was capable of evoking. And if sentiment and feeling are not accounted for, there is no reason for the figure of the infant to "flicker before the (mind's) eye as a memory image."[43] What Kobayashi hoped to emphasize with this example was the conviction that historical reality portrayed by historians was always incomplete because it recorded only the existence of the event at the expense of forfeiting experience. The mother knows this lesson, he remarked, and she understands that the death of the child will fail to qualify as historical reality unless it is also invested with genuine feeling. Meaning comes not from the event, as such, but from those who feel its force, which strangely becomes the event to be remembered. The love of the mother is the source of this meaning, and the child thus continues to exist because she still loves it "today," long after it has died. For this reason alone, it is not necessary to appeal to the details surrounding the cause of death to remember the child in the heart. In the mother's thinking, the facts are not reliable or even necessary for restoring the memory of the child. Kobayashi complained that the easy invocation of historical consciousness and objectivity made by historians attests only to abstraction and vagueness. These things experienced everyday, he believed in his "gut," are what really constitute history and are generally omitted from historical accounts. "Are we being paradoxical," he asked, "when we talk about things experienced in daily life?"[44] Everyday life is both the setting of experience whose meaning is supplied by those who lived it and the reservoir of memory that historical narrative must forget in the interest of communicating reason. Owing to its obligations to reason, historical practice resembled a large bamboo basket that scoops up from the "great sea of history" nothing more than minnows.[45] In this way, history misses the vast spectacle of human experience taking place before its eyes. Contemporaries find the contingent and "unreasonable" in history to be inconvenient, unacceptable, since only progress is necessary and desired. Causal relationships the brain invents to tell this story have nothing to do with the experience close to everyday life that creates fresh historical emotions in the heart. It was for this reason that Kobayashi invested everydayness with the power to imagine and recall the common, as opposed to a history driven by reason and the will to forget. History, Kobayashi concluded, is a "classic," and literature shows that history occupies a place that never moves; it is the "mystery of the place that never moves" that is precisely the indeterminate space of everydayness of common feeling and sentiment, not for acquiring a knowledge of but for restoring the spirit.[46] It is this commonness of experience lived in the everyday in which history appears motionless, timeless, and eternal and as the sign of a common tradition of emotional life derived from the ancient past. Kobayashi put this sentiment more assertively in his dialogue with the historian Suzuki Shigetaka during the conference on overcoming modernity. To an exasperated Suzuki, who had already complained that the conference was avoiding complexity that required abstraction, Kobayashi responded to his questioning of an "unchanging history" or statics. "The experience of appreciating the classics by even ordinary folk teaches the fact" that no time and development intervenes in the creative work of any artist who is able to stand in the position to experience the "route of the ancients" as a model. "It is the experience of our everyday."[47]

But in the end, Kobayashi managed only to mystify everyday life, making it impenetrable to all but a few who, like poets and artists, could understand the "mystery of the place that never moves," which required recalling—signifying—the commonness of feeling and emotion. By reidentifying everydayness with the auratic, he ran the danger of arriving at the same place contemporary fascist theorists had already reached. Whereas Tosaka saw everydayness "anywhere" welded to the larger processes of world history and the temporalizing of modernity, Kobayashi saw in it an alternative to history, a free-floating everydayness always calling forth the recurrence of common feeling fixed in a specific space, without time or duration, a complete and completed history.

In many ways, Kobayashi's postwar masterpiece, *Motoori Norinaga*, completed the argument for eternalizing a native aesthetic endowment, which had miraculously succeeded in exceeding history itself. Such a society, one Tosaka never lived to see, would be better served by the idea of culture prefigured in Kobayashi's conception of everyday life, and its celebration of eternal core values that promised to transcend past and present (history itself) and elevate culture over social formation. This perspective, it was believed, would reinforce an arrangement that drove a wedge between everyday life and history, removing custom from its conditions of production and aesthetics from politics and even ethics. But this solution would resolve nothing and empty society of everything but consumption rather than the possibility of actualizing critique in the interest of a genuinely participatory politics, one that he—Kobayashi—has already dismissed during the war because he had no knowledge on the subject. During the war, he continued to carry on the project to naturalize history into the space of timeless cultural form and repository of enduring value, which had escaped the demands of time. This elision of history and culture into what he had earlier called "second nature" was finally realized in the text on Motoori Norinaga. In this text, he returned to an exploration of "seeing" and "vision" and appealed to Buddhist modes of "knowing," which he contrasted with Western "realism" based on "observation." But it was the great eighteenth-century nativist Motoori (with Bergson standing behind him) who provided him with the methodological and philosophical means with which to envision "spirit" and "thingness" in "direct experience." It was Norinaga's own conception of empathic understanding of things, *mono no aware*, embedded in native everyday life, language, and culture that supplied the model for "seeing" and "knowing" that could not be grasped by other theories of cognition. Motoori had been certain that true Japanese emotionality, before it had been clouded over by the Chinese language, still existed in the sedimented residues of national life, despite the long dependence on imported and alien principles of knowledge. According to Kobayashi, the restoration of this natural emotionality as envisaged by Motoori invited a determinate stand against "rational norms" and the domination of abstraction in conduct and cognition. Motoori had already dismissed the "Chinese mind" as an expression of abstraction that had actually imprisoned the natural, affective life of the Japanese and was thus prompted to underscore the importance of resuscitating the spoken language (before the importation of ideographs) as the surest way to escape confinement in order to express true emotionality. But the great appeal of this theory of cognition was its promise to repress time altogether by fixing on the place where negotiation between knower and known was carried out, whereby the speaker of Japanese used a language that called attention to a particular place that was capable of interpellating the speaker as its subject. What this aesthetic mode of cognition produced was thus a static affirmation of the "way things are," not movement but the primacy of space over time, an acceptance of any historical givenness and any present as it has been received. In this regard, there would be no distinction between present, past, and future—echoing a form of fascist temporality already configured in Mircea Eliade's myth of the eternal return. What apparently attracted Kobayashi to Motoori's hermeneutic was the prospect of realizing a natural emotionalism freed from artificial, normative, and abstract constraints of the social, politics, and history— one more fully passive than active, always prepared to receive what was immediate, sentient, and, presumably, concrete. But it was reached through the exercise of a "spirit" embodied in language. "We take to language," Kobayashi wrote, "as we take to our own body."[48] He feared, like Motoori before him, that in his own time word and thing had been divided, and that this separation would remove speakers from precisely the world that had made them a community interacting with nature and each other through the medium of a sacralized language (*kotodama*). It would also alienate them from themselves, their own bodies. "People," he remarked, "should not confuse a daily life that walks the path of . . . free emotional expression with the way of rationalism (representation)."[49] For the "pure power of expression that inheres originally in language makes possible a stout-hearted community life for us." Kobayashi's conception of language, as the basis of communal life, reflected only a unique endowment and "a possession of this place," indistinguishable from its speakers. Language is the same as place because "it is closest to us" and "most like our bodies."[50]

Neo-fascist Spectacle: Transforming the Nation into a Theme Park of Cultural Memory

The escape from a debilitating abstractness and the desire to resituate the concreteness of timeless living cultural forms in the postwar period preoccupied the writer and would-be activist Mishima Yukio. With Mishima the representational but constitutive aporias faced by modernism and fascism came together to blur the line between a cultural politics and a political culture. Mishima's rejection of postwar history stemmed from a conviction that the times demanded a rearticulation of a theory of cultural holism that would center pure form, once more, unmediated by the demands of history. The model he offered of a culturally whole Japanese order distinct from the history of the "postwar" required a break with the West, even though he was Japan's most "Western" writer. The backdrop of his anticommunist manifesto, "Bunka bōeiron (Essay on the Defense of Culture)" was the emerging Japanese "super state" of the late 1960s, which, according to his text, was now compelled to defend culture against its destruction by socialism.[51] But Mishima did not really need the alibi of socialism to authorize his call to arms, since he was already complaining about his present, the showy "culturalism" of the 1960s that incessantly transformed culture into "things." Often he echoed the anxious plaints of cultural critics of the 1930s who worried about the loss of spirit to the machine and consumption. Everywhere he saw only "ornamentation," "exhausted emotionality," and the "elimination of the real." Contemporary cultural life was counterfeit, "diluted for mass consumption," revered as a thing and removed from the source of all things and value—the emperor—which had given meaning to all things but had managed to remain free from the alienating and abstracting world of commodification.[52]

Like many of his contemporaries and successors, Mishima was persuaded that cultural and aesthetic form offered a glimpse of national spirit and thus provided the surest defense against the erosions inflicted by time and history. In this regard, he was convinced that timeless form was manifested in continuities and repetitions, which, like the punctual rebuilding of the Grand Shrine at Ise every twenty years, have always defied mere history.[53] But the greatest sign of repetition, continuity, and the autonomy of form was the emperor, who was always present even when absent in certain periods of Japan's history. The emperor represented a "free creative subjectivity" who acted as a transcendental subject that authorized cultural meaning but who was not bound to a signification. He was always capable of transmitting form itself on its endless itinerary through time. If the rule of consumption and commodity form introduced interruption into national life, precipitating a genuine crisis in the cultural order of things, it could only be overcome by appealing to the agency of an emperor, who embodied the principles of both repetition and "free creative subjectivity" necessary for realigning culture to form. This image was intended to directly challenge the Shōwa emperor (Hirohito), who, according to Mishima, was indistinguishable from the content of contemporary everyday life.[54] The contemporary crisis involved a struggle over competing claims of cultural conduct and the defense of an idea of timeless culture as form.

To defend culture meant ridding society of egoism and encouraging self-sacrifice to conserve the "continuity of destiny."[55] Accordingly, the "mother's womb" of the vast cultural idea, whose surplus always escaped being assimilated to the logic of history, exemplifying a general economy of excess and expenditure, was performed as an imaginary community, itself a form remaining immune to history. The lynchpin in this vision of cultural wholeness was the emperor—the Tennō, as Mishima preferred to call him— representing fully the "ideal of cultural continuity." For Mishima, the Tennō incorporated into his person irreducible heterological elements opposed to mere utility, the useful, and abstract exchange and presented an alternative to the homogenous and safe world of contemporary commodity culture. The Tennō existed for himself first, before community and nation, as a kind of pure "having-to-be." With this understanding, Mishima challenged a recent history that had fixed on the identity of the Tennō and the "political body" to demonstrate that, even though the heterological force of emperorship relied on the homogenous existence of the state, it still had to remain apart from it. The state had to be seen as the abstract and degraded form of the living body of "having-to-be"; separation from impurity guaranteed the preservation of the continuity even when the political system had been disrupted. But an emperor unconstrained by time, that is political time, was free to enter it at will and "make a sudden outburst in time," which, in Mishima's scheme, entailed the Tennō's joining "absolutistic ethical values" to an "undifferentiated inclusive culture." For Mishima, the present was the appointed moment for the emperor to enter time to act decisively in the interest of making culture anew and to enact an age-old repetitive gesture aimed at destroying culture, only to re-create it. Such an intervention would combine the "national polity (kokutai)" of the Tennō's "state" with some form of economic order that, more often than not, resembled "capitalism and a system of private property," the classic equation already proposed before the war by fascist theorists now reformulated for the postwar present.[56] The act, he was convinced, would reveal the connection between temporal and spatial continuity in the performance of rituals and the identity between archaic divine authority and political disorder, eroticism, and anarchism.[57] Yet behind this appeal to imperial intervention in contemporary history from outside of time was also the attempt to articulate the classic reunion between art and everyday life—by making life into art and art into life in one stroke through the act of divine destruction and creation. To achieve this ideal, Mishima staged his last, great spectacle: suicide by ritual decapitation, which, far from moving his countrymen and -women to follow his call to action, was simply another commodity that was rapidly consumed and forgotten. We must acknowledge that nearly thirty years after the event of Mishima's suicide, the writer and critic Kato Norihiro revisited his conception of emperorship and its authorization of a holistic cultural state, which he juxtaposed to the Shōwa emperor, Hirohito, as a reminder of precisely what modern Japan had once gained but lost to forgetfulness demanded by commodity culture and unguarded Americanization.[58]

Modernism and fascism, like modernity itself, were constituted as historical temporalizations through which capitalism gained access to lived experience, the mediate forms through which a specific history is lived as the continuous historicization of existence. Through these forms, we are able also to identify the aporias of representation provoked by the constituent ambiguity produced by capitalism, which has continually marked Japan's modernity to the present. Peter Osborne has argued that these are not necessarily products of competing totalizations of historical material but, rather, coeval temporal structures, coexisting temporalizations that seek to find modes of relating past, present, and future in diverse and different ways yet also resolve the aporias and ambiguities created by capitalism and its ceaseless production of unevenness.[59] What this struggle has underscored has been the singular importance of this critical relationship between politics and time in modern society and, especially, how the central task of politics must always account for the experience of time. But it also illustrates how a society such as contemporary Japan has moved away from the modernist project imagined by people like Tosaka Jun, who saw in the present the promise of political possibility in the register of historical time that starts with the everyday. But Tosaka also looked to the political significance of a culture of formation based on an understanding of the now of everydayness and its critique positioned in such a way as to offset the reified claims of core value as culture and its consequent dependence on fixed space. Spatializing culture as core value, without considering process and temporality, which was promoted by Kobayashi and acted out by Mishima, risked making culture look like the mysterious commodity form and its relationship to value and exchange. We know that this critique vanished in the postwar desire to substitute economic well-being for political accountability, which insisted on cementing cultural "essence" to the realization of successful performance as a natural coupling. In this way, the effort to figure the now as temporally marked presentation—a showing of itself—gave way to the act of representing a reified past and its identity with the present. Its greatest outcome was to seek a realignment of a discrepant culture and politics, where in the past it had been recognized that the restricted nature of the latter could never metabolize the former. The effect was literally to eliminate both the incommensurability that had once divided these temporalizations—culture and politics—and the source of their respective productivities. Under these new circumstances, the constituent ambiguity produced by capitalist modernization and its penchant for a discrepant politics and culture capable of generating alternative but coeval forms of temporalization has probably come to an end. This generative force will have been removed from the place originally assigned to it in the overdetermined historical field and re-emplotted in a less charged configuration. The new configuration will now be composed of an image of a different and distant social order in the past designated to continually produce nostalgia for what has been lost; such a move is made in the interest of actualizing an ecstatic dissolution of time itself rather than seeking to find modes of relating past, present, future in politically distinct ways and alternative temporalizations of history. In the interminable prolongation of the postwar in Japan and the steady incorporation of politics into culture, we have, I believe, the sign of an obsessive desire to forestall the temporalizing process that has endangered the survival of politics altogether and opened the way to converting the social imaginary into a vast theme park of bad cultural memory. But the staging of bad cultural memory today still qualifies to fulfill the older penchant for spectacle manifest in the mass rallies, pageants, and marches undertaken with fascism's first appearance in the historical field.

Notes

My thanks to Alan Tansman for his reading and suggestions for revision and Hyun Ok Park for comments made on an earlier version.

Epigraphs: Theodore Adorno, *Minima Moralia*, trans. by E. F. N. Jephcott (London: Verso, 2005), 144. Also, Neil Larsen, *Modernity and Hegemony* (Minneapolis: University of Minnesota Press, 1990), 6; and Yoshimoto Takaaki, ed., *Kobayashi Hideoshū* (Tokyo: Chikuma Shobō, 1977), 221; see note no. 8.

1. T. J. Clark, "Origins of the Present Crisis," *New Left Review*, March–April, vol. 2, 2000, 88. The problem of aporias was raised by any number of thinkers during the 1930s, and notably bv the philosopher Miki Kiyoshi. In the postwar period an inventory of Japan's modern aporias was compiled by Takeuchi Yoshimi in "Kindai no chōkoku" (1959), in *Kindai no chōkoku*, ed. Matsumoto Kenichi (Tokyo: Fuzambo, 1979), 338–41. The list includes the antimonies of restoration and renovation, imperial loyalty and xenophobia (jōi), seclusion and opening the country, national essence and civilization and enlightenment, East and West.

2. Samir Amin, quoted in Larsen, *Modernism and Hegemony* (Minneapolis: University of Minnesota Press, 1990), xxxiv. See also Samir Amin, *Unequal Development* (New York: Monthly Review Press, 1978).

3. Larsen, *Modernism and Hegemony*, xxxiv–xxxv.

4. Ibid., xxxv.

5. Ibid., 10.

6. Ibid., 6; Adorno, *Minima Moralia*, 144

7. See Larsen, *Modernism and Hegemony*, 10.

8. Yoshimoto Takaaki, ed., *Kobayashi Hideo shū*, vol. 29 of *Kindai Nihon shisō taikei* (Tokyo: Chikuma Shobō, 1977), 312.

9. *Tosaka Jun zenshū* (Tokyo: Keikusa Shobō, 1977), vol. 3, 101.

10. See Kristin Ross, *The Emergence of Social Space: Rimbaud and the Paris Commune* (Minneapolis: University of Minnesota Press, 1988), 88, 129.

11. See esp. "Ningengaku to rekishi tetsugaku" (1935), in *Miki Kiyoshi essensu*, ed. Uchida Hiroshi (Tokyo: Kobushi Shobō, 2000), 209–23.

12. Uchida, *Miki Kiyoshi essensu*, 211.

13. Ibid., 229–30.

14. Ibid., 214.

15. The wording is from Peter Osborne, *The Politics of Time* (London: Verso, 1995), 140. This formulation is the argument of Yanagita Kunio's "Minkan denshō," in *Teihon Yanagita Kunio zenshū* (Tokyo: Chikuma Shobō, 1962–71), vol. 25.

16. Clark, "Origins of the Present Crisis," 88.

17. Ibid., 92–93.

18. See Francis Mulhern, *Culture/Metaculture* (London: Routledge, 2000), 174.

19. See Yoshida Masatoshi, *Yuibutsuron to Nihon ideorogi* (Tokyo: Sekibunsho, 1980), 176–76; see also *Tosaka Jun zenshū*, vol. 1, 36–37.

20. *Tosaka Jun zenshū*, 1, 40.

21. Ibid., 3, 80.

22. Yoshida, *Yuibutsuron to Nihon ideorogii*, 177; see also *Tosaka Jun zenshū*, vol. 2, 23; vol. 3, 260–64.

23. See Harry Harootunian, *Overcome by Modernity: History, Culture, and Community in Interwar Japan* (Princeton, N.J.: Princeton University Press, 2000), 145.

24. See Yoshida, *Yuibutsuron to Nihon ideorogii*, 179–80, for this observation.

25. See *Tosaka Jun zenshū*, vol. 4, 145–61, for a working though of this theory of criticism.

26. Ibid., 125–31.

27. For this observation, I am indebted to Manu Goswami's reading of Nicos Poulantzas, *State, Power, Socialism* (London: Verso, 2000), 93–122.

28. *Tosaka Jun zenshū*, vol. 3, 493.

29. Ibid., 488–89.

30. See ibid., 492.

31. Ibid., 485.

32. Ross, *The Emergence of Social Space*, 88–89.

33. "Bi no mitomeru kokoro," in Takaaki, *Kobayashi Hideo shū*, 321, 389,

34. See "Bungaku to rekishi," in ibid., 280.

35. *Tosaka Jun zenshū*, vol. 3, 483.

36. Ibid., 487.

37. Yoshimoto, *Kobayashi Hideo shū*, 274.

38. Ibid.

39. Ibid., 221.

40. Ibid., 221–23.

41. Ibid., 289.

42. Ibid., 288–89.

43. Ibid., 277.

44. Ibid.

45. Ibid., 275.

46. Ibid., 289.

47. Matsumoto, *Kindai no chōkoku*, 231.

48. Kobayashi Hideo, *Motoori Norinaga* (Tokyo: Shinchōsha, 1977), 312.

49. Ibid., 422.

50. Ibid., 312, 428.

51. *Mishima Yukio hyōron zenshū* (Tokyo: Shinchōsha: 1989), vol. 3, 223–51.

52. Ibid., 233.

53. Ibid., 228–46.

54. Ibid., 240–48.

55. Ibid., 233.

56. Ibid., 243–45.
57. Ibid., 244.
58. See Kato Norihirō, *Sengoteki shikō* (Tokyo: Kōdansha, 2000), 376–456, an essay that seeks to show the connection between prewar and postwar by pitting Mishima against Hirohito.
59. Osborne, *The Politics of Time*, 200.

PART II

KIM BRANDT

The Beauty of Labor:
Imagining Factory Girls in Japan's New Order

■   In early 1941, leading members of Japan's largest and most influential folk art organization, the Mingei Kyōkai (Folk-Craft Association),
published a proposal to reform the dormitory life of female workers at a
spinning factory. Much of the March issue of the organization's magazine
Gekkan mingei (Folk-Craft Monthly) was given over to the proposal and to
various articles and editorials in connection with it. Yet the factory girl
project, which centered on the construction, furnishing, and use of a special dormitory, appears never to have been realized. After the one special
issue, there was little further mention of the project or even of the factory
in the magazine, or in other association publications. And even in the pages
of the special issue itself, the editor, Shikiba Ryūzaburō, expressed doubt
that the project would ever be anything more than a "paper plan" (he was
quick, however, to add, "We have grasped a truth," and "I believe the day
will come when this material is put to use in some way").[1]

Nevertheless, the association's approach to what it called the "Problem of
the Daily Lifestyle of Female Workers" is worth considering in some detail.
A recognizably fascist effort to employ aesthetics as a means of increasing
industrial productivity for total war, the factory girl project helps to illumi-

nate several important but as yet under-studied aspects of the Japanese fascist experiment. Most discussions of the question of Japanese fascism have focused on political institutions and movements or on economic policy. There has been some study, also, of fascist ideology and literature.[2] However, it remains to assess the crucial question of the role played by aesthetics in fascist policymaking. As has long been stressed in the study of European fascism, aesthetic considerations were central to the fascist project. Not only were fascist politics characterized by the deliberate manipulation of spectacular new forms and symbols, such as architecture, film, mass festivals and rallies, posters, and uniforms, but the fascist renovation of society and the state was framed in explicitly aesthetic terms.[3] In Japan as well as in Germany or Italy or France, one of the central goals of fascist thinkers and policymakers was to create a beautiful new society in which individuality could be both exalted and sublated by the exquisite discipline of national unity and sacrifice. This vision had very concrete uses in mobilizing national subjects and resources for wartime labor and privation, but it was also held out as an end in and of itself. The ideal of "one hundred million hearts beating as one," as one of the most often quoted slogans of wartime Japan put it, was presented as a source of aesthetic gratification, as well as of virtue and strength.

The factory girl project points to the presence within wartime Japan, as in Nazi Germany, of a campaign to resolve some of the contradictions created by capitalism and industrialization through the beautiful rationalization of factory labor. Only recently have scholars begun to explore the cultural dimensions of industrial labor policies and practices during the late 1930s and early 1940s and the extent to which Japanese officials and agencies sought to create cultural programs for industrial workers comparable to those of the German *Kraft durch Freude* (Strength through Joy) organization or the *Opera Nazionale Dopolavoro* (National Organization of Afterwork) endeavor.[4] The efforts of the folk-craft or *mingei* activists in particular, and the interest and support those efforts received from key members of the so-called renovationist bureaucracy within Japan's New Order (*shintaisei*), suggest that in addition to the more familiar initiatives to entertain and uplift workers through traveling theatricals, sporting events, hiking trips, factory choirs, and the like, there was also attention to the possibility of a more thoroughgoing reconstruction of worker culture along the aestheticizing lines marked out by the architect Albert Speer's "Beauty of Labor" office within "Strength through Joy."[5]

Yet even as the factory girl project highlights the existence of yet another important set of ideas and programs linking wartime Japan to the fascist regimes of continental Europe, it also offers insight into the distinctive nature of fascism in Japan. The fact remains, for example, that the Folk-Craft, or Mingei Association's plan was never realized. To some degree, the failure of the factory girl project is emblematic of the larger failure of fascist planners to impose their ideals of managed productivity on Japanese industry. For a variety of reasons, the technocrats who dreamed in the late 1930s and early 1940s of rationalizing worker culture had far less scope or capacity to enact their plans than did their counterparts in Italy and especially in Germany.[6] But in addition, close study of the particular nature of the Mingei Association's factory girl proposal, along with the interest it elicited from various government and semi-governmental groups, makes it possible to see that the ideas about managing worker culture put forward by Japanese planners in the early 1940s were in fact distinctive. In their special emphasis on the aesthetics of a self-sufficient domestic creativity, or what they called *seikatsu bunka*, New Order officials and their collaborators sought to adapt fascist practices and ideals to the circumstances peculiar to Japan as a non-Western nation attempting to secure an Asian empire through total war.

The Factory Girl Proposal

For all fascist polities, folk art was useful as an impeccably indigenous aesthetic resource that evoked the social harmony of premodern communal forms. It is not surprising, therefore, that the bureaucrats who directed the key agencies of Japan's New Order from 1940 regarded favorably the complex of mingei institutions and organizations that had developed over the previous decade. Both of the monthly magazines put out by the Mingei Association were allowed to continue publication without apparent interference until late 1944. Only official complaisance on the part of such key state organs as the Cabinet Information Bureau and the Ministry of Commerce and Industry could have ensured the survival of not one but two mingei magazines during a period when forced consolidations and even outright dissolution drastically reduced the number of periodical publications.[7] Moreover, the Mingei Association grew significantly during the early 1940s, establishing its first three regional branches in 1942 in Tōhoku, or northeastern Japan, with the official approval of local branches of the national Taisei Yokusankai (Imperial Rule Assistance Association, or IRAA).

One important aspect of mingei's appeal to the wartime state is sug-

gested by an editorial entitled "Principles and Policies for the Establishment of Regional Culture," which appeared in early 1941 in the IRAA newspaper. Declaring that "the correct tradition of Japanese culture exists more
today in the regions than in the culture of the center, which has developed
under the influence of foreign culture," the article proposed that, properly
developed, regional culture would form the basis of a new national and
East Asian culture. Mingei was included as a separate category in a brief list
of those aspects of traditional regional culture to be preserved and developed.[8] It is not surprising that the association of mingei with an indigenous
way of life in the Japanese countryside gave it special legitimacy within the
context of escalating war and nationalism. Much in the way that folk culture and folk arts were conspicuously celebrated and promoted by official
agencies in Italy and Germany, or in Vichy France, mingei was taken up by
a Japanese state increasingly concerned to mobilize a national and imperial
identity founded on blood and soil.[9]

But there was another, rather different way in which it might be argued
that mingei appealed to the renovationist bureaucrats who came to prominence during the heady days of the New Order. The Japanese handicraft
objects identified as mingei offered access to international modernity, as
well as to the preindustrial, folkloric past of the native landscape. Indeed,
they joined the two, much in the way that Japan's "left fascists" hoped to
join industrial productivity with premodern, indigenous social forms and
ideals.[10] For one thing, there were strong affinities between the mingei
aesthetic, as developed during the 1920s and 1930s by the art critic Yanagi
Muneyoshi and his closest associates, and that of design modernism,
which was fast becoming an international aesthetic orthodoxy throughout
the industrialized world. Like the founders of such classic modernist institutions as the Bauhaus art and design school (1919–33), Yanagi and his
cohort were inspired by selected handicraft objects to insist on the unity of
art and craft and to exalt simplicity, functionality, and artisanal community
as the guarantees of true beauty.[11] In the late 1930s, the affinities between
mingei and modernity were lent special credence for bureaucrats in the
Ministry of Commerce and Industry by the pronouncements of modernist
foreign experts. Both the architect Bruno Taut and, especially, the designer
Charlotte Perriand, hired by the ministry to advise on craft production for
export, waxed enthusiastic about the timelessly modern beauty of mingei
and the possibilities it offered for a uniquely Japanese contribution to modern design.[12]

Ministry of Commerce and Industry officials and engineers were clearly intrigued by the idea that mingei might help to expand export markets in the industrialized West for Japanese consumer goods.[13] But finally, it was the activities of the Mingei Association itself that were most effective in persuading "managerial fascists," during the latter's brief ascendancy in the early 1940s, that mingei might have other, more practical uses in the difficult task of reconciling agrarian Japaneseness with industrial modernity.

Beginning in late 1940, the leaders of the Mingei Association eagerly embraced the premise of a New Order for Japan — announced in August by the newly formed Konoe cabinet — as an opportunity to promote their organization and ideology and to demonstrate mingei's relevance to Japanese society and culture in the broadest possible terms. The October 1940 issue of *Gekkan mingei* was devoted to the theme "The New Order and Mingei" and opened with a proposal for the establishment of an official organization to encourage regional handicrafts. This agency, in which the proposal's authors envisioned the participation of various government ministries (Agriculture and Forestry, Education, Commerce and Industry), was to represent an expansion and recognition of the Mingei Association's work of the past decade.[14] The October issue also included a long article by Yanagi titled "The New Order and the Question of Craft Beauty," a discussion of German handicraft organizations by Graf von Dürckheim, and the first mention of a new project on the dormitory life of female workers at a spinning factory, to be the subject of a special issue of the magazine only a few months later. "It is just this sort of problem, of a social nature, that the true mingei movement takes on," commented the reporter.[15]

Although the factory girl project was first mentioned only in October 1940, planning by the Mingei Association leaders seems to have begun in the summer of that same year, possibly during meetings in July with the factory owner Ōhara Sōichirō.[16] It soon eclipsed other initiatives. In early 1941, the special issue devoted to the project opened with a statement declaring that the "problem of the daily lifestyle of female laborers" represented the mingei movement's first major undertaking since it had begun, the previous fall, to become a powerful new cultural movement "for the purpose of constructing a new cultural order, by means of actively integrating with aspects of present-day society."[17]

The factory girl project demonstrates very specifically how activists worked to demonstrate the capacity of mingei to overcome contradictions between the farm village and the industrial city, or premodern handicraft and modern machine manufacture. The project reveals, moreover, that Mingei Association leaders were willing to adapt mingei ideology and practice to a significant degree in their efforts to aid in the construction of the New Order. Despite an earlier stance sharply critical of machine industry, mass production, and the lifestyle associated with these for both workers and consumers, for example, now even Yanagi seemed to support the idea of association work within the modern factory.[18] Perhaps most interesting about the factory girl project, however, is the insight it offers into the concept of "daily life culture (seikatsu bunka)," a watchword for Japanese fascist policymakers and ideologues in the late 1930s and early 1940s. By aestheticizing the seikatsu—or the objects, architecture, gestures, and routines of dormitory life—for teenage girls working at a nylon-spinning factory, the Mingei Association proposed not only to resolve the basic contradictions underlying the fascist ideal of Japanese society, but to ensure the managed hyper-productivity that was arguably its ultimate end. "The culture of daily life," in this context, became a way to suggest a beautiful, native discipline of maximal production and minimal consumption that would smoothly integrate city and country, industry and agriculture, and work and leisure, as well as women's roles as wage laborers and as wives and mothers.

The most immediate concern addressed by the association's plan was that of potential conflict between "farm village culture (nōson bunka)" and the culture of the urban factory. The nylon-spinning plant studied by the association, one of several large factories owned by the Kurashiki Silk Company, was located in the city of Kurashiki, in Okayama Prefecture. A survey conducted by the association of about half of the approximately 900 girls and women working at the plant (out of a total worker population of over 2,000 in 1940) revealed the unsurprising fact that the vast majority—about 85 percent—came from farming households in rural villages.[19] The association stressed the importance of its finding that well over half of the 359 female workers who had left the factory had done so to return to life in farming villages.[20] One goal of the proposed reform of dormitory life, therefore, was to reduce the presumed shock of the factory girls' re-entry into small-village farming life.[21] This was only part of a larger, related problem, however. The opening statement published in the special issue of Gekkan mingei devoted to the factory project noted that a national initiative was under way to disperse urban factories to rural locations, and that "even now we can see the great and intractable confusion to lifestyles that will occur in future. . . . Indeed, it is our urgent duty to plan for the contact between modern factory culture and traditional farm village culture, and to establish a path for their integrated development."[22]

Dormitory architecture and furnishings provided one obvious point of integration. The dormitory planned by the Mingei Association, and handsomely illustrated in *Gekkan mingei* by Serizawa Keisuke's woodblock prints, was modeled on the Okayama farmhouse, or *minka*. In what was claimed to be the characteristic Okayama style, the building was to be one story, with a gabled roof, and it was to be surrounded by a well-tended hedge "such as is often seen in Okayama Prefecture." Inside, the dormitory—scaled to house approximately ten workers at a time—was to be organized around two central rooms: a main common room, or *hiroma*, immediately accessible from the earth-floored entrance, and a combined kitchen and dining room. The rest of the plan was composed of two sleeping rooms for the workers, the matron's room, a guest room, and a bathroom. Most of these, except for the kitchen and dining room, which was envisioned with a wooden floor, were to be *tatami* (mat-floored) rooms (the *tatami* of Okayama manufacture).[23]

By building the dormitory in farmhouse style, and by furnishing it with a broad assortment of mingei objects—from the cushions the girls were to sit on, to the bowls and plates they used at mealtime, to the altar shelf (*kamidana*) in the main room—the association planners expected to instill in workers an appreciation of the "culture of daily life" of rural Japan generally, and of their own, specific farm villages in particular. As they put it, "The family-style dormitory (*katei ryō*) we have planned chooses its furniture and fittings, as well as utensils and other small items, from the mingei now extant in the various regions of Japan. We want thus to establish the facilities and the guidance that will give female workers, when they return to their villages and begin their lives there, the knowledge that will enable them to identify the things of their own village comparatively with respect to the mingei of other Japanese regions, and also so that they themselves understand the value of the culture of daily life in their own village."[24] It is worth noting here that the mingei from "other Japanese regions" included stencil-dyed cloth (*bingata*) from Okinawa, which was to cover cushions in the matron's room; Korean flooring (*ondoru*) paper for the sliding doors of the guest room; and various other items in the "Korean style."[25] Thus, a reformed culture of daily life might serve to integrate not only farm and factory, but also colony (or semi-colony) and metropole.

But the mingei aesthetic was to shape not only the housing and furniture of the female workers' after-work lives, but also the way they passed their time. The reformed "culture of daily life" imagined by association planners would integrate not merely the material culture of the Japanese periphery into its metropolitan center, but also the rhythms of rural productivity into the industrial leisure created by factory time. For example, it was noted with disapproval that the many girls at the Kurashiki plant who chose to spend some of their earnings and leisure time on needlework tended to favor French-style embroidery. And yet, the authors of the initial report pointed out, there still existed in Japanese farm villages a beautiful style of embroidery known as *sashiko*, which had developed as a means of reinforcing clothing. The implication was that somehow factory girls could and should be induced to take pleasure in the useful native art of *sashiko* rather than in foreign furbelows.[26]

By offering to replace decadent, consumerist, Westernized tastes and habits with an active appreciation for the homely arts of rural Japan, the Mingei Association's proposal advertised the disciplinary and educational as well as integrative potential of mingei. Not only would workers be protected by reformed dormitory life from the urban and foreign influences that boded ill for their reacclimation to the village, but mingei would train them to become more useful, productive farmwives. By learning how to mend and strengthen work clothes in an austere if attractive indigenous style, for example, factory girls would develop a skill that enhanced farm productivity, rather than one that diverted them (as well as scarce cash resources) with colored silks and urban fancies. Similarly, the authors of the proposal bemoaned the common practice of attracting rural workers to factories by promising such urban amenities as Western-style dormitories and after-hours cooking classes in kitchens equipped with gas lines and electric burners.[27] By contrast, the reformed dormitory would serve as a rustic classroom where factory girls would learn how to perform household chores—cooking, cleaning, and so on—in a manner and setting more appropriate to their final destinations. Along the same lines, the dormitory grounds were to include facilities for kitchen gardening and animal husbandry: a vegetable garden, a chicken coop, and a pig sty. Female workers would receive training at these sites in the "subsidiary industries (*fukugyō*)" appropriate to the farm household and increasing its self-sufficiency.[28]

Yet there was a certain ambiguity about the ends to which after-hours training was to be put. Was it only after leaving the factory, back on the farm, that mingei-inspired discipline and productivity would be useful? The culture of daily life promoted by mingei reformers is notable for a degree of surveillance and bodily discipline that, while meant to suggest the orderly harmony of the preindustrial household, has somewhat more dystopic implications within the context of what was, after all, an industrial labor camp. Tanaka Toshio, a young journalist and textile researcher who became increasingly involved with the Mingei Association during the late

1930s, was one of the chief planners of the factory project and the probable author of the initial report. In it, and in the roundtable discussion (*zadankai*) published in *Gekkan mingei*, he expressed concern that those female workers who lived in company dormitories—by far the majority at the Kurashiki plant—ordinarily spent as many as four hours a day as they pleased, without guidance or observation. He imagined that, by contrast, the minority of female workers who commuted to the factory were never left to their own devices when at home. Instead, "as soon as they return home and open the door, they are monitored in the way they open and close the door, in the way they take their coats off, in how they make their greetings, how they put down their parcels, how they sit, how they stand up, and in such ways an entire training in daily lifestyle occurs."[29] This was the sort of training that ought to occur, Tanaka asserted, in the reformed, mingei dormitory. "If a girl were at home, then for example to take a teacup, her parent might talk during mealtime about where the teacup was made, or teach her about whether it was good or bad. Or she would be taught how to hold the teacup, and how to eat, and further how to wash and dry it after the meal, and how to put it away. And then after eating, if she was sprawling about (*nesobette ireba*), she might be reprimanded, and even warned about opening and shutting doors. Well, I think this is the kind of education in living that is missing in factory dormitories at present, and that would be conducted at the family-style dormitory."[30]

It is unclear whether or not Tanaka was interested in the obvious advantages to factory managers and owners of a workforce under the constant, paternalistic surveillance he admired. But other Mingei Association members were readier to acknowledge the relation between reforms they proposed and enhanced factory productivity. Shikiba Ryūzaburō, for example, the editor of *Gekkan mingei*, wrote up for the special issue the results of an elaborate questionnaire on daily life he and another leading association member had composed and distributed among 362 female workers at the Kurashiki plant in January 1941. In his commentary on the section of the questionnaire dealing with music, Shikiba suggested that radio music and songs might be used in the factory to increase productivity. Noting that "Germany and other 'musical nations' are skillfully making use of industrial music," Shikiba wrote, "I think it would be good if at this factory as well, songs were selected appropriate to the various work stations, and [workers] were made to sing them or listen to them while working."[31]

Shikiba's questionnaire also included a section dealing with the topics of "Romantic Love," "Marriage," and "Menstruation." The questions subsumed under these categories, and particularly Shikiba's discussion of them, suggest that at least some of the association planners also sought to address one of the most difficult conflicts inherent in the fascist social model. Female factory workers were a particular node of anxiety in New Order Japan, as they were in Nazi Germany and fascist Italy, because of the threat they posed to a social ideology that claimed to value women first and foremost as a means of social and racial reproduction. Women, in short, were to be wives and mothers in the home, not laborers in the factory. Yet female labor was increasingly indispensable to industrial productivity, particularly in the context of total war and the military mobilization of ever growing numbers of men.[32]

The mingei proposals for dormitory reform, with their explicit intention of training the factory girl for a contented and productive life in a farming household, downplayed the contradiction by emphasizing the relative brevity (about five years) of the average factory girl's term of employment and the near inevitability of her fate as a village bride.[33] Nevertheless, Shikiba's questionnaire reveals worry about the possibility that the industrial labor experience might compromise the smooth fulfillment of feminine destiny as wife and mother. For example, he commented on the (alleged) paucity of the girls' experience of romantic love and their inability or unwillingness to describe an ideal marriage partner.[34] Shikiba blamed these responses, which he believed to reveal the belated development of passion (aijō), on the infrequency with which factory girls watched movies and on the rigid segregation of the sexes imposed by factory dormitory regulations. While he conceded the importance of guarding against "immorality," he insisted on the need for some education in sex and a "proper love life." As he put it, "At present, when early marriages are being encouraged, an environment that is overly indifferent to romantic love and marriage is not good."[35] There was further, if implied, criticism of the factory experience in Shikiba's discussion of menstruation. An active and well-known psychiatrist specializing in gynecology, Shikiba wrote with authority on the subject. "Most of the young girls at this factory [first menstruate] at the age of sixteen, and this is close enough to the Japanese average. But it is dreadful that as many as twenty-two are so delayed as not yet [to be menstruating] at the age of seventeen, nor even at eighteen, nineteen, and twenty, and this is something that must be attended to (chūi seneba naranai)."[36]

Perhaps Shikiba's attention to what he considered the low level of factory girls' interest in their own appearance should be understood in this context of concern about their reproductivity. In his commentary on the final section of the questionnaire, which dealt with the issue of clothing, Shikiba deplored the fact that the majority of respondents (sixty-six) expressed a lack of desire for any particular dress. He wrote, "As a rule, for women there is no such thing as too many dresses. Especially for young women. How sad this lack of desire is, then! . . . A diminished interest in clothing is certainly not a good thing."[37] Elsewhere, in commenting on responses to questions about the purchase and use of cosmetics, Shikiba expressed similar worry about what he perceived as an unusual lack of interest in makeup. The solution, he opined, was to educate workers on the nature of simple yet feminine beauty. He concluded, "It is important that [workers] be plain and yet that they not be permitted to lose their womanly flavor (*onnarashii nioi*)."[38]

Some of the education Shikiba called for to remedy the inadequate femininity of factory workers was to be provided in the context of classroom instruction. At the Kurashiki factory, workers were supposed to spend an hour most evenings in *shōnen gakkō* (youth school). It may be presumed, however, that like other mingei planners, he expected life in the family-style dormitory, with its watchful matron, carefully chosen furnishings, and round of homely farmhouse chores, to give workers a much more pervasive educational experience. The simple beauty of a reformed culture of daily life would teach workers femininity as well as discipline and productivity, thereby helping to ensure the reconciliation of their labor function with biological function. Shikiba wrote with approval of the sight of workers after they had returned to the dormitory at the end of the workday and had changed out of their Western-style uniforms and into "colorful" kimono. As he put it, "At last their femininity comes forth, giving the viewer a sense of relief." He added, in conclusion, "The rooms and the uniforms are too colorless, too cold. Shouldn't there be more color in the life of young women?"[39]

By proposing to aestheticize the "daily life," or life before and after the factory shift, of female industrial workers, Mingei Association leaders hoped to demonstrate the broadly useful potential of mingei in New Order Japan. They worked to show that the mingei aesthetic, far from being the plaything of urbane antiquarian dilettantes, was an authentically indigenous tool that might serve to help integrate, manage, and finally increase factory production, farm production, and social reproduction. Even if the factory reforms were never realized, therefore, they might be said to have served their true purpose after all. By helping to publicize a gritty, activist, even industrial image of the Mingei Association and its mission, the factory girl project contributed to its continued survival and even growth in the context of national crisis. Certainly the increasing tempo of collaboration in 1941 between the Mingei Association leadership and various official and semiofficial agencies was at least in part a direct outcome of the project. Several months after the special factory girl issue of *Gekkan mingei* came out, for example, a roundtable discussion was held at the Mingeikan (Mingei Museum) in Tokyo, with official participants from the Information Office, the Culture Section of the IRAA, the Ministry of Agriculture and Forestry, and the Sangyō Hōkoku Kai (Industrial Patriotic Organization). Most of the discussion revolved around the possibility that the mingei organization might aid the state in helping to design worker housing and, more generally, a new lifestyle for factory laborers.[40] Two more roundtable discussions on worker housing and culture were sponsored by the Mingei Association during the summer of 1941; government officials were conspicuous at both.[41]

Fascist Leisure, East and West

For some decades, European and especially North American scholars have persisted in dismissing the idea of a Japanese fascism. While the mainstream of postwar Japanese historiography in Japan has generally operated on the assumption that the central structures as well as ideology of rule in wartime Japan were recognizably fascist, the North American scholarship that dominates postwar Japanese studies outside Japan has tended to proceed instead from the conclusion that Japanese "militarism" or "ultranationalism" produced a form of government fundamentally different from the fascist regimes of Italy and Germany.[42] Yet as Andrew Gordon has pointed out, many of the Western critics who reject the fascist label for Japan are vulnerable to charges of "an implicit Eurocentrism and an explicit nominalism"; they rely on European cases, usually Germany, to generate a list of characteristics indispensable for "fascism." To the extent, then, that Japan lacks such features as a charismatic dictator, takeover by a mass fascist party, or genocidal domestic policies, it is said to be disqualified from fascist status.[43] However, as Gordon has argued persuasively, despite clear differences "we can find similarities in the historical contexts to the rise of fascist systems in Italy, Germany, and Japan, the ascendant ideas that justified the new order in each society, and the programs that resulted."[44]

Recently, Japanese historians have begun to study one particular set of ideas and programs concerning the state's management of workers' leisure that may be argued to provide another link between the Japanese wartime system and the fascist polities of continental Europe.[45] The Mingei Association's factory girl project, along with the discussions and proposals about worker housing and worker culture to which it gave rise, gives further evidence of both official and nongovernmental interest in a specifically fascist resolution to what had come to be seen throughout much of the industrialized world as the "problem of worker leisure."

By the 1930s, a variety of movements had emerged in the United States and western Europe to organize and manage the leisure time created by the widespread adoption of the forty-eight-hour work week. However, only in Mussolini's Italy, and later in Germany and other European right-wing dictatorships, was the effort to manage leisure first initiated, and then largely controlled, by the state through large agencies designated for that purpose.[46] Fascist Italy and Germany, in particular, pioneered efforts to enhance productivity by means of national, state-directed institutions dedicated to the authoritarian organization of mass leisure.[47] As Takaoka Hiroyuki has pointed out in his study of managed recreation in Japan, it was the European fascist model that would become particularly influential in Japan from the late 1930s.[48]

Beginning in 1938, the hodgepodge of recreational organizations and movements that had already emerged in some of Japan's larger cities and industrial plants—hiking clubs, the youth hostel movement, factory sports programs, and so on—were brought together under the Nihon Kōsei Kyōkai (Japan Recreation Association), which had been created by the newly established Kōseishō (Welfare Ministry).[49] The initial impetus driving the formation of the Japan Recreation Association (and, arguably, the Welfare Ministry itself) was alarm within the military about the poor physical condition of the nation's conscriptable youth and the need to combat— largely through exercise and outdoor activities—what was perceived as the particularly deleterious effects of city life and factory work on Japan's war effort in China. As the conflict in China escalated into the all-consuming total war of the late 1930s and early 1940s, however, the Japan Recreation Association, along with several other state-directed agencies, became concerned not only with the physical health of military recruits, but also with the larger goal of managing and systematizing leisure throughout Japanese society. There was special worry in the late 1930s about the need to curb excess consumption and frivolity on the part of urban workers, who were using their relatively high wartime wages to help create what authorities considered an "unhealthy" consumer culture in the cities, and there was special interest in the possibilities offered by emulation of the Italian and German examples.[50]

Yet the discussions of worker housing and culture organized by the Mingei Association in 1941 illustrate some of the problems as well as the attractions associated with the effort to rationalize factory leisure according to established, Western models. One difficulty concerned the content of the various entertainments and activities commonly used to divert workers and to raise their morale. The Italian and German programs for worker recreation prominently featured modern, even American-style, forms of mass entertainment, such as movies, jazz revues, and tourism. Japanese efforts to improve worker morale and productivity—both the earlier initiatives in individual plants, as well as the later, more coordinated programs directed by semiofficial agencies—also relied heavily on traveling theatricals and revues, movies, and other types of modern mass entertainment. Participants in the mingei roundtables worried, however, about the impact of such materials on workers, many of whom were presumably impressionable teenagers from rural villages. Tanaka Toshio, one of the chief planners of the Kurashiki dormitory, complained of the practice of having cabaret-style revues performed at provincial factories: "I heard of one nylon-spinning plant where they brought in a group from the Takarazuka. The result was that the workers decided to put on their own theatrical, [singing] in strange voices and performing an imitation revue. They've stopped this, and I do think that theatrical groups are a very good thing, but isn't there also a danger?"[51] Or, as Yamamoto Shōzō, a representative from the Japan Technological Education Association, put it: "when you suddenly bring into the dull existence of the factory dormitory a bunch of pretty girls to perform a revue, then doesn't that factory life become even more unbearable [to workers]? I think it's very dangerous simply to give them entertainment culture (goraku nari bunka), and especially strange, urban culture."[52]

One of the highest-ranking government bureaucrats present at the roundtables was Kamiizumi Hidenobu, the assistant director of the Culture Section of the IRAA. He concurred with the criticism of the entertainment approach to worker recreation, noting that "officials in the Welfare Ministry" see only the immediate gains in productivity that seem to result from giving workers entertainment. "But I think that we will pay for it in two or three years, or in five years, or ten," he said. "They don't consider this and use these methods to ensure labor power in the moment. We must revise this way of thinking." Kamiizumi went on to suggest that the true consequence of the entertainment approach was simply to increase workers' desire for escapist leisure.[53]

Kamiizumi's comments reveal a more fundamental dissatisfaction with the very premise of a separation or opposition between work and leisure. Not only were conventional factory-sponsored diversions disturbingly exotic and decadent, but they encouraged workers to find labor hard and dull. In other words, not only was the usual sort of organized worker recreation alien, but it was alienating. Kamiizumi noted that until recently, the Culture Section of the IRAA had been preoccupied with the rural culture of farming people and had only just come to recognize that the culture of factory workers needed to be considered on a separate basis. His characterization of the difference between farm and factory work is revealing: "People in factories think that they work in order to conduct their daily lives (seikatsu), that they work in order to eat, and that their work in no way enters into their daily lives. But people in farm villages consider their own work to be a pleasure. That is very different from factory workers. People who work in factories and mines do not think that way. . . . I believe that work must be integrated within daily life."[54] Unlike farming, industrial labor was somehow conducive to a fragmenting of life experience. As a result, factory workers found themselves leading an existence divided between labor, on the one hand, and "daily life"—or the hours before and after the work shift—on the other. The goal, Kamiizumi suggested, was to find a way to reintegrate work and leisure for factory laborers in a manner comparable to that of farm workers.

Kamiizumi's views reflected the position on "work culture (dōrō bunka)" associated more generally with the IRAA and the Cabinet Information Office, as distinct from the Welfare Ministry's Japan Recreation Association or the Recreation Section of the Industrial Patriotic Organization. While the latter agencies, which had undertaken to organize and direct worker leisure since the late 1930s, tended to define an appropriate work culture in terms of ordinary forms of recreation and relaxation, the more radical, "renovationist" vision promoted by officials in the Information Office and the IRAA during the early 1940s was of a new, "healthy" culture actively created by workers themselves in a manner that would integrate and "clarify" their daily lives. Takaoka Hiroyuki has shown that the latter view came to prevail in the early 1940s, replacing the previous emphasis on recreation with a new campaign to have cultural "specialists" guide factory workers in the spontaneous creation of new types of music, theater, or literature that would "renew worker daily life."[55]

In one sense, the objections to the recreational approach to worker leisure, and to the opposition between work and daily life apparently promoted thereby, represented an impulse to break away from the Western, specifically Italian and German models of leisure management. Yet it is also true that the ideal of integrating work and leisure within a more organically unified daily life was very much a part of the National Socialist program for industrial labor in Germany. Indeed, as Shelley Baranowski points out, the directors of Strength through Joy criticized the Italian program of worker recreation for seeking only to manage workers' time off the shop floor, and they insisted that "leisure unconnected with work would result in mindless entertainment rather than the 'elevation of personality.'"[56] It was precisely to demonstrate Strength through Joy's commitment to the integrated whole of workers' lives that the organization showcased a Beauty of Labor office, which was dedicated to aestheticizing the work experience itself through improvements in plant architecture and layout, the provision of specially designed furniture and decorations for canteens and recreation rooms, the organizing of cultural events for work breaks, and so on.[57]

It is clear that many of the Japanese who occupied themselves with the question of a properly managed worker culture were favorably impressed by the efforts of Strength through Joy, and particularly of Beauty of Labor. Admiring references to the German example, and specifically to Beauty of Labor projects, were scattered throughout the discussions sponsored by the Mingei Association. Taniguchi Kichirō of the Tokyo Industrial College, for example, spoke at enthusiastic length about the model barracks constructed in 1934 by Beauty of Labor for construction workers on the Autobahn, or national highway system. Apparently, Taniguchi had toured the barracks during a visit to Germany; he dwelled on the hygiene and recreational facilities provided and noted with approval that workers marched in lines from recreation hall to canteen, "singing songs and beating a drum." He concluded, "I think they are giving workers a degree of guidance in their daily lives that is extremely rational, culturally."[58] At another roundtable, there was animated discussion of the desirability of the joy in work that one speaker insisted was experienced by German workers at a machine company.[59]

And yet the Kurashiki dormitory proposal and the discussions hosted by the Mingei Association suggest that, even as Japanese embraced the ideal of a managed leisure that was somehow seamlessly integrated with work, and that might produce the sort of regimented, communitarian joy prized in Nazi Germany, there were those who gravitated toward a somewhat different model of integration. For some Japanese planners, the emphasis seemed to fall less on the effort to aestheticize the industrial work experience than on the notion of a more beautifully productive daily life, by which they meant the space and time occupied by laborers when they were not at their workstations. Rather than seeking to integrate leisure or recreation into work, in other words, they sought to integrate productive work into leisure. Thus, for example, Mingei Association leaders and their supporters were primarily interested in the possibility of "guiding" a new worker culture through the design and furnishing of worker housing, whether dormitories for single men and women or individual homes for families.[60]

The preference among at least some Japanese for a means of managing workers that focused less on the factory and more on the home may help to explain why Japan never saw the full development of anything like Strength through Joy or the Italian National Organization of Afterwork. Recent research has shown that the Japan Recreation Association attached to the Welfare Ministry, along with the Recreation Section of the Industrial Patriotic Organization, were larger and more effective in their efforts—which were often explicitly modeled on the Italian and, especially, the German examples—than has previously been acknowledged. Nevertheless it remains true that the Japanese agencies committed to managing "work culture" received little direct state support and never achieved anything approaching the scale and influence of their European counterparts.[61]

A variety of factors contributed to the failure or unwillingness of Japanese policymakers to rationalize worker leisure in the manner of the European fascist regimes. The political philosopher Maruyama Masao has argued in a classic essay that the relative absence in Japan of anything like Strength through Joy revealed the much greater influence of agrarianism in Japanese fascism and the comparative weakness in Japan of the "democratic movement" and the proletariat "prior to the fascist structure." It was also connected, as Maruyama noted, to the lesser degree of capital accumulation in Japan.[62] Moreover, it seems likely that opposition from private industry to any significant interference with labor management was too great for the state bureaucracy to overcome.[63] In the roundtable transcript published in the special issue of *Gekkan mingei* on factory girls, Ōhara Sōichirō, owner of the Kurashiki spinning factory, expressed his own objections to the German and Italian models quite forcefully. Arguing that the European systems entrusted all welfare and recreation functions to state agencies, thereby leaving the individual company and its managers little responsibility for guiding workers' "healthy daily lives," Ōhara asked rhetorically,

"Isn't it the case that if all recreation functions are left to some agency, then the true, integrated, cultural mission of the company as a social being will be impossible?" Ōhara went on to argue that the nature of the leisure activities promoted in "foreign countries," which involved individual workers' leaving the company to "travel, or go to the theater, or engage in sports," was inappropriate for Japan, whose "special circumstances" included the accommodation of the great majority of female workers, especially, in factory dormitories.[64]

But another possibility suggested by the mingei dormitory project, and the discussions about worker culture and housing to which it led, is that the rationalization of leisure in New Order Japan was not so much thwarted or neglected as it was pursued somewhat differently, by means of an emphasis on the beauty of a daily life culture that, while authentically native and non-Western, was as regulated and productive as modern, industrial labor. The German historian Anson G. Rabinbach has written that the historical function of Nazism "was to exorcize the traditional patterns of culture which conflicted with modern modes of production."[65] Rabinbach studied the Beauty of Labor office to show that, during the late 1930s, a cult of productivity and efficiency eclipsed an earlier emphasis on pre-industrial, völkisch forms and modes to give mature Nazi ideology and culture a distinctively modernist cast. In Japan, however, preindustrial folk forms and modes were not so much eclipsed as they were transfigured, to create a culture of daily life that was both non-Western and modern in its managed productivity. Faced with the challenge of mobilizing an only partially industrialized economy, and by the ambivalent associations of modern industry with the racist West, Japanese fascists made a virtue — or, rather, a beauty — of necessity.

Notes

I thank Cathy Ciepiela, Margaret Hunt, Mark Jones, Sean Redding, Jordan Sand, and Alan Tansman for their extremely helpful comments and suggestions on various drafts of this essay. All errors of fact and interpretation are my own.

1. Shikiba Ryūzaburō, "Joshi rōmusha no seikatsu chōsa," Gekkan mingei, vol. 3, no. 3, March 1941, 146.
2. On fascist ideology and literature, see Kevin M. Doak, Dreams of Difference: The Japan Romantic School and the Crisis of Modernity (Berkeley: University of California Press, 1994); William Miles Fletcher, The Search for a New Order: Intellectuals and Fascism in Prewar Japan (Chapel Hill: University of North Carolina Press, 1982): Harry D.

Harootunian, *Overcome by Modernity: History, Culture, and Community in Interwar Japan* (Princeton, N.J.: Princeton University Press, 2000); Gregory J. Kasza, *The State and the Mass Media in Japan, 1918–1945* (Berkeley: University of California Press, 1988).

3. The classic essay on the fascist aestheticization of politics is Walter Benjamin's "The Work of Art in the Age of Mechanical Reproduction" (1936). Another, more recent but also very influential discussion of the topic is Susan Sontag, "Fascinating Fascism," in *Under the Sign of Saturn* (New York: Farrar, Straus and Giroux, 1980). There is a large literature on questions of aesthetics in National Socialism. More recently, studies have begun to appear on aesthetics in Italian fascism. See, e.g., Simonetta Falasca-Zamponi, *Fascist Spectacle: The Aesthetics of Power in Mussolini's Italy* (Berkeley: University of California Press, 1997); Ruth Ben-Ghiat, *Fascist Modernities: Italy, 1922–1945* (Berkeley: University of California Press, 2001).

4. See the various publications by the historian Takaoka Hiroyuki, in particular his essays "Dai Nippon sangyō hōkokukai to 'dōrō bunka'—chūō honbu no katsudō o chūshin ni—," in *Senjika no senden to bunka* 7 (2001); "Sōryoku sen to toshi—kōsei undō o chūshin ni—," in *Nihon shi kenkyū*, no. 415, (March 1997). On the German Strength through Joy organization, see Shelley Baranowski, *Strength through Joy: Consumerism and Mass Tourism in the Third Reich* (Cambridge: Cambridge University Press, 2004). On the Italian Opera Nazionale Dopolavoro (OND), see Victoria de Grazia, *The Culture of Consent: Mass Organization of Leisure in Fascist Italy* (Cambridge: Cambridge University Press, 1981).

5. For more on the Beauty of Labor office, see, Baranowski, *Strength through Joy*; Anson Rabinbach, "The Aesthetics of Production in the Third Reich," *Journal of Contemporary History* 11 (1976); Paul Betts, *The Authority of Everyday Objects: A Cultural History of West German Industrial Design* (Berkeley: University of California Press, 2004), chap. 1. By "renovationist" bureaucracy, I refer to those influential career bureaucrats known as the *shin kanryō* (or *shin shin kanryō*) who came to prominence in Japan after 1932, and especially after 1937. Robert M. Spaulding Jr. discusses what he calls "revisionism" and "revisionist bureaucrats" in "The Bureaucracy as a Political Force, 1920–1945", in *Dilemmas of Growth in Prewar Japan*, ed. James William Morley (Princeton, N.J.: Princeton University Press, 1971). See also idem, "Japan's 'New Bureaucrats'" in *Crisis Politics in Prewar Japan: Institutional and Ideological Problems in the 1930s*, ed. George M. Wilson (Tokyo: Sophia University Press, 1970).

6. I thank Sean Redding for suggesting that I frame the point in this way.

7. See Kasza, *The State and the Mass Media in Japan*, chaps. 7–8.

8. "Chihō bunka kensetsu no rinen to hōsaku," *Taisei yokusankai kaihō*, vol. 10, February 19, 1941, 3. The other two categories were traditional customs and rituals expressing Japanese communal life and local arts (*kyōdo geijutsu*), such as theater, folk song and dance, *waka*, and haiku.

9. For Italy, see De Grazia, *The Culture of Consent*, 201–16.

10. Fletcher, *The Search for a New Order*.

11. Frank Whitford, *Bauhaus* (London: Thames and Hudson, 1984). See also Joan Campbell, *The German Werkbund: The Politics of Reform in the Applied Arts* (Princeton, N.J.: Princeton University Press, 1978).

12. See Kim Brandt, *Kingdom of Beauty: Mingei and the Politics of Folk Art in Imperial Japan* (Durham: Duke University Press, 2007), chap. 4. This is also discussed in Yuko Kikuchi, *Japanese Modernisation and Mingei Theory: Cultural Nationalism and Oriental Orientalism* (London: Routledge Curzon, 2004), chap. 2.

13. Brandt, *Kingdom of Beauty*.

14. Nihon mingei kyōkai, "Shintaisei no sho kōgei bunka sōshiki ni taisuru teian," *Gekkan mingei*, vol. 2, no. 10, October 1940, 2–4. Presumably, the Mingei Association's leadership expected to play a substantial role in the proposed new organization.

15. Tanaka Toshio, "Mingei kyōkai dayori," *Gekkan mingei*, vol. 2, no. 10, October 1940, 61.

16. Nihon mingei kyōkai, "Joshi rōmusha no seikatsu yōshiki no mondai," *Gekkan mingei*, vol. 3, no. 3, March 1941, 3; Tanaka Toshio, "Mingei zakki," *Gekkan mingei*, vol. 2, no. 8, August 1940, 33.

17. Nihon mingei kyōkai, "Joshi rōmusha no seikatsu yōshiki no mondai," *Gekkan mingei*, vol. 3, no. 3, March 1941, 2.

18. Yanagi was an active participant, for example, in the roundtable discussion published in the special issue "Nōson to rōmusha no bunka," *Gekkan mingei*, vol. 3, no. 3, March 1941), 46–63. In the same discussion, Tanaka Toshio, one of the Mingei Association organizers of the project, concluded, "With this [project], we have come into contact, up to a point, with modern industry; in future, shouldn't we really go much further to consider also the creation of machine-made crafts?": ibid., 63.

19. Nihon mingei kyōkai, "Joshi rōmusha no seikatsu yōshiki no mondai," *Gekkan mingei*, vol. 3, no. 3, March 1941, 2–3.

20. Ibid., 4.

21. Ibid., 7

22. Ibid., 10.

23. "Katei ryō sekkei zu," *Gekkan mingei*, vol. 3, no. 3, March 1941, 12–18.

24. Nihon mingei kyōkai, "Joshi rōmusha no seikatsu yōshiki no mondai," *Gekkan mingei*, vol. 3, no. 3, March 1941, 7.

25. "Katei ryō sekkei zu," *Gekkan mingei*, vol. 3, no. 3, March 1941, 12–17.

26. Nihon mingei kyōkai, "Joshi rōmusha no seikatsu yōshiki no mondai," 7. The special issue contained, therefore, a long illustrated article on the subject of *sashiko* as mingei.

27. Ibid.

28. Ibid., 13.

29. Ibid., 9.

30. Statement by Tanaka Toshio in the roundtable discussion "Nōson to rōmusha no bunka," *Gekkan mingei*, vol. 3, no. 3, March 1941, 59.

31. Shikiba Ryūzaburō, "Joshi rōmusha no seikatsu chōsa," *Gekkan mingei*, vol. 3, no. 3, March 1941, 121.

32. For a useful discussion of this dilemma in Japan, see Yoshiko Miyake, "Doubling Expectations: Motherhood and Women's Factory Work under State Management in Japan in the 1930s and 1940s," in *Recreating Japanese Women, 1600–1945*, ed. Gail Lee Bernstein (Berkeley: University of California Press, 1991), 267–95. On Germany, see Renate Bridenthal, Atina Grossman, and Marion Kaplan, eds., *When Biology Became Destiny: Women in Weimar and Nazi Germany* (New York: Monthly Review Press, 1984). On Italy, see Victoria de Grazia, *How Fascism Ruled Women: Italy, 1922–1945* (Berkeley: University of California Press, 1992). The special issue of *Gekkan mingei* included an article, translated from German, on female factory workers in Nazi Germany and the importance of reconciling their productive and reproductive roles.

33. Nihon mingei kyōkai, "Joshi rōmusha no seikatsu yōshiki no mondai," *Gekkan mingei*, vol. 3, no. 3, March 1941, 3–4.

34. Only 11 out of 362 respondents were willing to claim experience of romantic love. Shikiba was inclined to believe this figure, as the questionnaire was anonymous. To the question, "What sort of person would you like to marry?" 136 gave variants of the answer, "I don't know." The next most common answers were "a healthy person" (29), "a soldier" (25), "an earnest (*majime*) person" (17), no response (15), "a kind (*yasashii*) person" (10). One respondent wished for "a silent person," and another ventured to say that she did not want to marry: Shikiba, "Joshi rōmusha no seikatsu chōsa," *Gekkan mingei*, vol. 3, no. 3, March 1941, 127–29.

35. Ibid., 127–28.

36. Ibid.

37. Ibid., 140.

38. Ibid., 140, 136–37. Shikiba's concern was elicited, presumably, by the responses to the following question: "What cosmetics do you buy?" The top two responses were: "cream" (192) and "I don't buy cosmetics" (69). Cream, as Shikiba pointed out, referred to hand cream, which was actually so necessary to work at a spinning factory that some felt it should be supplied by the company.

39. Ibid., 140.

40. A transcript of the discussion appeared as "Seikatsu bunka to shomondai," *Gekkan mingei*, vol. 3, no. 5, June 1941, 2–21.

41. Transcripts were published as "Dōrōsha no jūtaku ni tsuite," *Gekkan mingei*, vol. 3, no. 6, July 1941, 10–30, and "Dōrō bunka o kataru," *Gekkan mingei*, no. 29, August 1941, 40–60.

42. For critiques of the North American and, especially, the U.S. resistance to considering wartime Japan as fascist, see Herbert Bix, "Rethinking 'Emperor-System Fascism': Ruptures and Continuities in Modern Japanese History," and Gavan McCormack, "Nineteen-Thirties Japan: Fascism?" both in the *Bulletin of Concerned Asian Scholars* 14, no. 2 (April–June 1982): 2–33.

43. Andrew Gordon, *Labor and Imperial Democracy in Prewar Japan* (Berkeley: University of California Press, 1991), 333–39.

44. Gordon, *Labor and Imperial Democracy in Prewar Japan*, 338.

45. I am thinking of the work by Takaoka Hiroyuki, in particular.

46. Takaoka, "Sōryoku sen to toshi—kōsei undō o chūshin ni—," *Nihon shi kenkyū* (March 1997): 148–49. See also De Grazia, *The Culture of Consent*, 238–40.

47. De Grazia, *The Culture of Consent*, 237–40.

48. Takaoka, "Sōryoku sen to toshi," 151–54.

49. The term *kōsei* is conventionally translated as "welfare," particularly in connection with the Welfare Ministry founded in 1938. However, it can also be translated as "recreation," as in the instance of the Japan Recreation Association.

50. This narrative is drawn largely from Takaoka, "Sōryoku sen to toshi," 150–56. Takaoka discusses key government officials' admiration for and emulation of the Italian OND and the German Strength through Joy organizations not only in "Sōryokusen to toshi," but also in the essay "Dai Nippon sangyō hōkokukai to 'dōrō bunka.'"

51. Statement by Tanaka Toshio, "Atarashiki seikatsu bunka no shomondai," *Gekkan mingei*, vol. 3, nos. 1–2, January–February 1941, 50. Presumably, Tanaka was referring either to the female workers at the Kurashiki nylon-spinning factory or to female workers at a similar plant. The Takurazuka Gekidan is a well-known cabaret revue, based in Osaka, in which all roles, male and female, continue to be played by female performers: see Jennifer Robertson: *Takarazuka: Sexual Politics and Popular Culture in Modern Japan* (Berkeley: University of California Press, 1998).

52. Statement by Yamamoto Shōzō in "Dōrō bunka o kataru," *Gekkan mingei*, vol. 3, no. 7, August 1941, 47.

53. Statement by Kamiizumi, "Dōrō bunka o kataru," *Gekkan mingei*, vol. 3, no. 3, August 1941, 50.

54. Ibid., 49.

55. See Takaoka's discussion of the recreation versus reconstruction positions on work culture in "Dai Nippon sangyō hōkokukai to 'dōrō bunka,'" 52–61. Takaoka notes that the effort to "reconstruct" worker culture was largely abandoned after 1943 in favor of a return to "recreation."

56. Baranowski, *Strength through Joy*, 46.

57. See ibid., chap. 3. An important earlier discussion of the Beauty of Labor office is in Rabinbach, "The Aesthetics of Production in the Theird Reich," *Journal of Contemporary History* 11 (1976). See also chap. 1 of Paul Betts, *The Authority of Everyday Objects: A Cultural History of West German Industrial Design* (Berkeley: University of California Press, 2004).

58. Statement by Taniguchi Kichirō, "Seikatsu bunka to shomondai," *Gekkan mingei*, vol. 3, no. 5, June 1941, 9. The model barracks for the Autobahn is discussed in Baranowski, *Strength through Joy*, 77–78. She notes that Speer, director of Beauty of Labor, received the contract thanks to his close relationship to Hitler, whose

pet project the Autobahn was. She also points out that in fact Autobahn workers endured "dismal working conditions."

59. "Dōrō bunka o kataru," *Gekkan mingei*, vol. 3, no. 7, August 1941, 53–55. Tellingly, this discussion of joy in work was accompanied by several comments to the effect that female workers should not feel excessive joy in their work, since they must marry and rear children.

60. Perhaps the most concrete achievement of all the talk and planning was the establishment, in July 1941, of a Worker Housing Research Group, with head-quarters at the Mingei Association. See "Rōmusha jūtaku kenkyūkai shuisho," *Gekkan mingei*, vol. 3, no. 6, July 1941, 32–34.

61. Takaoka Hiroyuki, "Kankō—kōsei—ryokō—fuashizumu ki no tsuurizumu," in *Bunka to fuashizumu*, ed. Akazawa Shirō and Kitagawa Kenzō (Tokyo: Nihon Keizai Hyōron Sha, 1993), 28.

62. Masao Maruyama, "The Ideology and Dynamics of Japanese Fascism," in *Thought and Behavior in Modern Japanese Politics*, ed. and trans. Ivan Morris (London: Oxford University Press, 1969), 50.

63. On the successful opposition by private industry to state efforts at economic rationalization circa 1940, see Gordon, *Labor and Imperial Democracy in Prewar Japan*, 320–30. See also Fletcher, *The Search for a New Order*, 150–54.

64. Ōhara Sōichirō, statement in the roundtable discussion "Nōson to rōmusha no bunka," in *Gekkan mingei*, vol. 3, no. 3, March 1941, 47–48.

65. Rabinbach, "The Aesthetics of Production in the Third Reich," 43.

NORIKO ASO

Mediating the Masses:
Yanagi Sōetsu and Fascism

■ In 1944, Yanagi Sōetsu (also known as Yanagi Muneyoshi), founder of the Japanese Folk-Craft Movement, wrapped up an essay summarizing his organization's achievements with a solemn reminder that "aesthetic questions are not simply about beauty."[1] While Yanagi was simply reiterating an argument he often made that aesthetics and spirituality were inseparable, his observation also serves as an occasion to set his writings in relation to larger historical currents. Yet the essay "Mingei undō wa nani o kiyo shita ka? (What Has the Folk Craft Movement Contributed?)" presents a curious dilemma when we try to fix it within its historical context. Written in 1944 but first published in 1946, the production of the essay spanned what was arguably the deepest rupture in modern Japanese historical consciousness. Read as a relic of 1944, the essay clearly supports such aspects of the wartime government's ideological dictates as anti-individualism: "I am one who sees greater depth in the beauty of the public (kō/ooyake than in the beauty of the individual (ko)."[2] Read as an artifact of the era of American occupation, Yanagi's claims made on behalf of crafts appear very postwar in their championship of ordinary folk over the establishment: "the people (*minshū*) are regarded as banal (*bon'yō*) . . . but we see a positive beauty within those thus abandoned."[3]

This is not a problem confined to just the one essay. Many of Yanagi's writings uneasily shift shape under this kind of double vision, aspects of Yanagi's discourse lending themselves equally to interpretation as liberal-leaning and humanist or as fascistic in tendency. Moreover, this slippery quality was far from being Yanagi's personal idiosyncrasy.[4] Such discursive ambiguities suggest points of articulation between mid-twentieth-century humanist and fascist discourses that made slipping from one to the other all too easy for many Japanese intellectuals at the time.

The body of this paper will closely examine a number of Yanagi's essays, including "What Has the Folk Craft Movement Contributed?" in *Tami to bi* (The People and Beauty). Completed in 1944 but published as a whole in 1948, the collection is a historical curiosity in terms of its publishing history yet quite in line with the general thrust of Yanagi's theoretical writings. A couple of points emerge from this reading. First, while Yanagi's writings have generally been perceived as humanist, often of a romantic cast but with liberal moments, striking similarities exist between his folk-craft discourse and fascistic aesthetics of the wartime era. Second, Yanagi's discursive strategies were organized by a particular consciousness of the importance of the "masses" in the modern world, a group he sought to "represent" in an aesthetic and, broadly speaking, political sense. This form of discursive mediating agency constituted a bridge between a kind of reform-oriented humanism and fascism in the historical context of Japan in the 1930s and 1940s.

Yanagi as Cosmopolitan and Humanist

Yanagi Sōetsu (1889–1961) was a prolific writer, avid collector, and respected educator who founded a folk-craft movement in the early twentieth century, inspired in part by the earlier Arts and Crafts Movement of Great Britain led by John Ruskin and William Morris.[5] Not only did Yanagi coin the term *mingei* (folk crafts, an abbreviation for *minshūteki kōgei*, or "handicrafts of a popular character"), which has long since entered into common parlance, but his Japan Folk-Craft Museum is well frequented by both Japanese and international visitors today. Though not an artist or craftsman himself, he was instrumental in promoting the careers of several important figures in the Japanese art world, including the graphic designer Serizawa Keisuke

(1895–1984) and the potter Hamada Shōji (1894–1978), both of whom were designated Living National Treasures in the postwar era. Particularly noted by friends and followers for his discernment or "seeing eye,"[6] Yanagi was eulogized by Hamada this way:

> Critics, in general, may be divided into those who collect, and who get bogged down in collecting, and those who split hairs of aesthetics. Yanagi escaped both pitfalls. He employed no intellectual foot-rule. His was an immediate and intuitive faculty of an extraordinary kind.[7]

As this quote suggests, Yanagi has generally been portrayed as free from rigid ideology, political or otherwise. Equally well versed in Asian and European thought, his dogmatism appeared to lie only in his efforts to win recognition within the aesthetic canon for humble objects embedded in the daily life of ordinary people.

To provide some basis for understanding Yanagi's enduring reputation, I will provide a brief biographical sketch of Yanagi's background and career.[8] From a Tokugawa merchant class background, Yanagi's father rose to the rank of rear admiral in the Navy of the Meiji period (1868–1912) through his research into Japanese and Western-style applied mathematics. Yanagi himself was educated at the elite training grounds of the Gakushūin and Tokyo Imperial University. While at school, Yanagi joined with Mushanokōji Saneatsu (1885–1976), Shiga Naoya (1883–1971), and other future literary lights to publish the journal *Shirakaba* (White Birch), which introduced the latest in modern Western art, literature, and philosophy to a Japanese readership. After graduation, Yanagi made his living in the private sector by teaching topics ranging from English literature to Buddhist aesthetics at a number of academic institutions, including Meiji and Dōshisha universities. He also published numerous essays and books on philosophy, religion, and aesthetics, such as *Bureiku to Hoittoman* (Blake and Whitman).

In 1916, Yanagi was introduced by a friend to Yi Dynasty Korean ceramics. This led to nearly a decade of intense engagement with Korean crafts, involving annual trips to the peninsula and the eventual establishment of a museum in Seoul. Based on this close contact, Yanagi was moved to express direct criticism of the Japanese government after it brutally crushed the Korean independence movement in 1919 in what is one of his best-known pieces, "Chōsenjin o omou (Regarding the Koreans)."[9] Yanagi's deep love for Korean crafts initiated his general turn toward the East: until the end of the Second World War, Yanagi was constantly traveling and collecting throughout Japan and the rest of Asia. By the late 1920s, he had established a terminology and set of principles for advocating folk crafts. By the late 1930s, a genuine movement was picking up steam, with membership and donation rolls, two journals in publication, numerous exhibits held in department stores and other similarly prestigious venues, a museum that opened its doors in 1936, and invitations for Yanagi to lecture on Japanese aesthetics not only within Japan but also abroad—most notably, at Harvard University and the University of Hawai'i. He was also invited to talk in Okinawa, which soon became a cultural mecca for members in the Folk-Craft Movement. During one of his trips there, Yanagi again challenged government authority by criticizing the draconian measures taken in Okinawa to make local inhabitants speak "standard" Japanese rather than their native "dialect."[10]

His early immersion in the study of various cultures and his extensive travels marked Yanagi as thoroughly cosmopolitan, more so than many can claim even in this current age of "globalization." He also demanded respect as one willing to criticize the state precisely at a time when the risk for such actions was becoming greater and greater. He was not a radical, however. While the police kept a close eye on Yanagi during the wartime years, he was never sent to jail. In the words of his biographer, Mizuo Hiroshi, Yanagi pursued a more subtle path: "he sought to correct the mistaken direction of the times with beauty, by protecting regional culture and handicrafts."[11] The end of the war meant the end of an old order, while the arrival of the American occupiers suggested sweeping changes on the horizon. Despite the general atmosphere of uncertainty, Yanagi and the Folk-Craft Movement hit the ground running. Yanagi was invited in 1946 to become a member of a joint American and Japanese education committee, where he gave a talk on "Handicrafts in Japan." He continued to travel frequently within Japan; his publishing, if anything, picked up pace; and from 1952 to 1953, he served as a cultural ambassador to Europe for the *Mainichi* newspaper.

If we round out Yanagi's biography with an examination of his written work, we find ample evidence of not only his cosmopolitanism, but also of his humanism. While *humanism* is, of course, a term both familiar and vague, its roots stretch back to the European Renaissance, and it tends to be loosely associated with such social attributes as pluralism and such political formations as liberal democracy.[12] One succinct (if somewhat a-historical and partisan) definition is offered by Tzvetan Todorov: "the three pillars of humanist morality are, in effect, the recognition of equal dignity for all members of the species; the elevation of the particular human being other than me as the ultimate goal of my action; finally, the preference for the act freely chosen over one performed under constraint."[13]

A quick glance at "Chihōsei no bunkateki kachi (The Cultural Value of Regionality)," another selection from *The People and Beauty*, provides a number of humanistic statements in this vein. In that essay, Yanagi both acknowledges the unevenness of modern development separating urban from rural areas and demands that the countryside be accorded equal respect to, if not greater respect than, the cities: "cities advance with great speed. But we must admit upon reflection that there are many points in which the cities lag behind the regions, which have much to contribute to the healthy development of culture."[14] Yanagi insists that we not misrecognize mere change as essential progress, comparing the latest in women's fashion on parade at the city center of Ginza most unfavorably to the work clothes of the women of "backward" and impoverished Okinawa. Yanagi, in the same vein, further reiterates his criticism of the Japanese state's policy to stamp out native speech patterns: "our position is that, along with the encouragement of standard language, the value of Okinawan speech must also be respected."[15] Yanagi suggests that Okinawans not only have a right to freely choose how they speak, but that Japanese as a whole benefit from the existence of such differences. As for Yanagi's desire to contribute to the betterment of his fellow human beings, it is not hard to read his hopes from such statements as the following: "we whose hearts are attracted to regional crafts are necessarily drawn to ponder their aesthetic value. Accordingly, we must inquire into the social and ethical qualities that give birth to this kind of beauty, digging deep into the very essence of that lifestyle."[16] Promoting folk crafts, for Yanagi, was not just about urging the production and purchase of pretty objects. It was about spreading the message of a beautiful—in a visual sense, but also in an emotional, ethical, and even economic sense—way of life for all people, everywhere.

A Slippery Slope

However, another reading of Yanagi's writings is possible. Indeed, not only is it possible, but it is critically important to pursue this rereading to begin thinking about the conditions of prewar and wartime Japan that made it possible for a broad range of intellectuals to contribute, consciously or not, to the "fascistic" tendencies of the era. While various scholars argue that, properly speaking, *fascism* as a term should be strictly reserved for developments in early-twentieth-century Europe, Harry Harootunian points out that, taken to an extreme, such cautiousness "permits the easy presumption that what has been taken as fascism was mistaken for something else, that its historically specific appearance means it could not have occurred elsewhere and that it will not recur again (unintentionally reinforcing the exceptionalist claims fascisms usually employ to explain the superiority of their own agendas)."[17] In this spirit, I will explore certain congruences between Yanagi's theories and fascist currents of the day as a means of approaching the larger question of the "slippery slope" that can take one from respectable to unacceptable ideological formations.

Without replaying the entirety of ongoing debates regarding the definition of fascism and its application to prewar and wartime Japan, I will draw out a few points germane to a potential reassessment of Yanagi's work. Based on his magisterial review of literature on the subject, Stanley Payne provides the following definition of fascism as a historical movement:

> Above all, fascism was the most revolutionary form of nationalism in Europe to that point in history, and it was characterized by its culture of idealism, willpower, vitalism, and mysticism and its moralistic concept of therapeutic violence, strongly identified with military values, outward aggressiveness, and empire.[18]

Style was particularly important to fascist movements, which "went beyond spectacle toward the creation of a normative aesthetics . . . to create a 'politics of beauty' and a new visual framework for public life."[19] According to George Mosse, fascists themselves "described their political thought as an 'attitude' rather than a system," paying far more attention to the visual than the philosophical coherence of the movement.[20] In this way, the confused and often contradictory tenets of fascism were welded together with a powerful aesthetic aimed at binding the masses into a national body. Above all, the beauty of organic harmony—"transcending" modern alienation and divisions between capital and labor—was repeatedly extolled through paeans to healthy human bodies, an authentic everyday life, and meaningful work.[21]

The aggressive and militarist thrust of fascism and fascist aesthetics certainly had little to do with the generally pacifist values espoused by Yanagi and his Folk-Craft Movement. Moreover, the humble craftsmen and cheap, ordinary wares promoted by the man and the movement could hardly seem further from the monumentality of that touchstone of fascist aesthetics by Leni Riefenstahl, *Triumph of the Will*. Yet the core values promoted by Yanagi before, during, and after the Asia-Pacific War shared a number of tendencies with fascist aesthetics. Yanagi's work was marked by an ongoing aesthetic critique of modern alienation and decadence. Indeed, Yanagi's project can in various respects be described as "reactionary modernist," a term employed by Jeffrey Herf to make sense of the simultaneously past- and future-oriented drive of the German Nazi and Italian fascist regimes.[22] While in Yanagi's eyes the past rather than the present better represented a complete and harmonious way of life, he was certainly no fusty antiquarian, for he insisted that the past was important primarily as a resource to reform the present for a more fulfilling, or authentic, future.[23] Yanagi's proposed solutions to the ills of contemporary society included elevation of the community over the individual, a revalorization of native tradition in opposition to slavish Westernization (particularly in reference to the West of the Enlightenment), adherence to normative standards of un-selfconscious health and wholesomeness, and concomitant rejection of finicky frailty and intellectual indulgence. European fascists would have found little to quarrel with in this platform.[24]

Let us return to the essay collection *The People and Beauty*. Its title proclaims from the outset a faith in collective identity, while Yanagi's profound antipathy to the individualism he sees as characteristic of the modern age is made abundantly clear throughout. In the preface, Yanagi writes that his inspiration for the volume is a desire to contest the prevalent belief that beauty is solely the product of rarity (*keu*), genius (*tensai*), and, ultimately, individuality (*kosei*): "the Folk-Craft Movement challenges such individualist (*kojin chūshin*) views, claims to freedom (*jiyū*), and bias toward fine art [over craft]."[25] Indeed, while Yanagi quite carefully eschews any overt references to the state of war that engulfed him as he wrote this preface, a certain congruence with that era's propaganda is hard to miss in such statements as, "We must mature from individual (*kojin*) work to public (*kōjin*) work. Henceforth there will be no allowances for the pursuit of the way (*michi*) of the individual in the absence of social consciousness."[26] The stern quality of this prediction of a new social order is rather chilling, quite unlike the gentle tone of remonstrance usually associated with Yanagi,[27] and quite unlike the celebration of individualistic decadence that swept through Japanese popular culture in the immediate postwar period.[28]

This individualism to be challenged is portrayed by Yanagi as part and parcel of the problems brought on by allowing Westernization to go too far in the modern era. In "What Has the Folk Craft Movement Contributed?" he diagnoses the ills of the Japanese aesthetic world as follows:

When we examine Japanese aesthetics and art theory in recent years, they are almost entirely in the Western vein. . . . Why have Japanese not been able to pioneer their own Japanese aesthetics? Is it not because they have sought to form their opinions on the basis of Western style academic knowledge, rather than grounding themselves in Eastern aesthetic experiences?[29]

While Yanagi does not claim that Western influence has been all bad, he suggests that it has done a great deal of harm by clouding the ability of people to see objects directly rather than through a veil of misleading "knowledge." The solution Yanagi proposes for this dilemma is naturally to be found in folk crafts. They are not individualistic like the fine arts; nor are they foreign or "borrowed (karimono)." Rather, folk crafts visually inspire "a state of perception born from Japan itself."[30] While erudite cosmopolitanism is more commonly seen as characteristic of Yanagi, this should not be allowed to obscure the strong strain of nationalism that also informs his work. Indeed, in this particular essay Yanagi develops a nuanced discussion of British, French, and German aesthetic terminology precisely to make the (rather specious) case that the term "mingei (folk craft)" has no precise equivalent in any Western language. The corollary is that "there is no influence at all from foreign thought" on Japanese folk-craft theory.[31] The common assumption that cosmopolitanism and nationalism are antithetical undoubtedly contributed to the ease with which figures such as Yanagi were able to form amicable working relations with the American Occupation. However, this is clearly an assumption that does not take into account the ways in which the two positions can surreptitiously contribute to one another.[32]

Threatened by modern individualism, Yanagi as well as fascist thinkers looked with particular hope to aesthetics as a set of norms to bind and heal an alienated and ailing society. In 1933, Adolf Hitler complained in reference to modern rationality that "it is not chance that this age, propagated and protected by sick persons, necessarily led to a general sickness—not only to sickness of the body but also to sickness of the mind."[33] The occasion for these comments was a gymnastics festival, one among many programs promoted by Nazis to build up the body politic. In "Kenkōsei to bi (Healthiness and Beauty)," Yanagi hits some of the same notes in his criticism of the nervous (shinkeiteki) and sickly (byōteki) character of modern art, which no longer evinces interest in expressing the holistic nature of living (seikatsu zentai) and has even come to oppose reality (genjitsu ni taisuru hankō).[34]

As a remedy, Yanagi proposes that "healthiness (kenkōsei)" receive long overdue recognition as the foundation of true beauty: "'healthiness' is the measure of beauty. 'Health' constitutes aesthetic value. Is it not the duty of aesthetics in the future to deepen its perception of this value? And is it not the essence of art in the future to express this beauty?"[35]

What exactly is "health"? According to Yanagi, it is the unimpeded employment of god-given (ten'yo) faculties, which until the present day was a commonplace (jinjō) and taken for granted (ishiki shinai) state of affairs.[36] More broadly, however, health serves Yanagi as a synonym for normality (jōtai, heijō),[37] both in the sense of near-universal practice and in the sense of the supreme measure of social virtue. Not surprisingly, Yanagi believes that folk crafts as a category best embody the quality of health. While "too much consciousness (ishiki), taste (shumi), and assertion (shuchō) do not give rise to health in objects," folk crafts are "born from a more natural, simple, and peaceful world" in which "the producers do not have dirty ambitions" and "the customers do not lapse into individual preferences."[38] Ultimately, health is a norm rooted in survival (seizon) and daily life (nichijō no seikatsu) that Yanagi sees as a link between aesthetics and the world at large: "whether it be in physiology, in ethics, in society, or in aesthetics, health is the fundamental truth that must become the natural standard."[39]

Western individualism as a common enemy brought Yanagi and fascist thinkers uncomfortably close on a number of theoretical points. Earlier we saw resonances in the way in which Yanagi posited the nation as a natural and self-referential community and in his obsession with health as an aesthetic merging art and society into a single unified field. There are other areas of discursive overlap that could also be discussed if there were more time. However, must we say on this basis that Yanagi was a fascist in spirit? Was he simply being hypocritical in his more liberal-seeming moments? Or should we look instead to a larger historical movement that encompassed a wide range of possibilities, ranging from totalitarian fascism on the one hand to a democratic liberalism on the other?

Mediating the Masses

Yanagi's ongoing championship of folk crafts and their producers may have been humanist, even liberal on occasion, but during the 1930s and 1940s it strongly resonated with a fascistic ideology promoted at both state and popular levels.[40] How can we start to make sense of the seemingly contradictory way in which the same texts could work well in both the pre- and postwar environments? One approach is to step back and survey the general landscape. What was the area of overlap among these various ideologies that would allow someone like Yanagi to be embraced by differing camps at one and the same time?

George Mosse suggests that, as an object of desire, the "masses" provided just such a point of potential articulation among a broad range of political programs that otherwise might be quite at odds with one another.[41] Mosse sees fascism as a particularly naked, but by no means unique, manifestation of what he calls the "new politics" of the modern masses. The roots of these "new politics" go back to eighteenth-century Europe, where the emergent concepts of nationhood and popular sovereignty intertwined. As a result, "The chaotic crowd of the 'people' became a mass movement which shared a belief in popular unity through a national mystique. The new politics provided an objectification of the general will; it transformed political action into a drama supposedly shared by the people themselves."[42] While it was clear to many that the modern masses—industrial labor as well as national subjects—would play an increasingly prominent but unruly and undetermined part in reshaping society, many questions remained. How could this "general will" be known? To what ends would this "general will" be directed? Who would do this directing? In other words, "representation" was an open and contested field, with the definition and invention necessary to the political and aesthetic process shading all too quickly into questions of manipulation and control. Moreover, by the 1930s parliamentary politics, although they had opened the door to representation of the masses, were widely perceived as ailing or having failed in Italy, Germany, and Japan. Fascists, National Socialists, and "revolutionary" military and bureaucratic figures in Japan seized on this conjoined crisis and opportunity. So, too, did Yanagi in his own way.

The People and Beauty as a whole certainly raises the masses up as an object of veneration, and in such essays as "Hin to bi (Poverty and Beauty)," Yanagi stakes out a specific position for himself as their advocate. "When the world will not grant them recognition, I want to rise up and defend (*bengo shitai*) them."[43] As indicated earlier, specific terms of his defense include stressing such virtues as communal character and health. However, the dynamics of exclusion and inclusion within the defense reveal an unstated but abiding politics within Yanagi's program. Who is the prosecutor—that is, the oppressor? Who is the plaintiff—that is, the victim? Where does Yanagi belong within this dichotomy? What qualifies him to speak as an advocate? How do these power relations fit within Mosse's so-called new politics?

We might begin by noting that, in the quote, Yanagi characterizes his opposition as the "world" or general public opinion (*seken*). Indeed, Yanagi consistently presents his position as fiercely embattled, framing his essays either in anticipation of criticism or in response to actual critics. The latter certainly existed, including some contemporaries who at first glance might seem natural allies, such as Yanagita Kunio, who is generally credited with the founding of Japanese folk studies or native ethnology (*minzokugaku*),[44] or Kitaōji Rosanjin, restaurateur, potter, and craft aesthetician.[45] However sharp the words exchanged between Yanagi and his critics may have been, however, we need to take Yanagi's claims to iconoclasm with a grain of salt. Yanagi did after all found a movement that exists to this day, so it was hardly the case that he lacked listeners. Yanagi himself somewhat boastfully grumbles in *Shūshū monogatari* (Tales of Collection) that all too often he "discovered" a new craft genre only to soon find himself outbid for such objects at auctions by less discerning but better-heeled collectors capitalizing on his keen eye.[46] What is more, recent works by Harootunian, Leslie Pincus, Miriam Silverberg, and others have clearly demonstrated that the masses and everyday life were the object of intense scrutiny and celebration on the part of a considerable number of intellectuals during the prewar era.[47] While Yanagi offered an unusually concrete and active program to promote this vision, he was not alone. The embattled attitude did, however, add particular force to his expressions of alliance with the masses against their oppressors, discursively generating a fierce sense of "we" against "them." But can we say that he thus became one with the masses? After all, to do so might put at risk his very ability to protect or "represent" them.

It is telling that Yanagi speaks as a rule on behalf of and in dialogue with craft *objects* rather than with potters, weavers, woodworkers, and the like. In fact, the pronoun "them" in the "defense" quotation specifically refers to the *products* of the folk or masses. It is the humble class of dishes known as *kurawanka* that inspires a feeling of warmth and familiarity (*shitashisa*) for Yanagi. It is *kurawanka* that Yanagi imagines ascending to heaven to be placed near the sacred throne (*Kami no goza ni chikai tokoro ni*). It is *kurawanka* that suggests to Yanagi the very mind of the deity: "whenever I see such goods (*shina*), I have faith that some kind of salvation has been promised."[48] The linguistic conceit of attributing spirit or soulfulness to objects is hardly confined to this one essay. In "Bi to keizai (Beauty and Economics)," for example, Yanagi paints a picture of utopia as a place and time in which folk-craft objects have become the companions (*hanryo*) of everyone, regardless of social standing.[49] Over and over, Yanagi depicts objects as teachers providing lessons through their physical attributes, such as textures, designs, and durability. In contrast, he does not speak of literal lessons with a potter or weaver as the gateway to understanding. Even the essay "Omoidasu shokunin (Craftsmen I Have Known)," which would seem to promise some kind of dialogue, is in fact a melancholy account of how death prevented him from meeting various craftsmen except through their works.[50] In sum, in Yanagi's texts, folk-craft objects tend metonymically to replace their makers. What are the implications of this substitution? While people can speak, be quoted, and review their words, objects cannot. Objects must be read. Objects must be interpreted. Objects must be spoken for. And Yanagi takes upon himself the role of representing their virtues.

This kind of simultaneous celebration and silencing of the masses in "Poverty and Beauty" is further apparent in the essay's central argument regarding an intimate connection between these two conditions. Yanagi insists that the beauty of ordinary wares such as kurawanka should be understood as inseparable and deriving from the destitute circumstances under which they were created. While this does not mean that all things manufactured by poor craftsmen are necessarily beautiful, rich craftsmen are all too prone to cater to the whims of their wealthy patrons by adding extravagant decoration. Yanagi laments that such luxury goods (objects supplanting subjects once more) tended to be "clamorous (sawagashiku)" and "arrogant (takabutta)."[51] However, ordinary craftsmen "fortunately (saiwai ni)" lack lucrative contracts to lead them into temptation.[52] The goods they produce do not kick up a fuss or demand attention, but are instead "humble (kenkyo)."[53] Poverty enforces the rule of necessity and humility over craftsmen. According to Yanagi, in aesthetics, as in ethics, "Poor people are more closely associated with modesty (kenson), honesty (shōjiki), and simplicity (soboku) than rich people. Therefore, [they are] closer to a lifestyle that matches (kanau) the will of the deity (kami no i)."[54] When one is poor, there is no time to anguish over original designs or perfect structural symmetry. It is enough that the final product is sturdy, functional, and affordable. Conscious thought is erased and replaced by tradition, community, nature, and, ultimately, the sacred. In this way, poverty becomes a fundamental condition for beauty.

Having characterized the hardworking folk as a group that could not and should not engage in self-conscious thought and speech, to serve as their spokesman Yanagi necessarily had to distinguish himself from his objects of veneration. Yanagi's use of "we" is revealing: "we should repent (zange) that, in various ways, we rather than the craftsmen are deeply sinful human beings."[55] While Yanagi speaks on their behalf, he does not in the end identify with either the physical or the mental state of humble craftsmen. Instead, the lives and the material goods of the working classes are used as a mirror to inspire reform on high:

> When we look at the poor (mazushii) life of a craftsman deep in the countryside, we are especially struck by what we ourselves are lacking (jibun no tarinai mono). Those people do not have what could be called economic privileges. But they, not us (wareware), possess many superior privileges, with their hearts so far from sin.[56]

One of the main thrusts of "Poverty and Beauty" is to redefine a social perception of lack as its opposite, richness. Along with this, Yanagi seeks to shake up complacency among members of the middle or upper class regarding the quality of their "full" lives. There should be no question that Yanagi genuinely desires to pay honor to a class long overlooked in terms of aesthetic theory. However, we also need to recognize that Yanagi has staked out for himself a very distinct position as mediator between poor producers and wealthy consumers. Action and agency entirely lie in this middle ground, as the masses are mobilized as models to dislodge the hereditary privileges of more established socioeconomic classes.

This move reveals a key, and unfortunate, congruence with fascism: labor and the laboring classes are glorified without resulting in the actual liberation of workers. In reference to the way in which fascist regimes trumpeted the concept of "nation" to erase recognition of existing social divisions, Mark Neocleous points out that "the fascist 'resolution' of the problem of class is thus a mystification; it deals with class on an ideological rather than a material level."[57] As an illustration, he points to the Nazi "Beauty of Labor" campaign that aestheticized rather than significantly reformed the workplace. Similarly, it must be acknowledged that Yanagi's celebrations of folk virtues did not offer means to free or change anything for the poor or the producers. They were already perceived to be in a state of grace. Instead, Yanagi privileged consumption over production, both reflecting the socioeconomics of his middle-class background and returning the masses to a subordinate position. Action and power were reserved for the advocate, Yanagi, and a better future for his followers, the tasteful consumers. And yet it would be unjust to say that by positioning himself in this manner, Yanagi was in effect fascist. An abstract concept of the poor or the masses used to reproach the wealthy and powerful is equally characteristic of various liberal humanist projects of political and social reform. What links these positions together is the polymorphous "new politics" of the masses and the intoxicating opportunities opening up to those who claim to represent them.

Fascism in the Japanese Context

It has not been my goal in this essay to simply indict or acquit Yanagi on the charge of fascism: it should be clear by this point that both the prosecution and the defense in such a trial would have plenty of evidence to support their cases. My main concern has instead been to demonstrate the very ease with which Yanagi's work can be assimilated to different political discourses. This in turn suggests the dangers of depending too much on assumptions of internal coherence and logic transcending time and place in such systems of thought as humanism or fascism as they organize specific texts such as those of Yanagi. This is a truism, perhaps, but context remains critical for interpretation.

It is in this sense that I think we might still ask about the degree to which Yanagi bears responsibility for contributing to fascistic tendencies in wartime Japan—not, of course, to vindictively punish Yanagi after the fact by devaluing his tremendous contributions to the field of folk crafts, which constitutes a distinct and thriving aspect of Japanese aesthetic production today. However, serious consideration of his complicity can serve to highlight a couple of points. First, it should give us pause that Yanagi, known for championing the marginal and downtrodden, seems to have been led down a slippery slope that took him from respectable to unacceptable ideological formations by this very act of representation. The social critic Tosaka Jun pointed out at the time just how common this "downward" movement was in his classic work *Nihon ideorogiiron* (The Discourse of Japanist Ideology), his indictment of the Japanese intellectual world during the prewar and wartime years.[58] Yet the danger of such slippage is hardly relegated to the distant past. Second, the resonances between Yanagi's work and that of European proponents of fascism proper suggest that we should not feel bound to identify a critical mass of card-carrying fascists in wartime Japan before positing the existence of a fascistic culture. Just as context is important in reading Yanagi's work, so context is important in reading Japanese trends as part of world, not just particularist and national, history.

Notes

1. Yanagi Sōetsu, "Mingei undō wa nani o kiyo shita ka? [What Has the Folk Craft Movement Contributed?]," in idem, *Tami to bi* [The People and Beauty] (Tokyo: Shunshūsha, 1972), 366.

2. Ibid., 347.

3. Ibid., 340.

4. Other prominent examples that come to mind include Hasegawa Nyozekan and Watsuji Tetsurō.

5. For an insightful discussion of the movement as such, which of course should never be reduced to Yanagi's work alone, see the essay by Kim Brandt in this volume.

6. Phrase used in Bernard Leach, "Introduction," in Yanagi Sōetsu, *The Unknown Craftsman: A Japanese Insight into Beauty*, adapted by Bernard Leach (New York: Kodansha International, 1984), 88.

7. Hamada Shōji, "Yanagi and Leach," in ibid., 10

8. For more detail on Yanagi Sōetsu's life and work, see Tsurumi Shunsuke, *Yanagi Muneyoshi* (Tokyo: Heibonsha, 1987); Mizuo Hiroshi, *Nihon minzoku bunka taikei 6: Yanagi Sōetsu* (Tokyo: Kōdansha, 1978); Okamura Kichiemon, *Yanagi Sōetsu to shoki mingei undō* (Tokyo: Tamagawa Daigaku, 1991); Idegawa Naoki, *Mingei: riron no hōkai to yōshiki no tanjō* (Tokyo: Shinchōsha, 1988).

9. Yanagi Sōetsu, "Chōsenjin o omou" in idem, *Yanagi Sōetsu zenshū chosakuhen* [The Complete Collected Works of Yanagi Sōetsu], vol. 6 (Tokyo: Chikuma Shobō, 1982), 23–32.

10. See the various essays on this topic in Tanigawa Ken'ichi, ed., *Waga Okinawa* [Our Okinawa] (Tokyo: Mokujisha, 1970).

11. Mizuo, *Nihon minzoku bunka taikei 6*, 127.

12. Lamont Corliss, *The Philosophy of Humanism* (New York: Frederick Ungar, 1982), 11–19.

13. Tzvetan Todorov, *The Imperfect Garden: The Legacy of Humanism* (Princeton, N.J.: Princeton University Press, 2002), 232.

14. Yanagi Sōetsu, "Chihōsei no bunkateki kachi [The Cultural Value of the Regions]," in idem, *Tami to bi*, 331.

15. Ibid., 314.

16. Ibid.

17. Harry Harootunian, *Overcome by Modernity: History, Culture, and Community in Interwar Japan* (Princeton, N.J.: Princeton University Press, 2000), 417.

18. Stanley Payne, *A History of Fascism 1914–1945* (Madison: University of Wisconsin Press, 1995), 487–88.

19. Ibid., 13.

20. George Mosse, *The Nationalization of the Masses* (Ithaca, N.Y.: Cornell University Press, 1975, 1991), 9.

21. For synthetic analyses of the aesthetic preoccupations of fascist regimes, see

Harootunian, *Overcome by Modernity*, esp. the preface; Mark Neocleous, *Fascism* (Minneapolis: University of Minnesota Press, 1997), esp. the chapters "Revolution against the Revolution I" and "Revolution against the Revolution II."

22. Jeffrey Herf, "Reactionary Modernism: Some Ideological Origins of the Primacy of Politics in the Third Reich," *Theory and Society* 10, no. 6 (November 1981): 812–13.

23. Yanagi Sōetsu, "Fukkoshugi ni tsuite [On Revivalism]," in idem, *Tami to bi*, 250–51.

24. See, e.g., the list of fascist attributes drawn up by Emilio Gentile and cited in Payne, *A History of Fascism 1914–1945*, 5–6. What is more, Mosse points out that the German Arts and Crafts Movement had significant influence on such aesthetic arbiters of Hitler's regime as Albert Speer: Speer, *The Nationalization of the Masses*, 186.

25. Yanagi Sōetsu, "Shohan no jo" [preface to the first edition], in idem, *Tami to bi*, 2.

26. Ibid., 7.

27. An anonymous reviewer pointed out that "one could just as easily see a similarity in 'social consciousness' between Yanagi and many of those on the Left who resisted the apotheosis of *shutaisei* as individual subjectivity." I agree: resonance in Yanagi's discourse with how various leftists, pre- and postwar, problematized individual subjectivity merits critical analysis. However, my aim in this essay is to indicate how bridges existed between the conventionally opposed categories of "liberal" or "humanist" and "fascist," particularly in terms of what Mosse terms the "urge to organize the crowd": Mosse, *The Nationalization of the Masses*, 212.

28. See Yoshikuni Igarashi, "The Age of the Body," in idem, *Bodies of Memory: Narratives of War in Postwar Japanese Culture, 1945–70* (Princeton, N.J.: Princeton University Press, 2000).

29. Yanagi, "Mingei undō wa nani o kiyo shita ka?" 336.

30. Ibid., 337.

31. Ibid., 335.

32. An elegant account of this kind of dynamic can be found in Naoki Sakai, "Modernity and Its Critique: The Problem of Universalism and Particularism" in *Postmodernism and Japan*, ed. Masao Miyoshi and Harry D. Harootunian (Durham: Duke University Press, 1989).

33. Cited in Neocleous, *Fascism*, 82.

34. Yanagi Sōetsu, "Kenkōsei to bi [Health and Beauty]," in idem, *Tami to bi*, 236–38. Kano Masanao provides a broader picture of prewar and wartime Japan in terms of the "tyranny of health" in his illuminating *Kenkōkan ni miru kindai* [Modernity Viewed through Health] (Tokyo: Asahi Shimbunsha, 2001).

35. Yanagi, "Kenkōsei to bi," 242–43.

36. Ibid., 240.

37. Ibid., 240–44.

38. Ibid., 244.

39. Ibid., 243.

40. See Harootunian, *Overcome by Modernity*, for a compelling account of both the depth and breadth of such currents in prewar Japan. See also Leslie Pincus, *Authenticating Culture in Imperial Japan* (Berkeley: University of California Press, 1996), for an incisive examination of Kuki Shūzō's "national aesthetics."

41. Mosse, "The New Politics," in idem, *The Nationalization of the Masses*, 1–20.

42. Ibid., 2.

43. Yanagi Sōetsu, "Hin to bi [Poverty and Beauty]," in idem, *Tami to bi*, 216.

44. See Alan Christy, *Ethnographies of the Self: The Formation and Dissemination of Japanese Native Ethnology, 1910–1945* (Berkeley: University of California Press, forthcoming), on the tangled relationship of Yanagi's Folk-Craft Movement to *minzokugaku*, or Japanese native ethnology.

45. See my discussion of the relationship between Yanagi and Rosanjin in "New Illusions: The Emergence of a Discourse on Traditional Japanese Arts and Crafts, 1868–1945," Ph.D. diss., University of Chicago, 1997.

46. Yanagi Sōetsu, *Shūshū monogatari* [Tales of Collection] (Tokyo: Chūō Kōronsha, 1989).

47. Harootunian, *Overcome by Modernity*; Pincus, *Authenticating Culture in Imperial Japan*. See also Miriam Silverberg, "The Modern Girl as Militant," in *Recreating Japanese Women, 1600–1945*, ed. Gail Lee Bernstein (Berkeley: University of California Press, 1991).

48. Yanagi, "Hin to bi," 216.

49. Yanagi Sōetsu, "Bi to keizai [Beauty and Economics]," in idem, *Yanagi Sōetsu zenshū chosakuhen*, vol. 10, 61.

50. Idem, "Omoidasu shokunin [Craftsmen I Have Known]," in *Yanagi Sōetsu mingei kikō* [The Folk-Craft Travelogues of Yanagi Sōetsu], ed. Mizuo Hiroshi (Tokyo: Iwanami Shoten, 1990), 69–77. This article was first published in *Kōgei* [Crafts], no. 108, 1942.

51. Idem, "Hin to bi," 227.

52. Ibid.

53. Ibid.

54. Ibid., 228.

55. Ibid., 229.

56. Ibid.

57. Neocleous, *Fascism*, 41.

58. Tosaka Jun, *Nihon ideorogiiron* [The Discourse of Japanist Ideology], in idem, *Tosaka Jun zenshū* [Complete Works of Tosaka Jun], vol. 2 (Tokyo: Keisō Shobō, 1970), 223–438.

AARON SKABELUND

Fascism's Furry Friends:
Dogs, National Identity, and Purity
of Blood in 1930s Japan

■ Nearly everyone in Japan is familiar with the tale of Hachikō (1923–35). Better known as the "Loyal Dog" (Chūken) Hachikō, this Akita breed was born in the town of Ōdate in Akita prefecture in northern Honshu. About two months later, the puppy was shipped nearly twenty hours by rail to Ueno Eizaburō (1871–1925), a professor of agricultural engineering at Tokyo Imperial University. For the next fifteen months, the dog walked with his owner to the nearby Shibuya railway station in the morning and accompanied him home each evening until May 21, 1925, when Ueno collapsed and died while at work. For the next decade, Hachikō was said to appear each evening at the station to await the return of his master. In 1934, while Hachikō was still alive, his purported loyalty was memorialized with a life-size bronze statue just outside the station, which immediately became a destination for sightseers. It is now best known by Tokyoites as a favorite landmark near which to rendezvous in the fashionable shopping and entertainment district of Shibuya. An even more authentic likeness of Hachikō, preserved by taxidermy, is often on display at the National Science Museum in Ueno Park. Though long dead, Hachikō remains very much alive in popular memory. In a 1999 survey conducted by the national postal service for the selection of a series of commemorative stamps, the public chose Hachikō as one of one hundred and seventy images that most aptly illustrate the Japanese experience in the twentieth century.[1] The dog's story has been retold in many children's books over the past seventy years, in a Japanese motion picture and animated film in the late 1980s, and most recently in a Hollywood knockoff starring Richard Gere (scheduled for release in 2009 as *Hachiko: A Dog's Story*). It is no surprise that visitors, both young and elderly, frequently exclaim, "Ah, it's Hachikō!" when they spot his stuffed figure at the museum.

What few people realize is that Hachikō played a prominent role in the culture of fascism as experienced in Japan. To characterize the Hachikō phenomenon as a warm and sentimental episode in a country slowly submerging into political turmoil and militarism, as the literary scholar Edwin Seidensticker did in his masterly history of Tokyo, may be true to some extent, but in the context of the 1930s the story of Hachikō had complex, even disturbing, implications.[2] Hachikō became famous precisely because dog enthusiasts and government bureaucrats cast the dog as an exemplar of what they defined as the country's canine ideal: Japanese in character, pure in blood, loyal to a single master, and a fearless fighter.

In recent decades, scholars have written extensively about the deployment of the past and place in the imagination and invention of national communities and traditions.[3] Non-human animals, too, figured in the formation of national, ethnic, and racial identities. Perhaps their most obvious use is as national symbols, like the American Bald Eagle, the British Lion, and the Russian Bear. Another more, subtle example is the intimate connection that developed among fascism, nationalism, and canines in the course of the early twentieth century. The association goes beyond the clichéd image of Hitler's personal fetish for his Shepherd dog Blondie. Rather, within the cultures of fascism, which were characterized by an idealization and glorification of nation, race, loyalty, and violence, dogs played an important role in defining the patriotic, pure, faithful, and ferocious qualities that were expected of the state's human, and non-human, subjects.

As the linguist Ferdinand de Saussure has asserted, meaning can only be found in difference. What it means to be human is understood in relation to the non-human — whether the divine or bestial — so animals often serve as metaphors through which to assert the humanity and civilized nature of one's own group and the animality or barbaric character of "Others." While always based on supposed differences, such discourses usually place an emphasis either on defining the essential qualities of one's own group or the quintessential characteristics of "Other" people. As I have discussed elsewhere, Westerners in colonized and colonizable areas in the nineteenth century explicitly commented on the character of native dogs and, by extension, native peoples, but spoke less often of the admirable qualities of the "colonial dog" or human colonizers, which were usually taken for granted.[4] The reverse was the case in the imperial metropole, where discussions about canines usually centered on the admirable attributes of newly nationalized national dogs. This also occurred in the fascist rhetoric of the first half of the twentieth century. Domestic discourses about canines overwhelmingly concerned themselves with describing the character of the national dog while using foreign or mixed breeds as foils.

Canines provided a powerful if understated symbol in the language of fascism. Rapid industrialization, urbanization, and societal upheaval left many people uncomfortable with modernity. Suspicious of universalism, individualism, and cosmopolitanism implicit in liberal thought, fascists offered their own exceptional and indigenous versions of civilization, based on the prowess of race, nation, and community. Influenced by Darwinian thought, they feared bourgeois degeneration and racial miscegenation and celebrated violent struggle. As in the previous century, when people spoke about the character of dogs, they projected human attitudes about national and racial identity onto animals. The ubiquity, familiarity, and emotional connection of dogs, as well as their malleable symbolic power, made them an ideal vehicle by which to define identity. The nationalization of an everyday animal, purported to possess an ancient and intimate relationship with native place and people, served to bolster and to emotionalize allegiance to the nation-state; distinct, indigenous breeds provided a graphic and comprehensible way for those concerned about human racial purity to express their views; dogs, celebrated in many cultures for their fidelity, offered a prosaic device to encourage individual submission to and sacrifice for the nation; and violence unleashed with a single command epitomized the control that many people wished to exercise over their world. Indeed, the relationship between a master or breeder and his dog may be seen as an archetype of the discipline and unity revered by fascist cultures.

The link between fascism and dogs was most readily apparent in two countries, Japan and Germany, during the first half of the twentieth century. In the fascist discourses of other places, different animal metaphors may have been more prominent, even if they were deployed in similar ways and for analogous ends. In Italy, for example, predators such as lions seem to have been the animal figures of choice. Mussolini himself was frequently portrayed as a modern tamer of wild animals. He made a practice of being photographed "completely at ease visiting the cages of lions" and riding in the back of an automobile with a lion cub in his lap.[5]

Although some historians and political scientists have contested the characterization of 1930s Japan as authentically fascist, it is necessary both to recognize the particularities of time and place and to recognize the commonalities. Popular mass anti-liberal and anti-socialist nationalist movements and regimes that used a common language of unity, purity, and violence appeared in a number of modern nations that had previously seemed to be on a path toward expanding democracy in the early twentieth century.[6] Societies displaying these characteristics can be meaningfully grouped under the label "fascist" as long as we keep in mind that no two societies are the same. It is also important to remember that fascism's influence affected the entire globe, its thought and language infiltrating even such democratic countries as France, Britain, and the United States. Nevertheless, fascism's sway over Japan was far closer to the historical experience of Germany and Italy. This is especially true in the realm of culture. While politics and ideology in Japan differed in some ways from the situation in Germany, Italy, and other countries that took a fascist turn in the interwar period, the cultural landscape showed a strong resemblance to these two European counterparts. As in Germany and Italy, many members of Japan's urban and educated middle class yearned for a pure, indigenous cultural aesthetic. They believed that it could be found in a "national political essence (kokutai)," a "range of ideological virtues that defined what it meant to be Japanese, as opposed to the 'other,'" and thought these communitarian values of the countryside or the distant past could "restore" a cultural and spiritual alternative to the foreign-influenced decadence of the city and the recent history of modernization and Westernization.[7]

There were not only striking parallels but also significant interactions between Japanese and German movements to protect and promote indigenous dogs. German precedents influenced, and interacted with, Japanese government bureaucrats, military officials, zoologists, and dog enthusiasts on a number of levels. Many aficionados of "Japanese" dogs admired so-called German Shepherd dogs, and some were members of groups that promoted the latter breed in Japan. The Shepherd dog was frequently a benchmark of comparison for "Japanese" breeds, and some fanciers in Germany and Japan considered both Japanese dogs and German Shepards to be closely related, and therefore the purest and finest canines in the world. Finally, the two groups of enthusiasts spoke a shared language of fascism.

公 チ ハ 犬 忠

1. A photograph of the "Faithful Dog" Hachikō that appeared on the opening page of Kishi Kazutoshi's *Chūken Hachikō monogatari* (1934). The photo was probably taken in front of the home of Andō Shō, the sculptor who crafted the bronze statue of Hachikō that was unveiled outside the Shibuya railway station in central Tokyo in 1934. Unfortunately, neither Andō nor his statue survived the Second World War. Andō died in an American air raid in May 1945, and the previous fall government officials toppled Hachikō's bronze figure because of a shortage of metal needed to prosecute the conflict. On August 15, 1945, the three-year anniversary of Japan's surrender, a replica of the original statue by Andō's son, Takeshi, was dedicated outside of station, where it stands to this day.

As the historian Boria Sax has written, "The Nazis were constantly invoking dogs and wolves for the qualities they wanted to cultivate: loyalty, fierceness, courage, obedience, and sometimes even cruelty."[8]

Although it is hardly a cruel story, the legend of Hachikō provides a useful framework for probing the relationship between dogs and fascism in Japan. Hachikō was the key figure in the rediscovery and valorization of native dogs, long despised as disorderly, savage, and wolf-like. Through the joint efforts of a group of private dog enthusiasts and the Ministry of Education, the native dog of Meiji times was in the course of the early twentieth century transformed into the "Japanese" dog, an icon of purity, loyalty, and bravery, superior to both Western dogs and the native canines of Japan's colonies. Indeed, the creation of the "Japanese" dog, with Hachikō as its paragon, was one of the building blocks of a culture of imperial fascism that venerated the nation, celebrated purity, esteemed fidelity, and glorified violence.

Nationalizing Native Dogs

The association of native dogs with the nation-state in Japan of the 1930s was part of a trend that had developed in Europe in the second half of the nineteenth century and spread with imperialism and the global diffusion of Western modes of dog-keeping and the ideology of animal pure-bloodism. Yet given indigenous canines' recent history, the extolling of native dogs in Japan was no small irony. Foreigners and local elites alike from the mid-nineteenth century had regarded indigenous dogs as primitive, cowardly, and of mixed or wild breed. Within a remarkably short space of time, these same canines came to be cited as an example of what supposedly made Japan superior to the West. For decades rounded up for elimination by dog-catchers in the government's employ, "Japanese" dogs had by the early 1930s became immensely popular, serving as a status symbol for anyone with the means to acquire one. Once the target of derision, they were now a source of pride.

The radical reappraisal of native dogs in Japan paralleled, even if it slightly trailed temporally, the nationalization of the Shepherd dog in Germany. As with native dogs in Japan, the "Germanization" of the Shepherd dog occurred comparatively late and produced a dramatic shift in popular attitudes. Until Max von Stephanitz, a Prussian cavalry captain, established the Verein für deutsche Schäferhunde (Society for the German Shepherd Dog) in 1899, the breed was largely undefined and little valued. Within a decade of its establishment, the group achieved phenomenal success in registering, breeding, and popularizing what Stephanitz called the "primeval Germanic dog."

Although there were earlier expressions of pride for native dog breeds and dismay at their "mongrelization" in turn-of-the-century Japan, these sentiments did not crystallize until several decades later. There were probably several reasons for the delay. A clientele for canines—that is to say, a bourgeois middle class that was interested in and could afford to acquire and keep a dog—did not emerge in Japan until the 1920s. It was not until such a constituency appeared that the ownership of dogs, and in this case the keeping specifically of native dogs, became widespread enough for a reconsideration of the maligned canines to take place. Urbanization played

an important role in the revaluation of indigenous canines, as well. The isolation from the countryside that is characteristic of citified modernity led in
many countries to a desire to reconnect with the natural world, albeit in a
domesticated form—or, as the historian Kathleen Kete has put it, to install
a "beast in the boudoir."[9]

Shifts in the political and cultural climate during the late 1920s and
1930s made people more receptive to the promotion of native dogs. Nationalism and the veneration of native canine breeds were inseparable. The first
expressions of concern for indigenous dogs coincided with rising nationalism at the end of the nineteenth century, and their full manifestation corresponded with what the historians Tetsuo Najita and Harry Harootunian
have called the "Japanese revolt against the West" in the 1930s. During this
period, ideologues promoted national pride in a pure, indigenous culture
that was unsullied but supposedly threatened by foreign elements. The reclamation and praise of native dogs was a canine variant of this pervasive
and powerful political, intellectual, and cultural ground swell of resistance
against the purported corrosive influences of Western modernity.

In the realm of dogs, Saitō Hirokichi (who also used the pen name Saitō
Hiroshi; 1900–64), the founder of the Nihon Ken Hozon Kai (Society for
the Preservation of the Japanese Dog), led the revolt. Born and raised in
rural Yamanashi Prefecture in central Japan, Saitō graduated from the prestigious Tokyo Bijutsu Gakkō (Tokyo Fine Arts Academy; now the Tokyo Geijutsu Daigaku) and became a landscape architect. He later played a leading
role in the design of a garden at the National Museum of Modern Art in
Tokyo, which opened in 1952. An art lover, Saitō was instrumental in protecting precious medieval cultural artifacts of the aristocratic Konoe household from the bombing raids of the Second World War. Saitō's other love
was dogs. In 1927, he joined the Eighth Artillery Division but was soon
discharged because of health problems. Told by his doctor that he needed
plenty of fresh air, and perhaps feeling in need of a mission, he decided to
buy a dog and began to search, as he later recalled, for a pure indigenous
canine like "those depicted in ancient scrolls."[10]

Saitō was unable to find a dog that met his standards in Tokyo, where,
in his view, Western decadence and foreign blood had spread to the urban
canine population. Even in the mountainous northern prefecture of Akita,
soon to be known for a breed of the same name, he found it difficult to
locate a dog that met his satisfaction. Alarmed that, through interbreeding,
native dogs were following wolves to what he believed was tantamount to
extinction, Saitō established the society in 1928. He then spent much of

the next half-decade traveling to remote highland regions throughout the archipelago to locate purebred dogs and to campaign for their protection. It was only dogs in these areas that Saitō considered to be free of the legacy of Westernization that he believed to have defiled Japan both physically and spiritually.

While returning from one of those trips, Saitō encountered Hachikō somewhere in the vicinity of Shibuya station. After this meeting, he featured the dog on the pages of a society newsletter in 1929, but several years later, Saitō realized that Hachikō had a potentially wider appeal and proposed a story about the dog to an *Asahi* newspaper reporter. The paper prominently placed the piece and a large photograph of a forlorn-looking Hachikō in its October 4, 1932, morning edition. "The Story of a Lovable Old Dog: A Seven-Year Expectant Wait for the Return of a Master Who Is No Longer of This World" told of the dog's unfailing fidelity and portrayed him as a mediator of dogfights and a protective patron (*oyabun*) for smaller canines.[11] The article launched Hachikō's tremendous popularity, which probably escalated to a degree beyond what anyone, including Saitō, anticipated.

Saitō's timing could not have been better. There are good, historical reasons why this dog got his day in 1932 and why such an apotheosis occurring just a few years earlier is difficult to imagine. The Manchurian Incident, which began the previous year, marked the start of what was repeatedly proclaimed to be an extended "national emergency (*hijōji*)" and a time of tremendous national anxiety. On September 18, Japanese military officers used a staged explosion on a railway in northeastern China as a ploy to launch an attack on the troops of the local warlord. By January 1932, the entire region was effectively in the hands of the Kwantung Amy, and the following month Tokyo established the Japanese puppet state of Manchukuo. The insubordination of military officers in Manchuria and the inability, and unwillingness, of civilian authorities to constrain them, coupled with "government by assassination" at home, led to an end to party rule by mid-1932. After the May 15 killing of Prime Minister Inukai Tsuyoshi by a group of navy officers and ultra-rightists, top military leaders proceeded to dominate "national unity" cabinets. Thus began the country's descent into a long, dark valley of militarism and fascism. The unfolding, sentimental tale of Hachikō surely brought release from the uncertainties of the early 1930s, but its very appeal stemmed from the fact that its underlying message subtly reinforced the upsurge in patriotism that sang praises to the virtues of Japan's unique "national polity" and demanded strict allegiance to the "imperial way."

三面村探検のさい，民家に残された古式の狩衣を着けた著者（昭和6年11月）

2. Saitō Hirokichi, in traditional hunting attire, while searching for purebred "Japanese" dogs in the Sanmen region of Niigata Prefecture in November 1931.

As indicated by the name of his organization—the Society for the Preservation of the Japanese Dog—Saitō explicitly linked native canines to the nation. Just as Stephanitz had "Germanized" the Shepherd dog several decades earlier, Saitō effectively nationalized native dogs on the archipelago by declaring them to be "Japanese," or *Nihon inu*. This simple linguistic move transformed dogs that had previously been considered wild and uncivilized into worthy domesticated pets, desirable to the middle class. Some people even before the 1930s had used *Nihon inu* (Japanese dog), which more unequivocally tied native dogs to the nation-state, but thanks to Saitō's efforts, it quickly became an almost exclusively used label. By the early 1930s, native canines had become a proud symbol of Japan, something unthinkable a few decades earlier.

Saitō did not link native dogs to the nation in name only. "Japanese" canines, he claimed, possessed a personality similar to the country's human population because of a long and close association between the archipelago's people and dogs. In a radio address in 1937 titled "What Kind of a Canine Is a Japanese Dog?" aired by Nippon Hōsō Kyōkai (NHK), the government-controlled broadcasting company, Saitō made the following declaration: "[the] dog's temperament is strongly influenced by the character of its master, but because the Japanese dog has a long history the character of the nation has exerted influence on the entire breed. The various traits of the Japanese nation—difficulty in getting used to anyone outside its master's family, being intelligent but not adept in expressing emotions as compared to Western dogs, diffidence and stubbornness, and extreme courage—have been ingrained into the personality of Japanese dogs."[12] Here and elsewhere, Saitō adeptly used the mass media to spread the message that centuries of interaction between Japanese people and native dogs had caused the canines to acquire a disposition like their human companions and molded them into the dog of the Japanese family-state (*kazoku kokka*).

Equally important was Saitō's success in ensuring that government bureaucrats showed and maintained an interest in dogs. The Ministry of Education, at the recommendation of officials in its Bureau of Cultural Affairs, sanctioned the nationalization of native dogs by declaring seven different breeds as natural treasures worthy of government protection during the 1930s. The legal instrument through which this feat was accomplished was the Law for Preserving Scenery and Historic and Natural Monuments (*Shiseki meisho tennen kinenbutsu hozon hō*), a measure enacted in 1919 and modeled on similar regulations in the United States and Europe, particularly German precedents.

Although indigenous domesticated dogs were not the first animals to be given special status, they were probably the most celebrated. During the 1930s, the ministry named the Akita, Kai, Kishū, Koshino (soon considered extinct through interbreeding), Shiba, Shikoku, and Hokkaido breeds to be endangered national assets. A declaration of protection stringently regulated the sale, breeding, and movement of designated canines, all of which continue to this day. The Ministry of Education's rationale for preserving "Japanese" dogs echoed Saitō's argument that the character of the nation was ingrained in the personality of the country's canines. When the ministry announced its designation of the Shiba breed in 1936, its spokesperson proclaimed that the dogs were worthy of the honor because they "reflect the character of the Japanese people, and compared to foreign dogs demonstrate a particular vigor and have all the characteristics of a Japanese dog."[13]

As underscored by the ministry's insistence that the vigor of the Shiba breed surpassed that of foreign canines, fans of native dogs were anxious to show that their animals were as good as, if not better than, any pureblooded Western breed. Claims about the superiority of native dogs vis-à-vis Western canines often appeared in articles in the specialized enthusiast and general press. The point was even made for young readers by Kishi Kazutoshi, author of The Story of the Loyal Dog Hachikō. "Mention the 'Japanese dog,' and the dogs of Japan who in the past have been treated like strays come to mind. Mention a dog show, and only Western dogs such as the setter, pointer, and terrier come to mind. What the Society for the Preservation of the Japanese Dog is making Japanese aware of is that the Japanese dog is by no means inferior, but in fact far superior, to Western dogs."[14]

Dog enthusiasts and education bureaucrats asserted that the timeless relationship between the archipelago's canine and human races, especially between the dogs and the country's emperors, made "Japanese" dogs better than others. Stephanitz used similar language to recall how in "time immemorial . . . the warlike proud German held in high esteem his courageous hunting comrade."[15] Saitō and other commentators insisted that native dogs enjoyed a special bond with the people of Japan that had begun during the rule of the country's first (mythical) emperor, Jimmu. Such claims, however, depended on the (a)historical connection between native dogs and the Japanese throne, both of which were perceived as having preserved a constant, untainted bloodline since the dawn of time.

In addition to calling frequent attention to the alleged connections between the country's dog population and its imperial masters in the past, dog fanciers sought to create similar links in the present. Society officials eagerly encouraged the participation of royalty and nobility in its dog shows. The first Japanese-dog show was held at the Matsuya department store in Ginza in early November 1932 and coincided with a national holiday commemorating the birth of the late Meiji emperor.[16] The society invited several members of the imperial household and presented them and, in absentia, the emperor with small statues of Hachikō.

Hachikō, the embodiment of the pre-eminence of Japan's newly nationalized dogs, attended this and subsequent shows as a special guest. At the first exhibition, he appeared together with Koma-go, another Akita dog, whom the society had previously given to a relative of the emperor.[17] The society awarded both dogs special collars to celebrate the event. The broad band of leather, stamped with the words "Commemorative Memento as Honorary Participant of the First Japanese-Dog Show—The Society for the Preservation of the Japanese Dog," still encircles the stuffed Hachikō in the National Science Museum. In death, as in life, Hachikō was collared by the nation and tagged as Japanese.

Blood and Breed

The society's breeding standards and the government's moves to preserve native dogs reflected the complex nature of Japanese attitudes about racial identity during the 1930s. These attitudes were represented by two conflicting strains of thought, one of which regarded Japanese as a racially homogenous people, and the other of which considered Japanese to be of mixed racial origin. Reflecting the former view, the policies and rhetoric of dog enthusiasts and government preservationists betrayed a strident concern with the maintenance of pure blood. Society officials considered and government bureaucrats recognized as "Japanese" only those groups of canines whose pedigree had been attested in the archipelago since the beginning of (Japanese) time. The primary threat driving "Japanese" dogs to extinction, they contended, were canines of Western and mixed breed. Their actions and statements mirrored wider societal anxieties about human purity of blood, the superiority of the Japanese race, and the specter of miscegenation.

Reflecting the latter view, enthusiasts and scientists speculated that the ancestors of "Japanese" dogs had likely come to the archipelago thousands of years earlier from the Asian continent or the South Pacific. In this sense, they, like their human companions, ultimately possessed a mixed heritage, but had since been isolated from outside influxes of canine blood by the islands' geography. Such an explanation supported the government's efforts to assimilate and exploit the human population of Japan's formal and informal colonies. In this way, fanciers, scientists, and government preservationists enlarged the Japanese canine imperium even as Japan's empire expanded making the country's political rule seem natural and organic.

The most pressing task for Saitō in the late 1920s and early 1930s was to determine precisely what a "Japanese" dog was. The defining characteristic of the breeds that came to be considered Japanese was that their bloodlines were free of foreign adulteration. While recognizing that the archipelago's earliest canines may have arrived with humans from elsewhere thousands of years before, Saitō drew a clear distinction between those dogs and breeds that appeared on the peninsula more recently, even if their distinctive appearance had been shaped by breeders in Japan.[18] As explicated by the society's foreign secretary, Hata Ichirō, the only dogs that were truly Japanese were "native dogs" of an "ancient breed that have been living more or less in a similar form and shape from the days of our forefathers."[19]

For fanciers, this primordial connection to the archipelago was not the only reason that certain indigenous dogs outclassed purebred Western dogs. "Japanese" dogs, they claimed, had lived with humans but had not been interbred by them, so they remained in a natural and uncorrupted state.[20] Such language echoed contemporary rhetoric about the unbroken and undefiled blood ties of the Japanese nation and the imperial line. It also ignored the irony that breeders and eugenicists were now intervening to improve and maintain those same Japanese canine and human races that they claimed were superior because they had been formed naturally.

At the same time that Saitō and other society members praised native dog breeds for being free of foreign canine blood, they celebrated their resemblance to wolves and possible blood links to their lupine cousins. Such admiration for the wolf-like nature of native dogs was ironic. Westerners and local elites in Japan and other colonizable and colonized areas of the world had denigrated certain native dogs for their purported physical and behavioral similarities to wolves, and this disparagement led to efforts to eliminate indigenous canines—whether street, feral, or wild dogs or the wolves themselves.

During the interwar period, a new respect for wolves and other large predators emerged throughout the world, especially in areas where these animals were extinct and no longer an actual, or even imagined, threat.

Attitudes toward canines once despised as wolf-like changed, too. Possible biological links with wolves and a wolfish appearance and behavior became more appealing, particularly in those countries where fascism made the deepest inroads. Nowhere was this shift more apparent than in Germany. Hitler and other National Socialist leaders continually appropriated wolves for symbolic purposes, referring to themselves as wolves and their various headquarters as lairs.[21] And the Führer and many Nazis admired the Shepherd dog because of its supposed wild, wolfish nature. The relationship between the three—Nazis, lupines, and Shepherd dogs—is aptly captured by the name Hitler gave the first "German" Shepherd he owned: Wolf.

Similar cultural trends were evident in 1930s Japan. Wolves were not deployed in the political sphere so frequently as they were in Germany, but the reasons for their extinction and their relationship with native dogs became a much discussed topic. The folklorist Yanagita Kunio speculated in the pages of the Society for the Preservation of the Japanese Dog's magazine that wolves may not have completely vanished from the archipelago at all, and even if they had, they probably interbred with dogs, so that wolf blood could still be found in native canines.[22] While Saitō and others rejected Yanagita's explanation of lupine extinction and his theory of a recent biological link between wolves and native breeds, they celebrated the idea of the wolf-like nature of "Japanese" dogs, which made local varieties seem more natural, pure, and fearsome than their foreign cousins.

Although there were striking parallels with Germany in discussions of canine blood and breed, there were also marked differences. Specifically, because of Japan's relatively shallow experience with animal husbandry, discussions about breeding neither preoccupied fanciers nor wielded the influence that they did elsewhere. In many Western countries, "breeding" animals *and* humans for superiority was important, as highlighted by the widespread popularity of eugenics, but nowhere did such thinking become policy as under the Third Reich. In early-twentieth-century Germany, a number of advocates of eugenics and Aryan supremacy had backgrounds in zootechny or referenced animal breeding in their arguments for artificially improving human heredity. Stephanitz and National Socialist educators, for example, used dog breeds to explain in readily understandable terms ethnogeny, the supremacy of the Aryan race, and the dangers of miscegenation. In Japan, however, animal breeding had less impact on racial policies. Crossover between animal breeders and the relatively weak eugenics movement in Japan was much rarer, and any concern with human purity in the writings of canine enthusiasts was far more muted and implicit. That said, the rhetoric of Japanese dog enthusiasts clearly fed into wider societal concerns about racial identity, just as canine terminology helped to shape larger discussions of race.

In broader terms, as well, the politics of race and empire in Japan differed significantly from that in Germany. Because Western notions of race were intertwined with a belief in the superiority of white races, many Japanese were uncomfortable with eugenic and racial thought. Japanese nationalism, as the historian Tessa Morris-Suzuki has pointed out, was generally centered on the idea of *Volk*, or "national people (*minzoku*)," rather than "race (*jinshu*)."[23] One current of nationalism depicted Japanese as a racially homogenous people literally descended from a common bloodline whose uppermost branch was the Imperial Family. The competing mixed-blood view emerged only later, in the late nineteenth century, but grew rapidly along with imperial expansion. Japan's acquisition of an empire populated by ethnically similar peoples living in relatively close proximity to the metropole led some people to emphasize that Japanese were of diverse racial origins and to identify this hybridity as a source of national strength and imperial power.

Such political realities were reflected in and supported by popular and scientific discourses about dogs. During the 1930s, Saitō increasingly embraced theories that extended the Japanese canine realm even as the country's political empire grew. With the assistance of colleagues, he investigated canines in the Ryukyu Islands, Taiwan, Korea, Manchuria, and the South Seas. In colonial Korea, he gained the cooperation of Mori Tamezō, a professor of zoology at Keijō Imperial University (present-day Seoul University). In early 1937, an *Asahi* journalist reported that Saitō and Mori had discovered on Chindō, an island off the southwestern coast of Korea, what the article labeled "Japanese dogs raised in Korea," sporting pricked-up ears and curled tails. Saitō speculated that the dogs had originated either in the Japanese home islands (*naichi*) or in the northern part of the continent.[24] As a result of Saitō's and Mori's research, alongside the seven breeds that the Ministry of Education designated "Japanese" national treasures during in the 1930s, Japanese colonial authorities in Korea granted similar "Japanese" status to the Chindō and one other peninsular breed, the Bunsan, in the late 1930s. This bureaucratic canonization surely did not arise out of pure concern for the canines themselves, much less the Korean populace. Rather, like other facets of colonial modernity, such as industrialization and the spread of primary education, it served the purposes of the imperial power.

Whether with regard to dogs he deemed "Japanese" on the archipelago or on the Korean peninsula, Saitō repeatedly emphasized two physical traits. All "Japanese" canines, as he declared in his radio speech in 1937, had to have "small, triangular ears that stand erect" and a "large and powerful curled tail."[25] Any animal that did not show these features was immediately regarded as suspect. Some people suggested, based on this standard, that Hachikō was not purebred because his tail slumped down when he walked and, even more noticeable, because his left ear drooped. Then, and repeatedly over the years, Saitō emphatically defended the integrity of Hachikō's bloodline. He argued that the tail dropped and the ear flopped as a result of skin disease and not because of foreign contamination of the dog's pedigree.[26] Fortunately for Saitō, and indeed because of his influence, taxidermists at the National Science Museum mounted Hachikō with his tail curled and both ears standing erect, so that he emerged looking like a young, healthy, purebred "Japanese" dog.

Unflagging Fidelity

Preservationists were not the only bureaucrats in the Ministry of Education who were concerned about native dogs. Educators within the ministry, too, realized that native dogs like Hachikō—and other dogs in the service of the empire—could be elevated as icons of loyalty in imperial and wartime Japan. From the 1890s, the inculcation of the Confucian virtue of loyalty (chū) had been central to the mission of the national school system. Government officials and private spokespeople labored to instill in imperial subjects a strong sense of obligation and veneration for elders, teachers, superiors, the state, and, most of all, the emperor. Schoolteachers taught their pupils that they were part of a unique family-state, with the emperor at its head. Hachikō and other supposedly devoted dogs provided perfect pedagogical models for authorities to suffuse people, both young and old, with messages about duty to and sacrifice for the nation.

Many cultures have celebrated the faithfulness of dogs to humans. Perhaps nowhere, though, were faithful dogs deployed so prominently as symbols as in the fascist rhetoric of the 1930s. In Germany, proto-Nazi and National Socialist commentators and educators often venerated canines as paragons of fidelity. It was precisely this supposed devout dedication that endeared the German Shepard breed to Nazi officials.[27]

If the deployment of dogs to spread ideas about race in Japan paled in comparison to Germany, the metaphorical mobilization of "Japanese" canines to foster loyalty was probably unrivaled. Such discourses extended to military dogs of Western breed in the employ of the army, especially Shepherd dogs. However, "Japanese" dogs were singled out even more often for their unconditional devotion. Commentators repeatedly asserted that the fidelity of native dogs was unique among canines in that it was directed exclusively and unendingly to a single master. More than once, the faithfulness of Hachikō and other "Japanese" dogs was compared to the bushidō ethos that supposedly bound a samurai warrior to his lord and the allegiance that people felt for the emperor.

In addition to ideological motivations, a desire for economic profit buoyed Hachikō's rise to fame. In 1934, businesspeople took advantage of the zodiac in the Year of the Dog, and the following year they capitalized on Hachikō's death to cash in on the canine celebrity. Merchants manipulated the "Loyal Dog" to sell everything from toys to kimonos, postcards to kitchenware, phonographs to books. The commercial exploitation of Hachikō continued throughout the 1930s and persists to some degree to this day. Annual events, most prominently a memorial service in March and a festival in April, honor the dog, and until 2006 (when the space was taken over by the global chain store, The Body Shop) any number of Hachikō trinkets could be purchased throughout the year at a store called the Hachikō Shop located just outside the officially named Hachikō Exit of Shibuya station.

The Society for the Preservation of the Japanese Dog and its allies in the Ministry of Education reveled in the attention that Hachikō was generating but by the same token fiercely sought to maintain control over the manner in which dog was portrayed. In late 1933, for example, anticipating even greater publicity during the upcoming Year of the Dog, a group of private entrepreneurs announced its intention to construct a wooden statue of Hachikō. Angered by this attempt by outsiders to literally shape Hachikō's image and profit from it, Saitō and his influential backers swiftly launched a campaign in early 1934 to raise money to build their own statue. The committee asked Andō Shō to take on the task of sculpting, with but one condition. Andō had already created a plaster model of Hachikō the previous fall for an annual show at the Imperial Gallery of Art and in that work faithfully depicted Hachikō with a floppy left ear.[28] Such a design, the committee decided—at Saitō's insistence—would not do: Andō must depict the dog with both ears erect. Saitō's wish went unfulfilled, however, when the exigency of quickly completing the statue forced the sculptor to use his original model for the cast, and for perpetuity Hachikō was cast in bronze as a dog with a suspect ear.

3. The original bronze Hachikō outside the Shibuya railway station on the day of its dedication, April 21, 1934. The adult figure standing in front of the statue appears to be Saitō Hirokichi, who was primarily responsible for popularizing the dog. Notice the many children surrounding the statue, an indication of Hachikō's appeal to youngsters. Photograph courtesy of Mainichi Photo Bank.

The statue was dedicated in an elaborate hour-long ceremony on April 21, 1934. Arrayed in white and red ribbons but beginning to show his age, Hachikō was the guest of honor. After speeches by dignitaries who included Saitō; the chief of the Ministry of Education's Social Education Bureau; and Kishi, the author of *The Story of the Loyal Dog Hachikō*, Ueno's niece Sakano Hisako unveiled the statue. A poem written by Yamamoto Teijirō—who served as a Diet member, a minister of agriculture and forestry, and, from 1935 on, the leader of the reactionary Kokutai Meichō Undō (Movement for the Clarification of the National Polity)—praised "The Conduct of the Loyal Dog (Chūken kō)" and was inscribed on the statue's base. In a melancholy tone, Yamamoto's poem lauded the faithfulness of Hachikō and lamented the fickle nature of humans.[29]

Although Saitō gave birth to the Hachikō story and the business community cashed in on it, Ministry of Education bureaucrats largely dictated its interpretation and dissemination to a national, colonial, and even world-wide audience. Initially, ministry bureaucrats used Kishi's *Story of the Faithful Dog Hachikō* to spread their tailored message. Ministry officials promoted the book in classrooms by way of an army of teachers. One man half-joked years later that his teacher encouraged students so enthusiastically to buy the book that he wondered if the instructor was getting a percentage of the income.[30] Moral suasion, rather than financial profit, was a more likely motive. A newspaper advertisement proclaimed that the book was an "ethics primer that must reach every mountain and seaside village of the archipelago." Reading it, the ad declared, caused children to "feel the righteous heart of Hachikō, who embodies the Japanese spirit" and braced them to defy a "world gone decadent, where people wallow in luxury and idleness, and humanity has become thinner than paper."[31]

Official and popular media, artists, and performers joined forces with the ministry to celebrate the virtue of loyalty as embodied by Hachikō. Just weeks before the dedication ceremony, the Society for the Preservation of the Japanese Dog, the Ministry's Social Education Bureau, and the Kōkoku Seishin Kai (Imperial Spirit Society) sponsored a benefit concert of skits, songs, and comic acts that attracted more than three thousand people to the Japan Young People's Auditorium in the outer garden area of Meiji Shrine. NHK transmitted the story of Hachikō as part of its children's radio programming. Countless poems, books, and songs hailed the inexhaustible fidelity of Hachikō. A dance group performed a number called "The Marching Song of Hachikō"; one poem equated Hachikō with Mount Fuji, cherry blossoms, and the Rising Sun flag as a "national treasure" that "taught people never to forget their debts of gratitude"; another verse by the poet Noguchi Ujō likened the dog to the famous forty-seven samurai of Akō, who in the early seventeenth century demonstrated their devotion to their late lord by avenging his ritual suicide, and to samurai and soldiers from Nitta Yoshisada (1301–38) to General Nogi Maresuke (1849–1912), who showed their allegiance to emperors in life and death.[32]

The campaign was a rousing ideological and financial success. Although the committee secured large contributions from businesspeople, the fund-raising drive was primarily aimed at schoolchildren and enjoyed the full cooperation of the Education Ministry, school officials, and teachers. Even in the midst of a lingering economic depression, many children throughout the empire apparently responded. The committee raised about 1,864 yen (the average yearly salary of a prefectural employee was 737 yen in 1934), more than enough to cover the cost of the statue. More important for educators, adoration for Hachikō's loyalty appeared to capture the minds of many people.

Ministry intervention ensured that the focus of the story would be loyalty rather than some other virtue or cause. Animal-welfare activists, such as those in the Japanese branch of the Humane Society, attempted to mobilize the dog to improve the plight of Tokyo's stray-dog population, among whose ranks Hachikō sometimes wandered, and to promote more compassionate conditions in the city's notorious dog pounds.[33] The Humane Society made Hachikō an honorary member of its Pochi Kurabu (Pooch Club), and its constituents called for better treatment of canines through newspaper articles and letters to the editor. The group also attached an ornament adorned with the club's name to Hachikō's collar, which still dangles from the museum mannequin today. The message stressed by animal-welfare activists, however, was largely overwhelmed by official and private voices praising the dog's devotion.

In the same month that ministry officials helped raise the dog's bronze likeness outside Shibuya station, they incorporated Hachikō further into the school curriculum by including his story in a new national ethics (shūshin) textbook for second-year students issued in 1934. The painter Ishii Hakutei provided an illustration for the story, depicting Hachikō with both ears erect—much to Saitō's relief, no doubt—waiting vainly but alertly outside of Shibuya station. The tale "On o wasureru na (Don't Forget Your Debts of Gratitude)" was rendered in the following manner:

> Hachikō was a cute dog. Soon after he was born, a person far away adopted Hachikō and cared tenderly for him just as if he were his own child. As a result, his weak body became very strong. Every day when Hachikō's master departed for work, the dog would see him off at the train station, and every evening when he would return, Hachikō was there waiting to greet him at the station. Then one day, Hachikō's master died. The dog, because he did not understand, searched for him daily. Hachikō would look for his master among all the people who got off at the station each time a train arrived. Many months passed in this manner.
>
> Even though one, two, three, ten years passed, Hachikō—grown old searching for his master—can be seen in front of the station every day.[34]

On the surface, the story appeared innocuous. But its title and its context underscored the fact that Hachikō was a tool for indoctrination. The title did not capture the content of the story; rather, it didactically admonished children, "Don't Forget Your Debts of Gratitude." Other stories in the same reader exhorted youngsters to strengthen their bodies, to honor their ancestors and emperors past and present, and to be obedient.

Hints of how the text may have been taught can be gleaned from articles about the story in instructors' manuals and educational magazines. The author of one such column, Kobayashi Gen, asserted that although the episode was true, teachers should teach it as a fable and not explore the tale's veracity in the classroom. "Second-year students are meek," Kobayashi wrote, "and will meekly accept what you tell them." He challenged teachers to instill in youngsters a sense of their indebtedness because, "for children not to forget their debts, they must first feel them." The debts that Kobayashi had in mind were made clear in the following paragraph. He suggested that the story be read in class on March 6, the birthday of the Meiji empress. This day, he recommended, should be dedicated to the important task of encouraging children to "contemplate the magnanimity of the splendid virtues of the imperial throne and to nourish hearts that will repay this supreme debt."[35]

The use of Hachikō to foster devotion to authority in youngsters likely had its intended effect. Although measuring accurately how people respond to ideology is problematic, if not impossible, essays by second-year primary-school students living in the Shibuya area and preserved in the station's archive suggest that Hachikō did inspire in some children a desire to emulate his purported fidelity. Many students reported making a special visit to the statue, seeing huge numbers of bouquets and wreaths, and feeling grief at his passing. A number of the compositions mouthed set phrases—describing Hachikō waiting vainly in rainy, hot, and snowy weather—from a poem that appeared in Kishi's *Story of the Loyal Dog Hachikō*, and a few children linked Hachikō with other paragons of loyalty who appeared in their textbooks.[36]

Stories of dogs were ideal material for the government's efforts to inculcate the entire population with messages about duty to and sacrifice for the nation. More than anything, what made the Hachikō story so effective was that the protagonist was a dog, a seemingly benign, non-ideological, commonplace companion that nearly everyone could relate to. Because the heroes of the Hachikō narrative and other stories were canines, they were appealing to children as well as adults.

The image of Hachikō as a model of dutiful devotion, however, was not without its complications or its detractors, even within the Society for the Preservation of the Japanese Dog. Saitō's fellow society member and canine researcher Hiraiwa Yonekichi harshly criticized the projection of human motivations onto Hachikō. In the April 1935 edition of *Kodomo no shi kenkyū* (Research on Children's Poetry), a magazine he founded and edited, Hiraiwa wrote that the "devotion of dogs does not stem from a sense of obligation for kindness received, but is based entirely on pure love." Despite the "dumbfounding" fuss over his alleged commitment to his master, Hiraiwa noted, Hachikō was still an unhappy dog who had lost his master. What Hiraiwa objected to most sharply was the use of Hachikō for the edification of children:

> There have been many people who one after another appear to manipulate even Hachikō's name in a variety of ways. Now he is even being used as material to teach people's children. This is because from the standpoint of human morality, everyday occurrences in the world of dogs are seen as extraordinary acts of good that demonstrate immeasurable integrity. They clamor "Don't Forget Your Debts of Gratitude." However, because there are no debts of gratitude in the world of dogs, there can be no forgetfulness. It is pathetic that only now, "man"—that ingrate animal—is kneeling down to worship and plead for guidance from the law of dogs.[37]

Saitō, for his part, did not see the deployment of the story as troubling. Referring to Hiraiwa's criticism years later, he countered that the "greatest result . . . was that children throughout the country became very fond of dogs."[38] Saitō's statement may have been true, but if so, it also bolsters the possibility that educators could make use of children's affinity for dogs to foster allegiance to the state and to the emperor.

Some observers outside the dog-fancying community found the fascination with Hachikō to be troubling, as well. Perhaps the most prominent voice to speak out was the liberal critic Hasegawa Nyozekan. In the April 1935 issue of the literary magazine *Bungei shunjū*, Hasegawa criticized the uproar as sentimentalism gone awry. The public, he argued, influenced by a swirl of "rumor, sensational media reports, and theories," had entered a "self-hypnotic, collective psychotic" trance that allowed them to believe things that they had not experienced and that they could not rationally explain. This tendency, Hasegawa worried, might result in similar delusions about weightier social and political issues with more dangerous consequences than those created by the fervor over Hachikō. In his view, politicians, educators, and journalists had the responsibility to restrain this "national inclination" rather than take advantage of it. The nation's leaders, Hasegawa warned, were not doing so but instead manipulating popular energies for their own benefit. During the recent years of politics by assassination, he noted, elites had fallen into the dangerous habit of either condoning forces from below with their inaction or obliquely encouraging them through pardons or drastically reduced sentences.[39]

Without using the word, Hasegawa was all but describing the culture of fascism. In the late 1920s and early 1930s, he openly argued that Japan was becoming fascist, the culmination of which process he saw in the Manchurian Incident. Hasegawa, however, became less inclined to use the term after his book *Nihon fashizumu hihan* (Criticism of Japanese Fascism; 1932) was banned and then reissued after being strongly censored, and following a brief arrest in 1933 for allegedly making a contribution to the Japan Communist Party. In his criticism of the Hachikō affair, Hasegawa appeared to affirm his earlier position that Japan had become fascist without expressly employing the term.

While Saitō rationalized the objections of Hiraiwa, he dismissed offhandedly the criticisms of intellectuals such as Hasegawa and the "misunderstandings" that they created.[40] Because loyalty, like purity, was so central to Hachikō's public persona, Saitō and his allies strongly contested any doubts expressed about the dog's devotion and subtly expressed reservations about the "Japaneseness" of those who questioned the dog's motives. Inflated claims of Hachikō's fidelity, however, could not help but invite criticism, if not cynicism, in certain quarters. A number of observers ventured that the dog was not waiting for his master at all. On the contrary, they deduced, the dog was merely hanging around the station and its surrounding shops waiting to be fed. Hachikō, it was rumored, was especially fond of chicken kebabs, or *yakitori*. Saitō and others, however, rejected any notion that Hachikō was a mere stray loitering in search of handouts. Even in death—or, perhaps, especially because of the circumstances of his death—the controversy about the actual motivations of Hachikō persisted. The official story is that Hachikō died due to the effects of filariasis and old age. However, according to a widely circulated rumor attributed to the attending taxidermist, several *yakitori* skewers were discovered in the dog's stomach during his autopsy, a factor that may quite easily have contributed to his demise.[41]

Dogs Fit for Empire

In addition to purity and loyalty, "Japanese" dogs were often esteemed as being endowed with vigor and bravery. During the 1930s, they and some other breeds were militarized and, regardless of their biological sex, figuratively masculinized. Stephanitz and other National Socialists made similar attempts materially and metaphorically to mobilize "German" Shepherds. It was probably no coincidence that the breeds Saitō defined and the Ministry of Education recognized as "Japanese" were all powerful hunting dogs. They seemed to embody loyalty, martial strength, and courage, qualities in great demand, especially among males, as enthusiasm for imperialism and war pervaded the country. Is it any surprise that from the early 1930s ownership of "Japanese" dogs—as well as breeds frequently deployed by the military, such as the "German" Shepherd—became wildly popular?

Saitō stipulated that physical power and ferocity were defining elements of the "Japanese" dog. The official breeding criteria of the Society for the Preservation of the Japanese Dog specified that the "nature and expression" of "Japanese" dogs—whether of the large, medium, or small category— was "sharp and fierce."[42] Elsewhere, Saitō elaborated on what that standard meant. In a prominently positioned article in the Yomiuri Shimbun in 1929, he boasted that the incomparable courage and bravery of native dogs complemented their muscular build and was the source of a distinctive "masculine beauty."[43] As has been mentioned, Saitō and other commentators boasted that "Japanese" dogs were instilled with bushidō, the spirit of the samurai, and that ancient blood ties to wolves made "Japanese" dogs more fearless and fearsome than other canines.

In the second half of the 1930s, fears about imminent disappearance were replaced by anxieties about the proper role for "Japanese" dogs as it became clear that they had been successfully preserved. The question became all the more pressing as the conflict on the continent widened and military demand for canines increased in the mid-1930s. Imperial military authorities preferred three Western dog breeds—Shepherds, Doberman Pinschers, and Airedale terriers, in that order—but probably 90 percent of all army dogs were "German" Shepherds.[44] Many government and private dog trainers considered native dogs unfit for military and police work because of their relatively small size (except for the Akita) and because of their difficulty in obeying the commands of anyone other than the person who had trained them. Not surprisingly, fans of the dogs, including the former Army Minister Araki Sadao, thought indigenous canines were up to the task. Araki, Saitō, and other fanciers repeatedly urged the military to conduct more research and training and to mobilize "Japanese" dogs more widely.[45] Although few native dogs were actually conscripted, trained, and activated until the desperate final years of the war, this did not prevent authors from metaphorically militarizing them in popular children's literature and other media.

In a largely unresolved irony, just as Hachikō's floppy left ear and his appetite for kebabs undermined pronouncements about his purported purity and the breed's unrivaled fidelity, his temperament weakened claims about "Japanese" dogs' incomparable martial spirit and bravery. As was related in *The Story of the Loyal Dog Hachikō*, but subsequently went unmentioned, the canine who was touted as the model "Japanese" dog seems in fact to have been quite fainthearted. While taking walks, Hachikō was apparently unnerved by gunfire resounding from military exercises at the nearby army base in Yoyogi and was even rattled by children shooting toy guns.[46]

Conclusion

The creation of the "Japanese" dog sheds light on the relationship between animals and the formation of national and racial identities in the early twentieth century. This history exposes the interconnections among humans, canines, environmental protection, animal breeding, national education, and identity formation. It is clear that "fascism's furry friends" were not restricted to the Japanese archipelago. Parallels with the German experience, in particular, are conspicuous. One reason for such historical contiguities is that both countries emulated the late-nineteenth-century nationalization of dog breeds elsewhere. Another reason for the commonalities is that Saitō and other enthusiasts sought inspiration in Stephanitz's efforts to promote the "German" Shepherd. A final similarity is that both countries were pervaded by the culture of fascism, which radicalized and intensified nationalism and racism and that explicitly glorified the loyalty and violence that were implicit in earlier civilizationist discourses.

One may be tempted to see Saitō and other fanciers of "Japanese" dogs as intellectuals schooled in European science and culture who retreated to the apolitical pursuit of launching a kennel club and passively adapted to the political climate of the 1930s. This may have been the case. They may simply have liked dogs. However, Saitō's and his colleagues' search for and creation of a pure "Japanese" dog untainted by and superior to foreign canines, along with their emphasis on the purported devotion and fierceness shown by Hachikō and other native dogs, suggests that their hobby was anything but a withdrawal from politics. The Western ideas that they drew on—of purebred dogs as representatives of nations—harbored underlying assumptions of racism and nationalism that could not easily be erased; nor did Saitō and his colleagues attempt to do so. Instead, Saitō and his allies combined these ideas with a notion of Japanese uniqueness, obsessions with purity, and an admiration for loyalty and bravery to produce what on the surface were mere dog-breeding standards and a heart-warming story of a faithful dog. A closer look, though, indicates that the story of Hachikō and the movement to preserve "Japanese" dogs contributed, perhaps unintentionally but nevertheless powerfully, to the construction of an imperial fascist culture that would breed the destruction of human and animal life on an unprecedented scale, both within and beyond Japan's borders.

Notes

Earlier versions of this paper were presented at Columbia University, Seton Hall University, and Utah Valley State College, as well as at the Association of Asian Studies annual conference in 2003. I am grateful to the organizers and participants at each of these forums. I express special thanks to Carol Gluck, Konrad Lawson, Ian Miller, Lee Pennington, Gregory M. Pflugfelder, Julie Rousseau, Alan Tansman, and two anonymous readers for their trenchant critiques and heartening encouragement.

1. Ministry of Finance, Printing Bureau, *20-seiki dezain kitte*, February 23, 2000, no. 7.
2. Edward Seidensticker, *Tokyo Rising: The City since the Great Earthquake* (New York: Knopf, 1990), 123.
3. Benedict Anderson, *Imagined Communities: Reflections on the Origin and Spread of Nationalism* (London: Verso, 1983); Eric Hobsbawm and Terence Ranger, eds., *The Invention of Tradition* (Cambridge: Cambridge University Press, 1983); Anthony D. Smith, *The Ethnic Origins of Nations* (Oxford: Basil Blackwell, 1987), 175–208.
4. Aaron Skabelund, "Can the Subaltern Bark? Imperialism, Civilization, and Canine Cultures in Nineteenth-Century Japan," in *JAPANimals: History and Culture in Japan's Animal Life*, Gregory M. Pflugfelder and Brett. L. Walker, eds. (Ann Arbor: Center for Japanese Studies, University of Michigan, 2005), 195–243.
5. See Simonetta Falasca-Zamponi, *Fascist Spectacle: The Aesthetics of Power in Mussolini's Italy* (Berkeley: University of California Press, 1997), 68–70, 149–62.
6. Robert O. Paxton, "The Five Stages of Fascism," *Journal of Modern History* 70 (March 1998): 1–23.
7. Tetsuo Najita and Harry Harootunian, "Japanese Revolt against the West: Politi-

cal and Cultural Criticism in the Twentieth Century," in *Cambridge History of Japan*, vol. 6, ed. Peter Duus (Cambridge: Cambridge University Press, 1988), 714.

8. Boria Sax, *Animals in the Third Reich: Pets, Scapegoats, and the Holocaust* (New York: Continuum, 2000), 75.

9. Kathleen Kete, *The Beast in the Boudoir: Petkeeping in Nineteenth-Century Paris* (Berkeley: University of California Press, 1994).

10. Saitō Hirokichi, *Nihon no inu to ōkami* (Tokyo: Sekkaisha, 1964), 331.

11. "Itoshi ya rōken monogatari," *Asahi Shimbun*, October 4, 1932, 8.

12. Saitō, "Nihon inu to wa donna inu ka," in idem, *Nihon no inu to ōkami*, 271.

13. "Wakentō yorokobe," *Asahi Shimbun*, October 11, 1936, 13.

14. Kishi Kazutoshi, *Chūken Hachikō monogatari* (Tokyo: Monasu, 1934), 463–64.

15. Max von Stephanitz, *The German Shepherd Dog in Word and Picture* (Jena: A. Kämpfe, 1923), 196–97.

16. Hayashi Masharu, ed., *Hachikō bunken shū* (Tokyo: Hayashi Masharu, 1991), 210–11.

17. Ibid.

18. Saitō, *Nihon no inu to ōkami*, 269–70.

19. Hata Ichirō, "Nihon inu kaigai shinshutsu," *Nihon inu* 3, no. 7 (July 1934): 147–48.

20. Ibid., 134–40.

21. Sax, *Animals in the Third Reich*, 75–76.

22. See Yanagita Kunio, "Ōkami no yukue" and "Ōkami shi satsudan," in *Yanagita Kunio zenshū* 24, (Tokyo: Chikuma Shobō), 584–630. The second article was originally published in *Nihon inu* in two parts in September 1932 and January 1933.

23. Tessa Morris-Suzuki, *Reinventing Japan: Time, Space, Nation* (Armonk, N.Y.: M. E. Sharpe, 1998), 87.

24. "Chōsen ni 'Nihonken,'" *Asahi Shimbun*, March 29, 1937, 15.

25. Saitō, *Nihon no inu to ōkami*, 271.

26. Ibid., 334–35.

27. Wolfgang Wippermann and Detlef Berentzen, *Die Deutschen und ihre Hunde: Ein Sonderweg der deutschen Mentalitätsgeschichte* (Berlin: Siedler Verlag, 1999), 69, 76.

28. Saitō, *Nihon no inu to ōkami*, 337.

29. For a complete rendering of the poem, see Hiraiwa Yonekichi, "Hachikō no shōgai," *Dōbutsu bungaku* 154 (June 1988): 3–4.

30. Miyawaki Shunzō, *Shōwa hachi nen: Shibuya eki* (Tokyo: PHP Kenkyūsho, 1905), 110.

31. "Chūken Hachikō monogatari," *Asahi Shimbun*, April 23, 1934, Hachikō shinbun kiji album, Tōkyō-to Shibuya-ku Shirane Kinen Kyōdo Bunkakan Archive, Tokyo, n.p.

32. Noguchi Ujō, "Chūgi o tataeru uta," in Kume, *Dōbutsu bidan chūken Hachikō* (Tokyo: Kin no hoshisha, 1934), 1–3; Ono Susumi, *Chūkon ode: Chūken Hachikō* (Ōdate-Chō, Akita Prefecture: Ono Susumi chosaku hankōkai, 1932), inside front cover page; Saitō, *Nihon no inu to ōkami*, 338–39.

33. Imagawa Isao, *Inu no gendai shi* (Tokyo: Gendai Shokau, 1996), 163.

34. Kaigo Tokiomi, Ishikawa Ken, and Ishikawa Matsutarū, eds., *Nihon kyōkasho taikei, kindai-hen, dai-2-kan: Shūshin 3* (Tokyo: Kōdansha, 1962), 245.

35. Kobayashi Gen, "Sangatsu no kakka gakushū shiryō," *Gakushū kenkyū* 15 (1936): 115–16.

36. *Chūken Hachikō kiroku*, n.p.

37. Hiraiwa Yonekichi, "On o wasereru na," *Zenshū Nihon dōbutsu shi*, 26 vols. (Tokyo: Kōdansha, 1983), 9:69–70.

38. Saitō, *Nihon no inu to ōkami*, 338–9.

39. Hasegawa Nyozekan, "Hachikō o chūshin to shite," *Bungei shunjū* 13, no. 4 (April 1935): 144–46.

40. Saitō Hirokichi, "Chūken Hachikō no hakusei," in *Shadan hōjin Nihon inu hozon kai sōritsu gojū shūnen shi*, ed. Nihon inu hozon kai, (Tokyo: Nihon inu hozon kai, 1978), 108.

41. Hayashi, *Hachikō bunken shū*, 300.

42. "The Standards Points of the 'Nippon Inu' Adopted by the Nippon-Inu Hozonkai," *Nihon inu* 3, no. 7 (July 1934): 149.

43. Saitō Hirokichi, "Nihon inu no hanashi," *Yomiuri Shimbun*, April 29, 1929, 3.

44. Imagawa, *Inu no gendai shi*, 60.

45. Araki Sadao, "Hōken jidai no gun'yōken, Nihonken no seinō o kenkyū shitai," in Nihon inu hozon kai, *Shadan hōjin Nihon inu hozon kai sōritsu gojū shūnen shi*, 109–10. Araki's article was originally published in the Osaka edition of the *Mainichi Shimbun*.

46. Kishi, *Chūken Hachikō monogatari*, 46.

PART III

EXHIBITING FASCISM

AARON GEROW

Narrating the Nation-ality of a Cinema:
The Case of Japanese Prewar Film

■ When Walker Conner posed the important question, "When is a nation?" he was not simply reasserting the historicity of a concept that, almost by definition, has often feigned amnesia about its historical production,[1] he was reminding us that national consciousness is fundamentally a mass phenomenon that cannot simply be studied through written artifacts mostly created by social elites. The nation may be, as Benedict Anderson says, an imagined community, but even in Anderson's scheme what is crucial is not simply the form of that imagining, but its material extent. That is one reason Anderson closely ties the emergence of the nation with the development of print capitalism, to him a means of spreading and standardizing the vernacular and enabling the simultaneous imaginings of community by mass populations.[2] Ernest Gellner similarly makes industrialization and modernization a condition for nationalism, although his emphasis is on the development of an exchangeable labor population rendered nonexchangeable with those of other nations by a language and knowledge shaped by nationwide education systems.[3]

This only underlines the necessity of a double-pronged approach to analyzing nationalism or its extreme form, fascism, defined by Roger Griffin as "a genus of political ideology whose mythic core in its various permutations is a palingenetic form of popular ultra-nationalism."[4] Fascism's aestheticization of politics, stressed by Walter Benjamin,[5] does, as Andrew Hewitt emphasizes, actually function "on the basis of one of the most radical reaffirmations of the *autonomy* of the aesthetic—*l'art pour l'art*" because it renders politics—as well as the ultimate pursuit of politics, war—a disinterested object of contemplation.[6] Yet that subsuming of politics to the cultural realm does not deny the fact that Susan Sontag's mass spectacles of "fascinating fascism,"[7] or the processes of "internal colonization" that Mabel Berezin sees as essential in the creation of fascist identities,[8] require national forms of material organization and mobilization to be realized. Just as cultural analysis is essential in understanding the phenomenon of fascism, so must we delineate the sociopolitical enactment of that culture, the extent of a hyper-nationalism usually predicated as "popular" and "mass."

I will use this two-pronged approach to focus on the question of fascist cinema, concentrating more specifically on the degree to which film in Japan achieved a degree of nation-ality—the state of being a national phenomenon—in an age of ultranationalism.[9] In alignment with Anderson and Homi Bhabha,[10] much work on national cinema has focused on the relation of nation-state and film in terms of intertextual imaginings of community. Including problems of intertextuality in the study of national cinema has allowed scholars to work against the ideological tendency of reinforcing the nation through film (studies) and instead reveal the contradictory dynamics of the national cinema enterprise. The recent focus on deconstructing the conceptual category of national cinema can itself, however, occasionally lead to a dead end. A scholar of British cinema such as Andrew Higson, for instance, can offer many reasons for how the concept of national cinema is problematic (e.g., it emphasizes unity over diversity, home over homelessness, and presumes imagined communities are bordered and national not diasporic),[11] but his ultimate "deconstruction" of the idea leaves us with little room to understand either the historical conditions behind the emergence of the concept of national cinema or the material struggles over time in the realms of production, distribution, and exhibition to create or tear down national borders in the motion picture world.

In the field of Japanese film studies, Darrell Davis's *Picturing Japaneseness* has offered an important contribution to the study of wartime militarist cinema but one that is similarly hampered by its historical blinkers.[12] His study of Mizoguchi Kenji's *Genroku Chūshingura* (*The Loyal 47 Ronin*; 1941–

42) powerfully describes the film's aesthetic sacramentalization of the nation through what Davis calls the "monumental style"—a style that could be termed fascistic if only because of Mizoguchi's contemporary written praise for Goebbels's cultural policies.[13] He also argues that the film's Japaneseness—its status as the epitome of a national film (kokumin eiga)—is a product of its textual appropriation of traditional aesthetic forms, its ideological project of expanding bushidō into the realm of women,[14] as well as, importantly, its efforts to teach spectators to perceive in a more purely Japanese way. Here national cinema is not simply a set of textual or conceptual features but a practice of spectatorship. Unlike Noël Burch, who assumes that the film embodies age-old Heian aesthetics even in wartime Japan,[15] Davis historicizes to the degree he recognizes the film as a conscious product of the state's effort to reconstruct Japaneseness during the war. Nevertheless, Davis never fully addresses either the material or the discursive implications of the fact that this most "Japanese" of films was not only a box-office failure, but was also cited by some critics as a specific example of what should not represent the nation.[16] The problem is not simply Davis's failure to address mass consciousness, but his tendency to make assumptions about what is Japanese—in this case, Mizoguchi's version of Genroku aesthetics—and thus about the nation-ality of a cinema, when it was precisely these issues that, as I will show, were still subject to intense debate and struggle on various planes even during the war. Such inadequacy in delineating the enabling environments for a national cinematic textuality prompt us to join Mitsuyo Wada-Marciano in her call for more specificity in accounting for the relation between modern mass culture and nationalism.[17]

This essay will adumbrate these struggles and conflicts over the form and meaning of a Japanese cinema from the arrival of motion pictures in Japan in 1896 through the Second World War. My intention is to specify and historicize the conditions that (dis)enable a national cinema in Japan and thus clarify how these varied antagonisms were a definitive aspect of the national-ization of film in the period. Not only were conceptions of national cinema torn between such opposites as the Western eye and national tradition or high culture and mass entertainment, practical issues such as the national-ization of the film industry and the "training" of spectators hampered the national cinema enterprise. Such a picture should complicate any attempt to term wartime Japanese film a *fascist cinema* both by relocating the texts in larger conditions of production and reception and by re-emphasizing militarist Japan's contradictory stance between tradition and modernity, the local and the national, and the Japanese and the Western. In the end, I will argue, it is the very gap—as well as interactions—between a cultural aesthetics and its material conditions that define the question of a fascist cinema in Japan; the difficulty, even impossibility, of nation-alizing film during the war was in many ways the condition for the (im)possibility of a fascist cinema, rendering a fascist cinema less an aesthetic than a process attempting to overcome the hybrid contradictions that were at the source of such futility, and realize through force the ideal of a total, mass, and hyper-national cinema.

Stealing the Western Cinematic Gaze

In some senses, the cinema was from its beginning an international medium, albeit one clearly centered in Europe and the United States. Films traveled the globe, and no nation indisputably dominated their domestic market. Where a movie came from was not yet important: until around 1910 in Japan, film magazines would often report on the newest films without even mentioning where they had been made (despite the fact that in those days the vast majority were from abroad). National difference only became discursively significant in Japan around 1910, when intellectual reformers began targeting the domestic cinema for critique, arguing that its use of theatrical acting, *onnagata*, and immobile, long-shot, long takes, in addition to its reliance on the *benshi* (lecturers who explained every film shown during the silent era) for narrative enunciation, was inherently uncinematic. These "pure film" reformers called for a form of cinematic modernization that would rid Japanese cinema of these impurities. Just as the conception of film as a problem to be solved (given its perceived pernicious effects) helped distinguish between the filmic and the non-filmic and formulate a unique meaning for the term *cinema*, the boundaries of nations aided the mapping of the limits of cinema (and vice versa).[18] These are discursive structures that would shape the national-ization of Japanese cinema through the Second World War. Japanese cinema thus appears on the map through discourses differentiating exciting, liberating foreign films from the lackadaisical, seemingly uncinematic Japanese output, a map with the legend note: Japan equals non-cinema.

The state of Japanese film was taken by many to be a source of national shame, so much so that one senses Japanese cinema being articulated as subject to a gaze that was not just Japanese. This was not unique to film: modernization in Japan was itself a kind of performance before the gaze of the other, one conscious of potential embarrassment yet intended to earn the recognition of that foreign spectator. Given such a discursive context, it is not surprising that most reformers proposed exporting Japanese cinema. Acceptance in the eyes of foreign audiences became the sign of cinematic achievement; in the words of one writer, "Only when Japanese-made films are exported abroad as commodities can we say that they have for the first time reached the stage of completion."[19]

The aggressive calls for export largely coincided with the rise of American- and European-made films featuring stories centered on Japanese characters and situations (performed by Caucasians or, in the case of films by Thomas Ince, by Japanese-born actors such as Sessue Hayakawa). Many considered this proof that well-made Japanese films could succeed abroad and chastised producers for wasting a good business opportunity. Yet the stereotypes and racism evident in such works provided reasons for many to prevent importation or, at least, censor them. With such films gaining worldwide popularity, there was an almost national urgency to the project of producing and exporting more accurate films on Japan. The following words by Kaeriyama Norimasa, the polemical leader of the reformers and later a director in his own right, indicate how complex these burgeoning national feelings toward the cinema were:

> Look! Has not the U.S. Kay-Bee Company created a six-reel epic on the eruption of our Sakurajima Island, using immigrant Japanese actors and boldly selling the film on the market?[20] Did not the Pathé cameraman Meneaux [?] photograph the volcanoes of Japan, braving in particular the dangers at the time of Sakurajima's eruption to boldly shoot an excellent film that Japanese cameramen were incapable of making? . . . Although Japanese producers possess this unique and splendid land called Japan, they do not make a single film aimed for overseas. Isn't it a colossal loss that they let it be stolen from them by the hands of foreigners?[21]

It is interesting that Kaeriyama's discourse renders Japan not only a commodity to be traded on the world market, but also the object of theft. This recalls, but puts a different spin on, Slavoj Žižek's discussion of the nation in terms of "theft of enjoyment." To Žižek, what is at stake in national or ethnic oppositions is "possession of the national Thing. We always impute to the 'other' an excessive enjoyment; s/he wants to steal our enjoyment (by ruining our way of life) and/or has access to some secret, perverse enjoyment."[22] Kaeriyama's comments make a public issue of this theft of the national "Thing," but his central anxiety was that foreigners want something that Japanese neither appreciate nor know they have. As such, the nation involved less "our Thing"—"something 'they,' the others cannot grasp"— than something that was easily taken because it was unacknowledged. It is this ability to take what technically is theft-proof that underlines a difference between Japan and Žižek's situation. Žižek considers the West's current fascination with Eastern Europe, wherein Eastern Europe's gaze functions as the means by which the powerful West fantasizes its superiority in the eyes of others. Japan's West, like the West's Eastern Europe, is in some ways Japan's ego ideal, cited to urge Japanese filmmakers to be more conscious of their own territory. But the bearer of the gaze here, unlike Eastern Europe, is in a position of geopolitical superiority; the West in many ways also functions as Japan's superego. The thieving gaze of Western cinema is more threatening, taking what is normally not its own with the backing of a colonialist world system; its vision is more parental, as Japanese (often rendered childlike in reformist discourse) strive to gain the recognition of the Law (of the Father, of cinema). The Western gaze can also objectify Japan, making it impossible for it to assume the gaze as a full-fledged subject (unless it adopts that same gaze itself). It is here that shame before the Western gaze enters the national cinema picture.

This is first reflected in what was ultimately an ambiguous attitude toward foreign-made "Japanese" pictures. While roundly criticized for their inaccuracies, they were still termed more "cinematic" than Japanese-made films and thus were also an object of admiration. Any effort to teach foreigners about the truth of Japan was imbricated with—or even undermined by—the simultaneous quest to earn their approval, both as the other that constitutes the self and as the producers of this more cinematic cinema. The success of the export policy always depended on acceptance on the part of foreign spectators. "If we can just make films even foreigners can understand," said *Kinema rēkodo* (Kinema Record), "then we should be able to export our works abroad for a long time."[23] Here the quest for a Japanese cinema (to truly represent Japan) closely intersected with the desire for a cinematic cinema. For a vision of Japan to be recognized abroad, it had to be represented in a supposedly universal language comprehensible on its own to other spectators, one that, to reformers, necessitated eliminating such uncinematic markers of Japanese uniqueness as the benshi. Japanese cinema was to be particular to the degree it first assumed the universal form of the exchangeable commodity. Reformers in effect emphasized that a pure film was a necessary condition for a purely Japanese film: Japan was possible in film only if it first became cinematic (which implies that Japan is partially a product of cinema). The inherent paradox of Japanese cinema was that for it to become different, it first had to negate its cultural distinctness; for it to become a national cinema, it was required initially to become the "translation" of foreign film style.[24]

Žižek notes that "what we conceal by imputing to the Other the theft of enjoyment is the traumatic fact that *we never possessed what was allegedly stolen from us*,"[25] but in Kaeriyama's discourse, the traumatic lack of ownership is ultimately disavowed less by accusing foreign cameramen of stealing images of beautiful Japan than by putting the ultimate blame on Japanese film producers who failed to take them themselves. That which reformers wanted "back" in Japan, then, were not the images of landscape themselves but the way they were filmed, the attitude toward cinema itself. In a perverse way, the stolen object that must be "returned" was that which properly belonged to the other in the first place: the film style of Hollywood and Europe. (If this was to found a Japanese cinema, then perhaps the origin of Japanese cinema lies more in Thomas Ince than in Kabuki.) Resentment over the theft of mere images of Japan thus masked a desire to possess the stylistic means by which those images were turned into cinema. The theft of enjoyment was (or was to be) actually committed by Japan and not the other. Perhaps we can say that guilt over this crime helped construct much of future Japanese cinema.

Such guilt was quickly displaced away from reformers advocating "translation" of Western cinema and onto the body of Japanese film itself. Domestic motion pictures were made the source of shame that seemingly necessitated the transgression of stealing film style from the other. The blame for this crime was also directed at those audiences—often composed of lower-class workers, women, or children—who were seen to favor such Japanese fare. The justification of modernization through discourses labeling these audiences vulgar and ignorant reveals how class divisions were essential to constructing a more cinematic Japanese film—a national cinema. This perception of the vulgarity of Japanese movie fare and its audience was in many ways a confirmation of how the West would supposedly view current Japanese movies. The quest for pure film reform, pitting a true Japanese film against the socially vulgar fare, then, marked the internalization of the other into the Japanese self, the adoption of the foreign mode of looking as the mirror image of the national cinema. If we just substitute "national cinema" for "national identity," the following statement by Yoshioka Hiroshi would fit well the case of Japanese film: "the very core of the national identity was constituted through the internalized eye of the West."[26]

National-izing Japanese Cinema

This equation of the Japanese with the uncinematic, the internalization of the cinematic gaze of the West, the adoption of its so-called universal cinematic language to obtain recognition of Japanese national cinema, and the class-based division of the universal and modernized versus the local and backward were all discursive moves that gave significance to the term *Japanese* in Japanese cinema. Yet this linguistic shaping of the country's motion-picture output by intellectuals was not sufficient to mold a national film industry. Reformers were painfully aware that their revolution in criticism—to be followed by practical efforts like those of Kaeriyama— was hampered by the current mode of production of Japanese motion pictures. In spite of the potential of this mechanical means of reproduction, Japanese film producers throughout the 1910s were mostly making only one print of every film produced.[27] To reformers, this ignorance of the potential of the medium proved that contemporary producers were hopelessly unable to vie for the foreign market and right the mistaken views of Japan circulating abroad. Worse yet, they were failing to use cinema as a reproductive medium capable of unifying the nation. Cinematic texts in Japan of the 1910s were more local than national since they were shown only in one place at one time, accompanied by a benshi and other elements in an exhibition space, which produced meaning deeply rooted in local experience. In the end, exhibitors and their theaters were more powerful in the industry, both economically and semiotically. Since no film possessed significance that transcended those local differences, cinema in Japan was far from being the kind of medium Anderson imagines bolstering the shared imaginations of a national community. Critics were profoundly aware that industrial reform was necessary for the cinema to be national. This contributed to what would be a long-running discourse on "modernizing" the industry in line with Fordist rationality. Eliminating such practices as developing a sole print was part of a larger effort to institute a clear division of labor in the industry, separating production, distribution, and exhibition, and to centralize both power and signification in the space of production. Kaeriyama Norimasa's model for the film industry was the publishing business, where publishers/studios would create the product that was distributed to the readers/spectators, leaving it such that "exhibitors are [like] retail book stores."[28]

A post-1918 history of Japanese cinema could paint a picture of this modernization, this national-ization of the domestic industry. Kaeriyama's first films, *Sei no kagayaki* (*The Glow of Life*) and *Miyama no otome* (*Maid of the Deep Mountains*)—both made in 1918 and released in 1919)—are often credited in orthodox movie histories as the first cinematic Japanese films, ones that began to adopt the motion-picture techniques of Hollywood. This trend in reform was accelerated in 1920 by the formation of two studios, Taikatsu and Shōchiku, both of which claimed as one of their goals the export of Japanese films, in part through a film style (they brought in Japanese film-making talent who had worked in Hollywood) and a studio structure that emulated the Hollywood example (Shōchiku officials, for instance, traveled to California to inspect that industry's layout). The number of films per print increased, and a burgeoning national film press helped to assert universal meanings for individual texts. As Hase Masato has argued, early censorship also targeted local, "live performance" aspects of exhibition (especially the benshi) to facilitate a film text that would have the same meaning in the theater as it did in the sterile censorship room—and thus in any other locality.[29] Nationalization of censorship by the Home Ministry in 1925 in effect assumed that local differences no longer mattered in the regulation of the motion pictures. The coming of sound in the early and mid-1930s also encouraged, as Fujii Jinshi has argued, both a concentration of capital that enabled a shift from craft to Fordist production and the articulation of film as medium, molding the film work as a standardized product founded in a naturalized style that hides technique.[30] It was as if cinema was being well prepared for its role as the bearer of the nation during the war.

Quite a number of factors complicate this linear narrative of nationalization, however. First, industrially, studios would continue to produce a small number of prints into the late 1930s, opting, as their predecessors did in the 1910s, for increased production of films over multiple reproduction of prints. Studios were mostly capital poor, protracting their reliance on powerful local exhibitors to keep afloat. Thus, even though Fujii's example of a capital-rich studio like Tōhō (backed by Kobayashi Ichizō) presented one model of respectable modernization in the industry, other studios such as Daito were headed by figures tied to Yakuza and exhibition bosses, who churned out films cheaply without rationalized management practices. While companies like Shōchiku could present, as Mitsuyo Wada-Marciano argues, a "light" vision of urban modernity that ideologically accommodated traditional national identity,[31] that image was always contrasted with a "vulgar" entertainment that critics still decried as a national disgrace. Such hybridity, in which different modes of production and conceptions of cinema mixed and conflicted, underlines how the multiple facets of cinema—industry, style, reception, discourse, and so on—were all sites for struggle over the meanings of cinema, the nation, and the modern.

Much had changed since the 1910s, but hybridity hampered the imagining of a homogeneous national cinema. Even as late as 1941, well into the state's total mobilization for war, the critic Imamura Taihei could express in writing his deep worries over the possibility of a Japanese national cinema, a concern directed less at textual than at material problems. According to the statistics Imamura cited, as of July 1940 only 10 percent of the cities, towns, or villages in Japan had cinemas, which meant that, while a country such as the Soviet Union had a population of 4,362 people per cinema, Japan had 29,625. Japan could boast 400 million admissions to movie theaters in 1939 (about four times a year per capita), but most were concentrated in the city.[32] Clearly, most Japanese did not attend movies often, and when they did, they were confronted with an extremely divided industry, with ten feature-film companies producing a total of about five hundred pictures a year—second in the world. Even if a splendid cinematic aestheticization of the nation like The Loyal 47 Ronin was produced, it would be drowned out in the flood of movies and become a kokumin eiga unseen by most of the kokumin (national citizenry). Given these conditions, in the words of the film director Kurata Bunjin, "The majority of Japanese films could not develop and grow as national films either in name or in reality."[33] The argument of Imamura and Kurata was in effect that cinema was not the kind of shared medium envisioned by Anderson and thus could not (to their chagrin) contribute to the formation of common Japanese imaginaries, fascist or not, or to the effective aesthetic expression of the nation.

This problem was not lost on authorities. Wartime film policy never simply pursued the utilization of an existing tool for the propaganda purposes of war and nation; it always involved a reformation of the medium to make it more capable of representing or even constructing the nation. If a national cinema was industrially problematic, given the number of studios, the excess of films, and problems in distribution, bureaucrats used their powers under the 1939 Film Law to consolidate the industry in several stages (reducing, for instance, the number of feature-film companies from ten to three), regulate the use of film stock and shorten program length (thus reducing the number of films made while increasing the number of prints produced), and, finally, in the waning days of the war, to streamline distribution so that audiences effectively had only two films to choose from a week. Given the lack of resources, the construction of extra theaters was impossible, but mobile projection units were created to show appropriate films in rural locations. These measures did effectuate state influence over the industry, but they also put into practice longstanding proposals on how, through material reform, to improve the films, rationalize and modernize the industry, and, it was hoped, enforce the true national-ization of Japanese cinema.

An Un-Japanese Cinema

Limitations on material resources in part prevented the realization of the ideal of a nationwide film industry. Film theaters, for instance, would be scarce until well after the end of the war. One could argue that such material restrictions were particular to film; that the inability of cinema to national-ize signifies little about the condition of fascist nationalism in Japan. It is my argument, however, that what complicated the national-ization of cinema involved discourses extending beyond cinema into the core of the nation itself. To consider this, I would like to discuss two other factors that hampered efforts to perfect a national film industry: the issue of spectator-ship and contradictions inherent in the discourse on film and nation. I will consider the latter first.

Longstanding arguments by critics about the deficiencies of Japanese film laid the foundation for government-led reforms, again providing evidence of the role that speaking about cinema historically has played in the construction of both the textuality and the industrial conditions of Japanese film. It was inevitable, then, that policies on kokumin eiga suffered from the same contradictions that had been borne by discourses on national cinema since the 1910s. One such contradiction was the fact that cinema was still predominantly conceived as a problem—that its definition in part depended on it being a social dilemma. While leading government bureaucrats had been conscious of the propaganda potential of the medium since the 1920s, this was always coupled with a concern for—and, one could say, fear of—its deleterious effects, the unknown impact of these flickering shadows in dark theaters surrounded by neon (the less rational side of its modernity). Cultural elites remained ambivalent toward film's capacity to express "nation-ality." The government may have encouraged roving projection units, but the low number of theaters in the country was partially the result of longstanding efforts by the police to curb theater construction. And even though government agencies were recommending films to be seen by the entire nation, the majority of schools, fearing the ill effects of the cinematic apparatus, still maintained a policy (begun around 1920) of prohibiting students from seeing movies without adult accompaniment.[34] Young Japanese were being told simultaneously that they had to see certain films and that movies as whole were bad for them.

This is one reason the nation was inherently difficult to represent in film: to many, cinema was too alien a medium to be entrusted with constructing the nation. Consider, for instance, the image of the emperor, himself represented in propaganda as the father of the family state, the embodiment of the kokutai. While films, especially newsreels and bunka eiga, were encouraged to represent the nation, the emperor was a problematic symbol. Censorship regulations, designed in part to protect the emperor from this fearful medium, strictly curtailed cinematic representations of his figure. When he did appear on film, it was usually in extreme long shots, in a car, or through metonymic emblems such as the imperial crest. There was thus a contradiction between the need to represent the kokutai through the emperor and the need to deny cinematic representation of the emperor (so as not to sully his divine status), a situation that produced an endless deferral of signification as the kokutai was represented by the emperor who was represented by the crest and so on. The paradox was that the sign meant to represent the nation in film was itself unrepresentable in cinema.

Much of this reflects continued ambivalence over the modernity film did or could represent, ambivalence perhaps inevitable in an Asian culture confronting modernity. But it also relates to lingering conflicts over the shaping of a modern Japan. A central contradiction complicating the nationalization of film was the fact that Japanese cinema could only be constructed on the basis of the equation Japan equals non-cinema. Even after the pure film reform of the late 1910s and early 1920s, and the appearance of such widely praised directors as Itō Daisuke, Ozu Yasujirō, Mizoguchi Kenji, Yamanaka Sadao, Itami Mansaku, Uchida Tomu, and Tasaka Tomotaka, the majority of Japanese film critics still held the domestic output in low esteem. The liberal critic Hazumi Tsuneo, for instance, began an essay entitled "The Tradition of Japanese Cinema" (1941) with the bold declaration that Japan was below even the second rung of national cinemas in quality.[35] This attitude, however, became less tenable as official policy came to frown on the foreign films (eventually banning their exhibition after Pearl Harbor) and to put the stamp of approval on certain domestic films. This prompted a sort of tenkō (apostasy) in film critics who had to reevaluate the standards by which they judged motion pictures. Hazumi, for instance, speaks of this change in opinion when he compares the anger he felt around 1920 toward Japanese spectators who had laughed at the first reformist films with his eventual appreciation of the reason for their laughter—the absurdity that the Japanese on screen were mere copies of Westerners. The founding premise of Japanese cinema—that it was to be a translation of Western film—was now under question, as was the assumption of a universal language essential to cinema. Hazumi came to reject the statement that there is a tempo inherent in cinema and instead asserted a national difference in tempo—and thus, cinema. He, like other critics around him, now had to conceptualize the difference of Japanese cinema—for example, a slower, more leisurely tempo—not as a violation of cinematic essence or quality, but as an authentic expression of a unique culture. They had to renegotiate the relationships not only between the universal and the particular, the Western and the Japanese, and the cinematic and the uncinematic, but also between modernity and tradition, as Japanese cinema's uniqueness was often tied to the legacy of ancient arts.

This renegotiation, however, was rarely without problems. While recognizing the slower tempo of Japanese films as an expression of Japanese life, Hazumi nonetheless openly admitted his desire for Japanese society to speed up; he could not completely free himself of the suspicion that slow Japanese films were simply not good cinema. Almost by definition, their conception of cinema's universalist modernity could not totally allow for Asian alterity. One thus sees such figures as Imamura Taihei, who, while devoting considerable amounts of his writing to the relation between cinema and Japanese traditional arts, sought in these arts not an explanation for the national cinema's difference but, instead, the markers of universal cinematicity.[36] Hazumi's somewhat confused solution to the contradiction between cinema's universality and its particular nationality was to resort to a humanism in which belonging to a nation was itself the universal human essence.[37] To him, rootless (*nenashigusa*) films devoid of national identity were based neither in human life nor in cinema, a charge he often leveled against contemporary Japanese cinema.

What these discursive conflicts between universality and particularity, modernity and tradition, and Japan and the West reveal is a fundamental uncertainty over the definition of the nation Japan to which cinema is supposed to be attributed. This is reflected in Hazumi's hope that Japan itself would speed up, a future he believed might come true, since "cinematic traditions cannot but have some sort of influence over everyday sentiment."[38] It is also, I would argue, expressed in a basic indeterminacy in the articulation of kokumin eiga. Peter B. High has documented the seemingly endless contemporary debates over the definition of kokumin eiga, especially revolving around such poles as education versus entertainment and propaganda versus pleasure, debates, he correctly notes, that never reached a conclusion.[39] Hana Washitani takes these same debates as the intertext for the contradictions that are textually evident in a *kokusaku* (national policy) films such as Makino Masahiro's *Ahen Sensō* (The Opium War; 1943), which incredibly was both a critique of Western imperialism and a celebratory imitation of the Hollywood musical.[40] Such conflicts over the cinematic articulation of the nation reveal that the struggle in wartime Japan was not simply over how to use the cinema to represent the nation, but over what nation the cinema should represent and how to place Japan in the oppositions between universal and particular, East and West, and tradition and modernity.

Training Imperial Spectators

The fact that many Japanese spectators stayed away from kokumin eiga such as *The Loyal 47 Ronin* indicates how they, too, were involved in conflicts over the definitions of both cinema and nation. Their participation, however, also made them one of the primary problems in articulating a national cinema, for while various regulatory forces could promote films representing the *kokutai*, there was no guarantee that audiences would correctly read the meaning inscribed in such works.[41] Especially given that the picture of a Japanese cinema catering to vulgar tastes was still vivid into the wartime, many felt that not only the films, but also the spectators, had to be improved to facilitate national consciousness through film. In the words of the director Itami Mansaku, "Half of what determines the quality of cinema is the people who make it, but the other half is the society that makes them make it. Therefore, the true meaning of improving cinema must involve upgrading not only the films, but at the same time, the culture of regular spectators who are the foundation of those films."[42] Spectators were acknowledged as a power capable of "changing, revolutionizing, and moving the cinema,"[43] and this is in part why those in charge of film regulation, like the Information Bureau's Fuwa Suketoshi, spoke of "training (*kunren*)" spectators.[44] A consciousness of the need to more actively construct "correct spectators"[45]—or, at least, to direct them in their viewing—had been evident since the early 1920s. I have written about how censors conceived of the benshi as a potential educator and censor, responsible for instructing spectators about the film at the same time that they checked on the propriety of their reactions. Benshi were articulated as the force in the theater that inserted public meaning into private fantasies to bring about both the absorption of national meaning and the internalization of self-regulatory functions. Parents and educators were also envisioned as substitute ben-shi who would watch over their children as they viewed movies and ensure that they received the proper meaning.[46] Such trained viewers would pre-sumably read films as imperial subjects within a cultural milieu defined by the fascist "political ideal that denies the separation of the public and the private self."[47]

Some argued that Japanese spectators in fact were already well trained by wartime. In a fascinating article dating from 1941, the critic Mizumachi Seiji, pointing to cinema audiences who dutifully stood in line awaiting the film, argued that "they line up without even being conscious of order, and that itself creates a splendid order." His example implies spectators as imperial subjects who had so internalized the regulation of meaning that they established their own "correct order of entertainment," even when Mi-zumachi thought the film was a poor one. Assuming a different position from those who stressed that films, as weapons in the "film war (eigasen)," must not be "unexploded bombs (fuhatsudan)," he highlighted the specta-tor's own service to the state:

> For better of worse, films must be made. But in the case of cinema, an "unexploded bomb" can be impossible depending on the beliefs of the people. As long as a film exists here, we spectators can have the reso-lution to follow it as a splendid piece of entertainment. As long as we follow it, it cannot be an unexploded bomb, since we conceive that fol-lowing a film can render our daily life an element in our service to the state. It is when film spectators do not think of it as a service that they become dangerous.[48]

True imperial subjects thus render any film imperial. In this case, propa-ganda is less a rhetorical means of convincing the unconvinced than an occasion to answer the hail of the state and confirm one's place in the imaginary community, this time by completing films for the country as part of one's "service."

The last sentence of the quote, however, expresses both the potential threat of misreadings and the continual necessity to "train" spectators. If one of the conditions articulating the formation of a national cinema was spectatorship, one of the problems confronting wartime film bureaucrats was that, to have a cinema that was truly nationwide, it had to show to audiences who were not yet "trained" to confirm the ideology of a film. Presumably one could imagine a point at which all the "people" would be trained, but Japanese cinema was too imbricated in class differences to allow equality among viewers: if Japanese film was always a problem, so were some of its spectators. Consider, for instance, the liberal theorist Hasegawa Nyozekan's writings on film. When most professional film critics were still extolling the superiority of foreign film, Hasegawa valorized a difference in Japanese cinema that he located in a certain relaxed tempo, an atmospheric line (*jōchō no sen*). Hasegawa found this tone in everything from contemporary film (his example is *Tsuchi to heitai* [*Mud and Soldiers*], dir. Tasaka Tomotaka, 1939) to Noh drama and everyday speech, thus considering it less an artistic creation than an ethic, "The condition of the heart and form of Japanese everyday life." Yet despite attributing this slow atmosphere to "the Japanese," he nonetheless points to a different Japanese: "in drama, it is the speech of servants that is curt, contracted, and suddenly quickens. Their line of movement is poor in atmosphere, becoming extremely constricted spatially and temporally. This symbolizes the fact that they are of a morally low class."[49] What is supposedly representative of the nation is seemingly lost on some of "the people" (here represented on stage), classes who logically must be less Japanese than those of higher status. Hasegawa reproduces this structure with regard to Japanese cinema as he criticizes the fast-tempo *jidaigeki* films popular at the time (usually with lower-class audiences) for "lacking the morality that constitutes the internal condition of Japanese aesthetic sense," a lack that is "impossible for a Japanese art." By drawing borders within Japanese cinema that are mapped onto a social hierarchy, he denies the Japaneseness of much of Japanese cinema and creates the necessity for filmmakers both to train in the proper form of Japanese cinema and to "cultivate Japanese life."[50]

While such divisions in morality and Japaneseness, backed by assertions of necessity, serve to legitimize an ethical social hierarchy—which we can call the emperor system—they also create an imperative to work at being a good Japanese (film), to submit to training. That the end of this training is none other than the internalization of the emperor system implies that to become Japanese is always predicated on an inadequacy of being Japanese.[51] The same is true of Japanese cinema: to be a national cinema, Japanese film must always fall short of being Japanese and thus must always be subject to state authority to be more Japanese. The Japaneseness that spectators help articulate in a film is thus perpetually deferred, as those audiences themselves are continually working at being Japanese while always being one step short of it.

The problem of spectatorship was exacerbated when, with the creation of the Greater East Asia Co-Prosperity Sphere, new imperial subjects who had never before viewed Japanese films were compelled to watch them.[52] Export, of course, had been one of the defining myths of prewar cinema, yet despite fitful attempts in the 1920s and 1930s, it remained just a myth. The Second World War, then, was the first time Japanese cinema was actually being viewed by non-Japanese on a mass scale, an occasion that sparked immense interest and concern on the part of the industry, bureaucrats, and the press in how other spectators were viewing these films.[53] While a central question was what films were appropriate for representing the nation to its new subjects, the issue frequently shifted into a consideration of how Asian spectators would read these texts. Audiences in China, the Philippines, Indonesia, Vietnam, and elsewhere became the objects of dozens of magazine reports. On the basis of these, some, like Kawakita Nagamasa, who became the head of occupied Shanghai's film industry, argued that local spectators did not possess the tools to read Japanese films and thus that, at least at the start, local staff should produce films under the direction of Japanese.[54] Other commentators contended that Japanese-made films could speak to other Asians but only if they used the universal language of cinema.

Washitani surveys these debates and argues that they were inconclusive. Nonetheless, it is clear that in many cases, the dream of export from the 1910s, now backed by wartime necessity, was again called forth to regulate the domestic industry and further prompt reform. As one commentator argued, "The problem of exporting films to Southeast Asia is, simply, the problem of domestic cinema."[55] Mori Iwao, the head of Tōhō's studio, proposed as a means of correcting what to him was a mistaken trend in Japanese cinema:

> I worry that at this rate, Japanese film will progressively take up forms of expression that not only Japanese but also people of other nations will find difficult to adapt to. There wouldn't be a need to worry if the forms of expression of Japanese film were only more straightforward and distinct in form, polishing an American film technique understood by anyone; that is, if it had the simple charm of old silent movies.[56]

To Mori, this Americanization of Japanese film style was in part necessary to capture an audience trained in American cinema. The paradox was that to expel both Western colonialists and their cinema from Asia, Japan had to adopt the film technology of the colonialists.

As occurred with film discourse in the 1910s, the strategy of spreading Japan abroad through its cinema called into question the Japaneseness of its cinema. Many like Mori complained of the slow tempo, wordiness, and excessive use of allusion in contemporary Japanese film—qualities that some critics like Hasegawa were identifying as the defining characteristics of Japanese cinema. Speaking from his own experience in Southeast Asia, a former military press officer argued for replacing the "Japanese characteristic" of suggestiveness with a more visual and concrete language and proceeded to cite Mizoguchi's *The Loyal 47 Ronin* as the prime example of which films not to send abroad.[57] It was again necessary for Japan to become cinema before its cinema could be consumed. In the words of the film critic Tsugawa Shūichi, "To capture the interest of [all the peoples of the Greater East Asia Co-Prosperity Sphere], who have not yet experienced familiarity with the customs, traditions, and ways of thought of the Japanese people, one can only depend at first on the technological superiority of cinema itself."[58] After some time, many from the field were reporting that Asians in occupied territories were watching and understanding Japanese films—works such as *The Opium War*, *Shina no yoru* (*China Night*, dir. Fushimi Osamu, 1940) and *Hawai marē oki kaisen* (*The War at Sea from Hawaii to Malaysia*, dir. Yamamoto Kajirō, 1942) were particular hits—as long as they were good cinema.

In contrast to the Western gaze postulated in the 1910s, other Asian spectators could serve as Žižek's form of ego ideal for the Japanese nation, confirming the superiority of its cinema. Their position as subjects to Japanese rule helped articulate this role, but the problem was when, as with Mori, they were simultaneously recruited to solve the errors of Japanese cinema, a fact that complicated the power relationship. Such audiences were often pictured as simple peoples in need of Japanese leadership, but their gaze was nonetheless essential to improve Japanese film, as if behind their mask of ignorance lay a superior knowledge of cinema. One writer spoke of Manchurian spectators viewing an inferior Japanese product in the following, suggestive terms:

> When we Japanese stare at the eyes of the young Manchurian crowd devouring the screen, an indescribable shame runs through our bodies if the film is something worthless. . . . In the faces of those Manchurians who have come to see these films—works unbearable to watch and a

disgrace to the nation—rises a strangely wry smile impossible to explain. When they chance to exchange glances with a Japanese, they immediately return to a stern, expressionless visage reminiscent of a mud snail. Most of them will in no way speak what is really on their mind. . . . They are critics (hyōronka) who neither speak nor debate. But their eyes are as merciless as a snake's and their critical spirit refuses all forms of compromise.[59]

One sees here the same shame for the national cinema evident in the 1910s, the same idealization of a foreign spectator with a masterly cinematic eye, but with a difference: Japanese are now supposed to be the "leading nation (shidō minzoku)" and the foreigners (Manchurians), the followers. Cinema clearly upsets this hierarchy and leads to an almost paranoid surveillance of the Asian spectator. Film, it seems, threatens to both belie Japanese pretensions (that it is the leading Asian nation; that it is a modern nation) and expose the reality of Japan (such as its class differences—the poverty the commentator said should never be shown in film to Manchurians). Remember that many Asian spectators were skilled in the Hollywood cinematic code—a fact often stressed in the film press—and thus could compare Japanese cinema to the Western film it first hoped to emulate. The paranoia is that the quiet, mud-snail-like faces of Manchurian spectators conceal, if not the "secret, perverse enjoyment" that exceeds that of the self, at least the perception that Japan—and its cinema—is a poor copy of the West, or, perhaps more precisely, a facade of nation-ality covering over the lack of nation-ality. Perhaps behind the wry smile of these Manchurian viewers is the realization of the irony of Japan's stealing the cinema of the West in order to steal Asia for its own.

Not only these spectators, but also those working-class audiences of districts such as Asakusa who mystified film intellectuals just as much, seemingly withheld the proper judgment on the national film product. Andrew Higson has rightly asked, "What is a national cinema if it doesn't have a national audience?"[60] but in the Japanese context, a factor complicating the construction of a national cinema during the war was the simultaneous need for two different audiences: one defined as imperial subjects capable of completing the construction of a national film; the other, inexperienced in Japanese film, who could recognize Japanese national essence when addressed in a language clean of the marks of nationality. This contradiction between the internal and the external definition of the nation could be metaphorically linked to contemporary ambiguity over what constituted the inside and the outside of the state and who was an imperial subject and who was not, and it expressed one of the fundamental incongruities cutting through the often contradictory ideologies of nation and colonialism in the Greater East Asia Co-Prosperity Sphere.[61]

Conclusion: Enforcing a Fascist Cinema

A growing amount of research emphasizes that national cinemas are never unified or distinctly national, that they are always subject to hybridity and contamination.[62] My research in many ways confirms this, underlining the contradictions evident in the notions both of film and of the nation that complicate any account of a monolithic fascist cinema in Japan.[63] Yet this is not the crucial issue; what matters is how cinema responded to these conditions. I argue that fascist cinema in Japan attempts to overcome hybridity as much as it politically enforces a given national aesthetic.

Certainly, there was a discursive framework for the production of stylistically fascistic texts. In one essay in 1941, Imamura Taihei defined kokumin eiga as the "aesthetic expression in cinema of the entire nation (kokumin sōryoku no eiga geijutsutekina hyōgen),"[64] a conception that all too closely echoes Walter Benjamin's view of fascism as the aestheticization of politics. Here national film is defined less by referential content (the representation of national things or ideas) than with textual processes, rendering national cinema a primarily textual—or intertextual—issue. Yet we have seen that the conditions surrounding Imamura's statement render it confused, if not contradictory. "Aesthetic" was torn between notions of the entertaining and the educational, the traditional and the modern, the Western and the Eastern, all the while implying divisions between low and high culture that obviated any aesthetic for the "entire nation." "Expression" itself focused attention on cultural production, but never to the extent of hiding the perpetual crisis in the nation-ality of the both the creators and the readers of those expressions. "Cinema" was intersected by various forces that, on the one hand, internationalized filmic expression at the same time as industrially limiting its extent, and, on the other, aimed to elevate a spectacle of nationhood at a time when film remained to many an object of distrust. Finally, the "nation," attempting to encompass intellectuals bearing the Western gaze and lower classes eternally less than Japanese, or a Westernized modernity and Asian colonialism, could only turn to media like the cinema to imperfectly imagine itself as a community.

If these were the conditions that complicated the formation of a fascist cinema—some unique to Japanese cinema, some incumbent on the concept of the nation and national cinema—it is not surprising to see that wartime Japanese cinema was materially different from Nazi cinema. The industry was never nationalized, as it was in Germany, in part because Japanese bureaucrats largely frowned on nationalization, but also because cinema never enjoyed the wholehearted favor of government officials as it did with Goebbels. The case of Japanese national cinema also lends a cautionary note to the narration of the modern Japanese nation-state. While it is certain that many of the intellectual and government apparatuses of the nation were in place by the late Meiji period, my contention is that mass entertainment was not easily recruited into these apparatuses until much later. At least in the case of the nation-ality of cinema, history appears to be multilayered, with numerous, often conflicting strata operating in different temporalities. Disjunctions between different layers can constitute forms of hybridity and enable opportunities for struggle and opposition. While I am hesitant to declare a manifestation of "resistance" in certain forms of prewar Japanese culture, it is clear that conflicts existed not only between elites, but also between sectors of the industry and audiences over the meanings of cinema, modernity, and the nation.

Citing these and other problems, I deny neither the pertinence of the concept of fascism to wartime Japanese cinema nor the reality of the nation, in effect deconstructing both into oblivion. I have not taken the framework of national cinema as a given (so as to show how cinema constructed the nation), but rather focused on the historical operations, pursued by forces often conscious of the contradictions I have shown, which attempted to create the conditions to enable a national cinema itself. The fact they did not really "succeed" does deny the effect of these operations, or the oppression they often created. It is these processes of creating nations and national cinemas that, I believe, reveal much more historically than an account of their conclusions. One can argue that any fascistic element to Japanese cinema lies less in the vision of the nation represented or the cinematic aesthetic itself than in the process involved creating a national cinema.

Hase Masato's study of the film critic Tsumura Hideo proves instructive in this regard. Hase's central question is how Tsumura, who in the 1930s was a champion of the director's artistic freedom from commercial constraints, could become one of the primary mouthpieces for the government's totalitarian (*zentaishugitekina*) film policy. His description of one of the engines of Tsumura's *tenkō* is provocative. To Hase, the effects of capitalism and industrial technology on the purity of cinematic expression produced an anxiety (*fuan*) in Tsumura and others that, since they were not willing to accept such impurities, "called on totalitarianism when they tried to overcome that anxiety through strong 'will-power' and a 'struggle of the spirit'"[65]—the buzzwords of Tsumura's articulation of national spirit. The problem is that the sources of this anxiety were, at least at the time, nearly insurmountable, a fact that demanded the intervention of even more power—total mobilization of the nation itself. Hase's framework suggests to us that fascism in the wartime Japanese cinema world is less an aesthetic of the national spirit in film, than the total reliance on power to surmount the contradictions and obstacles I have described here and construct a pure national cinema. Tsumura actually relied on such power as means to "correct" Asian spectators who showed an inability to understand Japanese film. To him that power involved forced dissemination of the Japanese language and things Japanese,[66] but we can add that it also involved the power of cinema, using the "technological superiority of cinema itself"[67]—the cinema as war machine—to overwhelm the spectator.[68] It thus is no surprise that wartime Japanese cinema made tremendous advances in the fields of special effects (e.g., *The War at Sea from Hawaii to Malaysia*), animation (e.g., *Momotaro no umiwashi* [*Momotaro's Sea Eagles*, dir. Seo Mitsuyo, 1943]), and spectacle (*The Opium War*).

Hase's mention of the problem of purity is telling, because it reminds us that historically the notion of purity in Japanese film has always called for the intervention of power. It was the pure film reformers who, from the 1910s on, looked to the power of capital (marketing films abroad), the independent artist (not catering to the common denominator), the cinematic text (unmoved by extra-cinematic intertexts and spectator play), the government censor (ridding the industry of riffraff), and especially the power of the gaze of the West and the Westernized intellectual to purge the cinema of uncinematic elements, ensure the clear transmission of cinematic meaning, rationalize the industry, cleanse the medium of lower-class influences, and create a national cinema. The fact that these projects never quite succeeded—in fact, some could not possibly succeed—and that the Japanese cinema world remained hybrid into the war only accelerated calls for even more power. In this sense, fascism is a *process* in wartime Japanese cinema, less a state; one that finds its roots in the 1910s but gained its form in the very obstacles and contradictions specific to the historical narrative of Japanese prewar film. That many of these contradictions and impurities were inevitable—were, in fact, the product of the very same desire for purity— means that the fascist ideal of a pure, controlled cinema was based on its own impossibility.

Notes

1. Walker Conner, "When Is a Nation?" *Ethnic and Racial Studies* 13, no. 1 (1990): 92–100.
2. Benedict Anderson, *Imagined Communities: Reflections on the Origin and Spread of Nationalism* (London: Verso, 1983).
3. See Ernest Gellner, *Nations and Nationalism* (Oxford: Basil Blackwell, 1983).
4. Roger Griffin, *The Nature of Fascism* (New York: St. Martin's Press, 1991), 26.
5. This is the famous statement that concludes Walter Benjamin's "The Work of Art in the Age of Mechanical Reproduction," in *Illuminations*, ed. Hannah Arendt (New York: Schocken Books, 1969), 217–51.
6. Andrew Hewitt, "Fascist Modernism, Futurism, and 'Post-modernity,'" in *Fascism, Aesthetics and Culture*, ed. Richard J. Golsan (Hanover, N.H.: University Press of New England, 1992), 44.
7. Susan Sontag, "Fascinating Fascism," *New York Review of Books*, February 6, 1975.
8. Mabel Berezin, *Making the Fascist Self: The Political Culture of Interwar Italy* (Ithaca, N.Y.: Cornell University Press, 1997).
9. My use of the hyphenated term "national-ity" is intended to distinguish the act of branding a cinema as a product of a particular nation (nationality in its strict sense) from the process of making a specific entity a shared object of national consciousness.
10. See Homi Bhabha, "Introduction," in *Nation and Narration*, ed. Homi Bhabha (London: Routledge, 1990).
11. Andrew Higson, "The Limiting Imagination of National Cinema," in *Cinema and Nation*, ed. Mette Hjort and Scott MacKenzie (London: Routledge, 2000), 63–74.
12. Darrell William Davis, *Picturing Japaneseness* (New York: Columbia University Press, 1996).
13. Mizoguchi Kenji, "Kokumin eiga no kokoro—*Genroku Chūshingura ni kanrenshite*," *Eiga hyōron* 1, no. 9 (September 1941): 71–73.
14. Yomota Inuhiko disagrees with Davis on the role of women in *Genroku Chūshingura*, ultimately claiming for them the function of critiquing the male discourse of bushidō: see Yomota Inuhiko, "*Genroku Chūshingura ni okeru joseitekinaru mono*," in *Eiga kantoku Mizoguchi Kenji*, ed. Yomota (Tokyo: Shinyōsha, 1999), 177–223.
15. Noël Burch, *To the Distant Observer* (Berkeley: University of California Press, 1979).
16. Murao Kaoru, "Nanpo kara mita Nihon eiga," *Eiga Hyōron* 1, no. 7 (July 1944): 5–7.

17. See Mitsuyo Wada-Marciano, "The Production of Modernity in Japanese National Cinema: Shōchiku Kamata Style in the 1920s and 1930s," *Asian Cinema* 9, no. 2 (spring 1998): 69–93.

18. The following thesis on 1910s Japanese film discourse was first expounded in my "Writing a Pure Japanese Cinema: Articulations of Early Japanese Film," Ph.D. diss., University of Iowa, Iowa City, 1996.

19. Yanagi, "Shokan: Zoku," *Katsudō shashinkai*, vol. 12, August 1910, 18.

20. Kaeriyama is probably referring to *The Wrath of the Gods* (1914), a dramatization of the eruption starring Sessue Hayakawa and Thomas Kurihara and directed by Reginald Barker. It was, however, produced by Ince's New York Motion Picture Company.

21. Kaeriyama Norimasa, "Jiko o shireri ya," *Kinema rēkodo* 19 (January 1915): 2.

22. Žižek points to enjoyment in the psychoanalytic sense as that "real, non-discursive kernel . . . which must be present for the Nation qua discursive-entity-effect to achieve its ontological consistency." The Nation is then a "Thing," "Enjoyment incarnated"—a means by which a community "organizes its enjoyment" by delineating a set of pleasures that only it, by definition, can have, but which the other perpetually menaces: Slavoj Žižek, "Eastern Europe's Republics of Gilead," *New Left Review* 183 (1990): 53–54.

23. "Nihon eiga yushutsu no koki ni saishite," *Kinema rēkodo* 40 (October 1916): 428.

24. Kaeriyama's agreement with Murata Minoru before making the reformist production *Sei no kagayaki* (*The Glow of Life*; 1918–19) stipulated, "We will make a film different from all other Japanese films until now, using dialogue titles instead of *kagezerifu* [the practice of the benshi speaking character dialogue] and resembling a Japanese translation of a Bluebird film." Bluebird films were relatively minor U.S. melodramas produced at Universal that proved extremely popular in Japan: quoted in Kondō Iyokichi, "Yukeru Eiga Geijutsu Kyōkai," in *Kaeriyama Norimasa to Tomasu Kurihara no gyoseki*, Nihon eigashi soko 8 (Tokyo: Firumu Raiburari Kyōgikai, 1973), 63.

25. Žižek, "Eastern Europe's Republics of Gilead," 54. Emphasis in original.

26. Yoshioka Hiroshi, "Samurai and Self-Colonization in Japan," in *The Decolonization of Imagination*, ed. Jan Nederveen Pieterse and Bhikhu Parekh (London: Zed Books, 1995), 104.

27. For more on this phenomenon, see my "One Print in the Age of Mechanical Reproduction: Culture and Industry in 1910s Japan," *Screening the Past* 11 (2000).

28. Kaeriyama Norimasa, "Katsudō shashin no shakaiteki chii oyobi sekimu," *Kinema rēkodo* 41 (November 1916): 479.

29. Hase Masato, "Ken'etsu no tanjō," *Eizōgaku* 53 (1994): 124–42.

30. See Fujii Jinshi, "Nihon eiga no 1930-nendai," *Eizōgaku* 62 (1999): 21–37.

31. Wada-Marciano, "The Production of Modernity in Japanese National Cinema."

32. Imamura Taihei, "Senjika no eiga goraku," in idem, *Sensō to eiga* (Tokyo: Daiichi Geibunsha, 1942).

33. Kurata Bunjin, "Eiga tōsei no kikō seibi," *Eiga Hyōron* 1, no. 12 (December 1941): 19.

34. Ōtsuka Kyōichi, "Eiga to seinen," *Eiga Hyōron* 2, no. 3 (March 1942): 56–59.

35. Originally published in *Shin eiga*, and included in Hazumi Tsuneo, *Eiga no dento* (Tokyo: Aoyama Shoin, 1942), 17–47.

36. See, e.g., Imamura Taihei's essay "Nihon geijutsu to eiga," in idem, *Eiga geijutsu no seikaku*, 2d ed. (Kyoto: Daiichi Geijutsusha, 1941), 120–136. In looking for cine-maticity in such arts as *emakimono* (picture scrolls), Imamura rarely cited Japanese cinematic examples, instead comparing Japanese art mostly with European film. His discourse can be considered nationalist to the extent that it valorizes Japa-nese tradition through universal/Western standards, praising its modernity, but it does not question modernity itself from the standpoint of Japanese alterity.

37. We must remember that this nationalist humanism, which became the dominant discourse on film in postwar Japan, was well represented during wartime.

38. Hazumi, *Eiga no dentō*, 30.

39. Peter B. High, *The Imperial Screen: Japanese Film Culture in the Fifteen Years War, 1931–1945* (Madison: University of Wisconsin Press, 2003).

40. Hana Washitani, "*The Opium War* and the Cinema Wars: A Hollywood in the Greater East Asian Co-Prosperity Sphere," *Inter-Asia Cultural Studies* 4, no. 1 (2003): 63–76.

41. I first introduced some of these issues surrounding wartime spectatorship in "*Miyamoto Musashi to senjichu no kankyaku*," in *Eiga kantoku Mizoguchi Kenji*, ed. Yomota Inuhiko (Tokyo: Shinyōsha, 1999), 226–50.

42. Itami Mansaku, "Omoi," *Eiga Hyōron* 1, no. 10 (October 1941): 43.

43. Yamazaki Isamu, "Kankyaku no shinpan," *Nihon eiga* 8, no. 11 (November 1943): 25.

44. See, e.g., his comments in the roundtable discussion "Kanyakusō no kakudai kyōka zadankai," *Eiga Junpō* 43 (April 1, 1942).

45. The term *tadashii kanshū* was used by the psychologist Hatano Kanji: see Hatano Kanji, "Kankyaku shinri to kankyakusō," *Eiga Junpō* 44 (April 11, 1942).

46. See my "Kankyaku no naka no benshi: Musei eiga ni okeru shutaisei to kazoku kokka," in *In Praise of Film Studies*, ed. Aaron Gerow and Abe Mark Nornes (Yoko-hama: Kinema Kurabu, 2001).

47. Berezin, *Making the Fascist Self*, 25.

48. Mizumachi Seiji, "Rinsen taiseika no kankyaku ni tsuite," *Eiga Hyōron* 1, no. 12 (December 1941): 60–62.

49. Hasegawa Nyozekan, *Nihon eigaron* (Tokyo: Dai Nippon Eiga Kyokai, 1943), 93.

50. Ibid., 95.

51. This is evident in the internalization of censorship that Peter High notices among wartime filmmakers. High cites the repeated demands by filmmakers and pro-ducers that authorities provide even more specific definitions of *kokumin eiga* as not only a relinquishing of creative control to the state, but also as evidence that,

in a climate of uncertainty over what would be approved or disapproved, creators were afraid to act without state approval and thus censored their own actions (see his *The Imperial Screen*). I would argue that this supplements the process in which filmmakers, never in complete grasp of the Japaneseness of film, must always continue to rely on authorities to make their films, if not their selves—that is, to train the filmmakers.

52. A longer version of some of this section's arguments are available in my "Tatakau kankyaku: Dai Tōa Kyōeiken no Nihon eiga to juyō no mondai," *Gendai shisō* 30, no. 9 (2002): 139–49.

53. Japanese films were being viewed by Koreans and Taiwanese before that, but their gaze was rarely a matter of great concern in the film press or the industry.

54. See Kawakita Nagamasa, "Chūgoku eiga no fukkō to Nanpō shunshutsu," *Eiga Junpō* 43 (April 1, 1942): 6–7.

55. Ueno Ichiro, "Nanpo eiga kōsaku no konpon mondai," *Eiga Hyōron* 3, no. 1 (January 1943): 25.

56. Mori Iwao, "Yume to hyōgen," *Eiga Junpō* 43 (April 1, 1942): 5.

57. Murao, "Nanpo kara mita Nihon eiga."

58. Tsugawa Shūichi, "Nanpō eiga kōsaku no konpon mondai," *Eiga Hyōron* 3. no. 1 (January 1943): 27.

59. Watanabe Hisashi, "Manshu kokkyo no eiga kankyaku," *Nihon Eiga* 8, no. 7 (July 1943): 86.

60. Andrew Higson, "The Concept of National Cinema," *Screen* 30, no. 4 (1989): 46.

61. See, e.g., Tessa Morris-Suzuki, "Becoming Japanese: Imperial Expansion and Identity Crisis in the Early Twentieth Century," in *Japan's Competing Modernities*, ed. Sharon Minichiello (Honolulu: University of Hawai'i Press, 1998), 157–80. Oguma Eiji considers the conceptual model of the *ie* as one of the ideological means for accommodating (assimilating) Koreans and Taiwanese as imperial subjects while still separating them as outside the "main house" (*honke*) of mainland Japan: Oguma Eiji, *The Genealogy of "Japanese" Self-Images* (Melbourne: Trans Pacific Press, 2002). I have yet to see evidence of a similar ideological model in wartime discussions of spectatorship, but perhaps one could pursue this issue using Sumita S. Chakravarty's notion of "imperso-nation" when discussing national cinema. Imperso-nation's slippages between the mask and identity, the cinema and the real, or surface and depth, could also be connected to these tensions between creating a national cinema and "translating" the Hollywood style: Sumita S. Chakravarty, *National Identity in Indian Popular Cinema* (Austin: University of Texas Press, 1993).

62. See, e.g., Tom O'Regan, *Australian National Cinema* (London: Routledge, 1996), or Darrell Davis, "Reigniting Japanese Tradition with *Hana-bi*," *Cinema Journal* 40, no. 4 (2001): 55–80.

63. Jeffrey Schnapp has found similar contradictions in Italian fascist culture: see Jeffrey T. Schnapp, "Epic Demonstrations: Fascist Modernity and the 1932 Ex-

hibition of the Fascist Revolution," in *Fascism, Aesthetics and Culture*, ed. Richard J. Golsan (Hanover, N.H.: University Press of New England, 1992), 1–37.

64. See the chapter "Kokumin eiga to wa nani ka," in Imamura Taihei, *Nihon geijutsu to eiga* (Tokyo: Suga Shobō, 1941), 140–47.

65. Hase Masato, "Nihon eiga to zentaishugi: Tsumura Hideo no eiga hihyō o megutte," *Eizōgaku* 63 (1999): 18. Hase's description of Tsumura's *tenkō* is problematic, if only because he mistakenly describes Tsumura's position in the 1930s as "Nouvelle Vague" instead of locating it in the traditions of prewar reformist film criticism and their idealization of art as uninterested in capital.

66. Tsumura Hideo, *Eiga seisakuron* (Tokyo: Chūō Kōronsha, 1943).

67. Tsugawa, "Nanpō eiga kōsaku no konpon mondai."

68. Paul Virilio argues that the warlike nature of the cinematic machine was inherent, but I have stressed the historical construction of that nature: see my "Tatakau kankyaku."

MICHAEL BASKETT

All Beautiful Fascists?:
Axis Film Culture in Imperial Japan

Amakasu said, "What a miserable race this is [Italians]. If we don't make our move now then we'll have to suffer through three weeks of sightseeing in Italy. Let's put them in their place here and now." Amakasu walked right up to Mussolini stopping abruptly in front of him. The small 5′3″ man on the one side of the room faced the 6′1″ giant on the other. For an instant, the two glared at each other. Amakasu faced Mussolini in silent protest, "Don't mess with the Japanese! Manchuria doesn't just belong to a bunch of Chinamen." Mussolini smiled a wordless reply as if to say "My apologies."
—Muto Tomio, *Manshūkoku no danmen*

■ Muto Tomio, a former high-ranking Japanese civil servant in the Manchukuo government, was part of the economic delegation in attendance at the meeting in Rome in 1936 between Amakasu Masahiko, future head of the Manchurian Motion Picture Company Studio, and the fascist Italian dictator Benito Mussolini. Written exactly twenty years after the event, Muto's musings on what the two men may have been thinking raises more questions than it answers regarding the motivations for interaction among Axis member nations. If Axis solidarity was based, as historians suggest, mainly on political, economic, or military needs, then what if any room existed for possible cultural exchange and interaction that was not simply superficial or negligible?[1] What common ideologies could be employed to legitimize a basis for cultural exchange? Fundamental ethnic differences and outright racism, clearly present in the preceding quote, question the very possibility for meaningful cultural exchange between Imperial Japan and its Axis allies, and they support assumptions that such divisions made Hitler's regime "embarrassed by [its] alliance with one of the *Untermenschen* and led the Japanese to either ignore or express contempt for their German and Italian allies."[2]

Although interactions among the Axis nations might have been, they were far more than just empty ceremonies. They underscored a common need among allies to recognize one another's national sovereignty, thereby legitimizing their prestige as both regimes and empires. Increasingly from the 1930s onward, Axis nations showed an almost absolute faith in the ideological power of film that, like stockpiled weapons, had "no other reason for existence than to be brandished and quantified in public [as] active elements of ideological conquest."[3] Axis film cultures had ideological goals in common, including an obsession with the discourse of racial purity and imperialist expansionism, as well as a belief in the ability of the medium of film to create (or destroy) national prestige on a mass level.[4] The interactions among Axis film cultures were imperfect and sometimes failed, but they help us understand the impulses to attempt to create an Axis film culture.

This essay examines the role of Imperial Japan in Axis film interaction on government, industrial, and commercial levels to understand the considerably comprehensive cultural interaction among the Axis powers across a variety of sociopolitical spheres. Imperial Japan proactively cooperated with fascist Italy and Nazi Germany as an active member of the Axis, with widespread official and unofficial interaction on nearly every level. While such interactions did not lead to the successful creation of a collective "fascist" identity, examining cultural cooperation among these regimes broadens our understanding of the politics of culture at the time, discernible in the interaction between film and government, ideology and entertainment, and nation and empire.[5] This essay investigates this interaction through film legislation and censorship, distribution and exhibition practices, and production and critical reception.

Interaction on the government level was evident in the Imperial Japanese government's study of German and Italian film legislation, which formed the basis of Japan's first comprehensive Film Law in 1939. Early attempts to articulate a collective Axis identity were manifest in the creation of anti-Anglo-American "film blocs" that censored or banned films offensive to Axis nations in response to economic and ideological threats from the United States and Great Britain.

Secondly, the distribution and marketing of Axis films fostered interaction in which the programming and exhibiting of Axis films at such specialized venues as the Venice International Film Festival attempted to create new distribution routes and markets to compensate for those to which Hollywood denied the film industries of the Axis access. Amid rising anti-Western and Pan-Asian rhetoric of the interwar era, distributors in Imperial

Japan had to find a way for audiences to distinguish between friendly Axis nations and "dangerous" Western nations such as Britain and the United States. Paradoxically, they chose to emphasize Japan's shared colonial identity with its Axis allies.

Finally, interaction can be seen through the short and troubled history of the production and reception of the Japanese–German co-production *Atarashiki tsuchi* (*The New Earth*; 1936), which revealed the common ideologies and basic fissures between Japan and Germany and the backlash by Japanese film journalists against German misrepresentations of their culture. The critical failure of the film brought to the surface culturally exclusivist attitudes, with each criticizing the other side. However, these attitudes were not the result of any East–West split, as critics then argued. Rather, they indicated the broader impossibility of mediating ideological differences within the Axis, to which the failed Italian–German co-production *Condottieri* attests.

In the Service of the State: Legislation,
Film Blocs, Cooperative Censorship

Japan's 1939 Film Law placed nearly every aspect of film production under the scrutiny of the Japanese government. The law was partly inspired by Nazi film legislation, but the impetus can be traced back to years before the Japan–Germany Cultural Pact (1938) and even the Tripartite Pact (1940).[6] Factions within the Japanese government and the Japanese film industry studied official film policies from Great Britain, France, fascist Italy, and particularly Nazi Germany for ways to consolidate and modernize Japan's film industry into an export-driven international enterprise.[7] The earliest studies of national film legislation in Japan reveal that Japanese policymakers were chiefly concerned with two issues: the possible adverse effects that representations of foreign customs may have had on the Japanese populace (especially women and children), and the possibility of "incorrect" interpretations of Japan in foreign films that might damage the national dignity of the Japanese empire.[8]

In 1933, the Proposal Concerning a National Policy for Films was presented at the Sixty-Fourth House Assembly to enable greater government control of the Japanese film industry and remove "various obstacles that interfere with its development." Passed within one week after its introduction, this proposal became the impetus for the creation the following year of the Cabinet Film Regulatory Council, chaired by Minister of Home Affairs Yamamoto Tatsuo. The council was formed just two weeks after Nazi Germany implemented the *Lichtspielgesetz*, or Film Law, and its mission was to "regulate film and legislate other important issues relating to film." Concerned that Japan would be left behind other industrial nations such as Germany, council members and politicians intently scrutinized German film legislation to enact a series of film-related laws that eventually would become incorporated into Japan's first comprehensive cultural law, the Film Law.[9]

Much broader in scope than its German counterpart, the Japanese Film Law was created with an international perspective. The implementation of strict rules for the import and export of films, measures for pre- and post-production censorship, and the compulsory registration of all film-industry personnel reveals the extent to which the government was aware of its power to articulate a domestic national identity as well as the need to officially regulate representations of other nations in Japan. The Japanese Film Law was directly responsible for motivating the stipulation that all film personnel were subject to mandatory examinations to qualify for licenses to work in the industry. Some examination questions had little or nothing to do with the applicant's technical expertise; they were designed to gauge the individual's ideological leanings. Applicants were evaluated in the following five areas: knowledge of standard Japanese, knowledge of national history, level of "national common sense (*kokumin jōshiki*)," general knowledge of film, and personality. Anyone who failed to answer any of the questions satisfactorily was denied a license and effectively shut out of the industry.[10]

Japan's Film Law imported the German Film Law's anti-Semitic rhetoric and the notion of a "Jewish Problem." It may seem odd to find a discussion of a "Jewish Problem" in a nation with a negligible Jewish population, but this rhetoric, in combination with the examination system component of the Japanese Film Law, clearly functioned as a useful mechanism by which the government could—and did—effectively exclude undesirable elements from the film industry. Postwar Japanese film critics have argued that government and film-industry leaders had to adapt the notion of a "Jewish Problem" to apply to what were called "ideological Jews" within the culture industry. These "Jews" were said to pose a threat to the nation and thus needed to be ferreted out for either re-education or eradication.[11]

The Japanese Film law was also influenced by Italian legislation. The Italian law was established in 1934, the same year that Germany's *Lichtspielgesetz* was passed and Japan's Cabinet Film Regulatory Council was formed. Italy's law was a comprehensive cultural law that regulated every form of Italian media, including publishing, theater, and film. The film critic Yamada Eikichi wrote in 1940, "The Italian Fascists treat film as a vital organ by which national policy is achieved and there is much that we can learn from the solid results that they have been accumulating." Particularly appealing to Yamada was the model of a state-run film industry such as Italy's L'Unione Cinematografica Educativa (LUCE), which he identified as a veritable model of successful symbiosis between the needs of the state and private industry. LUCE's structure resembled a combination of Hollywood-style vertical integration with Japanese "national policy corporations," such as the Japanese-run Manchurian Motion Picture Studios (Man'ei).[12]

All of the film laws discussed here shared the strong desire to legislate the right of the government to censor or ban any films deemed to be offensive to the national dignity. This could be, and was, extended to include the protection of the national dignity of one's own ideological allies and their territories. Censorship policies proliferated after the advent of sound film, but it is important to recall that silent film also was a source of great multilateral concern for the world's film-producing nations and often incurred diplomatic protests that resulted in the altering or shelving of problematic films.

One example was Cecil B. DeMille's *The Cheat* (1915). Its protagonist was a Japanese exporter who was represented as a misanthropic slaver. After the Japanese government lodged a formal complaint with the U.S. government against the negative representation of the Japanese, the film was withdrawn. By the time it was reissued in 1916, Japan had become America's ally in the First World War, and political pressure convinced Paramount Studios to change both the name and nationality of the protagonist to avoid any possible political friction. Thus, the Japanese character Torii became a Burmese named Arakau, and a precedent was established: governments would not leave national images to private enterprise.[13]

Exchanges such as this were not isolated, and nations regularly used whatever political clout they possessed to attempt to control the reception of their national image abroad. After the First World War "Hun" film cycle and throughout the 1930s, the political ramifications of being a nation "out of favor" with any or most of the major film-producing nations had serious consequences. Hollywood, as the largest producer and distributor of films internationally, wielded great influence over which races would be portrayed as "villains" to its global audience. America's adversary nations formed loose alliances or film blocs partially in response to this threat of being negatively represented as "bad guys" in American films (and to keep from being shut out of lucrative markets). Alliances like these articulated a practice that I call cooperative film censorship, developed to counteract the totalizing influence of Hollywood by seeking a way to exist outside it.[14]

U.S. consular and trade reports of the time reveal that Japan actively offered support to, and received support from, other Axis nations to censor damaging film representations of its national images. At a time that the national borders of the Axis nations were rapidly expanding, political alliances shifted with startling fluidity and sometimes resulted in diplomatically tricky situations. One such example occurred one year before the Nazi occupation of France in early 1939, when the French Embassy in Japan requested that the Japanese government ban a German film titled *The Accursed Ship*. Japan replied that it would "exercise great caution" in censoring the film but stopped short of an all-out ban to avoid offending its Nazi allies. The Japanese government only granted the request out of "consideration for the French action in cutting anti-Japanese propaganda out of Chinese films shown in France."[15]

Official promotion of intra-Axis cultural ties was established in 1937, with the Japan–German Cultural Film Exchange Agreement. Thereafter, Japanese officials found even more reason to honor requests from their Axis allies to censor or ban negative representations.[16] A string of such requests was indeed submitted by the Nazis to the Japanese government, leading to the banning of *La Grande illusion* (1937, France), *Confessions of a Nazi Spy* (1939, U.S.), and *The Great Dictator* (1940, U.S.).[17] Nor were feature films the only target of cooperative censorship requests. Newsreels were a primary target. William Randolph Hearst's *March of Time* series appears with the highest frequency in Japanese film censorship records. The following is a partial list of official actions taken by Japanese film censors with regard to various installments of *March of Time* from 1936 to 1937:

> *March of Time*, No. 16 (RKO-Radio). Total rejection. Part deals with assassination of a Japanese minister, and Japanese censor objects to anything dealing with political assassination or murder.
>
> *March of Time*, No. 21 (RKO-Radio). Relating to students at Princeton claiming bonus [as Veterans of Future Wars]. Delete subtitle "Cannon fodder"; delete word "nuts"—Rewritten title to read: "At Princeton University three undergraduates generate an idea."
>
> *March of Time*, No. 23 (RKO-Radio). All scenes of Mussolini and Ramsay MacDonald deleted.[18]

As these records clearly indicate, Japanese censors consciously excised scenes or entirely banned problematic representations of Imperial Japan as well as those of fascist Italy. The Japanese also made requests of other nations such as Lithuania and the Philippines for similar consideration. Lithuania appeared anxious to oblige Japan by promptly banning the Soviet-produced *The Days of Volotsayev* (1939), which represented the Japanese presence in Asia as "aggression."[19] Apparently most offensive to the Japanese were unauthorized representations of Japan's war in China. Perhaps out of deference to the substantial local Japanese population, film censors in the Philippines aggressively removed scenes of Japanese soldiers cruelly shooting Chinese civilians in the backs from the feature films *Thunder in the Orient* (1939) and *Fight for Peace* (1939, U.K.) five years before the Japanese military occupation of the islands.[20]

Japan's requests were respected by industrialized and developing nations alike, and its power to influence the production and dissemination of cultural products worldwide cannot be underestimated. As both a leading industrialized film-producing nation and an Axis member nation, Japan could not be entirely ignored even by Hollywood, which was known for its unfair representations of other cultures. Producers in Hollywood were afraid not only of diplomatic pressure, but also of the possible loss of lucrative foreign markets. In September 1937, their worst nightmares were realized when Japan placed a comprehensive embargo on the importation of all U.S. feature films and froze all of U.S. assets throughout its rapidly expanding empire.[21] This was a serious blow to Hollywood's hegemony in Asia, and contemporary American film journalists were swift to place Japan's action within the larger context of the Axis alliance:

> Up to the outbreak of the Sino-Japanese War, some 35% of the films shown in Japan were from Hollywood. However, Hollywood began to lose ground with the enactment of the German–Italian–Japanese "cultural" and economic pact, and eventually all Hollywood imports were barred. Control of the motion picture in Japan now completes control by and in the tri-cornered German–Italian–Japanese Alliance. The Nazis effected control several years ago, and Italy established a Government film monopoly on January 1.[22]

But cutting Hollywood out of Asia did not result in the complete disappearance of Western faces on Asian screens. European films would begin to replace American ones as Imperial Japan turned to its Axis allies to supplement domestic film production and as a possible source of new markets.

Marketing Axis Solidarity: Film Festivals and Exhibition Practices

Finding themselves shut out of many of the largest film markets, government and film-industry leaders in the Axis nations proactively searched for new markets and new venues in which to market their films while promoting their ideologies. The idea of exploiting nascent colonial film markets appealed in principle to government ideologues but in reality these markets often lacked infrastructures and offered the promise of only minimal financial return. Axis-sponsored film festivals, which included the Venice International Film Festival from 1934 to 1944, promised greater visibility for high profile films and possible new film markets.

Japanese filmmakers were enamored with the idea of Japan becoming an export film nation from at least the 1910s; many believed this was necessary to raise the level of the Japanese film industry, as well as that of the nation, to an international standard. Kawakita Nagamasa, president of Towa Studios and a major distributor of European films in Japan, was one of the most vocal exponents of such "internationalization" policies. Kawakita was one of very few Japanese with a practical working knowledge of the European film industry. The Axis alliance facilitated opportunities to use his extensive connections in the German film industry to help Japan break into the international market.

Kawakita proceeded to make his mark in production through a series of co-productions based on several successful European "multi-language version" films in the early 1930s in Europe. Kawakita was encouraged by the international success of the German producer Erich Pommer and made his first project the Japanese–German co-production *The New Earth*.[23] The film was meant to publicize Japan's "New Asia" to the world at a time when few outside the Axis formally recognized it. Ultimately the film's failure to pioneer an international market or start a new genre of Japanese export films led Kawakita to search for other strategies, such as the exploitation of Japanese films on the nascent international film festival circuit.[24]

The Venice International Film Festival was established in 1932 by General-Secretary Luciano De Feo of the Educational Cinema Institute to introduce the Italian people to films from around the world, publicize Italian films abroad, and spur tourism in Italy. From the festival's inception, its organizers wanted it to remain politically and artistically independent and consciously programmed artistically important films regardless of their country of production. Just two years later, in 1934, with the implementation of *Il Cinematografo e il Teatro nella Legislazione fascsita*, or Italy's Film Law, state control over the festival required that considerations of a film's political ideology take precedence over its artistic merit in the selection process, which naturally led to the preferential treatment of those films produced in Axis nations (especially Hitler's Germany and Franco's Spain). Yet preferential treatment did not necessary translate into winning the festival's highest honors.

Kawakita entered two Japanese feature films in the competition of 1937: *Kaze no naka no Kodomotachi* (*Children in the Wind*; 1937) and *Kōjō no tsuki* (*Moon over the Ruins*; 1937).[25] Although the Japanese entries received unprecedented international critical acclaim, Japan's status as an Axis nation alone was not enough to ensure victory; both films lost to Julien Duvivier's *Un carnet de bal* (1937, France). Undaunted, Kawakita returned the next year in 1938 and entered *Gonin no Sekkohei* (*Five Scouts*), a war film set in China that glorified the Japanese military presence there. Contrary to all expectations, *Five Scouts* won the Popular Culture Prize, becoming the first Japanese film to win a major award at a prestigious international film festival (a full thirteen years before journalists would make the very same claim for Kurosawa Akira's *Rashomon*).[26]

Recognition at Venice, however, did not necessarily lead to greater Axis cultural interaction. Despite the fact that all of the Japanese film entries were favorably reviewed in the Italian film press, there is no record of whether they were ever distributed or shown outside the main urban centers in Italy.[27] However, that same year, the German film *Olympia* (1938) and the Italian film *Luciano Serra Pilota* (1938), jointly awarded the Mussolini Prize, were widely released in Japan to great commercial and critical success. Japanese film critics particularly praised *Olympia* for its outstanding camerawork and rhythmic editing. The film's enthusiastic reception in Japan can be explained in part by its being feted at Venice as well as by its having been produced by Leni Riefenstahl, whose *Triumph of the Will* (1934) was also well received in Japan.

That Benito Mussolini's son Vittorio was also director of *Luciano Serra Pilota* drew Japanese audiences, but equally appealing was the man-as-machine imagery associated with the film, as well as its connections to the Italian Futurist Movement. Mechanical and technological themes appear to have more generally resonated with an obsession over similar representations of Imperial Japan's own empire-building activities in Asia. Moreover, Italy's Ethiopia was an exotic colonial setting that represented a worldview with which many Imperial Japanese subjects could relate.[28] Italian imperial epics were familiar to older Japanese filmgoers, who remembered early epics such as *Quo Vadis?* (1912) and *Cabiria* (1914), both of which also espoused expansionist rhetoric and idealized the Roman Empire. Those films laid the foundation for the box-office success of Italian colonial epics of the 1930s like *Condottieri* (1936, Italy–Germany), *Scipione l'africano* (1938), and *Abuna Messias* (1939), which revisited the myth of empire at the same time that contemporary films like *Luciano Serra Pilota* rearticulated the notion of *impero*, or a hereditary birthright to imperial expansionism, in a modern context.[29] Within this context, Italy's colonial films did not represent grand imperial adventures, as Alexander Korda's British colonial epics did. Rather, they revealed what one historian has called the natural expression of Italy's "imperialistic nature" grounded in its traditions inexorably linked to the Roman Empire.[30]

The colonial film as a shared genre linked Axis film cultures in the common assumption that in the New Order, certain nations were rulers by birthright and others were to be ruled. Japanese distributors chose to market Italian colonial films in the Japanese film market because they were aware of a pre-existing taste among the audience for such popular genre films with exotic settings and characters, which had been in great demand worldwide since the silent era. Colonial films produced in Axis nations also shared narrative and stylistic links with the Foreign Legion film (or desert film) genre that similarly presented a worldview from the point of view of the colonizer. Japanese film critics of the 1930s were keenly aware of the differences among colonial regimes, often comparing and contrasting the colonial worldviews represented in such films as *Beau Geste* (1926, U.S.), *Morocco* (1930, U.S.), or *Le grande jeu* (1933, France) with those of Imperial Japan.[31] Such comparisons led film critics such as Shibata Yoshio to the uncomfortable conclusion that, despite its moral superiority, the Japanese empire had not seduced the imaginations of Japanese youth as effectively or completely as foreign colonial films:

> Japanese often debate whether or not Foreign Legion films, marked by Feyder's human experiments or Duvivier's excessive atmosphere, are dreams or reality. When you think of it, urban Japanese know more about the Foreign Legion in Morocco than they do about their own border patrol guards in Manchuria. Japanese urbanites are a sad lot. Imperialist capitalist expansionists may scoff at Manchuria's Kingly way, but how do those nations justify their Foreign Legions terrorizing local people at gunpoint?[32]

The process of naturalizing the expansion into and seizure of foreign lands was essential to the imperial project. Japanese film distributors marketed the common experience of empire building as a trope of modernity to which most urban Japanese could relate.[33] It may come as no surprise, then, that in the wake of the embargo of Hollywood films and within the context of mutually exclusive Axis doctrines of racial and cultural purity, Japanese distributors were left with little else to exploit other than the shared experience of possessing empire.

Japanese film distributors manufactured a resonance between Japanese audiences and imported Axis films through the creation of film titles that could universalize, naturalize, and ultimately popularize the concept of expansion. The Japanese release title for *Luciano Serra Pilota* was *Sora Yukaba*, or "Should We Go to the Skies," a direct reference to the popular early-twentieth-century war song "Umi Yukaba," or "Should We Go to Sea."[34] Japanese distributors marketed this film about fascist Italian pilots fighting a colonial war in Africa by aesthetically linking Italian fascism and the Japanese martial spirit. This provided domestic audiences with a readily understandable metaphor that did not destabilize Japanese ideology.[35] The careful selection of film titles was not just an ideological ploy. It made good business sense, as well.

Even in the early 1940s when Japanese Pan-Asianist rhetoric was at its xenophobic height in denouncing Western colonialism, the lure of cinematic colonial modernity in foreign colonial films remained firmly entrenched—neither audiences nor distributors turned away from the genre. The enduring appeal of the colonial film genre with audiences might lie in the ambivalence inherent in its narratives, which could be reappropriated across cultures and political regimes for entirely different purposes.[36]

For example, the genre functioned to instruct Japanese film audiences about their Axis allies. The Japanese film critic Tsumura Hideo found the film style and narrative of Italian colonial films inferior to those of Germany, France, or even America. Nevertheless, he argued, "They let those of us in a corner of East Asia, far from Southern Europe, imagine what the conditions in the film culture of our Axis Allies were like," and they provided viewers with insights into Italian politics and social conditions. Tsumura thought that in these films one could measure the pulse of a nation—even if they were not accurate reflections of that nation. Tsumura also found even in these imperfect films a model that domestic production of nationalistic (*kokkashugiteki*) documentary films could productively adapt for the representation of Japan's "development" of the neo-colonial space of Manchuria.[37]

Nazi colonial films such as *La Habanera* (1937), *Ohm Krüger* (*Uncle Krüger*;

1941), and *Carl Peters* (1941) were imported into Japan but marketed in a significantly different manner from Italian films such as *Luciano Serra Pilota*.[38] The Japanese marketing of the film *Uncle Krüger* is an illustrative example. Co-scripted by Nazi Propaganda Minister Joseph Goebbels, *Uncle Krüger* was to have been the definitive German exposé of "British–Jewish imperialism" in South Africa. The film stylishly retells the history of the Boer War through a mixture of historical fact, fiction, and highly anti-British caricature. The veteran film and stage actor Emil Jannings played an idealized version of Krüger as a solitary hero who stands up to the British and the Jews. In opposition to the film's representation of Cecil Rhodes as a "Golden Calf of Africa," Krüger is portrayed as the ideal melding of "Boer, citizen, and patriarch." By emphasizing Krüger's Prussian ancestry (i.e., Mark Brandenburg), his usefulness as a model for wartime Nazi Germans becomes even more potent, and the Afrikaner State under Krüger appears as a precursor to the order and efficiency of the Nazi regime. Krüger's loss of power is highlighted in the film by representing him as an increasingly passive figure whose vigor dwindles away before viewers' eyes.

In Japan, distributors advertised the film as a warning of the horrors of British imperialism in an advertising tag line that could have been written for the Greater East Asian Co-Prosperity Sphere:

THIS!! is the real British Empire that hides behind a mask of chivalry. Judge for yourselves this page in the history of British imperial aggression painted red with the blood of women and children slaughtered in the name of Queen Victoria in a corner of South Africa!!

Stills from the film accompanying this advertisement show prison camps encircled with barbed wire, filled with Boar refugees. The camps looked eerily similar to Nazi concentration camps. The film's themes of anti-capitalism and anti-Semitism are driven home by projecting onto the British enemy precisely the same sort of ethnic prejudices behind the Nazis' violence practiced against the Jews in Germany.[39]

As with *Luciano Serra Pilota*, Japanese film critics discussed *Uncle Krüger* less for its intrinsic value as entertainment than for its ideological merit. Ozuka Kyoichi suggested that Japanese filmmakers and, by extension, Japanese audiences should watch the film to learn valuable lessons from the Nazis. In an article published in 1944 in the leading Japanese film journal *Eiga Hyoron*, titled "What I Expect from Films That Encourage Hate for the Enemy," Ozuka praised *Uncle Krüger* as setting the standard for the future of anti-Western Japanese films:

Uncle Krüger's crude tone and extremely obvious mode of expression has a certain kind of appeal, a filmic beauty, as a German anti-enemy film, which I believe is one of its strengths. There is more to its filmic expressiveness than simply the richness of the actors. While I do not advocate that every Japanese film encourage hatred for the enemy in that way, it does seem only natural that explicit anti-enemy films should overflow with raw energy.[40]

This was a restrained review. Many of the same critics who only a few years earlier had lavished praise on Jannings's performances in *Varieté*, *Faust*, *Der Blaue Angel*, or *The Last Command* were now cool to his work in *Ohm Krüger*; some even calling his acting "overblown."[41] What becomes clear from the preceding example is a realization that simply tailoring foreign films to suit the tastes of Japanese audiences was not enough. Producers such as Kawakita Nagamasa and Nagata Masaichi concluded that true multilateral understanding and cooperation had to be created through international co-productions. Kawakita was the first to move into this area with a big-budget, high-profile German–Japanese co-production on Japanese agricultural colonies in Manchuria.

Empires of a Kind? The Ideological Limits of Co-Productions

Well before the Anti-Comintern Pact was ratified in 1936, Imperial Japan, Nazi Germany and fascist Italy were anxious to prove that their impending alliance was based on real solidarity and motivated by more than mere military, political, and economic expediency. This flurry of high-profile official and unofficial cultural exchanges resulted in some particularly intriguing film projects. In Germany, Leni Riefenstahl directed and edited the film coverage of the 1936 Olympics, which prominently featured the participation of the German, Italian, and Japanese athletic teams and would become a highly acclaimed international success when it was released two years later. In Italy in 1936, the film director Giacomo Gentilomo and the German film director Luis Trenker gathered together a German and Italian crew to shoot the super-production *Condottieri* on location with a cast of thousands. *Condottieri* told the story of the rebellion of Giovanni di Medici's knights against Ceasar Borgia during a bid to unify Renaissance-era Italy. The problems surrounding the production of *Condottieri* and disagreements between the film's directors led to separate releases of the Italian and German versions of the film and foreshadowed the fate of similar co-productions. Con-

dottieri was pulled from German theaters only one week after its release, when censors lodged formal complaints regarding the film's representation of religion.

In Japan, this was the same year that the producer Kawakita Nagamasa invited the German filmmaker Arnold Fanck and his cameraman Richard Angst to Tokyo to begin production on *The New Earth*. Fanck, who had achieved international fame for directing a series of critically acclaimed *berg*, or mountain, films and for his discovery of a young actress-turned-director named Leni Riefenstahl, began writing the script for what he claimed would be the first film to "capture the true essence" of Japan. Kawakita explained in an interview with Japan's largest film journal that the title of the film referred to more than Manchuria. "We have named this film *The New Earth*, and it certainly is new earth both for ourselves and for the Japanese film industry," he said. "We pray that this new earth will be fertile soil that gives rise to many different forms of plants and will eventually bear magnificent fruit."[42] Fanck said that he wanted to make a film that would satisfy the expectations of Western audiences, an approach that seemed entirely consistent with Kawakita's desire to create a new type of Japanese export film for international distribution.

In *The New Earth*, a young Japanese university student, Teruo, who returns to Japan after several years studying modern agriculture in Germany supported by his wealthy Japanese stepfather. While in Germany, Teruo falls in love with Gelda, with whom he returns to Japan. Gelda hopes to convince Teruo's stepfather (played by the screen legend Hayakawa Sessue) to release Teruo from his betrothal to his stepsister Mitsuko. Aboard a steamship headed home, claustrophobically decorated with Nazi and Japanese flags, cherry blossom branches, and Japanese lanterns, Teruo seems reluctant to marry his stepsister Mitsuko. Teruo's apprehension is never represented as being much more than a flirtation with the West; gradually he discovers himself through his conversations with Gelda and comes to believe in the possibility of farming his own land in Manchuria. In the following sequence, Teruo and Gelda are physically positioned at opposite sides of a globe map as they discuss the creation of this new empire. Teruo says:

> I'm Japanese and want to live for Japan. Manchuria is twice the size of Germany and Japan with an abundance of land more than enough to support a large population . . . that is, if it is properly cultivated. But first we must bring order and peace to the land. That is Japan's intention. Japan must construct a nation on this land. And we believe that the con-

struction of a nation not only requires real men, but also real women. We don't need any who have been raised as spoiled dolls.

Japan's new earth of Manchuria would be settled by a new breed of imperial subject—one that is a hybrid of both rural and urban, epitomized by Teruo. Teruo's return to Japan is presented as a dilemma and expressed by his seeming reluctance to make a decisive choice between the traditional and the modern. Initially, his temptation comes less from an infatuation with the West, as his ambiguous feelings for Gelda might indicate, than from a general desire for urban, modern life itself. Teruo's confusion is visualized most dramatically in a sequence set in a modern Tokyo nightclub where, flanked by a loud jazz band, he is served *sake* by a Japanese hostess and red wine by a Caucasian. He first drinks the wine, but when he drinks the *sake*, the blaring jazz soundtrack is instantly replaced by a pastoral symphony, and Teruo nods approvingly to the Japanese hostess. When Teruo looks at the Caucasian, viewers see a montage of images of dancing and drinking set to an increasingly faint jazz melody. Unable to find his roots in the urban decadence of either Berlin or Tokyo, Teruo returns to his parents' farm, where he experiences an epiphany. He plunges his hands deep into the rice paddies and intently smells the handfuls of earth as his father smiles approvingly and says, "It's good earth but . . . it's become very old." Teruo decides to remain in Japan and marry Mitsuko, and Gelda returns to Germany. In the final scene, Teruo and Mitsuko and their baby son have immigrated to Manchuria, where Teruo happily farms the "new earth" with a new tractor under the protective gaze of an Imperial Japanese soldier.

Almost immediately after his arrival in Japan, Fanck personally selected Itami Mansaku, father of the late film director Itami Juzo, to co-script the film and serve as a consultant based on the strength of his work in the period-film genre. Ironically, Itami's films until then had humorously criticized precisely those sorts of government ideologies that Fanck wanted to propagate, and he was determined to prevent the film from becoming either an Orientalist travelogue or outright Nazi propaganda.[43] Itami's fears proved to be well founded, as it soon became clear that Fanck's vision of the "true" Japan bore very little resemblance to the one in which most Japanese lived.[44] Fanck's obsession with exterior shots of the natural beauty of Japan's countryside contrasted with his slipshod and uneven representation of the urban metropolises of Tokyo and Osaka. Similarly, Fanck's treatment of his actors—in particular, that of sixteen-year-old Hara Setsuko in the role of Mitsuko—is indicative of a matter-of-fact racism of which Fanck would later be accused. In a lecture to the Japan Motion Picture Foundation, Fanck stated that he had Hara speak her lines in German "in her own style," which he suggested was grammatically incorrect but produced an "inexpressible charm for us [Germans] when we heard her pronouncing the German language with a foreign accent. In other words, she made a better impression than if she had spoken German fluently."[45]

Increasing creative differences between Fanck and the Japanese staff were the result of this sort of attitude, which many felt was symptomatic of a larger problem having to do with stereotypical Western interpretations of Japan and eventually led the Japanese producer to demand that the film be re-shot in two separate release versions: a "German version" shot and edited by Fanck and an "international version" edited and partially re-shot by Itami. This only complicated matters. Some critics complained that Itami's version was not "Japanese" enough, while others argued that it was more "inconsistent, conceptual, and unfocused" but still felt like a Japanese film, whereas Fanck's definitely did not.[46]

Japanese film critics were particularly disturbed by Fanck's apparently indiscriminate application of Nazi ideologies (particularly those of blood and earth) to the Japanese case. At first glance, Fanck's representation of the Japanese soil as almost divine seemed an apt interpretation of the importance of land to Japan's farmers, who were then struggling with crop failure and crushing poverty. This was a familiar topic in Japanese left-wing "tendency film" filmmakers of the late 1920s and 1930s. Within two years, Uchida Tomu would begin filming *Earth*, which was based on Nagatsuka Takashi's novel about the destitute lives of Meiji-era farmers, and after that Toyoda Shiro would produce *Ohinata-mura*, a film about the mass immigration of a Japanese agricultural colony to Manchuria.[47] It is not difficult to see how Fanck and his crew might have linked Manchuria, and the emotional investment in land that it represented, with the Nazi aesthetic of soil. But the implication that Nazi aesthetics were interchangeable with Japanese aesthetics profoundly disturbed the Japanese press:

> The scenery that appeared on screen was definitely Japanese, but the way it was shown was Western (*batakusai*), exhibitionist, and queer. Holding up a Buddhist *manji* to resemble a Nazi swastika, he portrayed temples as if they were the sole repository of the Japanese spirit. Great Buddhist statues were treated as if they wielded an absolute power. He applied the Nazi spirit of self-sacrifice indiscriminately to the Yamato spirit. . . . [W]hile claiming to praise the Samurai spirit he was really praising the

German spirit. He openly recognized Manchuria, but it is Germany that is requiring this New Order.[48]

The New Earth looked like a German film from its opening sequence, which recalled the opening of *Triumph of the Will*, with its camera moving through the mists of ages, gradually revealing the mythic islands of Japan through the clouds. Fanck's use of graphic matches between Nazi swastika and Buddhist *manji*, which was roundly criticized in the Japanese press, was an attempt to apply his visual style to Japanese material in order to articulate a fascist aesthetics linking Nazi and Japanese iconography. Ironically, it was precisely the exterior shots of the countryside of Japan for which Japanese critics reserved their greatest praise and criticism. They praised their technical beauty but were disappointed at Fanck's inability to see Japan's "true essence" as being anything more than picturesque representations of cherry blossoms and Mount Fuji. Certainly, Orientalist film representations of Japan were nothing new. Japanese audiences had endured similarly exotic images produced by filmmakers in Hollywood and Germany for decades.[49] But as this film was meant to foster Japanese–German goodwill, it seemed to raise the question of the very possibility of finding any mutual understanding among Axis nations.[50]

Iwasaki Akira, a leading Japanese film critic, suggested that the fault may not entirely lie with either Fanck or his crew: "It is almost an impossible task for anybody to describe proportionally and properly a complex country like Japan, which contains all of the complications and contradictions that result from the juxtaposition and harmony of the past and the present, East and West, nature and modern science." Understood in this context, Fanck's inability was symptomatic of a universal problem facing any "foreigner, however understanding and sympathetic," who similarly attempted to represent Japan.[51] Iwasaki's language may be diplomatic, but his critique is clear: the film was a failure not because of any insurmountable cultural divisions between "East and West" but, rather, because of the impossibility of Germans' understanding the Japanese experience of modernity. The same argument might have been made about the production of *Condottieri*, which was plagued with similarly fatal intercultural misunderstandings but in which no East–West division could be blamed for the breakdown among Axis allies.

Such exclusivist attitudes must be understood within the context of a history of indignity over what many Japanese felt were repeatedly patronizing misrepresentations of Japan by the West. Ironically, however, it was also at this time that the Japanese film industry was similarly Orientalizing other Asian races under the auspices of building a "new order" in East Asia, to be led by the Japanese and ruled with mutual understanding and "goodwill." Japanese representations of bilateral goodwill toward Japan's "Asian brothers" were no more legitimate than Fanck's vision of a "pure" Japan.[52]

Despite debate in the Japanese film press over German misrepresentations of contemporary Japan in The New Earth, the subplot of Manchuria as Japan's "new earth" was almost ignored. Critics were far more upset by mistakes in continuity, such as Fanck's inexplicably editing shots of Osaka's Hankyu Department Store with shots of downtown Tokyo, than they were by the theme of a Japanese return to a nativist past not in the Japanese countryside but, instead, in the semi-colonial space of Manchuria.[53] Only the critic and screenwriter Sawamura Tsutomu speculated on the possible political effects of setting the story in Manchuria on the film's marketability in non-Axis territories:

> At the end of the film Teruo and Mitsuko leave the narrow rice fields of Japan to go to Manchuria where, under the protection and peace guaranteed by the Japanese army, they joyously plough the earth of a new continent with a tractor. This is one of the most important themes of the film. But won't showing this be a problem in countries that do not officially recognize Manchuria?[54]

Ultimately, the film never created any of the political problems anticipated by Sawamura, but it did spark a boom of interest in Nazi cultural policy and filmmaking in Japan. It also led to numerous translations of articles and monographs, such as the director Karl Ritter's "Theory of Nazi Film Aesthetics," and to the publication of original essays by influential film critics offering detailed discussions of how the German system might best be adapted for use in Japan.[55] The New Earth was not a box-office failure in Japan or Germany, but after failing to live up to expectations, its international marketing campaigns (the most ambitious ever planned for a Japanese film until then) had to be drastically scaled down.[56] Given the large production budget, the high-profile cast, and official backing by both governments, it would have been difficult, if not impossible, for The New Earth ever to have lived up to the hype.

<mark>MICHAEL BASKETT</mark>

Epilogue

Axis co-productions produced no masterpieces of lasting value and received scant critical acclaim even in their time. But to read intra-Axis film exchange as a failure, an empty symbol of a unity that never existed, is to miss the point. The significance of intra-Axis collaboration lies not in its success, but in the very fact of these nations having attempted to collaborate and in their concern for how they were represented. Unlike the enduring images of an Axis united in power and purpose churned out by wartime Allied propagandists, Imperial Japan, Nazi Germany, and fascist Italy were not all cut from the same political or cultural cloth; nor did any single entity ever truly dominate over another. In fact, Hollywood may have had more responsibility for uniting these nations into a film bloc than did any single ideology. The U.S. government's "film follows the flag" policy endowed Hollywood with a nearly totalitarian power of which other film-producing nations could only dream. The need to respond to that power through such means as cooperative censorship and film embargos ultimately created a fluid but useful common bond that Axis rhetoric built on but could never have produced itself.

In this context, film legislation and government communiqués circulated like the films themselves, traversing borders and influencing a broad range of people and institutions on official and unofficial levels. Looking at any one level exclusively presents a skewed picture of the partnership. Examining film culture in Imperial Japan from the relatively conventional point of view of official film policy would suggest that the influence of Nazi Germany in Japan dwarfed that of Italy. However, as the example of the Venice International Film Festival would seem to suggest, by shifting one's perspective to include distribution and exhibition venues, the opposite appears to be true. This shift in perspective is not simply an intellectual conceit. Much of the postwar scholarship on Japanese film history is grounded on the assumption that the era of Japanese film as an international industry started at the 1951 Venice International Film Festival and with Kurosawa's *Rashomon*.[57] But even if the history linking Japanese film to fascism and imperialism is obscured, it can never totally be forgotten, as director Kitano Takeshi demonstrated in 1997 after winning the Grand Prix for *Hana-bi* at Venice. He quipped to the Italian media, "Why don't we team up again and declare war on some country?" Kitano's "joke" can only be understood within the context of a history that has been evacuated by mainstream film scholarship. It also makes the eerily familiar assumption that contempo-

rary mass audiences are both able and willing to make relevant links between film, Axis solidarity, and Japan's imperial past.

Notes

Epigraph: Muto Tomio, *Manshukoku no danmen: Amakasu Masahiko no shogai* (Tokyo: Kindasha, 1956), 54–55.

1. Exceptions include Gunter Bergaus, ed., *Fascism and Theatre: Comparative Studies on the Aesthetics and Politics of Performance in Europe, 1925–1945* (New York: Berghaus, 1996); Akazawa Shiro et al., *Bunka to Fuashizumu* (Tokyo: Nihon Keizai Hyōron Sha, 1993); Dojidai Kenchiku Kenkyukai, ed., *Hikigeki 1930 nendai no kenchiku to Bunka* (Tokyo: Gendai Kikakushitsu, 1990).

2. John W. Dower, *War without Mercy: Race and Power in the Pacific War* (New York: Pantheon, 1986), 207.

3. Paul Virilio, *War and Cinema: The Logistics of Perception* (New York and London: Verso, 1989), 6–7.

4. Nicholas Reeves, *The Power of Film Propaganda* (New York: Cassell, 1999), 4–6. In 1922: Richard Taylor, *Film Propaganda* (London: I. B. Tauris, 1998), 35; Margaret Dickinson and Sarah Street, *Cinema and State: The Film Industry and the Government, 1927–84* (London: BFI Publishing, 1985), 19; Jean Gili, *L'Italie de Mussolini et son cinéma* (Paris: Henri Veyrier, 1985), 47–55.

5. The term *fascist* rarely appears in prewar Japanese film sources with regard to Japan. More often, these sources differentiate between German *nachisu* (Nazis) and Italian *fashisuto* or *fasho* (fascists). Postwar Japanese film journalists typically, and uncritically, apply the term to the Japanese military: Okada Susumu, *Nihon eiga no rekishi* (Tokyo: Sanichi Shinsho, 1957), 196–210. Yomota Inuhiko's *Nihon eigashi 100 nen* (Tokyo: Shueisha Shinsho, 2000) calls Hara Setsuko a "beautiful fascist maiden" in *The New Earth* without differentiating "Japanese fascism" from other "fascisms."

6. Gregory Kasza, *The State and Mass Media in Japan, 1918–1945* (Berkeley: University of California Press, 1988), 241; Uchikawa Yoshimi, ed., *Gendaishi shiryō*, vol. 41 (Tokyo: Misuzu Shobō, 1975), 234–36. The Anti-Comintern Pact was concluded between Germany and Japan in September 1936; Italy signed in November. The Tripartite Pact was ratified in Berlin on September 27, 1940.

7. NHK Dokyumento Showa Shuzai, ed., *Dokyumento Shōwa: Sekai eno tōjō* (Tokyo: Kadokawa Shoten, 1986), 111–20.

8. *Film Education in Japan* (Tokyo: Department of Education, 1937), 21.

9. Iwasaki Akira, *Hitora to Eiga* (Tokyo: Asahi Sensho, 1975), 86.

10. Tanaka Eizo *Eiga haiyū junbi dokuhon* (Tokyo: Eiga Nihonsha, 1941).

11. Iwasaki, *Hitora to Eiga*, 86. See Shibata Yoshio, *Sekai Eiga Sensō* (Tokyo: Toyosha, 1944), on the "Jewish Problem" and the monopolization of finance capital in Western (predominantly U.S.) film industries.

12. Yamada Eikichi, *Eiga kokusaku no zenshin* (Tokyo: Koseikaku, 1940); Dai Nippon Eiga Kyokai, ed., *Itari Eigaho* (Tokyo: Dai Nippon Eiga Kyōkai, 1938). Writing in 1940, the film critic Yamada Eikichi examined the influences of Italy's *Il Cinematographo e il Teatro nella Legislazione fascsita*, or the Italian Film and Theater Law, on the Japanese Film Law.

13. Kevin Brownlow, *Behind the Mask of Innocence* (Berkeley: University of California Press, 1990), 348–49. Sumiko Higashi, *Cecil B. DeMille and American Culture* (Berkeley: University of California Press, 1994), 101.

14. Andrew Higson et al., *"Film Europe" and "Film America"* (Exeter: University of Exeter Press, 1999). Ruth Vasey *The World According to Hollywood, 1918–1939* (Madison: University of Wisconsin Press, 1997).

15. John Harley, *Worldwide Influences of the Cinema* (Los Angeles: University of Southern California Press:, 1940), 154–55.

16. *Cinema Yearbook of Japan 1938* (Tokyo: Kokusai Bunka Shinkokai, 1938), 60.

17. Harley, *Worldwide Influences of the Cinema*, 156.

18. Ibid., 157.

19. Ibid., 160.

20. Ibid., 174.

21. *Cinema Yearbook of Japan 1938*, 54. Tanaka Junichiro, *Nihon eiga hattatsushi*, vol. 3 (Tokyo: Chuo Koronsha, 1980), 65–70.

22. *Motion Picture Herald*, June 3, 1939, 27.

23. For more on Pommer's success abroad, see Ursula Hardt, *From Caligari to California: Eric Pommer's Life in the International Film Wars* (New York: Berghahn Books, 1996).

24. Ibid.; Sato Tadao, *Kinema to hosei* (Tokyo: Liburopoto, 1985), 20–26; Tsuji Hisaichi, *Chuka den'ei shiwa* (Tokyo: Gaifusha, 1987).

25. Towa Shoji, ed., *Towa shoji goshikaisha shashi* (Tokyo: Towa Shoji, 1942).

26. Ibid.

27. Other Italian winners included *Abuna Messias* (dir. Goffredo Alessandrini, 1939); *L'Assedio di Alcatraz* (dir. Augusto Genina, 1940); and *La Nave Bianca* (dir. Roberto Rossellini, 1941): *Almanacco del Cinema Italiano*, vol. 17 (Rome: Bestetti, 1939).

28. *Luciano Serra Pilota*, supervised by Mussolini's son Vittorio, emphasized the fascist fascination for machines, especially airplanes, as the technological basis for victory in the Ethiopian War. Based on the life of the national hero Amedeo Nazzari, *Luciano Serra Pilota* presented a new sort of hero: a man who is part pioneer, pilot, and modern-day gladiator. He sets out to find his fortune in the exotic environs of South America after abandoning his family. Reunited by chance with his son on the battlefields of Ethiopia, Luciano sacrifices his life to save his son. Japanese critics cite *Luciano Serra Pilota* and *Only Angels Have Wings* (1939, U.S.) as having inspired *Nankai no Hanataba* (dir. Abe Yutaka, 1942): *Hikoki/Sensō eiga* (Tokyo: Haga Shoten, 1977).

29. Hay, *Popular Film Culture in Fascist Italy* (Bloomington: Indiana University Press, 1987), 182–83.

30. Ibid.

31. *Lo Squadrone Bianco* (*White Squadron*; 1936) was adapted from the French novel *L'escadron blanc* by Joseph Peyre: see Gianfranco Casadio, *Il grigio e il nero* (Ravenna: Longo, 1989).

32. Shibata, *Sekai eiga sensō*, 144.

33. It was precisely this desire for the colonial and the modern from which Shōwa intellectuals such as the writer Kobayashi Hideo created a sense of "lost home" and that made the deserts of Morocco that they have never seen more familiar to young Japanese than the Ginza right before their eyes: quoted in Seiji Lippit, *Topographies of Japanese Modernism* (New York: Columbia University Press, 2002).

34. Komoto Nobuo et al., *Shinpan Nihon ryūkōkashi*, vol.1 (Tokyo: Shakai Shisōsha, 1995).

35. Gian Piero Brunetta, ed., *L'ora d'Africa del Cinema Italiano 1911–1989* (Rome: Lavoro, 1990). This process by which Japanese film distributors attempted to localize the alien to Japanese audiences recalls previous attempts by journalists of the 1920s who wrote of their travels in China, naturalizing Chinese place names by assigning them Japanese equivalents such as "the Kyoto of (Hangkow)": Joshua Fogel *The Literature of Travel in the Japanese Rediscovery of China, 1862–1945* (Stanford, Calif.: Stanford University Press, 1996).

36. When the Italian–German co-production *Condottieri* premiered in Japan in 1937, it was released under the Japanese title *Arupus no sokitai* (*The Alpine Lancers*). This was a reference to the Japanese release title for the American colonial-themed film *Lives of a Bengal Lancer* (*Bengaru no sokihei*) released the year before.

37. Tsumura thought that even films like *Luciano Serra Pilota* compared favorably to "frivolous" Japanese films set in China such as *Shanhai no tsuki* (*Moon over Shanghai*; 1941), *Byakuran no uta* (*Song of the White Orchid*; 1939), and *Shina no yoru* (*China Night*; 1940): Tsumura Hideo, *Zoku eiga to kanshō* (Tokyo: Sogensha, 1943), 64–73. *Shanhai no Tsuki* (dir. Naruse Mikio, 1941), *Byakuran no uta* (dir. Watanabe Kunio, 1939), and *Shina no yoru* (dir. Fushimizu Osamu, 1940).

38. The German Kolonialfilm genre began with the 1896 colonial exhibition in Berlin, when the government integrated films that "instilled colonial spirit" into the education curriculum: Guido Convents, "Film and German Colonial Propaganda," in *Prima di Caligari*, ed. Lorenzo Codelli (Pordenone: Edizioni Biblioteca dell'Immagine, 1990), 58–76. Sabine Hake, "Mapping the Native Body," in *The Imperialist Imagination*, ed. Sara Friedrichsmeyer (Ann Arbor: University of Michigan Press, 1998), 163–87.

39. Advertisement in *Eiga junpō*, August 1, 1943, n.p.

40. Ozuka Kyoichi, "Tekisaishin koyo eiga ni nozomu," *Eiga hyōron* (August 1944): 7.

41. Ibid. *Varieté* (dir. E. W. DuPont, 1925), *Faust* (dir. F. W. Murnau, 1926), *Der Blaue Angel* (dir. Josef von Sternberg, 1930), and *The Last Command* (dir. Josef von Sternberg, 1928).

42. Kawakita Kazuko, "Atarashiki Tsuchi," *Eiga no Tomo* (December 1936): 67.

43. Tanaka, *Hattatsushi*, 2:350–56; *Towa shoji goshi kaishashi* (Tokyo: Towa Shoji, 1942), 93–103.

44. Janine Hansen, *Arnold Fancks Die Tochter des Samurai* (Wiesbaden: Harrassowitz Verlag, 1997); Yomota Inuhiko, *Nihon no joyū* (Tokyo: Iwanami Shoten, 2000).

45. Arnold Fanck, "On the Exportation of Japanese Motion Picture Films," *Cinema Yearbook of Japan 1936–1937* (Tokyo: KBS, 1937), 30–31.

46. Sawamura Tsutomu, *Gendai eigaron* (Tokyo: Tokei Shobō, 1941), 261–62.

47. Suzuki Naoyuki, *Uchida Tomu den, shisetsu* (Tokyo: Iwanami Shoten, 1997). *Tsuchi* (dir. Uchida Tomu, 1939); *Ohinata mura* (dir. Toyoda Shiro, 1940).

48. Sawamura, *Gendai*, 261–62.

49. China had been a favorite setting for German filmmakers since the 1910s: see *Harakiri* (dir. Fritz Lang, 1919), *Das Weib des Pharao* (dir. Ernst Lubitsch, 1921), and *Das Indische Grabmal*, (dir. Joe May, 1921). After the Manchurian Incident in 1931, German films took a political interest in Manchuria: see *Kampf un die Mandschurei* (1932), *Alarm in Peking* (1937), *Das Neue Asien* (1940), and *Geheimnis Tibet* (1943). Alfred Bauer, ed., *Deutscher Spielfilm-Almanach 1929–1950* (Berlin: Filmblatter Verlag, 1950).

50. Some Japanese film critics suggested that Fanck's use of actors may have been influenced by his extensive work in the mountain film genre. Mountain films were more than the mere glorification of mountains but approached a personification of nature in which the natural setting becomes the main protagonist and human actors are relegated to a secondary status. Fanck said that what he liked most about Japanese actors was that he did not have to talk to them; they "just understood" what he wanted: Hansen, *Arnold Fancks Die Tochter des Samurai*, 62–86; Yomota, *Nihon no Joyu*, 35–36.

51. Iwasaki Akira, "The Japanese Cinema in 1937," in *Cinema Yearbook of Japan 1937* (Tokyo: KBS, 1937), 18.

52. Elsewhere I have argued that the Japanese "goodwill film" genre was unable to either locate or create true Japanese–Chinese mutual understanding precisely because the stereotypical attitudes underlying the representation of the characters was based on a colonial (or neo-colonial) hierarchy that always found its way into the film: Michael Baskett, "Goodwill Hunting: Rediscovering and Remembering Manchukuo in Japanese 'Goodwill Films,'" in *Crossed Histories: Manchuria in the Age of Empire*, ed. Mariko Tamanoi (Honolulu: University of Hawaii Press, 2005).

53. Fanck returned to Germany after completing *The New Earth*, but Angst, the cameraman, stayed to write *Kokumin no chikai* (dir. Nomura Hiroshi, 1938) and direct *Senyū no uta* (1939).

54. Sawamura, *Gendai Eigaron*, 260.

55. *Doitsu eiga o ikani manabu bekika* (Tokyo: Aoyama Shoin, 1942); *Doitsu no eiga taisei* (Tokyo: Doitsu Bunka Shiryōsha, 1941).

56. In 1936, the average Japanese film cost 50,000 yen to produce, less than one-tenth *The New Earth*'s 750,000 yen budget.

57. Donald Richie, *A Hundred Years of Japanese Film* (Tokyo: Kōdansha, 2002).

AKIKO TAKENAKA

Architecture for Mass-Mobilization:
The Chūreitō Memorial Construction
Movement, 1939–1945

■   Since antiquity, war memorials, such as the triumphal arches of the Roman Empire, have celebrated empires, commemorated victorious battles, venerated heroes, and glorified leaders. In the modern era, especially from the latter half of the nineteenth century, memorials have proliferated in Europe—under the French New Republic and the Second German Empire in particular—to celebrate new regimes and reinforce their new national identities. During and immediately after the First World War, the common European soldier came to be recognized in memorial structures, leading to the construction of prominent monuments such as the tombs of unknown soldiers in London and Paris, as well as less known structures in town squares and on street corners. These added a new function to war memorials: a place to memorialize and mourn the death of individuals on a personal level. Whether built to commemorate an individual or a group, these structures gave physical form to the collective or national memory that needed to be created, maintained, or sometimes even reshaped following a military conflict.[1]

In Japan, just as in most other countries that experienced modern wars, numerous war memorials have been dedicated to military leaders, common soldiers, and civilians. Political and military leaders constructed Yasukuni Shrine in 1869 to centrally, collectively, and continuously memorialize the fallen members of the Imperial Army. The practice of memorial building for the common soldier started at the local level with the Russo-Japanese War of 1904–1905, during which almost every town and village suffered losses. Local memorial building for military deaths was further popularized during the Pacific War (1931–45),[2] and many continue to be built even today for military and civilian deaths.

Until 1945, war memorials in modern Japan had an important function in addition to honoring and preserving the memory of the dead: they were tools for motivating young men to fight in war with little concern for their lives. Children were taught from a young age that death in battle as a member of the emperor's army was the most honorable deed a man could accomplish. This notion was epitomized at Yasukuni Shrine, where military dead were enshrined as gods to protect the nation (*gokokushin*) and on occasion received tribute from the emperor himself.[3] At the local level, as well, war death in the family was transformed from a tragedy to be mourned into an honor to be celebrated. Memorial services for war dead became public events that took place in school yards and town halls and included many new features not conducted during traditional funeral rites, such as a chorus by schoolchildren, a memorial address by a dignitary, and the display of a photograph of the deceased.[4] Local war memorials, too, came to symbolize honor. Since the Sino-Japanese War (1894–95), the government had required local groups to seek permission when building war memorials; consequently, enshrinement in those memorials came to be considered a privilege.[5] It can be argued, then, that Japanese war memorials played a more politically influential role during the war than after. In the case of the set of memorials I examine here, it was not only their actual presence but the very act of their planning and the community's involvement that contributed to wartime mass-mobilization.

Chūreitō, which translates literally as "towers to the loyal spirits," were constructed throughout Japan from 1939 to 1945.[6] Typically made of stone or concrete, these memorials were built in a range of scales (their height varying from five feet to over one hundred feet) and situated in diverse sites, from large plots of land dedicated exclusively to the memorial to a corner of a schoolyard.[7] Most chūreitō memorials are identical in design: a simple, slender tower, inscribed with three characters that stand for the word *chūreitō*, rises from a rectangular base. On most memorials, the base is flanked by panels on which names of the memorialized are engraved.

The rectangular base has a function distinct to chūreitō: it is an ossuary for stowing the ashes of the war dead—or, in cases where the body was never recovered, the clippings of hair and nails that soldiers heading off to the battlefield left behind. Also unlike most other memorials, chūreitō were built by the hands of local people in a nationwide construction movement.

Chūreitō memorials have not received adequate scholarly attention because their design, which Japanese architects of the 1930s likened to a typical Japanese tombstone, has been considered mundane. This lack of interest has been compounded by the inability of historians of modern Japanese architecture to view architecture as a tool to propagate national ideology in wartime Japan.[8] They have compared what little was built in Japan in the last years of the Asia-Pacific War with contemporary projects in Germany and Italy and have used differences in style and quantity as proof that Japanese architecture of the time was not political.[9] To focus exclusively on style, however, does not sufficiently appreciate the political significance of cultural works.

The relationship of style to politics is complicated. There is no fixed one-to-one relationship between political regimes and styles of cultural production; nor is there stylistic consistency among cultural products created under one political regime. In her study of the relationship between politics and architecture in Germany between 1918 and 1945, the historian Barbara Miller Lane argues that stylistic consistency never emerged in German architecture during this period.[10] In Italy, where most architects were ardent fascists in the 1930s, scholars have noted Mussolini's reluctance to designate a specific architectural style to represent his regime.[11] And according to the architectural historian Francesco Dal Co, it is not even possible to identify a consistent trait in the works of a single architect for the same client during a short period of time, including those designed by the Nazi state architect Albert Speer.[12]

However, similarities in architectural styles have been recognized across diverse political systems. For example, while stripped neoclassicism has often been associated with Nazi Germany, a similar style can be found in the democratic state architecture of Washington, D.C., and elsewhere in the United States. The architect Giuseppe Terragni, when designing the Casa del Fascio in Como, Italy—perhaps the most famous piece of Italian fascist architecture—is known to have taken design inspiration from both the competition entry by Hannes Meyer for the headquarters of the League of Nations and that of Le Corbusier for the Palace of Soviets. Since similar design concepts can serve to represent Italian fascism, democracy, and communism, it can be argued that, regardless of the nature of the political regime, architectural styles meant to convey political messages can have shared characteristics that make them, theoretically, more alike than not.

Since the style of cultural production is not the Rosetta Stone of ideology, many scholars, particularly those who specialize in fascist cultural production in Europe, have pushed beyond style in their attempts to classify the aesthetic qualities of politically persuasive cultural works. In cases where it is possible to identify an artist or author who created a specific work of art, a biographical approach examining the political commitments of the artist or a thematic approach focusing on particular features of an artist's thought has been helpful in understanding the politics behind the object.[13] The chūreitō project, however, because it was not created by a single artist figure but (according to media reports) by people of all ages from across the country, requires a different sort of examination to uncover its political force in successfully mobilizing the nation. The chūreitō functioned like an icon in the civic religion of fascism, which, according to George Mosse, draws "its strength from an already present consensus."[14] Mosse's argument is confined to the visual expressions of fascist culture; the chūreitō project, however, helped create political consensus through its process of creation even more so than through its actual appearance. That consensus, fostered through education and mass culture, placed ultimate value on one's sacrifice through death to the emperor and was demonstrated not by the physical appearance of the memorials, but by individuals working throughout the process of design and construction. A concept of sacrifice was aestheticized not so much visually as through people's actions — actions that were coerced yet understood as voluntary only because a consensus already had been created.

The process of chūreitō memorial construction became a movement that functioned as a powerful propaganda tool for the promotion of nationalism in wartime Japan. It engaged people from Tokyo and regional cities, as well as small towns and rural villages, in a project to build monuments that represented the unparalleled significance placed on military death. Each monument was to be an icon that symbolized sacrifice by the war dead and by those who participated in the memorial construction. The nature of the project, which included a design competition and extensive campaigns for donations of money, material, and labor for construction, created the impression that it was being undertaken voluntarily by the will of the people when it had, in fact, been initiated by the military and enforced by the regional organizations put into place during the war as a surveillance mechanism to prevent unpatriotic thoughts and actions.[15] More important, most who participated by submitting design entries or donating money, labor, and material had been led to believe that they were acting on their own initiative. For those conditioned to believe that sacrifice for the emperor was the finest deed possible for a Japanese citizen, contributions to the construction of the memorials dedicated to the war dead, who were regarded as having committed sacrifices of the highest order, came naturally.

The memorial design—mundane as it may seem—had its significance, as well. Its tombstone-like design, representing death and mourning, possessed what the historian Daniel Sherman, discussing the war memorials of interwar France, has described as the "power of familiarity": it was a universal type that enabled people from varied social, cultural, and educational backgrounds to easily comprehend its symbolism.[16] The use of familiar or religious symbols associated with war, death, and mourning has been a common technique used for memorial design in Europe since the First World War, where memorials often used the Pietà composition, with the fallen soldier in the arms of a female figure or a comrade. Such familiar religious images possessed the power of "kitsch," so central to the aesthetics of fascism, which Clement Greenberg has defined as a predigested form of art that enables easy appreciation by the masses.[17]

The chūreitō memorials were the outcome of a nationwide construction movement of the late 1930s that took place amid an all-out war against China that was resulting in an unprecedented number of Japanese casualties.[18] This movement, initiated by the Dai-Nihon Chūrei Kenshō-kai (Greater Japan Committee to Exalt the Loyal War Dead)—a group composed of representatives from Interior, Army, Navy, Education, and Welfare ministries—aimed to construct a monument in every Japanese city, town, and village, as well as at major battlefields and occupied cities in China and Manchuria. The prototypes for monument designs of varying scales were selected through a competition co-sponsored by the committee and the Asahi Shimbun. The construction of the memorials was to be undertaken with the money, material, and labor of the local residents.

The design competition for the chūreitō memorials took place in late 1939. Ten major newspapers announced the "Official Regulations for the Chūreitō Design Competition," which called for three design prototypes: type one to be built on overseas battlefields; type two to be built in six major Japanese cities; and type three, consisting of three ranks—large, medium, and small—for Japanese cities, towns, and villages. Specific guidelines outlined the desired size and construction budget for each prototype. All prototypes were to incorporate an ossuary, and the design was to be "simple and plain in principle and symbolize the spirits of the fallen heroes in a grand and solemn manner."[19] The jury consisted of five established architects, five members of the military, and Masaki Naohiko, president of the Tokyo School of Art. The deadline for the submissions of competition entries was set for November 30 of the same year, and the Asahi Corporation was to provide the prize money for the winners.

The mass media, including major newspapers as well as state-sponsored and mass-market magazines, played a major role in the promotion of the chūreitō project. Even before the official announcement of the competition was made, newspapers started to feature chūreitō-related articles. Architects shared their thoughts on memorial design and encouraged readers to submit entries.[20] In early August, a three-part article in *Asahi Shimbun* chronicled the history of war memorials in Manchuria, Europe, and Japan.[21] The *Tōkyō Nichi Nichi Shimbun* published a series of eleven articles titled "Chūreitō tales (*Chūreitō monogatari*)," with contents ranging from the historical background behind the establishment of the committee and surveys of Japanese war memorials in China to various anecdotes regarding fundraising and volunteer work.[22]

Following the announcement of the competition, the media's focus shifted to design entries submitted to the committee. Rather than on well-executed entries by professional architects, most articles focused on submissions by amateurs, as they provided good subject matter for the "tales of virtue (*bidan*)" being published to inspire readers to participate in the project. It did not matter to the reporters or the readers that most of the amateur entries had been rejected by the committee. For example, the *Asahi Shimbun* reported on an entry by a very young boy drawn on a piece of construction paper. The article noted that the drawing "demonstrated his young dedication to honor the loyal heroes," but added that, unfortunately, the entry needed to be "respectfully sent back, because it did not meet the requirements."[23] The *Asahi* also published a photograph of a fifteen-year-old boy's perspective drawing. The boy had spent months of hard work on his design of a tower featuring a realist representation of a wounded soldier struggling to advance with the help of his comrades. This entry did not meet the competition requirements, either, but the committee announced that it planned to display it along with the winners.[24] Another media favorite was the submission sent from the front by an active soldier through the branch office of the *Asahi Shimbun*. Readers were told that the soldier had drawn his entry under candlelight with makeshift tools such as a compass made by attaching a pencil to a needle and thread and a ruler made from a piece of sharpened bamboo. The *Asahi* reported that the impressed committee members were in the process of retrieving the tools used by the soldier.[25]

Fund-raising to construct the memorials began even before the competition's winners were announced. Newspapers spilled a considerable amount of ink over the names of contributors and the amount of money donated. The committee generated public donations with the slogan *ichinichi senshi* (literally, "war dead for a day"). The slogan persuaded every civilian and soldier to donate one day's wage to express gratitude to the fallen heroes by imagining for one day that they had died in war.[26] To demonstrate the slogan, the Army and Navy announced their plan to deduct a day's wage from the salary of all their troops.[27] Soliciting donations was crucial, as the construction of the memorials depended primarily on them, and here again the mass media capitalized on "tales of virtue." A young man donated 2 yen that he had received from the police as a reward for saving a drowning child.[28] An impoverished orphan who had no money donated coins from the Tenpō era (1830–43) that he had inherited from his parents.[29] According to media reports, even prison inmates, the handicapped, and very young children donated their hard-earned money.

Not all design submissions and donations were voluntary. Many schools incorporated chūreitō design into their curricula, compelling students to draw war memorials during art classes.[30] Architecture firms and university design instructors were encouraged to adjust their work schedules so that employees and students might submit design entries.[31] Families were pressured to restrain from constructing individual tombstones for fallen family members and instead donate their savings to the chūreitō fund.[32] One Kyoto high school collected as much as 500 yen by forbidding the students from spending money on snacks and leisure and the faculty from buying tobacco and alcohol. A village in Toyama Prefecture took advantage of the nationwide reduction in land tax by collecting the original amount from its residents and using the difference for chūreitō construction.[33] These episodes, however, were framed as tales of virtue in media publications, creating the impression that they were undertaken voluntarily and willingly.

Media publicity for the chūreitō project proved successful. In Tokyo alone, donations reached 700,000 yen by early October 1939.[34] According to the announcement of winners published in major newspapers in January 1940, competition entries from 1,679 people had been received by the committee. (By way of comparison, typical architectural design competitions at the time attracted 60 to 80 entries.)

The media promotion of the memorial project was part of a larger phenomenon of competitions sponsored by newspapers and mass-market magazines in Japan of the 1930s.[35] Particularly during the war, newspapers and magazines held numerous competitions to promote patriotism through mass participation by soliciting war-themed slogans, songs, and essays. Like many of these contests, the chūreitō competition was sponsored by a newspaper and ostensibly did not require special qualifications for participants. But the drawing requirements imply that the competition was seeking entries from professional architects. Each entry was to consist of a series of drawings that included a site plan, a floor plan, three elevations, one or more sections, and a perspective. Drawings were to be done in ink, with shading applied to the elevations and colors to the perspective. Further instructions designated lettering, labeling, and other details. Newspaper articles reveal that many non-professionals submitted entries only to be rejected because they did not fulfill the requirements. Although professionals were solicited, the organizers actively solicited non-professional entries to engage a much larger population. The selection of a design from a competition that encouraged all Japanese to participate and the mass media's emphasis on submissions from amateurs created the impression that the entire nation took part in the design process.

However, we cannot get a full view of the chūreitō project from mass-market media targeting the general audience, as the project involved a design competition aimed at professional and aspiring architects, as well. At the time the chūreitō competition took place, architecture competitions had long been a source of contention between generations of architects. Younger architects who championed European-inspired modernist designs struggled for acceptance by the jury, which was composed of older architects who preferred more traditional styles often referred to as Nihon shumi (Japanese taste), characterized by the formulaic use of traditional Japanese roofs capping buildings of neoclassical design.[36] In most of the competitions for public architecture, such as those for city and town halls and museums that took place in the 1920s and 1930s, a Nihon shumi–style entry had been selected as the winner. Weary of the typical outcome, many young modernists had begun to boycott architecture competitions. In the case of the chūreitō competition, however, many of these modernists had participated, including the young elites who would come to represent postwar Japanese architecture—in part from patriotism and in response to the overwhelming publicity. These young modernists' entries typically incorporated bold geometric shapes such as a pyramid or expressionistic, free-form designs. As a stark contrast, the first prize for the type-three design, which became the model for most of the memorials built in Japan, was a simple design featuring a tall, slender tower rising from a pedestal that also functioned as an ossuary.

For the young elites, the outcome of the competition was truly disappointing, as none of their modernist entries was selected. The unsuccessful entrants used professional architecture journals to voice their disdain. Numerous journals championed the modernist entries by dedicating generous numbers of glossy pages to their photographs. At the same time, these articles disparaged the winning entries, criticized the competition as futile, and called for another competition. For example, an editorial in the architecture journal *Gendai kenchiku* (Contemporary Architecture) expressed concern over the "banality and lack of skill in the winning designs" and commented that the fallen heroes deserved better.[37] One architect described his experience viewing the exhibition of winning entries as "irritating" and "extremely unpleasant" and wondered "how in the world such abysmal designs were selected as winners." In a bitter tone, he proposed that the competition be considered a trial run and that the process be repeated.[38] The disgruntled architects mockingly labeled the winning designs "tombstone" style for the resemblance of their compositions—several lower layers of base structure topped with a high-rising monolith—to common Japanese tombstones.

It has been argued that these elite architects were detached from politics in wartime Japan and that the competition was rigged by the military, whose members had pre-selected the winning entries before the other jury members had a chance to examine all the entries, thereby completely dismissing the architectural significance of the winning designs.[39] But from newspaper articles and diary entries of one of the jury members, I have found that, while the competition indeed took a two-step process, the first round of selections was completed by a sub-jury composed of four senior architects.[40] In other words, it was the architect sub-jury, rather than the members of the military, who had selected the "tombstone"-style entries. These senior architects had typically served as jury members for competitions for public architecture, which usually called for designs that expressed Japaneseness while using floor plans, material, and technology imported from European architecture. In the previous contests, they had always favored entries that employed *Nihon shumi* designs, because the conspicuous Japanese tiled roof, even when used with otherwise Western-style building design, spelled out Japaneseness to the untrained eye. The selection criteria of this competition, then, were no different from those of the previous competitions. Trained before the advent of high modernism in Japanese architectural culture, these senior architects were capable of acknowledging the power of kitsch: they understood that just as the Nihon shumi style was easily recognizable as Japanese in public architecture, the "tombstone" style most effectively communicated death in war memorials.

The military, then, had little input in the selection of a design. In fact, the military had little interest in the project itself. A series of documents distributed by the military and the police in the early stages of the project indicates that their interest in supporting the chūreitō project had diminished considerably during the first year. In fact, by November 1939 the recommended budget for the construction of the local memorials had been drastically reduced to an amount that made their construction unfeasible.

Not that the military had always been uninvolved. Before the founding of the Greater Japan Committee to Exalt the Loyal Dead in May 1939, representatives from the Interior, Army, Navy, Welfare, and Education ministries had met on January 18 of the same year to discuss a nationwide project for the construction of war memorials.[41] This was in response to a growing demand from people living far from Yasukuni Shrine in Tokyo for a local memorial that they could call their own and visit daily.[42] The outcome of the meeting was distributed to governors throughout Japan on February 2, 1939, in the document "Matters Regarding Memorial Building Associated with the China Incident," which outlined the basic principles of local memorial building.[43] The Army initially showed strong enthusiasm for the chūreitō construction movement by promising financial assistance and offering to provide land for the memorials in military cemeteries.[44] By November, however, its stance had changed dramatically. The Army's public notice "On the Construction of Structures Associated with the China Incident," issued in November, stated that the memorials would be built only when financially feasible. The notice further downsized the scope of the project at the local level by discouraging the establishment of new committees for memorial construction and recommending the use of military cemeteries instead of constructing new memorials. The recommended budget was cut drastically from the amounts originally noted at the announcement of the design competition (50,000 yen for cities, 20,000 yen for towns, and 5,000 yen for villages), to a minimal amount of 200 yen to 300 yen, which effectively made it impossible to build them.[45] The last item on the document warned, "Prepare cautiously for construction with the above items in mind. Do not start construction until the time is right." Coupled with the head note indicating the main objective of the project was to build memorials on "the major battlefields of the Imperial Army," and several items that all but discouraged the construction of chūreitō, it might be safely concluded that, even before the deadline of the competition, the committee no longer intended to support the actual construction at regional levels—a drastic change from the enthusiastic support that the Army showed in its internal memo of February 1939. Nevertheless, by engaging in the broad public discussion of memorial building, the military was taking part in the maintenance of a political consensus focused on the memorial project.

In fact, the Army already had plans to construct chūreitō memorials in each garrison city throughout Japan prior to the establishment of the Greater Japan Committee to Exalt the Loyal Dead. The blueprint to be used for these memorials had already been completed by the Army Ministry long before the design competition was announced in August 1939. In Wakayama City, for example, local newspapers announced on February 2, 1939, the Army's plans to build a memorial inside the local military cemetery, and on April 8, 1939, it announced that the local Army troop had received the set of drawings issued by the Army Ministry.[46] For a year, the Wakayama edition of the *Asahi Shimbun* followed the memorial project with a focus on fundraising and the voluntary labor of local residents. Since the ongoing Wakayama chūreitō project design would have conflicted with the outcome of the competition, those in charge of the Wakayama project quietly replaced their design with the competition result. On April 20, 1940, the *Asahi*, without reference to its earlier announcement of the completion of chūreitō design, noted once again that the military had just completed its design for the memorial (figure 1).[47]

The project to construct memorials in small towns and villages was, then, not a priority for the military and the state. The chūreitō construction movement had developed as a solution to popular demands for local memorials. By establishing the Greater Japan Committee to Exalt the Loyal War Dead, which organized an open competition for memorial design as well as fund drives for memorial construction, the military and the state successfully reassured people of the viability of the project by creating the impression that they were responding to the demands of the competition while, in fact, they expended little on it.

Despite the military's lack of interest, the project, boosted by media publicity, developed into a mass movement that resulted in the actual completion of a number of memorials in various areas throughout Japan. Even the restriction of materials due to the ongoing war did not dampen strong

1. Chūreitō memorial, Wakayama City, Wakayama Prefecture, 1941. Photograph by the author.

local enthusiasm for memorial building. By February 1941, when four-teen memorials following the type-three prototype designed by Hoshino Shōichi were completed, it had become impossible to secure the steel and iron required to construct the structures according to the original plan. One valiant effort to work against these conditions was Satō Kōichi's revision of the prototype to allow it to be built without the unavailable materials.[48] The blueprint for the modified memorial was distributed on request to local committees that had received approval for construction.[49] But due to lack of time and resources, the goal to construct chūreitō memorials in every city, town, and village was not achieved before the end of the war. As of October 1, 1942, only 124 chūreitō memorials had been completed; 140 were near completion; and 1,500 cities, towns, and villages had plans to build one, though they never did (figures 2 and 3).[50]

Despite this lack of actualization, the ideological work of the competition had been done. The effect of the project did not depend on its actual execution. Even in regions that were not able to complete a chūreitō memorial before the end of the war, the project enabled the residents to act together and to sacrifice for something national that they could call their own. For many, simply taking part in the project was a way to mourn a loss. The mass media aestheticized all sacrifices that contributed to chūreitō construction as noble deeds that honored those who had given up their lives for the country. By selecting a design from a competition that encouraged all Japanese

2. One example of a chūreitō memorial completed before the end of the Asia-Pacific War, Atsugi City, Kanagawa Prefecture (formerly Echi Village), 1943. Photograph by the author.

3. Immediately after the end of the Occupation, many towns and villages resumed their effort to construct chūreitō memorials. Chūreitō memorial, Koayu Village, Kanagawa Prefecture, 1957. Photograph by the author.

to participate, rather than limiting participation to professional architects, the project created the impression that the entire nation took part in the design process. Each resulting memorial, then, was easily recognizable by the general public as a chūreitō.

If the physical presence of these memorials symbolized the sacrifice of men who lost their lives in battle, their process of creation demonstrated a different type of sacrifice: the donation of money and labor by the home-front civilians who were instructed to endure their sacrifices by imagining for a single day that they had lost their lives in battle. Through this communal effort invested in a state-organized project, personal memories of loss and sacrifice were transformed into a collective memory of the community tied to the state and its imperialist endeavors. Feelings of grief and mourning were channeled into a collective aspiration to succeed in the war effort. The memorialization of deceased family members in these monuments was also recognized as the highest honor bestowed on the common man. It was meant to both console those left behind and encourage young men to follow in the footsteps of those memorialized. With the collaboration of the mass media, which followed every step of the projects' development at the national and local levels, the chūreitō movement functioned as a powerful political tool for mobilizing home-front communities through the later years of the Asia-Pacific War.

Notes

1. Studies of war memorials have often focused on their artistic qualities and political symbolism, thus excluding many that were not deemed worthy of examination based strictly on design. More recently, such studies have begun to examine the process of memorial creation, as well as the rituals and ceremonies of mourning that took place. For example, in his study of the cultural legacy of the First World War in Europe, Jay Winter examines war memorials as "foci of the rituals, rhetoric, and ceremonies of bereavement." Kristin Ann Hass has studied private rituals surrounding the Vietnam Veterans Memorial in Washington, D.C. —in particular, the mementos that people leave at the wall. Others, such as James Young and Daniel Sherman, have taken a more biographical approach by focusing on the processes through which memorial projects were proposed and executed. See Jay Winter, *Sites of Memory, Sites of Mourning: The Great War in European Cultural History* (Cambridge: Cambridge University Press, 1995); Kristin Ann Hass, *Carried to the Wall: American Memory and the Vietnam Veterans Memorial* (Berkeley: University of California Press, 1998); James Young, *The Texture of Memory: Holocaust Memorials and Meaning* (New Haven, Conn.: Yale University Press, 1993); Daniel J. Sherman,

The Construction of Memory in Interwar France (Chicago: University of Chicago Press, 1999).

2. No consensus has emerged regarding the proper term for the wars that Japan undertook from 1931 to 1945. "Pacific War (*Taiheiyō Sensō*)," coined by the Allied Occupation forces in place of the official Japanese name, "Greater East Asian War (*Daitōa Sensō*)," fails to include the invasions in East Asia. In the 1980s, the cultural critic Tsurumi Shunsuke proposed "Fifteen-Year War (*Jūgonen Sensō*)" to include the Japanese aggression in China. I prefer to use the more recent "Asia-Pacific War (*Ajia Taiheiyō Sensō*)," which signifies by its name alone the wars that Japan fought with Asian countries as well as with the United States. On the naming of the Asia-Pacific War, see Kisaka Jun'ichirō, "Ajia Taiheiyō Sensō no koshō to seikaku," *Ryūkoku hōgaku* 25.4 (March 1993): 386–434. For a summary in English, see Lisa Yoneyama, *Hiroshima Traces: Time, Space, and the Dialectics of Memory* (Berkeley: University of California Press, 1999), 220, fn. 3.

3. Numerous writings on Yasukuni exist in Japanese, yet most scholars have approached the subject with a political bent. For an overview of the so-called Yasukuni problem, see, e.g., Ōe Shinobu, *Yasukuni Jinja* (Tokyo: Iwanami Shoten, 1984); Murakami Shigeyoshi, *Irei to shōkon: Yasukuni no shisō* (Tokyo: Iwanami Shoten, 1974); Tanaka Nobumasa, *Yasukuni no sengoshi* (Tokyo: Iwanami Shoten, 2002). English sources on Yasukuni Shrine include John Breen, "The Dead and the Living in the Land of Peace: A Sociology of the Yasukuni Shrine," *Mortality* 9, no. 1 (February 2004): 76–93; John Nelson, "Social Memory as Ritual Practice: Commemorating Spirits of the Military Dead at Yasukuni Shinto Shrine," *Journal of Asian Studies* 62, no. 2 (May 2003): 445–67; Klaus Antoni, "Yasukuni-Jinja and Folk Religion: The Problem of Vengeful Spirits," *Asian Folklore Studies* 47 (1988): 123–36; Cyril Powles, "Yasukuni Jinja Hōan: Religion and Politics in Contemporary Japan," *Pacific Affairs* 49, no. 3 (fall 1976): 491–505.

4. Tanakamaru Katsuhiko, *Samayoeru eirei tachi: Kuni no mitama, ie no hotoke* (Tokyo: Kashiwa Shobō, 2002), 52–53.

5. For the role of war memorials in the promotion of nationalism in modern Japan, see Awazu Kenta, "Kindai Nihon nashonarizumu ni okeru hyōshō no hen'yō" *Sociologica* 26.1–2 (December 2001): 1–33.

6. Some twenty Japanese terms are used to refer to war memorials, although in most cases the difference in how they are named does not necessarily translate into a difference in the nature of the memorial. The particular type that I focus on here, however, is distinct. Although they have never commanded political attention comparable to Yasukuni Shrine, the chūreitō have been scrutinized in the postwar years for their association with the military and with State Shintō in the years before 1945. Few historical studies of chūreitō exist, however. Ōhara Yasuo has published the book *Chūkonhi no kenkyū* and several articles on the subject. But Ōhara's works focus primarily on the fate of the memorials after the Shintō Directive (1945) that separated religion and state. He also attempts to dissociate chūreitō from Shintōism in an effort to recover a pure image of the

religion: Ōhara Yasuo, *Chūkonhi no kenkyū* (Tokyo: Akatsuki Shobō, 1984); idem, "Zoku chūkonhi no kenkyū: Gokoku jinja no seiritsu to chūreitō kensetsu undō ni shōten o atete" *Nihon bunka kenkyōjo kiyō* 52 (September 1983): 47–104. Other historical works on chūreitō include the following by Kagotani Jirō: "Sengo no chūkonhi, ireihi tō ni tsuite," *Rekishi hyōron* 329 (September 1977): 89–107; "Senbotsushahi to 'chūkonhi': aru chūkonhi soshō ni yosete," *Rekishi hyōron* 406 (February 1984): 27–55; "Sensōhi ni tsuite no kōsatsu: Ebine Isao shi 'Chūkonhi,' 'Sensō no ishibumi' o sozai ni," *Rekishi hyōron* 444 (April 1987): 96–107. Also, Hirano Takeshi, "Chūkonhi to irei-sai o meguru rekishi ninshiki," *Ryūkoku hōgaku* 16, no. 1 (June 1983): 1–34.

7. Photographs of existing chūreitō memorials can be found in several volumes of war-memorial inventories compiled by Ebine Isao, with sponsorship from Yasukuni Shrine: Yasukuni Jinja, ed., *Tōkyō-to chūkonhi tō kenritsu chōsashū*; Ebine Isao, *Kanagawa-ken chūkonhi tō kenritsu chōsashū* (Tokyo: Jinja Shamusho, 1995); idem, *Chiba-ken no chūkonhi* (Tokyo: Jinja Shamusho, 1995); idem, *Chūkonhi*, vol. 1, 2 (Chiba: Chiba-ken gokoku jinja, 1998); idem, *Sensō no ishibumi* (Saitama: Saitama shimbun-sha, 1985); and idem, *Gunma-ken no chūreitō nado* (Takasaki: Gunma-ken gokoku jinja, 2001). Similar research on a nationwide scale is currently under way by a team organized by the National Museum of Japanese History. Its progress was published in March 2003 under the title *Hibunken shiryō no kiso kenkyū hōkokusho: Kingendai no sensō ni kansuru kinenhi* (Chiba: National Museum of Japanese History, 2003).

8. In summing up the chapter "What Is ideology?" Terry Eagleton offers six definitions of ideology varying from the general to the specific. My interpretation and the general use of the term is derived from his fourth definition, in which ideology is used for the promotion and legitimating of sectoral interests through the activities of a dominant social power not only through importing ideas from above but also by securing the complicity of subordinated classes and groups. When censorship and propaganda were involved, ideology in wartime Japan started to take on the meaning of Eagleton's fifth definition, in which ideology "signifies ideas and beliefs which help to legitimate the interests of a ruling group or class specifically by distortion and dissimulation": Terry Eagleton, *Ideology: An Introduction* (London: Verso, 2007), 29–30.

9. Examples include Inagaki Eizō, *Nihon no kindai kenchiku: Sono seiritsu katei* (Tokyo: Kajima Shuppankai, 1979); Fujimori Terunobu, *Nihon no kindai kenchiku* (Tokyo: Iwanami Shoten, 1993); Inoue Shōichi, *Senjika Nihon no kenchikuka: Aato kitchu japanesuku* (Tokyo: Asahi Shoten, 1995).

10. Barbara Miller Lane, *Art and Politics in Germany, 1918–1945* (Cambridge, Mass.: Harvard University Press, 1985).

11. Dennis P. Doordan, *Building Modern Italy: Italian Architecture, 1914–1936* (New York: Princeton Architectural Press, 1988), 129. Diane Ghirardo, "City and Theater: The Rhetoric of Fascist Architecture." *Stanford Italian Review* 8, nos. 1–2 (1996): 165–93.

12. Francesco Dal Co, "The Stones of the Void," *Oppositions* 26 (spring 1984): 99–116. Barbara Miller Lane supports Dal Co's analysis in her review of Albert Speer's memoir, *Inside the Third Reich* (New York: Macmillan, 1970), writing, "If one takes all the buildings and projects together what emerges is an extreme eclecticism": Barbara Miller Lane, review of *Inside the Third Reich*, *Journal of the Society of Architectural Historians* 32, no. 4 (December 1973): 341–46.

13. Richard J. Golsan, "Introduction" in *Fascism, Aesthetics, and Culture*, ed Richard J. Golsan (Hanover, N.H.: University Press of New England, 1992), xiii.

14. George Mosse, "Fascist Aesthetics and Society: Some Considerations," *Journal of Contemporary History* 31 (1996): 245–52.

15. For a study of neighborhood organization in early-twentieth-century Japan, see Sally Ann Hastings, *Neighborhood and Nation in Tokyo, 1905–1937* (Pittsburgh: University of Pittsburgh Press, 1995).

16. Daniel J. Sherman, *The Construction of Memory in Interwar France* (Chicago: University of Chicago Press, 1999), 183. In the case of interwar France, such desire for familiar types was more prevalent in the lower and middle ranges of the monument market.

17. Clement Greenberg, "Avant-Garde and Kitsch" in *Clement Greenberg: The Collected Essays and Criticism. Vol. 1 Perceptions and Judgments 1939–1944* (Chicago and London: University of Chicago Press, 1986), 5–22.

18. In 1937 and 1938 alone, more than 61,000 Japanese soldiers died in the war against China. In 1939, 42,000 more lost their lives: Eguchi Keiichi, *Taikei Nihon no rekishi, vol. 14, Futatsu no taisen* (Tokyo: Shōgakkan, 1993), 340.

19. *Asahi Shimbun*, August 25, 1939. The same announcement was published in *Asahi Shimbun* (Osaka), *Mainichi Shimbun* (Osaka), *Kokumin*, *Chūgai sangyō*, *Tōkyō Nichi Nichi Shimbun*, *Hōchi Shimbun*, *Miyako Shimbun*, *Yomiuri Shimbun*, and *Dōmei Shimbun*, as well as the in September 1939 issue of *Kenchiku zasshi*, the journal published by the Architectural Institute of Japan.

20. Satō Takeo, "Manshū no chūreitō," *Asahi Shimbun*, August 2–4, 1939; Kishida Hideto, "Chūreitō shikan," *Asahi Shimbun*, August 6–8, 1939.

21. *Asahi Shimbun*, August 2 (Manchuria), August 3 (Japan), and August 4 (Europe), 1939.

22. The series was later published as a book under the authorship of Army General Hishikari Takashi: Hishikari Takashi, *Chūreitō monogatari* (Tokyo: Dōwa Shunjūkai, 1942).

23. *Asahi Shimbum*, October 7, 1939.

24. Ibid., November 24, 1939.

25. Ibid.; see also *Asahi Shimbun* (Osaka), November 18, 1939.

26. *Asahi Shimbun*, July 1, 1939.

27. Ibid., August 9–10, 1939.

28. "Chūreitō kenshō no shingi to kangeki o kataru," *Ie no hikari* 15, no. 11 (November 1939): 116–23.

29. Ibid.; see also Hishikari, *Chūreitō monogatari*, 234–35.

AKIKO TAKENAKA

30. E-mail correspondence with Kurita Kōji, May 16, 2004.

31. Lecture by Satō Kōichi at the Architectural Institute of Japan; transcript published in *Shinkenchiku* 15, no. 10 (October 1939): 489–95.

32. Hishikari, *Chūreitō monogatari*, 148–62.

33. Ibid., 233–34.

34. *Asahi Shimbun*, October 3, 1939.

35. The nature of the competition varied, ranging from acclaimed annual competitions targeting aspiring future professionals to one-time events for the general public. The annual music competition sponsored since 1931 by the *Tōkyō Nichi Nichi Shimbun* and *Mainichi Shimbun* (Osaka), for example, provided skilled amateur musicians a gateway to success. Far more popular were the competitions sponsored by newspapers and magazines to increase readership.

36. For a further description of the style as well as its significance in prewar architecture competitions, see Ōmi Sakae, *Kenchiku sekkei kyōgi: Konpetishon no keifu to tenbō* (Tokyo: Kajima shuppan-kai, 1986).

37. "Chūreitō kenshō sekkei nyūsen an happyō" (part of the monthly editorial "Kōsaku bunka"), *Gendai kenchiku* 8 (January 1940): 63.

38. Kishida Hideto, "Chūreitō kyōgi sekkei nyūsen an o miru," *Gendai kenchiku* 9 (February–March 1940): 2–4.

39. Inoue Shōichi, *Senjika Nihon no kenchikuka*, 168.

40. On December 3, 1939, *Asahi Shimbun* announced that a preliminary meeting of the jury members had taken place on December 2, during which a sub-jury group was formed by four architects and an army engineer. The article further noted that the sub-jury was to meet on December 3 and start its selection process immediately. The December 2 meeting is confirmed in the diary of one jury member, Masaki Naohiko. Masaki, who was not a member of the sub-jury, only participated during the final selection process that took place for three days from December 12: Masaki Naohiko, *Jūsan Shōdō nikki*, vol. 4 (Tokyo: Chūō kōron bijutsu shuppan, 1966).

41. *Asahi Shimbun*, January 19, 1939.

42. Of the over 2.3 million lives lost between 1931 and 1945, only 189,261 had been officially enshrined by the end of the war. I calculated these numbers based on data in *Yasukuni Jinja hyakunenshi*, vol. 1 (Tokyo: Yasukuni Jinja, 1983).

43. The document instructed against lavishness and prohibited religious symbolism in memorial design. Keiho-kyoku keihatsu kō dai 10 gō, Keiho-kyokuchō jinja-kyokuchō tsūchō, "Shina Jihen ni kansuru hihyō kensetsu no ken," February 2, 1939. Documents issued by the police and the military during the war are available at the National Archives of Japan and the Military Archives in the National Institute for Defense Studies, respectively. Military documents issued prior to 1945 are also available at Japan Center for Asian Historical Records, National Archives of Japan. I provide a full translation of the documents included in this essay in "The Aesthetics of Mass-Persuasion: War and Architectural Sites in Japan, 1868–1945," Ph.D. diss., Yale University, New Haven, 2004.

44. Rikufu dai 1110 gō Rikugunshō fukukan tsūchō, "Shina Jihen ni kansuru hihyō kensetsu no ken," February 27, 1939.

45. Keiho-kyoku keihatsu kō dai 178 gō Keiho-kyokuchō Jinja-kyokuchō tsūchō: "Shina Jihen ni kansuru hihyō kensetsu no ken," November 11, 1939.

46. *Asahi Shimbun* (Wakayama), February 2, 1939, April 8, 1939.

47. Ibid., April 20, 1940. The budget had increased to 17,000 yen by this time. The Wakayama chūreitō, inaugurated on January 15, 1941, features a thirty-three-meter-high tower of steel-reinforced concrete finished with granite, which follows the winning design by Hoshino Shōichi. The final budget amounted to 101,000 yen. The planning and construction process of the Wakayama City memorial is outlined in the booklet published by Wakayama-ken Chūreitō Go-jikai, a foundation that maintains the memorial today. The foundation operates out of the Peace Hall (Heiwa Kaikan), located on the memorial site, which includes a small exhibition room displaying belongings of those memorialized: Wakayama-ken Chūreitō Gojikai, *Heiwa no ishizue: Wakayama-ken chūreitō enkakushi* (Wakayama: Wakayama-ken chūreitō gojikai, 1990).

48. *Asahi Shimbun*, February 21, 1941; *Asahi Shimbun* (Osaka), February 21, 1941. Hoshino had specified steel-encased reinforced concrete for the larger structures to be built in cities and towns and reinforced concrete for those to be built in villages. It can be argued that the state never had serious plans to construct the type-three monuments. Steel, included in the initial requirements, was already restricted in 1938.

49. An original copy of Satō's plan is preserved at the Saitama Prefectural Archives, along with documents associated with the construction of the monument at a local elementary school.

50. Dai Nihon Chūrei Kenshōkai, *Naichi chūreitō kensei chakkō jōkyō ichiranhyō*, cited in Ōhara Yasuo, *Chūkonhi no kenkyū*, 142–43 (Tokyo: Akatsuki shobō, 1984). Numbers vary depending on the source. Hishikari Takashi, for example, noted in his book *Chūreitō monogatari* that by August 1942, 150 structures had been completed and 130 more were under construction: Hishikari, *Chūreitō monogatari*, 180. Most chūreitō structures that were built faithfully followed the prototype design by Hoshino (later revised by Satō), although their size and proportion varied. Construction of chūreitō memorials continued after the Allied Occupation following the prototype design.

JONATHAN M. REYNOLDS

Japan's Imperial Diet Building
in the Debate over Construction
of a National Identity

■ During the 1930s a new monument slowly emerged on the
Tokyo skyline. The Imperial Diet Building commanded a prominent site on
a hill rising to the southwest of the Imperial Palace grounds. Even before
Japan's national legislature occupied the structure, the government seized
on it as a banner for national unity and promoted images of it abroad as
proof of the nation's democratic government. This was an especially difficult claim for this particular government to make, and the Diet was an
unlikely centerpiece for such a propaganda campaign. The Diet itself was a
comparatively weak organ of the state, and the repressive civilian government teetered on the brink of destruction. The government for nearly a decade had been engaged in the brutal suppression of communists and other
dissidents. Japan had for five years been fending off international criticism
for its seizure of Manchuria and the installation of a puppet regime there.
Only a few months before the building opened, a group of army officers
staged an abortive coup and stationed troops at the Diet and other sites
throughout central Tokyo. The following year, the military launched its full-
scale invasion of China. The building's design itself was the equivocal prod-

uct of prolonged negotiations and was incapable of presenting a compelling visual argument capable of transcending the problematic institution that it housed. In the end, the building was unable to meet the unrealistic demands placed on it. The Diet building emerged from the war as an unhappy reminder of failed military adventurism and ineffectual political leadership.

From the earliest planning stages in the 1880s, people recognized the future Diet Building's potential to represent a vision of Japanese national identity both domestically and internationally. Yet no consensus was ever reached on how the Diet could most effectively fulfill that role. The protracted debates over the Diet's design testify to the complex cultural contradictions generated by the process of appropriation of Western ideas as part of an ambitious project of modernization.

In 1881, the Meiji emperor (r. 1867–1912) promised to provide a constitution and establish a parliament within ten years. After careful study of several European models, especially that of Germany, the emperor promulgated a constitution in 1889.[1] The new bicameral legislature, the Imperial Diet, met for the first time the following year. The Japanese leadership chose to form a parliament along Western lines to solidify a sense of national unity and defuse pressure from the emerging people's rights movement. At a time when there was also deep concern about the image of the Japanese government in the West, the formation of a parliament, it was thought, might help to convince Western powers that Japan was ready to deal with them on equal terms.[2]

However, the Meiji oligarchs did not intend to surrender their power to this new institution. The constitution affirmed the emperor's sovereignty and included many safeguards to ensure that the oligarchs would retain actual control over the government through their dominance of the Privy Council. The Diet was formed as a consultative body. Nonetheless, the Diet attained some measure of autonomy as the first generation of Meiji leaders began to pass from the scene and as political parties working within the Diet solidified their position. This culminated in the formation of the first party cabinet in 1918. Despite the Diet's growing role, it was by no means the most respected institution in Japanese public life. The very process of party politics that brought the Diet newfound influence was widely perceived as corrupt and ineffectual. As a result, until the end of the war there was little enthusiasm for party politics, and the Diet as an institution was held in relatively low esteem.[3] The history of the Diet buildings reflects this tentative status. For the first forty-seven years of its existence, the Diet met in a series of temporary structures as politicians and architects debated over the design for a more permanent building.

The Imperial Diet Building was only one component of a much broader program of government-sponsored public construction during the Meiji period. When the Meiji government came to power in 1868, it was deeply committed to transforming Japan into a modern nation. Architecture played an important role in that effort. The government needed modern office buildings to house a burgeoning bureaucracy and looked to the West for practical solutions. The Meiji leaders also embraced Western architectural styles, not to deny their Japanese cultural identity but, rather, to assert that their identity now needed to be firmly rooted in modernity. Western styles projected a contemporary yet dignified image and were tangible expressions of these aspirations.

The first plans for a building to house the new Diet began to take shape at a time of transition for the architectural profession in Japan. Japanese architects trained in the government's own architecture program within the newly established College of Engineering were beginning to take on significant public commissions, but government leaders still looked to Western advisers for certain critical commissions. As a result, the earliest designs for the Diet, a building intended to embody the spirit of national unity, were produced by foreign architects.

A government commission under the leadership of the pro-Western foreign minister, Inoue Kaoru, invited the German architectural firm of Ende and Böckmann to develop a government complex at the Hibiya Parade Grounds directly south of the Imperial Palace in Tokyo. The choice of a German firm is not surprising, given the pro-German sentiments in Inoue's circle at this time.[4] Wilhelm Böckmann spent several months in Japan in 1886, and his partner Hermann Ende visited in 1887. The architects proposed a sweeping transformation of a large portion of central Tokyo. In its final form, their plan called for a large central ring of government ministries linked by broad avenues radiating out to the palace, other government buildings, and a main train station. An elevated site to the southwest of the palace was reserved for the future Diet Building. Parliament Avenue would have offered a grand vista down to the palace moat and the ministries. Ende and Böckmann also worked up detailed plans for several of the individual buildings that were to fit into this grand scheme, including the Diet, the Ministry of Justice, and the High Court of Appeals.

The German firm produced two plans for the Diet Building. The first

PABLAMENTSHAUS FÜR JAPAN · KOKUKUWAI GIJIIN · HOUSE OF PARLIAMENT FOR JAPAN

PERSPECTIVISCHE ANSICHT · YENKENDZU · PERSPECTIVE VIEW

ARCHITEKTEN: ENDE & BÖCKMANN, KÖHLER

LICHTDRUCK DER REICHSDRUCKEREI

1. Hermann Ende and Wilhelm Böckmann, proposed design for the Japan Imperial Diet Building, version 1, 1887. Archives of the Architectural Institute of Japan.

2. Hermann Ende and Wilhelm Böckmann, proposed design for the Japan Imperial Diet Building, version 2, 1887. From *Deutsche Bauzeitung* (March 14, 1981).

proposed design, developed by Böckmann, would have been a masonry structure measuring 180 by 70 meters. The facade was bilaterally symmetric with a grand entrance set in a central pavilion capped by a dome, and with flanking wings for the two houses of parliament. The dome, mansard roofs, attached columns, pedimented windows, and other architectural details placed the design squarely within the framework of contemporary European practice. In fact, many specific characteristics of the design can be traced to the architects' own entries in architectural competitions for the German Reichstag in 1872 and 1882.[5] There was no effort to accommodate the architectural style to its Japanese context.

Ende produced an alternative version of the design. The overall disposition of the second proposal was similar to the first; however, there were some significant alterations. The architectural details that had so clearly marked the first design as "Western" were replaced by architectural features intended to allude to Japan's architectural past. Groups of engaged columns that had punctuated the main facade became buttresses of rusticated masonry surmounted by tiled gables. The two pairs of small towers that flanked the legislative wings lost their neo-baroque oculi and mansard roofs and were replaced by upswept tiled roofs. The roofs over the legislative halls became hipped-and-gabled tiled roofs characteristic of monumental architecture in premodern Japan. The Roman arched main entrance of the central pavilion in the original design was now marked by a bow-shaped gable (karahafu) and above that by a triangular gable (chidorihafu). The stately dome above the central pavilion was transformed into a multistory tower with spired pinnacles and more triangular gables. Ende also created Japanese-style designs for the Tokyo Court, the Ministry of Justice, and the Navy Ministry.

The chameleon-like substitution of architectural ornament had precedent in contemporary European practice. One might speculate that Ende hoped to introduce a Japanese style that could be integrated into modern architectural practice in Japan along with imported Gothic or Renaissance styles. The exotic hybrid of Western planning and building methods with Japanese architectural ornament is also analogous to efforts by Japanese builders to combine Western and Japanese ornament using indigenous materials and construction techniques.[6] What is distinctive about this design is that it was for such a prominent government building and was produced by formally trained Western architects working under the auspices of the government.

There are several possible explanations for this experimentation with

Japanese forms. Undoubtedly, at some level Ende wished to reflect his admiration for Japanese architecture, an admiration that was cultivated through extensive tours of great monuments in Japan's architectural heritage.[7] Ende and Böckmann came to Japan at a time when resident Westerners such as Gottfried Wagener, the German consultant to Japan's ceramics industry, and the American philosopher Ernest Fenollosa found themselves in the ironic position of advocating traditional Japanese culture in the midst of Japan's Westernization. Although there is no evidence that Ende met Wagener or Fenollosa, Böckmann did, and it is likely that both architects would have been aware of the other men's ideas. Ende and Böckmann also knew Josiah Conder, who avidly studied Japanese culture and sought to preserve what he thought of as Oriental architectural elements in contemporary practice.[8] These contacts may have encouraged Ende to acclimate his Diet design by adding the gables and tiled roofs.

The German architects were aware of mounting resistance to the pro-Western policies forwarded by Foreign Minister Inoue and others. A passage in Böckmann's account of his visit to Japan describes a shift in the political winds in the short period between his visit in 1886 and Ende's trip in 1887. Böckmann mentions criticism of Inoue's decision to leave the enormous government building project solely in the hands of foreigners as being contrary to national interests.[9] As the architectural historian Horiuchi Masaaki has suggested, Ende may have presented the alternative designs for the Diet and other government structures in part to deflect this mounting hostility.[10] Ende may have thought that "Japanicizing" the proposals would minimize the foreignness of the project as a whole, thus reducing nationalist objections. Inoue himself was receptive to Ende's second plan, possibly hoping that it would mitigate further opposition to German participation in the building project, as well as to his other policies.[11]

In the end, only a small portion of Ende's and Böckmann's government complex was built.[12] One important obstacle to the realization of the ambitious project was money. There were also concerns that it might not be possible to manufacture sufficient brick and other modern building materials to meet the project's demands, and the soil in critical sections of the proposed building site was too marshy to support large-scale masonry construction.[13] It is also likely that a lack of consensus concerning both the role of foreign architects and the problem of architectural style contributed to the demise of the proposals. These plans were being formulated at a turning point in cultural politics among the Japanese elite. While there was little chance that the government would backtrack on its support for modernization, the voices insisting on a degree of cultural independence from the West would grow stronger from the late 1880s onward.

Ende's and Böckmann's second Diet design was not the last effort by Western architects to offer an Orientalized design for the Diet to the Japanese government. Ralph Adams Cram, an American architect best known for Gothic revival designs, was contacted by a Unitarian minister based in Japan named Arthur May Knapp. Both "deplored the very terrible new architecture then being perpetrated under third-rate German influence." One wonders whether their concern was motivated more by the loss of a tradition or by American chauvinism about the German role in the new designs. Knapp convinced Cram to execute a design for the Diet Building that would "be based on the indigenous architecture of the Ashikaga and Fujiwara periods, but sufficiently adapted to modern conditions."[14] In 1898, Cram traveled to Japan with his design and through Knapp's offices was able to secure an interview with Prime Minister Itō Hirobumi. According to Cram, Itō was impressed and indicated that the government would be willing to pay Cram to draw up plans; however, his cabinet had fallen by the time Cram had returned to the United States. Cram did not pursue the Diet design any further.[15]

Cram referred to the project as an "Oriental dream," and the rendering of the design by Cram's colleague Bertram G. Goodhue does indeed have an oneiric quality. The perspective drawing is very delicately rendered, with the trees, shrubs, and Japanese lanterns of the garden setting contributing to his "Oriental" atmosphere. A man and woman in Japanese dress pause on a stone bridge over a river.

Cram's scheme, like both of the Ende and Böckmann designs, had a central pavilion and two wings for the houses of the Diet. However, Cram was more insistent about incorporating "Japanese" features into the design. His Diet was to be surrounded by a huge enclosure of walls and gates, perhaps following the precedent of the palace compounds of earlier Japanese capitals. Again we see bow-shaped gables, plover gables, and multistoried tiled roofs that were intended to mark the design as Japanese. This Orientalist fantasy was far removed from the realities of urban Tokyo in the 1890s. Cram's Oriental dream was a Western nostalgic mission to restore an unambiguously "Japanese" Japan through a self-conscious construction of Japanese tradition. Cram was anxiously attempting to re-sharpen the increasingly blurred distinctions between East and West threatened by Japan's modernization. In the years to come, such efforts would be carried out by Japanese architects.

3. Ralph Adams Cram with B. G. Goodhue, "A Proposal for the Parliament Houses in Tokyo," 1898. From Ralph Adams Cram, *My Life in Architecture* (Boston: Little, Brown, 1936).

4. Adolph Stegmueller with Yoshii Shigenori, First Imperial Diet Building, Main Facade, Tokyo, 1890. Archives of the Architectural Institute of Japan.

In 1888, as the deadline for the opening of the Diet approached, work began on a temporary structure to house the future Diet. Adolph Stegmueller, who had come to Japan as an architect from Ende's and Böckmann's firm, was the principal designer. He was assisted by Yoshii Shigenori, a graduate of the Imperial Engineering College who served as an architect from the Home Ministry. The building was completed in November 1890 in time for the first session of the Diet.[16] Since this new Diet was designed primarily by a German architect in Western style, it could have raised some of the same objections the earlier designs had, but perhaps because it was temporary and cost considerably less than the earlier proposals, the government was able to move forward with the construction.

The two-story wood clapboard building was a much more modest affair than Ende's and Böckmann's stately designs. It was constructed not on the elevated site that Ende and Böckmann had designated but to the south of the Hibiya Parade Grounds. The plan was close to the earlier designs, with a central entry and wings for each of the two legislative chambers. The pavilions rising over each chamber were lit with Roman-arched windows and covered with simple gabled roofs. There was a minimum of ornamentation.

This building burned down as a result of an electrical fire in January 1891, just two months after it was completed. A replacement designed by Yoshii and another Ende and Böckmann associate, Oscar Tietze, was completed by October of the same year. The second Diet Building closely followed the first except that it was somewhat larger and used exposed half-timber rather than clapboarding. This large but undistinguished temporary building housed the national legislature until it, too, was destroyed by fire in 1925.

With the completion of a temporary Diet Building, the government and the architectural community had time to debate more permanent solutions. The Home Ministry formed a series of commissions to study the issue. In 1899, one of these groups recommended that a competition be organized to select a design for the future Diet Building. Reflecting growing cultural nationalism, the commission proposed that the competition be limited to Japanese architects. In response to doubts about the maturity of the Japanese architectural profession, the commission indicated that it might be necessary to open the competition to non-Japanese if the Japanese entries were inadequate. The winning design would be chosen by a jury of five foreigners. The commission adjourned without further progress in 1901.[17]

The Russo-Japanese War of 1904–1905 tabled further consideration of the

5. Kobayashi Kiyochika, "Burning of the Japanese Diet Building," 1891. Woodblock print, Tokyo Metropolitan Central Library Special Collections Room.

6. Yoshii Shigenori and Oscar Tietze, Second Imperial Diet Building, Main Facade, Tokyo, 1891. Archives of the Architectural Institute of Japan.

Diet Building for several years. After the war, the Treasury Ministry sought to wrest control of this important public project from the Home Ministry. Members of the Treasury Ministry and representatives of both houses of the Diet went to Europe and the United States in 1908 to study Western legislative buildings, considered appropriate models for the Diet. In 1910, the Treasury formed its own commission on the Diet Building, with Prime Minister Katsura Tarō as chair.[18] This commission considered the Italian Renaissance style to be the most appropriate for the Diet, a recommendation that was immediately attacked in the architectural press. One anonymous author insisted that the "national spirit and the spirit of the age must be manifested through the architectural style of the building. . . . [A]fter all, one would not expect to manifest the spirit of sixteenth century Italy in Japan's Meiji-period Diet Building." The author called for a style that more accurately reflected contemporary "Japanese national spirit." This article was just one reflection of the intense debate within the architectural community over the issue of style.[19]

The ongoing study of the design for the Diet Building offered an excellent opportunity to explore this thorny problem. In May 1910, the Kenchiku Gakkai (Architectural Institute) sponsored a panel discussion on an appropriate future architectural style for the nation. Although the panel discussion was couched in general terms, the timing was such that the style of the future Diet was on the minds of all participants. Opinions varied dramatically. One participant advocated a purely Western style as the most appropriate choice for a modern nation. Another took a more traditionalist position. Several panelists proposed forging a new style that would draw on both Western and earlier Japanese architectural forms.[20] Speakers agreed that the choice of style mattered, since Japan's future public architecture would communicate something about its national ideals. The panelists could not agree, however, on a single, clear vision of Japan's community identity.

The Treasury Ministry created yet another commission, in 1918, to organize an architectural competition to select a design for the Diet Building. Initially, 118 entries were submitted, and of these, twenty designs were selected for the second stage of the competition. The finalists' designs were then put on public display. The commission awarded first prize to Watanabe Fukuzō of the Imperial Household Ministry. Watanabe's entry followed the same basic arrangement that Ende and Böckmann had introduced, with a central entry pavilion and two flanking wings. A pedimented portico marked the main entrance, and an ungainly domed tower rose high above the center of the structure. The roofline was flat, and the ornamentation was more subdued than its German predecessors.

The architect Shimoda Kikutarō had entered a design in the competition of 1918, but it was not included in the second round, and he was not satisfied with the designs of the finalists. He submitted a petition and design directly to the Diet. Shimoda argued that contemporary Japanese architects had lost touch with the "sublime poetic beauty that had characterized Japanese architecture since ancient times." He proposed combining European classicism with "pure Japanese style" in a new style that he called the "Imperial crown synthesis style (*teikan heigō shiki*)."[21] Shimoda illustrated his ideas with a design close to Watanabe's first-prize neoclassical work up to the cornice line. On top of this neoclassical structure, Shimoda placed pavilions with hipped-and-gabled roofs. The pavilions over the legislative chambers even sported bow-shaped gables and plover gables. The combination of a modern masonry structure and Japanese architectural details was nothing new, but Shimoda's brash juxtaposition of neoclassical forms and Japanese elements was striking. Shimoda pressed his case unsuccessfully for several years.

So much was at stake in the choice of styles for this important building that Shimoda was vigorously attacked by many of his colleagues. Curiously, Itō Chūta, who advocated incorporating elements from Japan's architectural past into contemporary practice, was one of Shimoda's harshest critics. Itō's critique is clearly reflected in an unfinished manuscript of 1921 in which he argued that Shimoda's work violated the structural logic of building materials and undermined the spirit of both the European classical and Japanese styles. He went so far as to declare Shimoda's design a "national disgrace."[22]

Members of the Treasury commission were not entirely satisfied with any of the competition designs. They settled on a compromise plan following negotiations with representatives of the Diet, and construction began soon thereafter.[23] This was an enormous undertaking that required a total of sixteen years between the groundbreaking in 1920 and the opening of the first session in the completed structure in December 1936.

The new Diet was constructed with a steel and reinforced concrete frame faced with gray granite. Its overall disposition is strikingly similar to Watanabe's competition entry, and it is likely that the commission drew heavily from that design in the development of its own.[24] The Diet has a stouter tower than Watanabe's, and it is capped with a stepped pyramidal roof rather than a dome. The commission may have borrowed this distinc-

7. Watanabe Fukuzō, proposal for the Imperial Diet Building, first-prize design for the Imperial Diet Competition of 1918–19. From *Kenchiku sekai* no. 134 (1919).

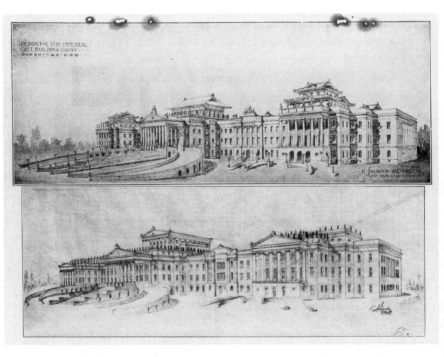

8. Shimoda Kikutarō, proposal for the Imperial Diet Building, design for the Imperial Diet Competition of 1918–19. From Shimoda Kikutarō, *Shisō kenchiku*, self published, 1928.

tive feature from the third-place entry by Takeuchi Shinshichi.[25] Recently, Suzuki Hiroyuki has argued that this architectural form was associated with the Meiji oligarch Itō Hirobumi and that the building might at one level be interpreted as a memorial to this longtime advocate for the Meiji constitution and the Diet.[26] The massing of the building is vaguely neoclassical in feel but lacks the extensive neoclassical detailing that characterized Watanabe's work.

At the time of completion, sources described the building as "modern style (kinseishiki)." It is likely that the designers arrived at this modern style through a process of suppressing potentially problematic European and Japanese historicizing detail rather than through a positive affirmation of simplified form in line with contemporary modernist thought.

How did the form of the new Diet Building, which was consonant with international architectural practice, address the concerns that this symbol of national unity be Japanese? By the 1920s one bone of contention—the nationality of the designer—did not present the problem it had in the 1880s. One frequently proposed strategy for situating the building culturally had been to appropriate historicizing detail from Japan's past. The design does include such Japanese decorative motifs as the phoenixes (a symbol closely associated with imperial rule) carved in shallow relief over the main entrance to the Diet and the chrysanthemums (the imperial crest) carved into the woodwork in the legislative chambers, but these represent a relatively minor aspect of the building design as a whole. The divisive issue of Japaneseness was also addressed by a requirement that all building materials be from Japan, a fact emphasized in contemporary government publications.[27] A headline in an Asahi Shimbun article covering the ceremonies celebrating the completion of the building read "The Crystallization of the People's Twenty Years of Effort: The Dignity of This Great Architecture Constructed Purely from Domestic Products."[28]

The Diet was described as a "modern" building produced by means of the latest technology. One government publication documented at great length the dimensions of the structure and offered a chart comparing them with those of other great structures in Japan and elsewhere, including the Great Buddha Hall at Tōdaiji, the Egyptian Pyramids, and the airship Graf Zeppelin.[29] This was clearly an appeal to national identity through pride in Japan's technological accomplishments. Instead of asserting national identity by distinguishing Japan from other cultures, this was a claim for including Japan among the great builders of the world. This interpretation of national

9. Special Diet Architecture Office, Treasury Ministry, Imperial Diet Building, Main Facade, Tokyo, 1936. Archives of the Architectural Institute of Japan.

少年倶樂部　帝國新議事堂大模型　十二月號附錄

10. Paper model of the Imperial Diet Building made by Nakamura Seika, published by *Shōnen kurabu* (Youth Club Magazine), 1935.

identity was much more in line with such Meiji modernizers as Inoue who first began the search for a Diet design.

It should be noted that even as the new Diet took shape in the late 1920s and early 1930s, the battle continued to rage over the issue of style and national identity in architecture. The competitions for the Kanagawa Prefectural Offices (1926), Nagoya City Hall (1930), Tokyo Imperial Household Museum (1931), and other prominent public buildings specifically called for entries reflecting what was termed "Japanese taste" and awarded commissions to architects who provided designs that incorporated hipped-and-gabled tiled roofs or other easily identifiable Japanese architectural features into their designs. In these cases, the decorative programs were better integrated than in Shimoda's Diet design, but the basic strategy for Japanicizing these buildings was the same.[30]

As the Diet Building neared completion, there were many efforts to promote it as a national symbol. The newspapers included articles on various stages of the new Diet's debut. In December 1935, the young people's magazine Shōnen kurabu (Youth Club), which regularly sent do-it-yourself projects to its members, issued an elaborate paper model of the Diet for them to build.[31] That same year, one could purchase a marble commemorative mantle clock in the shape of the Diet Building.[32] The Diet Building even entered the realm of mass advertising. The soy sauce manufacturer Kikkoman placed an advertisement in Asahi Shimbun a few days before the ceremony marking the completion of the Diet that showed a striking black silhouette of the building's tower overlapped at one corner by the company logo. Through this image, Kikkoman expressed its public spirit and promoted its products at one stroke.[33]

There was also an effort to draw international attention to the new monument. As early as 1935, the English language annual Japan Illustrated featured a photograph of the building shot at a distance, with the caption "The Imperial moat and the new Diet towering in the background."[34] In 1938, the Western-language publication Nippon, which published in multiple languages, though privately produced, enjoyed official support, included the Diet as one of the featured stops on a hypothetical bus tour of Tokyo tailored to foreign tourists.[35] The International Tourist Bureau of the Railroad Ministry commissioned several photomontages of Japan, including one for the International Exposition in Paris (1937) with layered images of the Diet Building, the Great Buddha at Kamakura, Himeji Castle, modern steel bridges, Mount Fuji, downhill skiers, and a profusion of cherry trees.[36] The Tourist Bureau was attempting to entice foreign visitors with an exciting, modernized Japan—as represented, in part, by the new Diet—enhanced by carefully selected signs of the nation's exotic traditions.

The opening of the new Diet received some attention in the architectural press. There was a special issue devoted to it in the profession's longest established journal, *Kenchiku Zasshi*, and a few short articles appeared in other venues, as well. As Yamaguchi Hiroshi has pointed out, however, the coverage was surprisingly thin given the size of the project and the extraordinary energy that architects had poured into it. Yamaguchi explains this lukewarm reception by arguing that the final design did not resolve longstanding conflicts over style within the profession and that architects felt some measure of responsibility for that failure.[37]

Conclusion

The Diet Building is the product of a process of design by committee—or, rather, a long series of committees. It is a compromise—a neoclassical design denuded of much of its neoclassical detail—created for a time and place in which any fully articulated architectural style would have generated opposition from one camp or another. When it was first completed, the Diet Building attracted attention because of its novelty and scale. Yet despite the publicity surrounding it at home and abroad, there is little evidence to suggest that the building ever achieved the status of a national symbol that resonated with the Japanese public.

Since the Meiji Restoration, many architects had advocated the adoption of certain Western styles for public buildings because they were believed to be transnational or "universal." Others willingly employed modern building methods but sought to apply them in designs perceived to be uniquely local.[38] This tension was present in the history of the Diet Building from the moment designers and politicians first began to speculate about the structure in 1880s. Both camps laid their claim on the final result. The building was branded with imperial crests, and newspapers defensively hailed the domestic materials that went into the construction. On balance, however, the current building represents a victory of the "universal" over the particular—the simplified classicism of the Diet Building allowed it to function, if equivocally, as a symbol of modern governance legible both at home and abroad.

When discussing the political message conveyed through the construction of Japanese government buildings in the late 1920s and 1930s, comparisons with Japan's Axis ally Nazi Germany are perhaps inevitable. Did an architectural style emerge during this period that can be clearly and un-ambiguously linked to the regime? To what degree did the Diet Building become an emblem of the repressive policies of the Japanese state? Even in Germany, it is difficult to isolate a single "Nazi style." The classicism of Speer's monumental Zepplinfeld in Nuremberg would have to compete for that title with the steeply pitched roofs of the "Heimat style" employed in housing, schools, and other publicly sponsored construction under the Nazis. And if the effort to locate a national style under the Nazis is com-plicated, the prospect is just as challenging in Japan. The Japanese govern-ment not only sponsored the bland classicism of the Diet but also promoted structures designed in the so-called Japanese taste, such as the Imperial Household Museum, and constructed some of the best high-modern de-sign of the prewar and wartime period, such as the central post offices of Tokyo (1931) and Osaka (1938). No one political message is communicated by such diverse designs. The government did not have a single planning agency forwarding an official style: the committee under the Treasury Min-istry that developed the plans for the Diet operated apart from the Imperial Household Ministry as it built its new museum building. The Communica-tions Ministry often chose modernist designs for its post offices, telegraph offices, and schools with relative autonomy. And in each of these cases, the responsible government agency answered to different political constituen-cies and designed for different target audiences.

The Diet Building's stripped classicism and intimidating scale can be equated with the work of the Nazi architect Albert Speer. Yet it shares these characteristics with significant examples of public architecture of the 1930s in the Soviet Union, the United States, and other countries with widely di-vergent political systems. It would be difficult to argue that there is one clear meaning embedded in this generalized architectural style. It is not capable of expressing a political ideology with great precision. Rather, it is more helpful to interpret the popularity of this style as a more generalized response to the crisis facing many modern nation-states. As Barbara Miller Lane has argued in her discussion of this "stripped classicism," "Each gov-ernment felt the need to assure its citizens of its strength and durability, and each wanted a building style which was both modern and somehow old."[39] It is only at this much more amorphous level that the Diet Building was able to communicate effectively.

Throughout the 1930s, the Japanese government faced mounting criti-cism for its repressive policies at home and its expansionism abroad. In this context, the government was anxious to deploy images of its newly

JONATHAN M. REYNOLDS

completed legislature to venues around the world. The Diet Building rather than the Imperial Household Museum was selected to anchor photomontages in Japanese pavilions in Chicago and Paris. Both the constitution and the Diet originally had been formed, in part, to assuage the concerns of foreign governments. One is tempted to conclude that whether this effort was successful or not, the Diet Building was chosen to represent Japan not as an intimidating assertion of military ambitions and authoritarian will, but as a reassuring symbol of stability, modernity, and constitutional governance.

Even in the first years after its completion, the building never entirely transcended the associations attached to the institution that it housed, an institution that before and during the war was neither powerful nor popular. That ambivalence is vividly expressed, for example, in Matsumoto Shunsuke's gloomy image of the Diet painting during the dark days at the end of the war in 1944.[40] After the war, the Diet's role in the national government expanded considerably, but as a result, the Diet Building became the site of bitter political struggles and a ready target of the public's frustrations when it failed to meet their needs.[41] In the 1954 science-fiction film classic, the charismatic monster Godzilla attacks Tokyo at night. During his rampage through the city, he melts electrical towers and crushes the Waco Department Store and the Japan Theater. Godzilla looms threateningly over the Diet Building, then trudges through the structure, which crumbles in his wake. Despite desperate efforts to stop Godzilla, the government is powerless in the face of this awesome phenomenon.[42] The famous aerial photographs of massive demonstrations in front of the Diet protesting the renewal of the U.S.–Japan security treaty in 1960 are just as vivid and disturbing as the scenes in Godzilla, although they are, perhaps, less cathartic. The impression of the Diet emerging from these pictures is of a stony and aloof fortress protecting high-handed politicians from an angry citizenry. The Meiji leaders' dream of a unifying and transcendent symbol of national identity was inevitably lost to the bureaucratic process and the realities of political life in a diverse society.

Notes

This essay is a revised version of an article that appeared in *Art Journal* 55, no. 3 (fall 1996): 38–47.

1. For a discussion of Japanese leaders' study of European constitutional models, see Ian Nish, "Some Thoughts on the Origins of the Meiji Constitution, 1889," in

Rethinking Japan, vol. 2, ed. Adriana Boscaro et al. (Sandgate: Japan Library, 1990), 42–47.

2. See Peter Duus, *Party Rivalry and Political Change in Taishō Japan* (Cambridge, Mass.: Harvard University Press, 1968), 2; George Akita, "The Meiji Constitution in Practice: The First Diet," *Journal of Asian Studies* 22 (November 1962): 31.

3. Duus, *Party Rivalry and Political Change in Taishō Japan*, 24–27.

4. It is not clear why the commission chose Ende and Böckmann in particular. This may have been the result of a recommendation from the government architect Matsugasaki Tsumunaga, who had studied in Germany for an extended period of time and may have known Böckmann at that time, but it may have been the consequence of other personal contacts: see Horiuchi Masaaki, *Meiji no oyatoi kenchikuka Ende to Bekkuman* [Ende and Böckmann: Foreign Architects in Meiji Japan] (Tokyo: Inoue Shoin, 1989), 172–76.

5. For an analysis of the relationship between this Diet design and the earlier designs by Ende and Böckmann, see Horiuchi, *Meiji no oyatoi kenchikuka Ende to Bekkuman*, 240–44.

6. Examples of such structures are the Tsukiji Hotel (1868) and the Mitsui House (1872) built in Tokyo by the carpenter-contractor Shimizu Kisuke II.

7. See Hasegawa Takashi, "Gijidō e no keifu [Toward a Genealogy of the Diet Building]," in *Nihon no kenchiku: Meiji, Taishō, Shōwa* [Japanese Architecture: Meiji, Taishō, Shōwa], vol. 4, ed. Muramatsu Teijirō (Tokyo Sanseidō, 1981), 126–27.

8. See Horiuchi, *Meiji no oyatoi kenchikuka Ende to Bekkuman*, 299–301. Horiuchi is drawing on the research of Suzuki Hiroyuki.

9. Wilhelm Böckmann, "Reise nach Japan," in *Reise nach Indien* (Berlin, 1893), 85, cited in Japanese and discussed in Horiuchi, *Meiji no oyatoi kenchikuka Ende to Bekkuman*, 203.

10. Horiuchi, *Meiji no oyatoi kenchikuka Ende to Bekkuman*, 293–98.

11. Hasegawa, "Gijidō e no keifu," 126–30.

12. Although Ende's and Böckmann's urban-planning proposal was abandoned, the permanent Diet Building that was finally constructed decades later used the site that Ende and Böckmann had set aside for it. The firm completed Western-style designs for the Tokyo Court and the Justice Ministry with the aid of Japanese associates.

13. See, e.g., Muramatsu Teijirō, *Nihon kindai kenchiku no rekishi* [The History of Modern Japanese Architecture] (Tokyo: Nippon Hōsō Shuppan Kyōkai, 1977), 148.

14. Ralph Adams Cram, *My Life in Architecture* (Boston: Little, Brown, 1936), 98. It should be noted that Cram was a great admirer of Fenollosa and his colleague Okakura Kakuzō.

15. Cram recounts this story in his autobiography. Even though his design for the Diet never materialized, Cram wrote a successful book on Japanese architecture on the strength of his visit: see Cram, *Impressions of Japanese Architecture and the Allied Arts* (Rutland, Vt.: Tuttle, 1981).

16. For a discussion of this design, see also Dallas Finn, *Meiji Revisited: The Sites of Victorian Japan* (New York: Weatherhill, 1995), 99–101.

17. Hasegawa, "Gijidō e no keifu," 165; Yamaguchi Hiroshi, "Nihon no kindai gendai [Japan in the Early Modern and Modern Period]," in *Kindai gendai kenchikushi* [The History of Early Modern and Modern Architecture), *Shin kenchikugaku taikei* [New Survey of Architectural Studies], vol. 5, ed. Suzuki Hiroyuki and Yamaguchi Hiroshi (Tokyo: Shōkokusha, 1993), 309.

18. Intense professional rivalries between Tatsuno Kingo and Tsumaki Yorinaka played a role in the outcome of these various commissions that cannot be pursued in this essay: see Hasegawa, "Gijidō e no keifu," 169–76.

19. This article was originally published in *Kenchiku Zasshi* 289 (January 1911); quoted in Yamaguchi, "Nihon no kindai gendai," 310, n. 17.

20. See Yamaguchi, "Nihon no kindai gendai," 311–312.

21. From Shimoda's *Shisō to kenchiku*, privately published, 1928, as cited in Hasegawa, "Gijidō e no keifu," 179.

22. Itō Chūta, "Giin kenchiku no yōshiki ni tsuite [Concerning the Style for the Architecture for the Diet]," in Itō Chūtta, *Ronsō zuihitsu manpitsu* [The Collected Writings of Itō Chūtta), vol. 6 (Tokyo: Genshobo, 1982), 99.

23. See Hasegawa, "Gijidō e no keifu," 177–78.

24. As Muramatsu Teijirō suggests, it was not unusual in this period to hold a competition, then not commission the winning entries and yet use those entries as a starting point for the final design: Muramatsu, *Nihon kindai kenchiku no rekishi*, 153.

25. Takeuchi's design resembles the Tomb of Mausolus at Halicarnassus, which was a model for many designs in Europe and the United States at this time.

26. For a discussion of possible explanations for the choice of the stepped pyramidal form, see Suzuki Hiroyuki, "Kokkai gijidō no ishō [Design for the National Diet Building]," *Kindai gasetsu* no. 9 (2000), 10–18.

27. Ōkurashō Eizen Kanzai Kyoku, ed., *Teikoku gijidō kenchiku no gaiyō* [A Summary of the Architecture of the Imperial Diet] (Tokyo: Ōkurashō Eizen Kanzai Kyoku, 1936), 27.

28. *Asahi Shimbun*, November 9, 1936, 6.

29. Ōkurashō Eizen Kanzai Kyoku, *Teikoku gijidō kenchiku no gaiyō*, 115.

30. See my *Maekawa Kunio and the Emergence of Modernist Japanese Architecture* (Berkeley: University of California Press, 2001), 89–101.

31. Illustrated in *Nitchū sensō e no michi: Shōwa jyū nen-jyū ni nen* [The Road to the War with China, 1935–37], in *Shōwa niman nichi no zenkiroku* [Shōwa: The Complete Record of Twenty Thousand Days], vol. 4 (Tokyo: Kōdansha, 1989), 2. *Shōnen kurabu* had a readership of 750,000 in 1936.

32. Illustrated in *Nitchū sensō e no michi*, 115.

33. *Asahi Shimbun*, November 5, 1936, 11.

34. *Japan Illustrated*, 1935 (Tokyo: Nippon Dempo News Agency, 1935), 470.

35. The publication received support from the Kokusai Bunka Shinkōkai and other

government agencies. For an analysis of this innovative and controversial magazine, see Gennifer Weisenfeld, "Touring Japan-as-Museum: NIPPON and Other Japanese Imperialist Travelogues," *Positions: East Asia Cultures Critique* 8, no. 3 (winter 2000): 747–93.

36. The montages were designed by Hara Hiroshi, with photographs by Kimura Ihee, Koishi Kyoshi, and Watanabe Yoshio. The Paris montage is reproduced in Dai ichi āto sentā, ed., *Nihon shashin zenshū* [Collection of Japanese Photography] (Tokyo: Shōgakukan, 1986), fig. 27; a similar montage for the Chicago Trade Fair (1938) appears in Japan Photographers, ed., *A Century of Japanese Photography* (New York: Random House, 1980), fig. 457.

37. Yamaguchi overstates the lack of coverage to some degree. He acknowledges coverage in *Kenchiku zasshi* and *Shinkenchiku* but does not cite articles in *Kenchiku chishiki* 3, no. 3 (March 1937) or *Kenchiku to shakai* 20, no. 1 (January 1937): Yamaguchi, "Nihon no kindai gendai," 397.

38. These two groups were not always mutually exclusive, as the career of Itō Chūta vividly demonstrates.

39. Barbara Miller Lane, "Architects and Power: Politics and Ideology in the Work of Ernst May and Albert Speer," in *Art and History: Images and Their Meaning*, ed. Robert Rotberg and Theodore K. Rabb (Cambridge: Press Syndicate, 1988), 307.

40. See a discussion of this painting in Mark H. Sandler, "The Living Artist: Matsumoto Shunsuke's Reply to the State," *Art Journal* 55, no. 3 (fall 1996): 81.

41. In a recent interview, the film critic Kyoko Hirano suggested that many Japanese viewers welcomed Godzilla's "stomping on the Japanese establishment" (including the Diet Building): see James Sterngold, "Does Japan Still Need Its Scary Monster?" *New York Times*, July 23, 1995, D5. I thank Emiko Ohnuki-Tierney for this reference.

42. The English-language version of the film, which included significant cuts and additions, was released in the United States as *Godzilla: King of the Monsters* in 1956. The makers of *Godzilla* returned to the theme in the 1992 sequel *Godzilla versus Mothra*, in which a gigantic larva crashes through the Diet Building, then weaves a huge cocoon around itself and what remains of the Diet to metamorphose into Mothra.

ANGUS LOCKYER

Expo Fascism?:
Ideology, Representation, Economy

■ If one wanted to look for fascism in Japan in the 1930s, exhibitions would be a good place to start. Mass spectacle, it is clear, was a political priority in fascist Italy.[1] The repeated commemorations of the March on Rome, the monumental staging of the 1932 Exhibition of the Fascist Revolution, the mass kinaesthetics of 18 BL in the same year (an experimental theatrical performance celebrating and starring the first truck mass-produced by Fiat), and the plans for the Esposizione Universale di Roma (EUR) in 1942 were all state projects. They were designed to ensure that their audience would identify with the nation, in the person of Mussolini, and so produce a new fascist subject, which the revolution had promised and on which the regime would be based. In each case, an architectural sanctum enabled a processional sacrament. By rehearsing in material form the ideological tropes and revolutionary narrative of the movement through which the regime had come to power, they promised to transform the spectator into willing participant, both actor within the spectacle itself and acted on by their viewing of the event. The epiphanic abolition of the usual distance between viewer and viewed would produce an ecstatic union with the leader, and thus with the regime. Nor was Nazi Germany slow to recognize the potential of such events. Nuremberg rallies and Berlin Olympics, not least in Leni Riefenstahl's filmic representations, have long been recognized as one key to understanding that regime.

Fascists were not alone in their enthusiasm for spectacle, however; nor were Italy and Germany the only countries to show signs of fascism. Great exhibitions had long been used by states to mediate the shock of the new, whose iteration and amplitude following the First World War were fast becoming insufferable. As Harry Harootunian has noted, the interwar crisis of capitalism was a global one, fracturing everyday convention and traditional certainties throughout the world. Fascism therefore took its place among a number of proposed solutions that promised "capitalism without capitalism"—that is, the liberating modernity that capitalism enabled without the corrosive externalities that it had also produced. Envisioning this alternative was the work of culture, which could conjure a foundation upon which to re-establish the sense of identity and community that had been set adrift. Fascist culture shared many of its own panaceas with other visionaries. Given the anxieties of the time, it is not surprising to find a recurring and general preference for community over individual, nature over history, and form over content, or to discover Japanese thinkers among those who sought indigenous solutions to the global crisis.[2]

In conjuring up mythic pasts or possible futures for popular consumption, however, cultural producers everywhere had to confront the present absence of the desired alternative. The imagined community could not be assumed but had to be represented; spectacle promised to do so in style. The French and the Americans were quick to turn again to exhibitions after the First World War, while Los Angeles in 1932 provided the blueprint for a modern Olympics, which Hitler sought to build four years later in Berlin.[3] The fascist regimes in Germany and Italy were innovators, overcoming the inherently diffuse nature of mass spectacle by disciplining the narrative, regimenting the audience, and animating the display, as noted earlier. But the benefits of such total environments were obvious and quickly sought elsewhere. The World's Fair in New York in 1939–40 sought to produce a world of tomorrow, nowhere more than in the Futurama exhibit by General Motors, in which its audience was rapt by a panorama of the automobilized future. Fifteen years later, fair and pavilion inspired the creation of Disneyland, wherein imagined worlds were enclosed for good. No less than fascist mass spectacle, the capitalist version sought to incorporate spectators in a world from which uncertainty had been banished. Abolishing the distance between viewer and viewed not only removed the consumer from the anxieties of the present, but also encouraged him or her to buy the trademarked future on display.[4]

Generalized anxiety, common solutions, and the use of spectacle were not by themselves enough to make the icons of American corporate culture fascist. Emphasizing commonalities and genealogies in this way suggests only the extent to which the fascist regimes in Germany and Italy shared their context, preoccupations, and some procedures with others at the time. Put differently, fascism did not arise beyond the modern pale; the potential for fascism was not limited to the countries that would later become an Axis or to the 1930s. Only in Italy and Germany, however, did fascism progress from potential to proclivity, ideology, movement, and finally regime. Analyzing fascism requires that we acknowledge the potential but also mark the differences that characterized the progression. Here, too, spectacle is useful. On the one hand, fascist culture inflected familiar themes in distinctive ways, emphasizing particular solutions to the common problems of the present. Nature, community, and nation were to be restored by a rupture with the immediate, degenerate past; the recovery of a founding national endowment; the identification of the nation with its heroic leader; and an ongoing militarization through which a new national subject might be forged.[5] On the other, fascist regimes, as noted earlier, were distinguished by the extent to which the production of culture became the work of the state, rehearsing these tropes in an attempt to yoke subject to regime.[6] Spectacle is therefore one point at which to connect fascist culture to fascist politics.

It is hard to find such a spectacle in Japan, however. In what follows, I will use the small story of an exhibition that did not take place to mark the difference between Italian and German solutions to the interwar crisis and what was happening in Japan in the 1930s. The Japan World Exhibition to commemorate the 2,600th year of the Imperial Era (*Kigen 2600 nen kinen Nihon bankoku hakurankai*; hereafter, Banpaku) was planned for 1940, to take place on a couple of reclaimed islands in Tokyo Bay. Together with the Olympics, it was to be the centerpiece of a range of events commemorating the anniversary of the putative ascension of Jimmu, the first emperor, to the chrysanthemum throne in 660 B.C.E. (hereafter, Kigen 2600). Banpaku and the Olympics were both cancelled in the summer of 1938 in the wake of the invasion of China, but until then the exhibition had fit easily enough with the rhetoric and initiatives that affirmed Japan's increasingly strident self-identity and place in the world.[7] In retrospect, too, it has proved easy enough to fold it into a familiar narrative about the dark valley of early Shōwa Japan. Banpaku, like most of the decade, can be seen to have led to war, Axis, and inevitable defeat. The teleology is tempting, collapsing the exhibition and the decade as a whole into the tale of an omnipotent state exploiting the fascist potential in a society under economic siege in order to build an authoritarian, if never quite fascist, regime.[8] But it is wrong.

A close analysis reveals that this exhibition attracted interest and investment not because it promised to forge a fascist subject, but because it could seem, albeit with some effort, to be all things to all people. That is, the exhibition was one of many ways in which Imperial Japan, almost until its end, could provide a sufficiently inclusive imaginary space, inscribed on an appropriately expansive physical area, to accommodate radically diverse, even ideologically opposed, interests. As such, it may also suggest some broader conclusions for our understanding of Japan in the 1930s and of the place of fascism within it. Japan certainly shared in the general anxieties of the time, but for solutions it was able for the most part to draw on older configurations of ideology, institutions, and initiative. It may be that these were enough, in the end, to achieve similar results to those achieved by fascist regimes: the mobilization that was possible under conditions of total war and the uses that were eventually made of the anniversary both suggest affinities between Japan and its Axis allies.[9] The differences in the process by which they arrived at these solutions, however, as well as similarities between Axis and Allied representation and practice, suggest that we need to widen the frame and place at least this exhibition, but also Japan—and even, perhaps, fascism itself—within a more general, if no less troubling, history of modern political economy, as well as mass spectacle.

Origins Narratives and Imperial Destiny

The theme of the exhibition was a predictable one. As summarized in the official prospectus, the exhibition promised to "humbly commemorate the 2,600th year of the imperial era by gathering and displaying the flower of industry from home and abroad, and so contribute to the fusion of cultures east and west, the development of global industry, and the advance of international peace."[10] This was elaborated elsewhere in the promotional literature to reaffirm a set of relationships between ancient national history, recent modern accomplishments, the contemporary international situation, and future global prospects. The ritual invocation of four-character slogans served to underwrite an evolutionary account of national destiny, but one that sought to banish the possibility of change over time and so confirm the self-identity of the Japanese nation and its historical mission.[11]

The starting point was Jimmu's accession to the "imperial" throne. The mythical first monarch had thus planted the "seed" not only of the Japanese people (*ikkun banmin*) and their "unsurpassed" national spirit, but also of Japan's successful recent modernization.[12] The present was thus the "autumn," industrial development and international standing the fall crop of Jimmu's initial planting, the inevitable fruit of the original spiritual endowment, guaranteed by the unbroken imperial line (*bansei ikkei*).[13] Finally, the organic unfolding of the national genetic code would itself bring about international harmony (*bankoku kyōwa*)—sometimes glossed as the infamous "eight corners of the world under one roof (*hakkō ichiu*)"—which was both the spiritual core of the founding (*chōkoku no seishin*) and therefore the national faith (*kokumin no shinnen*).[14] All that was required, and the goal of the exhibition, was to reaffirm the basic principles of their national destiny to the Japanese people and to reveal the true meaning and pacific nature of that destiny to the world at large.[15]

The theme was susceptible to any number of variations. One of the most elaborate was the lyrics of the official exhibition march, published in March 1938:

At the dawn	of a young Asia,
A new Japan	with bright life.
Look!	Piercing the ages
The essence	of Japanese spirit

Gorgeously unfolds today.

The Japan International Exhibition.

Three more stanzas elaborated the lesson, invoking familiar symbols ("pure Yamato cherry," "graceful Fuji") to anchor the "pure history" and "great mission" of a nonetheless "young Japan."[16] Again, an unfolding but unchanging essence, buttressed by nature and seasonal metaphors, served to anchor Japan's place at the center of Asia and modernity.

Much of the rhetorical content here was shared with the slightly later promotion of the Greater East Asia Co-Prosperity Sphere. Rather than rehearse the iterations of Japan's imperial destiny, however, and damn the exhibition by rhetorical association, it seems more useful to unpick the thoroughly generic form—the very model of a modern national narrative—that structures the particular Japanese content. Briefly, such a narrative begins by assuming a point of (divine) origin freed from the contingencies of the historical environment. This assumption of autopoesis allows subsequent historical experience to be rewritten as the inevitable self-realization of a genetically programmed destiny: one studies the past to anticipate the future.[17] Temporal and spatial distinctions are collapsed: the articulation of organism and its environment and the resulting change over time are characterized as the extension across time and space of the unchanging, self-same code and so the heroic yet effortless creation of a world by the organism. Thus the exhibition's president, Ushitsuka Kotarō, could note that the absorption of Western science and civilization since the beginning of Japan's rapid modernization in the Meiji period (1868–1912) was in fact the realization of the essence of Japan's own spirit and culture.[18] The origins narrative, sustained often by a metaphor of seasonal transformation, subsumes difference, both within and without, under Japan, naturalized as the world. Modern Japanese development is not understood as the outcome of an intricate pattern of interaction with the contemporary world; rather, a world of international harmony will result from the natural development of the Japanese empire.

Such an origins narrative was hardly unique to Japan. It differed little from the autobiographies of almost all imperial powers, in which the imagined distinction of the modern nation authorized manifest destiny and civilizing mission. Nationalism imagined a unitary identity (a spiritual essence, great culture, pure history) not only as a means of defence in a competitive international system, but also to transcend the differentiated interest of a pluralist, capitalist society. International competition and capitalist interest, however, both ensured that identity and system were expansive. The universal pretensions of a civilizing mission prescribed what was profitable for some as good, if not yet to be implemented, for all. Here was one difference with the distinctive posture of fascist rhetoric. Where the latter began with rupture (from both past and world), demanded personification, expelled difference, and generalized violence, imperial nationalism asserted continuity, abstracted personality, incorporated difference, and tended, at least in rhetoric, to peace.[19] This is not to argue that either set of attributes should be read as the truth of their respective regimes. But it is to claim that the ideological means toward their acquisitive ends were distinctive.

It also suggests that both rhetoric and exhibition need to be understood within a longer history. Nowhere were the projections and evasions of modern nationalism on more obvious display than the international exhibitions of the late nineteenth century and early twentieth century. Delusional patriotism and imperial destiny were their stock in trade. The Philadelphia Centennial Exhibition of 1876, the Paris Exposition Universelle of 1889, and the Chicago World's Fair of 1893 all sought to tie universal aspirations to national commemoration. Nor had Japan been slow to explore the possibilities of their newly invented imperial tradition. Unrealized plans for an international exhibition in 1890 had also exploited the putative ascension of the first emperor, although in that case the anniversary had been the 2,550th. Late Victorian bombast and national origins were less obvious by the interwar period, but both the United States and France continued to insist on their imperial birthright and civilizing influence, even as the focus shifted to tomorrow's worlds and modern art.[20] In other words, the constructed and contradictory nature of such narratives may have been more apparent in Japan in the 1930s, but the latter still relied on the conventions of the form.

Material Form and Commemorative Space

In the linear prose of public relations and official statements, exhibition organizers and supporters could have recourse to time-honored tropes and a familiar rhetorical structure. Origins narratives provided a simple solution for bridging particular and universal by collapsing distinctions, absorbing contradiction, and so freeing the thereby imagined community from any temporal or spatial specificity. It is not surprising that problems came when the rhetoric was obliged to take specific material form, as two-dimensional graphics or three-dimensional architecture. The rhetorical sleight of hand afforded by narrative—reading modern science as ancient destiny, for example—could not be sustained in more stable media, wherein signifiers were valuable precisely for the specificity of their historical and cultural reference. The contradictions inherent in reconciling Japan and the world, the effort required to do so, and the ambivalence of the final result were apparent at every stage of the process.

The basic outlines of the problem were apparent in the jury responsible for choosing the official exhibition posters. Its discussion of the submissions was bedeviled by an uncertainty as to whether the design chosen should express the "spirit of the age," emphasizing the exhibition's international dimensions, or the "spirit of the founding," highlighting its commemorative nature. A degree of interaction with the outside world, coded as "Westernization," seemed unavoidable: many of the posters copied foreign examples, and the Chinese characters used on all of the posters were unambiguously modern. In the end, the jury was saved by being able to reward and recommend the dissemination of several posters. The winners were united in suggesting that they had sought to produce something uniquely Japanese ("Nihon-teki toiu koto," "Nihon dokuji no kanji o dashitai"), although their designs ran the gamut. At one end, a decidedly futurist dove carried a globe in a sling of national flags, emblazoned with "2600." At the other, a white Mount Fuji floated on a red ground, while a bird flew across its face. The first prize must have seemed a safe bet, finally going to a portrayal of an ancient Japanese warrior standing, facing out over an expansive plain. Even here, however, one of the jurors suggested that there was no way of knowing whether or not he was standing in Japan or, perhaps, the whole universe.[21]

The poster competition revealed a simple version of the problem that was by now wracking design in general, architecture above all, and that caught the exhibition authorities in a multiple bind. On the one hand, the ascent of international modernism had rejected cultural specificity in favor of universal form. On the other, rising nationalism, not least among the bureaucrats responsible for overseeing architectural competitions, demanded a more identifiably Japanese architecture, especially on those occasions when Japan itself was on display. Fascist architects in Germany and Italy resolved a similar dilemma by framing the functional imperatives of modernism within the dictates of neoclassical style. Japanese architecture in the 1930s also saw an updating of tradition, known as Nihon shumi (Japanese taste), which involved the use of traditional Japanese elements to ornament modern building construction. But where fascists could pass off their atavism as the heir of earlier developments, and therefore an embodiment of genuine modernity, the Japanese reversion to type marked itself as a throwback to tradition defined against the modern, an embrace of the particular against the universal.[22] The problem was particularly acute given this particular context. The anniversary demanded a visual rubric that was clearly Japanese, but an international exhibition had to incorporate the world.

The solution came in two parts, combining architectural style and site planning. First, the authorities determined that a Memorial Hall should anchor the site as a whole. The regulations for the prize competition stipulated that the hall was the "main sign" of the exhibition and therefore its style should be "sublime and majestic, symbolizing the Japanese spirit."[23] After ruminations as tortured as those of the poster committee, the judges finally picked a design by Takanashi Katsushige, who explained his entry as "pure Japanese architecture," an attempt to modernize the Sumiyoshi style, the oldest of the "globally incomparable" traditions of shrine architecture. Sano Toshikata, the chairman of the judges, noted that the architects' task had been a difficult one, the traces of the struggle visible in the variety of submissions, which had mimicked castles and temples, as well as shrines. The simplicity of the latter model had carried the day, however. The great staircase, pillars, and roof combined elegance and dignity.[24] Inside the hall, frescoes would re-create the scene at the accession of Jimmu and the subsequent development of the Japanese people from ancient times to the present.[25]

Where the Memorial Hall could solve the puzzle by divorcing steel-frame structure and throwback style, the site plan had to resort to disaggregation. Early plans had the exhibition occupying four reclaimed islands at the mouth of the Sumida River, but the final site comprised only two (present-day Toyosu and Harumi), together with a small subsidiary site devoted to marine-related exhibits in Yokohama.[26] An artist's impression with accompanying commentary, spread over four pages of the official magazine, suggested the architectural panorama that would unfurl before the visitor. He or she would approach the main gate as if visiting a shrine. Beyond it sat the Memorial Hall, a modern rendition of the most ancient of Japanese architectures. To its right were halls relating to "spirit and culture" (including Society, Health and Hygiene, Education, and the Arts); to its left, exhibits of industry and natural resources (including Mining, Engineering, and Communication and Transportation). The island would be unified throughout by a "sublime" Japanese architecture before yielding to a miscellany of exhibits and facilities on the second, executed in a "free, modern" architectural style and including Agriculture, Chemical and Manufacturing Industries, the Foreign Pavilion, various entertainments, and parking. The exhibition's unique synthesis of East and West would further underwrite Japan's claims to possibly global and certainly Asian leadership.[27]

The plans as a whole neatly recapitulated the characteristic tropes of generic exhibition design. International exhibitions had early outgrown the original single-building model of the Crystal Palace in 1851. By the late nineteenth century, the movement had developed a standard repertoire: central axes, spatial symmetry, and officially endorsed, historically pedigreed architecture for the most important buildings, as the standard against which foreign styles were set off. By the 1930s, architectural style had moved on, but the other principles remained. They were ideally suited to accommodate the evolutionary and imperial principles that still informed such exhibitions, the spatial embodiment of the narrative structure outlined earlier. Narrative and exhibition might begin with a statement of national origins but quickly moved on to provide a panorama of the world beyond the nation. This was far removed from the national sacrament for which fascist architecture was designed. There, the original covenant was reaffirmed by creating a sanctum, excluding the world, and choreographing space and time as a processional, which would culminate in the ecstatic union of subject with leader and so the state.[28] In Tokyo, by contrast, site plan and architecture had to incorporate rather than exclude, making space for multiple ways of representing the world and, perhaps most important, experiencing the exhibition.

International exhibitions, in other words, were as much about pragmatics as ideology. Nowhere is this clearer than in the discussions of the Site Planning Committee, which began meeting in January 1937.[29] Later meetings of the committee touched on questions of representation and style, but much of this labor could be delegated, or subcontracted, to juried competitions. The committee began with the study of blueprints from Paris and Chicago and spent much of its time shuttling backward and forward between visitor numbers and site plans, tinkering with plans to maximize numbers and extrapolating from numbers to address the question of how people were going to get to and move around the exhibition.[30] The most basic imperative in site planning was traffic flow and crowd control, important enough to spawn a separate transportation committee and to produce the only permanent legacy from the exhibition, the Kachidoki bridge linking Tsukiji on the mainland, southeast of the Imperial Palace, to the reclaimed islands on which the exhibition would be staged.[31] This constraint also meant that the artist's impression would remain just that. There were multiple possible entrances to the exhibition, including one that led straight into the amusement zone on the second island. After this, and the novelties of the foreign exhibits, the unique architectural synthesis of the first island may perhaps have seemed merely antiquarian, its orchestrating symmetry didactic and dry.

At the most general level, in other words, planning for the exhibition betrayed the awareness that an exhibition had to work to attract people, that attractions at an exhibition therefore had to be adequately differentiated, and that its audience had to be accounted for. There could not be only one route around the exhibition, and there would certainly not be only one kind of visitor. As ideology and representation confronted the lessons of experience, in other words, the exhibition entered the world of tradeoffs, accounting, and interest.

Interest Aggregation and Numbers Games

What is most striking about this and other exhibitions in Japan during the 1930s, as well as the initial plans for the imperial anniversary, is that they were not state projects. In the 1870s, the early Meiji state had embraced exhibitions as a central initiative in its efforts to promote industry, but its initiatives at home had been quickly supplemented and soon replaced. By the turn of the century, municipal governments had turned to exhibitions for urban development and renewal, while the emerging consumer industry seized on them following the First World War as a powerful medium for commercial expansion.[32] This combination of local government, business interest, and an emerging exhibition industry was the context for the original plans for 1940. In 1926, a consortium of local politicians, industrialists, and exhibition promoters came together to form an Exhibition Club. Three years later, it was this group that first proposed an international exhibition, to be held in 1935, as a way to attract exhibitors, visitors, and above all capital to a local economy still reeling from the aftershocks of the Great Kanto Earthquake of 1923. The initial discussions ran aground in 1931, but the initiative re-emerged the following year as the locally organized centerpiece of a government-supervised celebration of the imperial anniversary. The lead advocate was Sakatani Yoshiō, a former minister of finance and mayor of Tokyo, and with his energetic promotion and extensive connections the proposal took off.[33]

The imperial anniversary provided an ideal opportunity for such an event. As suggested earlier, national commemoration had long proved a profitable rationale for international exhibitions, precisely because of its ability to satisfy diverse imperatives: national prestige and international respectability; local development and business opportunity; foreign tourism and popular entertainment. On the one hand, given this particular occasion, it is no surprise that the exhibition employed much of the rhetoric through which the population was mobilized for empire and, eventually, war. On the other, the capacious structure of that vocabulary, suggested earlier, could bear multiple investments, by private entrepreneurs as well as state ideologues.[34] The concerns of capital were indifferent to the putative content of the brands through which it sought a return on investment, and the opportunity of an imperial anniversary promised a higher-than-usual rate of return.[35] To understand how it did so, however, requires turning from words to numbers. In pitching the 1940 event, it was the latter that were paramount, but the same figures could be cut differently for different audiences. At the national level, organizers explained how the exhibition would benefit the national balance of payments, generating at least half as much foreign currency as textiles, Japan's leading export, but at twice the profit rate.[36] To regional audiences, however, they emphasized the influx of capital to the Kanto economy, relying on the example of Paris in 1889 to suggest that the exhibition would generate twenty-seven times its own budget for local businesses.[37]

At the same time, the fact that the brand was an imperial one, and the possibility of monopolizing its value, guaranteed that the battle for marketing rights was a keen one. Sakatani and the federation were not alone in producing visions of Kigen 2600. As early as October 1933, there were reports of plans by the Home, Education, Army, and Navy ministries for a "great national festival" commemorating the anniversary as a way of "overcoming the emergency."[38] The Home Ministry, in particular, was a persistent critic of any aspect of the exhibition that might detract from the solemnity it believed appropriate to the commemoration of the nation's founding. The advance guard of these concerns was the Nihon Bunka Renmei (Japan Culture Association), which had been formed in 1933 by Matsumoto Manabu, a Home Ministry bureaucrat, and which soon sought to promote an alternative vision of the anniversary. In January 1936, the association proposed a survey of Japanese culture together with four other projects, and a year later it published a comprehensive "Outline of Publicity Policy for Kigen 2600."[39] However, despite the organization's efforts, only the survey, of the five projects, was taken up by the government, its authorized budget of 1 million yen only a third of that initially proposed, and dwarfed by the expected 50 million yen cost of the exhibition. Although the Ministry of Education did subsidize the Japan Culture Association, the association remained on the periphery of the official plans for Kigen 2600, for which the exposition and the Olympics remained the centerpiece.

The Home Ministry and its allies were able to gain more leverage, though never the upper hand, by translating their concerns into the budgetary language of the exhibition's promoters. Financing an exhibition was never easy. Other decisions could be made in-house, but an international exhibition always required government funding, implying trade-offs with other bureaucratic interests and so providing an opening for possible compromise. In his proposal in 1932, Sakatani had emphasized that the success of earlier international exhibitions, notably at Paris in 1900, had rested in large part on advance ticket sales, which could finance the substantial expenses that fell due before the exhibition opened. To get potential visitors to buy tickets in advance, however, there had to be some incentive. A lottery seemed ideal.[40] Over time, however, this proposal ran into problems, with the Home Ministry leading the charge against the damage that speculation would do to the national spirit.[41] The association counterattacked, using the pages of the official magazine to claim that the exhibition itself was Jimmu's dying wish. The rhetoric was eye-catching, but the Home Ministry was fighting a rearguard action. In the cabinet and government committees, the lottery had been accepted as a fait accompli, with the point at issue being how far in advance the tickets should be sold and the financial value of the prizes. The debate rumbled on for another year, but all parties finally and predictably agreed to meet somewhere in the middle, the Diet passing the necessary law in August 1937. In March 1938, the first one million advance tickets were sold, many seemingly swept up in the dreaded speculative "fever," and in May the prize winners were announced. Among the ten first-prize winners, each of whom received 2,000 yen, was Sakatani, who immediately assured reporters that he would donate his prize to the Celebration Committee.[42]

The lottery was not the only issue on which entertainment and industry had to compromise with commemoration. In February 1938, the president of the exhibition spoke to the Tokyo City Council. He began by noting that while previous exhibitions had always had an aristocrat or bureaucrat as their president, the government had realized that this exhibition required the experience of the private sector. He then turned to numbers, citing the economic impact of the Chicago fair in 1933. His audience could expect the same of Banpaku. Given the war in China, they predicted only half the normal number of foreign visitors, but nonetheless the exhibition could be expected to generate 355 million yen in demand for the region. The number might be even higher if the exhibition could do what it wanted: special theme days and a slew of entertainments would certainly attract the crowds. But given the solemn significance of Kigen 2600, it would be difficult to make the exhibition as lively as one might want. Entertainment had to be kept within limits, and so, perhaps, the exhibition's attraction would be limited. Still, he promised, it would be a success.[43]

Conclusion

In the end, of course, national concerns trumped global outreach. On July 15, 1938, the cabinet announced that the exhibition, together with the Tokyo Olympics, were to be postponed indefinitely. At this point, Japanese essence proved incompatible with international affairs: material and meaning were restricted, devoted to the prosecution of the war. But while the exhibition was eventually swept away by the Japanese invasion of China, it is important not to subsume it within a narrative governed by that aggression. Until then, Kigen 2600 imposed limits, but it was not yet enough to overwhelm or even transform the exhibition itself. The latter, I have argued, needs to be understood not primarily in terms of a state mobilizing a nation for war, but in terms of a local economy seeking investment and recovery through the proven medium of international exhibition. From the late nineteenth century on, exhibitions had been adept at reconciling private, local, and state interests, putting national history and imperial destiny alongside modern industry and popular attraction. Like the origins narratives and capitalist economies of the empires in which they took shape, exhibitions could accommodate any number of players, providing some basic rules but requiring only a sufficiently expansive area within which to resolve the inevitable contradictions. The exhibition planned for Tokyo in 1940 was no different.[44]

In this light, the planning for the exhibition also suggests some broader conclusions for our understanding of Japan in the 1930s. Fascism may help us identify certain features of cultural production during that time, the clarity of whose constellation in Italy and Germany reveal both their utility in covering the fractured nature of contemporary experience and the eagerness with which they were also adopted elsewhere. Fascist culture, however, differs in key particulars from the emphases evident in the rhetoric surrounding at least the initial plans for the imperial anniversary. Moreover, analyses of fascist culture alone cannot explain how and why aesthetics and ideology could become regime. Spectacle suggests one way in which fascist culture was linked to politics but again marks the difference between contemporary developments in Japan and the countries that would later become its allies. Rather than using fascism to mark Japan as exceptional, therefore, and so confine it to an Axis that was yet to appear, it may be more useful to emphasize the extent to which developments in Japanese political economy, society, and culture during the 1930s were similar to those elsewhere in the world.

Two patterns seem significant here. The first dates to the late nineteenth-century world of industry and empire, of which international exhibitions were one self-congratulatory expression. Here, origin narratives justified hierarchy as the consequence of progress, rather than conflict and conquest, scripting development as the outcome of unique endowments and singular histories. As imperial commemoration, then, Banpaku echoed familiar themes, providing grandiose justification for municipal initiative and business interest. Japan in the 1930s, by this account, was a particular blend of a familiar brew of capitalist economy, differentiated society, and imperial polity, with its distinctive notes of nationalist bombast and exceptionalism. At the same time, however, a second pattern was emerging, born in large part of the consequences of the first. Globally, colonial nationalism was beginning to throw the rules of the imperial club into question, while socialism refused to accept the distributions of capital. Domestically, economic dislocation and social unrest provided the incentive and 1929 the opportunity for massive, unprecedented state intervention in the economy, ranging from Stalinist planning through Rooseveltian New Deal to fascist corporatism. This second pattern is also faintly visible in the planning of the exhibition as a local response to the dilemmas of uneven development.

Here, however, Banpaku points for the most part past 1945. Given the economy's relative resilience in the early 1930s and subsequent subordination to the unproductive demands of total war, the full-blown emergence of the developmentalist state had to wait until after the war, unlike its welfare counterparts in Europe and the United States.[45] When it did arrive, however, exhibitions were again part of the arsenal of development, milled by the bureaucrats of the Ministry of International Trade and Industry. The early postwar reiterated the prewar pattern, the state concentrating its efforts overseas through the newly minted Japan External Trade Organization and municipalities and newspapers seizing on exhibitions as a catalyst for recovery. By the 1960s, however, in the wake of liberalization, the government had to supplement export promotion with domestic demand. Big events became the means of choice not only to prime the economic pump, but also to provide the social capital with which to plan development and so even out the concentrations and distortions of unprecedented economic growth.[46]

In this sense, Tokyo's plans for 1940 came to fruition in the 1964 Olympics and the 1970 Osaka Expo. Given the innovations in mass spectacle during the 1930s and '40s, it was no surprise that the Olympics took precedence. But while the Olympics transformed the capital, it was the Osaka Expo that got people onto the new bullet trains, leading to a national campaign to "Discover Japan" and a boom in domestic and international tourism.[47] The 64,218,770 visitors to the Senri Hills in the summer of 1970, 15 billion yen in profit, and estimated 1.244 billion yen the expo generated in demand suggests that the Exhibition Club may well have been on the right track in the 1930s.[48] Prewar nationalism and imperial bombast may have been absent, but broader continuities remained. An evolutionary theme, "Progress and Harmony for Mankind," together with an expansive site, still proved able to accommodate not only the diverse interests of national and corporate exhibitors but even the Cold War rivalry of the United States and the Soviet Union. Expo '70 may not have been an exact replica of its predecessor, but anyone who still had his or her tickets from the Tokyo event was welcome to use them in Osaka, thirty years after the fact. Given the similarities between the two events, it was perhaps only appropriate that the backers of development should see some return on their investment.

Notes

1. The following draws on Jeffrey T. Schnapp, "Epic Demonstrations: Fascist Modernity and the 1932 *Exhibition of the Fascist Revolution*," in *Fascism, Aesthetics, and Culture*, ed. Richard J. Golsan (Hanover, N.H.: University Press of New England, 1992); *Staging Fascism: 18 BL and the Theater of Masses for Masses* (Stanford, Calif.: Stanford University Press, 1996); Mabel Berezin, *Making the Fascist Self: The Political Culture of Interwar Italy* (Ithaca, N.Y.: Cornell University Press, 1997); and Simonetta Falasca-Zamponi, *Fascist Spectacle: The Aesthetics of Power in Mussolini's Italy* (Berkeley: University of California Press, 1997).

2. Harry Harootunian, *Overcome by Modernity: History, Culture, and Community in Interwar Japan* (Princeton, N.J.: Princeton University Press, 2000); idem, *History's Disquiet: Modernity, Cultural Practice, and the Question of Everyday Life* (New York: Columbia University Press, 2000).

3. On exhibitions, see Robert W. Rydell, *World of Fairs: The Century-of-Progress Expositions* (Chicago: University of Chicago Press, 1993); Sylviane Leprun, *Le Théâtre des Colonies: Scénographie, acteurs et discours de l'imaginaire dans les expositions, 1855–1937* (Paris: L'Harmattan, 1986). On the Olympics, see Allen Guttmann, *The Olympics: A History of the Modern Games* (Urbana: University of Illinois Press, 1992).

4. On Futurama and for a picture of visitors "assessing the future," see Rydell, *World of Fairs*, 133–35. On Disney, see Steven Watts, *The Magic Kingdom: Walt Disney and the American Way of Life* (Boston: Houghton Mifflin, 1997); Stephen M. Fjellman, *Vinyl Leaves: Walt Disney World and America* (Boulder, Colo.: Westview Press, 1992).

5. This is only a partial list, which references an extensive literature devoted to identifying the differentia specifica of fascism. Two excellent recent surveys are Stanley G. Payne, *A History of Fascism, 1914–1945* (Madison: University of Wisconsin Press, 1995); and Roger Griffin, *The Nature of Fascism* (London: Pinter, 1991).

6. On Italy, see the sources in n. 1. On Germany, see Stephanie Barron, ed., *Degenerate art: The Fate of the Avant-Garde in Nazi Germany* (Los Angeles: Los Angeles County Museum of Art, 1991); Jonathan Petropoulos, *Art as Politics in the Third Reich* (Chapel Hill: University of North Carolina Press, 1996).

7. See Shōkōshō, "Kigen 2600 nen Kinen Nihon Bankoku Hakurankai ni tsuite," *Shūhō* 82 (May 11, 1938): 13–19.

8. See, e.g., Imai Shin'ichi, "'Hakkō Ichiu' no kage de," in Asahi Jānaru, ed., *Shōwa shi no shunkan 2* (Asahi Shinbunsha, 1974), 325–33.

9. For recent arguments along these lines, see E. Bruce Reynolds, ed., *Japan in the Fascist Era* (New York: Palgrave Macmillan, 2004).

10. Nihon Bankoku Hakurankai Jimukyoku, *Kigen 2600 nen Kinen Nihon Bankoku Hakurankai Gaiyō*, 1.

11. Four-character phrases, or *cheng yu* (lit., formulated expressions) were and are widely used in Chinese and were also eagerly adopted into Japanese. From the beginning of Japanese modernization, in the Meiji period, they provided a convenient medium through which government and ideologues could trumpet broad national goals. In the late nineteenth century, the chief of these was *fukoku kyōhei* (rich country, strong army).

12. *Banpaku*, no. 1., May 1936, 5. *Banpaku* was the official monthly magazine of the exhibition association, combining statements of support by prominent public figures and essays on the significance of the exhibition with updates on the work of the various committees.

13. The autumnal metaphor appeared early and lasted long: See Nihon Bankoku Hakurankai Kyōkai, *Kigen 2600 nen Kinen Nihon Bankoku Hakurankai*, 6, and *Banpaku*, no. 21, February 1938, 5. For attributions of recent developments to Jimmu's founding of the nation and its attendant spiritual bequest, see *Banpaku*, no. 1, May 1936, no. 2, June 1936, 7, 28.

14. Nihon Bankoku Hakurankai Jimukyoku, *Kigen 2600 nen Kinen Nihon Bankoku Hakurankai Gaiyō*, 4; *Banpaku*, no. 1, May 1936, 4.

15. *Banpaku*, no. 1, May 1936, 5, no. 2, June 1936, 28.

16. Ibid., no. 22, March 1938, 2.

17. Ibid., no. 3, July 1936, 22.

18. Nihon Bankoku Hakurankai Kyōkai, *Kigen 2600 nen Kinen Nihon Bankoku Hakurankai*, 20.

19. On the former, see Payne, *A History of Fascism*; Griffin, *The Nature of Fascism*.

20. Rydell, *World of Fairs*, esp. chap. 3, "Coloniale Moderne"; Leprun, *Le Théâtre des Colonies*. James D. Herbert, *Paris 1937: Worlds on Exhibition* (Ithaca, N.Y.: Cornell University Press, 1998), emphasizes that empire was hardly absent even when the nominal focus was art.

21. *Banpaku*, no. 15, July 1937, 10 ff.

22. See Inoue, "Pari Hakurankai Nihonkan, 1937"; Jacqueline M. Kestenbaum, "Modernism and Tradition in Japanese Architectural Ideology, 1931–1955," Ph.D. diss., Columbia University, New York, 1992; Jonathan M. Reynolds, *Maekawa Kunio and the Emergence of Japanese Modernist Architecture* (Berkeley: University of California Press, 2001).

23. Nihon Bankoku Hakurankai, ed., *Kigen 2600 nen Kinen Nihon Bankoku Hakurankai*

Chōkoku Kinen Kan Kenshō Kyōgi Sekkei Zushū. The desired permanence of the hall—and of what it signified—required modifications in the traditional signifier. The building was to be steel framed and would include a suite of rooms for the emperor and his attendants, facilities for the VIPs, a large hall including a stage for two thousand, committee rooms, dining rooms, a movie theater, and a viewing platform.

24. *Banpaku*, no. 19, December 1937, 4–5. The judges chose another submission by Takanashi as their runner-up. They claimed to have been surprised to discover the common authorship, although a brief glance at both reveals an obvious family resemblance. Sano commented that the innovative insertion of windows into the roof was a striking feature but detracted from the building's elegance and splendor. As Takanashi noted, his second design was not as faithful to the ancient model as his first.

25. *Banpaku*, no. 27, July 1938, 20.

26. The earlier plan included much of the reclaimed land to the west of present-day Daiba and north of Tokyo Big Site. The first island after the main gate (present-day Toyosu 4 and 5 chome) was devoted to exhibit halls; the next (Shinonome 1) had a memorial hall to the founding of the nation, two large, hangar-like exhibit halls, and an amphitheater for musical performances; the third (Shinonome 2) had circular exhibit halls, two outdoor theaters, and a pleasure garden; and the fourth (Ariake 1 and 2) had foreign pavilions, concessions, stalls, a theater, and an airstrip: Nihon Bankoku Hakurankai Kyōkai, *Kigen 2600 nen Kinen Nihon Bankoku Hakurankai.*

27. *Banpaku*, no. 27, July 1938, 15–18. See also Nihon Bankoku Hakurankai Jimu-kyoku, *Kigen 2600 nen Kinen Nihon Bankoku Hakurankai Gaiyō*, 18–19.

28. See, e.g., Schnapp, "Epic Demonstrations."

29. Reports of the meetings can be found in *Banpaku*, but the agenda and somewhat telegraphic minutes are available as *Kigen 2600 nen Kinen Nihon Bankoku Hakurankai Kaijō Keikaku Iinkai* in the Tokyo Metropolitan Archives. These files seem to have belonged to Uchida Yoshikazu, who was also a member of the committee.

30. It is this that seems to have led to the decision to abandon the first, four-island plan for the final, two-island solution. Earlier exhibitions were on the table at the first meeting (January 1, 1937); the four-island blueprint, dated March 20, 1936, at the second (February 1, 1937); and visitor predictions, at the third (February 12, 1937). The file includes a version of the two-island blueprint dated July 15, 1937, and labeled *mi-kettei* (undecided), but I assume this was adopted. Preliminary rules for the Memorial Hall competition were drawn up at the fourth meeting, whose records are missing. The rules were amended at the fifth meeting (August 11, 1937), and the committee began to discuss general questions of style at the sixth meeting (October 27, 1937).

31. The transportation committee's records can also be found in the Tokyo Metropolitan Archives.

32. See Yoshida Mitsukuni, *Bankoku hakurankai: gijutsu bummeishi-teki ni* (Nihon Hōsō Shuppan Kyōkai, 1970); Yoshimi, Shun'ya, *Hakurankai no seijigaku: manazashi no kindai* (Chūō Kōronsha, 1992).

33. The narrative is well chronicled in Furukawa Takahisa, *Kōki, banpaku, orinpikku,* much of which can also be found in idem, "Kigen 2600 nen hōshuku kinen jigyō o meguru seiji katei," *Shigaku zasshi* 103, no. 9 (September 1994): 1573–608.

34. Exhibitions and empire had long proved attractive to entertainment entrepreneurs: see, e.g., Breandan Gregory, "Staging British India," in J. S. Bratton et al., eds., *Acts of Supremacy: The British Empire and the Stage, 1790–1930* (Manchester: Manchester University Press, 1991), 150–78.

35. In using the idea of brand, I am following Furukawa, *Kōki, banpaku, orinpikku,* 19, 58, 217–18, 230–34. In other words, the anniversary and the slogans that surrounded it can be seen as valuable pieces of conceptual real estate, which could be turned to a variety of ends. Furukawa suggests that the predominance of private initiative requires that we classify the anniversary itself within an unproblematic history of economic development. This overstates the case; it also underestimates the usefulness of the idea of a brand as something that can encourage both loyalty (in this case, national service) and investment (the expectation of economic return).

36. *Banpaku*, no. 21, February 1938, 13–15.

37. Ibid., no. 13, May 1937, 6–7. This level of aggregate demand also promised individual windfalls. Land speculation had long been part and parcel of exhibition history, and Sakatani spent some time in his original proposal advocating a site in Kawasaki belonging to the Tokyo Bay Reclamation Company, of which he was one of the directors: Furukawa, *Kōki, banpaku, orinpikku,* 78–82. See pp. 3–8 for the land speculation surrounding an earlier exhibition, planned for 1912.

38. Furukawa, *Kōki, banpaku, orinpikku,* 93, citing *Denki Nippō*, November 30, 1933.

39. The latter suggested that the government should take the opportunity to "strengthen our national self-awareness of the true Japan, and display a correct Japan at home and abroad. Thus by contributing to the maturation of our national strength and proclaiming our national authority throughout the world, we can expect the achievement of our national destiny": ibid., 110–16.

40. Ibid., 82.

41. The objections were elaborated by Matsumoto in a pamphlet published privately in April 1936. The imperial anniversary, he argued, was essentially a religious ceremony in honor of the country's ancestors and as such should be supported by the family purse, however straitened its finances. Borrowing, or gambling, would compromise the integrity of the ritual: ibid., 112.

42. Ibid., 117–18, 122 ff., 138 ff. See also *Banpaku*, no. 21, February 1938, 4 ff.

43. *Banpaku*, no. 22, March 1938, 11–14.

44. The pages of its official magazine provide striking witness to this chameleon-like ability of the event to be all things for all people. The occasional advocate

for Esperanto could thus appear among the admittedly more frequent calls for renewing.

45. See Chalmers A. Johnson, *MITI and the Japanese Miracle: The Growth of Industrial Policy, 1925–1975* (Stanford, Calif.: Stanford University Press, 1982).

46. For the place of big events within the discourse of development, see Tada Osamu, *Okinawa imēji no tanjō: aoi umi no karuchuraru sutadīzu* (Tōyō Shinpōsha, 2004).

47. See Tada, *Okinawa imēji no tanjō*, 24–29.

48. *Official Report of the Japan World Exposition*, vol. 1, 16–19, vol. 2, 362–73, vol. 3, 124.

ELLEN SCHATTSCHNEIDER

The Work of Sacrifice in the Age of Mechanical Reproduction: Bride Dolls and Ritual Appropriation at Yasukuni Shrine

■ Yasukuni Shrine and its companion, the Yūshūkan Museum of Military History, located immediately north of the Imperial Palace in Tokyo's Kudan district, are among postwar Japan's most controversial sites. Within Yasukuni are enshrined the souls of approximately 2.5 million persons who have died in service to Japanese military since 1868, including fourteen Class A war criminals executed by the victorious Allies in the wake of the Second World War. Visits to the shrine by leading Japanese politicians, including the prime minister, inevitably unleash a firestorm of criticism across East Asia, especially in China and Korea. Critics of Japan's conduct during the war are no less outraged by the contents of the Yūshūkan Museum, which celebrates Japan's modern military history and pointedly denies any ethical wrongdoing by the Imperial Army or Navy during the 1931–45 conflicts in Asia and the Pacific.

To what extent may these two institutions be understood as coherent ideological and aesthetic undertakings? To their critics in mainland East Asia and among the Japanese left, these institutions exemplify unrepentant rightist nationalism. They are often denounced as anachronistic instruments of militarist State Shintō, through which the mainstream Japanese populace is encouraged to absolve their nation and their leaders of accountability for mass atrocities during the 1931–45 Asia-Pacific War. In turn, the defenders of the shrine and the museum present the complex as unambiguously dedicated to the principles of "peace," venerating the apotheosized souls of those who died in military service so that Japan may enjoy the postwar blessings of security and prosperity. In this essay, I will complicate these now familiar arguments by closely examining one specific development in the modern history of Yasukuni. Since the 1980s, about one hundred fifty bride dolls (*hanayome ningyō*) have been dedicated at Yasukuni by bereaved families to the souls of soldiers and sailors who died before marriage. Although senior priests at the shrine were initially reluctant to accept the dolls, the figurines are now displayed in the shrine's receptions halls and are viewed by the many hundreds of thousands of worshippers who come each year to pay their respects to the war dead. Six of these dolls were incorporated into the penultimate gallery of the Yūshūkan Museum during its renovation in 2002 and now occupy a place of honor within the museum.

The bride dolls pose several puzzles. To begin with, for most of its history Yasukuni (and its forerunner institution, the Shōkonsha) was dedicated to the principle that people who died in military service to the emperor were swiftly elevated to the status of national-level divinities (*mikoto* or *kamigami*) and were in effect separated from their prior domestic and familial identities. During the war, bereaved families were actively chastised by Yasukuni priests for addressing the dead by name; instead, they were instructed to pray collectively to all of the sacralized national war heroes.[1] Individuated prayers, it was argued, carried popular Buddhistic associations, unbecoming to State Shintō practice. Yet each modern bride doll at Yasukuni is emphatically dedicated to a specific dead man and often bears the names of specific bereaved relations. What is more, the postwar practice of bride-doll dedication was developed in popular Buddhist institutions and initially carried antimilitarist associations. In popular Buddhist establishments in northeastern Japan, the beauty of the bride dolls is widely understood as an offering to the unquiet dead, a propitiatory intervention aimed at lost souls (*muenbotoke*) whose tortured spirits would otherwise wander restlessly between this world and the other world.

Yet Yasukuni's supporters resolutely maintain that all the war dead, by virtue of their death in service to the emperor, have been transformed into divinities and are in no sense wandering or unquiet spirits. Why, then, have these memorial dolls been so extensively incorporated into the modern shrine and museum complex? In this chapter, I will argue that the growing popularity of the bride dolls at Yasukuni alerts us to important ambiguities and tensions in the shrine's contemporary ideological and aesthetic dynamics. Like national-level institutions the world over, Yasukuni has long celebrated the triumph of the state over the level of the domestic and kinship-based units of affiliation. Through shedding blood in national service, the military war dead symbolically help re-constitute the nation as a mystical community that transcends the conventional consanguinal and affinal ties of the family. Yasukuni powerfully functions as a grand theater of nationalist communion, incorporating its living and dead players into a cyclical state-centered drama of death and collective regeneration that echoes other fascist aesthetic projects in Japan and elsewhere.

Yet although Yasukuni Shrine and the Yūshūkan Museum unquestionably draw extensively on the broad repertoire of fascist aesthetics, the institutions' mass appeal to a sizable section of the Japanese populace is not entirely reducible to the drawing power of fascist aesthetics or fascist ideology. The shrine has unexpectedly emerged as a kind of alternative stage on which its lay visitors have projected more personalized dramas of family and kinship. The bride dolls in effect are suspended between competing moral and aesthetic registers, partially encompassed within Yasukuni's dominant symbolic and political narrative while also affording the possibility of alternative, unresolved stories of family loss and trauma. In important respects, I will argue, many of the laypeople who worship at Yasukuni have produced partially alternative and idiosyncratic sites of family grief that stand at odds with the homogenizing force of the shrine's dominant fascist aesthetic.

Political Aesthetics, Kitsch, and the "Optical Unconscious" in the Yūshūkan Museum

Through successive incarnations over the years, most display strategies in the Yūshūkan Museum have profoundly resonated with general principles of fascist aesthetics. The principles may be fruitfully approached through Walter Benjamin's classic discussion of modern experiences of the image, "The Work of Art in the Age of Mechanical Reproduction." Benjamin argues that modern technologies of mass image reproduction, especially photography, have deprived objects and artworks of their original "aura" of authenticity and of their seeming, primary anchoring in lived experience. Into this void has stepped fascism, which renders politics aesthetic, a process that culminates in mechanized war on a mass scale. Benjamin quotes

F. T. Marinetti's Futurist Manifesto, written in support of Italy's invasion of Ethiopia in the first decade of the twentieth century:

War is beautiful because it initiates the dreamt-of metallization of the human body. War is beautiful because it enriches a flowering meadow with the fiery orchids of machine guns. War is beautiful because it combines the gunfire, the cannonades, the cease-fire, the scents of putrefaction into a symphony. War is beautiful because it creates new architecture, like that of the big tanks, the geometrical formation flights, the smoke spirals of burning villages.

Remarks Benjamin, "Mankind, which in Homer's time was an object of contemplation for the Olympian gods, now is one for itself. Its self-alienation has reached such a degree that it can experience its own destruction as an aesthetic pleasure of the first order."[2]

Photographic and film technologies, for Benjamin, operate to produce what he termed an *optical unconscious*, holding great potential for both liberation and oppression. In the modern world, photographs, of course, do have an aura, although of a rather different kind than that once possessed by singular premodern "irreproducible" works of art. Even Benjamin, who saw photography as undercutting the ritual functions of the image, acknowledges that early portrait photographs had uncanny, numinous qualities, survivals of archaic ancestral cults. He observes, "The cult of remembrance of loved ones, absent or dead, offers a last refuge for the cult value of the picture. For the last time the aura emanates from the early photographs in the fleeting expression of the human face."[3]

Benjamin's insights are consistent with the more recent literature on kitsch as a privileged form of fascist aesthetics. For the sake of convenience, let us define kitsch as aesthetic representations (often mass reproduced through industrial techniques) organized according to the lowest common denominations of accepted beauty, fabricated to elicit singular and uncomplicated emotional responses. In Nazi artistic and aesthetic projects, some scholars have argued, kitsch suppresses or neutralizes the profoundly disturbing and disruptive features of death, "turning them into sentimental idyll."[4] The reliance on clichéd, stereotypical imagery; the avoidance of subtle or ambiguous evocations of pain; and the redundant emphasis on familiar conventions of representation all serve to render death seemingly knowable and comprehensible within the framework of sentimental pieties.

Kitschy representations of war dead, in particular, serve to reassure the viewer that the nation, on whose behalf the honored dead have sacrificed themselves, will triumph and live eternally. The standardized qualities of kitschy memorial objects are thus highly conducive to nationalist projects. As Susan Sontag argues, kitsch intimately links "beauty" to a kind of timeless death forever associated with youth and outside the normal process of aging and the conventional human community.[5] Familiar, sentimentalized works of art in effect proclaim: who among us cannot feel the same emotional response to the spectacle of duty and noble sacrifice? This inferred common, populist emotional response is simultaneously representative and constitutive of the dreamed-of homogenous national imagined community that is exemplified by fascism, and that appears to some extent in all modern societies.

In many respects, the renovated Yūshūkan Museum celebrates the merger of flesh and metal, body and machine, image and spirit dreamed of by futurist and fascist aestheticians. Visitors initially pass by a great Manchukuo-era locomotive and fighter plane in the entrance foyer before ascending to the second floor to view a long, elaborate film celebrating the living spirits of the heroic war dead. Numerous black-and-white photographs of martyred soldiers and sailors, especially the *tokkōtai* (Special Attack Forces, known in the West as kamikaze), are superimposed over cinematic pans of contemporary Japanese men and women. The narrator explains that all living Japanese are protected by the supreme sacrifice of the war dead, who continue to "look after and defend the living and all of Japan (*Nihon o mamoru tameni*)." In looking at the kamikaze, the film in effect argues, "we" see a transmuted, reflected vision of ourselves.

In this respect, the film replicates the standard experience of prayer at Yasukuni in the shrine building immediately adjacent to the museum. Worshippers are brought to the highest level of the shrine to offer their respects to the deified soldiers. There they look into a great mirror, much larger and much lower than in other shrines. As they look into the inner sanctuary of the main shrine (*honden*), where the deified dead are believed to reside, visitors are immediately confronted by their own reflections staring back at them. This implicit transposition between shrine and museum is intensified halfway through the museum, as visitors enter a darkened room that is centered on an elaborate model of Yasukuni as it appeared at night during the Asia-Pacific War, from 1931 to 1945. In the background plays an audiotape of the State Shintō ceremony of enshrinement (*shōkonsha*) broadcast repeatedly during the war on NHK, the national radio service, through which the souls of dead soldiers were raised to the status of divinities (*mikoto*). Delicate laser-filament technology replicates the nocturnal procession of lit lanterns through the shrine precincts, from the "Shoka" garden in the northwestern shrine precincts to the inner sanctuary itself. Visitors are encouraged, in effect, to participate vicariously in this animated simulacrum of the invisible deification of the honored dead. The final galleries of the museum again emphasize the enduring, uncanny presence of the kamikaze, hovering between their preserved visible images and subtle evocations of their invisible presence. Hundreds of photographs of the dead heroes, specifically identified as divinities (*kamigami*), line the walls of several rooms; beautifully arranged cases display personal objects left behind by the kamikaze, tangible evidence of their absence. One especially popular case displays a mirror case (to which I will return later) given to the Navy pilot Lieutenant Sumida Tetsuo by his mother instead of a photograph.[6] Accompanying text asserts that his mother told him that because he looked like her, he would see her each time he looked into the mirror.

The museum's final hall, which was largely unaltered during the museum's most recent (2002) renovations, is a particularly pointed illustration of fascist aesthetics as characterized by Benjamin. Here, the instruments of self-willed death and destruction used by kamikaze, including the "cherry-blossom" gliders (*okha*) and human torpedoes (*kaiten*), are lovingly displayed. Death in the service of the nation, especially death classified as voluntary and freely chosen, is unambiguously glorified. Celebrating syntheses of flesh and metal, of spirit and technology, these installations invite the visitor to participate vicariously in the martyrdom and apotheosis of the kamikaze. Self-destruction is indeed presented as supreme aesthetic pleasure. Visitors are invited, in effect, to imagine themselves inside these vehicles on their final missions of no return. At the end of hall is displayed a popular panoramic painting depicting the Kaigun Jinrai Butai (Navy Divine Thunder Squadron) heading across the sea near Okinawa into the rosy rising sun on its final attack run toward American naval targets. The pilots, a caption proclaims, vowed to meet one another beneath a special cherry tree on the grounds surrounding Yasukuni. The tree still stands, marked with a sign, to be visited by museum-goers after they have toured the exhibition. In this manner, the symbolic identification between dead kamikaze and living Japanese visitors is further reinforced. Like a pilgrim honoring a revered saint, the visitor retraces the physical and spiritual journey of the late martyr.

Dolls, War, and Memorialization in Japan

Before considering how the bride dolls have been situated over the past two decades within this rightist landscape of military memorialization, it is helpful to review the broader ritual functions of doll figurines in Japanese culture and history. For centuries, perhaps millennia, dolls and human figurines in Japan have been understood as prophylactic guardians of living persons, warding off and absorbing dangerous influences that would otherwise have polluted or injured their human charges. These practices are a feature of the long history of substitute or vicarious (migawari) image making in Japan, in which images have been apprehended as semi-animate substitutes of divinities or persons. These mimetic forms are believed to ease people through personal and cosmological transitions.[7] The dolls displayed by Japanese families on the March 3 festival of Girls' Day (hina matsuri), for example, are transformations of ritual paper or straw dolls (kata shiro and nagashibina) that, having absorbed people's sins and illnesses, were placed in rivers or other bodies of running water during an important purification ceremony on the third day of the third lunar month. To this day, families express gratitude to the children's dolls, which have in effect soaked up the pollution, disease, and dangers to which the young have been exposed. Doll symbolism was modified following the Meiji Restoration in 1868 as the doll market was increasingly rationalized and industrialized, as dolls became metonymic of "Japaneseness" in an internationalist framework, and as the Imperial Family (increasingly represented in doll forms) was presented as the idealized model for all Japanese families.

During the Meiji period (1868–1910) and Taishō period (1910–24), European techniques were incorporated by Japanese doll artisans to produce the forerunners of the modern kimono-clad bride doll, developed initially for overseas and tourist markets. Dolls took on increasingly militarist associations in the early decades of the twentieth century. From the early 1930s onward, schoolgirls and female relatives of Imperial Army soldiers were encouraged to make small cloth dolls, known variously as care dolls (imon ningyō) or mascot dolls (masukotto), for serving military personnel. For most of the war period, these figurines functioned as protective talismans, in a manner similar to amulets (omamori). But in the war's final months, these dolls were increasingly sent to kamikaze fighters to serve as ritual "companions" on their missions of no return. In some instances, unmarried pilots were given gifts of elaborate dolls, specifically termed "bride dolls (*hanayome ningyō*)," as symbolic wives in the other world.[8] Significantly, these objects were often termed "*migawari ningyō* (vicarious or substitute dolls)." The figurines, it was often said, would allow their makers to accompany the pilots in their final missions while absorbing the pain and suffering of the martyrs' lonely deaths.

At times, dolls took on explicit memorial functions for recently deceased pilots; in some cases they were dropped from the air by comrades over the sites where dead pilots were believed to have crashed. Letters written by military personnel late in the war sometimes hint at the dolls' capacity to mediate relations between the worlds of the dead and of the living. For example, an elementary-school girl, Shizue, who had made a doll and sent it to her brother, Kiyoshi Oishi, a kamikaze pilot, received this letter from one of his comrades:

> Miss Shizue Oishi, I suppose you are surprised at the sudden letter from a stranger. I am a soldier who is in charge of Corporal Oishi's plane. Corporal made a sortie splendidly today. Before he takes off, he left this letter. I send it to you. Corporal used to cherish a doll you had made for him very much. He always carried the small doll on the back of his cloth. Other pilots all hang dolls from their waists or from their parachutes' belts, but Corporal carried the doll on his back as if he was giving it a piggyback. He said that he would pity the doll if it gets scared when his plane is about to attack. When everyone was running toward the planes to get on, I could easily notice Corporal at a glance, because the doll was swinging as if it was clinging to him. I suppose Corporal always felt as if he was with you, Shizue-chan. To go together—this is a word of Buddha. Whenever you feel pain, or you feel lonely, you are not alone. There is always Buddha right beside you, cheering you up. I suppose Corporal's Buddha was you. But from today, Corporal will be your "Buddha" and always will watch over you. Corporal bravely crashed on an enemy carrier. I hope that you, Shizue-chan, would cheer up and study hard so you can be as your great brother. Goodbye.[9]

The letter presents a fascinating transposition. The doll initially evoked the presence of the young sister; the pilot even carried the doll on his back like a young child. Yet after her brother's death, the doll seemed to help the brother's spirit return to his sister, and she is exhorted to become "like" her brother: "A doll functions as a kind of switch-point between living and dead family members in a letter written by one of the first kamikaze pilots, who died 26 October 1944 in the Philippines. The letter is addressed to his daughter, 'The toy doll you had as a child I took with me in my airplane as a good-luck charm—this way you are always with me. I tell you this because I think it would be wrong for you not to know'."[10] The pilot added a post-script: "I want to see you grow up to be a splendid bride. . . . When you get older and want to see me, come to Kudan [i.e., to Yasukuni] and pray with all your heart and my face will appear before you. . . . You resemble me very much. When people see you, they often say how much you look like me."[11] The dolls in these instances appear to have functioned not simply as protective talismans or as comforting companions but as complex ritual operators, linking the kamikaze, who were themselves liminal beings suspended between the domains of life and death, to the living and to the dead. The doll made by the little girl Shizue allowed her older brother to feel, while he was alive, that she was always with him. Once he died, it enabled the living sister to feel that her dead brother was always with her. Similarly, the second writer carries his daughter's doll in his airplane to sense her presence. After death, he reassures her, she will be able to see his face at Yasukuni.

The contemporary ritual power of the bride dolls at Yasukuni partially derives, as well, from the postwar usages of the mascot dolls that survived the war, which took on memorial functions for dead. Many mascot dolls are preserved in museum displays dedicated to the kamikaze; one such doll is even featured in one of the final galleries of the Yūshūkan Museum, along with the letter that a kamikaze pilot wrote as he returned the doll and other objects to a mother and daughter who had given them to him. A Yasukuni publication shows a photograph of a pilot (who died in May 1945) in front of his plane, holding a large doll. In turn, a shrine video displays a photograph of a group of kamikaze holding up their mascot dolls, in a curious evocation of children's play. An often reproduced photograph shows a pilot holding a puppy, with a kimono-clad doll tucked into his parachute belt. The photograph was the basis of a painting by a war veteran, exhibited on the shrine grounds during a recent summer festival. Suggestively, this painting was displayed near a painting of a group of kamikaze moments after their fatal impact as they are raised into the sky under the protective aura of a heavenly maiden. The implicit symbolic logic may be, at least in retrospect, that the beautiful doll that the pilot carries with him as he journeys out of this world anticipates the beautiful female companion that will welcome him after he has crossed over to the other world. In effect, the doll bridges the great divide between life and death, and perhaps helps the pilot return to Yasukuni.

Dolls and Postwar Memorialization

The decades that followed the Second World War saw an intensifying affinity between dolls and memorial practices throughout Japan. Over the course of the 1970s and 1980s, dolls of all sorts were increasingly subjected to elaborate memorialization rites at major national shrines and temples. Doll-store owners and some priests have increasingly asserted that all dolls are repositories of "spirit (*tamashii*)" and therefore entitled to formal rites of spirit separation before being discarded. The growing popularity of doll memorialization and bride-doll spirit marriage during this period was largely conditioned by the emerging "memorialization boom (*kuyō būmu*)" that characterized the bubble-economy period and its immediate aftermath. Today, dolls that loyally served their human charges are respectfully disposed of in elaborate doll memorialization rites (*ningyō kuyō*), which are said to separate the dolls' "souls" from their "bodies." At such venues as Meiji Jingu and Kiyomizu-dera Temple in Tokyo, Hōkyōji (also known as Ningyō-dera) in Kyoto, and Awashima shrine in Wakayama, dolls are burned, sent out to sea, or otherwise removed from normal human contexts. Over the course of the 1960s and 1970s, bereaved family members in northeastern Japan (Tohoku) began to dedicate bride dolls to relatives who died during the war in the service of the Imperial Army and Navy.[12]

A transformation of older northern Japanese and mainland East Asian rites of spirit marriage, the practice of bride-doll (*hanayome ningyō*) dedication is usually characterized as Buddhist memorialization (*kuyō*) for souls who might otherwise wander forever in the void between the worlds. Numerous informants have told me that this practice developed because mothers and sisters of the military war dead were not fully satisfied with the forms of veneration performed at Yasukuni or at the related "Defense of the Nation" official Shintō shrines located around the country. The practice of bride-doll dedication was quickly extended from military casualties to memorialize postwar civilian victims of illness or of road accidents who had died before marriage. To this day, in several Tendai and Shingon Buddhist establishments in northern Tōhoku, rituals of doll consecration are still undertaken to ease the fraught cosmological predicament of young people who have died before marriage, who are considered to be lost souls (*muenbotoke*).

The dedicated dolls are nearly always kimono-clad bride dolls (or groom dolls) encased in glass boxes, of the sort sold to tourists and sometimes presented to Japanese brides upon marriage. In Aomori Prefecture, the practice of bride-doll dedication is deeply embedded in the veneration of the Boddhisattva Jizō and popular forms of female spirit mediumship. Speaking through mediums, the dead child may plead with his parents to "buy me a bride" for comfort in the great void between the worlds. Within the glass boxes holding the dolls (which are the opposite sex of the deceased youth) family members place a photograph of the deceased, a paper giving the Buddhist memorial name (*kaimyō*), and various offerings to the dead, such as toys, cigarettes, beer, or underwear.[13] The dolls, informants emphasize, must not become too attached to the homes of the living relatives who have dedicated them. The night before a doll is taken to the temple it may be brought home to be placed on the family's Buddhist domestic altar (*butsudan*). Throughout this time, the doll remains blindfolded so that it will not be able to "find its way back" to the house. In contrast to the wartime militarist deployment of dolls, strongly associated with State Shintō practice, these Tohoku rituals of doll dedication are usually glossed by my local informants within an explicitly Buddhist, pacifist, and antimilitarist frame. Informants emphasize the sorrow and futility of war and often discuss their hope that comfort given the dead by the opposite-sex doll will still the anxious wanderings of the displaced soul. In time, the companionship given by the doll spouse may allow the dead soul to attain Buddha-hood or reincarnation. In the late Shōwa period (c. 1970–89), bride-doll marriage allowed local family members, especially women, to grant their lost relatives a measure of peace in distinctly alternative, if not explicitly critical or oppositional, registers that stood outside prevailing neo-nationalist narratives. As noted earlier, the beauty of the dolls' faces and clothing is said to "calm" and "pacify" the rage and anguish of those who died without knowing the joys of married adulthood and without posterity.

The Dolls at Yasukuni

Given this historical background, it is perhaps not surprising that Yasukuni priests were initially uneasy when a woman from Hokkaido first requested permission to dedicate a bride doll in 1982. Sato Nami was the mother of the late Lieutenant Sato Takeichi, an infantryman who died in the battle of Okinawa in 1945. Her relatives recall that for nearly four decades she had refused to accept her son's death and held out hope that he would return. But as she approached her final years, she decided she needed to take steps to "take care of him" in the other world. She thus made a sizable monetary donation to the shrine. The following year, she dedicated the bride doll; made a further financial donation; and donated several objects from Hokkaido, including tourist sculptures on the parent–child theme of a mare and foal as well as an adult bear and a bear cub. She also presented a letter she had written to her son and to the bride doll, which she had named "Sakurako (Cherry Blossom Child)" in which she explained that she had always dreamed of her son's marrying.

Sato Nami's surviving relatives insist that she had not been aware of the practice of bride-doll dedication at Buddhist establishments in Tohoku; nor had she known about the wartime practice of presenting bride dolls to kamikaze pilots. Rather, they state, she and her sister-in-law had been motivated solely by "a mother's feeling" in deciding that a bride doll would be the most appropriate memorial gift for the late soldier. After this unusual gift was highlighted in the shrine's newsletter, several other families were inspired by her example and gave bride dolls, as well, in some cases accompanied by letters or poems written to their dead relatives. The fiftieth anniversary of the war's end in 1995 saw a marked increase in doll dedications, including by some prominent members of the Nihon Izokukai (War Bereaved Families Association). In 1999, the Yūshūkan Museum put up a temporary display of some of the dedicated dolls, which attracted more public attention. As of this writing, in 2005, approximately one hundred fifty dolls are visible in the reception rooms of Yasukuni's main shrine building. After considerable internal discussion, the shrine's priests have developed a policy of rotating the dolls through these rooms each three months, so that during the season in which a given soldier died, his doll will be closest to the shrine's inner sanctuary, the Honden, in which the spirits of the dead are believed to reside. All the priests with whom I have spoken insist the doll dedications are not instances of spirit marriage (shiryōkekkon) as such and cannot be considered Buddhist memorialization (kuyō). They are simply offerings by bereaved families to the deified dead soldiers.

During the extensive renovation of the Yūshūkan Museum in 2002, six bride dolls were selected for inclusion in the museum's penultimate gallery, viewed by visitors just before they enter the great hall containing the airplanes and submersibles of the Special Attack Forces, or kamikaze. Two walls of this room are adorned with photographs of the military war dead, primarily kamikaze. An entire wall is devoted to the first doll, dedicated by Sato Nami. A large glass case contains photographs of the dead soldier and of his mother, the doll clad in a white kimono, the sculptures of the parent–child pairs of bears and horses, and Nami's letter to her son and his doll bride.

Facing this large display are five exquisite bride dolls. In contrast to the many bride-doll cases next door within the Yasukuni shrine reception halls, these dolls are displayed not with photographs inside their glass boxes or with letters by family members, but only with tiny glasses of pure water and simple labels identifying the deceased soldier and the dedicating family members.

Propitiating the Dead

Why has the practice of bride-doll dedication, which emerged in partial contrast (perhaps even in opposition) to forms of memorialization associated with nationalist State Shintō, been so extensively grafted into Yasukuni ritual practice and into the new Yūshūkan Museum? Why have over one hundred fifty bereaved families chosen to dedicate bride-doll boxes at Yasukuni over the past two decades, and why is there deep public fascination with the practice? Why, in short, in spite of their rather divergent histories have bride dolls and neo-nationalist Shintō proved to be such a good fit in recent years? And how has a ritual practice previously embedded in a popular, antimilitarist aesthetic been so extensively incorporated into an overarching fascistic aesthetic?[14]

I suggest that in a curious fashion the growing practice of bride-doll dedication at Yasukuni marks an implicit, unacknowledged return to the shrine's largely repressed origins. In an insightful essay, Klaus Antoni proposes that Yasukuni does not simply glorify the war dead. It also, in a subtle sense, seeks to propitiate the unquiet spirits of those who died untimely or unusually violent deaths. The tortured souls of those who have died in unnatural fashion (goryō) have long been believed to haunt the living, especially the living relations of the dead. Those who died unmarried or experienced a "bad death" will become dangerous, wandering spirits. An Imperial Rescript presented by Emperor Meiji at the founding of Shōkonsha Shrine (Shrine for Calling the Spirits of the Dead) in 1869, the forerunner of Yasukuni Shrine, specifically sought to sooth and pacify the dead. Hence, proposes Antoni, "The country becomes a yasukuni, a peaceful land, because the warriors as 'bad dead' are no longer a threat and danger to it." He writes, "[The] country is protected from, instead of being protected by the spirits of fallen warriors."[15]

Antoni observes that Yasukuni and neo-nationalist Shintō have not been entirely successful in the initial cosmological project of propitiating the restless dead. In emphasizing the collective unified aspects of the apotheosized soldiers, these ritual complexes have not given sufficient attention to popular anxieties over the variegated dangers of individuated angry spirits (*goryō*) who each had specific, unresolved rage and hostility toward living people. Although Antoni does not precisely put it in these terms, a fascist aesthetic that seeks to appropriate the dead into the totalizing and homogenizing will of the state has proved incapable of addressing the specific apprehensions of individual families and of all those who sense that the military dead are potentially unruly and dangerous.

The adoption of bride-doll-marriage symbolism at Yasukuni over the past two decades, I suggest, has offered a ritual solution to these enduring cosmological challenges of soothing the unsettled dead and redressing proximate crises in kinship and family organization. Although official ritual action at Yasukuni is nearly entirely practiced by male priests, it has long fallen in Japan to women, especially to mothers, to tend to the unquiet spirits of children who died before their time. It is in this light that we may appreciate the leading role played by mothers and sisters in dedicating dolls at Yasukuni and the prominent symbolism of mother–child relations in these displays. The assertions in the shrine's publications notwithstanding, the bride dolls are not mere "symbols" honoring the dead; rather, these offerings would appear to console those who were deprived of the joys of marriage and of earthly posterity. Through these offerings, parents, siblings, descendants, and collateral relations are able to comfort specific dead people and protect themselves and their family members from potential spiritual retribution in a way that conventional neo-nationalist Shintō practice cannot. Shrine officials may continue to insist that Yasukuni exists only to exalt and honor the enshrined gods of the martyred souls that protect the nation. Yet the recent proliferation of bride dolls in the shrine and in the Yūshūkan Museum suggests otherwise. In an era of seemingly unending economic crisis, amid the emergence of ever more troubling questions about the conduct and legacies of the Asia-Pacific War, thousands, perhaps millions, long to propitiate these potentially dangerous beings and to protect themselves from the traumatic memories that they embody.

Death and the Problem of Kitsch: Sameness and Specificity

To a considerable extent, this cosmological project of propitiating the potentially unquiet dead is served by the kitschy, mass-reproduced qualities of the bride dolls. Dolls also feature in the veterans' paintings of kamikaze (often exhibited on the grounds of Yasukuni during festivals), which are themselves rather kitschy productions, usually representing the sacrificed young men in the hours just before death as they write final letters home or socialize with fellow soldiers. Like the often painted moment of death, these moments of acute collective anxiety demand repeated representations of already well-known photographic images. The naive, inexpert quality of these paintings by veterans, reproducing extremely familiar, mass-reproduced propaganda images, underscores the fact that each image is a sincere offering to the spirits of fellow soldiers, exemplifying the survivors' dedicated and reassuring service to the divinities.

The general tendency of kitsch everywhere to ease or neutralize the complexities of trauma and loss takes on particular force in Japan. This is true in part, I suggest, because of the psychodynamics of *amaeru*, an interpersonal emotional exchange that is usually glossed as "indulgence" or "dependence." The psychoanalyst Doi Takeo has argued that, in large measure, social relations of interdependence in Japanese society are constituted through the expanding exchange of *amaeru* between social actors, modeled on the formative exchanges of indulgence between mother and child. Schoolmates, workmates, and friends of all sorts continue to give and receive *amae* throughout their lives. These enactments of moments of unconditional indulgence return actors to the pure solidarity of early childhood experience while constituting ever more complex forms of interdependent sociality.

Doi notes that for mature actors, the longing for *amae* is sublimated through increasingly elaborate and aestheticized media, especially beautiful objects or forms that stress the inevitably transient nature of emotional fulfillment. To produce, view, or give a beautiful thing is to become, momentarily, one with that thing and, by extension, to become one with the recipient.[16] By dedicating beautiful bride dolls to the deceased relatives, the living are allowed to indulge (*amaeru*) the dead, giving them that which they most long for. The bride doll, a simultaneously maternal and erotic companion, is emphatically not a work of high art associated with specialized skill or restricted connoisseurship. The dolls, of the kind that are often given to actual brides, are suffused with eminently familiar sentimental and domestic associations. Clad in kimono, developed in the prewar era for the tourist trade, they are supremely knowable, conventional, and mundane and are coded as "typically Japanese." What better gift to ease the souls of those who died in unspeakable torment, far from home, in the service of a war whose origin and purposes most would prefer not to dwell on?

Memorial kitsch, after all, tends to be homogenous, to smooth out the complex specificities of actual lost lives, enduring pain, and broken families. In that respect, the mass-reproduced dolls offer useful symbolic affordances, in effect, for the standardizing fascist aesthetic of Yasukuni, which attempts to reduce all loss to a normative narrative of heroic self-sacrifice. Yet at the same time, the dolls offered by families to Yasukuni pose some challenges for a totalizing narrative frame. They are usually accompanied by photographs of the lost young man and sometimes contain haunting letters and poems to the dead. In this light, it is perhaps not surprising that the Yūshūkan Museum's curators decided to display five dolls that lacked photographs or accompanying documents. The accompanying caption explains that the dolls have been given to comfort all military personnel who died unmarried. The attempted effect, then, is to dull or neutralize the specificities of the original gifts and to recast the dolls as generic offerings to the collective assembly of the honored dead.

Alternate Narratives: Pain, Kinship, and the Uncanny

Nonetheless, the visceral impact of the dolls often transcends such attempts to appropriate them into a conventional fascist aesthetic scheme. In many conversations with Japanese visitors to the museum, I have been struck that the bride dolls elicit thoughtful mediations on the specific and unresolved conditions of their family's pain in a manner that seems deeply at odds with the museum's overarching triumphalist narrative and its celebration of wartime fascist culture. For example, in July 2002, as I stood contemplating the bride dolls in the Yūshūkan Museum's penultimate gallery, I was approached by an elderly Japanese gentleman, Abo Seichi, who asked if he might speak with me in German. Once he ascertained that I spoke Japanese, Abo explained that his brother had been a kamikaze pilot who had died in Okinawa in May 1945. He had occupied the second seat of a three man Tenzan (Heaven-Mountain) bomber. His brother's photograph, he showed me as he visibly shook with emotion, was hanging on the adjacent wall. When I asked Abo to explain the meaning of the bride dolls, he said, "It was hardest for the mothers; they were the ones who really suffered terribly." He talked of his own late mother's inconsolable pain and said that he had been considering dedicating a bride doll in his brother's memory at Yasukuni Shrine. Such an act, he speculated, would not only help his brother's soul, but it might also grant a measure of peace to their mother in the Other World.

Many of those who have dedicated dolls at Yasukuni similarly frame their action in terms of specific domestic obligations to their close kin. Consider, for example, the case of the two Tanaka sisters, currently in their eighties, who in 1997 dedicated one of the bride dolls displayed in the Yūshūkan gallery in memory of their elder brother, who died as an infantryman on the Eniwetok Atoll on the Marshall Islands. They specifically refer to the doll as an instance of Buddhist memorialization (kuyō); over the decades, they have undertaken numerous memorial pilgrimages to the Marshall Islands, taking their brother's favorite foods and other offerings to the location where they believed he died. Neither sister, it should be noted, ever married; they have devoted their postwar lives to caring for one another and for their dead brother, who was to have been the head of the family. In marrying the doll to their brother, they emphasized, they were simultaneously honoring and comforting their late parents, who had not been able to leave behind a conventional family line.

Complex and highly specific kinship dynamics are also poignantly evoked by one of the most striking doll assemblages in Yasukuni: an elaborate, large glass box contains two "cherry blossom" dolls, of a weeping mother and a weeping small girl who holds on to her mother's shoulder. The dolls were made by Sumida Yuko, the younger sister of Lieutenant Sumida Tetsuo, who died on a kamikaze mission in April 1945 and whose mirror case (given by his mother) is preserved in one of the Yūshūkan Museum's final galleries.

When I spoke to Sumida Yuko, she explained that the dolls took a year of intense effort to make. She, too, referred to them as kuyō for her dead brother, specifically using the Buddhist term for memorialization (a term that would, of course, never be used by the Shintō priests at Yasukuni, who insist that the dolls are merely offerings to the apotheosized military dead). Noting that her brother, a student at Tokyo's elite Rikkyo University, had been an accomplished amateur photographer and draftsman, Yuko explained that in part because her brother was an artist she in turn had a special obligation to create a work of beauty in his memory.

Tetsuo and Yuko, it should be noted, were their parents' only children, and Tetsuo's death left Yuko responsible for caring for her parents and for the butsudan, the family's domestic Buddhist altar, which remains in her home. When she finally married, at the relatively late age of thirty-nine, she married an "adopted husband" who took on her family's name so that her natal line would endure.

Sumida Yuko's assemblage may be considered in light of Melanie Klein's discussion of mourning as a re-enactment of the process of weaning. The artist appears to re-enact the loss of her brother, and her own loss of childhood, through a three-dimensional representation of herself facing her mother, yet not fully embraced by her. Here the toys of childhood, transitional objects that in normal childhood would have eased the trauma of weaning and separation from the mother, sit abandoned, tangible evidence of the loss of the brother and of the sister's own vanished childhood. One might even interpret this piece as an attempt by the artist to reclaim her mother's attention, so long directed toward the son (to whom she had, after all, given a mirror in lieu of her own photograph). In the void of his absence, paradoxically, the son is an ever stronger presence, displacing the daughter, who seeks in this haunting piece to return to a full maternal embrace even as she signals the impossibility of such return.

When I first viewed these dolls, I assumed that they straightforwardly represented Sumida Yuko's mother and Yuko herself embracing after learning of Tetsuo's death. But in our conversation, Yuko adamantly resisted such a specific reading, saying only that she felt that making the dolls was an important act of kuyō for her late brother. She did tell me that the seated doll of the adult woman was emphatically "not a bride doll," since as Tetsuo's sister she could not properly offer him a wife. She also recalled that she had initially only made the seated adult female figure and had added the standing girl only after her doll-making teacher suggested that a second figure would be appropriate.

It is striking in this regard that the little girl depicted is much younger than Yuko was in 1945 when Tetsuo died. The ambiguities here, I think, are significant. Yuko and Tetsuo were extraordinarily close, and his death was devastating for her. She did not marry until age thirty-nine, seventeen years after his death. When she did marry, she married an adopted husband, who took on the name and ancestors of the Sumida house and family line. The dolls thus carry multiple associations for her; they evoke Yuko and her mother but also Yuko as an adult, as well as her memories of herself as a young child. And although Yuko insists that the female doll is not a "bride doll," she did donate it to Yasukuni in a context in which it joined scores of marked bride dolls. The net effect is that the two dolls would appear to evoke a great range of identities and relationships, confounding mother–daughter, brother–sister, and husband–wife relations. Perhaps because of these ambiguous and uncanny associations, shrine official and curators chose not to include Yuko's dolls in the renovated gallery in the Yūshūkan Museum. Yet for many visitors with whom I have spoken to over the years, her dolls remain the most poignant and compelling of all the displayed offerings in the shrine complex. Although most viewers do not know the specific details of the doll maker's loss, they clearly sense that her assemblage emerges out of a specific, unique history of pain that cannot be subsumed with the conventional pieties of nationalist sacrifice.

Conclusion: The Ambiguous Aesthetics of Yasukuni

For some, the bride dolls displayed in Yasukuni and the Yūshūkan might seem a minor sideshow to the shrine. Yet the figurines cast an interesting light on the extraordinary tenacity of the shrine's mass appeal in Japan, a popularity that continues to baffle and infuriate Japan's neighbors as well as its progressive intelligentsia. Although shrine priests were initially reluctant to accept these highly personalized offerings, the dolls over time largely have come to resonate with the overall aesthetic project at the shrine, including its many fascist and neo-nationalist elements, through which potentially complex meditations on war and accountability are re-cast into standardized, sentimental emotional responses. The dolls help to establish a reassuring distance from the pain of personal and collective loss, holding out the promise of conjugal comfort for the military war dead. The eternally young faces of the bride dolls unquestionably evoke, for some, an image of the eternal, unblemished youth of the sacrificed soldiers, forever frozen in a tableau of noble sacrifice. In this respect, we might say, the shrine has incorporated extensive elements of kitsch and fascist aesthetic principles in keeping with the nationalist imperative to reanimate the "beautiful" youthful war dead.

Yet over the past several decades, Yasukuni has also in effect been domesticated by local, individually oriented, and feminized forms of memorialization that are somewhat at odds with the overall ideological and aesthetic tenor of postwar neo-nationalism and neo-fascism. The bride dolls cut across a broad spectrum, incorporating kitschy qualities as well as their antithesis, evoking both sentimental and uncanny responses to mass death in warfare. While the dolls' deployments are largely consistent with the neo-nationalist agenda of the shrine's leadership, the figurines have also enabled creative, idiosyncratic acts of memorialization by individual family members, directed more toward the ritual resolution of highly specific domestic-based problems of memory work than toward homogenizing fascist and militarist memorial undertakings. The Tanaka sisters, for example, understand their decision to dedicate a doll at Yasukuni as simply one component of their lifelong commitment to easing the predicament of their late brother's soul, as well as the souls of their parents, and deny any interest in the broader political dimensions of Yasukuni. Abo, in turn, anticipates that dedicating a bride doll to his brother would, first and foremost, ease the pain of his late mother.

For Benjamin, photographic and mass-reproduced forms hover between diverse social and cultural projects. They may be easily co-opted by rightist and fascist enterprises that offer simulated, dangerous compensations for the loss of the authentic "aura" under conditions of alienated modernity. Yet the faces of the deceased in photographs, he writes, can simultaneously summon up archaic cults of the ancestors that are grounded in deeply meaningful premodern structures of kinship, the family, and community. New optical technologies of mass reproduction, he insists, thus carry destructive and libratory potential. Recall, in this light, the facial symbolism of Sumida Yuko's memorial assemblage for her dead brother, who carried to his death the mirror in which he saw himself and his mother conjoined. Regardless of whether the seated adult woman is his mother, his sister, his unrealized bride, or some combination of all three, enormous care went into the making of her face, which entrances the viewer. Significantly, the face of the little girl, which may be Yuko's remembered childhood self, is turned from our view and remains forever enigmatic. In some respects, these memorial figurines may have enabled their makers to move beyond the immediate pain of trauma toward productive acts of mourning and social reproduction; significantly, Yuko made the doll assemblage just before she married an adopted husband, thus structurally replacing her long-lost brother so that she could carry on their family name. For Yuko, dedicating the doll at Yasukuni can scarcely be reduced to an act of neo-nationalist obeisance but was, rather, first and foremost, a meaningful act of symbolic action within the context of her specific domestic responsibilities to the dead and to the living.

Like other popular commentaries about the bride dolls, Yuko's insistence that her dolls were offered to Yasukuni solely as acts of Buddhist memorialization (kuyō)—as personalized, heartfelt expressions of family feeling—should alert us to a significant undercurrent of popular engagement with the shrine. Rather than speaking of a singular aesthetic at Yasukuni, fascist or otherwise, we should instead understand that the institution emerged as a staging ground for overlapping, partially inconsistent aesthetic projects. To be sure, the family domain is powerfully encompassed with a resurgent nationalist framework at Yasukuni and related political and religious enterprises. Yet at the same time, the signifying practices of the postwar state are partly encompassed within the aesthetic sensibilities of the domestic sphere. Future research on Yasukuni and the memorialization of the Japanese military war dead, I suggest, should pay careful attention to these unresolved dialectics between the fascist, sacrificial, and standardized demands of the nation-state and the private, specific obligations of kinship. Each public youthful visage of an unmarried male martyr, sacrificed in service to the vanished empire, remains obscurely bound to the less visible faces of his mother, sisters, and hoped-for bride. These reflected faces and the paradoxes they embody pose enduring puzzles for Yasukuni's defenders and detractors alike, as they confront the unresolved legacies of war, traumatic loss, and truncated family lines.

Notes

1. John Nelson, "Social Memory as Ritual Practice: Commemorating Spirits of the Military Dead at Yasukuni Shinto Shrine," *Journal of Asian Studies* 62, no. 2 (May 2003): 445–67.
2. Walter Benjamin, "The Work of Art in an Age of Mechanical Reproduction," in *Illuminations*, ed. Hannah Arendt (New York: Schocken Books, 1968), 242.
3. Ibid., 223.
4. Saul Friedlander, *Reflections on Nazism: An Essay on Kitsch and Death* (Bloomington: Indiana University Press, 1993), 27.
5. Susan Sontag, *Under the Sign of Saturn* (New York: Farrar, Straus and Giroux, 1980).
6. In most instances, I have used pseudonyms in this essay.
7. Masao Yamaguchi, "The Poetics of Exhibition in Japanese Culture," in *Exhibiting Cultures: The Poetics and Politics of Museum Display* (Washington, D.C.: Smithsonian Institution Press, 1991), 57–67; Ellen Schattschneider, *Immortal Wishes: Labor and Transcendence on a Japanese Sacred Mountain* (Durham: Duke University Press, 2003), 55–58; idem, "Family Resemblances: Memorial Images and Faces of the Dead," *Japanese Journal of Religious Studies* 31, no. 1 (2004): 141–62.
8. Idem, "The Bloodstained Doll: Violence and the Gift in Wartime Japan," *Journal of Japanese Studies* 31, no. 2 (summer 2005): 329–56.
9. Kosaka Jiro, *Kyo ware ikite ari* [Today We Are Still Alive] (Tokyo: Shinchōsha, 1985), 42–45.
10. "Kamikaze Pilots, Last Letters," trans. Nicholas Voge, in "Silence to Light: Japan and the Shadows of War. New Writings from Japan" *Mânoa* 13, no. 1 (2001): 121.
11. Ibid.
12. Before the mid-twentieth century, northern Tōhoku spirit marriage was centered on the production of votive painted tablets (*mukasari ema*). A bereaved family seeking to memorialize a dead unmarried male would commission the painting of the face of a specific living young woman on the tablet, sometimes paired with a painted image of the dead young man.
13. Ellen Schattschneider, "Buy Me a Bride: Death and Exchange in Northern Japa-

nese Bride Doll Marriage," *American Ethnologist* 28, no. 4 (November 2001): 854–80.

14. In her recent book on the kamikaze and cherry-blossom symbolism, Emiko Ohnuki-Tierney makes passing reference to the 1999 temporary exhibition of bride dolls at Yasukuni: Emiko Ohnuki-Tierney, *Kamikaze, Cherry Blossoms, and Nationalisms: The Militarization of Aesthetics in Japanese History* (Chicago: University of Chicago Press. 2002), 178–82. She dismisses the display as a cynical appropriation, by shrine officials, of folkloric "ghost marriage" practices. Yet such an explanation accounts for neither the early history of the dolls at the shrine nor the widespread popularity of the practice among those who worship at Yasukuni. As we have seen, Yasukuni officials did not actively seek out bride-doll dedication in the 1980s; rather, they reluctantly acceded to women's efforts to dedicate dolls and have only slowly become reconciled to the practice.

15. Klaus Antoni, "Yasukuni-Jinja and Folk Religion: The Problem of Vengeful Spirits," *Asian Folklore Studies* 47 (1988): 133.

16. Takeo Doi, *The Anatomy of Dependence* (Tokyo: Kōdansha, 1981).

PART IV

LITERARY FASCISM

NINA CORNYETZ

Fascist Aesthetics and
the Politics of Representation
in Kawabata Yasunari

■   Kawabata Yasunari (1899–1972) was the first Japanese writer to win the Nobel Prize for Literature, which was awarded to him in 1968. He was renowned for his deep concern with "the beautiful," or aesthetics, as the title of his Nobel Prize acceptance speech, "Utsukushii Nihon no wata-kushi (Japan, the Beautiful, and Myself)," suggests.[1] According to Ueda Makoto, Kawabata "repeatedly made the same point in his critical essays. . . . [H]e suggested that literature recorded nothing but . . . encounters with beauty."[2] Tachihara Masaaki put it this way: "Kawabata was always looking for beauty everywhere. When he discerned a beautiful object he relentlessly laid it bare in an attempt to get close to its true essence. His eyes were trained toward (nozomi) immortality and turned away from things of the earth."[3] As a matter of fact, Kawabata's literature is beautiful, but that is not the end of my discussion. Rather, it is where it begins.

This focus on aesthetics in so many secondary sources on Kawabata overwhelmingly ignores or denies the impact of any political ideology, as Tachihara also intimates by claiming Kawabata was "turned away from things of the earth." In a nutshell, Kawabata has been read as an aesthete unconcerned with politics (or current events) for whom the war constituted a personal, artistic, and cultural trauma.[4] This essay, to the contrary, attempts to reintegrate his aesthetics with the political context in which they arose—in particular, with fascist ideology. I ask: What are the politics of representation underlying Kawabata's literary aesthetics, and how do those politics of representation compare with those of fascist aesthetics in general? I will argue that many attributes of his aesthetic indeed colluded with fascist ideology and that those attributes came to dominate his aesthetics at the same time that Japan was becoming politically fascist. Moreover, against the reevaluation of their wartime ideology by most writers and artists in the postwar, Kawabata instead became more aestheticist in the manner that I believe, and hope to show here, is a system of representation collusive with fascist ideology.

However, let me also state up front what this essay is not attempting: to claim that Kawabata, as an individual, was a card-carrying fascist who enthusiastically and uncritically supported the fascist-imperialist actions of Japan's military in the Second World War. But I do believe that it was his very (celebrated) aesthetics—or what I will be calling a nationalized, acculturating aestheticentrism—that made possible his (largely disavowed) enthusiasm for Japanese imperialism and colonialism, an enthusiasm revealed in some of his wartime writings and convincingly argued by Charles Cabell.[5] I would go so far as to argue that, even if there were no texts by Kawabata that literally voiced support for Japan's "mission" in Asia, the theoretical analysis of the *signifying system* that underpins Kawabata's aesthetics, which I pursue here, will reveal aspects shared by the various and different political forms of fascism.

Because the word *fascism* means different things to different people, I devote a fair percentage of this essay to a discussion of how I understand and am using the term. I begin with the problematic of the term; follow with an equally general description of Kawabata's aesthetics; and conclude by integrating the two.

On Fascism

First, I do not want to limit the term *fascism* to, as some have espoused, the geophysical and temporal specificities of European fascism beginning in the 1920s and ending in 1945. Instead, I agree with Mark Neocleous, who argued (following Walter Benjamin) that such a conception of (European) fascism "ignores the fact that this development [fascism] was rooted in a particular set of philosophical debates rather than in a coherently organized political party or movement."[6] As Peter Osborne wrote:

> As an object of reflection and inquiry, "fascism" is notoriously resistant to conventional forms of political and ideological analysis. Herein, in part, lies its significance: fascism problematizes "the political," while presenting itself as its truth. As such, it opens itself up to philosophical forms of interpretation and analysis which, while based on its history as a political movement, nonetheless of necessity exceed its bounds. From this perspective, fascism is no *merely* political form—one among a series of alternatives to be listed in the catalogues of comparative politics as competing forms of organization or rule—but a manifestation of deep-rooted historical, or even metaphysical, tendencies or possibilities of the age.[7]

Borrowing from Osborne the characterization of fascism as "no *merely* political form," and in the spirit of Roger Griffin and others, in this essay I am interested in an analysis of the aesthetics of fascism as a signifying system that bears certain common markers across its otherwise variously particular historical manifestations, including Nazi Germany, fascist Italy and France, as well as Japan.[8] I understand fascism to be a historical development specific to the massification of society in relation to the rise of modern, industrial capitalism that attempts to solve the problem of class struggle ideologically rather than economically. I also understand fascism as a signifying system that employs a specific *typology* of images, sentiments, and slogans (although the *content* of these may vary) to enlist the masses in a nationalist, collective, vitalist movement. As a reactionary modernism, fascism has a specific politics of time—or, as Griffin puts it, it is palingenetic, moving forward toward "regeneration" as it looks nostalgically backward toward a mythic past.[9] And, of course, at its core fascism is dependent on nationalism. To quote Neocleous at greater length:

> Fascism is a politics implicit in modern capitalism, involving mass mobilization for nationalist and counter-revolutionary aims, militarized activism and a drive for an elitist, authoritarian, and repressive state apparatus, articulated through a nebulous vitalist philosophy of nature and the will.
>
> [Fascism is] a counter-revolutionary phenomenon engaged in the prevention of communism, but which seeks none the less to provide an alternate revolutionary impetus to the social forces of mass society by

mobilizing them through an aggressive nationalism. . . . [I]t is a form of reactionary modernism: responding to the alienation and exploitation of modern society but unwilling to lay down any serious challenge to the structure of private property central to modern capitalism, fascism can only set its compass by the light of reaction, a mythic past to be recaptured within the radically altered conditions of modernity.[10]

Second, as already suggested, although fascism can certainly be approached (and, of course, has often been so approached) by concentrating on its more concrete manifestations in political and military institutions and activities, here I am concerned with the aspect of fascist ideology that makes itself known as "aesthetics" and "culture" (but that is "political" in effect), which, as Benjamin insisted, are equally integral to fascism. In their introduction to *Fascist Visions: Art and Ideology in France and Italy*, Matthew Affron and Mark Antliff explain,

> As Walter Benjamin argues in his seminal essay, "The Work of Art in the Age of Mechanical Reproduction" (1936), fascism can be seen as a form of aestheticized politics in which aesthetic issues permeated all aspects of society; and the political, economic, and cultural realms should not be considered separately when discussing fascism. Rather than dismissing fascist ideology as a form of "false consciousness" as [Robert] Soucy does, *one should recognize the very real role of cultural production in the formation of groups and constituencies favorable to fascism.*[11]

In Benjamin's own words:

> The growing proletarianization of modern man and the increasing formation of masses are two aspects of the same process. Fascism attempts to organize the newly created proletarian masses without affecting the property structure which the masses strive to eliminate. Fascism sees its salvation in giving these masses not their right, but instead a chance to express themselves. . . . The logical result of Fascism is the introduction of aesthetics into politics. . . . Communism responds by politicizing art.[12]

Although it might appear at first glance that Benjamin sees fascism as a conflation of domains, it is actually the opposite. Andrew Hewitt has written that here Benjamin "is arguing not simply that fascism somehow confuses aesthetics and politics but rather that maintaining a traditional differentiation between the two is itself potentially fascistic."[13] That is, art, be it literary, filmic, or visual, is always produced and received or consumed in a political circumstance with its attendant ideological context. The commingling of politics with aesthetics can produce a potentially murderous disinterest. War can be perceived as beautiful, and death may be divested of affect. More simply still, it can also be taken to suggest that there is no artistic stance or production that is purely objective or freed from interest of any sort. Fascism is the potential, final culmination of the purification of domains that lies at the heart of art for the sake of art, or the attempt to ignore the sociopolitical and historical context of artistic production.

Third, it is also important to acknowledge what Susan Sontag called the beauty of fascism,[14] or what Rey Chow termed fascism's positivism and positivity:

> The most important sentiment involved in fascism is not a negative but a positive one: rather than hatefulness and destructiveness, fascism is about love and idealism. Most of all it is a search for an idealized self-image through a heartfelt surrender to something higher and more beautiful. Like the Nazi officer who killed to purify his race, the Japanese soldier raped and slaughtered in total devotion to [his] emperor and in the name of achieving the "Greater East Asia Co-Prosperity Sphere." Like the Nazi concentration camp official who was genuinely capable of being moved to tears by a Beethoven sonata being played by Jewish prisoners, the Japanese officer, we may surmise, was probably also genuinely capable of being moved by the delicate feelings inscribed in cultured practices such as haiku poetry, calligraphy, or the tea ceremony. In each case, what sustains the aesthetics of monstrosity is something eminently positive and decent.[15]

Fourth, I understand fascism to be about a crisis in representation at perhaps its "deepest" level—or about the anxiety over the potential slippage between reality and how that "real" is represented, in image, slogan, or text. This anxiety is, of course, first and foremost the anxiety and sense of alienation over the radical social, political, economic, and other shifts that marked the entry into modernity (and capitalism). As Harry Harootunian explains:

> What modernist discourse in Japan, and elsewhere, confronted was the crisis of modernity over the stability and reliability of forms of representation. While this crisis was manifested throughout the moderniz-

ing world . . . in Japan it was inflected in discussions over the form best suited to represent lived experience in social circumstances dominated by the ever new in the ever same . . . the auratic endowment of culture-memory . . . and the experience of the communal body. . . . This crisis, then, was over the forms most capable of relaying and communicating the lived experience—the experience of genuine difference—and securing accessibility to a memory that was being shattered into splinters by speed, shock, and sensation. . . .

[In Japan] the crisis was inflected into claims of cultural authenticity and diverse efforts to recall the eternal forms of community outside of history (and thus immune to the social abstractions of capitalism). Yet this particular inflection of the crisis of representation invariably worked to yoke modernism (seeking to resolve the question of representation) to fascism (aiming to resolve the problem of political representation), combining ideologemes the state subsequently but selectively appropriated for national mobilization and war in the late 1930s.[16]

Moreover, as many have argued, fascism masquerades as that which it is not—it is narcissistically invested in its own representation for the sake of representation.[17] Within the fascist order, "signification" itself (meaning) and "true" subjectivity founded on self-recognition through the radical difference of the other is replaced with a performative identification with the other (refusal of difference). Hence, meaning itself is "evacuated." In semiotic terms, this evacuated subjectivity mirrors the evacuation of "content" in fascist slogans and images.

The fascist solution to the anxiety caused by radical alterity (the Other) constitutes a wholesale rejection of dialogue for a combination of images of sublation (the shared mission and communalism of the *Volk*, or the Japanese equivalent of *minzoku*, that functions to elide class distinctions) and annihilation strategies (the Jews, communists). Permitted, then, is only the ("false") image of the same. This is, in other words, a sort of short-circuiting of the constitutive instability of the sign in an attempt at fixing signification. However, fascism itself remains "unrepresentable": "if fascism somehow defies representation, it has nevertheless been represented with obsessive frequency at any number of discursive levels—not least of all as a marker (if not a representation) of the historical dilemma of unrepresentability."[18]

Finally, I want to note a distinction between what I am calling fascist aesthetics and fascism proper. Although I leave further elaboration of just how

I am conceiving of fascist aesthetics to the following sections, I will simply state here that by *fascist aesthetics*, I mean the ideals of beauty that work well within fascist systems but that are certainly not limited to regimes that are politically fascist. With this distinction in mind, I will argue that Kawabata's literary aesthetics grew more, not less, fascist in the postwar era.

Kawabata's Aesthetics

Kawabata's expository writings on literature and many of his narratives—both the earliest and some of his last—were decidedly "modernist," influenced by Western modernist stream-of-consciousness writers such as James Joyce and Marcel Proust.[19] It is curious, then, that he insisted that it was the Japanese classics alone that inspired him. Kawabata fiercely distinguished his ideal associative narrative from the Western avant-garde because they, Kawabata felt, reveled in psychological depravity and neglected the "real," so-called natural world.[20] However, by "natural" Kawabata meant something quite specific: Japanese classical poetics, insisted Kawabata, were rooted in mediated impressions of the material—rather than purely psychic—world and were thus superior to Western modernism (which reveled in mental unbalance). From the 1920s forward, Kawabata sought a "new mode of Japanese literature" inspired by Japanese literary conventions. In 1934, he insisted:

> I believe that the classics of the East, especially the Buddhist scriptures, are the supreme works of literature of the world. I revere the sutras not for their religious teachings but as literary visions. I have had in mind for the last fifteen years the plan for a work to be entitled "The Song of the East," which I would like to make my own swan song. In it I will sing, in my fashion, a vision of the classics of the East. I may die before I can write it, but I should like it at least to be understood that I wanted to write it. I have received the baptism of modern literature and I have myself imitated it, but basically I am an oriental, and for fifteen years I have never lost sight of my bearings.[21]

Such a rejection of things "Western" and valorization of things "Eastern" in the arts and literature was by no means uncommon for Kawabata's generation. As did many of his contemporaries, against the perception of excessive Westernization, Kawabata sought to find in Japanese tradition (before Japan had been tainted by Western materialism and rationalism) a "spiritual" superiority to offset perceptions of Japanese technological inferiority.[22]

For Kawabata, this Japanese inspiration began with formal concerns (although it did not end there). Throughout his corpus are woven citations of, references to, and other markers of Japanese literary and art forms from the Heian period (794–1185) through the Edo period (1600–1868) that in the modern era have been canonized as signifiers of Japanese convention. For example, the separate poetic episodes and images that together make one text—most notably, perhaps, in *Yukiguni* (Snow Country; 1948), begun in 1935, added to over the years, and then rewritten many times—are not necessarily cumulative; each is intricately related to the words and imagery immediately surrounding it but not bound to the overall shape of the narrative. Thus, Kawabata's writing has been likened to *renga* (long sequences of multi-authored linked verse originating around the twelfth century).[23] Kawabata's writing is highly referential to the classic Heian-period *monogatari* (tale fiction) tradition, as attention is lavished on decorative details— the scent of perfectly brewed tea or the crane pattern adorning a kimono.[24] Causal or plotted elements are subordinated to descriptive aspects. This is the sort of "fetishization of the trivial" that also informed so much classical *monogatari*, such as the famous *The Tale of Genji*.[25] From Kawabata's *Senbazuru* (Thousand Cranes; 1949): "when a red oleander floods into bloom, the red against the thick green leaves is like the blaze of the summer sky; but when the blossoms are white, the effect is richly cool. The white clusters swayed gently, and enveloped Fumiko."[26] Kawabata's episodic brevity and reliance on contrastive images are believed born of early modern Japanese poetics such as the haiku. Edward Seidensticker wrote,

> Kawabata has been put, I think rightly, in a literary line that can be traced back to seventeenth-century haiku masters. Haiku are tiny seventeen-syllable poems that seek to convey a sudden awareness of beauty by a mating of opposite or incongruous terms. Thus the classical haiku characteristically fuses motion and stillness. Similarly Kawabata relies heavily on a mingling of the senses.[27]

An English translation of *Snow Country* was illustrated by the contemporary Japanese artist Kuwamoto Tadaaki with stark, bold, abstract shapes in red, white, and black.[28] Kuwamoto's visual interpretation of the text suggests that *Snow Country* indeed uses a prose narrative to explore the play of contrasts, colors, and shapes, and not simply to tell a story. In this sense Kawabata's reference to a literature that was as much about extra- and non-narrative textualities, such as visual, aural, or figural elements, is clear.[29] Yet I believe that Kuwamoto's rejection of illustrations representative of traditional art forms in favor of modern abstract art was brilliant. What Kuwamoto appears to have understood is that Kawabata's references to convention are never recapitulations of the same but thoroughly modernist in their redeployment of signifiers of tradition in innovative and nontraditional contexts.

Accordingly, characterizations of Kawabata as continuous with tradition must, I believe (as do many others who have written about Kawabata), be countered with the fact that Kawabata was also affected by contemporary literary issues and debates. The indeterminate, or overdetermined, nature of Kawabata's fragmentary mining of Japanese literary and artistic convention is, of course, clearly modern and even modernist.[30] This fact did not escape all Kawabata commentary. Kosai Shinji mused:

> As I lay down my pen, now, I think, maybe, Kawabata Yasunari's symbolist aesthetics are, however, after all, dependent upon a tradition of "Japanese verse (*Yamato uta*)" that permeates throughout the *Kokinshū*, the *Shinkokinshū*, Basho's *haikai* [*renga*]. Nonetheless, that fact that I think the passage in *Snow Country* looks like Mallarmé's symbolism, *The Lake* assimilates George Bataille's eroticism, and moreover *House of the Sleeping Beauties* even seems like it is a sort of Platonism [means that] this "essence" of our Heian aesthetics is imbued throughout with the essence of French symbolism.[31]

It is well known that prior to the war, Kawabata was affiliated with the Neo-Perceptionalist literary coterie (*Shin kankaku ha*, sometimes translated as Neo-Sensualist or New Senses School) during its formative stages in the 1920s. The coterie rejected the then dominant naturalist literature that followed the principles of scientific observation and reportage. Kawabata's narratives emerge as influenced by, yet distinct from, the group. In his "Shinshin sakka no shinkeikō kaisetsu (On the New Directions of Up and Coming Writers)," Kawabata elucidated his belief that foregrounding sensory perception in the writing of literature would originate a *new* mode of Japanese literary expression.[32] Faithful to his own literary ideals as influenced by the Neo-Perceptionalists, Kawabata's narratives access the world through the varied perceptual senses. Accordingly, his characterizations are vibrantly tactile, auditory, and visual: a woman is described by the contrasts of black hair and white skin, the sound of her voice, or the touch of her finger. Perhaps inspired by the haiku and renga, contrasts are indeed everywhere: stillness is offset by sudden movement, sadness by a moment of joy, the brightness of red against black, purity against the soiled:

> Shimamura glanced up at her, and immediately lowered his head. The white in the depths of the mirror was the snow, and floating in the middle of it were the woman's bright red cheeks. There was an indescribably fresh beauty in the contrast.
>
> Was the sun already up? The brightness of the snow was more intense, it seemed to be burning icily. Against it, the woman's hair became a clearer black, touched with a purple sheen.[33]

At the end of his life, Kawabata returned to an abbreviated form of impressionistic writing that he had experimented with toward the beginning of his writing career—short, descriptive, and often surrealist vignettes he called "palm of the hand stories (tanagokoro no shōsetsu)." Hence, one can easily characterize Kawabata's literary project as one that moved forward while gazing backward—or one that incorporated and combined signifiers of premodernity in a quest for innovation and originality—yet was one that he troped as a return to tradition.

This incorporation or combination of references to or signifiers of now canonized conventions is perhaps most overt in his Nobel Prize acceptance speech, which wound its way through references to one traditional Japanese art form after another, including poetry, landscape painting, and the tea ceremony; art forms that range over time from Heian to Edo and even into the twentieth century. "'The ancients arranged flowers and pursued enlightenment.' Here we see an awakening to the heart of the Japanese spirit, under the influence of Zen"; two pages later, on the topic of Heian-period tale fiction (monogatari) written by women, Kawabata holds: "so was established a tradition which influenced and even controlled Japanese literature for eight hundred years."[34] In between a discussion of the Buddhists Ryōkan (1758–1831) and Ikkyū (1394–1481) he quotes the twentieth-century writer Akutagawa Ryūnosuke: "nature is for me more beautiful than it has ever been before. I have no doubt that you will laugh at the contradiction, for here I love nature even when I am contemplating suicide. But nature is beautiful because it comes to my eyes in their last extremity."[35] On the tea ceremony he wrote:

> The snow, the moon, the blossoms, words expressive of the seasons as they move one into another, include in the Japanese tradition the beauty of mountains and rivers and grasses and trees, of all the myriad mani-

festations of nature, of human feelings as well. That spirit, that feeling for one's comrades in the snow, the moonlight, under the blossoms, is also basic to the tea ceremony.[36]

These different arts and personages are linked as continuous in signification over history, in large part, because of the dominance of the "natural" or "nature" as a conceit or inspiration. Elsewhere Kawabata put it: "To be natural, to be true to nature—this has been the basic principle pervading all the arts in Japan, both past and present."[37] *Thousand Cranes* laments the deterioration of the (traditional art of the) tea ceremony in contemporary, modern, declining Japan; the mountainside to which the protagonist Shimamura travels in *Snow Country* is facilely interpreted as symbolic of preindustrialized Japan—a quest reiterated within the text in Shimamura's (unfulfilled) desire to find Chijimi linen—purported to still be snow-bleached in the preindustrial manner. *Snow Country*, written before and during the war, valorizes a preindustrial, pre-mass Japan in which nature dominates, albeit neatly transposed into the periphery of a modern bourgeois context.

Kawabata's insistence that his literature, and that of the canon, is about "nature" notwithstanding—as he himself may have intuited, given his description, that classical Japanese literature celebrated *mediated impressions* of the material world—premodern Japanese literature was less about "nature" itself than about a *cultured* notion of "nature."[38] For example, Andrew Feenberg has noted: "Haiku . . . are often said to be concerned with the experience of nature. But in fact they articulate the natural world poetically in all its rich emotional and historical associations without distinguishing a purely material content from the contributions of culture and the subject."[39]

The aesthetic rendering of the natural world in Kawabata's writings likewise celebrates a nature anchored in a cultural specificity—and his acculturated apprehension and representation of nature has at its core a Zen Buddhist sensibility. Throughout his Nobel Prize speech, Kawabata quoted poems about Zen written by Zen monks connecting them to a putative timeless essence of "the deep quiet of the Japanese spirit," "the emotions of old Japan, and the heart of a religious faith." Claiming that the premodern "Ikkyū of Zen comes home to me with great immediacy," Kawabata concluded the speech with the following:

Here we have the emptiness, the nothingness, of the Orient. My own works have been described as works of emptiness, but it is not to be taken for the nihilism of the West. The spiritual foundation would seem to be quite different. Dōgen entitled his poem about the seasons "Innate Reality," and even as he sang of the beauty of the seasons he was deeply immersed in Zen.[40]

Kawabata's rendering of Zen as the aesthetic sentiment of Japan throughout the ages is, however, a modern construct.

Let me digress for a moment. From the Meiji period onward, Western theories on aesthetics and other philosophic inquiry poured into Japan (alongside Western novels; texts on science and technology and on health and hygiene; and other discursive and material imports), with aesthetics becoming a field within the university by 1881.[41] However, the high academic discourses tended toward explications of Western aesthetic theory; there were apparently only limited philosophical treatments exclusively dedicated to inquiry into so-called traditional Japanese aesthetics. Among these were several essays, and later a thick study by the philosopher Onishi Yoshinori attempting to apply logical rationalism to, and integrate with Western aesthetical discourses, the three categories he identified as the core of Japanese aesthetics: yūgen (mysterious depth), aware (strong emotive sense of the sad and beautiful transience of all things), and sabi (restrained melancholy or loneliness). Ueda Makoto notes that his studies were met with hostility. There was no need to dissect these categories, held one reviewer, and, moreover, was not everything that Onishi discovered in this contorted logical approach already self-evident to all Japanese?[42] The point I want to make with this short digression is not that Japanese aesthetics were unimportant to Japanese of the time. Rather, the objection to the separation of aesthetics from discourses on ontology and culture, I think, pinpoints an important aspect of how aesthetics were then conceived in a rapidly modernizing Japan. That is, it shows the prewar naturalization of an environmentally and ethnically particular "sensibility" as a constitutive component of Japanese being.

Aesthetics was of paramount importance; it was inseparable from (Japanese) being itself in a manner not unlike that of the (in)famous National Socialist philosopher Martin Heidegger, whose analysis of temporality in Being and Time Peter Osborne has summarized as "an aestheticization of ontology or ontologization of transcendental aesthetics."[43] In the works of eminent modern Japanese philosophers such as Nishida Kitarō, Miki Kiyoshi, and Watsuji Tetsurō, Japanese being is not only aestheticized, but it is also conceived as intertwined with an experiential aesthetic immediacy.[44]

By 1968, when Kawabata accepted his Nobel Prize, as Robert Sharf has convincingly argued, Zen Buddhism in particular signified something quite different from what it had before the twentieth century and had, in fact, become the favored vessel for this aesthetic-ontic constellation. With modernity, Zen had become commingled with Japanese being in a newly individualized formulation well suited to the modern subject. The result was that, unlike in premodern Zen Buddhism, the "heart" of modern Zen now lay "in a private, veridical, often momentary 'state of consciousness.'"[45] But this private "state of consciousness" is simultaneously communal and national because it is perceived to be (potentially) shared by all Japanese. In other words, with Japan's modernity, the meaning of Zen shifted from an institutionalized religious practice by a dominant aristocratic-military minority to a subjectively individual, yet culturally communal, ontology available to the masses and linked to nationalism. In short, Zen Buddhism had been re-conceptualized as "the ground of Japanese aesthetic and ethical sensibilities. Virtually all of the major Japanese artistic traditions are reinterpreted as expressions of the Zen experience, rendering Zen the metaphysical ground of Japanese culture itself."[46] Because the various arts are now all linked to Zen, and Zen is linked to Japanese being, both Zen and being are at once aestheticized, nationalized, and bound to a type of contemplative experientialism.

Kawabata's Nobel Prize speech expressed this sentiment as follows:

Seeing the moon, he [the poet Myōe (1173–1232)] becomes the moon, the moon seen by him becomes him. He sinks into nature, becomes one with nature. The light of the "clear heart" of the priest, seated in the meditation hall in the darkness before the dawn, becomes for the dawn moon its own light.[47]

Kawabata gestures toward defining this aesthetic as "Pan-Asian" when he includes references to Chinese poets and substitutes the word "Oriental" for Japanese here and there.[48] But this gesture toward a common Asia must be recognized as an imaginary (mythic) Asia, not only because by 1968 China had become the People's Republic of China, but also simply because Ch'an Buddhism (the progenitor of Japanese Zen, originated in the early seventh century) and Buddhism in general in China had overwhelmingly yielded to the philosophic dominance of Neo-Confucianism by the fourteenth century.[49] Kawabata's "Asia" that is (still) unified through a Zen sentiment is therefore a thoroughly Orientalized Asia—frozen in its antiquity, completely aestheticized, stunningly a-historical, and originating in negative difference from the so-called West. The Zen beliefs and practices that Kawabata discovers everywhere as he meanders (discursively, of course) through China and Japan, from Japan's earliest recorded writings to the present day, are all read as signifying homogeneity. The speech—in its modern interpretation of Zen—disavows the radical differences that history would discover in the various places, periods, and poets, let alone the differing meaning and practice of Zen itself over time and regime. (One might also argue that this Pan-Asianism has an ominous undercurrent when one remembers how the mission of unifying all of Asia under Japan during the Second World War made use of similar notions of an "Asian" spiritualism.)

It is, then, as a particularity unique to being Japanese that Kawabata drew inspiration from Zen in the form of an individualized (yet nationally communal), subjective sensory experience of contrast, transience, internal negation (or the dialectic of self-negation described by Nishida in which the temporal-[human]-historical self comes into being in relation to its simultaneous negation in space, and vice versa).[50] This aesthetic-ontic construct is, moreover, grafted onto a culturally particularized nature and manifested in the mythicized Japanese (Pan-Asian) past—but a past that can be, and should be, reborn in the present and future. As Nishida put it during the war, "The return of the past in our nation has always been the character of a renewal. It has never been a mere return to the past but always a step forward as the self-determination of the eternal present. . . . In this history of our country, there was always a return to the Imperial Throne, a return to the past. This has never meant a return to the systems and culture of antiquity but has involved taking a step ahead in the direction of a new world."[51]

Fascist Aesthetics

The question remains, however, as to how this avowedly peaceful, compassionate, and contemplative core of Kawabata's mobilization of signifiers of convention—from an acculturated nature to Zen—might be particularly amenable to a fascist agenda. First, I will recall Walter Benjamin's claim that fascism relies on an aestheticization of politics. As Andrew Hewitt explains,

> The "aestheticization of politics," which seems to entail a confusion of discourses, actually functions on the basis of one of the most radical reaffirmations of the autonomy of the aesthetic—l'art pour l'art. Thus,

when Benjamin recommends "politicizing art," he is arguing not simply that fascism somehow confuses aesthetics and politics but rather that maintaining a traditional differentiation between the two is itself potentially fascistic.[52]

Hence, it is an epistemological structure of purification of domains, including aesthetics as aesthetics, that Benjamin identifies at the base of both fascism and modernism. This is not to facilely and inaccurately claim no distinction between fascism and modernism (fascism is, of course, a *reactionary* modernism).[53] The critic Karatani Kōjin coined the phrase "aestheticentrism," to describe the *inflexible* purification (or bracketing off) of aesthetics as a domain (that also undergirds Orientalist fascination with an aestheticized Asia) and that helps distinguish modernism proper from fascism. While modernism relies on a bracketing off, or purification of domains, the "aestheticentrist" naturalizes, and fixes that purification:

> The aesthetic stance is established by bracketing other elements, but one should always be prepared to remove the brackets. . . . However, the characteristic of aestheticentrists is that they forget to remove the brackets. They confuse the reality of the other with what is achieved by bracketing. Or they confuse their respect for beauty with respect for the other. . . . Furthermore, aestheticentrism is at the core of fascism. Appearing to be anticapitalist, it attempts to aesthetically sublimate the contradictions of the capitalist economy.[54]

Because the act of bracketing, or the purification of domains, depends on the isolation of certain attributes for appreciation or investigation, the object that emerges from that bracketing is of necessity partial. As Karatani points out, while this bracketing is essential for the advancement of many fields (such as science or mathematics), it is also essential that the bracketing be flexible, and that such bracketing must be conscious and perhaps deliberate. Otherwise, the partial object of purification may be confused with the object in its totality and context. Kawabata, I think, was an aestheticentrist in this sense. As such, he refused to unbracket his rendering of Japanese traditional culture. Or, as Benjamin might have put it, he refused to politicize art—that is, he refused to refuse the de-politicization of what is already always political—but held steadfastly to the decadence of art for art's sake.

Second, if fascism is understood to be a nationalistic reactionary modernism—that is, a reaction against the threat to the dominant classes brought on by modern mass society; a reactionary modernism that mobilizes those masses toward a new future that is overtly nostalgic for the past, moreover, one that attempts to unite the masses and obscure class struggle through an ideology (propagated by images) of national homogeneity and superiority against an encroaching pollution threatened by modernity, then Kawabata's mobilization of tradition can be easily understood as amenable to appropriation by fascist agendas or, more simply, as complicit with fascist aesthetics.

Let me be more specific. I have characterized Kawabata's relationship with premodern literature as one that looks backward as it moves forward and as replete with a host of canonized signifiers of Japanese tradition in its quest for innovation. Roger Griffin has argued that at the mythic core of fascism lies its "lowest common denominator"—"a palingenetic form of populist ultranationalism."[55] Griffin uses the term *palingenetic* to refer to "the sense of a new start or of regeneration after a phase of crisis or decline which can be associated just as much with mystical . . . as secular realities."[56] Palingenetic, then, connotes "a backward-looking nostalgia for a restoration of the past (in the sense of rebirth)" that "refers to the *future* as much as the past . . . while appearing to be a reactionary turn to the past, in fact constitutes an orientation to the future."[57] Hence, fascism calls for a new order with terms such as restoration, or regeneration; this restoration, of course, is to a purer time of "national" glory.[58]

In this sense, fascism also counters the progressive temporality of the modern with a "simultaneity of the non-simultaneous" (and vice versa; i.e., the non-simultaneity of the simultaneous).[59] Peter Osborne has argued that this is a "politics of time" that underpins both conservative revolutions and reactionary modernism.[60] As Jeffrey Herf has pointed out, the apparently paradoxical nature of this politics of time stems from an awareness that what conservative revolutions and reactionary modernist political movements mobilize to revitalize is believed to be something already lost but may in fact never have existed as more than a possibility.[61] Hence, Osborne paraphrases Herf to postulate that reactionary modernism seeks "to realize this 'past' *for the first time*."[62] Moreover, it is this politics of time in reactionary modernism that leads Osborne to claim:

> Reactionary modernism may be understood as a bad modernism; not (or not primarily) in a moral or political sense, but in terms of the contradiction internal to its temporal structure. This structure—the structure of radical reaction within and against modernity—is of necessity contra-

dictory, since one of the things it aims to reverse is the production of the very temporality to which it is itself subject. Radical reaction cannot but reproduce, and thereby performatively affirm, the temporal form of the very thing against which it is pitted (modernity). Hence the necessity for it to misrepresent its temporal structure to itself as some kind of "recovery" or "return."[63]

That this politics of time requires, at its core, a sense of loss should be obvious. Griffin stresses the importance of a perception of decay, decadence, and corruption of the present moment as integral to the development of palingenetic myth.[64] Benjamin has suggested that the experience of loss in the First World War—and the attempt to represent that loss—was an integral element fertilizing the growth of German fascism.[65] Rephrasing Benjamin, Hewitt terms this the "ontologization of a (historical) loss" whereby,

> in the reconstruction of a (national) identity, the very concept of "loss" is already recuperative: implying something that has been lost, it posits lack as the absence of a historical and ontological (or national) presence. More than this, however, the ontologization of loss ensures that loss can never be lost, since it becomes the very condition of national identity.[66]

Quite unlike Germany, Japan entered the Second World War the military victor of its recent wars (in Russia and China). But Japan was in the midst of a *cultural* crisis that was widely experienced as loss. From the Meiji era through the early 1920s, Japan had eagerly and enthusiastically embraced modernity and the Westernization with which it was inextricably intertwined. But by the late 1920s and early 1930s, the mood had radically changed. Tetsuo Najita and Harry Harootunian write, "It was precisely because Japanese saw the urgency of keeping their culture uncontaminated and hence preserving its essence against the threatened external pollution that many felt justified using militant forms of political and cultural action."[67] It is important to add that this urgency felt toward protecting cultural purity was the result of a perception *of loss that had already happened*, as the writer Tanizaki Jun'ichirō's words from 1933 perhaps best describe:

> *What losses we have suffered*, in comparison with the Westerner. The Westerner has been able to move forward in ordered steps, while we have met superior civilization and have had to surrender to it, and we have had to leave a road we have followed for thousands of years.

In recent years the pace of progress has been so precipitous that conditions in our own country go somewhat beyond the ordinary. The changes that have taken place since the Restoration of 1867 must be at least as great as those of the preceding three and a half centuries.[68]

In Kawabata's fiction, this sense of loss is communicated primarily through a melancholic *mood*—a sense of loss and decay—rather than in blunt, straightforward statements lamenting loss. Kawabata's *Yama no oto* (Sound of the Mountain; 1949) explores the decline toward old age and impending death of the protagonist. Or, for example, from *Snow Country*:

> He spent much of his time watching insects in their death agonies.
>
> Each day, as the autumn grew colder, insects died on the floor of his room. Stiff-winged insects fell on their backs and were unable to get to their feet again. A bee walked a little and collapsed, walked a little and collapsed, It was a quiet death.[69]

Or in the concluding pages of *Thousand Cranes*, when the daughter of a tea-ceremony master breaks an antique tea bowl:

> The broken Shino lay on the stepping stone before the stone basin.
>
> He put together four large pieces to form a bowl. A piece large enough to admit his forefinger was missing from the rim.
>
> Wondering if it might be somewhere on the ground, he started looking among the stones. Immediately he stopped.
>
> He raised his eyes. A large star was shining through the trees to the east.
>
> . . .
>
> It seemed dreary in contrast to the fresh glimmer of the star, to be hunting a broken bowl and trying to put it together.
>
> He threw the pieces down again.
>
> The evening before, Fumiko had flung the Shino against the basin before he could stop her.
>
> He had cried out.[70]

This sentiment of loss and an encroaching doom, hinted at in the darkening mood of much of Kawabata's fiction, took many different manifestations throughout Japanese society—philosophic, political, literary, to name a few—which collectively expressed the anxiety that something that must be retrieved had been lost to Japanese culture with the precipitous process of modernization/Westernization. It was this cultural loss that laid at least a portion of the ideological groundwork for the support of the Asia-Pacific War by many intellectuals and politicians. In his short article on the Pan-Asianism of the Western-educated liberal politician Nagai Ryūtarō, Peter Duus places this perception of cultural loss at the matrix of Nagai's (surprising) support of the Asia-Pacific War. Nagai called for a unified Asia against white imperialism because,

> Like others of his generation, Nagai did not regard the "successes of Meiji" as a source of undiluted pride as a Japanese. . . .
>
> Success in war did not necessarily establish the nation's cultural worth. To Nagai, it seemed that although Japan had been a military and diplomatic victor, she *remained a cultural loser*. . . . [T]he defeat of China and Russia made Japan a great power, but not a great civilization.[71]

In this sense, one might adapt Hewitt's argument and claim that the Japanese nation-state ontologized that cultural loss—that is, positioned loss as intrinsic to current Japanese being. Hence, loss became a sort of "presence" that "stood in" for that which was absent (i.e., traditional culture itself) as the Asia-Pacific War began.

Moreover, the link between the perception of cultural loss and the sanctification of nature in Japan (which, it must be reiterated, is "second" nature, or acculturated nature, not nature itself) could not be more clear: as modernity/Westernization had irrevocably altered the relation of human to nature, Japanese traditional culture, which supposedly resided still in remote, preindustrialized provinces like that of *Snow Country*, was imagined to be a potential source for a new age of Eastern sensibility. Against the "divisiveness of modern political and social relations" from Meiji through the 1930s, nationalist activists such as Kita Ikki and the fundamentalist agrarianists Gondō Seikei, Inoue Nisshō, and Tachibana Kōsaburō called for a new "return" to an agrarian and communalist Asia in which the people were bound naturally to the Japanese emperor (at the same time that Kawabata was celebrating such locales in his fiction).[72] The more radical of the agrarianists advocated violent means to achieve these ends, but even for those who sought peaceful change,

> The people were seen as an embodiment of a common essence that derived from the local land and the tutelary shrines that defined all within a marked-off space as "brothers" under the divine protection of spiritual entities. Far from the corrupt cities and the sites of industrial capitalism, the possibility of communal brotherhood, the agrarianists believed, *con-*

tinued to exist as an accessible reality, even though in recent times it had been attacked by the forces of modernity.[73]

Maruyama Masao wrote that Tachibana Kōsaburō, a leading fascist ideologue, praised "the life bound to the soil in the following words":

Man's world will be eternal so long as the bright sun is over his head and his feet are planted on the ground. . . . What is tilling the soil if not the very basis of human life? . . . Only by agrarianism can a country become eternal, and this is especially the case with Japan. Japan never could, and never can, be herself if she is separated from the soil.[74]

As in Nazi Germany, the "naturalization" of culture by the prewar Japanese agrarian-communalism did not halt at landscape but endeavored to conceive of the nation itself as a "natural entity rather than an imagined community."[75] Modernity is believed to have "polluted" nature, while

focusing on the natural allows fascism to highlight the issue of land and its importance to the people and the nation. The Nazi "blood and soil" doctrine, for example, is suggestive of an intimate connection between the blood of the people (nation) and the soil of the land (nature), expressing the unity of a racial people and its land. . . . [I]deologically fascism does not merely "respect" nature: it sanctifies and spiritualizes it. For fascism the philosophical distinction between man and nature is an artificial product of rationalist philosophy and science.[76]

Moreover, a naturalized connection between the land of Japan and its ethnic populace was being made in philosophical discourses. The most famous example is that of Watsuji Tetsurō, whose Fūdo (Climate and Culture; 1935) linked natural environment to national character.[77] The Kyoto school Buddhists attempted a similar naturalization of nation and support of (ultra)nationalism, "explicitly connecting 'blood and soil' with the Japanese state."[78] In these renderings, nature becomes the hallmark of the spiritual in a manner that I think is quite similar to how nature is configured in Kawabata's valorization of Zen as the "natural essence" of the Oriental sensibility. (And, of course, fascist ideology valorizes vitalism and faith over rational doctrine in a way that is not unlike religions, including Zen.)[79] While Zen itself was not, of course, intrinsically fascist, it met fascist ideology's need to sanctify nature and the nation:

The sanctification of nature is simultaneously the sanctification of the nation as the natural collective unit. The integral connection between the idea of a national spirit and the spiritual concept of nature focuses attention on this nature, that is, the land of this nation, and the role it plays in shaping national character and identity. A geographically specific nature forms the mediating link between the sanctification of nature and the nationalist impulse. . . .

To mobilize the masses in an anti-communist fashion, fascism "nationalizes" the masses, that is, reconstitutes the working class as part of the nation, presenting the struggle of the nation in terms of a mysticism of nature; the nation in motion fulfils its historic role by realizing its natural spirit—the will to power.[80]

The "natural" in Kawabata's texts, however, is nowhere wild and rampant; it is the cultured garden, tamed by the human hand, or the mountains made docile in poetry. Objects (and women) seen in mirrors or through glass, for example, are transformed into what they "should" or "could" be, which surpasses what they are. *Snow Country* opens on Shimamura aboard a train traversing a snowy countryside. He sees a woman, Yoko, reflected over the passing scenery in the train window. A light projected from the mountains, shining in the reflection of Yoko's face, is to Shimamura "inexpressible beauty."[81] As the modern train travels the old country, the shape and contours of the landscape and Yoko's face, the play of changing light, the sensations of coldness and steam, the high pitch of Yoko's voice in the dark night, and the flow of time and space are all given equal narrative attention. A sample passage yields:

In the depths of the mirror the evening landscape moved by, the mirror and the reflected figures like motion pictures superimposed one on the other. The figures and the background were unrelated, and yet the figures, transparent and intangible, and the background, dim in the gathering darkness, melted together into a sort of symbolic world not of this world. Particularly when a light out of the mountains shone in the center of the girl's face, Shimamura felt his chest rise at the inexpressible beauty of it.

The mountain sky still carried traces of evening red. Individual shapes were clear far into the distance, but the monotonous mountain landscape, undistinguished for mile after mile, seemed all the more undistinguished for having lost its last traces of color. There was nothing to catch the eye and it seemed to flow along in a wide, unformed emotion. That was of course because the girl's face floated over it. Cut off by the face, the evening landscape moved steadily by around its outlines. The face too seemed transparent—but was it really transparent? Shimamura had the illusion that the evening landscape was actually passing over the face, and the flow did not stop to let him be sure it was not.[82]

This mediated nature, to reiterate, is particularized as "naturally" Japanese. Representation repeatedly surpasses reality, hence again recalling fascist politics of representation in a short-circuiting of the sign and the fixing of signifiers.

A reactionary politics of time (looking backward while moving forward and a simultaneity of the non-simultaneous), aestheticentrism (or *inflexible purification of domain*), and spiritualized nature are clearly present in the mythic re-conceptualization of Zen as the "ground" of Japanese culture evident in Kawabata's Nobel Prize speech. The speech sanctifies a specifically Japanized acculturation of nature as well as aestheticizes Japanese being (or ontologizes transcendental aesthetics). So do his essays that call for (and literature that attempts to formulate) a new mode of Japanese literature inspired by the canon. This reactionary politics of time, aestheticentrism, and spiritualized nature are also evident in his ontologization of loss, and in his disavowal of Western modernist influences. In addition, it can be argued that the form of Zen embraced by Kawabata also has a "politics of time" that postulates a simultaneity of the non-simultaneous.[83] It is no stretch to postulate that against precipitous modernization that was in Japan essentially intertwined with Westernization, and a growing proletarian movement in the 1920s through the early 1930s, Kawabata proposed a reactionary modernism. In place of political praxis, Kawabata retreated into the purified domain of a culturally exceptionalized and essentialized aesthetic of the past to be regenerated in the present and guard the future against the pollution of modernity and rationalism.

The myth at the core of Kawabata's reactionary modernism—that invents a non-changing over time, culturally particular, Japanese past imbued with a nature bound to the Zen aesthetic and thus takes the place of history—much like that of National Socialism, is the notion of the past glory of harmony between nature and human that becomes fixed in the notion of the *Volk*.[84] Indeed, Neocleous argues that this is endemic to fascist ideology: "having emptied reality of history, fascist myth fills it with nature."[85] The varied class violences of the empowered aristocracy of the Heian, the warring factions of Muromachi- Kamakura (which included religious wars between the various sects in the battle for power), and the centralized feudalism of the Edo period are obliterated in the recirculation of "tradition" divested of history: class struggle and the brutality of the samurai class; the dehumanization of the outcastes; the abuses of the various temples; the starving peasants and the rice riots—all disappear alongside the contemporaneous march toward fascism. As Kawabata retreated into an aestheticized past imaginary, the current moment and its modernity were simultaneously disavowed. Kawabata's mission, so to speak, was precisely to realize this past in the present—in terms of *representation*. One can also describe this as a tension in which the real, or material reality (history), is disavowed and replaced with an aestheticized, acculturated, mediated, and subjective representation of the real (myth).

Of course, the aesthetics and politics of representation that I am describing, although they may well share much structurally and even thematically with those of fascist systems, might not seem particularly sinister in the absence of a fascist movement. But these aesthetics become potentially monstrous when they are used to justify brutality. Here one should remember that at the same time that Kawabata resolutely turned rhetorically to the Japanese past, the Japanese nation-state was resolutely marching toward fascism. In 1934, Kawabata was appointed a member of the Literary Discussion Group, a group organized by the Public Security Division of the Japanese Home Ministry to ensure literary cooperation with ever tightening government control of literature in its fascist-imperialist interests. His aestheticentrism was at the very least not viewed as threatening to fascist interests, and more unsettling is the fact that an early version of *Snow Country* was awarded the third annual literary prize by this same (fascist) Literary Discussion Group in 1937.[86] In fact, Kawabata, like so many others of his generation, supported the war: "Kawabata indicated that now as the 'Japanese race' which had situated the emperor at its center, there was nothing to be done but participate in the war."[87]

Importantly, Kawabata fiercely *sharpened* his insistence that the essence of his own writing was grounded in the tradition of "Japanese verse" during the Second World War.[88] Many of Kawabata's wartime publications, such as *Bokka* (Pastoral Song; 1937–38) and *Tōkaidō* (The Tokaido Highway; 1943), seek peace and solace in a mythic past that is nationalized in a search to revitalize premodern Japan. These narratives did reference (as did *Kōgen* [Heights; 1943–45]), and even appeared to lament (through the voices of various characters), the context of Japan at war, encouraging some critics, including Kobayashi Yoshihito, to argue that alongside the wartime turn toward Japaneseness and nature, *Pastoral Song* in particular made an "antiwar" gesture.[89] However, this retreat into an acculturated, specifically Japanese nature should now be understood as in itself complicit with fascist ideology. Moreover, on closer consideration, it turns out that what look like "references to the war" in these wartime narratives are not exactly references to the existing war. Rather, as Hatori Tetsuya wrote:

> In order to make the contemporaneous war accommodate his notion of the spirit of Japanese culture, the war [that Kawabata wrote about in these narratives] could not be one in service to Japanese supremacy and the domination of another ethnic group (*minzoku*) by the Japanese race (*minzoku*). To the contrary, it would have to be a war in which the [Japanese] self perishes and dissolves into the other, or one could equate it with a war of sublation in which the self is fused with the other. This notion is there in both *Pastoral Song* and *Heights*, and in *The Tokaido Highway*, I think, you can see it [the notion of this spirit] in [Kawabata's] attempt to introduce it as a solid foundation in the archaic basis of Japanese cultural tradition.
>
> Kawabata could not oppose the war during the war. He had to accept it like one accepts fate. But while accepting the war, he hoped it would not be a war [fought] to promote the ego[ism] of the Japanese race (*minzoku*), but instead be a war that took the form of dissolving Japan into the world. However, because there was a gap between his hope and his ideal and the real war, Kawabata never finished writing (*chūzetsu*) *Tōkaidō* or *Bokka*—[texts] that, at least to some degree, tried to deal honestly with the age and the war. In the end, caught up in the flow of history that no single individual had power over, Kawabata could only fix his gaze on the sadness of individual (*hitotsu hitotsu*) lives that were tossed about in that flow.[90]

Hatori Tetsuya's description of how Kawabata substituted his "ideal" war for depictions of the actual war is part of his attempt to exonerate Kawabata from complicity with Japan's imperialism and militarism in the Second World War. However, in the context of my argument about fascist aesthetics, this very substitution indicates precisely a fascist aesthetic. This is structurally similar to substituting "myth" for "history," or "image" for "depth narrative"—a purposeful transformation of even *current militarism and its events* with idealized images of subject–object sublation. Even those texts such as *Pastoral Song* that (originally) resisted a complete "bracketing" outside the sociopolitical context (as *Snow Country* did) merely turned the actual war into a fictitious one after Kawabata's personal preference. What looks like an attempt to grapple with the war is more accurately the replacement of the "real" war with an imaginary one. Against the background of soldiers being called into service and deployed, Suda, the protagonist in *Heights*, sinks into reverie, imagining a world peopled with biracial (mixed-blood) children, inspiring Hatori Kazuei to dub this (in *katakana*) "cosmo-politanism."[91] The imaginary war of *Pastoral Song* and *Heights* disavows Japanese "egoism" and in its place proposes a deflection away from the real, or material, political reality and toward a mediated, imaginary transformation of this real (world). As Hirakawa Sukehiro has argued, it was during the war that Kawabata's aesthetic sensibility was sharpened, to the point that, "like waving a magic wand, his pen and eyes totally transformed the ugly, or that which one expects to be filthy, into something beautiful and pure,"[92] The aestheticization of war in some of his narratives is, I believe, ominous, given the context of actual war in which he wrote and published those texts. Thematically, or contextually, this short-lived gesture toward writing the "war" (which must be understood as I have described it and not confused with any attempt at historicization) is thus in Kawabata constitutively paired with a reactionary modernism. Increasingly his protagonists sought solace in mythic representations of Japan's past and an aestheticization of war. The real war of "egoism" and tyranny is transformed into a more acceptable, even "pure," war of self-depreciation and apparent cosmopolitanism (dare I say, a beautiful war?), and death becomes one of Kawabata's favorite occasions for the celebration of beauty.[93]

In contrast to the harsh postwar self-reevaluation undertaken by the majority of Japanese intellectuals, artists, and writers, Tsuji Kunio quotes Kawabata as fortifying this positioning *after* the loss of the war: "from now on I will probably tend toward Japanese style traditionalism and classicism."[94] In his Nobel speech, he spoke of a friend for whom "there is no art superior to death . . . to die is to live."[95]

But where, one might ask, are the "real" politics in this acculturation of nature and aestheticization of death and war? (Kobayashi, after all, finds this aestheticization and retreat into nature to constitute a resistance to the war.)[96] It helps to remember that fascist propaganda largely *downplays* economic and political issues in favor of foregrounding feelings and affects and aims to incite the masses by using images, intuition, and sentiment.[97] The aesthetic construct at the core of Kawabata's politics of representation encompasses many elements that this essay, following such theorists as Benjamin, Chow, Griffin, Hewitt, Neocleous, and Sontag, has analyzed as integral and endemic to fascist ideology, aesthetics, and propaganda: a mythic, naturalized past in the present (palingenetic myth), aestheticentrism (that also aestheticizes death), the dissolution of self into community, an ontologization of cultural loss, and more.

I will conclude this essay with a brief comparison of the depictions of two young women in Kawabata's *Snow Country* and his much later *Nemureru bijo* (House of the Sleeping Beauties; 1960–61), an account of protagonist Eguchi's visits to a unique brothel where elderly, impotent men fondle drugged, unconscious virgin girls. In the last pages of *House of the Sleeping Beauties*, Eguchi is put together with two drugged girls: one is pure, fair, and beautiful; the other is described as a dark, oily girl. She sweats; her body and breath exude an unpleasant odor; and, Eguchi imagines, she is tough and wild:

> She seemed to be lying with her legs spread wide. She lay face up, her arms flung out. The nipples were large and had a purplish cast. It was not a beautiful color in the light from the crimson velvet curtains. Nor could the skin of the neck and breasts be called beautiful. She had a dark glow. There seemed to be a faint odor at the armpits.
>
> "Life itself," muttered Eguchi.
>
> The oily skin of the dark girl was unpleasant behind him. It was cold and slippery.[98]

She cannot be Japanese, he surmises. After passing much of the night alternately touching the two girls and lapsing into one troubled memory-dream state after another, Eguchi awakens to discover that the dark girl lies dead beside him.[99] There is nothing beautiful or erotic in her death. "Old Eguchi awoke with a groan. He shook his head, but he was still in a daze. He was facing the dark girl. Her body was cold. He started up. She was not breathing. He felt her breast. There was no pulse. He leaped up. He staggered and fell. Trembling violently, he went into the next room."[100]

The "foreign" oily girl's terrifying and revolting death makes a vibrant contrast with that of Yoko, the perfectly aesthetic and thoroughly Japanese beauty of *Snow Country*. Yoko's death in a burning warehouse is conversely the stunning vehicle for oneness with the "universal." Hastening toward the fire, Shimamura is distracted by the skies above:

> The Milky Way. Shimamura too looked up, and he felt himself floating into the Milky Way. Its radiance was so near that it seemed to take him up into it. *Was this the bright vastness the poet Bashō saw when he wrote of the Milky Way arched over a stormy sea?* The Milky Way came down just over there, to wrap the night earth in its naked embrace. There was a terrible

voluptuousness about it. Shimamura fancied that his own small shadow was being cast up against it from the earth. Each individual star stood apart from the rest, and even the particles of silver dust in the luminous clouds could be picked out, so clear was the night. The limitless depth of the Milky Way pulled his gaze up into it.[101]

On his way to witness Yoko's apparent death, the limitless depth of the Milky Way literally "sucks up" Shimamura's gaze (*shisen o suikonde itta*).[102] Shimamura begins to disintegrate into a vast "nature": "and the Milky Way, like a great aurora, flowed through his body to stand at the edges of the earth. There was a quiet, chilly loneliness in it, and a sort of voluptuous astonishment."[103] The motif of the Milky Way that carries through these final passages is introduced as an experience related by the canonized, revered, medieval poet, Matsuo Bashō (1644–94). Great, universal nature—the heavens themselves—flow down into Shimamura in much the same way that Bashō experienced the stars. The coming together of human and nature is culturalized, particularized, and de-historicized and requires the ultimate disinterestedness of an aestheticized, (Japanese) female corpse. Successfully aestheticized in *Snow Country* (looked at disinterestedly, or "bracketed"), Yoko's death facilitates Shimamura's communal, nationalized, spiritual diffusion. Unsuccessfully aestheticized, the oily, non-Japanese girl of *House of the Sleeping Beauties* functions as the repository for Eguchi's objects of abjection. Although the aesthetic annihilation of the other (as in Yoko's death) is easily understood as a fascist aesthetic, the other side of this configuration, or the diffusion of the self into a fiercely mediated reality, can also be a fascist aesthetic when at its foundation it requires a reconfiguration of the real (in the Lacanian sense) into this same "reality"[104]—that is, reconfigured into a culturally particularized and communal "reality qua second nature," or the relentless mediation of reality with a mythicized "Japanese convention" in a disavowal of historical and individual difference. This is where Emmanuel Lévinas calls for invocation: it is an integration of self and other that obliterates the otherness of the other.[105] On the level of social discourse, this appears as the denial of history and an elevation of myth, the mediation (to a degree that it equals annihilation) of "real things" (especially the representation of women) with aesthetics and an imaginary Japaneseness. On an interpersonal level, it is the sublation of the other and the self but in the image of the nationalized-aestheticized subject. It is this process—the specific manner in which mediation of reality is obsessively attempted through all the aesthetic-acculturated devices (the culturally exceptional aestheticization of ontology) I have described—that I understand to be collusive with fascist aesthetics.

Notes

1. Kawabata Yasunari, *Utsukushii Nihon no watakushi* (Tokyo: Kōdansha, 1968). A translation by Edward G. Seidensticker is included.
2. Ueda Makoto, "Kawabata Yasunari," in idem, *Modern Japanese Writers* (Stanford, Calif.: Stanford University Press, 1976), 174–75.
3. Tachihara Masaaki, "Kawabata bungaku no erotishizumu," in *Gunzō Nihon no sakka 13, Kawabata Yasunari* (Tokyo: Shōgakukan, 1991), 116.
4. Almost everything that has been written on Kawabata in English and Japanese could be cited here. To choose a few, see, e.g., Van C. Gessel, *Three Modern Novelists: Sōseki, Tanizaki, Kawabata* (Tokyo: Kodansha International, 1993); David Pollack, "The Ideology of Aesthetics," in idem, *Reading against Culture: Ideology and Narrative in the Japanese Novel* (Ithaca, N.Y.: Cornell University Press, 1992), 100–20; Okude Ken, *Kawabata Yasunari: Yukiguni o yomu* (Tokyo: Miiyai Shoten, 1989); Dennis Washburn, *The Dilemma of the Modern in Japanese Fiction* (New Haven, Conn.: Yale University Press, 1997). Exceptions to this tendency are few in number but include several attempts to read some of Kawabata's wartime publications in relation to the war: see Kobayashi Ichirō, "Kōgen ron: jidai haikei o chūshin ni," and Kobayashi Yoshihito, "Bokka ron," both in *Kawabata Yasunari kenkyū sōsho 5: Kyojitsu no himaku, Yukiguni, Kōgen, Bokka*, ed. Kawabata Bungaku Kenkyūkai (Tokyo: Kyōiku Shuppan Senta, 1979), 141–56, 157–71; Hatori Tetsuya, "Sensō jidai no Kawabata Yasunari," in *Nihon bungaku kenkyū shiryō shinshū 27; Kawabata Yasunari: Nihon no bigaku* (Tokyo: Yūseidō, 1990), 146–51; Hatori Kazuei, "Showa jyūnendai bungaku to kawabata," *Kokubungaku kaishaku to kyōzai no kenkyū 15*, no. 3 (February 1970): 109–13. Although these Japanese critics try to reconcile Kawabata's wartime writings within the context of Japanese fascism, they largely read Kawabata's wartime retreat into aesthetics and "nature" as a sort of protest against the war—a reading that, as this essay will show, I find deeply problematic. For historicizations of Kawabata more in keeping with my reading of him, see Harry D. Harootunian's brief comments on Kawabata in Najita Tetsuo and H. D. Harootunian, "Japan's Revolt against the West," in *Modern Japanese Thought*, ed. Bob Tadashi Wakabayashi (Cambridge: Cambridge University Press, 1998), 207–72; Matsuura Hisaki, "Miru koto no heisoku," *Shinchō* 6 (June 1992): 269–75; Charles R. Cabell, "Maiden Dreams: Kawabata Yasunari's Beautiful Japanese Empire, 1930–1945," Ph.D. diss., Harvard University, Cambridge, Mass., 1999.
5. Cabell, *Maiden Dreams*.
6. Mark Neocleous, *Fascism* (Minneapolis: University of Minnesota Press, 1997), ix. Neocleous's excellent, sweeping analysis covers virtually all of European fascism but completely excludes any reference to Japanese fascism.

7. Peter Osborne, *The Politics of Time: Modernity and Avant-Garde* (London: Verso, 1995), 160.

8. Roger Griffin, *The Nature of Fascism* (New York: Routledge, 1991).

9. Osborne, *The Politics of Time*; Griffin, *The Nature of Fascism*.

10. Neocleous, *Fascism*, xi; xii.

11. Matthew Affron and Mark Antliff, "Introduction," in *Fascist Visions: Art and Ideology in France and Italy*, ed. Matthew Affron and Mark Antliff (Princeton, N.J.: Princeton University Press, 1997), 9; emphasis added.

12. Walter Benjamin, "The Work of Art in the Age of Mechanical Reproduction," in idem, *Illuminations* (New York: Schocken Books, 1968), 241–42.

13. Andrew Hewitt, "Fascist Modernism, Futurism, and 'Postmodernity,'" in *Fascism, Aesthetics and Culture*, ed. Richard J. Golsan (Hanover, N.H.: University Press of New England, 1992), 44–45.

14. Susan Sontag, "Fascinating Fascism," in *Movies and Methods*, vol. 1, ed. Bill Nichols (Berkeley: University of California Press, 1976), 45.

15. Rey Chow, *Ethics after Idealism: Theory–Culture–Ethnicity–Reading* (Bloomington: Indiana University Press, 1998), 17.

16. Harry Harootunian, *Overcome by Modernity: History, Culture, and Community in Interwar Japan* (Princeton, N.J.: Princeton University Press, 2000), xxv–xxvii.

17. See Hewitt, who has written about this extensively in his article, "Fascist Modernism,"; in his book, *Fascist Modernism: Aesthetics, Politics, and the Avant-Garde* (Stanford, Calif.: Stanford University Press, 1993); and *Political Inversions: Homosexuality, Fascism, and the Modernist Imaginary* (Stanford, Calif.: Stanford University Press, 1996).

18. Hewitt, *Political Inversions*, 7

19. See Ueda, "Kawabata Yasunari," 201–14; Washburn, *The Dilemma of the Modern in Japanese Fiction*; Masao Miyoshi, "The Margins of Life," in idem, *Accomplices of Silence: The Modern Japanese Novel* (Berkeley: University of California Press, 1974), 94–121; Kosai Shinji, "Kawabata Yasunari shō," in *Nihon bungaku kenkyū shiryō shinshū 27*, 53–59.

20. Ueda, "Kawabata Yasunari," 206–208.

21. Quoted in and translated by Donald Keene, "Kawabata Yasunari," in idem, *Dawn to the West: Japanese Literature of the Modern Era*, vol. 1 (New York: Holt, Rinehart and Winston, 1984), 807. The original is in *Kawabata Yasunari zenshū*, vol. 33 (Tokyo: Shinchōsha, 1982), 87–88.

22. Almost any text dealing with the transition into modernity in Japan brings up this late Taishō–early Shōwa sense of excessive modernization and the trauma of the speed of transformation. One culminating moment was the symposium "Kindai no chōkoku (Overcoming the Modern)" in 1942 of Japanese intellectuals and writers on the problematic of Westernization and modernization. For a good overview in English, see Najita and Harootunian, "Japan's Revolt against the West."

23. See, e.g., Miyoshi, *Accomplices of Silence*, 111.

24. David Pollack, however, finds the structure of nō drama in *Snow Country*. See Pollack, "The Ideology of Aesthetics," 116.

25. If I remember correctly, it was Professor Paul Anderer who used the wonderful phrase "fetishization of the trivial" to describe *monogatari* when I was in graduate school.

26. Kawabata Yasunari, *Thousand Cranes*, trans. Edward Seidensticker (New York: Berkeley Publishing, 1965), 125.

27. Edward G. Seidensticker, "Introduction," in Kawabata Yasunari, *Snow Country*, trans. Edward G. Seidensticker (New York: Berkeley Medallion Books, 1956), 6–7.

28. Kawabata Yasunari, *Snow Country*, trans. Edward G. Seidensticker (New York: Limited Editions Club, 1990).

29. See Thomas LaMarre, *Uncovering Heian Japan: An Archaeology of Sensation and Inscription* (Durham: Duke University Press, 2000), for a fascinating and pathbreaking analysis of the figural and other extra-linguistic attributes of Heian-period poetics.

30. Following Harry Harootunian in his *Things Seen and Unseen: Discourse and Ideology in Tokugawa Nativism* (Chicago: University of Chicago Press, 1988), I make this argument in detail about Izumi Kyōka in my *Dangerous Women, Deadly Words: Phallic Fantasy and Modernity in Three Japanese Writers* (Stanford, Calif.: Stanford University Press, 1999).

31. Kosai, "Kawabata Yasunari shō," 59. In addition to *Snow Country*, Mizuumi (The Lake; 1954–55) and *Nemureru bijo* (House of the Sleeping Beauties; 1960–61) are narratives written by Kawabata. The *Kokinshū* and *Shinkokinshū* are Heian-period poetry anthologies; *haikai* is another term for *renga*, or linked poetry.

32. Kawabata Yasunari, "Shinshin sakka no shinkeikō kaisetsu," in *Kawabata Yasunari zenshū*, vol. 30 (Tokyo: Shinchōsha, 1982), 172–83.

33. Kawabata, *Snow Country*, 45.

34. Kawabata, *Utsukushii Nihon no watakushi*, 49, 47. Although the Japanese text follows Japanese convention by being paginated and reading from right to left, strangely the English text that appears at the end of the Japanese reverses the Japanese order (and, like conventional English, starts thus at the end of the book, reading left to right). Pagination, however, is continuous in the Japanese order. That is why the page numbers decrease (or appear backward) in multi-page citations to the English translation.

35. Ibid., 63–62.

36. Ibid., 68.

37. As quoted and translated in Ueda, "Kawabata Yasunari," 208.

38. I have written about this at length elsewhere, but to summarize briefly: landscapes described and painted in premodern texts were not attempts to represent "the real landscape." To borrow the critic Karatani Kōjin's description, landscape was more accurately "a weave of language" given signification by poetry: Karatani Kōjin, "One Spirit, Two Nineteenth Centuries," *South Atlantic Quarterly* 87, no. 3

(summer 1988): 619. Natural landscape, as described in medieval travel diaries or drawings, was depicted following canonized antecedent texts and paintings. The medieval artist or diarist did not try to capture the essence of landscape as he or she actually observed it; rather, the requirements of a variety of rigid rhetorical forms dictated the description and appreciation of famous sites previously celebrated in the literary canon. According to this logic, there were strict customs delineating how to express the putative "true essence" of the object—including appropriate and inappropriate combinations of particular birds, trees, and flowers, or such dictums as, for example, mountains in spring are best depicted with mist and clouds. Therefore the artist-diarist made sure to include mist in his depictions of spring mountains regardless of whether mist was present at the moment of viewing the physical site. This is what Karatani has called a "transcendental" vision of space. For Meiji-period artists and writers to see an actual landscape as an appropriate subject of artistic production, "this transcendental vision of space had to be overturned": Karatani Kōjin, *Origins of Modern Japanese Literature* (Durham: Duke University Press, 1993), 27. See also my discussion in *Dangerous Women*, particularly the chapters on Izumi Kyōka.

39. Andrew Feenberg, "The Problem of Modernity in the Philosophy of Nishida," in *Rude Awakenings: Zen, the Kyoto School, and the Question of Nationalism*, ed. James W. Heisig and John C. Maraldo (Honolulu: University of Hawai'i Press, 1994), 155–56.

40. Kawabata Yasunari, *Utsukushii Nihon no watakushi*, 69, 65, 58, 41.

41. Ueda Makoto, "Yūgen and Erhabene: Onishi Yoshinori's Attempt to Synthesize Japanese and Western Aesthetics," in *Culture and Identity: Japanese Intellectuals during the Interwar Years*, ed. J. Thomas Rimer (Princeton, N.J.: Princeton University Press, 1990), 284.

42. Ibid., 297–99.

43. Osborne, *The Politics of Time*, 161.

44. For critical commentary on these philosophers in English, see, e.g., Bob Tadashi Wakabayashi, ed., *Modern Japanese Thought* (Cambridge: Cambridge University Press, 1998); Rimer, *Culture and Identity*; Heisig and Maraldo, *Rude Awakenings*; Naoki Sakai, *Translation and Subjectivity: On "Japan" and Cultural Nationalism* (Minneapolis: University of Minnesota Press, 1997).

45. Robert A. Sharf, "Whose Zen? Zen Nationalism Revisited," in Heisig and Maraldo, *Rude Awakenings*, 45.

46. Ibid., 44–46.

47. Kawabata Yasunari, *Utsukushii Nihon no watakushi*, 71–70.

48. As was more evident in Kawabata's earlier eulogy to Yokomitsu Riichi, "Sufferer of the New Asia that fought the West / Pioneer of the New Tragedy in the Asian Tradition / You shouldered such a destiny / And you left the world sending a smile to Heaven / this tradition of beauty as part of a larger Asian whole": as quoted and translated in Yuasa Yasuo, *Watsuji Tetsurō*, in Najita and Harootunian, "Japan's Revolt against the West," 272.

49. Although some argue that Ch'an deeply affected Neo-Confucianism in China: see, e.g., Wing-Tsit Chan, trans. and comp., *A Source Book in Chinese Philosophy* (Princeton, N.J.: Princeton University Press, 1963), 425–30.

50. Nishida Kitarō, "Ishiki no mondai," in *Nishida Kitarō zenshū*, vol. 3 (Tokyo: Iwanami Shoten, 1988), 3–236.

51. As translated and quoted in Agustin Jacinto Z., "The Return of the Past" in Heisig and Maraldo, *Rude Awakenings*, 133, 144. The original is in *Nishida Kitarō zenshū*, vol. 12 (Tokyo: Iwanami Shoten, 1980), 136, 337.

52. Hewitt, "Fascist Modernism," 44–45.

53. For more on the question of fascism in relation to modernism, see Hewitt, *Fascist Modernism*; Osborne, *The Politics of Time*; Griffin, *The Nature of Fascism*.

54. Karatani Kōjin, "Uses of Aesthetics: After Orientalism," *Boundary 2* 25, no. 2 (summer 1998): 152–53.

55. Griffin, *The Nature of Fascism*, 32.

56. Ibid., 33.

57. Neocleous, *Fascism*, 72.

58. I put national in quotations here because the past to which many reactionary modernists refer predates the formation of modern nation-states.

59. Hewitt, *Fascist Modernism*, 188–93.

60. Osborne, *The Politics of Time*, 160–96.

61. As explained in ibid. See also Jeffrey Herf, *Reactionary Modernism: Technology, Culture and Politics in Weimar and the Third Reich* (Cambridge: Cambridge University Press, 1984).

62. Osborne, *The Politics of Time*, 164.

63. Ibid., 167.

64. Griffin, *The Nature of Fascism*.

65. Walter Benjamin, "Theories of German Fascism," in idem, *Selected Writings*, vol. 2, ed. Michael W. Jennings, Howard Eiland, and Gary Smith (Cambridge, Mass.: Harvard University Press, 1999), 312–21.

66. Hewitt, *Political Inversions*, 249.

67. Najita and Harootunian, "Japan's Revolt against the West," 207.

68. Tanizaki Jun'ichirō, *In Praise of Shadows* (New Haven, Conn.: Leete's Island Books, 1977), 8, 39; emphasis added.

69. Kawabata, *Snow Country*, 109.

70. Idem, *Thousand Cranes*, 140.

71. Peter Duus, "Nagai Ryūtarō and the 'White Peril,' 1905–1944," *Journal of Asian Studies* 21, no. 3 (November 1971): 42–43; emphasis added.

72. Najita and Harootunian, "Japan's Revolt against the West," 219. The texts by Kawabata I am thinking of here include *Kōgen*, *Bokka*, and *Tōkaidō*.

73. Ibid.; emphasis added.

74. And, against Marxist socialism, Tachibana insisted that "we must not be thrown into that most dangerous of errors: the rash dream of immediately establishing a new society and creating a new culture and a great revolution in world history

merely by means of the expansion of large-scale industry and the application of their productive power to achieve the level of the most advanced nations": as quoted and translated in Maruyama Masao, "The Ideology and Dynamics of Japanese Fascism," in *Thought and Behavior in Modern Japanese Politics*, ed. Ivan Morris (Oxford: Oxford University Press, 1963), 43.

75. Neocleous, *Fascism*, 75.

76. Ibid., 76.

77. Watsuji Tetsurō, *Fūdo* (Tokyo: Iwanami shoten bunko, 1979). For a thorough and compelling discussion of Watsuji, see Sakai, *Translation and Subjectivity*, chaps. 3–4.

78. Kevin Doak, "Nationalism as Dialectics," in Heisig and Maraldo, *Rude Awakenings*, 186.

79. Neocleous, *Fascism*, 14–15.

80. Ibid., 77, 15.

81. Kawabata, *Snow Country*, 9.

82. Ibid., 15–16.

83. At the heart of Nishida's Zen is what one might call a simultaneity of the non-simultaneous in the "delusion" of a split between the so-called physical and biological worlds that obscures their simultaneous mutual negation of one another. In the biological realm, time is both durative and progressive; it is the manifestation of the material world in its myriad forms and includes the human-historical world. The physical realm, to the contrary, is spatial, in which time is reversible rather than teleological. This is a realm of simultaneity in which the manifestation of the material individual is negated by the universal, or the One: see Nishida Kitarō, *Last Writings: Nothingness and the World View*, trans. David A. Dilworth (Honolulu: University of Hawai'i Press, 1987).

84. Of course, all history is narrative, and as such there is no one, singular, "real" history separated from narrative perspective. Here I use the word *history* essentially in the Marxist sense to signify class struggle and the violence of domination.

85. Neocleous, *Fascism*, 79.

86. On this award, see Gessel, *Three Modern Novelists*, 133–94.

87. Hatori Tetsuya, "Sensō jidai no Kawabata Yasunari," 149.

88. Tsuji Kunio, "Kawabata Yasunari ron," in *Nihon bungaku kenkyū shiryō shinshū 27*, 46–52.

89. Kobayashi Yoshihito, "Bokka ron," 170.

90. Hatori Tetsuya, "Sensō jidai no Kawabata Yasunari," 150, 151.

91. Hatori Kazuei, ""Showa jyūnendai bungaku to Kawabata."

92. Hirakawa Sukehiro, "Kawabata Yasunari ni okeru aestheticizing," in *Nihon bungaku kenkyū shiryō shinshū 27*, 105.

93. This is also evident in Kawabata's "Eirei no ibun," in *Kawabata Yasunari zenshū 27*, 338–82, a collection of letters from deceased soldiers at the front, to which Kawabata added his commentary. See Cabell, *Maiden Dreams*, for excerpts in English translation as well as commentary on this narrative.

94. Tsuji, "Kawabata Yasunari ron," 51.
95. Kawabata Yasunari, *Utsukushii Nihon no watakushi*, 62.
96. Kobayashi Yoshishito, "Bokka ron."
97. I have paraphrased Neocleous's quote from Georges Sorel, one of the influential French theorists on National Socialism whose writings influenced many fascists, on how to mobilize the masses to support a socialist movement: "use must be made of a *body of images* which, by *intuition* alone, and before any considered analyses are made, is capable of evoking as an undivided whole the *mass of sentiments* which corresponds to the different manifestations of the war undertaken by Socialism": Neocleous, *Fascism*, 8. The original quote is in Georges Sorel, *Reflections on Violence*, trans. T. E. Hulme (London: George Allen and Unwin, 1915), 130–31.
98. Kawabata Yasunari, *House of the Sleeping Beauties and Other Stories*, trans. Edward G. Seidensticker (Tokyo: Kodansha International, 1969), 86, 96.
99. I do not think, as Mizuta Noriko (Lippit) reads, because he has somehow killed her. See Noriko Misuka Lippit, *Reality and Fiction in Modern Japanese Literature* (New York: M. E. Sharpe, 1980), 141, 144.
100. Kawabata, *House of the Sleeping Beauties*, 97.
101. Idem, *Snow Country*, 165; emphasis added.
102. Idem, "Yukiguni," in *Shōwa bungaku zenshū 5: Kawabata Yasunari, Okamoto Kanoko, Yokomitsu Riichi, Dazai Osamu* (Tokyo: Shōgakukan, 1986), 81.
103. Idem, *Snow Country*, 168.
104. The real in the Lacanian sense refers to that which is constitutively unrepresentable in consciousness or language; it is also that which causes desire. The real must not be confused with reality. Our perception of reality is always filtered through our individual psyches and the cultural discourses into which we are born.
105. Emmanuel Lévinas, *Totality and Infinity: An Essay on Exteriority*, trans. A. Linguis (Pittsburgh: Duquesne University Press, 1969), 52.

JIM REICHERT

Disciplining the Erotic-Grotesque in
Edogawa Ranpo's *Demon of the Lonely Isle*

■ In the late 1920s, popular discussions of psychology, sexology, and criminology inundated the Japanese discursive field. Interest in these topics was closely connected to a highly commercialized formulation of modernism known as Erotic Grotesque Nonsense (*ero-guro-nansensu*), which revolved around explorations of the deviant, the bizarre, and the ridiculous. Capitalizing on the popularity of this stylishly modernist sensibility was a flood of publications, including magazines such as *Hentai shiryō* (Deviant Materials; 1926) and anthologies such as *Kindai hanzai kagaku zenshū* (Anthology of Modern Criminal Science; 1929–30). This trend in the publishing industry coincided almost exactly with the ascendancy in Japan of authoritarian political and social forces that strongly advocated the fascistic ideological fantasies of cultural harmony, ethnic purity, national power, and empire.[1] At first sight it might appear that these two trends existed in direct opposition to each other, with the decadent and deviant elements of the modernist erotic-grotesque sensibility offering a challenge to an increasingly fascistic vision of Japanese culture and society. As I will demonstrate in this essay, however, the relationship between these developments cannot be reduced to a simple binary opposition. The tendency of erotic-grotesque cultural products to treat the "bizarre" and the "deviant" in a simultaneously celebratory and alarmist manner resulted in a multivalent relationship with the fascistic outlook. On the one hand, erotic-grotesque celebrations of "deviant" practices and identities defied myths of cultural homogeneity and purity. On the other hand, the tendency in erotic-grotesque discourse to treat deviance as an unwholesome pathological condition to be cured, isolated, or obliterated mirrored the fascistic compulsion to assimilate, dominate, or destroy outlooks and subjectivities deemed incompatible with national interests and cultural hegemony.[2]

The Erotic Grotesque Nonsense phenomenon is rife with contradictions and inconsistencies. One of the distinguishing characteristics of this sensibility is its transgressive quality. Cultural products associated with this phenomenon conspicuously differentiated themselves from conventional moral and aesthetic standards. This would explain their appeal to urban sophisticates, who constituted their primary audience. For modern girls (moga) and modern boys (mobo) on the cutting edge, consumption of erotic-grotesque cultural paraphernalia, and the simultaneous rejection of "wholesome" values and "productive" behavior implicit in these choices, signified their participation in the cosmopolitan, self-consciously modernist lifestyle known as modern life (modan seikatsu). Adding to the cachet of these decadent cultural products was the vague air of science that surrounded them. Replete with pseudoscientific jargon and presented in the form of research, erotic-grotesque discourse cannily exploited the mania for science that was one of the defining features of modern life.

Complicating the signification of these consumer spectacles was the view, current in Japan during the 1920s and 1930s, that all orders of phenomena adhered to the principles of evolution.[3] That is to say, evolution was conceived not only as a biological process involving the modification of species over successive generations, but it also served as a theoretical model for interpreting and evaluating social and cultural phenomena. Within this framework, commonly known as Social Darwinism, one could distinguish between more evolved and less evolved societies and social practices. This tendency to view social distinctions through the prism of evolutionary theory shaped to varying degrees prewar disciplines such as sexology, eugenics, and criminology, all of which ultimately abetted efforts to regulate society and rid it of "undesirable" or "threatening" elements. In the specific context of erotic-grotesque cultural production, Social Darwinist assumptions revealed a comparable proclivity toward the fascistic turn, which manifested itself in the tendency to categorize individuals who deviated from normative standards of respectability, fitness, and morality as inferior to, and potentially problematic for, the imaginary community of "respectable," "wholesome" Japanese citizens.

The complex relationship between erotic-grotesque cultural products and fascistic visions of Japan is epitomized in the detective fiction (*tantei shōsetsu*) of Edogawa Ranpo (1894–1965). Ranpo's work celebrates the "bizarre" and the "deviant" aspects of society as it simultaneously articulates the necessity of containing and neutralizing these "dangerous" elements. One of the distinguishing features of Ranpo's detective fiction was the conspicuous manner in which it incorporated the latest criminological, medical, and sexological theories. This practice is most dramatically realized in the novel *Kotō no oni* (Demon of the Lonely Isle; 1929–30). Consisting of fourteen installments, which ran from January 1929 to February 1930 in the magazine *Asahi*, Ranpo's narrative renders an account of adventures experienced by a handsome young Tokyoite named Minoura Kinnosuke. Mining bits and pieces from contemporaneous discussions of evolution, psychology, eugenics, sexology, and criminology, the story involves a child assassin, a deranged villain, a gang of medically engineered freaks, a deviant sleuth, and a damsel in distress who suffers from an unusual physical disability. The impact of these various plot devices is further enhanced by the accompanying illustrations, created by Takenaka Eitarō.[4] A famous illustrator who worked with Ranpo on a number of occasions, Takenaka contributed otherworldly images that perfectly complemented the atmosphere of Ranpo's written narrative.

Although this fare might not appeal to everyone, the unqualified commercial success of *Demon of the Lonely Isle* leaves little doubt that there was among Japanese readers at the time a sizable audience for such material. The publication history alone attests to the remarkable popularity of the work. A few months after the story concluded its triumphant run in *Asahi*, the publishers at Kaizōsha rushed the novel out in book form. One year later, in 1931, the novel was published again as the fifth volume in Heibonsha's *Edogawa Ranpo zenshū* (The Collected Works of Edogawa Ranpo; 1931–32).

Clearly, then, there is no denying that conspicuous engagement with reigning pseudoscientific theories of the day, a practice that defines Ranpo's prewar oeuvre in general and *Demon of the Lonely Isle* in particular, resonated powerfully with consumers during the 1920s and 1930s. The question that arises, however, is why this kind of cultural product exerted such a strong hold over audiences. It could be argued that *Demon of the Lonely Isle* captured the Zeitgeist of the period and appealed to paranoid fascist concerns about ethnic purity, cultural homogeneity, military prowess, and imperial expansion. In other words, the account of Minoura's harrowing encounter with deviance and freakishness serves as a kind of fascist heroic narrative, one in which the protagonist skillfully marshals the latest advances in science to thwart "bizarre" and "deviant" elements that threaten the security and sanctity of Japanese culture and national community. In this reading, disciplines like eugenics, criminology, and sexology are useful tools that stand as a bastion against decadent, contaminating forces detrimental to Japan and the Japanese race. At the same time, one could also point to the attention lavished on characters who personify non-normative sexualities, psychologies, and physical bodies and argue that Demon of the Lonely Isle is a celebration of deviance and freakishness. From this perspective, the focus of the text would not be Minoura's triumph over his adversaries but, rather, his interaction with them; he would function as a substitute for the reader, undergoing one exhilaratingly "weird" experience after another. In this reading, science would serve as nothing more than a transparent legitimizing device, a means for justifying detailed discussions of otherwise inappropriate topics. With its ostentatious display (and implicit acceptance) of forces at odds with respectable, wholesome society, Demon of the Lonely Isle could be interpreted as a transgressive gesture against fascistic notions of timeless morality, pure culture, and natural sexuality.[5]

It is my contention, however, that in Demon of the Lonely Isle the production of meaning through signs and other symbolic means, or what I refer to hereafter as Demon of the Lonely Isle's signification, is far more complicated than either of these rigid formulae would suggest. Despite the fact that the novel plays on fascistic fears that the Japanese race and culture are under a state of siege, at risk of being contaminated or weakened by various transparent personifications of modern decadence, Demon of the Lonely Isle cannot solely be treated as a covert propaganda tool for reactionary nationalistic, militaristic, or imperialistic interests. By the same token, the text cannot be taken as an unambiguous celebration of difference, sexual experimentation, and other forms of transgression associated with extreme expressions of prewar modernism and urban consumer culture. Emblematic of the text's complex and unstable ideological position is how it evinces faith in repressive disciplines like sexology, eugenics, and criminology as it simultaneously conveys unabashed enthusiasm for various forms of sexual, physical, and psychological "deviance."

Rather than treat Demon of the Lonely Isle as a static crystallization of any single ideological perspective, it is more illuminating to highlight the "freakish" nature of the text itself. My use of this term is influenced by recent theoretical discussions of freak discourse, which define "freakishness" as the quality that fascinates and horrifies by "blurring identities (sexual, corporeal, personal)" and by "travers[ing] the very boundaries that secure the normal subject in its given identity and sexuality."[6] In other words, the distinguishing characteristic of *Demon of the Lonely Isle* is its resistance to easy categorization. Echoing the symbolic position inhabited by "freaks" of various stripes, including individuals who exhibit an extraordinary body, a "deviant" sexuality, or an "exotic" cultural identity, *Demon of the Lonely Isle* occupies an unstable position that blurs boundaries relied on to separate different discursive, literary, and ideological positions.[7] The result is a signifying field, by which I mean both Ranpo's written narrative and Takenaka's images, that simultaneously enraptures and repels. In this sense, then, the text of *Demon of the Lonely Isle* embodies in its own signification the freakish quality associated with its story and characters. It is a veritable Frankenstein's monster, a disturbing conglomeration of formal elements and ideological signs that have been removed from their familiar context and then stitched together in unexpected patterns.

Demon of the Lonely Isle

Emerging from the same cultural milieu as *Deviant Materials* and *Anthology of Modern Criminal Science*, Ranpo's *Demon of the Lonely Isle* also capitalized on the popularity of pseudoscientific erotic-grotesque discourse. Despite its status as one of the crowning achievements of this vibrant cultural movement, however, the novel has received almost no attention from literary critics or scholars.[8] The following statement from Ōuchi Shigeo suggests why: "No doubt, the novel's many shortcomings are a consequence of the story being serialized in a popular magazine. . . . Ranpo once declared that *Demon of the Lonely Isle* 'marked the beginning of my degeneration into a literary hack.' Elsewhere he commented: 'In contrast to the scrupulousness of my early days as a writer, I had become satisfied with producing mediocre work.'"[9] Ōuchi clearly perceives *Demon of the Lonely Isle* to be a step down from the more legitimate pieces of detective fiction that Ranpo produced as a young writer. Inscribed within this assessment, it turns out, are assumptions borrowed from the standard narrative history of Ranpo's prewar literary career. This master narrative typically charts a decline from intellectual and artistic integrity to crass commercialism. In the years immediately following his debut as a writer in 1923, Ranpo's output consisted mostly of short stories. Starting around 1927, he shifted to full-length novels.[10] The short stories written during the first phase of his career, often described as "pure mystery fiction (*jun tantei shōsetsu*)," are thought to be Ranpo's best work. The pleasure of these narratives is said to lie in their intricate plots, rigorous explorations of the criminal mind, and clever surprise endings.[11] Scholars have treated the novels composed after 1927 with considerably less enthusiasm. The main reason behind this disdain is the shared perception that these novels are excessively vulgar.[12] Ranpo's efforts to extend his appeal beyond a core audience of detective-fiction aficionados resulted in works of questionable taste and scant intellectual value. The plots became too fantastic; the crimes, too horrific; and the characters, too perverted.

Although a brief plot summary can never fully capture the bizarreness of *Demon of the Lonely Isle*, a basic outline of the narrative will facilitate later discussions of the text's signification. The fantastic events of the story are recounted in the first person by the novel's protagonist, Minoura Kinnosuke. The first half of the story centers on Minoura's efforts to solve the murder of his fiancée, Kizaki Hatsuyo, whose body is found in a room in which all points of entry have been secured from the inside. Minoura initially suspects that the crime was committed by a mysterious acquaintance of his, a research physician named Moroto Michio. Moroto is the prime suspect mainly because he is a homosexual man who has made no secret of his affection for the attractive Minoura. It turns out, however, that Moroto is not the perpetrator. To the contrary, he has been trying to solve the mystery on his own. Moroto, in fact, becomes the driving force behind the investigation, bringing his considerable intellectual faculties to bear on the case. He eventually discovers that Hatsuyo was murdered by a trained child assassin in the service of an ominous figure known as Ototsan (a variation on the word "father").

The second half of the story revolves around Minoura's and Moroto's attempts to bring the mysterious Ototsan to justice. Their determination is motivated by three additional factors. First, they are moved by pity after they uncover a diary written by a young girl named Hide-chan, who has been held prisoner by the evil Ototsan. Her plight is even more pathetic in that she is one half of a pair of conjoined twins. Second, Moroto gradually becomes aware that Ototsan is none other than his own father, Moroto Jgor. Third, the young men ascertain from another piece of evidence that a treasure is hidden somewhere on Ototsan's island. After infiltrating Ototsan's headquarters, they learn that he, too, is in hot pursuit of the treasure. He wants the money to finance a nefarious scheme to scientifically create a race of "freaks." The motivations behind this plot are complicated, but in essence Ototsan sees the production of freaks both as a source of profit (he ships his victims off to commercial freak shows) and a means for exacting revenge on "normal" humanity (as a hunchback, Ototsan has suffered numerous indignities in mainstream society). Due to Moroto's considerable resourcefulness, the two young heroes succeed in foiling Ototsan's plans and capturing the hidden treasure.

Their investigation also uncovers some critical information about the lineage of Hatsuyo, Hide-chan, and Moroto. It turns out that Hatsuyo was the rightful heir to the treasure that Ototsan coveted, which explains his decision to have her killed. It also becomes apparent that Hide-chan is Hatsuyo's younger sister and that Ototsan had surgically attached her to another child in an early experimental effort to create a freak. Finally, Moroto finds out, much to his relief, that he is a foundling and not Ototsan's actual son. Once matters on the island are settled, Hide-chan undergoes corrective surgery to separate her from her "twin." After recovering from the operation and claiming her sizable inheritance, she marries Minoura. The only remaining loose end in this happy scenario is Moroto, who still nurses an unrequited love for Minoura. This problem is resolved when a fatal illness claims Moroto's life.

The preceding plot outline helps to explain why critics have treated *Demon of the Lonely Isle* as a scandalous deviation from the parameters of "pure" detective fiction. Indeed, the defining feature of the novel is the erotic-grotesque atmosphere that suffuses the entire text. Examination of two specific story lines reveals more fully how the erotic-grotesque operates in *Demon of the Lonely Isle*. The first story line involves Moroto's unrelenting desire for Minoura. The text devotes a great deal of attention to this issue. The same basic scenario plays itself out on numerous occasions. Moroto expresses his desire, only to have his propositions rebuffed by Minoura. Significantly, the terminology used to describe Moroto shifts constantly. On occasion, he is depicted as an eminently desirable figure. He is referred to as "beautiful (*utsukushii*)" and "alluring (*namamekashii*)." With equal frequency, though, the text asserts the abnormality of Moroto's desire by utilizing such pathologizing sexological terms as "pervert (*henshitsusha*)" and "sexual invert (*seiteki tsakusha*)."

The characterization of Minoura's sexuality, as it manifests itself in his response to Moroto's advances, is equally indeterminate. There are times when Minoura seems open to the possibility of sexual relations with Moroto. For example, after Moroto first professes his love, Minoura indulges in a startling erotic fantasy: "this might sound weird, but for a moment it felt as though I had become a woman . . . and that this beautiful man were my husband."[13] Comments like this suggest that even the ostensibly "normal" Minoura can appreciate, at least on the level of fantasy, "deviant" sexual urges. Most of the time, however, he is simply perplexed by Moroto's feelings. On one occasion he comments, "I could not fathom the feelings in Moroto's heart. But I could tell that he was unable to rid himself of this bizarre love. In fact, over the course of time, it only became more intense. . . . Is it not difficult to comprehend why he would harbor these feelings for me?"[14] Here, as Minoura professes complete bafflement when confronted by a form of desire supposedly foreign to his own experience, his final rhetorical question is especially significant. Through this device, Moroto implicitly signals his inclusion in a larger interpretive community of "normal" readers that shares his views about what constitutes "deviance." That is, he emphatically aligns himself with a community of readers not susceptible to homoerotic desire. The persuasiveness of this gesture, however, is seriously undermined by his tendency to engage in erotic fantasies about Moroto.

Further militating against any neat interpretation of Minoura's and Moroto's relationship are Takenaka's stunning visualizations. This component of the text cannot be overlooked for the simple reason that these illustrations played a vital role in the marketing and consumption of the text as a piece of popular fiction. Indeed, the vast majority of popular-fiction texts from the 1920s and 1930s were prodigiously illustrated. The publishing industry realized that securing the services of a talented artist could dramatically heighten the impact of a narrative. Among the many illustrators working at the time, Takenaka was especially sought after because his images so thoroughly enriched the signification of the texts they accompanied. His images of Minoura and Moroto underscore the indeterminate nature of their relationship.

Figure 1 accentuates the erotic possibilities of the bond. It depicts the comrades as they languish in an underground maze. Not coincidentally, this illustration resembles a cinematic close-up, with many aspects of its composition recalling images found in still photographs taken from Western romantic films. The relative position of the two faces, for example, evokes cinematic conventions for composing the passionate "clinch" shot. In this particular image, the more assertive Moroto's face is on top, with the more submissive Minoura's on the bottom. The representation of their expressions is significant, as well. With his clenched teeth and staring eyes, Moroto conveys the crazed intensity associated with male heartthrobs of

1. Minoura and Moroto trapped in an underground maze. Originally published in *Asahi*, vol. 2, no. 1, 1930, 142–43. Reproduced with permission of the National Diet Library, Tokyo.

the era. With his slightly open mouth, closed eyes, and the backward tilt of his head, Minoura evokes the cinematic heroine, overwhelmed by her passionate lover. Comparison with figure 2, a photographic image from a 1931 series devoted to "erotic-grotesque" love scenes, reveals the degree to which Takenaka relied on the visual idiom of contemporary film to eroticize this encounter. Figure 3 offers a very different visualization of the two men. Specifically, it coincides with the moment when Moroto's umpteenth declaration of love devolves into an actual physical attack. Although most descriptions of Moroto focus on his physical beauty and sophisticated sense of style, this particular passage presents him as a grotesque monster. He is variously described as "snake," "dog," and "leech." The terms "beast" and "animal" are also applied to him.[15] In essence, Moroto is transformed into a freakish monstrosity, a chimera consisting of incongruous parts. The implication of these comparisons is obvious. They offer readers a metaphorical

2. This still photograph is taken from a pictorial series titled, "Eiga rabu shiin (Movie Love Scenes)," which appeared in the publication *Gendai ryōki sentan zukan* (Images from the Cutting Edge of Contemporary Weirdness; 1931). This still comes from the German film *Ungarische Rhapsodie* (Hungarian Rhapsody; 1928), starring Willy Fritsch and Lil Dagover. Reproduced with the permission of the Special Collections Division, Waseda University Library, Tokyo.

manifestation of Moroto's deviant sexuality. Figure 3 duplicates this operation by presenting Moroto as a terrifying monster. The monstrous nature of this incarnation is signaled by such details as Moroto's demented expression and his hand clutching at Minoura's throat. The horror of the moment is also conveyed by the image of the hapless Minoura, whose desperate expression and thrashing limbs suggest the intensity of his efforts to escape. The dark background in which images of bats and other ghoulish creatures are just discernible further highlights the frightening atmosphere.

The second erotic-grotesque story line to be examined here revolves around the conjoined twins, Hide-chan and Yoshi-chan. This plot device

3. Moroto attacking Minoura. Originally published in *Asahi*, vol. 2, no. 1, 1930, 146–47. Reproduced with the permission of the National Diet Library, Tokyo.

is particularly interesting because it offers readers what can be described as metacommentary on the exploitative nature inherent in most instances of erotic-grotesque cultural production. The narrative describes how Oto-tsan kidnapped two infants; stitched them together; provided them with a catchy moniker, Hideyoshi; and raised them with the intention of sending them to a freak show. The signification of this plot device is especially ambiguous because it implicates the erotic-grotesque industry as it simultaneously functions as a selling point for the erotic-grotesque commodity *Demon of the Lonely Isle*.

This complex dynamic is explored further through Minoura's response to Hide-chan and Yoshi-chan. Each twin elicits different reactions from Minoura. Hide-chan, the female twin, strikes Minoura as the epitome of pathos. With her gentleness and uncanny beauty, she inspires in him feelings of affection. Indeed, he is completely entranced from the first moment he lays eyes on her. "I blushed and looked away. Stunned by the young girl's strange beauty, my heart pounded."[16] The physicality of his reaction (the blushing and the pounding heart) suggests that there is an underlying element of erotic desire to his feelings. Intensifying and complicating Minoura's erotic attraction for Hide-chan are his feelings of pity and condescension. These feelings are mostly in reaction to her pathetic determination to rise above her miserable circumstances. The narrative contains numerous descriptions of Hide-chan as she gamely tries to conform to the images of "normal" humanity that she has gleaned from a small cache of books and magazines.

Yoshi-chan, by contrast, elicits feelings of contempt and hatred from Minoura. This antipathy is established immediately. "Kit-chan turned his dark, ugly face toward me, and glared at me with undisguised hostility. I'll never forget the frightening look on his face. It was a malicious expression, conveying his warped, petty character."[17] With just one glimpse, then, Minoura is able to recognize Yoshi-chan as a debased individual. Echoing the precedent established by more conventional pieces of erotic-grotesque discourse, the definitive marker of Yoshi-chan's debasement turns out to be his "excessive" sexuality; Hide-chan reports that he masturbates on a daily basis. Significantly, Yoshi-chan is never given an opportunity to articulate his position. This silence is essential, however, if he is to function in the narrative as the ultimate cipher upon which Minoura projects his darkest fantasies about the freakish denizens of the erotic-grotesque world.

Demon of the Lonely Isle thus offers a remarkably elaborate enactment of the erotic-grotesque spectacle. The text does not simply reify widely accepted categories, such as normal or freakish. Rather, it vitiates these categories as it cannily exploits their notoriety. When the text's signification is expanded to include a panoply of contemporaneous issues, a comparable dynamic occurs. That is to say, discursive systems such as political rhetoric, moral instruction, and scientific research are reformulated when they operate within the freakish signifying field of *Demon of the Lonely Isle*. As a result of this process, fundamental concepts that underpin some of the fascistic ideological conceits of the era are destabilized, although never completely elided. In the remaining sections of this essay, I will explore the complex manner in which *Demon of the Lonely Isle* thematizes two closely related issues of particular concern to fascist ideologues and their constituents: the impact of deviance on Japanese society and the utility of science to contain its detrimental effects.

The Meanings of Deviance

Demon of the Lonely Isle was composed at a historical moment when deviations from respectability were frequently treated as a social problem with wide-ranging implications. This tendency to consider various categories of deviance as forms of socially disruptive or dangerous behavior reflects a wider set of concerns that preoccupied the era. There was widespread concern, Donald Roden informs us, among early-twentieth-century Japanese ideologues that deviance was sapping the Japanese nation of its vigor. Moralists such as Nogami Toshio and Tokutomi Sohō predicted, for example, that the appearance of aggressive, "masculine" women and passive, "feminine" men would be the undoing of Japanese society.[18] Fueling these apocalyptic prophecies was the perception that modernism, and the resulting redefinition of gender roles, had overturned the "natural" sexual order and consequently threatened the basic fabric of society. Paralleling developments in the West, these alarmist claims were lent further credibility when they became linked with scientific "advances." The discipline of sexology offered an intellectually legitimate system for categorizing and evaluating different expressions of human sexuality. Despite their pretensions of scientific objectivity, Roden points out, most prewar studies of "deviant" sexuality amounted to nothing more than ideologically determined prescriptive tracts. Habuto Eiji's and Sawada Junjirō's influential *Hentai seiyoku ron* (The Theories of Deviant Sexual Desire; 1915) was typical:

> The format of the book bears a close resemblance to Krafft-Ebing's *Psychopathia Sexualis* (1886), to which the authors refer explicitly throughout the text. And like their Viennese predecessor, Habuto and Sawada seemed obsessed by the destructive threat that "unnatural desires" posed for the Japanese social order. At the most obvious level, aberrant sexual feelings underlay criminal acts of brutality, but of more concern to the authors was the less dramatic but more widespread pattern of antisocial behavior that arose from the confusion of the sexes.[19]

As Roden observes, prewar sexology differentiated "natural" or "respectable" (the two categories were interchangeable) expressions of sexuality from "unnatural" or "deviant" sexual activities and identities. Ultimately, these sexological tracts deployed science to reinforce fascistic visions of natural, respectable sexuality (and social order) and to decry the toxic effects modernism and urbanization had on this idealized prelapsarian state.

In its first few chapters, *Demon of the Lonely Isle* seems to unquestioningly perpetuate the most negative stereotypes associated with deviance. The focus of these paranoid fantasies is Moroto. As the specific circumstances surrounding Hatsuyo's murder are gradually revealed, all the evidence points to Moroto. It is revealed, for instance, that on more than one occasion he had tried to sabotage Minoura's relationship, even going so far as to pursue Hatsuyo's hand in marriage himself. After this plan failed, the narrative implies, Moroto in all likelihood became desperate enough to commit murder. Even more damning than this circumstantial evidence is the simple fact that Moroto is homosexual. Minoura explains:

> It might seem as though I were jumping to ridiculous conclusions [by accusing Moroto]. But you can't judge a pervert by normal standards. Wasn't he a man incapable of loving the opposite sex? Wasn't it more than likely that he had tried to interfere with my engagement because of his homosexual desire for me? Wasn't his campaign to win Hatsuyo's hand in marriage excessive? Didn't his love for me border on the insane?[20]

The reasoning here is echoed throughout the first few chapters of the novel. Moroto figures as the most likely suspect merely because he prefers men as his sexual partners. Variant sexuality, in other words, is tantamount to criminality, a recognizable threat to the smooth operation of a civil society.

There are occasions, however, when the text undermines the facile assumption that variant sexuality is inherently dangerous or socially disruptive. These instances mostly occur in the "treasure story" sections of the novel, after Minoura and Moroto embark on their expedition to find the buried gold. This pattern of imbuing male–male bonds with an implicit erotic component is not out of character for the genre of adventure literature. In fact, homoeroticism energizes texts ranging from Mark Twain's *Adventures of Huckleberry Finn* (1885) to Iwaya Sazanami's *Koganemaru* (1891).[21] In the particular case of *Demon of the Lonely Isle*, the text infuses the Minoura–Moroto partnership with erotic overtones by presenting them as an updated version of premodern samurai comrades. The model for this pattern of male bonding is derived from Edo-period (1615–1867) literary representations of an idealized form of samurai love known as the *shud* (Way of Young Men). By implying that Minoura's relation with Moroto conforms loosely to this ideal, the narrative eroticizes Minoura's and Moroto's relationship as it neutralizes the negative connotations associated with their sexually charged interaction.[22]

In *Demon of the Lonely Isle*'s reformulation of the *shud* couple, Minoura clearly plays the role of the youthful partner (*wakashu*). The text underscores this position by having Minoura regularly acknowledge the spiritual and intellectual superiority shown by the older, more experienced Moroto. Indeed, mirroring the dependence of a youth on his adult lover, there are numerous occasions during their quest when the callow Minoura actually relies on Moroto to save his life. The most striking instance of this dependence occurs when the two young men are trapped together in a cave that is filling with water. Just as Minoura is about to give up, Moroto revives his flagging spirit:

> Moroto put his arm around my waist and held me tightly. The darkness prevented me from seeing his face even though it was only about one or two inches away from mine. But I could hear his steady breathing and feel his breath upon my face. Comforting warmth from his muscular body passed through our soaking-wet clothes and enveloped me. I noticed that he gave off a pleasant scent, which wafted all about us. All of these things gave me the strength to carry on. Thanks to Moroto, I was able to stay on my feet. If it were not for him, I would certainly have drowned.[23]

Incidents such as this counteract the impression that Moroto's sexuality is inherently detrimental to the establishment and maintenance of constructive social bonds. To the contrary, the narrative suggests that his sexual attentions can have an energizing effect on Minoura. Without it, Minoura would never be able to contribute to the important task of finding the buried treasure and overthrowing Ototsan. The narrative thus implies that, under certain circumstances, intense, sexually charged male–male bonds can foster concrete, useful achievement.

The ambiguous way that the text thematizes male–male sexuality reflects the indeterminacy of its position on the meaning of abnormality in general. This uncertainty is played out most dramatically in the novel's concluding chapter. On one level, the denouement is noteworthy for its seemingly unproblematic valorization of the status quo. Like the grand finale (*daidan'en*) of Edo-period drama and fiction, an association that is underscored by the use of this outdated term as the title of the last chapter, *Demon of the Lonely Isle*'s conclusion seems to uphold the generic conventions of reward virtue and punish vice (*kanzen chōaku*). In this particular context, virtue equals "normality" and vice equals "abnormality." The grand finale consists of a rapid succession of events, including the apprehension of Ototsan, the discovery of Hide-chan's true lineage, the successful performance of Hide-chan's corrective surgery, the marriage of Hide-chan and Minoura, and the timely death of Moroto. Every one of these resolutions asserts the primacy of normative values; the threat of abnormal elements disrupting Japanese society is totally erased through death, incarceration, or assimilation. In a manner reminiscent of the Bakufu-endorsed literary convention of reward virtue and punish vice, *Demon of the Lonely Isle* appears to end on an appropriately orthodox note.

Of all the events recounted in *Demon of the Lonely Isle*'s grand finale, the transformation of Hide-chan seems to conform most completely to fascistic imaginings of "natural" gender and sexual roles. After all of his travails, Minoura proclaims that nothing could be more satisfying than the thought of Hide-chan becoming a "normal" woman who "styles her hair, puts on makeup, wears a beautiful kimono, and speaks in the standard Tokyo dialect."[24] With these changes, she becomes a suitable choice for his wife. The text implies that after years of suffering, she has finally achieved fulfillment through the triple intervention of corrective surgery, repatriation into mainstream society, and, most important of all, "normal" heterosexual love and marriage. In this manner the text overcomes the type of deviance and unnaturalness bemoaned by ideologues and sexologists and reasserts the more "natural" order. The final image of Hide-chan as a conventional housewife is a far cry from the young girl who once believed that "humans come in different forms" and assumed that a person with only one head was somehow deficient.[25] Once she is exposed to the values and aesthetics of respectable society, Hide-chan comes to realize the "error" of her youthful misconceptions. Only then, after she has come to accept the "shamefulness" of her previous condition, can she fully appreciate the gallantry of Minoura's actions.

The assimilation of Hide-chan is also reflected in Takenaka's illustrations. Figure 4 offers a reassuring vision of the new and improved Hide-chan. In physical terms, she is now part of the "normal human race."[26] The illustration also suggests that she has successfully taken on a "normal" social/gender role; she has been transformed into the picture-perfect bride, signaling her domesticity through her choice of traditional Japanese clothing and her sophistication through her stylish modern-girl bob. With her outstretched arms she displays the results of this successful metamorphosis to the paternalistic gaze of her husband (the cigarette-smoking figure in the lower-left corner of the composition) and, by extension, the viewer of the illustration. Significantly, this is the final image in the text, the last visual

4. Hide-chan showing off her new appearance to her husband, Minoura. Originally published in *Asahi*, vol. 2, no. 2, 1930, 181. Reproduced with permission of the National Diet Library, Tokyo.

impression made on the reader. The tone of this conclusion seems to suggest that, despite its gratuitous attention to the erotic-grotesque, *Demon of the Lonely Isle* endorses "normal" values and a "natural" social order. Specifically, it valorizes conformity to a rigid set of physical, sexual, and gendered standards. Heightening this impression is Minoura's decision to open a philanthropic institution. After returning from his quest with a beautiful wife and an immense fortune of about one million yen (approximately four billion yen in today's currency), Minoura decides to use a portion of his newfound wealth to establish a haven "where the latest advances in medicine can be used to turn freaks into normal humans."[27] This act is presented as the ultimate sign of Minoura's fundamental decency.

Yet the text simultaneously enables a more skeptical interpretation of this outcome by gesturing to its absurdity. The absurd nature of the situation becomes apparent when the reader recalls that at the outset of his retrospective narrative Minoura describes himself as a "white-haired demon (*hakuhatsuki*)."[28] This is an explicit reference to his "weird" appearance. The comparison refers to the fact that Minoura's hair has been permanently bleached white by the traumatic experiences he has undergone. The condition is so unusual that it elicits questions and comments from complete strangers. On an implicit level, the white hair also functions as a physical manifestation of Minoura's deep-seated deviance, which reveals itself through his tendencies toward male–male sexuality, teratism, and cannibalism.[29] It is highly ironic therefore that Minoura would appoint himself the patron of an institute whose sole purpose is to isolate or cure, both for their own sake and for society's, individuals who show deviant characteristics comparable to his own.

The text further opens the possibilities for an ironic reading of the final triumph of fascistic values by providing the reader with details of Moroto's death. The final lines of the novel read as follows:

> I anxiously awaited Moroto's return, since we had arranged that he would become the director of my new medical institute. But alas he passed away while still visiting his birth parents. After all of my recent good fortune, this alone turned out unhappily. His father wrote me a letter describing the last moments of Moroto's life: "As he drew his last breath, Moroto clutched to his breast a letter he had received from you. The last words on his lips were not the name of his father or his mother, but your name, repeated over and over."[30]

In practical terms, of course, Moroto must die to ensure a smooth conclusion to the story. His continued presence would only destabilize Minoura's domestic situation. At the same time, however, the manner in which Moroto's demise is presented conveys a certain aversion to the final turn of events. As his last words suggest, the most important presence in Moroto's life was not his biological family, the mythical foundation of fascist constructions of the national community, but Minoura, the object of his ceaseless affection. By closing with a reference to Moroto's love, the novel suggests that, although a world where the regime of normalcy prevails is inevitable, there is always a segment of the population that is sacrificed to this social order. By giving Moroto the last word, the narrative acknowledges the burdens endured by those who do not conform to an increasingly narrow vision of "natural" and "respectable" sexuality and identity.

Responding to widespread concerns about the impact that deviant individuals can have on society, the Japanese discursive field of the 1920s and 1930s was overrun with "scientific" proposals promising to contain this potential threat. One major source of these proposals was the discipline of eugenics, or the science of improving the hereditary qualities of a race or breed. As the historian of science Suzuki Zenji points out, eugenics exerted considerable influence on prewar Japanese social policy.[31] Among the proponents of these social programs, certain factions worked under the assumption that the sole application of eugenics was in modifying the hereditary composition of the national community through programs of selective breeding, birth control, and sterilization. But in its more popular formulations, eugenics dealt with questions of culture as frequently as it did with issues of heredity. The following statement issued by the Nippon Yūsei Undō Kyōkai (Japanese Eugenics Society) in 1928 typifies this tendency:

> The primary goal of the Japanese Eugenics Society is to ensure that in the future the Japanese people can maintain their position of world leadership. There are two essential steps that will allow us to achieve this goal. First, we must work to improve our mental and spiritual health, strengthen our physiques, extend our life spans, and create families without any trace of psychological weakness or hereditary illness. Second, we must commit ourselves to raising the level of our national culture, to familiarizing ourselves with the Imperial Constitution, and to realizing our full potential as law-abiding citizens.[32]

Showing a clear investment in the fascistic linkage of cultural purity, national health, and global domination, the Japanese Eugenics Society offered a blueprint for strengthening Japanese imperial subjects so they could contribute to Japan's success in the competitive arena of international relations. This process did not simply involve selecting the fittest members of a community and making sure that only they reproduced. It also entailed improving the character and vitality of society and national culture.

Criminology was another discipline that offered solutions to the deleterious effects that aberrant individuals have on society. In the prewar context, Japanese criminology operated in compliance with a set of assumptions remarkably similar to those of eugenics. For example, criminology was also predicated on the Social Darwinist belief that society is divided into two categories of people: the fit and the unfit.[33] In the case of criminology, the category of the "unfit" consisted of criminals, mostly denizens of Japan's urban centers, whose actions disrupted society, while the category of the "fit" consisted of law-abiding citizens whose behavior contributed to society's betterment. The two disciplines had in common another important characteristic: they shared the absolute conviction that science offered the best weapon in the battle against forces threatening to diminish society.

A comment by the cultural critic Hirabayashi Hatsunosuke exemplifies the widespread belief that science was an essential component of any serious crime-prevention program:

> In abstract terms, the necessary condition is the establishment of a civilization of science; in other words, the establishment of rationality, an analytical outlook, and a rigorous methodology. To put it simply, crimes and crime solving are by nature scientific, the investigation and conviction of suspects relies on the collection of physical evidence, and a carefully conceived body of laws maintains the order of the nation-state.[34]

Hirabayashi thus envisioned criminology as an intellectual discipline that ordered, and therefore empowered, the nation-state. As was the case with eugenics, the authoritarian overtones of this rhetoric were legitimated through the imprimatur of science. Actions committed in the name of these disciplines were rationalized by asserting their foundation in the infallible epistemology of science. Further linking the two disciplines was their mutual suspicion of the urban environment; eugenics treated the modern urban landscape as a source of physical enervation and cultural degeneration, while criminology treated it as a breeding ground for criminal behavior.

Significantly, Hirabayashi's commentary on criminological science occurs in the context of a discussion of detective fiction. This suggests that even fictional accounts of criminal investigations were expected to show a sufficient air of scientific rigor. Moreover, as Hirabayashi explicitly indicates, science continued to function, even in the fictional realm, as an intellectual justification for what typically constituted conservative promotions of law and order. As I mentioned earlier, *Demon of the Lonely Isle* was noted for its departure from this approach. This, not coincidentally, was one of the main reasons that critics dismissed it. I assert once again, however, that this deviation from the standard model of detective fiction is not grounds for characterizing *Demon of the Lonely Isle* as a failed literary exercise. Rather, it further demonstrates the complexity of the text's engagement with the position that scientific disciplines such as eugenics and criminology provided a way to achieve a more wholesome, harmonious society through the systematic containment and neutralization of the unfit and the criminal.

That is not to say, however, that *Demon of the Lonely Isle* dismisses science as a means of responding to problems caused by the unfit/criminal elements in society. To the contrary, the text frequently endorses the applicability of scientific rationality in such cases. These endorsements primarily appear in sections of the narrative that conform most faithfully to the contours of conventional detective fiction. They are conspicuously present, for example, in the scenes where Minoura and Moroto collect and analyze various pieces of evidence in the course of investigating Hatsuyo's murder. Interestingly enough, the character that best exemplifies a scientific approach toward life is not the novel's protagonist, Minoura, but his comrade, Moroto. On the most basic level, his profession as a research physician signals his investment in this system. This scientific background, he insists, is what makes him an ideal candidate to undertake a criminal investigation. He reassures an uncertain Minoura, "I might just turn out to be an exceptional detective. After all, didn't I study science in medical school?"[35] The reliability of the scientific method for Moroto is underscored constantly. During his lengthy explanation of how an intruder broke into Hatsuyo's room, murdered her, and then managed to escape leaving all the doors and windows locked from the inside, Moroto makes clear that all of his conclusions have been based on careful "deductive reasoning." He explains how he first conducted preliminary "research," then "developed a hypothesis," and finally "examined the existing evidence," before offering a solution to the crime. After listening to this report, Minoura can only marvel at the "systematic order" of Moroto's approach.[36]

The results of this deductive tour de force are far too elaborate to summarize here. Suffice it to say that a ten-year-old professional acrobat flexible enough to conceal himself in a large vase committed the murder. Of course, the premise is fantastic; this is precisely what makes the narrative so entertaining. What is interesting, though, is the way that scientific theories are used to shore up the plausibility of this incredible scenario. For example, when the dubious Minoura questions the likelihood of a ten year old committing such a heinous crime, Moroto explains, "Child specialists know that, contrary to our expectations, children are much crueler than adults. ... According to proponents of evolution, children resemble primitive man; they are barbaric and cruel."[37] Leaving aside the question of whether there is any truth to these "scientific facts," statements like this play a crucial role. They lend a patina of verisimilitude to Moroto's otherwise ludicrous theory. Science also figures prominently in the "adventure-story" sections of the narrative, which focus on Minoura's and Moroto's efforts to locate the hidden treasure and rescue Hide-chan. The ability to reason scientifically is ultimately what allows Moroto to accomplish these goals. The race to find the hidden treasure, for example, involves an elaborate process of decoding a secret message and then using the information to follow a trail of ingeniously concealed clues. Moroto's scientific expertise also proves invaluable in the quest to deliver Hide-chan from her misfortunes, for it is he who performs the surgical procedure that separates her from her lascivious worse half, Yoshi-chan, and allows her to begin life anew as a "normal person."

Throughout the novel, then, science is key to the resolution of various crises. In the first half of the story, things are resolved when Moroto deduces the circumstances surrounding the murder of Hatsuyo. More complete closure is achieved when the mysteries of the hidden treasure and Hide-chan's lineage are made clear. In short, science makes possible a progression from a state of chaos to a state of order. More important, the "natural" order of society is restored with the triumph of the "normal" over the criminal and the unfit. The legitimacy of this hierarchy is assured, because it is founded on truths attained through the incontrovertible logic of science.

Questions about the utility of science as a system for social management, however, emerge in the subplot involving Ototsan's plan to flood Japan with an army of freaks. The narrative makes clear that Moroto's medical experiments and research provide the intellectual foundation that ultimately enables Ototsan to inflict various physical deformities on human subjects. Ironically, Ototsan's efforts can easily be interpreted as a eugenics program gone awry. Like proponents of eugenics, Ototsan exploits science to engender hereditary changes in the Japanese race. To be sure, his scheme is motivated by hatred and desire for revenge and therefore involves "diminishing" the population rather than "improving" it. Yet the basic formula is the same: science provides the know-how that makes it possible to bring about lasting changes in the composition of a racial community. This threat was all the more credible for readers in the early 1930s because neo-Lamarckian theories of heredity were still in common currency. In other words, it was widely believed that acquired characteristics, such as those that Ototsan visited on his victims, could actually be passed on to future generations.[38]

Science, then, is represented as a double-edged sword. On the one hand, it offers solutions to perceived social problems. On the other hand, it is presented as a source of anxiety, the possible catalyst for a crisis of almost unimaginable proportions. In both cases, however, the perceived enemy is any threat to the vigor and purity of the Japanese bloodline. Moroto gives voice to these concerns in a speech vilifying Ototsan and his project: "what a hideous nightmare, flooding Japan with freaks until not a single normal person remains. If my father has his way, Japan will become crippled, a nation of cripples."[39] In diatribes such as this, the narrative expresses an unmistakable revulsion at the prospect of Japan being overrun by physically "deficient" freaks. The outrage elicited by Ototsan's plan is clearly premised on the conviction that the presence of unfitness, regardless of its origins, will seriously compromise the health of the Japanese national body. Indeed, suspense in the narrative's second half is generated entirely by the question of whether Moroto and Minoura will be able to foil Ototsan's plot and prevent this disaster from occurring. The text thus reveals a clear investment in the fascistic principles regarding the sanctity of the Japanese national body and the need to protect it from contamination and degradation.

At the same time, operating in accordance with the logic of the erotic-grotesque spectacle, Moroto's excessive rhetoric also invites titillation. Eugenic paranoia becomes grist for the mill of *Demon of the Lonely Isle*'s outrageous exploration of the bizarre. The text thus deflects serious contemplation of its more sober implications and encourages an ironic appreciation of its sensational pyrotechnics. This is a natural tendency for any piece of erotic-grotesque entertainment, since its success as a commodity is directly proportional to its capacity to attract an extensive audience.

Conclusion

Ranpo's *Demon of the Lonely Isle* was closely linked to the bourgeois consumer/cultural movement known as Erotic Grotesque Nonsense. The text embodied the spirit of this movement by tacitly authorizing the audience's pursuit of pleasure—or, at least, by providing the audience with a medium through which it could vicariously observe an assortment of "bizarre," "perverse" characters indulging themselves in unsanctioned activities. Challenging this permissive tone, however, was the text's subscription to currents of Social Darwinist thought that were the intellectual foundation for such disciplines as sexology, eugenics, and criminology, all of which endeavored to contain or eradicate perceived abnormalities within the Japanese population. Indeed, *Demon of the Lonely Isle* was produced at the precise moment when fascist concerns about issues such as respectability, racial purity, and productive morality were becoming ascendant in Japan.

Affiliation with these ideological fantasies is legible in sections of the text in which any deviation from accepted sexual, physical, and psychological norms is treated as a potential threat to the homogeneity and purity of Japanese society. At these moments, Demon of the Lonely Isle can be read as a form of covert propaganda that impressed on readers the need to monitor both themselves and those around them for signs of deviance and freakishness.

Notes

An earlier version of this article originally appeared in Journal of Japanese Studies 27, no. 1 (2001), 113–41.

1. For more on the specific character of this fascistic discourse in Japan, see Harry Harootunian, "Overcome by Modernity: Fantasizing Everyday Life and the Discourse on the Social in Interwar Japan," Parallax, no. 2 (1996): 79–84.

2. For more on Japanese manifestations of this fascist compulsion to assimilate, dominate, and destroy alternative outlooks and subjectivities, see O. Tanin and E. Yohan, Militarism and Fascism in Japan (New York: International Publishers, 1934), 184–203; Edwin Reischauer, Japan: Past and Present (New York: Alfred A. Knopf, 1947), 165–71.

3. Suzuki Zenji, Nihon no yūseigaku (Tokyo: Sankyō Shuppan, 1983), 136.

4. Takenaka was a leading illustrator for the Japanese detective-fiction industry of the 1920s and 1930s. For a more detailed account of Takenaka's life and career, see Fujikawa Chisui, "Kaiki e no naka no seishun: Takenaka Eitarō suiron," Shisō no kagaku 5, no. 30 (1974): 40–48.

5. Harootunian, "Overcome by Modernity," 82–83.

6. Elizabeth Grosz, "Intolerable Ambiguity: Freaks as/at the Limit," in ed. Rosemarie Garland Thomson, Freakery (New York: New York University Press, 1996), 64.

7. For a more detailed discussion of the manifold ways that the label "freak" is assigned to groups or individuals, see Rosemarie Garland Thomson, Extraordinary Bodies (New York: Columbia University Press, 1997), esp. 19–51.

8. Two noteworthy exceptions to this institutional oversight are Taguchi Ritsuo, "Kotō no oni ron," Kokubungaku: Kaishaku to kanshō 59, no. 12 (1994): 109–14; Mark Driscoll, "Imperial Textuality, Imperial Sexuality," Proceedings of the Midwest Association for Japanese Literary Studies 5 (1999): 156–74.

9. Ōuchi Shigeo, "Karei na yūtopia—Ranpo no chōhen shōsetsu" (1975), in Edogawa Ranpo—Hyōron to kenkyū (Tokyo: Kōdansha, 1980), 172.

10. Ranpo shifted his focus from short stories to full-length novels with the composition of Issun bōshi (The Midget; 1926).

11. Nakajima Kawatarō, "Ranpo bungaku no chōkan" (1954), in Edogawa Ranpo (Tokyo: Kōdansha, 1980), 60–62. Gonda Manji, "Tojikomerareta yume" (1973), in Edogawa Ranpo—Hyōron to kenkyū, 148–49.

12. Nakajima, "Ranpo bungaku no chōkan," 63–64; Gonda, "Tojikomoerareta yume," 148–49.
13. Edogawa Ranpo, *Kotō no oni* (Tokyo: Sōgensha, 1996), 33.
14. Ibid., 36.
15. Ibid., 366–67.
16. Ibid., 257.
17. Ibid., 263.
18. Donald Roden, "Taisho Culture and the Problem of Gender Ambivalence," in ed. J. Thomas Rimer, *Culture and Identity: Japanese Intellectuals during the Interwar Years* (Princeton, N.J.: Princeton University Press, 1990), 44–45.
19. Ibid., 45–46.
20. Ranpo, *Kotō no oni*, 85.
21. For a more detailed discussion of the homoerotic inflections of these narratives, see Leslie Fielder, "Come to the Raft Ag'in, Huck Honey!" (1948), in *Mark Twain's Adventures of Huckleberry Finn: A Case Study in Critical Controversy*, ed. Gerald Graff and James Phelan (Boston: St. Martin's Press, 1995), 528–34. Komori Yōichi, "Koganemaru no kanōsei: Nanshoku bungaku to shite no shōnen bungaku," in ed. Nihon Jidō Bungaku Gakkai, *Nihon jidō bungakushi o toinaosu: Hyōgenshi no shiten kara* (Tokyo: Tokyo Shōseki, 1995), 35–54.
22. For a more complete discussion of expressions of male–male sexuality in Ranpo's writing, see Furukawa Makoto, "Edogawa Ranpo no hisoka naru jōnetsu," *Kokubungaku: Kaishaku to kanshō* 59, no. 12 (1994): 59–64.
23. Ranpo, *Kotō no oni*, 346.
24. Ibid., 293.
25. Ibid., 177.
26. Ibid., 393.
27. Ibid., 393.
28. Ibid., 11.
29. In the lexicon of sexology, *teratism* refers to sexual attraction for extraordinary bodies. Minoura's initial obsession with Shū-chan can therefore be categorized as an example of this condition. As for Minoura's cannibalism, the incident occurs shortly after Hatsuyo's death. On departing from her funeral, Minoura absconds with a charred fragment of Hatsuyo's body, which in a moment of extreme despair he consumes.
30. Ranpo, *Kotō no oni*, 394.
31. Suzuki, *Nihon no yūseigaku*, 99–141.
32. Ikeda Shigenori, "Nihon Yūsei Undō Kyōkai no shui oyobi shinjō," *Yūsei undō* 3, no. 6 (1928): 18–19.
33. A representative example of this tendency to conflate the categories of the criminal and the unfit can be seen in Katsumi Atsuyuki's *Hanzai shakaigaku* (Social Criminology; 1922). Katsumi assumes that criminality is a sign of *kakusei iden* (inherent atavism) and consequently links it with traits such as bushy eyebrows, sloping forehead, prominent cheekbones and jaws, deformed skulls, brutish

strength, and left-handedness: Katsumi Atsuyuki, *Hanzai shakaigaku* (Tokyo: Ganshōdō Shoten, 1922), 162.

34. Hirabayashi Hatsunosuke, "Nihon no kindaiteki tantei shōsetsu: toku ni Edogawa Ranpo-shi ni tsuite" (1925), in *Edogawa Ranpo: Hyōron to kenkyū*, 9.

35. Ranpo, *Kotō no oni*, 121.

36. Ibid., 125–46.

37. Ibid., 142.

38. For more information on the impact of the French naturalist Jean de Lamarck's theories on the prewar Japanese understanding of heredity, see Suzuki, *Nihon no yūseigaku*, 45–97.

39. Ranpo, *Kotō no oni*, 359–60.

KEITH VINCENT

Hamaosociality: Narrative
and Fascism in Hamao Shirō's
The Devil's Disciple

> To order my story properly I should start with the time you and I split up.
> —Hamao Shirō, *Akuma no deshi*

■ The detective novelist Hamao Shirō's (1896–1935) family background, his education, and his profession gave him a privileged insight into the workings of the prewar Japanese state and legal system. His adoptive father, Viscount Hamao Arata, served as minister of education, as a member of the Privy Council, and as president of Tokyo Imperial University. Hamao's grandfather was Baron Katō Hiroyuki (1836–1913), the towering scholar who lectured the Meiji emperor on Western legal thought and served as the first (and third) president of Tokyo Imperial University. In modern Japan it would be hard to come by a more elite pedigree.[1] Hamao himself studied German law at Tokyo Imperial University and worked as a public prosecutor from 1919 until 1929. But in that year he gave up his prestigious position as a prosecutor to become Japan's first practitioner of legal detective fiction. By so doing, Hamao transformed himself from an enforcer of the law into one of its harshest critics. Thus, a former prosecutor and the grandson of one of the founders of the modern Japanese legal system ended up writing detective fiction shot through with what Gonda Manji describes as a "deep skepticism about [the possibility of] justice through the law."[2]

The theme of the arbitrary violence that lurks at the law's foundations is one that Hamao would turn to over and over in his fiction. It is his radical mistrust in the law that makes his work so different from the classic detective novel as it emerged in the late nineteenth century and that, by the 1920s, had gained wide popularity in Japan. Classic detective fiction is a genre that serves both to frighten and to reassure. However disturbing the crime and however gruesome the murder, the rules of the genre dictate that the criminal will eventually be brought to justice and the social order restored. Cast initially into a state of generalized paranoia in which "every external sign is given equal weight, meaning, and menace,"[3] the reader of the detective novel, like the detective himself or herself, works to distinguish clues from mere details, to fish a coherent narrative out of a pool of red herrings. In its classic "whodunit" form, the detective novel also strives for an airtight correlation of character with plot. Over the course of its narrative and through the application of scientific ratiocination, it fixes the criminal as a determinate subject by tying him tight to the predicate of his crime.

Hamao's novella *Akuma no deshi* (The Devil's Disciple; 1929) offers no such reassurance. Written just as the promise of so-called Taishō democracy was giving way to unchecked militarism and colonial expansion, it reverses the stabilizing work of modern detective fiction and stages an unresolved struggle between a homosocial heaven in which both narrative closure and juridical certainty are possible and a hell of perversion and addiction where the law is undermined and the national order is threatened. Suspended in such a purgatorial state, the reader of *The Devil's Disciple* is confronted with the same aporias of subjectivity and representation that the culture of fascism promises, disingenuously, to resolve. Such aporias are, of course, the problems raised by modernity itself. The culture of fascism, for our purposes, is that which responds to these problems with insistent certitudes. While there are many ways of producing such certitudes (such as myth, spectacle, architecture, or rhetoric), the focus here will be on the work done (and undone) by *narrative* in the transformation of subjects into identities and the reduction of language to communication. The complex narrative structure of *The Devil's Disciple*, I will argue, works as a kind of participatory theory of fascism. It exposes us to temptations that might lead us into fascist positions; but it also provides the instruction we need to avoid them. And yet the trick of *The Devil's Disciple* is not simply to follow the instructions but, rather, to stick with the text, to stay put in the dilatory middle of narrative. In *The Devil's Disciple*, this is a space in between a series of oppositions that its narrator works very hard to establish—between homosexuality and heterosexuality, instruction and seduction, insomnia and sleep, and speech and writing. It is also a space between the formal experimentation of modernist narrative and the blunt instruments of fascist melodrama.

Hetero-Narrative

The plot of *The Devil's Disciple* revolves around its narrator Shimaura Eizō's attempt to murder his wife Tsuyuko. Heavily addicted to sleeping medication, Shimaura tries to use subliminal messages to make Tsuyuko take the same amount of sleeping medication as he. Since a normal dose for him is an overdose for her, he hopes that Tsuyuko will die and the whole thing will look like an accident. With his wife out of the way, Shimaura plans to marry his mistress, Sueko, and settle down into a happy marriage based on genuine love and affection. But his attempt to use his own addiction to rid himself of his cloying wife takes an unexpected turn when Sueko takes the bait instead. While his wife, whom he despises for her abject dependence on him, turns out to be smart enough to know how much medicine she needs,[4] his mistress is dumber than he thought. Sueko dies of an overdose, and Shimaura ends up in jail charged with her murder.

Accused of a crime he did not commit but burdened with the knowledge of his murderous intentions, Shimaura can neither protest his innocence nor plead his guilt. Instead, he writes a letter to the public prosecutor in the court where he is being tried, one Tsuchida Hachirō, who also happens to be Shimaura's ex-boyfriend. The letter relates the events summarized above for the prosecutor's (and the reader's) benefit. But this narrative function is compromised by Shimaura's relentless diatribe against the prosecutor himself. Shimaura accuses Tsuchida of seducing him into a homosexual relationship and getting him addicted to the sleeping medication that has caused Sueko's death and landed him in jail. This letter to his former lover constitutes the entire text of *The Devil's Disciple*, thus placing a homosexual frame around what is otherwise a heterosexual story. More a stream of invective than an accusation of any specific criminal acts, the letter sets the integrity and character of Shimaura against that of Tsuchida, without giving us any means of knowing what to believe.

While Shimaura claims to have learned to love women since Tsuchida left him, he believes that Tsuchida remains exclusively homosexual. On the most basic level, then, Hamao's short novel shows us the attempt of one man to shore up his compromised heterosexuality by projecting the threat represented by homosexuality onto another man. "Tsuchida-san," writes

Shimaura, "You have no interest in the opposite sex. So I believe you must still be a bachelor (*dokushin*)."[5] While Shimaura has *moved on*, Tsuchida has *remained the same*. This belief not only anchors Shimaura's own narrative of "recovery" from homosexuality, but also equates the redemptive power of narrative with that of heterosexuality itself. The corollary of this equation is that homosexuality in *The Devil's Disciple*, through the phantasmatic figure of Tsuchida, is that which threatens to disrupt or unbind the (hetero-)normatizing work of narrative.

In its insistence on narrative as that which secures heterosexual identity, Shimaura's story follows the Freudian theory of sexual development. In his *Three Essays on the Theory of Sexuality* (1905), Freud crafts a narrative (much like Shimaura's) that begins with perversion and ends in genital heterosexuality. While Freud himself was careful in that text not to confuse the normal with the normative and insisted that "the disposition to perversions is itself of no great rarity but must form a part of what passes as the normal constitution,"[6] far too many of his epigones overlooked Freud's careful insistence on the pervert in all of us. And for those who later sought a psychoanalytic explanation of the rise of fascism, Freud's work was easily and often (mis)appropriated to read fascism in relation to sexual perversion (most typically embodied by the male homosexual). This made it possible to contain both fascism and homosexuality outside the interlocking domains of heteronormative domesticity and the liberal-democratic public sphere. The pervert or the homosexual was thus hypostatized as one whose story has stalled, as a person who has lost his way along the Oedipal path to normality and fortified subjectivity—now understood in both sexual and political terms. "The people who are most subject to the wiles of Nazi propaganda," argued Freud's biographer Ernest Jones in no uncertain terms, "are those who have neither securely established their own manhood and independence from the father nor have been able to combine the instincts of sexuality and love in their attitude toward the mother or other women. This is the psychological position of the homosexual."[7]

The "homofascist" subject is thus a case of failed development, a story of "not yet" that presumes there is only one happy ending.[8] Three decades later, Doi Takeo resorted to the same notion of the stalled Oedipal narrative to elaborate his theory of "dependence," or *amae*. It was *amae*, he argued, that accounted for the "childishness" of Japanese society and its "failure, *so far*, to develop individual freedom in the Western sense."[9] While Doi held out the possibility that the (heterosexual) Japanese might (yet) overcome this tendency toward "amae" by following that narrative through to completion, homosexuals were stuck by definition. "The essence of homosexual feelings," Doi wrote with the same flat-footed finality we heard from Jones, "is *amae*."[10] As I have argued elsewhere, not even Ōe Kenzaburō could resist the easy appeal of showing us a teenage "fascist" whose indifferent and (too) Americanized father turns him from the left to the right until he ends up masturbating over the image of his (too) beloved emperor.[11]

As all of these examples suggest (and I could cite many others), there is a whole mess of theories in which the Oedipal narrative of sexual development and gender differentiation is read alongside that of the development of the political subject. When the narrative stalls or goes astray, so the story goes, you get (homo)fascists, and when it comes to maturation, you have heterosexual, democratic subjects. What I want to argue here is that these narratives of narratives are themselves symptomatic of a paranoid fascist subjectivity. In my reading, the narrator of Hamao's novella is an example of such a fascist subject. He uses (or abuses) narrative as what Judith Roof calls "a structural defense against a chaotic world" to reassure and stabilize himself through the production/projection of an imagined male homosexual.[12] This imagined male homosexual is sexually predatory, politically dangerous, prone to addiction, and suffering from arrested development. Obviously, the production of such a fantasy is not the only way in which fascist subjects seek to stabilize themselves. Indeed, there is no end to the kinds of enemies a fascist culture can conjure up. But the figure of the homosexual proves particularly useful to those for whom *narrative* serves as a defense against chaos. As the introduction of difference into sameness, of the hetero into the homo, narrative serves as a means of differentiation and othering. Shimaura's desperate attempts to differentiate himself from Tsuchida through an insistent narrative of his own achievement of heterosexuality is clearly a means of warding off the "homo-ness" that threatens to engulf him.

From Instruction to Seduction

Yet things were not always this way in Japan. There was a time, not too long before this story was written, when male–male sex (as distinguished from "homosexuality") posed less of a threat to narrative coherence. If homosexuality remained a disease and an unspeakable sin in the West until well into the twentieth century, it had only recently become pathologized in Japan when Hamao was writing. Thus, in the larger narrative of Japanese cultural history, *The Devil's Disciple* occupies a moment when two very different ways of understanding male–male sexuality were still competing for dominance. This sets up a certain undecidability as to whether the relationship between Shimaura and Tsuchida is to be understood from the perspective of the premodern tradition of what was called *nanshoku*, or in the psychologized modern model of exclusive "homosexuality."[13] As we shall see, this interpretative undecidability is what makes it possible to hypostatize both ends of the tale, and both at Tsuchida's expense.

In its ideal(ized) form, the nanshoku model involved a hierarchical relationship of fictive fraternity between two men, where the older brother "offered the youth physical and social protection, a role model, and material aid," and the younger "reciprocated through obedience, respect, and intimate access to his person."[14] The older partner expected loyalty and monogamy from his younger brother, but the practice of nanshoku did not preclude marriage to a woman. As such, it retained the possibility of a narrative arc in the form of development toward "responsible," reproductive adulthood and participation for both parties in the homosocial corporate family system (*ie seido*). To the extent that Tsuchida fulfills the role of teacher and benefactor and remains faithful to Shimaura, he is an exemplary "older brother."

Echoes of the nanshoku model abound in *The Devil's Disciple* and may account for the fact that the two men's love story can be narrated in such an uncensored, if not undistorted, form. Shimaura refers to the beginning of their relationship as the moment when he became Tsuchida's "one and only younger brother (*muni no otōto*)." Tsuchida, who is a brilliant student, helps Shimaura with his studies, and for two years they are never apart. Their dorm mates refer to them as a "*Paar*," the German word for "couple," a contemporary (non-derogatory) student slang for male–male couples. "You were my older brother" and "my teacher," Shimaura writes. "I respect you and stand in awe of you."[15]

Of course, none of this can be read at face value, since it is all just a setup. Sharing space in the same letter and coming even *after* Shimaura's accusation that Tsuchida is "the most dangerous person in the world," this nostalgic evocation of the early days of their love affair is necessary for the narrative of seduction and corruption. But that does not make it true. To the extent that it also recapitulates on the personal level the historical "transition" from nanshoku to *dōseiai*, it works nostalgically to evoke the loss of something that exists only through the retroactive magic of narrative. This is the misogynous *but not yet homophobic* practice and discourse of *nanshoku* in which male–male eroticism was neither pathologized nor seen as a threat to one's masculinity or patriotic duties. But whatever kind of male–male relationship might have been possible in the context of historical nanshoku toward which Shimaura's reminiscence seems to gesture, it is clear that what we have here has as little to do with that (unknowable) historical reality as "samurai values" had to do with the conduct of the Imperial Japanese Army. This is an instance in which narrative's tendency to put things in order works to isolate what are in fact overdetermined and coexisting ideologies. The pair/series "instruction/corruption" is just one example of a set that also includes "nanshoku/homosexuality," "tradition/ modernity," and "modernism/fascism."

Thus it is that Tsuchida's ability (in Shimaura's letter) to appear as both an "older brother" in the discourse of *nanshoku* and as a "homosexual" outside the bonds of filiation in the discourse of modern sexology allows him to do double duty in figuring Shimaura's corruption. As an "older brother" in the nanshoku mode, he stands in for the misogynous ie seido in which women are considered objects of exchange, marriage for love is unheard of, and relations among men exist along a seamless homosocial continuum from friendship and mutual support to sexual relations. Shimaura believes at a certain point that heterosexual love will differentiate him from Tsuchida, both exonerating him from the misogyny of the ie seido and promoting him to modern and enlightened subjecthood. And yet it is only by accusing Tsuchida of being an exclusive "homosexual" rather than an "older brother" in the discourse of nanshoku that Shimaura can accomplish this differentiation. Thus, Tsuchida must be homosocial and homosexual, premodern and modern at once for Shimaura to assert himself as a modern heterosexual. When he was together with Tsuchida, he writes, "the opposite sex may as well not have existed for us." But after Tsuchida leaves him and he meets Sueko, he believes for a time that he has overcome Tsuchida's baneful influence by shedding his misogyny and learning to be a heterosexual. "I had come to know the beauty and sanctity of women of which you are utterly ignorant."[16]

Unfortunately, however, this first attempt at differentiation crashes and burns when his beloved Sueko succumbs to the pressures of that same homosocial family system by agreeing to marry the man her parents have chosen for her. Shimaura construes Sueko's acquiescence as a failure of heterosexual love to overcome the force of the patriarchal family system. "At the time Sueko said she was doing this for her parents' sake, but for me that made no difference. The point was that Sueko had chosen someone else to be her husband." Betrayed and disillusioned by Sueko, Shimaura loses his faith in heterosexual love and regresses to the homosocial misogyny of the ie seido. And, of course, this is all Tsuchida's fault. "I cursed women," he writes. "And Tsuchida-san, it was then that what you always said began to come back to haunt me. I cursed all women."[17]

As if to confirm his re-entry into the homosocial world, Shimaura rushes into a marriage with Tsuyuko, whom he does not love and only wants to exploit. "This marriage was not based on love (at least on my part)." Shimaura tells Tsuchida:

> It was because I required her loyalty, her kindness, and the little money she had saved. Tsuchida-san. I say this without any shame. I was a little devil. I'm sure you would agree that there was no reason not to sacrifice a woman or two so that I could grow up into a big one.[18]

Shimaura's renewed identification with Tsuchida is thus clearly mediated by the homosocial traffic in women exemplified by the ie seido. But the bitter irony evident in his tone makes clear that Shimaura also associates Tsuchida with something far worse than the evils of premodern patriarchy. From the very beginning of Shimaura's letter, mixed in with a language of respect and tutelage in which the two men's relationship, though hierarchically structured, remains uncoerced and mutually beneficial, there is another language of seduction and indoctrination. A benign paternalism of the older for the younger "brother" is now read in terms of quasi-religious enthrallment. In becoming Tsuchida's "disciple," Shimaura writes, "I sold my soul for knowledge. I will have to live with the fact that I sacrificed my body to your strange love, but I cannot bear the thought that I sold my soul as well." Tsuchida has turned Shimaura from an "innocent boy" who literally "wouldn't hurt a fly" into his "plaything." He has brought Shimaura under the sway of his "strong personality" and has impregnated him with his "seed."[19] He has also introduced him to alcohol and gotten him addicted to sleeping medication.

As the agent of seduction and corruption rather than instruction and guidance, Tsuchida has left the premodern sphere of nanshoku altogether to become a quintessential example of the modern homosexual. His transformation from loving pedagogue to perverted predator thus echoes that of the historical discourse of male–male sexuality in Japan more generally and, I would argue, that of the transition from a modernizing enlightenment to fascism. The endpoint of both of these transitional narratives is a form of identity (be it "homosexual" or "Japanese") in which development and instruction are superseded by seduction and indoctrination. And yet it is crucial to recognize that these "transitional" narratives are not in fact reducible to a series of discrete stages or events, however much they might present themselves as so. Shimaura's storyline is constantly undermined by his retrospective rancor, its beginning colored by its end. Vampire-like, Tsuchida has poisoned Shimaura with his "strange love," and they have both stepped outside of time.

Repetition and Recovery

As readers of the letter we have already gotten a glimpse of this other, poisonous side of Tsuchida in Shimaura's account of how the former unceremoniously dumped him for a younger boy. Shimaura's realization that he is only one of many younger men that Tsuchida has corrupted is another point when Tsuchida's position as the embodiment of the ie seido gives way to his identity as a modern homosexual. In this instance, homosexuality figures as a pathology of repetition and destruction:

> You told me that life wasn't a rose-strewn path. That it was a battle that I would have to learn to fight. But it isn't fighting you like. You get off on destruction . . . You take boys who've never had a drink and make them suffer while you stand back and watch. . . . You love nothing more than to watch them destroy themselves with alcohol while you never touch a drop.[20]

Rather than mentoring them into maturity, Tsuchida corrupts one promising young man after another for his own viewing pleasure. Both Tsuchida's serial seductions and the addictions that he foists on his victims are manifestations of what Freud calls, in *Beyond the Pleasure Principle*, "a compulsion to repeat . . . [which] exhibit[s] to a high degree an instinctual (*triebhaft*) character and, when they act in opposition to the pleasure principle, give[s] the appearance of some 'daemonic' force at work."[21] Tsuchida represents precisely such a demonic force for Shimaura.

Of course, repetition can also work as a means of mastering traumatic experiences or anxieties about the future. Recurrent nightmares are one example. Although they may not be pleasurable themselves, to the extent that they pave the way for mastery and pleasure Freud considers such repetitions "in the service of the pleasure principle." The example Freud gives is that of a little boy who tries to master the anxiety caused by his father's departure for war by repeatedly re-enacting the scene of that departure. These forms of repetition are attempts to master an actual or imagined trauma, to "get over it" and move on. And it is this kind of repetition, according to Peter Brooks, that drives narrative. In his reading of narrative dynamic through Freud's *Beyond the Pleasure Principle*, Brooks writes of a "binding of textual energies that allows them to be mastered by putting them into serviceable form, usable 'bundles,' within the energetic economy of the text."[22] But when such repetition fails to "bind" the excitations that set the narrative in motion (in the detective novel, this is most typically the murder and the mystery of "whodunit?"), it sets off a compulsion to repeat that has no end in sight. It is an addiction, a hunger that will never be sated, a *drive*. When an adult reads a narrative through to the end, "It is hardly possible to persuade [him or her] to re-read it immediately."[23] When we find out "what happens" we are able to put the book down and go to sleep, to close its *binding*. But children (and, as Roland Barthes adds, old people and professors) never tire of hearing or reading the same story over and over.[24] This relation to repetition is also what distinguishes the pervert from the paranoiac. While the former may linger unhurried over the "trivial" details of a text, the latter will recruit them all into "serviceable form," only to throw them away when they are no longer necessary for the narrative.

The fact that we do not know whether Tsuchida ever responded to Shimaura's letter, let alone whether he ever did or would receive it, makes of *The Devil's Disciple* itself an achingly (or deliciously) unbound and uncompleted narrative. That unbound quality thus reproduces in formal terms the perversion that Tsuchida figures for the paranoid Shimaura. Perhaps Shimaura has become addicted to sleeping medication because he fears a sleep in which he will be faced with those unconscious drives, in which the binding force of his recovery story will be weakened even further. This would explain his compulsion to repeat that narrative in a futile attempt at mastery. In this light, his addiction serves as a metaphor for the compulsion to repeat that Freud associates with the death drive.

The fact that sleeping medication is both what keeps Shimaura and Tsuchida alive and a means of murder and suicide in *The Devil's Disciple* also figures perfectly the contradictory nature of the death drive. Take just enough and you get the rest you need, but too much and it kills you. Shimaura (and Tsuchida) keep increasing their dosage as their tolerance increases, treading an ever thinner line between life and death. "These circuitous paths to death," Freud writes, "faithfully kept to by the conservative instincts, would thus present us to-day with the picture of the phenomenon of life."[25]

Shimaura is stuck somewhere between the unbound and a-temporal state of sleep and the narratives of the waking day. In this light, his insomnia emerges as a fear of the unbound energies of the drives, the a-temporal and thus non-narratable energies of the primary process ("with its hint of possession by some 'daemonic power'")[26] that threaten to undo the daytime (narrative) work of the ego instincts.[27] As a self-described "devil's disciple," Shimaura experiences Tsuchida as a "daemonic power" beyond his control and yet part of himself. Perhaps it is for this reason that his accusations of homosexuality and seduction fail to stick to the prosecutor. Instead, they linger in the air and threaten to undermine his narrative by boomeranging right back to him. Thus, the homosexual "frame" to his heterosexual narrative threatens to frame Shimaura himself.

The term *fascism* is of course rooted etymologically in the same notion of "binding" that appears as a central concept in Freud's *Beyond the Pleasure Principle* and functions as the motive force of narrative. In the face of an eminent collapse of identity and subject–object relations, the culture of fascism resorts to the force of narrative to bind errant drives into normative channels. Whether it takes the form of what Andrea Slane calls "nationalist melodrama" in her discussion of fascist culture in the United States,[28] or the more benign injunction to "share" narratives of recovery in a culture obsessed with addiction ("I will always be a recovering alcoholic"), narrative is that which keeps the drives in their place. For our purpose, fascist culture might be thought as one in which narratives of recovery themselves become compulsory and addictive.

Shimaura is culturally fascist to the extent that what he perceives as Tsuchida's "daemonic power" drives him to write his long, accusatory letter. His desire to tell his own story is both an attempt to "get his story straight" in the eyes of the law and, on a more fundamental level, to formulate an identity for himself that is separate from that of the prosecutor. He must tell the story of his own seduction by Tsuchida to contain and bind his past homosexual acts into a narrative that begins with his sexual innocence, moves through a homosexual "stage," and ends with his achievement of a differentiated (hetero) self:

> So we were lovers of a sort (*isshu no koibito dōshi datta deshō*), weren't we? And sure enough, I was dumped by that lover (*sōshite watashi wa sono koibito ni suterareta ni chigai arimasen*). But once I was abandoned by you and

moved away (*hanareta*) from you, I was able to look hard at myself (*wata-shi wa, jishin o mitsumeru koto ga dekita*), and at the same time to see every-thing about you, all the way through (*anata jishin o zenbu mitōshite shimatta no desu*).[29]

As this rather strangely worded passage suggests, Shimaura's narrative culminates in a self-knowledge attained through knowingness.[30] Shimaura can see himself because he can *see through* Tsuchida. By separating himself from Tsuchida, Shimaura is cured of blindness and able to see Tsuchida for what he *is*—a "devil" and a homosexual. This process is echoed in the verb forms used in the passage, which chart an emergence from a passive state into active subjectivity. Beginning with a conspiratorial copula (*datta deshō*), Shimaura moves on to two iterations of the passive verb "to be dumped (*suterareta*)," then to the intransitive "moved away (*hanareta*)," and finally to two active transitive verbs of seeing, the first, "to look hard (*mitsumeru*)," responsible and unflinching when the object is himself, and the second, "to see through (*mitōsu*)," contemptuous and withering when it switches to Tsuchida. The personal pronouns undergo a similar progression—from "we (*wareware*)" to an objectified "that lover (*sono koibito*)" that works to yank the narrator out of the dialogue and into a third person narrative.[31] Finally, fortified by the distance thus gained, he enters again into dialogue, but this time as a separate subject confronting its other: "I (*watashi*)" versus "you yourself (*anata jishin*)." The "I" does the seeing now. It can see itself and "you," too. And yet this assertion of Shimaura's separate (heterosexual) identity will not last long. Eventually his story will lead him back to the realization that he is indeed "the devil's disciple." He writes, "I felt the seed you planted inside me getting stronger and stronger. I became afraid of myself."[32]

The more afraid Shimaura becomes, the less certain he is of his own status as the subject of the gaze or of anything else. This is not helped by the fact that his former lover is now in the position of passing judgment on Shimaura as the prosecutor in his trial, thus blurring the boundary between public and private that would (or should) otherwise create the condition for unbiased judgment. As a prosecutor who cannot sleep, and with whom Shimaura has already slept, Tsuchida appears in Shimaura's imagination not as the embodiment of "blind justice" that a prosecutor should be, but as a relentless persecutor who will not stop looking at him.

Insomniac Homosociality

In Shimaura's account, insomnia is the only thing he and Tsuchida have always had in common. Hamao himself suffered terribly from insomnia, according to his friend Edogawa Ranpo,[33] but we need not resort to the biographical to appreciate the possible meanings of sleeplessness in his work. What was it, one wonders, that kept the author and his protagonists up at night?[34]

It was sleeplessness that brought Shimaura and Tsuchida together when the two were still at boarding school. Unaccustomed to life in the dormitories and overworked with preparations for college entrance exams, Shimaura finds himself unable to sleep for nights on end. Late one night as he wanders the campus, he meets Tsuchida, who also has trouble sleeping, and they immediately bond over their common affliction. Shimaura narrates their first meeting in language that evinces a clear connection between sleeplessness and homoeroticism:

> Until then you and I had never spoken a word to each other. But there is nothing strange in two dormitory mates having a conversation when they find themselves at two in the morning standing in a schoolyard overgrown with fall grasses. The first thing I said to you was that my nights had been made miserable for the previous month out of an inability to sleep. You were deeply moved by these words. You yourself had suffered from insomnia for two years already. Under the dark skies our conversation drifted towards those sleepless nights and as we spoke a warm intimacy grew between us. By dawn we two were bound in a beautiful friendship (utsukushiki yūjō).[35]

Insomnia in The Devil's Disciple serves Shimaura as a displacement for the homoerotic bond that once united the two men and continues to subtend his ambivalent relation to Tsuchida. The narrator goes on to explain that he complained of his insomnia on every occasion when he met Tsuchida. He refers to Tsuchida as the one "who showed me the way when it came to insomnia (fuminshō ni kakete wa senpai de aru anata)."[36] And soon he begins taking sleeping powder under Tsuchida's direction. This "education" in sleeping medication would lead to a terrible addiction and, as I mentioned earlier, progressively larger doses for both men. Here again we have a narrative of decline from education (staying up all night studying) to corruption. Not sleeping has been unmoored from its "use value" to become a perverse and solipsistic repetition. As insomnia, it is taken out of the narrative of self-improvement and sent spinning into the circle of drug addiction. Once again we hear echoes of the death drive, in the shadow of which perverse (homo)sexuality and addiction add up to the same thing.[37]

For a brief period in the beginning of his marriage to Tsuyuko, Shimaura gets a job as a translator, settles down in a "little house in the suburbs," and begins to imagine a comfortably heteronormative life for himself.[38] His father dies at the same time, and the small inheritance he receives supplements the couple's income. Having set up his own household and inherited his father's property, Shimaura further reconfirms his entry into the heteronormative family narrative. The idyllic coziness of this period as it is evoked in the text even suggests he might have gotten some sleep. All he and Tsuyuko need now is a child.

Misogyny Inside and Out

But that, Shimaura writes, "was just a daydream. I had forgotten that I was the devil's disciple." After just six months he grows tired of the very "chastity," "obedience," and "goodness" in Tsuyuko that had first attracted him to her. These "feminine" qualities begin to drive him mad. To test the limits of her submissiveness, he begins to treat her in the most abominable fashion, staying away from home for days on end carousing with other women, purposely sending her out on trumped-up errands in bad weather, and, employing an expression used earlier to describe Tsuchida's treatment of himself, selfishly turning her body and soul into his personal "plaything." But rather than fighting back, Tsuyuko only becomes more submissive, meekly permitting his every indiscretion. "In the end," he writes, "having tormented her mercilessly, I could no longer stand myself and began to wonder if I had not been possessed by my wife's living ghost (ikiryō)."[39]

When he finds out that Tsuyuko is pregnant, the baby appears to him not as a confirmation of his ability to carry on the family name but as a monstrous "gaybie" that materializes his connection to Tsuchida and reaffirms the homo-ness of which he is so afraid. He calls it both a "second me" and a "devil's seed."[40] It is at this point that he moves from merely fantasizing about murdering Tsuyuko to actually planning the deed. By doing away with Tsuyuko, he will be able to kill the fetus at the same time, making the murder an abortion and a kind of suicide, as well.

This "devil's seed" is both Shimaura himself (as the eponymous "devil's disciple") and the spawn of the devil ("I felt the seed you planted inside me getting stronger and stronger.")[41] His desire to murder the child/fetus is a negation of the homosexual fantasy Freud describes in his analysis of the Wolfman "to be copulated with by the father, and therefore both to be born of him and to present him with a child."[42] Freud's description of the Wolfman's "constant *ambivalence*" between the active and passive positions sounds like a description of Shimaura:

> No position of the libido which had once been established was ever completely replaced by a later one. It was rather left in existence side by side with all the others, and this allowed him to maintain an incessant vacillation which proved to be incompatible with the acquisition of a stable character.[43]

This is also, of course, a description of the failure of narrative, a failure to *move on*. It is Shimaura's "incessant vacillation" that both drives him to reach for certainties (whether they be sexual, historical, or otherwise) and prevents him from ever finding them.

But the "devil's seed," the "second me," is not really a baby born between two men, however much Shimaura might fear (and desire) it to be so. It is, after all, Tsuyuko and Shimaura's baby. Shimaura's revulsion at having been impregnated by Tsuchida (which we are reading as a negated desire for such impregnation) registers a threat both to his active masculinity and to his *differentiation* from Tsuchida. But when Tsuyuko is in the picture, this revulsion is transformed into a bond mediated by the misogyny that courses through the homosocial triangle among Shimaura, Tsuchida, and Tsuyuko. Indeed, as the misogynist crescendo of Shimaura's narrative grows, it becomes apparent that it is fueled by his desire to come as close to his former lover as a homosocial libidinal economy will allow—by bonding with him over their common hatred of women.[44] After explaining to Tsuchida how he would comfort himself on sleepless nights with images of Tsuyuko dying by disease, by suicide, or murder, how he would gaze smilingly on her sleeping face knowing that only her death would bring him satisfaction,[45] he addresses Tsuchida yet again in the second person. But this time around, rather than distancing himself from Tsuchida the devil, he pivots back into devilish identification. "What do you think? Tsuchida-san! Had I not become the perfect inheritor of your soul?"[46]

By this point, Shimaura's dead father, from whom he has inherited property, has been completely eclipsed by his former lover, whose very soul has passed into him. He has been infected by Tsuchida's soul and in the process the vertical narrative of succession and filiation has been replaced with a lateral, vampiric cloning. Shimaura shares his insomnia and his soul with his nocturnal companion, and now he imagines the two of them staying up all night together, relishing "devilish fantasies" of his murdered wife.[47]

As if in reaction to the description of such an intense and non-narratable bond between the two men, Shimaura picks up the thread of narrative almost immediately with the story of how Sueko came back into his life. In doing so, he returns to the work of differentiation. After first establishing that Tsuchida (who hates "sentimentalism") would find his continued attachment to her laughable,[48] Shimaura relates that Sueko's husband and entire family were killed in the Great Kanto Earthquake of 1923. Sueko alone survives, perversely freed, like the city of Tokyo itself, from the bonds of the past. Suddenly become a free agent able to make her own decisions outside the structure of the ie seido, Sueko gets back together with Shimaura, and their love returns stronger and hotter than ever. And once again, the heterosexual bond promises the freedom to grow and develop on a slate wiped clean.

But tragically, by falling into a trap set for someone else, Sueko once again reverses Shimaura's work of separation and identity formation. With her death by overdose, what began as an act (the intended murder of Tsuyuko) in which subjective intention was already made intransitive through "suggestion" ends up as an occurrence (Sueko's death) without a transitive subject at all. This ambiguity regarding agency is also in evidence in the strange wording with which Shimaura describes the moment he decides that he wants Tsuyuko dead. He seems to stumble initially over who will do the killing and who will die. "All I could come up with was a terribly prosaic way out of my dilemma. Only one way. Namely, death. To die. And according to our philosophy, she would be killed."[49] Sueko's death will simply substitute, as we will see later, one "she" for another in a kind of paroxysm of undifferentiated misogyny. It is this shared misogyny that Shimaura imagines will both implicate Tsuchida in Sueko's death and mediate his love for the prosecutor. The death of Sueko seems to have resulted from a strange mishmash of subjectivities and intentions, of unfinished sentences that bring the two men together beneath a cloud of guilt.

The Insistent Voice

To read The Devil's Disciple is to feel suffocated and embattled, as anyone might who has received a letter that is forty pages long. The ceaseless drumbeat of the second person positions the reader along with Tsuchida on the receiving end of Shimaura's fulminations, inevitably inspiring some level of sympathy and identification with the prosecutor. And yet to the extent that we take Shimaura's calumnies seriously, the prosecutor with whom we have just identified emerges as a diabolical figure all the same. Our sympathies are thus divided much as Shimaura's seem to be, whose hatred for Tsuchida is matched only by the intensity of his spurned affections.

The form of the letter makes it impossible for the reader to get outside Shimaura's head to find out how much of what he says is "true." Moreover, the paranoid and accusatory nature of the writing renders it suspect from the start and gives the impression that Shimaura is desperate to maintain control of how the text will be read. In fact, one senses that he does not want the text to be *read* at all. He wants to keep yelling at Tsuchida without being interrupted. All of this yelling paradoxically produces a rather hushed mood as the reader is put into an almost embarrassing position somewhere between that of an eavesdropper and a voyeur. Or perhaps we are simply theatergoers.

Hamao's choice to make a novel out of this letter is his way of *staging* Shimaura's desire for unmediated (and unreciprocated) communication. Shimaura depends on the possibility of such communication to make his narrative of recovery believable and to reaffirm his heterosexuality. He wants to make an identity out of a grammatical subject, to make *who he is* the ground of *what he says*. And the only way that this can happen is if he can get someone not only to believe what he says, but to believe (in) *him*. "You may be the only person who will believe what I have said thus far," Shimaura writes. "You will believe that I have told no lies. . . . I call out to you in the name of that friendship we once shared, please believe me. And in believing me, believe what I say."[50]

These are the last lines of a letter bound together by repeated apostrophes to its recipient: "Tsuchida-san!" "Tsuchida-san!" This use of apostrophe, a mode perhaps more suited to a lyric than a letter, is another way in which Shimaura struggles to push forth his own identity through the appeal to an absent other. Its vocative mood is the closest one gets to speech in writing. As what might be thought of as an *acute* or synchronic instance of the same binding that enables diachronic narrative, apostrophe is exemplary of political rhetoric in general, and fascist rhetoric in particular. Barbara Johnson has analyzed apostrophe in a way that sheds light on the way it functions in *The Devil's Disciple*. As a trope that "calls up and animates the absent, the lost, and the dead," apostrophe is, to paraphrase Johnson, the *mode* of Shimaura's letter and the *theme* of *The Devil's Disciple*. While the letter struggles to breathe life into Tsuchida as Shimaura's other, the homo to his hetero, the novel poses the question, "Can this gap be bridged? Can this loss be healed through language alone?"[51] The answer, of course, is "no," and the *novel* seems to know this. But Shimaura keeps trying. As readers of *The Devil's Disciple*, we watch him try as we might watch Pat Robertson denounce the "homosexual lifestyle."[52]

Escape from the Third Person

Shimaura's preference for speech over writing is also understandable, given that it was the ambiguity of writing that landed him in jail in the first place. He tells Tsuchida that after he discovered Sueko's death, he took the train to a small inn in Kiso, "where you and I went as a couple."[53] Here again we have a repetition and circling back of narrative, from the "heterosexual" to the "homosexual" position.

It is at this inn in Kiso that Shimaura resolves to kill himself after writing an account of all that had led up to Sueko's accidental death. But no sooner does he finish composing the document than he decides that "it is more interesting to leave behind a crime that will never be solved" and burns it.[54] Of course, as we have already noted, no actual crime has been committed. Sueko's death was an accident. But in what looks like a last grab at some stable form of subjectivity, Shimaura retroactively renders it a crime of which he is guilty. In penance, he takes an enormous overdose of sleeping powder and lies down to die.

But Shimaura's tolerance for the medication proves greater than even he had imagined. An unspecified number of days later, he wakes up in a police station accused of murder, somehow having neglected to destroy all of the pages of the letter in which he told of his plan to kill Tsuyuko. His memory of the whole affair is temporarily wiped out by the overdose but preserved partially in those surviving pages. Discovered by the maid who came into his room after he failed to emerge for so long, the pages tell only of a plan to kill "her (*kanojo*)," and this is what lands Shimaura in jail. With no memory and only the letter to go by, Shimaura at first believes that he has in fact killed Sueko. As for Tsuyuko, he does not even remember having a wife. But when she comes to visit him in jail, the sight of a packet of sleeping powder tucked into the *obi* of her kimono jogs Shimaura's memory, and he realizes that it was she and not Sueko whom he had planned to kill.

But by then it is too late. "If I had written 'my wife' or 'Tsuyuko' instead of 'her' the letter would not have served as evidence of homicidal wrongdoing in Sueko's death. My failure to write her name has brought about a bizarre result." The free-floating, third-person pronoun "she,"[55] like the un-specified guilt that suffuses the text, speaks of a crime without a clear sub-ject or object. "What a strange coming together of coincidences!" Shimaura writes to Tsuchida. "My hateful wife and the woman I loved! And from now on, when will I ever be able to really sleep?"[56]

The Hole Story

But there is one more twist to this tale. Shimaura's near-overdose on sleep-ing medication has introduced a black hole in the middle of the text that undoes (and indeed motivates) all of his efforts to bind it together. The let-ter we have been reading turns out (according, as always, to the letter itself) to have been written just after Shimaura began to recover from the total loss of his memory and his cognitive abilities. "Everything seemed shrouded in mist. I didn't understand myself," the letter says. "I couldn't even remem-ber who I was."[57] His brush with death and his loss of memory has thus cut his tale in two and rendered his narrative radically unreliable. Knowing the way the letter ends, if the reader goes back to the beginning (which is, of course, to treat the letter as a written narrative rather than the act of com-munication Shimaura wants it to be), we are reminded that Shimaura is not so sure of his story after all: "Prosecutor Tsuchida, I am imprisoned here on suspicion of murder. But I am probably not the guilty party. That's right. Probably not. . . . I regret that I have to say it in such a strange way. But if you read this letter to the end you will surely understand why."[58]

Read this letter to the end, writes Shimaura. The letter ends, as we have seen, with a plea to Tsuchida to believe him and to believe the story it tells. But it is precisely by reading it to the end that Tsuchida and the reader will under-stand the meaning of this "probably," this doubt as to whether the letter is believable after all. And now that the narrative is subjected to doubt, all that can anchor our belief is Shimaura himself. "Tsuchida-san! I call out to you three times in the name of that friendship we once shared. Please believe me. And in believing me, believe what I say."[59] Shimaura, of course, is very unlikely to be believed. But it is Hamao's genius to show us his attempts to *coerce belief* through a narrative that is both held together and pulled apart by the ambivalent force of a homosocial bond. Such is the seductively redemp-tive lure of fascist narrative.

The Devil's Disciple gives us a clear sense of the genocidal consequences of this narrative by showing us how Shimaura's story gets out of hand and starts to devour its own characters. The airtight plot of the detective novel here becomes a stranglehold. When Shimaura finds Sueko dead, he tells Tsuchida:

> I saw in it the result of the murder I had so carefully thought out (kangae ni kangaeta). Strangely, at that moment, I did not feel the sadness of having lost someone I loved. I just (tadatada) looked at this strange, happy-making lump of flesh, there before my eyes. And it was the result of all my planning (keikaku ni keikaku shita).[60]

In a stunning reversal of the structure of melancholy or nostalgia, in which the lost object is animated retroactively to make up for a lack felt in the present, Sueko (whose name means "last child"),[61] exists here in the pure present, unhinged from the narrative and indistinguishable from Tsuyuko or any other woman. To have lost a loved one would be a narrative. But to gaze on a "happy-making lump of flesh" is to enter the realm of repetition and the death drive. The Japanese text evokes this tension between narrative and repetition by doubling the very verbs that describe Shimaura's actions. He "just just (tada tada) . . . thought and thought (kangae ni kangaeta)" and "planned and planned (keikaku ni keikaku shita)." Like what Freud would call a sexual aim unsoldered from its object, Shimaura's machinations have become ends in themselves. As the "last child," Sueko's lump of flesh, indistinguishable from any other and outside the confines of time and narrative, figures the end of history. It is the ultimate unbinding that fascism both fears and brings about. "It was the result of all my planning."

The Perverted Persecutor

But what of the fact that the person with whom Tsuchida is trying to communicate (or trying to lie to) is both a homosexual and a prosecutor? And what of the fact that Shimaura believes that this homosexual prosecutor is the *only one* who will believe what he says? Shimaura blames the prosecutor Tsuchida not for the crime he has (not) committed but for the *person* he has become. "If I had not met you as a young boy," writes Shimaura, "I would not be in prison now. You may not have taught me crime, but you gave me the personality of a criminal."[62]

As the "devil's disciple," Shimaura has become who he is as a result of Tsuchida's instruction and seduction. As we have seen, the story he tells inside the letter of his attempted escape from Tsuchida's influence is a desperate attempt to differentiate himself from the prosecutor and to (re)claim his heterosexuality-as-identity. But the story that *The Devil's Disciple* as a novel tells suggests to the reader the impossibility of his ever extricating himself from that influence. I should emphasize that by this I do not mean to say that Shimaura is "really" a closeted homosexual. This is no more demonstrable from this text than the idea that Tsuchida is an exclusive homosexual. What the text shows is the attempt of one man to shore up his own identity by holding these two "orientations" apart. Indeed, there is no "homosexual" in this text (any more than there are in "reality") except to the extent that such a figure serves to isolate and contain the scourge of sexual perversion in the other. "Homosexuality is constituted as a category," writes Lee Edelman, "to name a condition that must be represented as determinate, as legibly identifiable, precisely insofar as it threatens to undo the determinacy of identity itself; it must be metaphorized as an essential condition, a sexual orientation, to contain the disturbance it effects as a force of de-orientation."[63]

Shimaura *needs* Tsuchida to be a homosexual. This is an essential part of the story he needs to tell. His is a story of recovery from homosexuality (and criminality, and perhaps even insomnia) that may or may not have been successful. But Tsuchida has no story. He simply *remains* a homosexual with a criminal personality who suffers from insomnia and addiction. Shimaura may be all of these things as well, but he is also addicted to *narrative* in the hope that it will tell him that he is not. And part of that narrative depends on casting Tsuchida as somehow outside narrative, like the death drive itself, circling around in the endless repetition of addiction and seduction, remaining *single* and thus outside the narrative of reproduction as well. If Sueko as a dead lump of flesh existed only in the present because severed from the past, Tsuchida lives only in the present because he has no future. "Tsuchida-san. I hear you're increasing your dosage as well. And not even you in all your brilliance can see where you'll end up."[64]

The homosexual predator Tsuchida is at the same time a prosecutor, the very embodiment of the law, the enforcer of social order. In a move that will be familiar from our earlier discussion of "homofascism," Shimaura intertwines the story of Tsuchida's sexual perversion with that of his alleged perversion of the social order. Not only has Tsuchida corrupted Shimaura; he has also weakened and poisoned the law itself. Consider the following passage:

> Not only did you mercilessly transform me into your plaything, but now you see me languishing in prison. But you, who taught me everything, have used your talents and intelligence to live your life without a single

misstep. I respect and admire you from the bottom of my heart. But at the same time I cannot help being appalled at the frailty of the laws of this nation that are powerless to do anything to stop someone as dangerous as you. You're the prosecutor and I'm the criminal. How perfectly appropriate.[65]

By contrasting his own powerless state with that of Tsuchida, who has so cleverly managed to dissimulate his homosexuality *while personifying the law*, Shimaura manages to homosexualize the arbitrariness of legal power. Or, rather, he is able to salvage his (impossible) ideal of justice by casting it as "frail" and "powerless" in the face of this Trojan horse of a homosexual. One cannot help but be struck by the resonance of Shimaura's claim to victimhood with the recent uproar on the right in the United States over "activist judges forcing their arbitrary will on the people" by shoving gay marriage down their throats.[66] Shimaura's hatred and homosexualization of Tsuchida seems almost to pale in comparison to the climate in the United States today, where judges' lives are threatened for the decisions they make.[67] This fear that the legal system and the government will take on a "daemonic" life of its own and cease to represent "the people's interest," that they will cease to hear its voice, is surely at the root of the fascist revolution that seeks to restore some fictive, unmediated form of political representation.

The fact that these anxieties over narrative, representation, and subjectivity surface so often around the person of the homosexual is both symptomatic and instructive. Occupying the constitutive outside of the naturalizing narratives of heteronormativity, and made to figure a fixation *past which* that reproductive and redemptive narrative can proceed, the homosexual as he is imagined by fascists like Shimaura and our own crusaders for "family values" is an indispensable figure.[68]

Conclusion

According to the Marxist critic Hirabayashi Hatsunosuke, writing in 1931, "love scenes"[69] in and of themselves are not interesting to the reader of a detective novel except to the extent that there might be something "behind them":

> Indulging oneself (*hitori de etsu ni itte*) in drawn-out accounts of [sex and love] is enough to destroy a work. . . . Details that do not relate to the crime and its investigation are not necessary in the detective novel. The

writer must work to make every line and every letter come together into a single point at the end, like the spokes of a radiating highway system (*hōshasen dōro*).[70]

The ideal reader of the detective novel should be able to stand firm against sexual temptation, like a spy who will not be waylaid by feminine charms. And the ideal detective novel should help him out by binding sexual and textual excess and waste (that which is "not necessary") into a rational and satisfying ending. For Hirabayashi, "every line and every letter" must be recruited to this end, lassoed in to close up some gaping hole in the heart of the city and the novel at once. Hirabayashi's "radiating highway system" might suggest such centripetal figures for narrative closure as a closing eye or the tightening of a sphincter if it were not for the fact that (1) "radiating" happens outward; and (2) the cars on the highway system are most likely going in both directions. Thus, his simile (inadvertently?) figures the impossibility of closure through written narrative. If the modern detective novel finds such clean closure indispensable, its precondition is to be found in another impossible project, described famously by Hirabayashi in an earlier essay as "the maintenance of the national order through a complete (*kansei sareta*) system of written laws."[71] The use of writing to "complete" a system of laws and to bring a novel to a single closural point is among the most cherished fantasies of modernity. For the fascist subject it becomes an obsession. The fact that it is a fantasy is a knowledge that most detective and legal fictions work to suppress. Their chronic failure or principled refusal to do so are symptoms of and resistances to a culture of fascism that seeks to cure itself through the production of increasingly implausible fictions.

Notes

I thank Nina Cornyetz, Douglas Crimp, and Kota Inoue for their rigorous and generous critiques of this essay. I am also extremely grateful to Alan Tansman for his unstinting help, encouragement, and criticism at every stage of what turned out to be a very long process.

Epigraph: Hamao Shirō, *Akuma no deshi* [The Devil's Disciple], 86.

1. Hamao's son is currently a Roman Catholic cardinal.
2. Manji Gonda, *Nihon tantei sakkaron* (Tokyo: Yūshisha, 1992), 179.
3. Marshall Needleman Armintor, "Paranoia: Schreber, Lacan, and The Sacred Fount," in idem, *Lacan and the Ghosts of Modernity: Masculinity, Tradition, and the Anxiety of Influence* (New York: P. Lang, 2004), 57.

4. Tsuyuko blithely replies to Shimaura's query as to whether she has taken as large a dose as he (as he hoped she would) with, "What? If I took that much it would kill me, silly! (*Ara, anna ni nondara shinjimau wa yo*)": Hamao, *Akuma no deshi*, 113.

5. Ibid., 98.

6. Sigmund Freud, "Three Essays on the Theory of Sexuality" (1905), in James Strachey et al., eds., *The Standard Edition of the Complete Psychological Works of Sigmund Freud*, vol. 7, (London: Hogarth Press, 1995), 171.

7. See Ernest Jones, "The Psychology of Quislingism," quoted in Andrea Slane, *A Not So Foreign Affair: Fascism, Sexuality, and the Cultural Rhetoric of Democracy* (Durham: Duke University Press, 2001), 116.

8. Despite Jones's misleading use in this passage of the gender-neutral term *people*, these subjects are almost always thought to be men. More precisely, they are thought to be not man enough.

9. Takeo Doi, *The Anatomy of Dependence*, trans. John Bester (New York: Kodansha International, 1981), 175; emphasis added.

10. Ibid., 118.

11. See "Seventeen," in Kenzaburō Ōe, *Seventeen and J: Two Novels* (New York: Blue Moon Books, 1996); Vincent, "Ōe Kenzaburō to Mishima Yukio no sakuhin ni okeru homofashizumu to sono fuman," *Hihyō Kūkan* 2, no. 16 (1998): 129–54.

12. Judith Roof, *Come as You Are: Sexuality and Narrative* (New York: Columbia University Press, 1996), xxxi.

13. I should point out that Hamao does not actually use the word *homosexuality* (*dōseiai*) in *The Devil's Disciple*. Neither does he use the term *nanshoku*. The two discourses are nonetheless clearly in evidence in the text. I use the terms *homosexuality* and *homosexual* here to designate those moments when the text represents male–male sex in the psychologizing terms associated with the newly emergent discourse of sexology. But Hamao's text, as I will demonstrate later, straddles two discourses of male–male sexuality. For example, he uses *onnagirai* (woman hater; Hamao, *Akuma no deshi*, 100), a term that belongs to the lexicon of *nanshoku* and implies an exaggerated masculinity rather than an effeminate passivity. But at the same time, the frequent use in the text of the neologism "opposite sex" *isei* points to the polarized notion of gender that informs the modern hetero–homo divide. In two articles written in 1930, Hamao used the term *dōseiai* but also the term *Urning*, derived from the work of the German writer and activist Karl Heinrich Ulrichs, the earliest advocate of what is now known as gay rights: see idem, "Dōseiai Kō," *Fujin Saron*, September 1930, 136–42; and "Futatabi Dōseiai ni tsuite," November 1930, 58–65.

14. Gregory M. Pflugfelder, *Cartographies of Desire: Male–Male Sexuality in Japanese Discourse* (Berkeley: University of California Press, 1999), 41.

15. Hamao, *Akuma no deshi*, 85–86, 90.

16. Ibid., 86, 93–94.

17. Ibid., 90.

18. Ibid., 96.

19. Ibid., 86, 88–90, 97.

20. Ibid., 88.

21. The *Standard Edition* uses the word *instinctual* to translate Freud's term *triebhaft*, perhaps because of the difficulty of forming an adjective out of "drive." As the editors note, the German term *Trieb* "bears much more of a feeling of urgency than the English 'instinct.'" For this reason, it is better rendered as "drive": Sigmund Freud, "Beyond the Pleasure Principle," in James Strachey et al., eds., *The Standard Edition*, 1–64.

22. See Peter Brooks, "Freud's Masterplot: A Model for Narrative," in idem, *Reading for the Plot: Design and Intention in Narrative* (Cambridge, Mass.: Harvard University Press, 1984), 101.

23. Freud, "Beyond the Pleasure Principle," in James Stracey et al., eds., *The Standard Edition*, 35.

24. "Those who fail to reread are obliged to read the same story everywhere": Roland Barthes, *S/Z: An Essay*, trans. Richard Miller, (New York: Hill and Wong, 1974), 16.

25. Freud, "Beyond the Pleasure Principle," in James Stracey et al., eds., *The Standard Edition*, 39.

26. Ibid., 36.

27. On the non-narratable and a-temporal qualities of the primary process, see Leo Bersani, "Pleasures of Repetition," in idem, *The Freudian Body: Psychoanalysis and Art* (New York: Columbia University Press, 1986); Brooks, "Freud's Masterplot."

28. See Slane, *A Not So Foreign Affair*.

29. Hamao, *Akuma no deshi*, 87.

30. I use the term *knowingness* here in the sense given it by David Halperin. He writes, "What our culture typically produces, or recognizes, as 'the truth' about gay men and gay sex is not a disengaged, serene, or politically innocuous 'knowledge,' but an array of contradictory and, it would now seem, murderous knowledge-effects: an illusory *knowingness*, that is, which is not only distinct from 'knowledge' but is actually opposed to it, is actually *a form of ignorance*, insofar as it serves to conceal from the supposedly knowledgeable the nature of their own personal and political investments in the systematic misrecognition and abjection of homosexuality": David M. Halperin, *Saint Foucault: Towards a Gay Hagiography* (New York: Oxford University Press, 1995), 16

31. One thinks of "that woman."

32. Hamao, *Akuma no deshi*, 97.

33. Ranpo Edogawa, "Hamao-shi no kotodomo," in ed. Oshita Udaru, *Hamao Shirō zuihihitsushei* (Tokyo: Shunjusha, 1936), 3.

34. In his memoirs of his career as a detective novelist, Yokomizo Seishi records his impression of Hamao. "Given his occupation as a prosecutor, I expected Hamao to have a dignified, if not a haughty demeanor. But the person whom I met was the very antithesis of haughty—a gentleman who radiated kindness, dressed casually in the simplest of kimonos and tall and thin as a crane. He had a nervous

disposition and was so plagued by insomnia that he had to consume enormous quantities of sleeping medication. What life was left in that scraggy, crane-like body seemed to waste away before one's eyes": Yokomizo Seishi, *Tantei shōsetsu gojūnen* (Tokyo: Kodansha, 1977), 161–62.

35. Hamao, *Akuma no deshi*, 91.

36. Ibid., 106.

37. Eve Kosofsky Sedgwick notes the same tendency to figure homosexuality through drug addiction in British literature. She writes, "In *The Picture of Dorian Gray* as in, for instance, *Dr. Jekyll and Mr. Hyde*, drug addiction is both a camouflage and an expression for the dynamics of male same-sex desire and its prohibition: both books begin by looking like stories of erotic tensions between men, and end up as cautionary tales of solitary substance abusers": Eve Kosofsky Sedgwick, "Epidemics of the Will," in idem, *Tendencies* (Durham: Duke University Press, 1993), 134. Hamao was certainly familiar at least with *Dorian Gray*. As Shimaura searches for a way to dispose of his wife's body, he wishes he had the powerful acid that Dorian used to dissolve Basil Hallward's body after he murdered him: Hamao, *Akuma no deshi*, 103.

38. Hamao, *Akuma no deshi*, 97.

39. Ibid., 97, 99.

40. Ibid., 102.

41. Ibid., 97.

42. This is a paraphrase from Kenneth Lewes, *The Psychoanalytic Theory of Male Homosexuality* (New York: New American Library, 1989), 29.

43. Sigmund Freud, "From the History of an Infantile Neurosis," in James Stracey et al., eds., *The Standard Edition*, 26–27.

44. While romantic rivalry over a single woman is the most common mode in which two men enter into a homosocial relation (as in the classic example of Sensei and K in Sōseki's *Kokoro*), I am arguing that virulent misogyny may work to draw the triangle even tighter without stepping over the line.

45. Later, when Shimaura discovers Sueko dead from the overdose he had planned for Tsuyuko, she is described as "sprawled out dead as if asleep" (*Nemutta yō ni taorete imasu*): Hamao, *Akuma no deshi*, 116.

46. Ibid., 99.

47. Ibid.

48. "That is the difference between your personality and mine": ibid., 100.

49. *Hidoku sanbun teki na hōhō de shika kono kyōgū kara nukederu michi wo miidasenakatta no desu. Sore wa tatta hitotsu no michi deshita. Sunawachi shi desu. Shinu koto desu. Shikamo wareware no tetsugaku ni shitagaeba, kanojo ga korosareru koto desu*: ibid., 99.

50. *Dōka watashi wo shinjite kudasai. Sōshite watashi no iu koto wo shinjite kudasai*: ibid., 123–24.

51. Barbara Johnson, "Apostrophe, Animation, and Abortion," in *A World of Difference* (Baltimore: The Johns Hopkins University Press, 1987), 184–99.

52. The repeated use of this term by the homophobic right is telling in the way it

immobilizes "homosexuality" as something that cannot be narrated (as opposed to a "life").

53. Hamao, *Akuma no deshi*, 118.

54. Ibid.

55. Significantly, *kanojo*, along with all the other words that are now considered "pronouns" in Japanese, is a modern neologism, an abstraction of personhood inconceivable in premodern Japanese, where people were nominated either through their relations to others or through proper names—in other words, the "my wife" or "her name" that would have proved Shimaura's innocence.

56. Hamao, *Akuma no deshi*, 118–19.

57. Ibid., 120.

58. Ibid., 84–85.

59. Ibid., 124.

60. *Watashi wa kangae ni kangaeta satsujin no hōhō no kekka wo koko ni miidashimashita. Watashi wa fushigi ni mo kono toki, ai suru mono wo ushinatta to iu kanashimi wa mattaku kanjimasendeshita. Tadatada, jibun wo yorokobasu fushigi na niku no katamari wo me no mae ni mita nomi desu. Shikamo jibun ga keikaku ni keikaku shita sono kekka desu*: ibid., 116.

61. Actually the *sue* of Sueko is written phonetically in hiragana, so we cannot know what character (if any) it is standing in for. But the sound does suggest the word for "last (or youngest) child." The phonetic rendering makes for yet another instance of undecidability in the text, hovering between speech and writing.

62. Hamao, *Akuma no deshi*, 90.

63. Edelman, "Homographesis," 14.

64. Hamao, *Akuma no deshi*, 107.

65. Ibid., 90.

66. George W. Bush, "State of the Union Address," January 20, 2005.

67. See John Files, "From Chicago Judge, a Plea for Safety and Softer Words," *New York Times*, May 19, 2005.

68. As Hamao himself pointed out in an article he wrote for the magazine *Fujin saron* in 1930, homosexuality was not subject to legal prohibition in Japan as it was in Europe at the time, and for this Japanese homosexuals might be thankful. Hamao cited this legal tolerance of homosexuality as a sign that Japan was more "cultured (*bunka-teki*)" than Europe. This did not mean, however, that homophobia was not an issue in Japanese *culture*. In response to this first article Hamao received letters from lonely, suicidal "Urnings" (see n. 13) all over Japan who wrote of the pressure their families put on them to marry, their sense of shame about homosexuality, and their fear that it should be revealed. Reading Hamao's accounts of these letters, it is perfectly clear that the unstigmatized *nanshoku* model of male same-sex relations had been largely overwhelmed by the modern discourse of homosexuality by 1930. Hamao's response to these letters came in the form of a second article published two months later as an open letter to all of Japan's "Urnings" that reads like a 1970s pamphlet on gay liberation. Hamao's

extraordinary understanding of the way homophobia functioned in Japanese culture at the time makes it no wonder that he was able to deal so intelligently with the theme in his detective fiction: see Hamao, "Dōseiai kō" and "Futatabi dōseiai ni tsuite."

69. Hirabayashi uses the English word in *katakana*.

70. Hatsunosuke Hirabayashi, "Tantei shōsetsu sakka ni nozumu" in *Hirabayashi Hatsunosuke bungei hyōron zenshū*, vol. 3, (Tokyo: Bunsendō Shoten, 1975), 401–4.

71. Idem, "Nihon no kindai teki tantei shōsetsu: Toku ni Edogawa Ranpo shi ni tsuite" (1925) in *Hirabayashi Hatsunosuke bungei hyōron zenshū*, vol. 2 (Tokyo: Bunsendō Shoten, 1975), 220–27.

JAMES DORSEY

Literary Tropes, Rhetorical Looping,
and the Nine Gods of War:
"Fascist Proclivities" Made Real

■   On March 6, 1942, Captain Hiraide Hideo, section chief in the
Kaigun Hōdōbu Kachō (Naval Information Bureau), delivered a radio address relating details of the top-secret submarine component of the tre-
mendously successful surprise attack that Japan had executed three months
earlier at Pearl Harbor. The story he told, and the manner in which he told
it, struck a cord with the Japanese people, setting off an avalanche of retell-
ings, additions, and commentaries across a wide spectrum of media out-
lets. A transcript of Hiraide's broadcast was carried in all of the major newspapers the following day; it was reproduced in a host of periodicals the next
month. There then followed a veritable flood of cultural artifacts dealing
with the men and the mission: nonfiction books, poems, essays, a Kabuki
play, short stories, novels, songs, and educational material. Perhaps the
most memorable was Iwata Toyoo's novel *Kaigun* (The Navy) and the director Tasaka Tomosaka's feature film based on it. The 1943 release of the film,
produced with the full support of the Imperial Navy, represents the completion of a circle: ideologically motivated government propaganda had inspired public participation in a discourse that was subsequently reclaimed
by agents of the state to further promote its agenda. This "looping" pattern

binding the public to the state is a distinguishing characteristic of cultural production in the opening days of the Asia-Pacific War, and it transformed what began as but another round in the public-relations competition between the Imperial Navy and Imperial Army into something much larger: a communal myth propagated and consumed by the entire nation.

While the individual articulations of the submariners' tale varied in genre, focus, and style, virtually all of them tapped into the same core of emotionally charged tropes. In a sense, the discourse was modular. The components were largely limited to those presented in the Navy's original announcement, but each retelling of the submarine mission would inflect the story by varying the particular configuration of the elements, adding texture to the overall portrait. Three components of the tale stand out for their prominence in the media firestorm: (1) the heroes as guileless agents, so pure in spirit that they transcend the political motivations of the war; (2) mother figures distinguished by their down-to-earth pragmatism and their unwavering devotion to both the nation and its warriors (their sons); and (3) points of rural origins, hometowns (*furusato*) noted for distinctive natural landscapes and customs that, paradoxically, bind their native sons all the more tightly to the nation as a whole.

This third feature also demonstrates the trope that is repeated at various levels of this cultural phenomenon: the concrete specificity of the hero's birthplace merges with the abstract concept that is the nation in much the same manner as each uniquely inflected reiteration of the story contributes to the communal myth. This looping action fuses the particular to the universal, and it is ubiquitous. It binds unique locales to an all-encompassing nation; it ties the present incident to historical precedents through both the mode and contents of the representations. The singular event of the submarine attack thereby becomes somehow also eternal, timeless. The task of telling, too, loops from the state to the citizenry and back to the state again, binding the two in a communal act of mythmaking. The very erasure of self through surrender to the state that is the subject of the myth is therefore embodied in the praxis generating and sustaining that myth.

The discourse surrounding the submariners of Pearl Harbor shows all the elements of a culture of fascism. In it one finds a large swath of the population assuaging the anxieties of modernity through participation in a totalizing myth that envelopes the individual in an eternal essence that is the state. Most important, though, the myth that is repeated endlessly in so many corners of culture, looping between the present and the past, between the citizenry and the wartime regime, between traditional genres of representation and new media, is one that invariably concludes in an apocalyptic act of glorious, violent self-destruction. Such acts were to become normal in the final year of the war as thousands upon thousands of Japanese military became "shattered jewels (*gyokusai*)" — the euphemism for those meeting a glorious death against hopeless odds — in either futile charges against superior forces or in kamikaze missions from which there was to be no return. Shocking and unthinkable as those episodes are to us at this historical remove, they were apparently not so to the participants. Such deaths had, after all, been rehearsed through the participation — sometimes as active producers and sometimes as passive consumers — in the communal myth.

The Initial Act of (Attempted) Violence

The radio address that so inspired the Japanese nation in 1942 took as its subject a military exploit that in the postwar years came to be all but entirely forgotten. While on both sides of the Pacific today the attack on Pearl Harbor is associated with the endless stream of fighter planes and bombers that attacked an unsuspecting Pacific Fleet early on a Sunday morning, in wartime Japan that opening salvo conjured up images of an attack from below, one designed to take advantage of Japan's secret weapon: a "midget" submarine. Measuring but twenty-four meters in length and two meters in diameter, these battery-powered vessels were armed with two torpedoes.[1] In the plan hatched by Squad Leader Captain Sasaki Hanku, these tiny vessels would be attached to full-size submarines for transportation to within striking distance of Pearl Harbor, where they would then be released into the waters under cover of darkness on the night before the aerial attack. Infiltrating the harbor by either squeezing under the anti-submarine nets or slipping through undetected in the wake of a U.S. vessel, the midget subs would then sink to the ocean floor and wait, attacking either in unison with the morning's aerial attack or, alternatively, after nightfall the next day, when they would target whatever U.S. ships remained afloat. After accomplishing this mission, the submariners were to leave the harbor and rendezvous with the mother ships at one of two points near Lanai Island, where the vessels would be scuttled and the crewmen would board the larger submarines for their escape.

Five such subs were deployed in the attack, and they were manned by crew members selected according to the following criteria. The submariners were to be (1) strong in mind and body; (2) enthusiastic and filled with an aggressive spirit; (3) single; and (4) without binding familial obligations.[2] Chosen for the mission were the following five two-man crews: Lieutenant Iwasa Naoji and Ensign Sasaki Naokichi, First Lieutenant Yokoyama Masaji and Ensign Ueda Sadamu, First Lieutenant Furuno Shigemi and Ensign Yokoyama Shigenori, Second Lieutenant Hiroo Akira and Ensign Katayama Yoshio, and Second Lieutenant Sakamaki Kazuo and Ensign Inagaki Kiyoshi.[3] The men were all young; Sasaki was the oldest at twenty-nine, and Hiroo was the youngest at only twenty-two. The officers were all graduates of the prestigious Naval Academy at Etajima, and, as if by design, all crew members were of rural origin.

As is well known, the attack on Pearl Harbor was a success. When day was done, three U.S. battleships had sustained heavy damage, and five others had been sunk completely, most notably the mighty *U.S.S. Arizona*. A number of cruisers, destroyers, and other vessels were also seriously damaged. Furthermore, large numbers of U.S. military aircraft on the island were rendered inoperable—having been grouped together for easy protection against anticipated sabotage from the Japanese Americans on the islands, these planes made easy targets for the bombing and strafing Japanese aircraft. Human casualties were devastating. More than 1,100 Navy, Army, and civilian personnel had been wounded, and more than 2,400 had lost their lives.

The first detailed report of the attack issued by the Naval Division of Japan's Imperial Headquarters came ten days later, on December 18, 1941. Here the aerial component of the assault was underemphasized, the only mention being of the twenty-nine airplanes lost. However, one entire section of this terse four-point bulletin is dedicated entirely to the submarines: "in this same naval battle our special attack force, composed of special submarines (*tokushū senkōtei*), exercised the utmost caution in a harbor infiltration that they realized could cost them their lives. Some attacked the heart of the enemy forces just as the Japanese planes fiercely struck from above; others acted independently to launch nighttime attacks. At the very least these submarines sank the aforementioned battleship *Arizona* and left the enemy fleet quivering in fear over their grand military feat." In its summary of Japan's losses during the attack, this report mentions the five submarines that "have yet to return."[4] This short news bulletin constitutes the first version of the mission that would attain mythic proportions in the months to come. Other than its (mis)representation of the submarines' grand success, it is most significant for its use of the label "Special Attack" Force (*tokubetsu kōgeki tai*; often abbreviated as simply *tokkōtai*). This label was to become the generic term used to describe all future military assignments carried out with the expectation that they would end in death. What are known in the United States as the kamikaze are in Japan universally referred to as the "Special Attack Forces (*tokkōtai*)."

The December 18, 1941, appraisal of the submariners' accomplishments remained the accepted version for the duration of the war. Almost none of it is true, however, other than the fact that no submarine returned from the mission. The U.S.S. *Arizona* was sunk by the aerial attack, and though it seems that two submarines did succeed in infiltrating the harbor, neither was able to use its torpedoes effectively. Furthermore, at least one of the midget submarines was spotted by a U.S. naval vessel outside the harbor hours before the aerial attack began and, had it been dutifully reported rather than dismissed as a false alarm, the Pacific Fleet might very well have been better prepared when the planes appeared in the skies above Pearl Harbor.

The most fascinating escapade of the submarine squad was undoubtedly that of Second Lieutenant Sakamaki Kazuo and Ensign Inagaki Kiyoshi. When last-minute preparations revealed their submarine's key navigational device as malfunctioning and beyond repair, their commanding officer asked Sakamaki how he wished to proceed. Sakamaki would later recall, "It was unthinkable that I abandon [the operation] at this point. A powerful feeling of responsibility and a sense of mission bound me tightly and gave me courage. With energy and enthusiasm . . . I answered, 'Commander, I will go!'"[5]

Not surprisingly, the mechanical problems rendered the men unable to stealthily enter the harbor, and they repeatedly suffered damage to their craft. Still, it was only after nightfall on December 7 that the crew of this submarine decided to abandon the mission. Floundering in search of the rendezvous point, however, their submarine ran aground on a coral reef, where its power supply then expired. While Inagaki did not survive the swim ashore, Sakamaki did, but only to fall unconscious as soon as he pulled himself up on the sandy beach. When he regained consciousness, Sergeant David M. Akui, a Nisei, stood over him with a pistol. Sakamaki Kazuo thus achieved the dubious honor of becoming POW number 1.[6]

Political Propaganda from Imperial Headquarters (I):
The Guileless Hero

By any objective account, the midget submarine "Special Attack Forces"
that participated in the attack on Pearl Harbor were a military failure, and
though the quality of military intelligence at the time is a matter of some
dispute, Imperial Headquarters back in Japan was almost certainly aware
of this fact. That knowledge, however, did not prevent the Imperial Navy
from declaring the mission a success and initiating a public-relations drive
that succeeded far beyond its wildest dreams. It began with the March 1942
press release providing details of the submarine squad, a curious document
stitched together from a variety of tones and rhetorical modes. It includes
not only a journalistic narrative of the mission but also vitriolic denuncia-
tions of Western imperialism and decadence. For example, Captain Hiraide,
the Navy spokesman, insists that the fallen seamen were

> enacting an annihilation of the England and America that lurks in our
> hearts; they were acting on their conviction that we must exterminate—
> destroy—the American and English egocentrism that through culture
> and philosophy has over long years wormed its way into the spirit of the
> citizens of Japan.
>
> We can hope for success in the Greater East Asian War only when we
> have both expelled the concrete, visible tyrannical influence exercised
> by England and American on East Asia and cleansed our hearts of their
> invisible concepts of egotism and materialism. From this perspective,
> too, our heroes have provided us all with a good example to follow.[7]

The deluge of media representations prompted by this press release, however, indicate that it was not the hackneyed diatribes in Hiraide's announcement that resonated in the communal psyche. Rather, the other dimensions
of Hiraide's bulletin exercised an appeal: specifically, the poignant anecdotes of the submariners in their final hours and the paeans to selfless supporters on the home front. It was here that the press release successfully
introduced two of the three emotionally charged tropes that would drive
the myth: that of the heroes as innocent, almost childlike agents immune
to the political dimensions of their act and that of the mother figures who
firmly grounded both the heroes and the nation. The third trope—that of
a specific rural locale serving as a synecdoche for the nation as a whole—
would only appear at the next stage of the communal mythmaking.

Hiraide's portrait of the Nine Gods of War (kyūgunshin),[8] as the fallen submariners came to be known, rendered them heroes more for their attainment of a spiritual, egoless state than for their military exploits or dedication to a political or ideological cause. The submariners, as Hiraide paints them, are utterly guileless to the point where they assume childlike qualities. Though Hiraide himself does acknowledge a political context for the attack on Pearl Harbor, painting it as the moment when "the sword of justice was lowered on the tyrannical United States, which has trampled on the great spirit of a Japan dedicated to world peace," nowhere does he attribute such consciousness to the submariners themselves.[9] Hiraide insists instead on an almost religious selflessness: "each and every one of them was completely without desire for promotion, and they had all rejected the concepts of glory, pleasure, personal comfort—even the very idea of the 'self.'"[10]

Interestingly, this selflessness is so complete that it transcends even a conception of surrendering themselves to a larger cause. As Hiraide describes them, the men do not sacrifice themselves for nation or race or liberty; such abstractions no longer have meaning for them. Instead, they engage the material world in a most concrete sense: through their corporeal being. "The squad truly transcended the question of life and death, and concentrated to the very end on the destruction of the enemy ships. There was no thought of returning alive in their heads. . . . There are more than a few examples of men who have in the heat of the battle gone willingly to their deaths. Still, the pinnacle of bushidō lies in that pure, sublime, and selfless realm wherein one's convictions are realized with the body."[11] Here the heroes are intent on their mission, but it is not a mission to free Asia from subjugation by the West, not an assignment to gain redress for Japan's treatment as a second-class citizen of the world, not an obligation to secure Japan's access to colonies and resources—all of which would imply a concern with the larger, abstract context within which they act. To the submarine crew, the mission is simply a matter of sinking ships.

This artless authenticity of the men is further developed through Hiraide's introduction of various anecdotes from their final moments, anecdotes that highlight their guileless nature by returning them to childhood and stripping them even of the marks of the military. This characterization appears when Hiraide describes the simple pleasure the men took in the special supplies provided them for the mission. "I am told that valiantly boarding his submarine, one of these young officers said, 'We've got our lunchboxes and some cider, and they even gave us some chocolate. I feel just like I'm going off on a hike.' Pleasant childhood memories of a school field trip (*ensoku*) must have come flooding back to the mind of this young hero for a moment. His heart filled with the dear memory of such field trips, this hero danced cheerfully towards the site of his death."[12] The political and ideological context framing their mission erased, the men are depicted as innocent children off on a "field trip."

A second telling anecdote related by Hiraide also serves to erase any abstract motivation that might sully the innocence of the crew. Hiraide tells of how one of the men, about to board his submarine, said, "I suppose we should wear our uniforms, but they're so hot that I'll just take the liberty of going in my work clothes."[13] By stripping the men of their military uniforms, the quintessential symbol of dedication to the abstract notion that is nation, Hiraide succeeds in further distancing these men from any conscious, reasoned motivation. Without uniforms, the men act for neither personal military glory nor national interests; in their work clothes they simply focus on the concrete task at hand. These depictions establish the image of an apolitical, genuinely selfless hero, one whose childlike artlessness suggests an unmediated, ingenuous interaction with the material world.

In this portrait of the heroes Hiraide is, consciously or unconsciously, tapping into a trope that had been infused with an enormous emotional charge by roughly contemporaneous literary and cultural trends. The philosopher Nishida Kitarō's conception of "pure experience (*junsui keiken*)," his student Nishitani Keiji's privileging of the "position of subjective nothingness (*shutai-teki mu no tachiba*)," the writer Hayashi Fusao's understanding of the significance of the widespread conversions (*tenkō*) away from a Marxist orientation, the critic Kobayashi Hideo's longing for a literary "home" antecedent to contrived narratological strategies—all of these ideas were responses to a perceived crisis of modernity, a crisis marked by a nagging suspicion that protracted intellectual discourse ultimately alienated humans from the very realities they were attempting to fathom.[14] In Hiraide's portrayal, the Nine Gods of War seem to embody all that these writers had been espousing: the submariners had transcended the desire to explain or rationalize their act by an appeal to any abstract "ism" and instead devoted themselves single-mindedly to a simple, concrete act—in this case, the sinking of enemy ships. Thus, Hiraide's anecdotes portray the squad as having achieved a childlike innocence.[15] The incorporation of this charged image into this early narrative of the mission is one of the primary reasons for the public's enthusiastic response to the myth.

Political Propaganda from Imperial Headquarters (II):
Mothers Serving Sons and the Nation

Hiraide's press release also taps into the potent literary trope of the mother. There were, to be sure, practical reasons for him to pay tribute to this sector of the home-front population. With the conscription of an ever increasing percentage of able-bodied men laying a onerous burden on the communities that depended on their labor, it was the women left behind who were called on to maintain production on the farms and in the factories. They were incorporated into the national agenda through the mobilization of the local chapters of the Kokubō Fujinkai (Women's Defense League), an organization charged with planning and executing the village-wide "celebrations" of military call-ups.[16] Depending on women for these duties, the propaganda bureaus of the armed services surely recognized the need to tend to their morale.

Still, in acknowledging the mothers of Japan in this ode to the fallen submariners, Hiraide is incorporating another charged image that would resonate in the public imagination. Hiraide's announcement included the following lines:

> I must point out here that this grand spirit of sacrifice in which the self is extinguished in becoming a martyr for the nation was made possible largely through the influence of exceptional mothers. As if by design, all of our heroes were famous for their filial piety.
>
> One of the heroes enjoyed nothing more than using his furloughs, no matter how short, to return home and spend a day in his mother's company. This gives us a glimpse of the devotion they felt to their mothers. Such devotion attests to the immensity of the behind-the-scenes strength with which these mothers lovingly raised these valiant heroes — they toiled endlessly and without thought for themselves, dedicating everything to their families, their husbands, their children, and therein finding a supreme happiness. The self-sacrificing spirit of these mothers lived on as a powerful force within the heroes. If not for these grand mothers of Japan we would be bereft of men capable of selfless service to the nation. In short, these egoless mothers who live on through their children are mothers who live for the nation itself.[17]

This tribute to the mothers, like the depiction of the submariners as guileless heroes, taps into tropes cultivated in more rarefied literary texts in the years leading up to the Asia-Pacific War. Unlike the model of the male hero (which includes the transcendence of an ultimately alienating analytical stance in a return to an unmediated engagement with the concrete world), women—and in particular mothers—had frequently been painted as firmly rooted in the realities of the material world, unperturbed by complex abstractions and keenly attuned to their emotions. This image of women is presented in a broad range of texts, including Kawabata Yasunari's *Snow Country* and Kobayashi Hideo's "Literature of the Lost Home" and "History and Literature." In Kawabata's work, it is the impetuousness and forthcoming character of the country geisha Komako that soothes the frayed nerves of the intellectual Tokyoite Shimamura. In Kobayashi's essays, it is a mother figure who embodies the "natural" mode of apprehension for which he longs.[18] By incorporating mothers into its account, the Imperial Navy had co-opted the emotional charge that such literary texts had infused in the image of mothers and nurturing women.

By weaving into its narrative both of these images—that of the pure hero and that of the selfless mother fully integrated into her world—the Imperial Navy succeeded in appealing to the populace more powerfully than if it had restricted itself to the facts of the mission and its clichéd assertions that Japan "must exterminate—destroy—the American and English egocentrism that . . . [has] wormed its way into the spirit of the citizens." As a pastiche of varying tones, perspectives, and rhetorical modes, the narrative of the mission served to invite popular participation in the continued construction of the myth of the submariners. The populace did respond, enthusiastically, and across a wide variety of genres.

The Popular Imagination Responds:
The Navy Fuses Local to National

Captain Hiraide's press release on the submarine mission prompted an avalanche of representations dealing with the subject. The Nine Gods of War were the subject of at least nine full-length books published in the year or so after Pearl Harbor: *Ah, The Special Attack Force!*; *Biographies of the War Gods*; *The Special Attack Force: Traces of the War Gods*; *War God Special Attack Force of the Seas*; *Aa, The Nine War Gods!*; *Submerged at Pearl Harbor: The Record of Lieutenant X*; *The True Story of the Nine Special Attack War Gods*; *Mothers of the War Gods*; and *The Mothers Who Gave Birth to the War Gods*.[19] Short stories and essays dealing with the topic were too many to count, and a seemingly infinite number of verses offered by patriotic poets appeared in the newspapers and magazines.[20] Even the recording industry capitalized on the craze: the *Yomiuri*

JAMES DORSEY

418

newspaper's recording division released both "The Special Attack Forces" and "Commander Iwasa, War God" in 1942. The latter included the following verse:

When I die for your sake, my lord,	*kimi no tame ni shisuru toki*
Consider it the fulfillment of my filial duty	*kō o togeshi to oboshimese*
Final lines written before my brave deed	*kaoru isao no zeppitsu o*
Taking them in hand, father smiles	*ste ni suru chichi ha hohoemite*
And the mother of a War God never weeps!	*aa gunshin no haha nakazu*[21]

These songs were later approved by the Ministry of Education and distributed to public schools for educational use.

Within this deluge, the most compelling and widely consumed reiteration of the myth was the novel *Kaigun* (The Navy; 1942), by Iwata Toyoo, and the film by the same name directed by Tasaka Tomotaka. Although Iwata had originally hoped to tell the story of the entire squad, he soon realized that such an undertaking was beyond him, and he opted instead to create a fictional composite character based largely on First Lieutenant Yokoyama Masaji. Because he was participating in a "communally owned" discourse, Iwata was cautious and waited nervously for over a month before his preliminary five-page treatment was cleared by Navy officials. This is not to say that he wrote as a spokesperson for the Imperial Navy. Quite the contrary: no naval official was enthusiastically behind the project, and it was only with serious reservations that Tomonaga Kengo, one of Hiraide's colleagues, agreed to help Iwata with the portrait of the Naval Academy at Etajima and the basic facts of a life in the Navy.[22]

Iwata began serializing the novel in the *Asahi Shimbun* on July 1, 1942, with the final installment published there on December 23 of the same year. After garnering the Asahi Bunkashō (Asahi Cultural Prize) for 1942, it was released as a single volume in 1943. The initial run of fifty thousand copies soon sold out. An edition published in December 1943, its cover decorated with a bluish demon (*oni*) straddling a torpedo coursing through the sea, indicates that the novel had already gone through six printings.[23]

Hoping to capitalize on the novel's success, the once wary Naval Propaganda Division of Imperial Headquarters performed an about-face and promptly commissioned a film treatment from the Shōchiku studios. Directed by Tasaka Tomotaka and starring Yamauchi Akira, the film was completed in December 1943. The film deviates only slightly from the novel; both incorporate at their cores the same anecdotes and suggestions introduced in Captain Hiraide's original statement. In both the novel and the film, the mother figure functions as an imperturbable touchstone through the vicissitudes of the historical moment, and the daring submarine attack on Pearl Harbor is executed by a pure, artless hero whose engagement with a concrete task is so single-minded that the process leading to his death is more a narrative of ego-effacing spiritual transcendence than an act of violent warfare. Contributing to this image of the hero is the depiction of his roots in a distinct rural locale (*furusato*) that serves as a synecdoche for the nation as a whole.

The Navy (novel and film) follows the life of Tani Masato through his birth and childhood years in Kagoshima, his studies at the Naval Academy at Etajima, and the early years of his career as a naval officer and submarine pilot. Like his model Yokoyama Masaji, protagonist Masato is born to a large Kagoshima family managed by a strict, hardworking mother. As is the custom for such families, she does not coddle her children, especially her sons — she refrained from accompanying Masato even to his first day of school. Her importance to the family's well-being and the production of the future war god is further emphasized by the complete absence of a father figure. As the novel and film open, Masato's father has already died from a sudden illness. We learn that Masato's mother has mourned for a week, then returned to work in the family rice shop, where she refuses the help of her sons who have started other careers. So hardworking is this mother that the family not only survives but flourishes: "in time the children forgot that empty feeling of being without a father. This was possible because at some point a new pillar had been erected. Waka [Masato's mother] was that pillar. She was not one of those women with a chip on her shoulder when it came to men, neither was she particularly adept. But her children grew to trust her and rely on her, and the world around her did the same."[24] Masato's mother is the ideal mother for wartime Japan. She is so industrious that she can replace the father, and yet her rise to the position of "pillar" of the family does not pose a threat to the males increasingly absent (due to death or military service) from the domestic landscape. She is the glue that holds not only the family but all of society together. As she appears in the film version, Waka is largely silent, offering little more than poignant facial expressions and quiet support of her son as he sets out on this dangerous career. She is the simple, salt-of-the-earth figure of Hiraide's statement;

she inculcates through example the simple sincerity and selflessness that eventually lead Masato to heroism.

Working in parallel with the mother figure is the trope of the *furusato*, the rural hometown. Masato is a native of Satsuma (Kagoshima), and in his youth he is painted as very much a part of the distinctive landscape of that locale. The movie, in fact, opens with a shot of Sakurajima, the off-shore volcano that spews an endless pillar of ash high into the air, and revisits this symbol of Masato's hometown repeatedly throughout the film. Iwata's novel, too, provides great detail on the landscape within which this hero was raised: "the sandy shores stretched out forever, and the children could roll about on them endlessly, without ever reaching their end. The flowers crinum and moonflower blossomed on the sands and there was nobody to object to the children skipping stones and snapping branches off the pines. The children were kept company by nothing but this exceedingly beautiful nature—the most beautiful scenery in the realm, the natural vistas of the Satsuma shores."[25] This rural locale allows Masato to grow up "naturally," free from the distractions and temptations of a Westernized urban setting.

The concrete rendering of this sylvan origin is necessary for a convincing depiction of a pure and wholesome childhood. In its specificity, however, it risks detracting from the appeal of Masato as a *national* hero. Both the novel and its film treatment engage this problem, and both are careful to craft a "dual citizenship" for this local boy–cum–national hero. While Masato comes of age in a distinctive rural locale, he is also painted into the landscape of the nation. When his naval training cruise takes him into the port at Yokosuka, Masato hurries into Tokyo proper to see the sites. The imperial palace sends shivers down his spine, and he visits the Meiji Shrine (*Meiji jingū*) and Yasukuni Shrine.[26] Most striking, however, is the site spied from the deck of his ship as it approaches the capital city:

> It was while they were gliding through the seas off the coast of Shimizu. After dinner Masato had made his way to the stern of the ship. It was already that time when the white, green, and purple running lights of the ship began to glow. Turning his eyes briefly towards the darkening shore, he discovered a most startling sight. "My God, it's Mount Fuji," he thought. It had been an overcast day, but fortunately the mountain alone had burst through the cloud cover. He had not seen the mountain except in photographs and paintings, and yet all the same it was a mountain landscape that he had known intimately since long ago. It was

a silhouette, and he could not determine whether or not it was covered in snow. Still, the mountain had a majesty that inspired in Masato a reverence. Seeing Mount Fuji, Masato felt that he had indeed arrived at the heart of Japan.[27]

The image of Mount Fuji, symbol par excellence of the nation, overlaps with that of Sakurajima, the mountain that marks Masato as a product of a particular rural locale. This same "dual citizenship" is forged in the realm of language as Masato learns to speak standard Japanese in addition to the dialect of Kagoshima. The construction of a "dual citizenship" for Masato through the layering of a national language (hyōjungo) and a Japanese landscape on top of his guileless dialect and pristine hometown inculcates the same emotional, nostalgic bond for the nation that has been established for the hometown.

Just as had been the case in Hiraide's naval press release, both Iwata's *The Navy* and its film treatment avail themselves of the emotional charge that had been infused by literary texts into the images of mothers and rural hometowns.[28] From these sources emerges the artless subjectivity that distinguishes the hero of the Asia-Pacific War. This subjectivity is, of course, embodied in the hero Masato, whose very name reflects his nature: the character *shin* (or, alternatively, *makoto*), meaning "true" or "honest," followed by the character read *hito*, meaning "person," mark Masato as the truly "genuine man." True to his name, he is always frank, honest, and true. The evolution of Masato toward this spiritually transcendent state is such a pronounced element of the film treatment that Peter B. High categorizes it as one of the wartime "spiritist (seishinshugi) films," works that "stake out for themselves a special psychological terrain, sealed away from modern rationality."[29]

Masato's guileless nature is attested to throughout the novel, and the signs of this innocence and spiritual purity actually increase as Masato becomes more deeply enmeshed in the military and the war. For example, as Masato and the new recruits in the Etajima Naval Academy are led off to the communal bath for the first time, an upperclassman tells them, "Be sure to wash off the dirt of the secular world (shaba)!"[30] Indeed, particularly in the film treatment of the novel, the Naval Academy at Etajima strikes one as more a temple for ascetic training than an institute promoting the mastery of higher learning or military strategies. Masato's visits to the academy's museum feature shots of him dwarfed by monumental, cathedral-like architecture, and he bows deeply before the icons of naval history on display there. In addition to the photos of heroes such as Tōgō Heihachirō, the museum is filled with samples of calligraphy, the jet-black ink on snowy white presented more as religious iconography or fetish than language producing meaning in the conventional sense. The spiritual training of the academy is rounded out by ascetic practices, the film including a detailed treatment of the annual boat race. The scene features young, beautiful male bodies covered in sweat as they move in unison and an endless line of countless bodies standing along the course as they scream encouragement to the rowers—all staples of fascist imagery.[31]

Masato's purity continues to grow even after graduation from the academy. Not only does his tendency to blush remain with him throughout his short life; he actually takes on more and more of the luster of youth as his fatal mission approaches.[32] In his press statement, Hiraide had emphasized the childlike innocence of the men by relating the anecdote of the crew member who compared the suicide mission to a "hike," and this episode is reproduced in both Iwata's novel and Tasaka's film. The original press release's muting of a military identity is here, too: Masato has a tendency to shed his naval uniform in favor of "civvies."[33] Finally, as this return to a childlike innocence precludes any sustained concern for the historico-political dimensions of the upcoming mission, such references are kept to a minimum. The film version only hints at the international situation by flashing newspaper headlines across the screen to mark the march toward Pearl Harbor. The only other references to Japan's increasingly problematic position in the world community come in the form of lectures delivered to Masato and his comrades by teachers, advisers, and military officers. As in Hiraide's original announcement, these diatribes against Western imperialism provide the viewer/reader with a context for the actions of the heroes while simultaneously divorcing the heroes themselves from such explicitly nationalistic stances and, more important, from that analytical mode of being. Peter High points out how this delicate balance is presented visually in Tasaka's film version. While a teacher lectures Masato and his classmates about Japan's predicament, "the camera views the scene from different places in the room, as if overcome by impatience. This is followed by an abrupt cut to a parade ground where thousands of white-clad cadets are singing and marching in a series of vast concentric circles. The whole sequence is a subtle subversion of the assertion that the war can (or should) be placed in a rational historical context. Although the boys listen and respond respectfully, they have already given themselves to the cause and feel no particular compulsion to reason out the 'why' of the matter."[34]

Everywhere the larger context is erased, and in its place the submariners' mission is portrayed as the pinnacle of a quest for spiritual purity. This lack of context is reflected, too, in Masato's personal motto: "where one treads with true conviction, both gods and demons withdraw (*danjite okonaeba kishin mo kore o saku*)."[35] The nature of the conviction is irrelevant.

So powerful is Masato's purity that under its influence the world around him is reborn. His childhood friend Takao, who had thrown himself into a life of debauchery as an artist, mends his decadent ways as he becomes re-acquainted with Masato the naval officer. In one of the many melodramatic turns of the novel, the reborn Takao ends up as the Navy's official painter and is required to paint scenes from the Pearl Harbor attack in which his friend perished. Takao's high-spirited sister Eda is also reborn. Once filled with dreams of a career or college education in Tokyo, her contact with Masato reforms her. At one point Takao notices the change: "she had never treated men with the respect that they deserve, so the only thing that could possibly have elicited such a violent change in her is love. Takao realized that Masato, without even knowing it, had transformed Eda into a traditional woman of Satsuma. Takao was also fully aware how these women of Satsuma could have their hearts wildly aflame with passion while all the while refraining from any self-assertion and continuing to be fully obedient."[36] Masato's purity permeates the world around him, turning that world and its inhabitants away from the decadent trends of urban, Westernized lifestyles and back toward the simple values of the *furusato*, the rural towns and villages untouched by the complexities of modernity.[37] The myth of the Nine Gods of War promised to do much the same: provide the nation with an alternative to the anxiety-ridden present in the form of a return to an authentic subjectivity lying dormant beneath their intellectualizing modern selves.

The Ties That Bind

The co-opting of the charged images outlined here (the pure hero, his roots in an idyllic, unchanging natural landscape, the support of a selfless mother) was one reason the discourse on submariners reached mythic proportions. The audience had been primed to respond by the development of those images through many literary texts produced over many years. The second distinguishing characteristic of this myth was its repetition of a looping rhetorical trope that bound the populace to a timeless national essence through the communal act of mythmaking. The looping, or spiraling, motion operated at many levels. It is evident in the manner in which these images were generated by literary texts, only to be appropriated by the Imperial Navy for clearly ideological purposes before being embraced once again by literary figures. Iwata's *The Navy* is but one example; even novelists as different as Yokomitsu Riichi and Sakaguchi Ango felt compelled to address the topic of the submariners in their writing.[38] This popular response then prompted the Navy to commission the film *The Navy* as the task of mythmaking looped back around to its origin. The state and the civilian population were thereby bound together in the production of the myth.

The looping motion whereby the civilian population is merged with the agents of the state is echoed within the tales of the Nine Gods of War. Just as each specific articulation of the story contributes to the entirety of the universally shared myth, so, too, does each representation of a unique individual or specific location contribute to the construction of archetypal heroes and the abstract concept that is the nation. In Iwata's novel and Tasaka's film, this process is evident in protagonist Tani Masato's "dual citizenship," his identity as both a native of Satsuma and a citizen of Japan. Sakurajima, the landscape feature that defines his roots in Kagoshima, is associated with Mount Fuji, that symbol of the nation, and Masato's local dialect is first traded for the standard Japanese he uses in the Naval Academy before later serving as an alternative language strategically employed in his ongoing negotiation of his identity as a native both of Kagoshima/Satsuma and of Japan. This looping action ties the particular with the universal, the local with the national, the individual with the state.

The rhetorical looping also works diachronically, fusing the singular act of the Nine Gods of War to heroes of earlier days. This looping is worked through the press release's invocation of the genre known as the *bidan* (beautiful tales of exemplary behavior) and, more specifically, the *gunkoku bidan* (beautiful tales of the militarized state). While the latter surely have roots dating back to the touching tales of warriors depicted in the thirteenth-century epic *The Tales of the Heike*, their modern lineage can be traced back to the Meiji state's strategic deployment of what Naoko Shimazu calls "the myth of the patriotic soldier." Novels such as Sakurai Tadayoshi's *Human Bullets: A Soldier's Story of Port Arthur* (Nikudan, 1906), Shimazu argues, were produced and disseminated for the purpose of instilling patriotism in rural populations not yet fully incorporated into the ideology of the nation-state.[39] At some level, the Navy's press release most certainly had similar intentions, and it employed similar means.

However, while the example from early in Japan's modern period suggests a unidirectional, top-down attempt at ideological indoctrination, subsequent "beautiful tales of the militarized state" demonstrate an increasing degree of communal interest, participation, and consumption. One such bidan was that told of the Russo-Japanese War hero Commander Hirose Takeo, who died at Port Arthur after searching valiantly for a missing crewman on his sinking ship. Hirose's tale was commemorated in poetry and song; it was later included in school textbooks and even memorialized in the construction of a bronze statue in Kanda, Tokyo.[40] An even greater popular response was elicited by the tale of the "Three Heroic Human Bombs (*Bakudan sanyūshi*)," the privates who, in 1932, died while detonating a crude explosive device deployed to open a hole in the enemy defenses for an attack. This bidan inspired not only songs, poetry, and schoolbook versions, but also a spate of representations in other media, including comics, puppet-theater productions, newspapers, radio, film, and even the Kabuki stage.[41]

Navy Captain Hiraide's press release concerning the submariners of Pearl Harbor is, in its portrait of the heroes, reminiscent of this genre. Curiously, in the next stage of the development of the myth, the tradition of bidan is explicitly incorporated into the works. In his novel, Iwata includes an extended, detailed rehearsal of naval submarine heroes, all of whom distinguished themselves by remaining diligently at their posts while waiting to drown as their damaged vessels fill with water.[42] In Tasaka's film version, the model for young Masato's budding bravery is the Russo-Japanese War hero Admiral Tōgō Heihachirō, himself a native of Masato's Satsuma and the subject of various heroic tales. Masato pays his respects at Tōgō's grave, studies for the Naval Academy's entrance exams beneath a portrait of the admiral, and bows reverently before that same portrait as it hangs on the walls of the academy's museum.[43] In this way, the bidan that is the tale of the submariners loops back to incorporate previous heroic tales, installing them as inspiration for new acts of selfless sacrifice. The layering effect renders the unique heroes and their singular event simultaneously a part of a timeless, cyclical tradition.

Evidence suggests that such "beautiful tales of the militarized state" did indeed inspire patriotism and self-sacrifice for the national cause. One of the submarine pilots who died at Pearl Harbor, twenty-four-year-old Furuno Shigemi, included in his final letter home an explicit comparison of himself to the Commander Hirose of bidan fame: "the crisis increasingly demands we face the autumn of our lives. . . . [What I am about to do represents] the height of glory. There is, of course, no hope that I will return alive. It is a task no less valiant than that undertaken by Commander Hirose; please treasure the memory of my act as something no less worthwhile than his."[44] Similarly, the twenty-two-year-old submariner Hiroo Akira, in the document he left behind, wrote that the mission they were setting out to accomplish was "like the suicide missions (shinjū) of Commander Hirose's blockade squad and the three heroic human bombs. Of course, the issue of life and death is something we do not consider."[45] Furthermore, just as their embodiment of the recurrent myth was inspired by those that came before, so, too, did the tale of the Nine Gods of War shape the subjectivity of those who were to follow: the journalist Ushijima Hidehiko, author of numerous works on the Nine Gods of War, recalls how, as a fifth-grader in 1945, he had been inspired by the story of Tani Masato and was deter-mined to follow in his footsteps.[46] Linking heroes past with heroes present through the invocation of the bidan genre propels the looping action into the future, guaranteeing an unlimited source of individuals ready to sustain the communal myth.

The myth of the submariners at Pearl Harbor shows in its contents, its rhetoric, and its mode of circulation all the elements of a culture of fascism. It is composed of emotionally charged images (the guileless hero rooted in a concrete world; the self-sacrificing, salt-of-the earth mother; the idyllic, eternally unchanging rural hometown) produced in the attempt to ease the anxieties of the hyper-conscious, alienated modern individual living in a cold, industrialized world, and it depicts an act of spiritual transcendence through a merging of the self with the collectivity of the eternal nation. This fusion of the individual (the particular, the contemporary) to the state (the universal, the eternal) is then replicated in both the rhetoric and the pro-duction of the myth. The allusions, both implicit and explicit, to the corpus of "beautiful tales of the militarized state" fuse the nine submariners to the pantheon of bidan heroes, creating as well the illusion that the present is the eternal. The depiction of a hero whose unique roots make him, para-doxically, a national "everyman" similarly functions to render all elements of a diverse population integral elements of a single nation. Finally, the innumerable rearticulations of the submariners' tale, for all their varied in-flections and points of origin, ultimately reify an increasingly textured, all-encompassing myth constructed and sustained through the joint efforts of the state and its population. This "looping" of the tale through time, space, and multiple discursive zones generates a centripetal force that draws all toward the aestheticized act of apocalyptic self-destruction that centers the myth. As such, the myth of the Nine Gods of War represents a rehearsal for

427

that actual merging of the individual with the eternal nation: the "shattering of the ten million jewels (*ichioku gyokusai*)" in desperate, suicidal attacks launched against insurmountable odds. In this myth and its physical re-enactment, the fascist proclivities often identified in Japan's cultural discourse are made real.

Notes

1. For a lively if somewhat sensationalist account of the mission from the American perspective, see Burl Burlingame, *Advance Force Pearl Harbor* (Annapolis, Md.: Naval Institute Press, 2002). Details on the history and uses of these midget submarines is also available in Richard O'Neill, *Suicide Squads: Axis and Allied Special Weapons of World War II* (London: Salamander Books, 1981), 21–54, and Shigeru Fukudome, "Hawaii Operation," in *Air Raid Pearl Harbor:Recollections of a Day of Infamy*, ed. Paul Stillwell (Annapolis, Md.: Naval Institute Press, 1981), 57–73.

2. Ushijima, *Kyūgunshin wa katarazu: Shinjuwan tokkō no kyojitsu* (Tokyo: Kōjinsha NF Bunko, 1999), 26. The same basic qualifications are listed in Sakamaki Kazuo, "Tokushū senkōtei hasshin su" [The Special Submarine Sets Forth] in *Taiheiyō sensō kaisen*, vol. 4 of *Shōwa sensō bungaku zenshū* (Tokyo: Shōeisha, 1964), 46.

3. Various sources transliterate the names differently. I follow the *furigana* readings provided on the front page of the 7 March 1942 edition of the *Asahi shinbun* (Tokyo). Some sources may refer instead to Yokoyama *Masaharu*; see Donald M. Goldstein et. al., *The Way It Was: Pearl Harbor, The Original Photographs* (Dulles, Va: Potomac Books, 1995). Others mention not Ueda but rather *Kamita Sadamu*; see Ushijima, *Kyūgunshin*, 241.

4. This press release from Imperial Headquarters is reproduced in Ushijima, *Kyūgunshin wa katarazu*, 83–84.

5. Sakamaki, "Tokushū senkōtei hasshin su," 48. Sakamaki's statement to his commander would enter the myth of the submariners but, for reasons explained below, was never attributed to him. By saying simply "I will go" (*ikimasu*) in this context rather than "I'll be back" (*itte kimasu*), which was the standard parting phrase for men sent off on a mission, Sakamaki was acknowledging the fact that there was virtually no chance he would return alive.

6. Sakamaki's story is fascinating. The account above is based mostly on his 1964 essay "Tokushū senkōtei hasshin su." His other publications include: *Furyo seikatsu yonkanen no kaiko* [Reflections on Four Years as a Prisoner-of-War] (Tokyo: Tokyo kōdankai, 1947), *Horyo daiichigō* [Prisoner-of-War Number One] (Tokyo: Shinchōsha, 1949), and *I Attacked Pearl Harbor*, translated by Toru Matsumoto (New York: Associated Press, 1949). On Sakamaki's fate in the days immediately after his capture, see also Gordon William Prange, *December 7, 1941: The Day the Japanese Attacked Pearl Harbor* (New York: Wings Books, 1991). After the war Sakamaki had a very successful career with Toyota, the automobile manufacturer,

rising eventually to head of operations in Brazil. He died on November 29 1999, at eighty-one. On the reaction to the submarine squad in the United States., see Jackson, *On to Pearl Harbor—and Beyond* (Dixon, Calif.: Pacific Ship and Shore, 1982).

7. I base my discussion of Hiraide's statements on the transcript that appeared in the journal *Murasaki* in April 1942, which has in turn been reproduced as Hiraide Hideo, "Ōkimi no hotori ni shinamu: Ikun kagayaku tokubetsu kōgekitai" in *Nihon daizasshi: Shōwa senchū hen* (Tokyo: Ryōdō Shuppan, 1979), 138–44. I have compared this transcript to that one that appeared on the front page of the Tokyo *Asahi Shimbun*, March 7, 1942, and the two are virtually identical. The lines translated here appear in Hiraide, "Ōkimi no hotori ni shinamu," 143.

8. The designation "Nine Gods of War (*kyūgunshin*)" was widely used by the media in spite of the fact that the Navy had asked explicitly that the squad be referred to consistently as the "Special Attack Force" in order to avert confusion. The fact that the ten-man squad yielded only nine heroes suggests that the Imperial Navy was at least partially aware of the fate of Sakamaki Kazuo, the officer who would have been the tenth had he but perished in the attack.

9. Hiraide, "Ōkimi no hotori ni shinamu," 138.

10. Ibid., 140.

11. Ibid., 141. *Bushidō* refers to the "code of the samurai" established during the Tokugawa period (1600–1868).

12. Ibid., 142.

13. Ibid.

14. See Nishida, *Zen no kenkyū* (Tokyo: Iwanami Shoten, 1950), or the translation by Masao Abe and Christopher Ives, *An Inquiry into the Good* (New Haven: Yale University Press, 1990); Nishitani, "'Kindai no chōkoku' shiron," in Kawakami Tetsutarō, et.al., *Kindai no chōkoku*, ed. Takeuchi Yoshimi (Tokyo: Toyamabō, 1990), 18–37; Hayashi, "Tenkō ni tsuite" in *Shōwa hihyō taikei*, vol. 2 (Tokyo: Banchō Shobō, 1978), 239–61; Kobayashi, "Kokyō o ushinatta bungaku," in *Shintei Kobayashi Hideo Zenshū*, vol 3, (Tokyo: Shinchōsha, 1978), 29–37.

15. This type of spiritual purity was a mainstay of wartime propaganda in Japan, as John W. Dower so convincingly argues in *War Without Mercy: Race and Power in the Pacific War* (New York: Pantheon Books, 1986).

16. On ways in which women were incorporated into the war machine, see Fujii Tadatoshi, *Heitachi no sensō: tegami, nikki, taikenki o yomitoku* (Tokyo: Asahi shinbunsha, 2000), particularly 10–21; Fujii Tadatoshi, *Kokubō fujinkai: Hi no maru to kappōgi* (Tokyo: Iwanami shoten, 1985); Yoshimi Yoshiaki, *Kusa no ne no fashizumu: Nihon minshū no sensō taiken* (Tokyo: Tōkyō Daigaku Shuppankai, 1996), 83–85.

17. Hiraide, "Ōkimi no hotori ni shinamu," 143. Hiraide seems oblivious to the irony of his statement: these were mothers who would most certainly *not* live through their sons, all of whom had died in the waters of Pearl Harbor.

18. See Kawabata Yasunari, *Snow Country*, trans. Edward G. Seidensticker (New York: Knopf, 1956) and Kobayashi, "Kokyō o ushinatta bungaku," and also "Rekishi

to bungaku," in *Shintei Kobayashi Hideo zenshū*, vol 7. (Tokyo: Shinchōsha, 1978), 200–223.

19. Kaedei Kinnosuke, *Aa tokubetsu kōgekitai* (Tokyo: Kokumin Shimbunsha, 1942); Hata Kennosuke, *Gunshinden* (Tokyo: Chōbunkaku, 1942); Fukuyu Yutaka, *Tokubetsu kōgekitai: gunshin no omokage* (Tokyo: Kikō Seinensha, 1942); Tsuchiya Ken'ichi, *Umi no gunshin tokubetsu kōgekitai* (Tokyo: Shunyōdō Shoten, 1942); Yamamoto Hatsutarō, *Aa gunshin kyūhashira* (Tokyo: Nihon Kōen Kyōkai, 1942); Yomiuri Shimbun Shuppanbu, ed., *Shinjuwan senkō: OO taii ki* (Tokyo: Yomiuri shinbunsha, 1943); Asahi shinbunsha, ed., *Tokubetsu kōgekitai kyūgunshin seiden* (Tokyo: Asahi Shinbun Tokyo honsha, 1942); Yoshio Natsuko, *Gunshin no haha* (Tokyo: Misaki Shobō, 1942); Seikanji Ken, *Gunshin o unda haha* (Tokyo: Kyōa Nihonsha, 1943).
20. One such poem is Fukuda Masao's "Shinjuwan no gunshin kyuchū: kaigun tokubetsu kōgekitai o utau [The Nine War Gods of Pearl Harbor: An Ode to the Navy Special Attack Force]," 1942. A partial translation of this poem is available in Steve Rabson, *Righteous Cause or Tragic Folly: Changing Views of War in Modern Japanese Poetry* (Ann Arbor: Center for Japanese Studies, University of Michigan, 1998), 186–87.
21. Quoted in Ushijima, *Kyūgunshin wa katarazu*, 208.
22. See ibid., 94.
23. The novel was perceived as such a Navy public-relations coup that the Army commissioned a novel of its own the following year: Hino Ashihei's *Rikugun* [The Army] (Tokyo: Asahi Shimbunsha, 1945). A film version, directed by Kinoshita Keisuke, was released in 1944.
24. Iwata, *Kaigun* (Tokyo: Hara Shobō, 1967), 19.
25. Ibid., 12.
26. Ibid., 177.
27. Ibid., 174.
28. The rural hometown (*furusato*) serves as a metaphor for unselfconscious, "natural" modes of existence and apprehension in a wide range of writers, including the aforementioned Kawabata Yasunari (*Snow Country*) and Kobayashi Hideo ("Kokyō o ushinatta bungaku").
29. High, The Imperial Screen, 388.
30. Iwata, *Kaigun*, 99. Referring to the civilian world as "shaba" was common among military men.
31. On fascist imagery in film, see Susan Sontag, "Fascinating Fascism," in *Under the Sign of Saturn* (New York: Farrar, Straus, Giroux, 1980), 73–105.
32. Iwata, *Kaigun*, 280.
33. Ibid., 131, 256. In the film treatment, Masato wears a suit on his final visit home, eliciting a puzzled remark from his sister.
34. High, *The Imperial Screen: Japanese Film Culture in the Fifteen Years' War, 1931–1945* (Madison: University of Wisconsin Press, 2003), 388–89.
35. Iwata, *Kaigun*, 347, but see also 38, 85. The motto is also featured prominently in the film version.

36. Ibid., 326.

37. Roger Griffin argues convincingly for the centrality of the myth of "purifying, cathartic national rebirth (palingenesis)" in all fascist movements; see Roger Griffin, *The Nature of Fascism* (London: Pinter, 1991), xi.

38. See Yokomitsu Riichi, "Gunjin no fu," originally published in *Bungei* (April 1942) and Sakaguchi Ango, "Shinju," originally published in *Bungei* (June 1942).

39. Naoko Shimazu, "The Myth of the 'Patriotic Soldier,'" *War and Society* 19, no. 2 (October 2001), 69–89, esp. 70. Shimazu writes that the Meiji government also intended these stories to instill a belief in Japanese exceptionalism among a Western audience, and notes how this novel by Sakurai, once a student of the novelist Natsume Sōseki and later head of the Army's propaganda division, was published in English translation by Houghton Mifflin in 1906. Shimazu does not explicitly link this "myth of the patriotic soldier" to the genre of *gunkoku bidan*.

40. On the statue and Yosano Tekkan's poem "Aa, Commander Hirose," see Rabson, *Righteous Cause or Tragic Folly*, 69–71; the military song, produced by the Ministry of Education, is "Hirose Chūsa"; on the inclusion of the tale in textbooks, see Nakauchi, *Gunkoku bidan to kyōkasho* (Tokyo: Iwanami shoten, 1988), 100–105. For an analysis of *bidan* produced following the Manchurian Incident of 1931, including a comparison of them with earlier tales such as Hirose's, see Louise Young, *Japan's Total Empire: Manchukuo and the Culture of Wartime Imperialism* (Berkeley: University of California Press, 1999), 90–114.

41. On this tale, see High, *The Imperial Screen*, 35–39; Emiko Ohnuki-Tierney, *Kamikaze, Cherry Blossoms, and Nationalisms: The Militarization of Aesthetics in Japanese History* (Chicago: University of Chicago Press, 2002), 113–14. Rabson includes a translation of the *gunka* (war song) detailing the men; see Rabson, *Righteous Cause or Tragic Folly*, 73–74.

42. Iwata, *Kaigun*, 288–302.

43. Cf. High, *The Imperial Screen*, 410.

44. Quoted in Ushijima, *Kyūgunshin wa katarazu*, 43.

45. Quoted in ibid., 46.

46. Ushijima, *Shinjuwan*, 17.

PART V

CONCLUDING ESSAY

ALEJANDRO YARZA

The Spanish Perspective:
Romancero Marroquí and the Francoist
Kitsch Politics of Time

■ In "Narrating the Nation-ality of a Cinema: The Case of Japanese Prewar Film" in this volume, Aaron Gerow argues that any fascistic
element to Japanese cinema "lies less in the vision of the nation represented
or the cinematic aesthetic itself than in the process involved in creating a
national cinema." For Gerow, Japanese national cinema was always subject
to hybridity and contamination; it is precisely this hybrid, contaminated
state of Japanese cinema that paradoxically constitutes for him the condition of possibility for a fascist Japanese cinema. As he writes, "The fascist ideal of a pure, controlled cinema was based on its own impossibility."
Therefore, fascism in wartime Japanese cinema, he concludes, is rather a
process than a state.

Michael Baskett's exploration of intra-Axis cooperation on film legislation also reveals similar cracks and fissures in what to the eyes of the
Western allies was supposedly a unified fascist aesthetic. Baskett's analysis of Arnold Fanck's *The New Earth*—a German–Japanese co-production
about the Japanese colonization of Manchuria—for example, shows how
the intra-Axis collaboration "did not lead to the successful creation of a collective 'fascist' identity." Although the colonial film genre created a strong

link among Axis film cultures for the Japanese film critic Iwasaki Akira, Baskett writes, *The New Earth* ultimately failed with Japanese audiences precisely "because of the impossibility of Germans' understanding the Japanese experience of modernity."

I would argue, however, that this failed attempt to create a state-sponsored totalizing "fascist" cinema aesthetics in Japan, a successful intra-Axis co-production policy, did not amount to an ultimate failure of the various fascist states to achieve a high degree of ideological hegemony. In fact, as Lutz Koepnick has observed regarding the Nazi case, the German state attempted to impose ideological hegemony on its citizenry using a variety of cultural channels; thus implying a higher degree of laissez-faire governance than is normally assumed.[1] This indicates that the cultural policies of the various national fascisms, as well as their attempts to reach out to one another, were weighed down by inner contradictions and substantial cultural differences right from the start. The Axis nations never formed the homogeneous political and cultural front that, as Baskett observes, Allied propagandists made them out to be. As he writes, "Unlike the enduring images of an Axis united in power and purpose churned out by wartime Allied propagandists, Imperial Japan, Nazi Germany, and fascist Italy were not all cut from the same political or cultural cloth; nor did any single entity ever truly dominate over another."

Focusing on Japanese cinema, Baskett naturally leaves Francoist Spain out of the collaborative and legislative intra-Axis film agenda. Although Franco's Spain did not have any official ties with wartime Japan's film industry, as early as 1938 it did collaborate in a variety of film projects with German and Italian production companies, resulting in five feature films made in less than two years through the Spanish–German joint venture Hispano-Film-Produktion, and in the shooting in 1940 of *Assedio dell'Alcazar*, a film by the renowned Italian fascist director Augusto Genina about the siege of the Alcázar of Toledo by Republican forces during the Spanish Civil War.[2]

Despite several grandiose but short-lived attempts to create a Francoist national cinema, Francoist film policy was even more relaxed than that of its German, Italian, or Japanese counterparts. The case of Francoist film politics helps illuminate the hybrid and apparently contradictory ways in which fascist regimes attempted to secure ideological hegemony. Much like the Imperial Japan described by Gerow and Baskett, Franco's Spain lacked a cohesive film aesthetic, produced early film legislation plagued by apparent contradictions, and attempted to stimulate the production of a line of colonial films that ultimately failed to fully address their intended audiences.

As we shall see in the following analysis of *Romancero marroquí* (dir. Carlos Velo and Enrique Dominguez Rodiño, 1939),[3] a documentary about Spanish Morocco, Francoism attempted to achieve ideological hegemony in post–Civil War Spain by means of what could be characterized as a totalitarian kitsch aesthetic, a kitsch aesthetic functioning in much of the cultural work done in Japan in the same years, as described in this volume. This kitsch aesthetic is best exemplified by a series of texts (a film script, a war memoir, a political treatise) written by Franco himself, as well as by a series of films, memoirs, and novels produced by several prominent Spanish fascist artists. By a totalitarian kitsch aesthetic, I simply mean an aesthetic that resorts to artistic cliché and erases, in Milan Kundera's words, "every display of individualism . . . ; every doubt . . . ; all irony."[4]

However, as we will see in the example of *Romancero marroquí*, the state-planned attempt to secure consent from the Spanish citizenry ultimately failed—as Gerow suggests it did in the Japanese case—as the ideological suturing that these Francoist kitsch fascist texts were supposed to attain ultimately unraveled. Through this failure, the inner contradictions—but, paradoxically, also the strength—of Francoism were made patently clear.

Romancero marroquí, a film with a clear political intent, was officially sponsored by Franco's provisional government.[5] In *Romancero*, religious iconography helped create a mythical representation of Morocco. By offering Moroccans a highly favorable portrait of themselves, the High Spanish Commission in Morocco aimed to pay homage to the Moroccans who had already enlisted in Franco's colonial army, but, more important, they also hoped to procure a constant flow of new recruits. By doing so, however, *Romancero* wrongly presupposed a Moroccan audience that would respond obediently to its kitschy message.

The kitschy mythical place the film evoked was precisely the Spanish Morocco where Francoism—that eclectic kitsch fascist ideology that established itself in Spain by means of a military uprising that began in Morocco and was waged against Republican legality—was born. For Francoism, Spanish Morocco was not a geographical reality but a mental space, an ideological fantasy—"the immortal cradle of the [Francoist] movement," as it was sometimes called. This was the ideological fantasy *Romancero* meant to signify and that was at the core of the Francoist kitsch politics of time and space.

As it turned out, *Romancero* was rejected by high Moroccan officials and was never dubbed into Arabic for its intended target audience. It is my contention, however, that its mythical representation served the Francoist goal of persuading conservative Spaniards of the legitimacy of deploying forty thousand Muslim "Moors" on Spanish soil during Franco's "crusade" against the Republicans.

Romancero's failure to connect with its intended audience—and its double-edged identificatory agenda—provides valuable insights into the question of how the state-planned attempts to secure consent from the Spanish citizenry seem ultimately to have failed. Through this "failure," the inner contradictions of Francoism were made clear: its lack of a unified social, political, and cultural agenda due to the vastly different political, economic, and ideological interests it tried to accommodate. In the cultural sphere, these contradictions were expressed most clearly in film legislation passed in 1941—such as compulsory dubbing—which almost single-handedly destroyed the Spanish film industry, seemingly undermining Franco's official cultural and political attempt to create a submissive Francoist subject. I would suggest here that the lack of a "unified" agenda behind Japanese fascism did not preclude it from similarly gaining forms of consent.

Francoism took the political potential of cinema seriously. As early as 1938, still in the midst of the Spanish Civil War, the Departamento Nacional de Cinematografía was created both to supervise "nationalist" cinema and to control the state's visual propaganda.[6] Important fascist leaders such as Ernesto Giménez Caballero, Franco's first press secretary, theorized about the role cinema should play in the construction of the new Spanish state. For Giménez Caballero, the goal of this new cinema would be to achieve a mystical synthesis between self and society to supersede both the disappearance of the self as it appeared in Russian film and the self's overwhelming predominance as it appeared in American film. These two powerful "empires," Giménez Caballero warned, were advancing over Europe "to the drumbeat of their camera shutters more than with cannons and armies."[7] The creation of such European, universal, and Catholic cinema, Giménez Caballero mused, could very well be the spiritual mission of Spanish cinema.[8]

I should point out that the idea of using film politically to advance the interests of the Spanish state, although fervently renewed by Francoist ideologues at the beginning of the Spanish Civil War in 1936, had begun as early as 1909 at the onset of the military conflict in Spanish Morocco. The Ministry of War enlisted cinema as part of its military effort against the "hostile Moroccan tribes" attacking Spanish positions in the city of Melilla. In requesting cinema's aid in this effort, the Ministry of War had a double objective in mind: to help create a patriotic mood in Spain "against the waves of protest that the conflict produced in a wide sector of Spanish society" and to propagate Spain's "mission civilisatrice" in North Africa abroad.[9] Thus, from the beginning, as Martin Corrales has suggested, "the movie camera aimed in the same direction as the Spanish rifles."[10]

As part of its recruitment effort, the Spanish Ministry of War supported and encouraged Spanish filmmakers to produce documentaries about the Spanish colonial army's fight against Moroccan tribes hostile to Spanish interests in Morocco. Even General Millán Astray, one of the most renowned Spanish generals of the time, used cinema as a medium to glamorize the Spanish Foreign Legion, the new military body he co-founded with General Franco in 1921.[11] Franco himself was enthralled by the seductive power of cinema. As a contemporary witness reported in 1924, he took the time amid enemy fire to personally film the withdrawal of Spanish troops from the Moroccan city of Xauen.[12]

Pre-Francoist films had depicted Morocco and the Moors through a typically self-righteous colonial lens. But the films of 1936 through 1942 could be characterized, oddly enough, as Domínguez Búrdalo has pointed out, as representing an attempt to replace old colonial clichés with a more nuanced and positive representation of Morocco and its inhabitants.[13] This was a radical move for Francoism, which had aligned itself ideologically with a Spanish ultra-Catholic and nationalist conservatism that had traditionally defined Spain's essence in radical opposition to the Muslim other, seeing it as a heretical foreign intruder.

It is in this historical context of the Francoist shift in the film representation of Morocco that I would situate *Romancero marroquí*. *Romancero* attempted to stage a mythical representation of northern Morocco to persuade Moroccans to enlist in Franco's army; this representation in turn helped convince conservative Spaniards of the moral soundness of enlisting "Muslims" in Franco's "Christian crusade."

According to the High Commissioner of the Spanish Protectorate in Morocco under whose auspices the movie was produced, and who was primarily responsible for its narrative concept, *Romancero* should capture in documentary format "all the natural and artistic beauties of the area," as well as its "regional traditions and costumes," while at the same time, "by means of its story line," pay homage to "the fervent participation of the Moroccan people in our glorious uprising."[14]

Because of this double objective, *Romancero* was a hybrid product. In its visual idealization of the Moroccan lifestyle, it was influenced by Robert Flaherty's visually stunning documentaries—*Nanook of the North* (1922),

Moana (1927), and *Man of Aran* (1934). The film portrays an organic community blending harmoniously with its environment—the Moroccan inhabitants from the Yebala area of the Spanish Protectorate—supposedly a spiritually unified community un-fractured by the alienating forces of modernity.

With a painstaking eye for detail, *Romancero* tries to capture the "mythical" world of these Moroccan "natives" through a highly choreographed visual composition, beautiful cinematography, and an extensive cinematographic repertoire in which dissolves and close-ups clearly stand out. However, unlike Flaherty's documentaries, *Romancero* adds a voice-of-God-style commentary over the images of its Moroccan natives; it is the commentary's function to cue viewers into how to best interpret the images. Trying to eliminate any possible ambiguity generated by the silent images themselves, the voiceover transformed an otherwise beautifully crafted, albeit kitsch, film into a perfect example of totalitarian kitsch aesthetics, with its ability to restrict meaning and close down visual signification. The tension generated by the friction between the visual images and the verbal commentary is paradoxically exemplified by exclusive visual means in the first shot of the film (see figure 1).

The opening still shot of the film joins the traditional Islamic decorative style in the background with "the yoke and the arrows," the Phalange's own visual icon, thus establishing a visual parallel between the Islamic tradition and the Francoist ideological cause. Following this initial shot, a written text also informs us that *Romancero* was made "thinking of Franco," and "with deep love and respect towards our Muslim brothers," to whom, in fact, it wants to pay homage "for their virtues" and their "generous loyalty." The text describes the Moroccan people, as well as the film's hero, not as barbaric tribesmen or as the heretic infidels of past traditional depictions, but as "noble and simple, brave and pure." Finally, it also reminds us that, like the protagonist, they took part in "our Crusade" voluntarily, guided by ancestral forces. The text ends with a poetic wish: "let the blood ties that unite our two 'peoples' flourish in a luminous future for both."

And yet, despite *Romancero*'s stated goal of paying homage to Moroccans helping in Franco's cause, its main goal was in fact to convince conservative Spaniards of the moral righteousness behind the decision to enlist Muslims—Spain's traditional enemies—in their "Christian" crusade against Republicans on Spanish soil. (*Romancero* did open in every major provincial town in Franco's Spain.)[15] It had to persuade conservative Spaniards that, unlike the old one, this new crusade was not launched to extermi-

1. Still from *Romancero marroquí* (dir. Carlos Velo, 1939).

nate "pious" Muslims brothers but to eliminate Spanish Republicans now labeled traitors to the fatherland and unworthy of the term *Spaniard*.[16]

Given its hidden propagandistic and ideological agenda, it is no surprise that *Romancero* did not really attempt to seriously explore the cultural and ethnographic differences of Moroccans living under Spanish rule. On the contrary, and without ever abandoning the use of ethnographic cliché, it set out to reveal the deep similarities between Christian and Muslim "believers." Thus, in *Romancero*'s representation, northern Moroccans resemble much more the biblical images of Semitic tribesmen in white flowing robes tending to their flocks, plowing their land, or playing their musical instruments — images that filled the standard Spanish Catholic catechisms of the time — than they do the more realistic images that would correspond to the starker reality of a hungry and disease-ridden Spanish Moroccan Protectorate in 1938 (see figure 2). For Francoism, Spanish Morocco was thus a kitschy mythical place, like the Japanese countryside that Nina Cornyetz describes in this volume. It was not a geographical reality but a mental space, an ideological fantasy that was at the core of the Francoist kitsch politics of time.

One of the defining traits of early Francoism was this politics of time. Specifically, *Romancero* is structured around a notion of messianic time,

2. Still from *Romancero marroquí* (dir. Carlos Velo, 1939).

characterized by what Benedict Anderson, following Walter Benjamin, called "prefiguring and fulfillment."[17] The film is subdivided into four main segments: the first one revolves around Aalami's family life in his native village around sowing time; the second focuses on Aalami's travels around Morocco in search for work; the third follows him to Spain, where he fights in Franco's colonial army; and the fourth depicts Aalami's return home from Spain in time for the harvest. Each segment prefigures and fulfills the preceding one. Aalami first feels compelled to leave his village after receiving an ancestral call while he is plowing his land, visually represented by the close-up of an ox's head underlined by a few musical chords on the soundtrack reminiscent of the music played at bullfights, which here is meant to underline the ancestral call Aalami receives back from Spain, his supposedly former fatherland.

He travels on foot around Morocco in search of work. The narrator's ethnographic excuse for photographing white mosques and villages, colorful markets and ritual weddings is nothing but a disguised pilgrimage toward his embrace of Franco's higher cause. After a brief encounter with a Francoist messenger riding a white horse—an obvious reference to Santiago "Matamoros" (Saint James of Compostela), patron saint of Spain and the mythical Moor slayer of the Spanish Reconquest—he finally stops his wandering at the recruitment office to join Franco's army; put simply, this has been a pilgrimage in search of a destiny that has already been determined for him. His fighting in Spain—where he receives three wounds—fulfills this predetermined "destiny." Finally, his return home in time for the harvest not only brings the narrative to a close but also implies that even nature itself rewards his courage for fighting for the right cause with a bountiful crop.

Romancero's narrative thus "moves" cyclically, revolving around agricultural events inextricably tied to the religious, the political, and the transcendental. Time is contained within an organic community of believers and never spills out into the empty, homogenous time of history, the linear historical time of the modern nation.

This circular, a-historical, Francoist temporality around which *Romancero*'s narrative is built is what Mark Neocleous sees at the heart of fascism, which can also be said to characterize all forms of kitsch.[18] At the heart of the power of fascist kitsch is its hallucinatory power, "its compulsion to escape from abstract sameness," to use Adorno's phrase, from the empty homogeneous time of modernity.[19] Kitsch, like Francoism (and like Japanese cultural fascism), promised a refuge against the passing of time, against the decay of the aura that Benjamin saw at the center of modernity. This fear of change and, ultimately, of the inevitability of death implied by the modern teleological conception of history accounts for the emergence of political kitsch as refuge, a "home"—as the Spanish avant-garde writer Gómez de la Serna calls it—looking into the past, not into the future.

Yet this notion of kitsch only goes so far in explaining the film's political aesthetic. To fully understand *Romancero*'s attempt to persuade Moroccans to join Franco's army, it is important to recall Saul Friedlander's crucial distinction between two different types of kitsch: "common kitsch," which "tends to universality," and "uplifting kitsch," which "is rooted, symbol-centered, and emotionally linked to the values of a specific group."[20] This uplifting kitsch, which exploits "obvious mythical patterns," has a clear mobilizing function: its emotionally coded and readily available message is presented aesthetically, not rationally, thus eliciting from its audience an automatic "unreflective emotional response," making that audience unaware of the ideology being imparted. It is the harnessing of the power of kitsch that, I suggest, Francoism shared with Japanese fascism.

Romancero's narrative, whose explicit goal was military mobilization, to make Francoist soldiers out of starving Moroccan peasants by promising them the "best roses watered with the generous blood of our people united in one ideal" is carefully constructed around this notion of uplifting kitsch; appealing to Moroccan "tribal" emotion in order to mobilize. *Romancero* attempts to link the pristine natural landscape of the Moroccan Rif to the traditional values of its inhabitants. It prepackages its own political message as a closed ideological system, which, to be made more effective, it renders aesthetically, producing that "confusion of the ethical with the aesthetic category" that for Hermann Broch is the essence of kitsch.[21]

The first section of the film introduces us to the harsh natural environment of Spanish Morocco and directly into the land of the mythical patterns of uplifting kitsch. The various shots of giant cacti and the mosque's white tower with the muezzin calling to prayer combine with shots of arid mountains and ocean waters through a chain of dissolves. These establishing shots visually conflate the natural and the spiritual in a series of "organically" linked shots—with hardly any visible cuts—rendered in that "curative imagery of unity" that for Kenneth Burke was so characteristic of fascism (see figure 3).[22] Immediately after these shots, the camera gives a long panoramic shot of Aalami's village, followed by a long panning take accenting the immaculate pure white dwelling against whose walls a few rural implements idly rest. The palm roof is metaphorically linked to the tree branches surrounding the small house, suggesting nature and civilization blending harmoniously (see figure 4). The camera comes finally to rest with a medium shot on two pairs of traditional Moroccan slippers in front of the house—metonymically indicating the people resting inside.

The next series of shots progressively introduces Aalami's family: a crying baby in the cradle; his oldest son, Ahmed, waking up and immediately transforming his blanket into a *chilaba* (robe), leaving the house moments later with his mother, Fatima; and finally, a shot of Aalami himself tightening his turban around his head. At this point, the voiceover, guiding the viewer on how to see the scene, makes its first utterance connecting the natural, the social, and the spiritual: "the Muezzin's voice, extending itself through mountains and valleys, the skies and the seas, has called to life. Morocco wakes up, the day has arrived, and the fields get flooded with light."

These first shots, then, visually follow the pattern set by films such as Karl Freund's *Berlin Symphony* or the opening of Dziga Vertov's *Man with a Movie Camera*. However, unlike those documentaries, whose opening shots emphasize new rhythms and patterns in celebration of modern technology and city life, in *Romancero* anything artificial that distracts from the organic

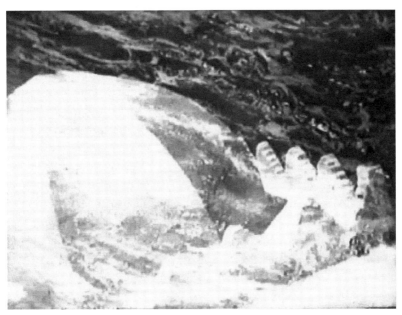

3–4. Stills from *Romancero marroquí* (dir. Carlos Velo, 1939).

flow of life has been removed from sight. The voiceover draws on an old narrative model, from the biblical Genesis, in an attempt to give the phrase "let there be light" a faithful visual representation. Therefore, from the very beginning *Romancero* frames an unfamiliar Moroccan reality for the Spanish audience within the parameters of an immediately familiar narrative structure—a structure that stands outside linear historical time. While in traditional colonial representations the colony becomes an alluring, albeit inferior, other to the colonizing metropolis in need of progress and civilization, paradoxically in *Romancero*'s representation, Spanish Moroccan society becomes a model to be imitated, a biblical kitsch paradise opposing—like Francoism itself—modern materialism and parliamentary democracy.

It is in this kitschy visual idealization of a premodern way of life that the Spanish Morocco depicted in *Romancero* becomes the ideal embodiment of the "scattered fragment" of the aura, to use Celeste Olalquiaga's term, that Franco hoped to restore and bring back to Spain by his new crusade of reconquest.[23]

In this kind of Francoist kitsch, the "empty space" opened up by the flattening out of a distinct geographical and cultural reality and its replacement by a historical cliché is metaphorically filled with moral and political content: with irrationality and blind faith, guilt, repentance, punishment, and the seemingly beautiful appearance of death. *Romancero* was, after all, a cry for war, an attempt to persuade young Moroccans to die for Franco's cause.

But as I already mentioned, *Romancero* failed to connect with its Moroccan target audience. Ironically, and much like the rejection of Fanck's *The New Earth* by Japanese critics because it failed to come to terms with Japan's modernity, high Moroccan officials ultimately rejected the film because it depicted northern Morocco as a poor, premodern, backward place.[24] *Romancero* had a very limited distribution within the Spanish protectorate; in fact, it was never released with its soundtrack dubbed into Arabic. It also had a very short run in Spain. *Romancero* was supposed to be the beginning of a soon to be abandoned new line of "Africanist cinema" that would help advance Spain's colonial expansion in Africa.

Romancero's difficulty in successfully addressing its intended audience, however, allows us a precious glimpse into the inner ideological contradictions that plagued Francoism right from the start—contradictions that are highly visible in the cultural and political arena in apparently self-defeating Francoist film legislation. In helping its own cause, Franco's regime could have created screen quotas or prohibited the import of foreign, ideologically suspect films. Instead, as early as 1941, and under the excuse of preserving Spain's imperial language from foreign contamination, it passed legislation enforcing compulsory dubbing and ruled that only producers of Spanish films could import foreign films. This legislation single-handedly struck a powerful blow to the Spanish film industry, from which it would never fully recover. As expected, Spanish audiences flocked to Hollywood films dubbed into Spanish and widely available in Spanish theaters.[25]

Such legislative measures undermined the efforts of the more genuine fascist elements within Franco's regime. As a result, their attempt to conduct a uniform process of ideological interpellation never really worked, though its effects were certainly not negligible. In this way, the Francoist case, riddled with internal contradictions and lacking a unified fascist cultural agenda, greatly resembled the Japanese case.

It has often been said that because Francoism (like Japanese fascism, as described by Alan Tansman in the introduction to this volume) was an "ersatz" form of fascism from the start formed by competing political interests, it might have outlasted other forms of fascism. Francoism was a perfect example of Ernesto Laclau's empty signifier, which can be filled with all kinds of contradictory content, and as such, it perfectly fit Ortega y Gassett's well-known definition: "fascism is A and B." In reality, Francoism, like Japanese fascism, was A, B, and C. Ultimately, Francoism, as seen in its film legislation, was an arrangement that suited all concerned: "the regime got its films, the producers massive profits and the public the Hollywood films they liked."[26] But perhaps in the end what the regime really needed was not its propaganda films, whose effect on audiences is at best dubious, but the Hollywood films Spanish audiences loved to watch. In the end, then, I would argue that Francoism, though lacking a systematic and cohesive cultural politics, was able to secure ideological consent less through centralized, grandiose projects such as *Raza*, a 1941 film based on Franco's script, and *Romancero* than through the popularity of American films and sentimental comedies. It might be argued that in this diffuse mode of securing consent, Francoist Spain shared much with Nazi Germany, fascist Italy, and Imperial Japan.

Francoism practiced above all a very successful politics of survival. It is not purely coincidental, after all, that while Mussolini was executed by Italian partisans and his body hung upside down in Loreto Square, and Hitler killed himself hidden in a lonely bunker, and Japan was transformed by its American conquerors into a democratic, neoliberal state, Franco died in bed at eighty-two, softly uttering the words, "How hard it is to die." He was buried with all the honors of a head of state.

Notes

1. See Lutz P. Koepnick, "Fascist Aesthetics Revisited," *Modernism/Modernity* 6, no. 1 (1999): 51–73.
2. The five films produced by Hispano-Film-Produktion were *El barbero de Sevilla* (dir. Benito Perojo, 1938); *Mariquilla Terremoto* (dir. Benito Perojo, 1938); *Suspiros de España* (dir. Benito Perojo, 1939); *Carmen la de Triana* (dir. Florián Rey, 1939); and *La canción de Aixa* (dir. Florián Rey, 1939).
3. I thank Javier Herrera of Filmoteca Nacional Española for his generosity in providing me with a copy of this film.
4. See Milan Kundera *The Unbearable Lightness of Being* (New York: HarperCollins, 1987), 252
5. See Alberto Elena, "Romancero marroquí, 1939," in *Antología crítica del cine español 1906–1995: Flor en la sombra*, ed. Julio Pérez Perucha (Madrid: Cátedra, 1997), 123.
6. See Ferrán Alberich, "Raza. Cine y propaganda en la inmediata posguerra," *Archivos de la Filmoteca* 27 (October 1997): 53
7. Ernesto Giménez Caballero, *El cine y la cultura humana. Conferencia pronunciada en la facultad de Filosofía y Letras de la ciudad universitaria de Madrid* (Bilbao: Ece, 1944), 32
8. Ibid., 33.
9. Eloy Martin Corrales, "El cine español y las guerras de Marruecos (1896–1994)," *Hispania* 55, no. 190 (1995): 708.
10. See ibid., 695. For an excellent overview of Spanish film production centered on Morocco, see José Domínguez Búrdalo, "El cine africanista español: 1925–1935 frente a 1938–1942. La racial singularidad de 'La canción de Aixa,'" *Revista Canadiense de Estudios Hispánicos*, forthcoming.
11. Domínguez Búrdalo explains how Spanish intellectuals such as Joaquin Costa and Miguel de Unamuno provided the "ideological arsenal" that ultimately would serve to justify Spain's colonial intervention in Morocco. From all of the members of the Spanish Generation of 1998 (various writers who reflected on Spanish national identity in response to Spain's loss of Cuba in the Spanish–American War), as Domínguez Búrdalo points out, Miguel de Unamuno was the one who provided the kind of double-edged reasoning that would be characteristic of Spanish colonial rhetoric about Morocco: Domínguez Búrdalo, "El cine africanista español," 11. In "El porvenir de España," for example, Unamuno offered a crash indictment of the Arabs: "I do not want to say anything about Arabs. I have a deep dislike for them, I do not believe in what has been called Arabic civilization and think that their stay in Spain has been the worst calamity we have endured" (*De los árabes no quiero decir nada, les profeso una profunda antipatía, apenas creo en eso que llaman civilización arábiga y considero que su paso por España como la mayor calamidad que hemos padecido*). But at the same time, Unamuno considers "Spain

and the Rif as one and the same": Miguel de Unamuno, "España y el Rif es uno y lo mismo," quoted in ibid. As Dominguez Búrdalo notes, "When it is convenient the Arab legacy is diminished; but also when is it convenient it is linked to Andalusia, endowing it with Spanishness, something that gets reiterated specially in the first Francoist filmography (*cuando interesa, el legado árabe es ninguneado; también cuando interesa, cautamente se lo emparienta con lo andaluz, dándole así carta de españolidad, algo que se reitera especialmente en la filmografía del primer franquismo*": ibid., 12. The translations are mine.

12. See Martín Corrales, "El cine español y las guerras de Marruecos (1896–1994)," 694, 696.

13. See ibid., 15. About this new, more favorable, representation of the moor, Dominguez Búrdalo writes, "The shift in the Maghreb's image is more acute and positive in the movies shot while the Civil War was still going on. It is only logical to assume that one of the reasons of this new representation resided in the decisive participation of Moorish troops on the Francoist side, but it was also part of a wider political strategy tending to consolidate the Spanish union . . . with the *Alawita* Kingdom, a goal toward which the Francoist troops rushed once the Civil War was finished" (*El cambio de imagen del magrebí es más agudo y positivo en las cintas filmadas mientras aún continuaba la Guerra Civil. Lógico es deducir que una de las razones de esta nueva representación radicaba en la decisiva participación de las tropas moras en el bando nacional, pero formaba también parte de una estrategia política de mayor calado tendente a consolidar la unión (la anexión) de España con el reino Alawita, algo a lo que se aprestaron las tropas franquistas finalizada la Guerra Civil*: ibid., 15.

14. See María Rosa de Madariaga, *Los moros que trajo Franco* (Madrid: Martínez Roca, 2002), 354.

15. In fact, very satisfied with its outcome, Franco himself gave *Romancero marroquí* the green light. Its Spanish release was set for July 17, the third anniversary of Franco's uprising against the Republic: See Elena, "Romancero marroquí, 1939," 123.

16. In Dionisio Viscarri's words, "The I and the Other got fused and confused. . . . The moors were now 'the good guys.' . . . Morocco was now what it was necessary to retain and Spain what it had to be conquered": see Dionisio Viscarri, "Political Ideology and Orientalism: The Pre-Fascist Narrative of the Moroccan War (1921–1923)," Ph.D. diss., Ohio State University, Columbus, 1999, 75.

17. See Benedict Anderson, *Imagined Communities: Reflections on the Origin and Spread of Nationalism* (London: Verso, 1983), 24.

18. See Mark Neocleous, *Fascism* (Minneapolis: University of Minnesota Press, 1997), 72–73.

19. Quoted in Matei Calinescu, *Five Faces of Modernity: Modernism, Avant-garde, Decadence, Kitsch, Postmodernism* (Durham: Duke University Press, 1987), 208.

20. Saul Friedlander et al., "On Kitsch," *Salmagundi*, nos. 85–86 (1990): 203.

21. See Herman Broch, "Notes in the Problem of Kitsch," in *Kitsch: An Anthology of Bad Taste*, ed. Gillo Dorfles (New York: Universe Books, 1975), 63.

22. Kenneth Burke, "The Rhetoric of Hitler's 'Battle,'" in idem, *The Philosophy of Literary Form: Studies in Symbolic Action* (New York: Vintage Books, 1957), 177.

23. Celeste Olalquiaga, *The Artificial Kingdom: A Treasury of Kitsch Experience* (New York: Pantheon Books, 1998), 95.

24. On the problematic reception the film had with Moroccan nationalists politically aligned with Franco, see Elena, "Romancero marroquí, 1939," 124.

25. For a discussion on Francoist film legislation, see Nuria Triana-Toribio, *Spanish National Cinema* (London: Routledge, 2003), 53.

26. Aurora Bosch and M. Fernanda del Rincón, "Franco and Hollywood, 1939–56," *New Left Review* 232 (1998): 112–27, quoted in Triana-Toribio, *Spanish National Cinema*, 53.

CONTRIBUTORS

NORIKO ASO is an assistant professor of history at the University of California, Santa Cruz. She has published essays on cultural history and is completing a study of late nineteenth- and early twentieth-century Japanese cultural institutions as they negotiated new forms of publicness.

MICHAEL BASKETT is an associate professor of film studies in the department of Theatre and Film at the University of Kansas, where he teaches courses in East Asian cinema and film history. He is the author of *The Attractive Empire: Transnational Film Culture in Imperial Japan* (2008).

KIM BRANDT is an associate professor of history at Columbia University. She is the author of *Kingdom of Beauty: Mingei and the Politics of Folk Art in Imperial Japan* (Duke, 2007).

NINA CORNYETZ is an associate professor of interdisciplinary studies at the Gallatin School, New York University. She is the author of *The Ethics of Aesthetics in Japanese Cinema and Literature: Polygraphic Desire* (2007).

KEVIN M. DOAK holds the Nippon Foundation Endowed Chair in Japanese Culture at Georgetown University, where he also chairs the Department of East Asian Languages and Cultures. He is author or editor of several books and has written over thirty articles on nationalism, ethnicity, and political thought in modern Japan. His most recent book is *A History of Nationalism in Modern Japan: Placing the People* (2007).

JAMES DORSEY is an associate professor of Japanese literature and cultural history at Dartmouth College. In addition to publishing essays on and translations from the writer Sakaguchi Ango, he has recently completed a study of the critic Kobayashi Hideo.

AARON GEROW is an assistant professor of Japanese cinema and culture in the departments of East Asian Languages and Literatures and Film Studies at Yale University. His publications include *Kitano Takeshi* (BFI, 2007) and forthcoming books on *A Page of Madness* (dir. Kinugusa Teinosuke, 1926), and Taishō film culture.

HARRY HAROOTUNIAN is the Max Paleusky Professor of History, emeritus, at the University of Chicago, and adjunct senior research professor at Columbia University. His most recent publication is a book of essays edited with Tomiko Yoda, titled *Japan after Japan* (Duke, 2006).

MARILYN IVY is an associate professor of anthropology at Columbia University. She is the author of *Discourses of the Vanishing: Modernity, Phantasm, Japan* (1995) and has published a range of essays on modernity and mass mediation in Japan.

ANGUS LOCKYER is a lecturer (assistant professor) in Japanese history at the School of Oriental and African Studies, University of London. His recent articles include "The Logic of Spectacle c. 1970," in *Art History* (2007), and "National Museums and Other Cultures in Modern Japan," in *Museums and Difference*, ed. Daniel Sherman (2007). He is completing a book on exhibitions and modern Japan.

JIM REICHERT is an associate professor of Japanese literature at Stanford University. He is the author of *In the Company of Men: Representations of Male–Male Sexuality in Meiji Literature* (2006). He is currently working on a history of nineteenth-century Japanese print culture.

JONATHAN M. REYNOLDS is an associate professor of art history at Barnard College and Columbia University. His research has concentrated primary on the history of twentieth-century Japanese architecture. He has also begun to work on Japanese photography.

ELLEN SCHATTSCHNEIDER is an associate professor in the Department of Anthropology at Brandeis University. A sociocultural anthropologist, she is the author of *Immortal Wishes: Labor and Transcendence on a Japanese Sacred Mountain* (Duke, 2003), a study of women ascetics in northeastern Japan. She is currently completing a book on Japanese war memory and material forms, *Facing the Dead: Japan and Its Dolls in the Mirror of War*.

AARON SKABELUND is an assistant professor of history at Brigham Young University. He is the author of "Can the Subaltern Bark? Imperialism, Civilization, and Canine Cultures in Nineteenth-Century Japan," in *JAPANimals: History and Culture in Japan's Animal Life*, ed. Gregory M. Pflugfelder and Brett L. Walker (2005).

AKIKO TAKENAKA is an assistant professor in the Department of the History of Art at the University of Michigan. She has taught and published on the use of architecture and visual cultures for wartime propaganda, memory works associated with war and other human and natural catastrophes, and the destruction and reconstruction of cities. She is working on a book manuscript on the collection, preservation, and politicization of Asia-Pacific War memories in Japan.

ALAN TANSMAN is a professor of East Asian languages and culture at the University of California, Berkeley. He is the author of *The Aesthetics of Japanese Fascism* (forthcoming 2009).

RICHARD TORRANCE is an associate professor in the Department of East Asian Languages and Literatures and director of the Institute of Japanese Studies at Ohio State University. He is the author of *The Fiction of Tokuda Shūsei and the Emergence of Japan's New Middle Class* (1994) and the translator of Tokuda Shūsei's *Rough Living* (2001).

KEITH VINCENT is an assistant professor of Japanese and comparative literature at Boston University. His research interests include modern Japanese literature, queer theory, the theory of the novel, and translation theory. He is currently completing a book on homosocial narrative in modern Japanese fiction.

ALEJANDRO YARZA is an associate professor of Spanish at Georgetown University. He teaches contemporary Spanish literature, film, and cultural history. He is the author of *Un caníbal en Madrid: La sensibilidad camp y el reciclaje de la historia en el cine de Pedro Almodóvar* (1999) and is completing a book on kitsch and fascism in Spanish literature and film.

Page references in italics refer to illustrations

France: exhibits, and nationalism in, 282, 292n20; fascism, and infiltration into, 158; Vichy, 116, 118, 221, 251n16

Franck, Arnold, 225–29, 234, 234nn50,53, 435, 446

Franco, Francisco, 26–27n45, 137, 139, 439, 446–49

Francoist film industry, 16, 20, 221, 233n33, 436, 437, 439, 447, 448–49n11. *See also* Morocco

freak discourse, 357–59, 361, 363, 365–66, 371, 376–78

Freud, Sigmund, 384, 389–91, 395, 400, 405n21

fuan (malaise), 6, 9–10, 11, 13, 25n29, 32, 206

Fuashizumu undō ron (Imanaka), 34

Fujin saron (magazine), 407–8n68

furusato, and components of, and components of submariners myth, 410, 414, 420–24, 430n28

Futurism, 10, 25n30, 220, 300

Futurist Manifesto, 10, 299

Fuwa Suketoshi, 198

Gakugei Jiyū Domei (Alliance for Freedom in Academic Research and the Arts), 60

Gassett, Ortega y, 447

Gekkan mingei (publication), 115, 118, 121, 123, 126, 131

Gellner, Ernest, 185

Gendai ryōki sentan zukan, 364

genjitsu reality, of daily life, 85, 145

Genroku Chōshingura (film), 186–87, 194, 198, 202

Germany: aesthetics for films from, 228, 234n49; architectural style, and ideology in, 237, 251n12, 270–71; artistic propaganda for shaping public opinion in, 14, 15, 26–27n45, 32, 436; Autobahn construction workers model barracks in, 130, 136–37n58;

Beauty of Labor campaign in, 130, 132, 150; colonial identity in films from, 222–23, 233n38; cultural worker programs in, 116, 117; dogs, and role in, 156–60, 164, 168, 170–71, 179; entertainment for workers in, 128; eugenics, and fascism in, 168; exhibitions, and role of mass spectacle in, 276–79; fascism in, ix, 24n23, 31, 32, 37, 38, 50n8, 51nn13,15, 337; female factory workers in, 135n32; folk culture, and social ideology in, 118, 132; joint film ventures with, 217, 436; legislation for film industry in, 215; leisure time for workers in, 127, 130; marketing films from, 222–23; nationalization of film industry in, 205; national socialism, and role in, 51n13, 78n30, 130, 168; Olympics in, 224, 277; politics of despair in, ix, 9; racial purity advocacy in, 15, 38, 51nn13,15, 168; Strength through Joy program in, 116, 130, 131; wolves as symbol in, 159, 168

"ghost" marriage, 305–6, 307, 316n12, 317n14

Gluck, Carol, 23n16

Godzilla (films), 272, 275n41

Goebbels, Joseph, 26n34, 26–27n45, 187, 205, 223

Gonin no Sekkohei (film), 220

goodwill film genre, 229, 234n52

Gordon, Andrew, 126

government. *See* state government

Gramsci, Antonio, 93, 96

Grande illusion, La (film), 217

Grand Shrine at Ise, 106

gratitude indoctrination, 175

Greater East Asia Co-Prosperity Sphere, 201, 202, 204, 280, 325

Greater East Asian War, 249n2, 297, 309

Griffin, Roger, 6, 185–86, 323, 336, 337, 431n37

gyokusai euphemism, 411, 428

Library of Congress Cataloging-in-Publication Data

The culture of Japanese fascism / edited by Alan
Tansman.

p. cm. — (Asia-Pacific)

Includes bibliographical references and index.

ISBN 978-0-8223-4452-0 (cloth : alk. paper)

ISBN 978-0-8223-4468-1 (pbk. : alk. paper)

1. Fascism and culture — Japan — History — 20th
century. 2. Japan — Civilization — 1926–1945.

I. Tansman, Alan, 1960– II. Series: Asia-Pacific.

DS822.4.C85 2009

335.60952′09043 — dc22

2008051102